THE S. MARK TAPER FOUNDATION

IMPRINT IN JEWISH STUDIES

BY THIS ENDOWMENT

THE S. MARK TAPER FOUNDATION SUPPORTS

THE APPRECIATION AND UNDERSTANDING

OF THE RICHNESS AND DIVERSITY OF

JEWISH LIFE AND CULTURE

The publisher and author gratefully acknowledge the generous contributions to this book provided by the following individuals and organizations.

LUMINARY CIRCLE
Richard and Rhoda Goldman Fund
Walter and Elise Haas Fund
Jewish Community Endowment Fund
Koret Foundation

PUBLISHER'S CIRCLE
Laura and Gary Lauder
William and Fern Lowenberg

The Jewish Studies Endowment Fund of the University of California Press Foundation, which was established by a major gift from the S. Mark Taper Foundation

LITERATI CIRCLE
Jewish Community Federation of the Greater East Bay
Keren Keshet/The Rainbow Foundation
Lucius N. Littauer Foundation
Roselyne Swig

CHAIRMAN'S CIRCLE
Stephen and Maribelle Leavitt
Alan and Susan Rothenberg

DIRECTOR'S CIRCLE
Warren and Chris Hellman
Robert and Anne Levison, Jr.

Cosmopolitans

Cosmopolitans

A SOCIAL AND CULTURAL HISTORY
OF THE JEWS OF THE
SAN FRANCISCO BAY AREA

Fred Rosenbaum

UNIVERSITY OF CALIFORNIA PRESS
BERKELEY   LOS ANGELES   LONDON

University of California Press, one of the most
distinguished university presses in the United States,
enriches lives around the world by advancing scholarship
in the humanities, social sciences, and natural sciences.
Its activities are supported by the UC Press Foundation
and by philanthropic contributions from individuals and
institutions. For more information, visit www.ucpress.edu.

University of California Press
Berkeley and Los Angeles, California

University of California Press, Ltd.
London, England

Library of Congress Cataloging-in-Publication Data

Rosenbaum, Fred.
    Cosmopolitans : a social and cultural history of the
Jews of the San Francisco Bay Area / Fred Rosenbaum.
        p.   cm.
    Includes bibliographical references and index.
    ISBN 978-0-520-27130-2 (pbk. : alk. paper)
    1. Jews—California—San Francisco Bay Area—
History.   2. San Francisco Bay Area (Calif.)—
Ethnic relations.   I. Title.

    F869.S39J57 2009
    305.8992'407946—dc22   2008047129

Manufactured in the United States of America

20   19   18   17   16   15   14   13   12   11
10   9   8   7   6   5   4   3   2   1

This book is printed on Cascades Enviro 100, a 100% post
consumer waste, recycled, de-inked fiber. FSC recycled
certified and processed chlorine free. It is acid free,
Ecologo certified, and manufactured by BioGas energy.

FOR SEYMOUR FROMER

CONTENTS

ILLUSTRATIONS

PREFACE AND ACKNOWLEDGMENTS

LIKE NEARLY 20 PERCENT OF the Jewish adults in the San Francisco Bay Area, I hail from the New York metropolitan area.[1] Since my arrival in 1969 as a graduate student at the University of California, Berkeley, I have been intrigued by Jewish life near the Golden Gate, very different from that of my native Queens. For more than a third of a century, while working as an educator in the Jewish community, I have investigated its history. The rich material I unearthed in my early study of the Jews of Oakland and my research for two subsequent books on San Francisco's Congregation Emanu-El[2] convinced me of the value of a narrative history encompassing the entire Jewish community rather than just one corner of the Bay Area or a single synagogue.

Until recent decades historians of the American West gave short shrift to the Jewish experience, and American Jewish historians long neglected developments west of the Mississippi. But in the past generation several scholars have written informatively and insightfully on Bay Area Jewry, and I have greatly benefited from their work. Yet most studies have emphasized the pioneer period or the sagas of a few German Jewish dynasties.[3] Far less attention has been directed toward such important topics in local Jewish history as the cultural creativity of the native-born second generation and its ambivalence toward Judaism; the lively neighborhoods of East European Jews in the interwar period; the Jewish role in the convulsive labor disputes of the mid-1930s; and the bitter internal debate about the proper response to the Holocaust and Zionism.

This work focuses on the first century, from the Gold Rush to 1948, the year of the birth of modern Israel and the eve of a demographic sea change for Bay Area Jewry, which still resided primarily within the city limits of San Francisco and Oakland. It concludes with an extensive epilogue on the legacy of these first hundred years for the much more populous and widely dispersed contemporary Jewish community.

The story told in these pages is in many ways an exception to the Jewish experience in the rest of America because the Bay Area as a whole has been unusual, largely owing to the extent and persistence of its cultural pluralism. San Francisco was born diverse during the Gold Rush, and the Bay Area has continued to be one of the most ethnically and religiously mixed spots in North America, its many cultures simultaneously resisting both eradication and parochialism.[4] Unlike in urban centers in New England, the South, or other parts of the West, no single denomination or ethnicity has gained hegemony in Northern California since the time of the Catholic missions during Spanish and Mexican rule.

Jews, fluctuating from about 3 to 9 percent of the Bay Area population since 1849, have related closely to a welter of groups, including not only white elites but also people of color. The relationship between Jews and African Americans, vital for many American communities, is addressed here, but I write at greater length about the complex connection between Jews and Asians (both groups far more numerous in San Francisco than blacks until World War II) and also touch upon relations with Mexican, Irish, Italian, German, and other communities. Moreover, the Jewish contingent has itself been remarkably variegated, and tensions (both creative and destructive) between subgroups—such as Bavarians and Poseners, Germans and Russians—can also be traced from the pioneer to the contemporary period. Local Jewish leaders have also originated from such places as Paris and Alsace, England and Ireland, the Caribbean and Central America, and, in recent decades, the Middle East and North Africa.

The community has been diverse in the range of its occupations as well, with Jewish farmers and miners, boxers and mountaineers countering occupational stereotypes. Jewish women have enjoyed a high profile in the professions and the arts since the turn of the century. One performed all the duties of a rabbi in the 1890s, another covered the Russian Revolution of 1905 as a foreign correspondent, and still another served in Congress in the 1920s and 1930s. Today, both United States senators from California are Bay Area Jewish women.

Since the Gold Rush, Bay Area Jews have encountered relatively little anti-Semitism. Being Jewish in the Bay Area—where Jewishness is less of a social category than it is in the rest of America—has usually proved little hindrance to economic and even social advancement. Indeed, Jews have been so deeply enmeshed in virtually every phase of local history that the following narrative often reads as a chronicle of the metropolis refracted through its Jewish inhabitants. They were prominent Gold Rush–era pioneers, Gilded Age tycoons, and Progressive era reformers. They suffered disproportionate losses in the 1906 earthquake and fire and were instrumental in rebuilding the city after the disaster, despite experiencing the sensational graft trials of one of their own during that time. They were leaders on both sides of the barricades during the Red Scare following World War I, the waterfront strike of 1934, and the student protests of the 1960s. Few individuals embody San Francisco more than its best-known entrepreneur (Levi Strauss), its most celebrated retailer (A. L. Gump), its preeminent civic leader (Adolph Sutro), its most dazzling musical prodigies (Yehudi Menuhin and Isaac Stern), its greatest newspaper columnist (Herb Caen), its most notorious influence peddler (Abraham Ruef), and its most lovable eccentric (Emperor Norton). Two Jews, an artful promoter (Joseph Strauss) and a brilliant engineer (Leon Moisseiff), were among the three people most responsible for the Golden Gate Bridge. And such landmarks as the Fleishhacker Pool and Zoo, Steinhart Aquarium, Sigmund Stern Grove, and de Young Museum all resulted from the generosity of the most magnanimous group in the city.

But beyond the achievements of individuals, what has been the effect of the group as a whole and how has it differed from that of Jews in other American communities? And may one also speak of a Bay Area Jewish identity, an inner sense of what it has meant to be a Jew there compared to other places?

These questions lie at the heart of this study. Two particular themes emerge in answer. First, Bay Area Jewish history is marked by a preoccupation with the visual and performing arts, especially in the last quarter of the nineteenth century, but in virtually every other period as well. I attempt here not only to delineate the Jewish impact on drama, painting, sculpture, music, literature, photography, architecture, and home interiors in the Bay Area but also to consider the place of the arts in the sensibility of Bay Area Jews.

A second theme is the key role of Northern California Jews in the fight for social justice from the pre-Progressives of the 1880s to our own day. Local Jews have been leaders in the battles for agrarian reform and humane prisons, women's suffrage and child welfare, union rights and integrated neighborhoods, free speech and gay liberation. To be sure, many gave little thought to their Jewish heritage as they embarked on such crusades. Others, however, were motivated by the ethics of the Hebrew prophets, considering the struggle to heal society's ills a supreme religious commandment.

Yet Jewish religious observance and synagogue affiliation and attendance have been consistently low in the Bay Area, and throughout the community's first century the level of education in Judaica was low as well. Before 1967 Jewish nationalism was weak too, and during the Holocaust the Bay Area produced the country's largest chapter of the anti-Zionist American Council for Judaism.

What, then, has been the essence of a Jewish community that is more universalist than particularist, artistically creative and economically powerful, philanthropic and civic-minded, borrowing freely from other traditions and interacting fully with non-Jews? The historian Glenna Matthews has used the term *cosmopolitan* to label the unique civic culture of Northern California since the Gold Rush, and I have found it a helpful organizing principle in interpreting the Jewish story as well.[5] Studies of the Irish, Chinese, and African Americans in San Francisco have also stressed the relative success, sophistication, and worldliness of these groups despite the discrimination to which they were subjected.[6] Like members of these and other communities, local Jews felt themselves the product of an age-old history and tied to the fate of their people throughout the globe. But they focused even more on their teeming port city, an instant metropolis, which brought the world to them.

I am grateful to many individuals and institutions for their help in making this book a reality. First and foremost is Stephen Dobbs, a specialist in San Francisco history and an expert in the internal workings of the Jewish community. He conceived and shaped this project along with me, shared his invaluable insights on local Jewry, and meticulously edited every page. This work would not have been possible without him.

Richard A. Goodman and Professors David Biale, Marc Dollinger, and Diane Wolf read the manuscript and provided helpful suggestions and hearty encouragement. I would also like to acknowledge four longtime Bay Area residents to whom I frequently turned for clarification when the paper trail ran cold: Rita Semel, John Rothmann, and my dear friends Seymour Fromer and Ze'ev Brinner. I also consulted with historians in the field such as Professors Moses Rischin and Ellen Eisenberg, and Ava F. Kahn. Time and again I asked questions of Jeremy Frankel, president of the San Francisco Bay Area Jewish Genealogical Society, and he never failed to respond with useful data and good humor.

I am thankful for the grants I received while I worked on this volume for almost a decade. Six local foundations, all of which have supported the educational initiatives of my school for adult Jewish education, Lehrhaus Judaica, also funded my work as a historian, and I am deeply appreciative of their confidence and trust: the Jewish Community Endowment Fund in San Francisco, the Koret Foundation, the Richard and Rhoda Goldman Fund, the Walter and Elise Haas Fund, Keren Keshet–The Rainbow Foundation, and the Jewish Community Endowment Foundation of the Greater East Bay. Sandra Edwards at the Koret Foundation and Phyllis Cook at the Jewish Community Endowment Fund were particularly encouraging. In addition, I benefited from the generosity of a number of local community leaders, including William and Fern Lowenberg, Laura Lauder, Cissie Swig, Warren and Chris Hellman, Stephen and Maribelle Leavitt, and Alan and Susan Rothenberg.

I worked in numerous libraries on both coasts, including the Bancroft Library of the University of California, Berkeley; the San Francisco Public Library; and the Jewish Division of the New York Public Library. But one archive stands out as the premiere repository in this field: the Western Jewish History Center of the Judah L. Magnes Museum. Established in the mid-1960s by Seymour Fromer, the museum's visionary co-founder, the WJHC, with its periodicals, books, photographs, personal correspondence, institutional records, and ephemera, is arguably the leading regional Jewish history center in the country. It was my privilege and pleasure to have worked in its serene confines on Russell Street in Berkeley, California, with a succession of dedicated head archivists over the years: Ruth Rafael, Susan Nemiroff, Susan Morris, Aaron Kornblum, and Lara Michels. I am also grateful to the WJHC and the museum for permission to reprint here several passages from two of my earlier works, which they published.

I am also indebted to my colleagues at Lehrhaus Judaica past and present, and above all Executive Director Jehon Grist, for the spirit of intellectual honesty, cultural and religious pluralism, and overall decency they have fostered over the decades.

My final word of thanks goes to my life partner, Dorothy Shipps, who not only read the manuscript with a discerning eye but also sustained me with her enduring love and patience.

F. R.
Berkeley and Brooklyn
June 2009

ONE

Boomtown

Tumult and Triumph in Gold Rush San Francisco

SAN FRANCISCO CAME INTO BEING with the suddenness of an explosion. The discovery of gold in the Sierra foothills in 1848 triggered an influx to Northern California of a quarter of a million people, and the initial destination for nearly all of them was the Golden Gate. A remote and inconsequential Mexican outpost of fewer than a thousand inhabitants was rudely transformed into a monstrous center of commercial activity.

San Francisco swelled to thirty-five thousand by 1851, and by the eve of the Civil War it ranked as the nation's fifteenth largest city and sixth busiest port. In New York and Boston the transition from settlement to city had taken around two centuries, but San Francisco was transformed in less than a decade. And "the volume of this migration must be multiplied by its velocity," writes Carey McWilliams. "Not only were the emigrants in a great hurry [but] the same energy kept them in motion, jostling them about and sweeping them here and there."[1]

Overwhelmingly young and male, they came from all parts of the country and the globe, an unprecedented confluence of peoples. Foreigners outnumbered the American-born, making San Francisco the most ethnically diverse city on the continent, a nineteenth-century Babel. Along with Southerners, New Englanders, and New Yorkers, virtually every European country was represented. There were Chinese and Latin Americans, Polynesians and South Africans, Australians and Moroccans.

Among this "medley of races and nationalities" described by Hubert Howe Bancroft were the "ubiquitous Hebrews."[2] Barely two-tenths of one percent of the American populace at midcentury, Jews "numbered in the thousands on ships' passenger lists,"[3] constituting a disproportionately high percentage of those daring enough to take part in this greatest adventure of its day.

Every argonaut entered a social environment without a past, only a future. "The traditional mold was broken," as a historian of San Francisco's Irish community has said, and "relations between native stock and immigrant were set free from the shackles of history to take a new course."[4] For no group was this truer than it was for the Jews.

PRIDE OF PLACE

The Jews who poured into multiethnic San Francisco were themselves a mixed lot. The overwhelming majority hailed from German-speaking lands of Central Europe—part of a migration numbering two hundred thousand that transformed American Jewry in the mid-nineteenth century—but this contingent was itself split into subgroups. The two largest, Bavarians and Prussian Poles, would be at odds in Northern California for more than two generations.

The Kingdom of Prussia had seized much of Poland in the late eighteenth century, and the province of Posen, conquered in 1793, became a large reservoir of Jewish immigration to California in the following century. Although Prussian subjects, Jewish Poseners lived among ethnic Poles and were more pious, parochial, and impoverished than Jews anywhere else in the German states.

But Berlin sought to "Germanize" the Jews. Beginning in 1833, Jewish children were required to attend Prussian elementary schools. By midcentury, although their religious rites remained East European, young Jews from Posen and other parts of Prussian Poland had much in common with their coreligionists from the western part of Prussia and other German states. They carried Prussian passports and spoke and wrote German as well as Yiddish.

In America, these Jews preferred to emphasize the German rather than the Polish element of their binational provenance for reasons of social status. Declaring themselves "Prussian" in official documents, they frequently concealed the names of their hometowns.[5] In 1858 two brothers from Posen even founded the San Francisco Turnverein, a gymnastic club that was a pure expression of German mass culture.[6] Yet none of this helped very much. To their chagrin, Prussian Jews from east of Berlin were widely known in the United States as "Polish Jews," and they were frequently derided as "Polacks" by the other major German-speaking Jewish group in America.[7]

These were Bavarians, among the first German Jews to emigrate and destined to achieve the most, particularly in business. Like Poseners, they came from devout towns and rural villages, spoke a variant of Yiddish as well as German, and chafed under discriminatory decrees. But in Bavaria Jews had nourished hopes of emancipation. As in neighboring Baden and Württemberg, the French Revolution had raised expectations that the chains of persecution would finally be broken. Instead, following Napoleon's defeat, reactionary German monarchs crushed all aspirations to legal equality, restoring medieval restrictions on occupation and residence and even limiting the annual number of Jewish marriages. Immigration for Bavarian Jewry thus became "a substitute for emancipation."[8] Particularly in the 1830s and '40s, it was the poorer Jews in the southern German states who chose to emigrate, young people who "could neither work nor marry."[9]

Socially acceptable to both Prussian Pole and Bavarian was the much smaller cohort of Sephardim, Jews of Iberian ancestry, established in America since Colonial times. Fully acculturated and often well educated, they would play a vital role in the city and its Jewish community, especially in the 1850s, as lawyers, judges, synagogue presidents, and community spokesmen.

There was also an important Jewish contingent from France, mainly from Alsace along the Rhine. Known for its Talmudic academies, Alsatian Jewry had been highly traditional before the French Revolution. But there, unlike in Prussia or Bavaria, the National Assembly conferred legal equality upon the Jews in 1791. Acculturation—and Gallic patriotism—grew at an astounding pace thereafter. Pioneer Alsatian Jews in San Francisco, although fluent in German and often Yiddish, proudly considered themselves French, and were perceived as such by Jews and non-Jews alike. They served in Jewish organizations (usually alongside the Bavarians) and held municipal posts, but much of their passion was reserved for establishing French cultural institutions in their adopted city.

Some Jews came from England, they or their parents (often from Posen or another part of Prussian Poland) having sojourned, usually in London, before immigrating farther west. In early San Francisco there was also a sprinkling of Jews from the Hapsburg Empire, czarist Russia, the Caribbean, and

South Africa. Just as "the world rushed in," as one eminent Gold Rush historian put it, so did world Jewry.[10]

THE JOURNEY

Like most who headed to California, Jews were lured by the desire for riches. Rumors of "gold in the streets," wild reports in newspapers, and hyperbolic accounts in guidebooks enticed thousands of people. One young Jew from Prussian Poland who had left his wife and children in mid-1849 to seek his fortune in New York remained there only a year and a half before undertaking the much longer voyage to California. What Abraham Abrahamsohn *thought* he had witnessed near the docks of lower Manhattan provided the impetus: "Everywhere the astonished eye saw people who . . . showed large chunks of gold or carried them braggingly around their necks."[11]

The Gold Rush also attracted established New York Jewish businessmen. Bavarian-born Joseph Seligman sent two of his seven younger brothers to San Francisco in 1850 with $20,000 worth of merchandise and the exhortation to be a supplier of goods, "not a gambler hoping to make a strike."[12] He urged them to mine men's pockets rather than the veins of the Sierra Nevada, not yet realizing that a purveyor incurred only slightly less risk than did a prospector.

Simply getting to California was perilous. In 1849 the Bavarian Louis Sloss, destined to become one of the most prominent corporate executives in America, traveled from Kentucky across the continent on horseback. At twenty-five, he partnered with two non-Jews and braved cholera, hunger, thirst, and floods before riding triumphantly into Sacramento.[13] Seventeen-year-old Fanny Bruck (later Brooks) was probably the first Jewish woman to cross the plains, in 1854. She and her husband walked alongside their wagon, which served as "a bedroom, parlor, kitchen, [and] sometimes boat."[14] From a sheltered, middle-class home in Silesia (another Prussian province that had been Polish), Fanny quickly learned to use a gun, drive a mule team, and bake bread over an open fire. She lost her baby, born en route, and snowstorms forced the couple to winter in Salt Lake City, but the following spring they reached El Dorado.[15]

Yet among Jewish migrants, Sloss and the Brucks were exceptions; the large majority traveled by sea. Already veterans of one ocean voyage and usually embarking from a coastal city, Jews also tended to bring goods in tow, and a ship generally offered more cargo space than did a covered wagon.

Early on, sailing "around the Horn"—a 16,000-mile-long journey lasting up to five months—was the favored route. Accounts of those on board reflect the wonder they felt when visiting the tropics for the first time: seeing birds and fish they had never encountered before, experiencing sunsets unlike any in the northern latitudes, and encountering exotic tastes and aromas. But this was little compensation for the monotony, disease, discomfort, and at times terror they endured aboard old vessels hastily put into service, an ordeal likened to "half a year in a floating tenement."[16] Myer Newmark, a fourteen-year-old Jewish New Yorker of Prussian-Polish ancestry who would become a prominent California attorney, embarked with his mother, brother, and three sisters in 1852. His diary reveals a near fatal disaster only one day out of port:

> A great storm arose against us . . . and we covered the blankets over us glad to get into our berths. . . . The sea was mountains high, and the two life-boats attached to each side of our ship were carried off, together with a large portion of fresh stores and, worst of all, our Christmas turkey. The seas came in our cabin and relieved us of our stovepipe. In attempting to save one of the life-boats, the captain almost fell overboard.[17]

The greatest danger lay in rounding the Cape, where ships could be smashed by waves more than eighty feet tall. Young Newmark was fortunate, recording merely "cold, stormy and disagreeable" weather and his mother's gastric distress.[18]

Fear of shipwreck and the desire to shorten the journey caused many to travel via the Isthmus of Panama or to cross Nicaragua, and a few even traversed southern Mexico. Panama's Atlantic port of Chagres, only a few weeks from New York by steamship, was the transfer point more frequently used. But once passengers disembarked, a hellish odyssey began as they passed through malarial swampland in canoes and then cut across mountains on muleback. Along the way they usually had to sleep outdoors, exposed to thieves, animals, and insects. When they finally reached the Pacific they often had to wait for weeks in wretched circumstances before boarding a steamer for San Francisco. By 1855, a railway across Panama eased this segment of the journey, but those who crossed earlier often ranked the experience as one of the worst of their lives. Abraham Abrahamsohn writes of a fire in the night:

> Worn out from the difficulties of the trip and the glowing heat, we fell asleep in the alleys of the village but were woken up . . . by dreadful cries and noises.

Several huts were going up in flames and after a few minutes the whole place. The copper-red Indians were running around like black goblins, trying to save what they could of their miserable possessions. After a quarter-hour the whole village was in ashes.[19]

Abrahamsohn's three-week delay in Panama City depleted his cash— $150—and now he lacked funds for the last leg of the trip. A glazier, he hoped to earn money installing windows, but he found the town's residents too poor to afford anything more than wooden venetian blinds. A San Francisco–bound ship would transport him only after he agreed to work on board as a dishwasher and bootblack.[20]

Nor were circumstances any better for well-off Adolph Sutro, a twenty-year-old engineer from Aachen, a Prussian town near the Dutch and Belgian borders, who was destined to become mayor of San Francisco in 1894. On a riverbank near Chagres he spent four nights sleeping inside his canoe, pistols close at hand. On the mule trail he slept in the open, wet from the rains and hungry because food could not be had at any price. His riding mule was stolen in the night, so he walked the last seven miles to Panama City, pack animals beside him.[21] Then his ship to San Francisco would not accept the bales of high-quality cloth he had brought from New York and they had to be abandoned. Late in life he told his friends he wouldn't live in Panama, "were [he] made sole proprietor over all of it."[22]

Those traversing Nicaragua benefited from a shorter ocean voyage but faced a longer trek across disease-ridden jungles by boat and mule. At age six Mary Goldsmith Prag, later one of San Francisco's leading educators and the mother of Florence Prag Kahn, the first Jewish congresswoman, came through Nicaragua with her family. She recalled:

We each and all paid tribute . . . in the form of "Chills and Fever." . . . I was fretful and sick, so father placed me before him on the saddle and we jogged along. By water we were transported in canoes through dense masses of verdure which clogged the streams. Most of the time the natives were in the water dragging and pushing the boat along. Finally we were across and reached the western coast where we waited wearily for the steamer. She came and a thousand passengers were crowded into accommodations intended for four hundred.[23]

The overbooked *Samuel L. Lewis* was typical of the fleet dubbed "the death line," owned by Cornelius Vanderbilt. On a run prior to the

Goldsmiths' voyage, the ship's unsanitary conditions and rotten food contributed to the deaths of nineteen passengers. The ill-starred boat ran aground less than a year later, in a fog several miles north of San Francisco.[24]

Jewish accounts of the journey are similar to the hundreds of other testimonies documenting the rigors of travel in the Gold Rush years. There is but occasional mention of a Sabbath or holiday observance, or the need for kosher food. Other religious groups, such as the Mormons, sometimes chartered entire wagon trains so that they would be able to enforce their own moral codes along the way and halt travel on Sunday. New England trade associations sometimes purchased their own ships to take their members as a group to California. But there were neither Jewish caravans nor Jewish vessels. Jews made up a disproportionately large percentage of migrants, but they were thrown together with everyone else in tight quarters. It would be good preparation for the Jewish experience in San Francisco.

TURMOIL AND TEMPTATION

When their ships finally docked in San Francisco, weary travelers first set foot on wharves almost two miles long, which stretched from the deep water of the bay to the mud flats of Yerba Buena cove. The original shoreline was Montgomery Street, but the tremendous growth of the city, which was hemmed in by sand dunes and hills, mandated expansion east, into the harbor. People lived and worked on wooden piers and in the abandoned boats alongside them, and already by 1850 most of the cove was filled with beached ships, sand, and debris.

Walking toward the city proper, new arrivals saw a jumble of highly flammable canvas tents and flimsy shacks; San Francisco during the first two Gold Rush years was ravaged by six citywide fires, most of them the result of arson. Floods and sandstorms were also frequent. Rats and other vermin infested the area, which suffered a severe outbreak of cholera in 1850. And litter was everywhere: garbage was routinely strewn in the streets and the bay, and large quantities of unsold goods lay rotting on the ground or washed up on the beach.

There were few street lamps, but the town was illuminated by its many saloons, centers for prostitution, gambling, and brawling as well as drinking. Popular sports included not only horseracing and bullfighting, but also cockfighting and bearbaiting. The muddy streets were rife with crime, including gang warfare and murder, and despite the formation of vigilante committees, justice was rare. The fifty-four homicides in the year ending in June 1851 all went unpunished.[25]

Aside from the onerous living conditions and recurring physical disasters, and apart from rampant vice and crime, new arrivals were astonished by the unbridled frenzy for lucre. As Abraham Abrahamsohn recalled,

> On all the faces of the people . . . I clearly read the desire to become rich quickly in order to leave their Eldorado even more quickly. Many were proudly and triumphantly wandering through the streets with large pieces of gold, which looked like yellow, iron dross, or with bags full of gold grains in their hands. They had come from the mines in order to lose either hard or easily acquired winnings in the gambling halls in one night, and then have the pleasure of grubbing again for the yellow metal in the mountains.[26]

The values the immigrants had learned about work and money often collapsed as they saw fortunes made and lost in a day, and masters and servants change places overnight. In fact, "ruin [became] so ordinary," wrote the French Jew Daniel Levy, "it no longer upset anyone."[27]

Pioneer women provided a certain grounding influence, and there are many accounts of their strength and resourcefulness in making a home and raising a family amidst such chaos. At times they ran their own small businesses or taught school in the city or gold country. On the western frontier, more than elsewhere in the country at midcentury, necessity demanded that women work outside the home, and the relatively fluid social structure permitted it.[28]

But this was a society largely without women, not only in the mining camps but even in San Francisco, where among adults men outnumbered women 6.5 to 1 as late as 1852.[29] As a local historian wrote, "a woman was almost as rare a sight as an elephant. . . . Whenever a woman appeared on the street, business was practically suspended."[30] The small female contingent included many prostitutes. Ladies of the night, mostly French and Hispanic, were the most elegantly dressed women in town and, as one scholar has said, were "admired" and "uniquely respectable."[31] Abrahamsohn remembers the "beautiful girls . . . with perfumed flowers in their hair and on their bosom [who] flirted with word, smile and look, and in each gambling hall they offered to everyone . . . ale, port, various wines, punch and grog, white bread, butter, cheese, all of it for free."[32]

"Everyone was affected by his own passions,"[33] Daniel Levy reported, including the Jews. He tells the story of a Jewish violinist from Hamburg who earned enough performing in the gambling houses to purchase a half-share of a $40,000 house—which he lost in a single card game.[34] Abrahamsohn, a certified *mohel,* or ritual circumciser, among other professions, used his skill to earn $60 needed to tide him over during a lean time, yet he too squandered it in a casino.[35] Other Jews gripped by the gold fever turned to crime, including theft, fraud, and even attempted murder. Some ran gambling dens, frequented brothels, and drank to excess.[36]

But overall, the Jewish pioneers—who were twice as likely as non-Jews to remain in the area permanently[37]—were a stabilizing influence on the frontier and essential to the burgeoning mercantile economy of Northern California. Often relying on a relative in the East to ship dry goods, for which there was terrific demand, they carried packs on their backs or opened small stores in San Francisco as well as in the coarse mining towns. They were also middlemen: importers and exporters, auctioneers and salvagers, brokers and agents. As one observer wrote in 1856, "Merchandise[,] from the time it is freighted on the clipper ships until it is consumed, passes through the hands of the Jewish merchants . . . without them now trade would become almost stagnated in the State."[38] Nor were they exclusively businessmen: as early as 1849 they served as lawyers and public officials, stevedores and water carriers.[39]

But most conspicuous were their clothing outlets, both retail and wholesale. By the mid-1850s one Jewish-owned textile warehouse stood next to another along Sacramento Street, in the heart of the business district. Just to the north, on Clay and Washington streets, were the smaller retail stores, called "cheap shops" or "Jew shops" (and, in the mining towns, "Jew slop shops"), even if owned by a Christian. Here Jews were known to "stand ensconced the livelong day, waiting for a customer, and satisfied to argue and show their wares for an hour at a time, if there be a chance of making but a nominal profit."[40] But the rent on even the most modest storefront could be prohibitive, so many sold their goods from a tent, stall, or even a box on the street or wharf.

"A MAN GOT ONE MISFORTUNE . . . AFTER THE OTHER"

Some of these humble Jewish vendors would become wealthy businessmen and community leaders, but others worked feverishly for years, eschewing every comfort, only to fail miserably and return east empty-handed. The letters of Alexander Mayer, a youth from the Rhineland, to his uncle in Philadelphia, who had capitalized him, reflect the despair felt by many.[41]

Mayer arrived in San Francisco via the Isthmus of Panama in early 1851, a portion of his goods waterlogged. Exhausted and running a fever he had contracted in Panama, he soon discovered the market glutted with pants and shoes—items he had intended to sell—and his spirits sank even farther. "There will be a great many failures here,"[42] he wrote home, directing his uncle not to send more wares. Oversupply—a problem because of poor communication with eastern shippers—worsened in the spring, and the sluggish economy required Mayer to extend credit to his customers, who soon fell into arrears. He struggled to repay part of his uncle's investment and, on March 31, he repeated in a letter home that "the times [are] getting every Day worse and worse."[43]

The Great Fire of May 3 dealt him the cruelest blow. In one night it destroyed eighteen city blocks, one fourth of the "cloth and board" city.[44] Property worth $10,000,000, much of it belonging to Jewish retailers, was lost. With no insurance companies operating in San Francisco, and with underwriters in the East covering only a portion of the value, many merchants were ruined. Mayer, who could not afford a brick building (at a rent four times that of his wooden store), lost almost $5,000 worth of merchandise as well as his personal effects. But in his letter home he stressed the human toll; he had just returned from a funeral for four Jews and reported that the fire had blinded another. His next missive, to his cousin, urged the youth not to follow in his footsteps: "I don't like to advise no man to such a Country. If a man makes a living at home [he] should be satisfied."[45] Two weeks later he added, "That was not the last [fire] we had. . . . It will come again, it can't be other wise."[46]

Indeed, within two months Mayer was burned out again. He was forced to flee the store after working up to the last instant to save some of his stock and had to "let [the rest of the] Goods Burne rather than my self."[47] Even then he determined to "try to make up [his] Losses. He wrote, "My wish is only to bring back Again [what] I brought Here. . . . Believe me Since I left Philadelphia I look ten years Older. In all my days . . . I have not been so down Hearted as I have been for the Last 6 weeks. . . . A Man got one Misfortune then Comes one after the other."[48]

By June 1851 the city was in the grip of a militant citizen's group that, in the wake of the frequent fires and unchecked crime, had seized control from ineffectual elected officials. Seven hundred men—among them about thirty Jews—joined the extralegal and self-appointed Vigilance Committee. Throughout the summer the vigilantes arrested suspected lawbreakers, tried them summarily, and then dispensed "justice." Their main target was the Sydney Ducks, gang members usually of Irish ancestry who had immigrated via Australia, where some had done time in that country's penal colonies. About half of the ninety men tried were acquitted, but one was whipped publicly and four others hanged.

Mayer, who witnessed the execution of two prisoners dragged from their cell, "was very Glad of it" and mailed home a leaflet printed by the Vigilance Committee and his own crude drawing of the hangings. "I tell you," he wrote, "[this is] a great Country."[49] But the vigilantes brought neither peace nor prosperity, and in the fall Mayer left for the mining towns. He would have rather gone back east but "couldn't, because [he'd already] lost too much."[50]

Mayer traveled to the Mother Lode, where he joined hundreds of Jews who in a few years would establish thriving businesses, benevolent societies, cemeteries, and synagogues. Yet at the outset there was no more stability near the diggings than in San Francisco. Mayer tried to sell a new consignment of clothing in the town of Columbia, but he failed again because drought had dried up the swift streams prospectors needed to wash the dirt and gravel from the gold.[51] His potential customers simply returned to San Francisco, where they would swell the ranks of the unemployed. It is not known what Mayer did next.

Abraham Abrahamsohn also set off for the gold fields in 1851 with the idea of becoming a miner. Because he had lived on the wharf, he had lost even more than did Mayer in the spring fires, when "the boardwalks turned to glowing coals" and he became "a beggar without clothes."[52] With $10 from a fellow Jew, he bought "pants, boots, a blue woolen overshirt, a wool blanket, a cap, a leather belt, a pick, spade, tin pan, [and] a strong wide knife."[53] For weeks he toiled at several sites near Placerville, one of several Jews who worked the mines, disproving the assertion of a few visitors[54] that all Jews in the gold country were merchants.* But the paltry return for such hard labor induced Abrahamsohn to leave the diggings. He would work at several other trades, but in the spring of 1852, his "luck . . . not blooming," he left California for the Australian gold rush with others

---

*Another was Bernhard Marks, who wrote his cousin in Philadelphia in 1854: "I wanted to see the Elephant [the gold fields]. . . . To the mountains I must go, and I went . . . to be a miner." He prospected near Placerville for several months (J. Solis-Cohen Jr., "A California Pioneer: The Letters of Bernhard Marks to Jacob Solis-Cohen," *Publications of the American Jewish Historical Society* 44 [September 1954–June 1955]: 31).

"who had sought their fortune here in vain." Of his year in El Dorado, he wrote, "Anyone who thinks that roast pigeons are flying around here on golden wings, just waiting to be plucked and eaten, should stay at home."[55]

Even those who later became successful in San Francisco invariably met with terrible adversity in the early 1850s. Louis Sloss lost all his assets when a raging flood killed his livestock. Michael Reese, later one of the richest men in America, lost nearly all the merchandise he had brought with him when the riverboat carrying it sank in the Sacramento Delta; he was stripped of his cash reserves when his bank failed, and his warehouse burned in the May firestorms.[56] Adolph Sutro opened a store in Stockton and miraculously escaped a horrific conflagration there. But a few years later, on San Francisco's mean streets, he was the victim of a knife attack that left his face disfigured. For the rest of his life he wore muttonchop whiskers to cover the scars.[57]

HOPE

The San Francisco economy began to recover in mid-1852, in part because the glut of unsold goods had gone up in flames. Prices rose and merchants who persevered were finally able to reap rewards. Business would turn down again eighteen months later, but the last two years of the momentous 1850s would usher in a long period of prosperity. Yet even during the most chaotic days of the Gold Rush there were businessmen and professionals who could see—"through the mud, stink, and immorality,"[58] as one historian has put it—that San Francisco had the potential to be the leading commercial center in the American West. They linked their future to the new city and sought permanence and security in their unstable surroundings.

Jewish merchants were a major part of that group. Some, like the far-sighted Seligmans, invested in brick warehouses and thereby withstood the fires. Others sent for wives or fiancées and began to raise families. Still others served as aldermen, legislators, and judges just as the city and state were being born. While most of the transients in town gave little thought to the welfare of their community, Jews were conspicuous among those who cared about the rule of law, and about education, parks, culture, and religion. As one Bavarian Jew later wrote about the longing to make order out of anarchy, "Hope's rosy finger beckoned us on to the joys she promised us in the future. Hope's siren voice told us pleasant stories of what was in store for us."[59]

Thousands of miles from their families, Jews also craved the emotional support their faith could provide: fellowship with their own kind, links to the past, and connections with home. These impulses led to the first Jewish services on the West Coast on Rosh Hashanah, September 26, 1849, when a group of perhaps thirty, including one woman, responding to a notice in a local newspaper, met in a wood-framed tent on Jackson Street near Kearny.* [60] By Yom Kippur their number grew to nearly fifty. As they had no *sefer Torah,* a sacred scroll made of parchment, a printed copy of the Pentateuch was used instead.[†]

The first Jewish organization in the American West came into existence soon after these services were held. At the end of 1849 the First Hebrew Benevolent Society, composed largely of Prussian Poles, was founded to care for the sick and needy. Soon one of its leaders, Henry Hart, raised the funds to acquire two lots at the intersection of Vallejo and Gough streets for a Jewish cemetery. In the fall of 1850 the Eureka Benevolent Society, with goals similar to those of the First Hebrew, was established primarily by Bavarian Jews. Its founder, the twenty-six-year-old dry goods dealer August Helbing of Munich, later reflected upon the mix of social needs and charitable obligations felt by "the Jewish young men":

> We had no suitable way of spending our evenings. Gambling resorts and theatres, the only refuge then existing in 'Frisco to spend an evening, had no attraction for us. We passed the time back of our stores . . . disgusted and sick from the loneliness. . . . Besides, our services were in active demand; every steamer brought a number of our co-religionists, and they did not always come provided with means. In fact, some came penniless, having invested their all in a passage to the Coast. Some came sick and sore, and it needed often

---

*Another version of the story puts the site of the first service on Montgomery Street, near Washington and Columbus, and the city has placed a plaque at that spot, but contemporary research tends to support the tent on Jackson.

[†] The partial list of those present reveals the diversity of the town's Jews. At least two were American-born: the Sephardi Joseph Shannon, soon to be elected county treasurer, and Albert Priest of New York, who had arrived by wagon from Sacramento. Englishmen included Benjamin Davidson, a future agent of the Rothschilds; Barnett Keesing, accompanied by his wife; and Lewis Franklin, of Silesian descent, whose tent-store housed the worship services. Abraham Watters was a merchant from Prussia; Samuel Fleishhacker was likely a relative of Aaron Fleishhacker of Bavaria, patriarch of the banking family. Joel Noah, a retailer, was Hungarian (Fred Rosenbaum, *Visions of Reform: Congregation Emanu-El and the Jews of San Francisco, 1849–2000* [Berkeley, 2000], 6n).

times a respectable portion of our earnings to satisfy all the demands made upon us.[61]

High Holiday services that autumn, now attracting a considerably larger group, were held in Masonic Hall, with "much pleasure felt at the cheering presence of many dark-eyed daughters of Judah." Twenty-nine-year-old Lewis Franklin delivered the Yom Kippur sermon. He hailed from Liverpool, but his Orthodox family's roots were in Prussian Poland.

Like the many Christian preachers during the Gold Rush whose favorite topic was the folly of greed, Franklin delivered a fiery oration, imploring each person present to "pause in [his] mad career ere it be too late. . . . Man thou art a very idiot! These shining baubles . . . will take unto themselves wings, and flee from thee, leaving thou as naked as when thou wert first created."[62] He noted the familiarity with Jewish teachings of most of his listeners (who indeed had been raised in traditional households) but railed at their lack of piety: "Your very knowledge makes you doubly culpable." He castigated "the Sabbath-breaker[, whose soul] shall be cut off from his people."[63]

In his thunderous demand for strict religious observance in the midst of libertine San Francisco, Franklin showed little interest in adapting Judaism to its new environment; his faith had to be rigid because it was a shield, offering protection against immorality, natural disaster, and loneliness. The presence in the city of kosher butchers and boarding houses, matzah bakers and *mohelim,* documented as early as 1851, is evidence that he was hardly alone in clinging to tradition.[64] Franklin left San Francisco that year and sailed back to Europe at decade's end. But in his sermon of September 1850, he issued a challenge to the Jewish community: "Shall there be no temple built to Israel's God?"[65]

Yet there were no services beyond the High Holy Days because of the deep rift between the Eastern and Western Europeans on liturgy. One of the two factions (probably the one led by the Bavarians, who objected to *minhag Polen,* the traditional Polish ritual that Franklin almost certainly used) even walked out of the Yom Kippur services.[66] The German and Polish rites were virtually identical textually, but evidently the distinctions in pronunciation, melodies, and minor procedures made all the difference to immigrants seeking to replicate precisely their childhood religious experiences.

A semblance of unity returned early in 1851, as the community prepared for Passover and even began raising funds for a synagogue. By March of that year, $4,400 had been collected from 182 contributors, more than half the Jewish households in San Francisco.[67] A meeting was called for April 6, inviting "the Israelites of San Francisco" to form a congregation and elect officers. Alas, the group proved deadlocked on the election of a community *shochet* (ritual slaughterer), with the German and Polish factions, comprised primarily of Bavarians and Poseners, respectively, each supporting their own countrymen. At the "stormy" public meeting, reported an eyewitness, dissension was so great that there could be no other decision but to establish *two* congregations, just as there were two benevolent societies.[68]

Such disagreements between Bavarians and Poseners were common across the United States and split many of the dozens of new synagogues formed at midcentury.[69] One might have expected San Francisco—almost two thousand miles from the nearest synagogue, in St. Louis, and in many respects a social and cultural anomaly—to have been different, but here, too, age-old customs as well as prejudice and mistrust prevailed.

Moreover, the regional pride—according to one scholar, the "arrogance"[70]—of the Bavarians was based on more than ritual or liturgy. Even at this early moment, social and class gradations were evident. As a rule, the Bavarians had arrived in America about a decade earlier than most Prussian Poles and, in part because of that head start, they were usually more successful in business. They also tended to have more of a mercantile background than the Poseners, who, although often retailers, were more likely to have been trained as artisans. The Bavarians could identify fully with German culture, in vogue in America at midcentury, whereas the *Hinterberliner,* those from "beyond Berlin" (meaning east of Berlin), were prevented by other Jews from shedding their Polish skins.

This fragmentation within a religious group was hardly unique in early San Francisco. French Catholics worshipped apart from their déclassé Irish coreligionists. Even American-born Presbyterians were divided along regional more than doctrinal lines, with Southerners and New Englanders early establishing separate churches.[71]

As for the two Jewish congregations born in the same room on April 6, 1851, they would be as rival siblings ever since. One was Emanu-El, meaning "God is with us," perhaps reflecting gratitude for a safe arrival on the West Coast, perhaps forging a link with its New York namesake, formed six years earlier by Bavarians. On April 8 it prepared a charter signed by sixteen men, mostly Bavarians but also at least three native-born Sephardim.[72]

The other congregation, Sherith Israel—also the name of a New York synagogue, the oldest in the nation—included Englishmen (largely of Prussian-Polish ancestry), Poseners, and Jews from Russian-occupied

Poland. A small group met on April 8 and prepared an advertisement for kosher meat, which ran in the *Daily Alta California* two days later. Sherith Israel's minute book (which, unlike Emanu-El's, survived the earthquake and fire of 1906) begins with a meeting held in a boarding house on April 13 at which officers were elected and a committee appointed to draft a constitution and bylaws. Emanu-El began with sixty members, Sherith Israel with forty-two. The founding document of the former explicitly required the German rite known as *minhag Ashkenaz;*[73] that of the latter mandated strict adherence to *minhag Polen.**[74]

A recent study of Emanu-El's founders reveals they were typically in their early twenties, significantly younger even than the youthful founders of comparable synagogues in other parts of the country.[75] Their wives (or future wives, because many were still unmarried) were younger still. Nearly all the founding members were in commerce.

Given their later orientation, it may be surprising that in infancy both congregations were Orthodox. But this was the form of Judaism with which most of their members had been familiar in the small towns of Europe.

---

*The controversy and confusion about which is the older congregation has never ceased. In 1900 Emanu-El's spiritual leader, Jacob Voorsanger, adamantly claimed that distinction for his synagogue, claiming it was founded in 1850, but in 1974 two researchers demonstrated that he based his conclusion entirely on a misdated document (Stern and Kramer, "A Search for the First Synagogue," *WSJHQ* 7 [October 1974]: 3–20). As they pointed out, no reference to either congregation—either in newspapers or municipal records—exists before April 1851. Their finding is corroborated by Alexander Iser's *Almanac* listing the local Jewish organizations. This earliest Jewish resource guide lists April 1851 as the founding date for both congregations (Alexander Iser, *The California Hebrew and English Almanac for the Year 5612, Corresponding with the Years 1851–1852* [San Francisco, 1851], in WJHC/JLMM).

Sherith Israel has claimed both 1849 and 1850 as its starting date, citing the High Holiday services of those years as its first service. But in fact few of those worshippers later joined the congregation; a large majority either became members of Emanu-El, left the area, or remained unaffiliated.

The strong desire to be considered the first congregation has led to tampering with Sherith Israel's founding documents. Although the opening page of the original, bound minute book is dated April 13, 1851, the words "Record of previous meetings held August to date lost" are written with a different pen and handwriting in the upper margin. On the title page of the congregation's constitution appears "Organized 1851," but the "1" is crudely changed to a "0" in a different hand and a differently colored ink (Minutes of Congregation Sherith Israel, in WJHC/JLMM).

Moreover, in the tumultuous early 1850s the desire for acculturation was neither fully awakened nor clearly directed. On the frontier most Jews felt forced by necessity to relinquish many religious practices in their daily lives, but this did not preclude pioneers from founding synagogues that would put them back in touch with the old-world piety they had left behind not so long ago.

In addition to attaching importance to the office of *shochet* and to the form of worship, both constitutions required members to attend a minyan, the quorum of ten men for prayer services, when notified. Also, no one married to a non-Jew could join, and any congregant taking a gentile wife automatically forfeited membership. At Sherith Israel membership was also contingent on a man and his sons being circumcised.[76]

While dues were only $2 a month, a great deal of lay involvement was required from both congregations. Sherith Israel's members were obliged to come up to the Torah when called, attend meetings, serve on committees, and (as at Emanu-El) accept election as an officer. Stiff fines were levied for any infraction. Each congregation also required the written permission of its board of trustees for a member to marry within the city of San Francisco.[77]

The two fledgling institutions struggled amid the horrendous fires of the spring and shocking vigilantism of the summer of 1851. Although they grew rapidly, each passing the one-hundred-member mark within the year, it was difficult to collect dues. Both groups met in plain rented quarters a few blocks apart on Kearny Street and engaged knowledgeable laymen to perform a variety of religious duties. Sherith Israel hired the versatile Alexander Iser as *shochet, shamas* (sextant), Torah reader, and bill collector, all for $60 a month. Emanu-El was even more parsimonious; its payroll consisted only of a nominal amount to a Torah reader.

But there were some encouraging signs, most notably the first marriage at Sherith Israel in late December 1851. Emanuel Linoberg, thirty-three, one of the earliest settlers of the mining town of Sonora, had been in San Francisco to purchase supplies for his several businesses when he met Pauline Meyer, whose parents belonged to the congregation.[78] Weddings occurred about every other month in 1852 and more frequently the following year. Due to the dearth of females, many men were less fortunate than Linoberg and had to send for a wife from the East, women known "only by reputation, or because her brother or friend recommended her."[79]

The early marriage records of Emanu-El are not extant, but the congregation received an invaluable gift in 1851: a Torah scroll, less than two feet tall, donated by the renowned British philanthropist Sir Moses Montefiore.[80] In later years it was used by the congregation on Yom Kippur, but it would be destroyed in the disaster of 1906.

As the economy improved in early 1852, each congregation sought to build a new synagogue, hoping to leave its rented storefront for a permanent home, but both made a point of not conferring with the other. In the end, they bought lots only a block and a half apart from one another in North Beach, a relatively fashionable area where many Jews resided and from which they enjoyed a short walk to the business district. The cornerstones were laid only two weeks apart in July 1854, and in September of that year both buildings opened their doors in the same week.

Not surprisingly, each board of trustees was preoccupied with its capital project almost to the exclusion of everything else. And because the next downturn in the city's roller-coaster economy began in 1854, both groups had been forced to scale back their original designs. Emanu-El, on Broadway between Mason and Powell, ultimately spent $20,000 and Sherith Israel, on Stockton near Broadway, about half that amount, each institution forced to take a large mortgage at a high interest rate.

Neither of the two utilitarian buildings conveyed a hint of the magnificent synagogue architecture that would grace San Francisco in future decades. Emanu-El, with a seating capacity of eight hundred, was the larger, a solid redbrick structure with a neo-Gothic façade and separate entrances for men and women. It had a modicum of elegance, with its Brussels carpet and handsome chandelier, but hardly impressed out-of-town visitors; there were thousands of similar houses of worship across the country. Sherith Israel, about half the size and covered only by gray cement, was even more modest.[81]

Yet given the obstacles faced by pioneers in such a distant land, the erection of two synagogues by the mid-1850s was an achievement. The emerging community also had cemeteries and benevolent societies, kosher meat and ritual circumcisers. But it still lacked rabbis, and attracting them would prove the greatest challenge of all.

THE SEARCH FOR SPIRITUAL LEADERSHIP

What kind of rabbis were the young laymen seeking? They had formed two Orthodox congregations in 1851, but within a few years many who had survived the trauma and disorientation of the Gold Rush began to feel comfortable in their new home and less in need of the same religious experience they had known as children. Now, as they became solid citizens, "the new focus of their lives was San Francisco," writes a Gold Rush historian of a change in sentiment found among most ethnic groups in the city by mid-decade, and "no hankering after the past could repel its demands." As Robert Lotchin continues, "The narrow streets jumbled people up together; business, pleasure, educational, and ceremonial life multiplied their contacts . . . and the growing use of English gradually wiped out the main European criterion of nationality."[82]

Religious insularity was beginning to erode as well. By 1855 there were twenty-two Protestant churches in the compact city, many of them with a high profile.[83] Jews had at least a passing acquaintance with the universal message of the Unitarians, the cultivated aestheticism of the Episcopalians, the tireless benevolence of the Methodists, and even the popular Sunday schools of the Baptists. They were annoyed at the handful of Christian proselytizers (a problem throughout America at this time) but also had to be aware of the broad-minded preachers among the Protestants, some with degrees from Harvard or Yale, who delivered inspiring sermons in the streets and wharves as well as in the churches.[84]

Particularly at Emanu-El the vision of an Americanized synagogue emerged, shorn somewhat of its Jewish and German distinctiveness. The Bavarians, Sephardim, and Alsatians were groping toward a rational and dignified religious expression that would not seem strange to the non-Jews with whom they had such close contact. They hoped as well to resolve the growing contradiction between lack of observance outside the synagogue and strict ritual practice within it.

For these reasons, Emanu-El sought for its first spiritual leader a reformer, a man in the coterie of Central European rabbis that had recently come to America seeking to bring Jewish life more into line with that of the host country. The leader of this new school of thought was Isaac Mayer Wise, who by the mid-1850s was ensconced in Cincinnati, an expanding young city that became the national headquarters of his new weekly, the *American Israelite,* and of the burgeoning Reform movement.[85]

As early as 1853, the twenty-five-year-old president of Emanu-El, Henry Seligman, sought to bring west a man in Wise's camp. Seligman convinced the membership, already hard-pressed by the building campaign, to pledge an additional $3,500 annually to retain a full-time rabbi.[86] Yet even at that lofty salary, almost triple the amount then earned by an experienced physician or lawyer, few ordained rabbis were available. Most of the nation's seventy-five congregations were led by cantors or laymen, because the yeshiva-trained rabbi—whether a reformer or not—was an unlikely candidate for immigration to the "American Babylon." Seligman offered San Francisco's first rabbinical post to several allies of Wise, but in vain.[87] In the end, the congregation reluctantly engaged a rabbi far more traditional than it had wanted.

The learned Julius Eckman had arrived "on his own hook" (that is, without a formal invitation and at his own expense) in July 1854, in time to perform the ceremonies of laying the cornerstones for both synagogues.[88] After leading High Holiday services at Emanu-El on a trial basis, he was given only a one-year contract at $2,000, far below the advertised compensation.[89] Perhaps the Emanu-El leadership was concerned that, since immigrating to America in 1849, he had lasted no more than a year at each of three congregations he had led in the South.[90] But with a swelling list of members, many of them now with wives and children, the board felt it could leave the pulpit vacant no longer.

Because Eckman had spent three years in London as a teenager, his English was flawless, and it was expected his sermons would rival those of any American rabbi. To be sure, he had been born and raised in low-status Posen, but he had earned a doctorate from the University of Berlin, usually sufficient, in the minds of Bavarians, to turn a Posener from a "Polack" into a German. In any case, the Bavarians had little choice: a large percentage of ordained Jewish clergy in America in the 1850s hailed from the devout communities east of Berlin.

Eckman would live on the West Coast until his death in 1874, but this first San Francisco rabbi remained at Emanu-El only one year. Clearly a major reason for his failure was that he was at best a halfhearted reformer. Even by mid-nineteenth-century standards, he was resistant to change when it came to the role of women. He abided the mixed classrooms and choir organized before his arrival, but women worshippers were still required to sit in the upstairs gallery of the new Broadway Synagogue. In contrast to Isaac Mayer Wise, who favored universal suffrage and allowing females to serve as synagogue board members, Eckman viewed the "so-called Emancipation" of women as "ridiculous foolery."[91] "In a woman," he wrote, "an ounce of heart is worth more than a pound of brains."[92] Claiming that a woman's ultimate goal ought to be matrimony, he opposed divorce in all circumstances.[93]

Eckman's temperament also clashed with his new surroundings. In a city of frenetic young men, his manner was calm and ascetic. A lifelong bachelor now past fifty, he lived in a garret on meager rations of food.* The only possession he prized was his library, comprised of books in the many languages he read and studded with illuminated Hebrew manuscripts.[94]

Eckman chastised the whole country for its excesses, claiming, "We eat and dance ourselves to death [more] than they do at the Sandwich Islands."[95] His advice to hard-drinking San Francisco was temperance, a cause taken up by few other Jewish leaders in the city's history.[96]

The gentle rabbi delighted in animals and related best to small children.[97] Shortly after his arrival he opened a supplementary Jewish school, the first on the Pacific Coast, which he headed for many years thereafter. Known as Hefzibah (referring to the people of Israel), it required attendance weekdays as well as at Sabbath services and a Sunday lecture. Although Hefzibah was a major achievement, Eckman's lack of administrative and business expertise and his reluctance to charge reasonable fees, or any tuition at all for the children of the poor, caused the school, like its director, to be in dire financial straits.

As for his congregational work, his tactlessness became obvious early. He published a haughty letter in the *Daily Herald* denying his synagogue's right to oversee its ritual butchers and claimed that prerogative for himself.[98] Many members demanded his resignation at a congregational meeting, and Eckman did not survive the rancorous annual assembly the following year.

What brought him down, though, was more a struggle over rabbinical authority than a disagreement about kosher slaughtering. Eckman had in mind a European model of tight rabbinical control over every religious matter. But America was different, he would painfully learn, for the ultimate authority was the lay leadership, not only at Emanu-El, but at all of the young synagogues across the country. His attack in the press on his own board of trustees showed that Eckman had no idea of the congregational rabbi's role in the New World.

But if Eckman was unsuited for the pulpit, other skills enabled him to make a deep impact on the pioneer Jewry for almost twenty years. After his

---

*His austerity and introspection bring to mind the Eastern religions, and in the 1860s he seriously considered ministering to the Jews of Kaifeng, China, although he never did so (Joshua Stampfer, *Pioneer Rabbi of the West: The Life and Times of Julius Eckman* [Portland, Ore., 1988], 127).

dismissal he turned even more vigorously to his first love, education, codirecting a secular day school and Jewish day care center along with the Hefzibah venture. Now lacking congregational backing, he was forced to move Hefzibah out of the Broadway Synagogue to shabby rented quarters a few blocks away. Yet the love the youngsters felt for their grandfatherly teacher overcame the squalid setting. As Mary Goldsmith Prag remembered:

> It was a ramshackle, weird old building, falling into decay, full of strange noises and haunted corners; its halls and stairways unswept, and decorated with cobwebs and dust. . . . How slowly we ascended the rickety old stairs . . . how we held our breath and shivered with fear as we heard the rats . . . scurrying across the rafters; how we finally made a rush for the door of the room, to be welcomed by our dear old friend; to forget all our fears and troubles in the charm of his presence and the magic of his instruction.[99]

At the same time, the irrepressible Eckman embarked on another consuming career: journalism. In 1857 he unveiled the *Weekly Gleaner,* for the next six years the most influential Jewish newspaper in the western states (predating the first viable periodical of the city's far more numerous Irish community). Circulating along the entire Pacific Coast, the *Gleaner* offered scholarly essays on Judaica as well as news from growing Jewish communities in the American West and around the world.

But the failure of subscribers to pay their bills often brought the *Gleaner,* like the Hefzibah school, close to bankruptcy. In order to maintain them both, Eckman worked long into the night, slept on a sagging couch in the newspaper office, and remained impoverished.[100]

For all of his later accomplishments, Eckman remained bitter about his removal from Emanu-El as well as the lack of an offer from Sherith Israel or any of the local congregations formed later. He complained, with some justification, that he had been "found wanting not in honesty, integrity, or energy, nor in zeal and knowledge—not in self denial and self-sacrifice [but rather in] pliancy, worldly policy, and hypocrisy—hence in popularity."[101]

Sherith Israel also engaged a full-time rabbi shortly after its first synagogue was completed. Rabbi Henry A. Henry, a Londoner probably of Prussian Polish ancestry, was brought from New York in September 1857. A large man with a long white beard, he strode through the streets in flowing black robes. Fifty-one years old when he arrived, Henry was strictly Orthodox, but if he was out of place in youthful, sinful San Francisco, he was much more suitable for his congregation than Eckman was for Emanu-El.

For Sherith Israel firmly rejected reform during the first decade and a half of its existence. An Americanized service seemed far from its members' minds, judging from the impression of a visitor to the Stockton Street Shul who praised its congregants as "more assiduous" than Emanu-El's but faulted them for the "unforgivable wrong of making their fervor too loudly vocal. [Like] the classical and venerable uproar in the synagogue in the good old days of the faith . . . the Poles have not fallen away."[102]

Henry, who served Sherith Israel for twelve years, meticulously followed the Polish rite. As early as 1859 he proposed a Jewish day school, an idea that gained almost no support even within his own congregation and predated the establishment of such schools in San Francisco by more than a century.[103] In the national Jewish press he sharply criticized Eckman (hardly a dangerous reformer) for laxity in performing conversions and suspending a few Talmudic laws regarding marriage.[104]

Yet Henry was not as parochial as all this suggests. The rabbi may have come west to be engaged with the non-Orthodox more than was possible in his native England or on the East Coast, where he had sometimes been sanctioned for his contacts with Christians and even liberal Jews. In San Francisco, of course, he had no fear of an attack from the right.

A powerful writer and sermonizer when many American rabbis were more comfortable in German than English, he made a compelling case for traditional Judaism in the many books he wrote while serving on Stockton Street. Trying desperately to reach the younger generation—he had nine children himself—he penned three handsome high school primers that reflected an educator in touch with the needs and abilities of his student-readers, hardly commonplace in Orthodox circles in the mid-nineteenth century. Henry, who spoke French and German fluently, was well versed in world literature and science and active in organizations ranging from the Freemasons to the Alliance Israelite Universelle. He appeared frequently as a dignitary at civic ceremonies.[105]

But in the 1860s, when even at traditional Sherith Israel the demand arose for some liturgical reform, the elderly Henry showed no inclination to comply. In a letter to the nationally respected Orthodox journalist and cantor Isaac Leeser of Philadelphia, he vowed to "suffer no innovations" and sounded almost like a warrior out of the Book of Joshua: "Although at times I have to go into the battlefield . . . [I] do not flinch."[106]

Henry was especially resistant to allowing men and women to sit together in the pews. However, as with Eckman at Emanu-El the decade before, the larger dispute was over rabbinical authority. Henry "has not only ignored and disregarded my orders," President Charles Meyer angrily reported to his board in April 1869, "but [he] seems to think that he . . . has a right to do so, for when I censured him for having disobeyed [me] he gave me the vulgar American 'I shall not play second fiddle,' insulting not only me and the whole Board but also [those] who have elected us to conduct the Congregation's affairs."[107] For this insubordination the venerable rabbi was soon terminated.

It is not clear if Henry, who worked primarily as headmaster of a Jewish school in England before immigrating to America in 1849, had ever been ordained, but the depth of his learning was never in question, nor was Eckman's. Both were solid scholars as well as devoted spiritual leaders. Yet the pioneer West also had its charlatans, untrained men who reinvented themselves on the coast as rabbis. The charismatic Herman Bien, who followed Eckman at Emanu-El for a year, feigned both rabbinical ordination and a doctorate and had only passing acquaintance with classical Jewish texts. He conducted services wearing a distinguished white neckcloth and a cap embroidered with the words *Kadosh L'Adonai,* or "Sacred to the Lord." But his sermons, though long on histrionics, were short on substance.[108]

Eckman was enraged at his successor, not least of all because "Reverend" Bien, half his age, had also decided to compete with him as a journalist, publishing the *Voice of Israel* when the rabbi launched the *Gleaner.* Bien's newspaper was short-lived, but, like many pioneers, he quickly switched to other things: running a jewelry store, staging two lavish productions of a play he had written, and then founding a second Jewish newspaper, the *Pacific Messenger.* When that went bankrupt, he simply started a successor, the *True Pacific Messenger.*[109] And before he left San Francisco in 1864 for Nevada, where he was elected to the first state legislature, he had opened— and closed—several different Jewish schools.[110] One can imagine what Eckman and Henry thought of him as an educator.

CIVIC DUTY

The emergence of an instant city did not ensure instant citizens. To most of the footloose young men who arrived from all over the world, San Francisco looked like "a traveling carnival," as one Gold Rush scholar has put it, "that would disappear when the festivities were over."[111]

But there was also a countervailing trend. From Alexis de Tocqueville on, observers have stressed the importance of voluntary associations in budding

American communities, and this was particularly true of San Francisco, where the municipal government was weak and corrupt. The organizations born in the early 1850s furthered self-interest of course; many members sought business contacts or useful information. But in bringing like-minded people together, religious groups, fraternal orders, civic societies, and cultural institutions served larger purposes. They strengthened the individual's sense of identity amidst his or her amorphous new surroundings and helped provide stability in the newly born metropolis by addressing social problems.

Each of San Francisco's ethnic and religious groups had its organizations, but the early network of Jewish groups was especially extensive and influential. First of all, the good-sized Jewish population offered a critical mass of potential members. By 1860 there were roughly ten thousand Jews in the West, half of them in San Francisco, where they comprised perhaps nine percent of the inhabitants, no small figure given that the entire country counted only 150,000 Jews.[112] About forty thousand of U.S. Jews lived in New York on the eve of the Civil War, but San Francisco, one of the nation's larger Jewish communities, was not far behind Baltimore and Philadelphia, numbering around eight thousand each.[113]

The city supported three synagogues: Emanu-El, Sherith Israel, and Shomrai Shabbes, a small group of Orthodox Polish Jews. In 1861 a fourth—Beth Israel, also traditional—would be founded. For a while in the early 1850s there had been a Sephardi congregation as well.

The two benevolent societies were established at the beginning of Jewish settlement, and as early as November 1850 they worked together to aid victims of the cholera epidemic, which killed almost 5 percent of the city's population.[114] By the decade's end the Eureka Benevolent Society (EBS), with three hundred members, was the largest Jewish organization in the West, its annual fundraising balls major events. Like the First Hebrew Benevolent Society and the Chevrah Bikkur Cholim Ukedusha (established in 1857), the EBS, forerunner of today's Jewish Family and Children's Services, aided the needy, cared for the ill and indigent, and buried the dead. Women organized mutual aid organizations of their own, including the Israelite Ladies Society.[115] And prominent non-Jews, such as San Francisco's mayor in 1854, C. K. Garrison, sometimes made significant financial contributions to the city's Jewish charities.[116]

In 1860, Emanu-El joined with the EBS to purchase a burial ground on Eighteenth and Dolores streets in the Mission District, then an undeveloped part of town. Known as the Home of Peace Cemetery, it adjoined a block bought at the same time by Sherith Israel and served the community for almost thirty years. The first lodge of B'nai B'rith in San Francisco, Ophir, was founded in 1855 by William Steinhart, a young native of Baden, who headed a thriving textile enterprise. For the next century, the B'nai B'rith would be one of the most powerful Jewish organizations on the Pacific Coast.

In the open atmosphere of the pioneer West, Jews also gained an early foothold in nonsectarian life. Even a man under as much stress as Alexander Mayer found time to belong to the Odd Fellows, and other Jews joined lesser-known fraternal groups such as the Red Men, United Workman, and Foresters.

But it was to the largest of these fraternities, the Masons, that Jews were especially attracted. Emanu-El's first president, the Sephardi clothier Abraham Labatt, was likely Master of California's first lodge, which also included many other Jewish leaders, including Rabbi Henry. The Masons, known at the time for their disdain of Catholics, reacted warmly to Jews who soon would account for 12 percent of the San Francisco membership, a high level of integration given that any lodge member could block a candidate by secretly casting the legendary black ball.[117]

Jews were also well represented in German cultural organizations and were the earliest pillars of the city's exclusive German social clubs. Joseph Brandenstein, the tobacconist who later led the German Benevolent Society, its hospital, and old age home, was devoted to the San Francisco Verein, or Association, founded in 1853, which became the Argonaut Club.[118] Levi Strauss and Martin Heller were among the earliest leaders of the Alemanian Club, later known as the House of Concord and eventually the Concordia.*[119] Central European Jews often spoke German at home in this first generation, and they basked in the respect most Americans had for German culture. Later, Jewish Francophiles became the backbone of key institutions such as the French Library, Hospital Society, and National League.

Jews were highly visible in the well-regarded Mercantile Library Association. Their own Hebrew Young Men's Literary Association, essentially a debating club, offered an opportunity for newcomers to improve their public speaking skills. The tremendous Jewish impact on the arts would

---

* Within only a few years, however, these German clubs consisted almost exclusively of German Jews.

await the second generation, but even in the 1850s Jewish patrons were a major element in the success of the opera—almost a hundred performances of Verdi's works were performed in San Francisco during the decade—the theater, and, later, the symphony. As one visitor observed, "Whenever an undertaking of public interest or benefit is to be carried out, the Jews are looked to first of all, because they are always ready to contribute."[120]

Jews served in the volunteer fire department as well, fulfilling a vital function in a city of so many devastating blazes. But another aspect of Jewish civic involvement has left a more controversial legacy. Armed vigilante groups (the largest in American history) claimed to benefit—indeed, to save—the entire city, but they used force and intimidation to advance the interests of one group in particular: the merchants. This extralegal militia suspended due process when it seized control of the city in 1851 and again in 1856, and in the latter instance it enlisted eight thousand members for three months in a move that was little short of a coup d'état. Sparked by the assassination of a popular anti-Catholic newspaper publisher, the vigilantes severely punished alleged killers, arsonists, and thieves, hanging four (as in 1851), deporting twenty-five, and intimidating hundreds more who left on their own.[121]

At Emanu-El the sanctuary was draped in black and kaddish was said for the vigilantes' martyr, James King of William, a Christian who added his father's first name to his own to differentiate himself from the other James Kings in the city.[122] The memorial service was evidence of the support enjoyed by the movement among Jews such as the well-known journalist and Emanu-El board member Seixas Solomons, who served as officers in the vigilantes' five-thousand-man military arm.[123]

Many other Jews simply hoped the militia would sweep the streets of the criminal element. According to one pro-vigilante newspaper, Jewish businessmen were vulnerable to "scoundrels and cowardly bullies," who "have omitted no opportunity to harass and vex and rob them." Referring by name to two Irishmen targeted and deported by the insurrectionists, the writer continued, "It was the pride of the Mulligans and the Billy Carrs to scoff at the Jews and in pure fun to appropriate their wares and merchandise. No wonder they rejoice at the expatriation of such pests. They can walk the streets of San Francisco today without being jostled and derided by cowardly shoulder strikers."[124] Modern scholarship, however, has revealed little support for the claim that the Vigilance Committee actually brought down the crime rate.[125]

The vigilantes also won the support of many Jewish merchants by forming a new party in 1856, intended not only to destroy Mayor Broderick's corrupt political machine, but also to reduce taxes and sharply curtail municipal expenditures. Jesse Seligman (brother of Emanu-El's president) was one of the powerful Committee of 21 that nominated the candidates of the pro-business People's Party, which remained in power until the mid-1870s and essentially ran the city on behalf of the merchants.[126]

Even before the vigilantes, however, Jews engaged in politics to a degree unusual in the United States at the time. Native-born Sephardim led the way, since the far more numerous Central Europeans were often not yet citizens nor in full command of the English language. Emanu-El's first two presidents, Abraham Labatt and Joseph Shannon, were also local office holders, and in 1852 two Jews were sent to the State Assembly from San Francisco: Isaac Cardozo, uncle of the future U.S. Supreme Court justice, and the half-Sephardi Elcan Heydenfeldt. Although the Southern-born Heydenfeldt shamelessly opposed the right of blacks to testify in court, this first Jewish California legislator also advocated some progressive causes, most notably a statewide system of public education.[127]

The most respected Jew in town was Heydenfeldt's older brother, Solomon. In 1851, soon after arriving from Alabama, he was nearly chosen by the legislature as a United States senator. The following year he became one of the three state supreme court justices, joining another Jew, Henry Lyons of Philadelphia. (Although born of Jewish immigrants from Frankfurt, Lyons does not appear to have practiced the Jewish faith or to have been connected with any Jewish institution.)* Heydenfeldt, deeply committed to the rule of law, was one of the few prominent citizens to speak out against the vigilantes. Regrettably, his outstanding career, like that of his brother, was blemished by his opposition to nonwhites being put on the witness stand: in 1854 he ruled against allowing the testimony of Chinese in any case involving a white.[128]

---

*The same may be said of two distant relatives of the Heydenfeldts: Washington Bartlett, who became governor of California in 1886, and his cousin Washington A. Bartlett, who, installed by the U.S. military in 1846, became the first *alcalde* (mayor) of the settlement by the bay and renamed the town known as Yerba Buena "San Francisco" on January 30 of the following year (Norton B. Stern, "Washington Bartlett: California's Jewish Governor," in *Sephardic Jews in the Western States*, vol. 1, ed. William M. Kramer [Los Angeles, 1996], 67).

In the 1850s Northern Californian Jews were numerous and easily identifi-able, influential, and, in some cases, conspicuously well off. Yet despite the frustration and violence that the boom and bust economy of the Gold Rush decade naturally brought in its wake, Jews were invariably spared their neighbors' wrath, with the exception of a few scattered incidents, mainly in the mining towns. As a contemporary commentator points out, they could not be viewed as "intruders." He continued, "There was no aristocracy . . . only a rag tag gang of money-hungry pioneers of heteroge-neous origins, welded together into a 'frontier brotherhood' community. As the 'first families' became encrusted, they became encrusted necessarily in amalgam with the 'first families' of the Jewish community."[129]

Other minority groups were racially excluded from that instant aris-tocracy and bore the brunt of the masses' discontent. American Indians were virtually exterminated, Mexicans and Chileans often driven off their mining claims, blacks prohibited from voting or testifying in court. The most common scapegoats were the Chinese, and their plight in California recalls the ordeal of the Jews in Russia during the same years. Persecuted because they clung to a distinct ancient and unfamiliar culture, they banded together for self-protection and were then accused of being inas-similable.

California, though, was not scarred by a millennium and a half of Judeo-phobia emanating from the Church. Of course, aggressive missionary ac-tivity could be found on the Pacific Coast, organized first by Catholic or-ders and then by Protestant evangelists. But the diversity of the population precluded the dominance of any one religious group (with the later excep-tion of the Mormons in Utah), and in this respect the West differed even from other regions in the United States.

Whether it was caused by the great distance from established religious centers, the emphasis on the individual, or even the dramatic landscape that lent itself to a personal spirituality, doctrinal and theological conflict some-how lost its sharp edge west of the Rockies. Race was determinative, as it was everywhere in America; religion was not.

Of course, antipathy to Jews could also emanate from a deep-seated fear of "Jewish influence" and innovation. In late nineteenth-century Europe Jews came under heavy attack for their growing activity in such fields as industry, banking, transportation, retail trade, journalism, and politics. Yet the entrepreneurial spirit that permeated the dynamic American West made this modern anti-Semitism a rarity. In California, Jews were admired precisely because of their efforts at modernization.

The most serious attack on pioneer Jews was provoked by the controversy over the Sunday Closing Law. In 1855 Assembly Speaker William Stow, originally from upstate New York, who represented Santa Cruz, attributed Jewish opposition to the blue laws to a desire to make a fast dollar and leave. Stow, an adherent of the antiforeign, secretive Know Nothing Party, powerful in California in the mid-1850s, urged a special tax on Jews to drive them away.[130]

When anti-Semitic incidents did occur, Jewish leaders met them forthrightly and adroitly. San Francisco assemblyman E. G. Buffum fiercely denounced the Speaker's remarks. The primary response, though, was prepared by Abraham Labatt's son Henry, who acted as the unofficial spokesman for the Jewish community. Only twenty-three, the Yale graduate was already one of San Francisco's most prominent attorneys. He authored a number of law books (welcome in these years, when "generally the lawyer carried his library in his hat and his office on the back of a mule")[131] and in 1855 was elected clerk of the superior court. Labatt's incisive letter to the Speaker, printed in several western newspapers, skillfully exposed both Stow's ignorance and his dishonesty. Labatt enumerated the Jews' many contributions on the coast and then asked,

Have the Jews squatted upon your lands? If so, I have yet to learn who; the Jews are not squatters.

Have they built grogshops to poison the people? Surely not; they are not rum-sellers. Have they filled your jails or taxed the state with criminal trials? Surely not; they are not robbers, murderers, or leading politicians [i.e., political bosses].

Have their females prostituted the morals of young men? Surely not; they are noted for the virtue of their mothers and the chastity of their daughters.

I do claim Mr. Speaker . . . that [the Jews] are good citizens, and better than you; and . . . worthy men, worthier than you; and that they would scorn to vilify the Gentiles as you have grossly and falsely vilified them. . . .

Pray on whom will you commence [to levy the special tax]? In the Supreme Court where sits on the bench . . . one Jew? . . . What will you do in the halls of legislation, or public offices, the bar, and medical fraternity? Surely Jews fill or have filled these positions in our state, and without the like disgrace . . . that hovers over yourself![132]

Labatt warned that "voters of this state will remember these facts, and . . . every Jew will bear it in mind a long day,"[133] and one local newspaper stated that Stow's anti-Semitism cost him the gubernatorial nomination.*

However, there emerged in the 1850s a more subtle form of anti-Semitism that eluded even those as watchful as Labatt. As urban historian Peter Decker has revealed, Jewish merchants seeking commercial loans were held to a much higher standard than non-Jews:

> R. G. Dun [forerunner of Dun and Bradstreet] almost always noted if a mer-
> chant was a "Jew" or "Israelite." If . . . not accompanied with a positive qual-
> ifier such as "White Jew" or "an Israelite of the better classes," the religious
> affiliation more often than not carried with it an assumption of bad credit. . . .
> A credit report on two German Jews who owned rather substantial assets
> warned: "They are Hebrews. May be good (for credit) *if well watched;* they
> are *tricky.*"[134]

But Jews usually prevailed, often borrowing from family members or other coreligionists. Like a number of Asian groups in America today, Jews were able to overcome economic discrimination through their social cohesion and close family ties.

Overall, San Francisco Jews achieved unparalleled standing in mid-nineteenth-century America, and one gesture in particular demonstrates the sensitivity to the "Israelites" shown by the city. In September 1858, "Steamer Day," when mail and packages were to be put aboard a ship to the East Coast, fell on Yom Kippur. So that Jews could observe the holy day, Steamer Day was officially postponed. The *Daily Alta California,* the city's leading newspaper, respectfully described the Day of Atonement and enthusiastically approved the "deference" paid to the Jews, "who occupy prominent positions and have won the respect and esteem of all."

---

*The Sunday Closing Law, less important to Labatt than the anti-Jewish tirade it trig-
gered, passed the legislature, but it was declared unconstitutional in 1858, when Solomon
Heydenfeldt, now in private practice, successfully defended a Sacramento Jew who had
kept his store open on the Christian Sabbath. The court held that because he shut his
shop on Saturday he should be exempt from having to close Sunday (William M. Kramer,
"The Earliest Important Jewish Attorney in California, Solomon Heydenfeldt," *WSJH*
23 [January 1991]: 154–55). Yet later the court overturned that decision, and blue laws
remained in force until repealed by the state legislature in 1883.

The paper concluded, "No other part of the world can instance a similar act of liberality."[135]

From the outset, San Francisco Jewry not only defended itself well but also felt committed to aid oppressed Jews elsewhere. By mid-decade ninety families in the city subscribed to national Jewish newspapers;[136] from these organs and the local Jewish press they were well informed about the condition of their brethren overseas. Early on they contributed to communities under pressure, such as the Jews in Morocco. In 1861, under the guidance of Rabbi Henry, Congregation Sherith Israel responded with warmth and generosity to the first *shaliach*, or emissary, from the Holy Land to visit San Francisco, Abraham Nissan.[137] A few years later another messenger from Jerusalem, Nathan Notkin, was rewarded for his long journey with a check for $460 from the Grand Lodge of the B'nai B'rith and smaller donations from Jews in Sacramento and the mining towns; he would return to Northern California in the late 1870s.[138]

Most impressive, though, was the mass meeting in January 1859 protesting an outrage in Bologna, Italy—the kidnapping of a Jewish child by papal guards. Edgardo Mortara, aged six, had been secretly baptized by his nurse and was therefore considered Catholic by Pope Pius IX, who placed him in a monastery rather than return him to his parents. The Vatican was flooded by a storm of criticism, and San Francisco's response was the largest in America.[139] More than three thousand people gathered in Musical Hall to hear a series of speeches and resolutions.

The deep regional and class differences within the Jewish community were bridged during this event, and the list of the event's conveners, which included the presidents of the two leading congregations, the three benevolent societies, and B'nai B'rith, reflected unity in the face of crisis. Justice Solomon Heydenfeldt, the meeting's chair, spoke of "the power of public opinion, which, if excited properly in this instance, [will make] the Mortara Case the last of its kind."[140]

A committee chaired by Rabbi Henry drafted resolutions, the most important of which urged the U.S. government to cooperate with European countries "to suppress religious intolerance and persecution, such as exhibits itself in the Mortara case."[141] The declarations were sent to Moses Montefiore in London, coordinating a global effort to have the Mortara boy released.

Rabbi Eckman, whose *Gleaner* covered the case extensively, was rarely so impassioned. His speech excoriated "the superannuated Roman Canon Law . . . antagonistic to civilization, progress and religious toleration all over the world." But he also sensed the danger of vehement anti-Catholicism overtaking the huge crowd of Christians and Jews. Mindful of the violence recently directed against Irish immigrants, he urged that "the deed of the Roman Executive [not be] instrumental in raising any ill-feeling against Roman Catholics."[142]

Like Eckman, Rabbi Henry also delivered one of the most important addresses of his career that night. Sherith Israel's spiritual leader declared that the purpose of his committee's eight resolutions was "to show the world at large that, even on this far western shore, the broad Pacific, humanity has found a home."[143] Echoing his colleague, he declared he "had not come to denounce Catholicism, but to denounce an act of outrageous cruelty."[144] The rabbis' prudence was in sharp contrast to the incendiary anti-Catholic remarks of Jewish leaders in other parts of the country, most notably Isaac Mayer Wise, who castigated all priests as hypocrites.[145] In the West, though, cooperation and mutual respect tended to characterize interfaith relations from the beginning. The event in Musical Hall revealed the goodwill of several Christian clergymen, including William Anderson Scott of Calvary Presbyterian, the leading minister in the city, who expressed their indignation at the Vatican and sympathy for the Mortara family.[146]

With the exception of the Catholic organs, the local press uniformly lauded the mass meeting. A *San Francisco Times* editorial declared it "*the sacred duty of our government* to protest against the Mortara *outrage*."[147] That editorial and many others, as well as the entire proceedings of the mass meeting, were soon published in a pamphlet circulated throughout the city—an early document of highly effective Jewish community relations.

Leading Jews, overwhelmed by such an ardent and ecumenical public response, realized perhaps for the first time that the diverse, open society taking shape on the West Coast could not only be a center of protest against injustice but also serve as a sanctuary for the politically persecuted. This was articulated in the evening's closing speech by Manuel Noah, who was soon to become editor of the *Daily Alta California*. Like his eminent father, Mordecai—diplomat, playwright, New York sheriff, and proto-Zionist—Manuel had a propensity for looking into the future: "This grand swelling voice of sympathy . . . will redound to the credit of California as the eyes of all . . . oppressed people may look toward this great State on the Pacific as a land of refuge."[148]

By the late 1850s it was clear that the Jewish community had played a key role in transforming a crude frontier outpost into a thriving center of commerce and culture. None of the groups in the diverse metropolis could match the upward occupational mobility of the Jews, who often made a rapid leap from peddler or petty shopkeeper to solid merchant. "Almost all of them are doing well," claimed the Jewish world traveler I. J. Benjamin, who arrived in 1860: "A large part of the wealth of California is in their hands; they have acquired it by thrift and sobriety, by steadfast industry and toil."[149]

As has been noted, San Francisco also produced many spectacular failures in its first decade, human wrecks ruined by the vagaries of nature or the economy. Peter Decker contends that economic opportunity was actually no greater in early San Francisco than in the East and that Thoreau had a point when he declared California "three thousand miles closer to hell."[150]

But using quantitative analysis, Decker has demonstrated that Jews were the exception. Despite the hard-luck stories of men like Abraham Abrahamsohn and Alexander Mayer, Jews as a group "were more successful than others. . . . For them, at least, the 'American Dream' was a reality."[151] The self-discipline and mercantile skills with which they came and the social cohesion and community consciousness they developed on the West Coast served them well in the Darwinian struggle that was nineteenth-century capitalism.

Daniel Levy may have romanticized the impact of the newly won prosperity on Jewish daily life, but his description of 1858 is nevertheless instructive:

> Anyone leaving California in those [Gold Rush] days, not so long ago in time, but far removed by events, and returning today, would certainly not recognize it. Instead of the social chaos he had left, he would be pleased and delighted to find about a thousand Jewish families with pure morals and with homes that contained all the conditions necessary for comfort and even luxury. In place of the old and miserable hovels, ravaged by vermin and constantly exposed to total destruction by fire, he would see elegant brick homes or dainty and graceful cottages, hidden among trees and flowers; charming nests for people, where Americans have learned so well to shelter their domestic bliss.
>
> The ladies, almost all of them young, well brought up, more or less musical (there is a piano in every parlor), get together either for Saturday or

Sunday visits, at the Temple, at dances or at the theater, or for their charitable meetings. All this creates a charming and serene social life. I do not think that many European communities can boast of as large a number of young and happy households living in affluence.[152]

In less than a decade a San Francisco Jewish identity had begun to emerge. Much of it, as Levy indicates, was a bourgeois mentality, the result of recently gained wealth and respectability. But also evident were the variations within the Jewish community. Politically, it tended to be centrist, yet conservative and liberal strains were noticeable too, sometimes in the same individual; socially, it was tightly bound by convention, though one could make out faint hints of a nonconformist streak to come; religiously, it was relatively unobservant, but pockets of Orthodoxy could be found. Money counted for a great deal in this Jewish community, and place of origin only slightly less. Yet from the very beginning Jews were also known for their generosity, both in taking care of their own and in improving the city as a whole. Perhaps most noteworthy was the uncommon degree of acceptance, indeed respect, accorded Jews by the larger society. As the well-traveled Benjamin wrote, "Nowhere else are they regarded with as much esteem by their non-Jewish brothers and nowhere else . . . so highly valued in social or political circles."[153]

It must have been exhilarating for the young immigrants, most of whom only a few years earlier had chafed under repressive regimes of European kings. Indeed, Jews in the American West in the second half of the nineteenth century were arguably the freest anywhere in the world. But they did not take that freedom for granted, as shown by the skill and unity with which they faced enemies both at home and overseas. The unprecedented conditions of life on the Pacific Coast, already evident in the 1850s, would allow for the development of a notably creative and adaptable Jewish community. And California in turn would be shaped to a remarkable degree by Jews. That mutual process would characterize the next century and a half.

TWO

Woven into the Fabric

The Confident Community of the Gilded Age

FOLLOWING THE GOLD RUSH DECADE the area west of the Rockies emerged as a mighty commercial region with San Francisco at its vortex, and the city's domination of the hinterland was aptly compared with that of ancient Rome.[1] By 1880 San Francisco's economy outstripped that of the other twenty-four western American cities combined; it manufactured 60 percent of the goods and handled nearly all the imports and exports of the three West Coast states.[2]

The city profited immensely from the Comstock silver strike in the eastern Sierras in 1859, which yielded hundreds of millions of dollars. Nevada, whose mines were controlled on Montgomery Street, was virtually a colony of San Francisco; soon Alaska and Hawaii would have almost the same status.

The War Between the States—because of the tremendous demand it generated for gold, wheat, and wool—also propelled California's economic climb in the 1860s. Technological advances spurred business activity even further; prior to the transcontinental telegraph in 1861, it had taken ten days by Pony Express to send a message to the East Coast. But the state's isolation was truly ended by the transcontinental railroad, completed in 1869. The train reduced the coast-to-coast trip from a month to a week—so fast, people marveled, that one didn't even have to take a bath en route.

Jewish merchants took advantage of the great opportunities that presented themselves in the Gilded Age. They opened department stores, as they did elsewhere across America, but in San Francisco some of them went much further, establishing colossal corporations reaching distant shores. Whether they made their money locally or internationally, the leading Jewish families amassed impressive wealth and stature. They built sumptuous Victorian mansions and collected fine art; they erected a magnificent synagogue and established an extensive network of communal organizations.

The new money, of course, widened the already-established gaps between Jew and Jew, which were based on pride of place: The Bavarians looked down on the Prussian Poles, who looked down on the Russians. Alsatians and Sephardim were close to the top of the pecking order, Hungarians and Czechs in the middle, and Rumanians near the bottom. The synagogues and benevolent societies reflected this stratification, which was similar to New York's.

Yet Jewish behavior was less constrained than it was in the East, the age-old question "What will the goyim think?" asked less frequently and less anxiously. Anti-Semitism was milder in the West than in the rest of the United States, and when it did appear it was roundly refuted by powerful Sephardi polemicists. Meanwhile, the town's leading Jewish journalist regularly ridiculed Christianity (and just about everything else), and few seemed to mind. The most hated family in San Francisco, headed by Jewish social-climbing newspaper publishers whose stock-in-trade was defamation, somehow escaped the wrath of anti-Semites. Even the looniest street person was a Jew, and the populace adored him.

In calmer Oakland a much smaller and more conventional Jewish community took root. There, too, Jews felt at ease in society, and this self-assurance helped to produce several mavericks who believed they could make a lasting impact on the world—and partially succeeded.

WAR IN THE EAST, EMBARRASSMENT AT HOME

Conscription was never enforced in California during the Civil War, largely because the government deemed the cost of transportation to the front prohibitive. Since the state was spared the "terrible and destructive [fighting] in the East," according to Henry Seligman, "peace reigns in our midst, our homes and firesides are blessed with plenty . . . commerce follows its usual channels, and is more prosperous than ever."[3]

The Seligmans were among the most outspoken supporters of President Lincoln in a city so patriotic that it named its central meeting ground Union Square. But there was also a degree of pro-Southern sentiment, some of which emanated from the Jewish community. The Alabaman Solomon Heydenfeldt closed his law practice when the state legislature required all attorneys to swear a loyalty oath to the Union.[4] And Rabbi Eckman, never averse to voicing unpopular views in his *Gleaner,* opposed the war and advocated independence for the rebels. He even labeled as "undignified" the local synagogues' practice of flying the Stars and Stripes.[5]

Eckman, who had held three Southern pulpits, was by no means a rabid secessionist, but his remarks triggered a serious controversy. His paper was often mistakenly regarded as an official Jewish organ, and it unwittingly provided ammunition for a local pro-Unionist daily, the antiforeign *American Flag,* which had earlier questioned the loyalty of the Irish and now impugned the Jews. In the spring of 1864 it declared, "A large majority of the wealthiest Jews of California and particularly of San Francisco *are Copperheads!* [poisonous snakes, and the name by which Lincoln's backers called northerners who supported the South]." It urged an economic boycott against "the Israelites."[6]

Such bigotry was commonplace across America late in the war, when Jews on both sides were subjected to attacks based on the stereotype of the rapacious Jewish smuggler, and nurtured by wartime inflation and food shortages. Jews were frequently accused of perfidy and profiteering, and General Grant issued an order (later rescinded by Lincoln) evacuating them "as a class" from three border states occupied by his army.

Yet during the Civil War Judeophobia was nowhere as thoroughly condemned as it was in San Francisco.[7] As early as 1861, the *Evening Bulletin* labeled the charge of Jewish disloyalty "base slander."[8] The *Flag's* assault three years later was countered by the *Morning Call,* which proclaimed the Jews among "the most ardent Unionists," adding, "in this country there can be no classification of patriotism or treason upon the basis of sectarian creeds."[9]

Unfortunately, the *Gleaner* made things difficult for the many allies of the Jews. Angered by the *Flag's* charges, it began to brag of Jewish "superiority," claiming "our children receive a better education, and our men and women lead more virtuous lives [than] the rest of American citizens." During the tense year of 1864, the Jewish paper held that "we [Jews] control the nations of the earth by virtue of our penetration [i.e., insight] and our means."* [10]

The boasts had immediate consequences. A popular athletic society, the San Francisco Olympic Club, expelled its eleven Jewish members. The *Gleaner* reacted with more foolishness: "We claim for the Jews more virtue, and more humanity, as we claim for them more penetration and more intelligence." It also heaped scorn on the young country even amidst the greatest emergency in its history: "When we speak of morality . . . we must certainly leave America out of the question . . . a nation running riot with itself."[11]

Now the *Flag* intensified its call for "every Christian . . . to avoid" Jewish stores: "Let no patriotic women gladden the heart of the reviling Israelite by the chinking of American coin, until he shall have made atonement for this unpardonable insult of her people." Other newspapers, mostly in the Gold Country, launched further attacks on the Jews.[12]

The furor subsided only when two hundred leading San Francisco Jews, including the rabbis of Sherith Israel and Emanu-El, signed a statement printed in the two largest local dailies. It condemned the *Gleaner*'s editorial, which "filled us with indignation and disgust [and is] an outrageous insult to a noble, generous and highly cultivated [American] people, of whom we are proud to form an integral part."[13] This expression of loyalty quickly caused the Olympic Club to reverse its ban on Jewish members, and even the *American Flag* tempered its stance. San Francisco Jewry recovered from its self-inflicted wound and again came to be regarded as a mainstay of Unionism.

This was especially evident when news of Lincoln's assassination came over the telegraph lines. Although the entire city was dismayed, the Jewish community, comprised of so many grateful immigrants, seemed particularly grief-stricken. A eulogy for the "Patriarch Abraham," delivered at the recently formed District Four Grand Lodge of B'nai B'rith, articulated this special sorrow: To "the household of Israel no calamity could be greater—for as the adopted citizens of this great country we have found it to be the liberal and natural home of all tongues, creeds, and nations of the

---

*Eckman himself, who was in Portland, Oregon, at the time, may not have been directly responsible for the offending editorial. It was evidently written by his interim replacement, Isidore Choynski, who was starting a career as one of the most aggressive and infuriating Jewish journalists in the country.

earth, and in Abraham Lincoln we have found the perfect representative of the generous principles of the Government."[14]

Emanu-El's Rabbi Elkan Cohn, like his Unitarian friend the Reverend Thomas Starr King a champion of the Federals, was informed of the president's death just as he mounted the pulpit for his Saturday sermon. He reportedly collapsed and wept before rising to deliver a moving impromptu tribute in his heavy German accent. Lincoln, he intoned in his sermon, which was printed in the *Alta California* as well as the Anglo-Jewish press, "stood among us like a mighty giant, holding with his hands the tottering columns of our great commonwealth and planting them secure upon the solid basis of general freedom and humanity."[15] Cohn was chosen as one of the thirty-eight distinguished citizens of the West who served as pallbearers in a procession through San Francisco.

"MUCHO DINERO"

In 1871, when postwar prosperity was near its peak, an article in the *Morning Call,* bluntly entitled "Mucho Dinero," listed the net worth of the hundred richest men in San Francisco.[16] Five hundred thousand dollars was the smallest amount appearing on this golden register, and eleven of those recorded as worth more than half a million dollars were Jews, all merchants hailing from Bavaria, Alsace, or other points west of Berlin. One need not accept the list as completely accurate to conclude that it represented a remarkable achievement for local Jews, given that the large majority of non-Jews on it—men with names like Ralston, Stanford, and Lick—had had the advantage of being born and educated in the United States.

Most of the Jewish fortunes were made by selling wholesale clothing and other dry goods, a sector of the economy almost monopolized by Jews. The Seligmans, Levi Strauss, and Strauss's brother-in-law and partner, David Stern (all high on the *Morning Call*'s list) were already established during the 1850s, as were August Helbing, William Steinhart, and many others. The following decade saw the rise of the Schwabacher brothers, Abraham Gunst, and Raphael Peixotto, one of the few Sephardim in an industry dominated by Bavarians.

Yet nothing testified to the city's explosive economic growth after the Civil War better than the new manufacturing sector, comprised of noisy factories and foundries that cropped up primarily south of Market Street. Levi Strauss and David Stern are examples of merchants who made the transition to manufacturing the goods that previously they had only sold. Rather than have their popular work clothes produced in New York by Strauss's brother, they opened a factory, first on Fremont Street and later on Battery, saving on labor and transportation costs. In 1873 the firm obtained the patent for the riveted pants destined to conquer the world. The Hecht brothers, meanwhile, were among the city's largest producers of boots and shoes, employing hundreds of workers, including many Chinese, in the 1860s and 1870s. Simon Koshland and William Steinhart owned the town's largest woolen mills. The manufacture of cigars (an industry as large as clothing) was dominated by Moses Gunst, Herman Heyneman, and the partners Mendel Esberg, Simon Bachman, and Julius Ehrman. In the 1870s, Aaron "Honest" Fleishhacker became a leading manufacturer of cardboard boxes. Producing paper was also the business of Anthony Zellerbach, who opened a one-room basement store in San Francisco in 1870 and lived to see his concern become one of the largest of its kind in the world.

Jews also established most of the city's leading department stores, which carried wares from all over the globe and almost resembled museums in their elegance. The bon vivant Raphael Weill of Alsace opened his famed White House, offering fine French imports, in 1870. Adolph and Achille Roos, Isaac Magnin, David Livingston, and Solomon Gump built mighty retail enterprises bearing their names until late in the twentieth century. Others, like William Haas and Frederick Castle, grew wealthy as wholesale grocers. Joseph Brandenstein established a thriving tobacco dealership, and one of his ten children, Max, founded the firm of M. J. Brandenstein and Company, the giant tea and coffee concern later known as MJB.

Some early San Francisco Jews made the leap from retailing to banking—still a crude industry during the Gold Rush years, when a strongbox in a saloon or store was a typical depository. The brothers Daniel and Jonas Meyer, originally tobacconists, entered banking as early as the 1850s, as did the former dry goods dealers Alexander, Simon, and Elie Lazard, Alsatian Jews who later transferred the headquarters of their famous bank, Lazard Frères, to Paris. Later Philip Lilienthal, who had worked closely with the Seligmans, major bankers in both New York and San Francisco, established his successful firm, the Anglo-California Bank of London. Most prominent in the realm of finance was Isaias W. Hellman, who in 1871 founded the Farmers and Merchants Bank in Los Angeles and much later moved to San Francisco to save the Nevada Bank, which he merged with Wells Fargo.

Jews were also conspicuous in securities. Adolph Sutro's cousin Charles was one of the city's first stockbrokers, and when a regulated stock exchange was finally formed in the early 1880s, more than half the charter members were Jews.[17] But invariably the best investment was urban real estate, and many Jewish businessmen multiplied their assets through the accumulation of residential and commercial property. The Bavarian Michael Reese amassed more than five million dollars in this way by 1871, putting him near the top of the *Morning Call's* clique of business barons.

Arriving in the city in 1877, America's leading rabbi, Isaac Mayer Wise, was amazed, writing, "Every other house, almost, in the wholesale quarter, is occupied by a Jewish firm. . . . They are very prominent in industry, finance and commerce, some living in princely mansions and occupying high positions in society . . . more prominent than the Hebrews as a class in any other city I have visited."[18]

Yet even he had not fully fathomed the breakthrough made by San Francisco Jewry's newly minted commercial elite. For Jews were widely engaged in dry goods, manufacturing, and retailing in many other American cities during the second half of the nineteenth century, and in New York they far surpassed their West Coast cousins as bankers and stockbrokers. In Northern California, however, Jews were distinguished by their great range of occupations and activity in arenas entered by relatively few of their coreligionists elsewhere. They were involved in enterprises from the fur trade in Alaska to wheat farming in the Central Valley, from sugar mills in the Philippines to vineyards near San Jose. The venturesome spirit of those who had come west, the extraordinary opportunities that awaited, and the relative lack of anti-Semitism combined to permit Jews to blaze new economic trails.

Among the most daring endeavors was the Alaska Commercial Company, founded in 1868 by the brothers-in-law Louis Sloss and Lewis Gerstle.[19] After selling groceries and later securities, they shifted their sights to Alaska soon after the United States purchased it from Russia. With several partners they bought a string of trading posts—including boats, wharves, warehouses, and merchandise—from Sitka to the Bering Sea. The real prize, though, was gaining control of the remote Pribilof Islands, rich in fur seals. Sloss and Gerstle bid for a twenty-year lease from the federal government that would allow them to harvest the animals. Aware, however, that as foreign-born Jews they would be at a disadvantage when those in Washington determined who received the concession, they enlisted the help of the well-connected general John F. Miller, who was later to become a U.S. senator. He obtained the concession at a favorable rate—and not for the highest bid, as it turned out.[20] Although Sloss and Gerstle's company was required to abide by a host of regulations protecting both the seals and the native Aleuts, it reaped annual profits of more than a million dollars on the seventy-five thousand skins it was allowed to take. It also harvested the rare otter seals—sold in London for $1,000 each—conducted a huge business in salmon, and opened new trading posts in the interior of the territory, operating ninety in all. The scale of their enterprise was such that Sloss and Gerstle considered privately financing a canal across Central America to speed the delivery of the skins and salmon to the East Coast and Europe. One of the nation's largest corporations, the entire empire was run from a modest office at 310 Sansome Street. Neither of the two principals ever visited Alaska.

Similarly ambitious was the towering Isaac Friedlander from Hanover, whose height was reported by a local newspaper to be almost seven feet. In the late 1850s Friedlander cornered the market in wheat, one of the most lucrative crops in California until the late nineteenth century.[21] Among the first to see the state's agricultural potential, he accumulated thousands of acres in the San Joaquin and Livermore valleys. He built a network of irrigation canals and commanded a fleet of twenty ships to send his produce as far as England and Australia. Friedlander suffered some serious setbacks, most notably the drought of 1860, and he died in 1878 at age fifty-four from a heart condition, probably worsened by his high-risk enterprises.[22] The acquisitive "Grain King" was one of the few Jewish tycoons who occasionally drew the wrath of anti-Semites, but at the same time he countered the stereotype of the overurbanized Jew with his single-minded focus on cultivating the soil.

Large-scale agriculture attracted other pioneer-period Northern California Jews. Simon Newman, with profits made in retailing, bought large tracts of land in the 1870s, where he grew wheat and barley and raised sheep and cattle. The town of Newman, named for him, reflects his influence in the Central Valley. Samuel Lachman, also a former storekeeper, was a pioneer in viticulture, and by the 1870s he was among the first to market California wines in the East.[23] Later his son Henry, who acquired extensive vineyards near Mission San Jose, founded a cartel known as the California Wine Makers' Corporation. Other pioneering Jews established wineries in the Napa Valley.[24] But it was I. W. Hellman who dominated the industry after 1900 by taking financial control of the California Wine Association, a syndicate that produced two-thirds of the state's output.[25]

And then there was David Lubin from Russian Poland, a highly successful merchandiser in San Francisco and Sacramento who, with his half brother, Harris Weinstock, went into wheat farming and fruit growing in the 1880s. Their holdings did not put them among Northern California's largest landholders, yet these self-educated visionaries had a high profile as advocates for their fellow farmers, and their initiation of cooperatives would change the course of agriculture in the American West and around the world.

Perhaps the most ambitious Jewish businessman was Adolph Sutro, who also excelled as an engineer, politician, book collector, and philanthropist. After a number of reverses during the turbulent 1850s, the muscular young man, a husband and father of three, established himself as a tobacconist in San Francisco. But in 1860, the discovery of gold and silver in Nevada drew him away from the comforts of home to the rough mining town of Virginia City. Sutro sold his three tobacco stores and went alone to the Sierras while his wife, Leah, remained in the city, helping to support the family by managing two boardinghouses.[26] He opened a refining mill near the mines to extract the silver quartz ore using an innovative method he and a partner had devised in a tiny laboratory on Market Street.[27]

The mill proved profitable, but within a few years he hit upon a much bolder idea: a four-mile tunnel, 1,500 feet below ground, through the Comstock Lode. For more than fifteen years he would be consumed by this mammoth project, which ultimately would make his fortune and reputation. Sutro had seen firsthand not only the miners' slow work pace but also the hazards to their health and safety. The shafts were unbearably hot and in danger of floods, fires, and cave-ins. His ingenious solution was a massive subterranean passageway to drain the mines, provide fresh air, and allow for the removal of ore in handcars.

The miners hailed the idea, but the problems Sutro faced were legion. In Washington he obtained the right-of-way for the tunnel, but he was denied federal financing. Turned down for government loans in Sacramento and Carson City as well, he sought private funding, a grueling nine-year effort that took him to New York and Europe. His chief obstacle was the all-powerful Bank of California, controlled by the unscrupulous William Ralston, who dazzled San Franciscans with his extravagant Palace Hotel and lavish lifestyle. His "Bank Ring" had acquired most of the Comstock's riches by over-mortgaging mining companies and then foreclosing on them. Ralston and his Nevada lieutenant, William Sharon, perceived Sutro a threat to their continued looting of the Comstock. They tried to block him by shutting his company out of the stock market that they manipulated, blackening his reputation among New York financiers, and even attempting to repeal his federal permit.[28] But Sutro defended himself through a series of persuasive reports outlining the tunnel's many benefits, which were distributed to public officials, potential investors, and the general public.[29]

In the summer of 1875 Ralston's empire crumbled, as his overextended bank, facing a run of nervous depositors, was forced to close. The next day, taking his daily swim in the bay, he mysteriously drowned. Sutro, who had already begun constructing the tunnel, had finally won his war against the Bank Ring. Three years later he completed one of the greatest engineering feats of the nineteenth century.

Ironically, the Sutro Tunnel, which functioned just as its inventor had predicted, fell far short of recovering its $6.5 million cost. By the time it opened, most of the high-quality silver had already been extracted. Sutro, however, had earlier sold his stock in the company and came away with almost a million dollars.[30]

With perfect timing he invested his profits in San Francisco real estate, depressed in the mid- and late 1870s. He bought prime downtown commercial property but also vast stretches of the "outside lands," the undeveloped, sand-covered southern and western sections of the city, all the way to the oceanfront. There he would rebuild the Cliff House (a far larger and more ornate building than the utilitarian tourist attraction that exists today) and construct the Sutro Baths and a vast estate known as Sutro Heights. In all, he purchased one-twelfth of the land of the entire city.[31] It was a tremendous wager on the future, but, like so many bets made by other pioneering Jewish entrepreneurs, it would pay off spectacularly.

A WEB OF INSTITUTIONS

Despite his world-famous library of Judaica, Sutro, a freethinker, had little connection with Judaism or Jewish institutions in San Francisco, save at the time of his wedding and burial. Yet he was the exception. The large majority of prominent Jews joined organizations such as Congregation Emanu-El, the Eureka Benevolent Society, the Concordia Club, and the B'nai B'rith.

At the apex was Emanu-El, which in 1860 finally engaged a liberal rabbi, forty-year-old Elkan Cohn. Like his predecessor, Julius Eckman, Cohn was a Posener with a doctorate from the University of Berlin. Even-tempered and methodical, neither a stirring sermonizer nor a powerful writer, Cohn would remain for three decades, transforming the synagogue into a Reform temple, the first in the West to join Isaac Mayer Wise's Union of American Hebrew Congregations. Early on, Cohn streamlined the liturgy, initiated Friday evening services, and allowed men and women to sit together in the pews. Later he went much further, banning head-coverings in the synagogue, and for a year holding Sabbath services on Sundays.[32] He even replaced the traditional *shofar* (the ram's horn, blown on the High Holidays in almost every synagogue in the world) with a cornet played by a professional musician. "Classical Reform," as it was later known, would become even more pronounced later in the century and would characterize Emanu-El for generations to come.

While Cohn's radical reforms were ridiculed as far away as Europe, there was also opposition at home from Rabbi Eckman and many Emanu-El congregants.[33] They were appalled when Cohn engaged a Catholic opera singer for High Holiday services in 1863.[34] The final indignity was the adoption of a new prayer book the following year, abrogating the time-honored *minhag Ashkenaz,* which most of the members had known since childhood. In 1864 it led to the defection from Emanu-El of fifty-five households, which soon formed a new congregation, Ohabai Shalome.[35]

The breakaway families were not strictly Orthodox—they allowed mixed seating during services—but they insisted that the prayers remain unchanged. Their deeply felt sentiments were articulated by the president of the congregation, Joseph Mayer, who "called God as his witness that he bore the old Congregation no malice . . . but [said] their principles and his own did not coincide. The memory of his deceased parents, his early education and childhood was still fresh in his mind. He honored and loved his parents and would do violence to his feelings if he did not follow their teachings and example."[36]

Ohabai Shalome enlisted many other prominent laymen, including Simon Koshland, patriarch of the philanthropic family, and although he eventually rejoined Emanu-El, the nascent congregation took long strides. Within one year it erected a substantial synagogue on Mason Street and grew to 125 households. A decade later it engaged the Hungarian scholar Albert Bettelheim as its first full-time rabbi, and in 1898 the congregation would construct an elegant house of worship, the redwood Moorish-style Bush Street Temple, near Laguna Street.*

---

* After the demise of Ohabai Shalome in 1940, its sanctuary served as a center for Zen Buddhism for many decades, but it was nearly reclaimed by the Jewish

Despite the loss of a fifth of its membership to the Civil War–period "secession," Emanu-El pressed ahead with its earlier plans for a new home. In 1860, President Seligman had predicted that his synagogue, not quite a decade old, could soon become the largest Jewish congregation in America.[37] Only one year later, a choice lot was purchased on Sutter Street between Powell and Stockton, today the location of a medical building at 450 Sutter Street.

The Sutter Street Temple, including its furnishings worth almost $200,000, was dedicated on March 23, 1866, only six months past its scheduled completion date. Considered by many the most impressive building on the West Coast, it was designed by the Englishman William Patton, who had grown up among Norman churches in Durham and York. In 1863 he had won recognition for his creation of Thomas Starr King's stately Unitarian church, but Emanu-El would become his magnum opus. The big, brick edifice—80 by 120 feet—was not merely plastered with Gothic features, as had been the Broadway Synagogue, but "the arches, the pillars, the buttresses were built into the structure, as they would have been in a truly medieval church."[38]

Atop the graceful octagonal towers was the distinguishing mark of the temple, two bronze-plated domes tapering upward into smaller shining globes. These gold-tipped spires, 165 feet high, would be an integral part of the San Francisco skyline for the next four decades, a prominent landmark for ships entering the Golden Gate and a sight for hikers across the bay in the Berkeley hills.* Fifty feet high, the sanctuary was one of the largest vaulted chambers ever constructed in the state. Its black walnut pews could seat 1,200 people.

––––––––––

community in the early 1990s as a home for the Western Jewish History Center of the Judah L. Magnes Museum. Those plans did not materialize, however, and today only the imposing façade of the original structure remains—on a Korean senior center.

* Eadweard Muybridge's famous panoramic photomontage of the city's skyline shows Emanu-El's imposing towers. At first glance the domes appear Moorish, in the style of major German synagogues built only a few years earlier. But the domes, described by Patton as "pomegranate capitals, which crown the towers," were probably meant to symbolize the headpieces of the Torah, known in Hebrew as *rimmonim,* or pomegranates. The broad central window, with its Shield of David, likely represented the breastplate of the Torah (Allan Temko, "Temple Emanu-El of San Francisco," *Commentary* 26 [August 1958]: 114–15).

The Sutter Street Temple was part of the boom in synagogue construction throughout America in the 1860s as German Jews reached a new level of wealth and acculturation and demanded majestic homes for their growing congregations. Most impressive was New York's Emanu-El, which spent an unthinkable $600,000 on a twin-towered sanctuary on Fifth Avenue. Isaac Mayer Wise's Plum Street Temple in Cincinnati, in a style reminiscent of the Alhambra, was also built at this time at a cost of more than $250,000.

But the grand scale of Emanu-El's edifice indicated that a Jewish elite had crystallized in San Francisco as well—and faster than anywhere else. It opened barely a decade after the membership had struggled to build its first synagogue, and only fifteen years after the birth of the congregation, when sixty young men had pledged dues of two dollars a month.

The more traditionally inclined Sherith Israel, most of its members from Prussian Poland, also did well during the economic upswing of the Civil War decade. Although none of its members had become merchant-princes, as a few dozen of Emanu-El's members had, the Stockton Street Shul, with about 125 families, included some affluent retailers and wholesalers.

The Sherith Israel congregants, too, were now ready to leave congested North Beach, where they had outgrown their plain Gold Rush–era shul, for a larger and finer synagogue in a better location. In 1867, persuaded by its forceful new president, Charles Meyer (who gave the largest donation to the capital project, $1,000), the board voted to purchase a parcel on the corner of Taylor and Post streets, near Emanu-El's new Sutter Street Temple.[39] Both pioneer congregations would now be in the center of the city (as was the new Ohabai Shalome, on Mason Street). Sherith Israel's site was only four blocks from the Western Addition (at that time stretching from Larkin Street out to Divisadero Street), which had formerly been filled with sand dunes but had recently opened for residential development. Streets around Bush, O'Farrell, Pine, and Polk were beginning to attract Jewish families, and congregants could thus easily walk to services.

Completed in 1870, the sanctuary cost $70,000 to construct, about a third the price of Emanu-El's. The large structure, however, with upstairs galleries for women, could accommodate more than a thousand worshippers.[40] A strong earthquake in 1868 convinced the builders to make only the foundation and basement of brick; most of the neo-Gothic structure was built of wood.[41] A notable Moorish feature was added: four slender turrets projecting from the façade, the two tallest about eighty feet high.

The capital project had been a struggle for the midsized congregation, which still charged only $24 a year in dues and whose annual budget was less than $9,000.[42] The old Stockton Street building, purchased by Shaare Zedek, a small group of Russian Jews, fetched only $7,000. When Sherith Israel's plan to solicit donations from other West Coast Jewish communities failed, the board sold part of the new lot to a commercial developer, scaled back the original plans, and delayed construction a year.[43] Finally, through the sale of life seats, guaranteeing the holder the same spot in the sanctuary for the rest of his days ($150 was the top price), the down payment was secured.[44] The $50,000 mortgage, however, would prove almost crushing in the decades ahead.

The new synagogue initially energized the congregation, and enrollment swelled to almost two hundred. Yet the economic downturn of the 1870s, combined with a series of bitter internal conflicts, sapped the shul's strength. After long-serving Rabbi Henry was dismissed in 1869, the congregation voted overwhelmingly to end segregation of men and women during services.[45] But the new spiritual leader, Aaron Messing of Chicago—hired without a trial sermon or even an interview—was much more set in his traditional ways than the board realized, and he frustrated most of the membership by blocking further reforms.[46] He also damaged the always-fragile relations with Emanu-El by bashing Elkan Cohn in the national Jewish press as "a 'messiah' who has converted the whole town into a Sodom. He rides around on the Sabbath with a cigar in his mouth and says that Moses and his generation invented the Torah and we have no part in it. He gets $6,000 a year and is a very rich man."[47]

Within three years Messing was replaced by the learned and dynamic Rabbi Henry Vidaver.* Though born and raised in Warsaw, he had gravitated toward liberal Judaism in his youth and confided in friends his doubts about the divine authorship of the Torah.[48] At Sherith Israel he was a moderate reformer until his untimely death in 1882. He inaugurated an organ and choir, reorganized the religious school, and delivered the most engaging sermons of any rabbi in town.[49] But even he could not win back the scores of members who had left in the early 1870s, nor solve the many difficulties plaguing the congregation. Not until the next generation would Sherith Israel enter a phase of growth and vigor.

The most traditional of the major pioneer congregations was Rabbi Nathan Streisand's Beth Israel, established on the eve of the Civil War.

---

*Messing later took the pulpit of the more Orthodox Beth Israel, which he held until 1890 with much more success.

Unlike the other three synagogues, it remained in rented quarters until 1879, and for decades it drew its members not from the respectable Western Addition but rather from the gritty South of Market area, which had the highest concentration of blue-collar workers in the city.[50] Here, in shabby wooden dwellings—interspersed among boardinghouses filled with single men who labored on the docks—were a good number of Jewish families headed by tailors and small shopkeepers. They were immigrants from Prussian Poland and areas further east, under czarist control. To be sure, some Western European Jews also joined Beth Israel, but in the 1860s and '70s, few of its members belonged to the middle class.

But much of Beth Israel's flock prospered by the 1880s, and it counted in its ranks the most successful Orthodox businessmen. The congregation moved up, first to Turk Street, then to Geary near Octavia in the heart of the Western Addition, and, soon after the turn of the century, further west to a capacious home on Geary near Fillmore.[51] Dedicated clergy—most notably Rabbi M. S. Levy and Cantor Joseph Rabinowitz, both of whom arrived in the early 1890s—aided by highly active laymen made Beth Israel a viable institution.

The four major synagogues established by the end of the Civil War—one adamantly Reform (Emanu-El), two in effect Conservative, although that term was not yet in use (Sherith Israel and Ohabai Shalome), and one Orthodox (Beth Israel)—would remain the leading congregations in the city for the next seventy-five years. There was also the tiny Orthodox Shaare Zedek and at least two worship groups meeting in rented halls or private homes.

But during the Gilded Age the synagogue was not the locus of the Jewish community's vitality. By the end of the 1870s the city's Jewish population had passed sixteen thousand, making it the second largest Jewish community in the country.[52] Yet only one-sixth of Jewish families belonged to a congregation, about the same percentage as were synagogue members in the city 125 years later.[53] Even Emanu-El, with one of the most august sanctuaries in America, in 1877 had a membership of barely 250, less than before it had opened the Sutter Street Temple.[54]

More popular were the charitable associations and social societies, a phenomenon also seen among San Francisco's German Catholics, only 5 percent of whom reportedly attended mass regularly.[55] The city's largest Jewish organization in the second half of the nineteenth century was the Bavarian-led Eureka Benevolent Society, with more than 500 members in the late 1870s and 831 a decade later. Its assets, including a special fund for widows and orphans, amounted to nearly $150,000 by 1889, the interest on which, along with additional donations, went to support the needy. That year seventy-five Jews received a small monthly stipend, and more than five hundred households obtained one-time cash grants.[56] The First Hebrew Benevolent Society, closely aligned with Sherith Israel, was smaller, counting three hundred members in 1877, but was also very active.

With the aid of the B'nai B'rith's western region, funds were raised to establish the Pacific Hebrew Orphan Asylum. The new facility, including playgrounds, was dedicated on Divisadero Street near Golden Gate Park in 1877. Its leadership was also concerned with sheltering the elderly, and in the early 1870s acquired land for that purpose on the city's outskirts. But the Hebrew Home for the Aged Disabled actually opened much later, in rented quarters on Lyon Street in 1889, and then moved to a larger home on Lombard Street when it merged with the orphanage.[57]

In 1887 a group led by Frederick Castle, nearly all of them Emanu-El members, founded Mount Zion Hospital, the first Jewish hospital in the West. A modest building of twelve beds along with surgical suites, it was dedicated in January 1897. Two years later a fifty-bed unit was opened on Sutter Street between Scott and Divisadero.[58] The hospital's planners faced the thorny philosophical question of whether it would serve only Jewish patients, but the notion that it should be a nonsectarian institution prevailed.

The city's Young Men's Hebrew Association, forerunner of the Jewish community center movement, came into existence in 1877 in rented rooms on Post Street near Sutter. It offered a strong cultural program, and its first lecturer was Oaklander Henry George, who was completing his seminal *Progress and Poverty*, a searing analysis of the great disparities in America between rich and poor.[59] After the turn of the century, the YMHA would purchase a building on Page Street near the entrance to Golden Gate Park.

Particularly vibrant was B'nai B'rith, ascendant throughout America at this time. In addition to the West Coast regional headquarters on Eddy Street (erected in 1879), it operated seven lodges in San Francisco. B'nai B'rith also operated a three-thousand-volume lending library that grew steadily until its destruction in the earthquake of 1906. Another Jewish fraternal order, Kesher Shel Barzel (Band of Iron), had eight lodges in town as well as its District Grand Lodge.

All of these groups were active in benevolent work, and the policies of Mount Zion Hospital demonstrated that the well-being of non-Jews was included as well. As Mary Watson wrote in her *San Francisco Society* in 1887, the Jews constituted the most charitable group in the city.[60]

Noblesse oblige was a paramount concern of Jewish merchant-princes, who became known for their munificence as well as their culture and refinement. In the late nineteenth century they built ornate Victorian and even more flamboyant Queen Anne residences on Van Ness Avenue, a beautiful boulevard before the 1906 earthquake; on sedate Franklin Street, one block west of Van Ness; and on the fashionable streets that crossed them, including Post, Sutter, Bush, Pine, California, Sacramento, Clay, Washington, Jackson, and Pacific.* In marbled drawing rooms and leather-walled libraries, surrounded by precious works of art and waited upon by live-in servants, they entertained themselves lavishly. They also frequented the theater and opera, social clubs like the Concordia, and, for two days in early fall, during the High Holidays, attended Temple Emanu-El, when they filled the Sutter Street Temple to capacity, alighting from carriages driven by liveried coachmen. Here in formal attire, the women in luxurious furs, they listened to a sermon and to exquisite liturgical music performed by a non-Jewish choir.[61]

By the 1890s, Sherith Israel had a few lordly families of its own, as the following reminiscence of a Yom Kippur service indicates:

> The Meyerfelds, the Friedenthals, and the Greens were the crest from which social grades radiated to the back pews and gallery. Among the flutter of the Friedenthals, Ella Green Meyerfeld sat in splendor beside her husband, Mrs. Friedenthal's brother. She was of the stem of the M. Greens who occupied the front row of the side seats on the right of the altar. Mr. Green possessed great wealth and well-favored daughters who gavé balls and fancy dress parties to which Bavarians came and mixed freely with Poles. The second daughter, a tall, beautiful blond, bore so unmistakably the stamp of high lineage that the judgment of the congregation differed only on a question of degree. "A queen," said some. Others said, "An empress."[62]

The children of the elite attended the best private academies, such as Madame Ziska's Finishing School, and were also tutored in French and

---

*The grand Haas-Lilienthal House on Franklin Street, which was built in 1886, exemplifies the Queen Anne style. It was donated to the San Francisco Architectural Foundation in 1974 and is open to the public as a museum.

music, often by the four Godchaux sisters, whose home, known as "Little France" was a cultural shrine. Others studied Greek and Latin. Many of them entered the University of California, Berkeley, but some enrolled at Stanford (where Louis Sloss was invited by Leland Stanford himself to join the board of trustees),[63] and a select group went to Harvard, where the class of 1892 alone had six San Francisco Jews.[64] A trip to Europe in the tradition of the grand tour was de rigueur for completing a young person's education. Often an entire family, with servants and a tutor for the children, would cross the Atlantic and live in high style in Germany or France for the better part of a year.

Those in the gilded circle formed an exclusive group. At Emanu-El, where annual dues were set at $100 as early as the 1870s, very few members failed to belong at least to the upper middle class. Indeed, a recent study has shown that 99 percent of the congregation were merchants or professionals by 1900; not one laborer or even "petty proprietor" could be found on the temple's rolls.[65]

One's birthplace also carried a great deal of weight with the status seekers. Many in the German Jewish aristocracy considered the Russian-Jewish refugees only one cut above the Chinese. And the haughtiness of the Bavarians toward the Prussian "Polacks," which had polarized the Jewish community at its inception, continued unabated decades later. A notable exception was the B'nai B'rith lodges, whose rosters reveal that young men from a wide variety of backgrounds belonged to the fraternal order after the Civil War.[66] Even so, it appears that Kesher Shel Barzel, whose members largely hailed from Prussian Poland and further east, served as an alternative for those uncomfortable among the many south Germans in B'nai B'rith.[67] In virtually every Jewish organization in town, membership seemed to be determined by a line of demarcation half a world away, somewhere to the east of Berlin.

Perhaps the keenest observer of this divide was Harriet Lane Levy, whose witty memoir *920 O'Farrell Street* describes the rigid social stratifications of the Gilded Age. Her parents had arrived in San Francisco in the 1850s and reached the upper middle class in the following decade. They lived with their three daughters on a good block in the Western Addition, in a richly furnished home with a live-in Irish servant girl. Pillars of Sherith Israel, they were model citizens in every way and spoke flawless German as well as English. But because Benish and Yetta Levy had been born in a province neighboring Posen (and that was Polish until 1772), the family regarded itself as inferior to the Bavarian Jews. "On the social counter the price tag 'Polack' confessed second class," Harriet wrote. "Upon this basis of discrimination everybody agreed and acted."[68]

She and her sisters befriended south German girls but felt "uncomfortable" in their midst: "Pleasure was rarely simple or unmixed with fear. I never completely belonged." Her mother put an end to any notion she might have of ever marrying a Bavarian: "No Baier marries a Pole unless he is *krumm* or *lahm* or *stumm* (crooked or lame or dumb)."[69] Levy's impressions are corroborated by Rebekah Kohut, daughter of Ohabai Shalome's Rabbi Albert Bettelheim, who also spent her adolescent years in San Francisco in the late 1870s and early '80s. She claims that Jews segregated themselves from other Jews even more than they did in the community from which her family had come, staid Richmond, Virginia.[70]

Rebekah and Harriet were aware that the Jewish elite admired the Christian families of money and power, and to a large extent the feeling was mutual. The Slosses and Gerstles, who were sometimes invited to parties thrown by the Crockers and Hearsts, are examples of pioneer Jews mixing with the gentile upper crust, a phenomenon much more common in San Francisco than in the East.[71] But both groups evidently drew the line at intimate social contact. While the socialite and author Gertrude Atherton beamed that Jews "are welcome members of the best society," she wrote in the same sentence that "they are clannish."[72] And even Harriet Levy, perched a couple of rungs below the top of the ladder, sensed this "pleasant disassociation which no one wished to change."[73]

Although the Bohemian Club had a Jewish founder and more than a dozen Jews as members by 1900, other exclusive haunts such as the Pacific and Union clubs (later to merge) and the Junior League admitted very few Jewish members.[74] The Bay Area's first *Elite Directory,* published in 1879, included more than two hundred Jewish households, 19 percent of the total and almost triple the proportion of Jews in the general population.[75] Yet nearly all of the Jewish names were printed on a separate list, with the exceptions of Levi Strauss and the importer of fancy lace Abraham Weil, who were on the Christian list only. Jews were interspersed among the general elite in the *Blue Book* by 1888,[76] but this did not increase their presence at the lavish parties thrown by the Christian plutocracy.

Not only were marriages between Jews and non-Jews unusual among the elite (although they would occur more frequently in the next generation), but marriages between elite Jews and anyone outside a circle of a few dozen German Jewish clans were also rare. It was not unusual for two siblings in one privileged family to marry a pair in another, as the Lilienthal, Stern, Meyer, and Gerstle genealogies reveal. By World War I the city's Jewish aristocracy had become so inbred it almost resembled European royalty. Holding themselves aloof from the Jews below them, and not quite accepted by the highest social circles of the Christian elite, they formed a very exclusive set indeed, an "inner group of their own," according to Gertrude Atherton.[77]

"THAT LURKING PREJUDICE"

Overall, though, in the post–Civil War period Jews were increasingly woven into the fabric of San Francisco life even as anti-Semitism gained strength in other parts of America. In 1879 an East Coast newsweekly, printing a lithograph of 299 of San Francisco's most prominent citizens, assured its readers it was not exaggerating "when the covenanting Presbyter is observed in happy contiguity with the Jewish Rabbi [Elkan Cohn], and when all together are met in the auditorium of a first-class theater, where nature and human nature and not schism and creeds are represented."[78]

Still, "that lurking prejudice" as one historian puts it, was not entirely absent in San Francisco.[79] An echo of the attacks on Jews voiced in newspapers during the Civil War was heard in 1869, in congressional hearings held in San Francisco on the chronic problem of smuggling at the bustling port. A key witness was John McLean, a supervisor of the harbor for the Treasury Department, who testified that "undervaluation [to avoid the heavy duty on imports] was very largely practiced [by] persons of foreign birth, and a large portion of them were Israelites."[80] Indeed, during the war a Jewish tobacco importer had been sued in federal district court for defrauding the Customs House by sneaking in more than half a million Cuban cigars.[81] But McLean's highly publicized generalization half a decade later, that Jews are "a little more prone to that sort of business than persons who are not of that *religious* persuasion" (original emphasis), was taken by Jewish community leaders as pure prejudice.[82]

They struck back with a widely circulated pamphlet entitled "Unfounded and Gross Slander." Signed simply "the Israelites of San Francisco," it held McLean accountable for "stigmatizing a whole community . . . because of their religion [and] because some of its professors [i.e., adherents] may have thought less of it than of coining money at the Government's expense." Evidently assuming a receptive audience, the leaflet asked rhetorically, "Does [McLean] intend to convey the impression that our religion renders us given to commit crime?—that it furnishes a school for immorality?"[83]

McLean's charges gained little traction, but more dangerous than the image of the Jew as wartime profiteer was that of Judaism as inferior to Christianity or, even worse, an ossified set of beliefs that had rejected the loving message of Jesus and killed him. And while evangelical Protestantism and conversionism were not as pronounced in San Francisco as elsewhere in America, a number of local ministers, most notably John Hemphill of the Calvary Presbyterian Church, publicly denounced the Mosaic faith.

In two sermons in 1875, Pastor Hemphill, with the stated intention of making the Jews see the error of their ways, advocated daily recitation of the Lord's Prayer in the public schools.[84] The issue of separation of church and state thus emerged as a major issue in the 1870s, and the city's public school system was its battleground. There zealous Protestants hoped to succeed where the Catholics (Hemphill's greatest nemesis) had failed in convincing the Jews of the "story of the Cross" and "true gospel."[85]

The minister's arguments were demolished by Joseph Rodriguez Brandon, referred to by a contemporary historian as a "one-man Anti-Defamation League."[86] In the tradition of Henry Labatt, who had ably defended the Jews during the Sunday Closing Law controversy two decades earlier, Brandon, also a proud Sephardi and respected attorney, penned a twenty-page rebuttal that silenced Hemphill. He wrote that Jews are in no need of Christian teachings:

Israel too, Mr Hemphill has a gospel of peace; Israel too, has a story of the cross. Our history is one long story of . . . patient endurance of persecution, suffering and death for humanity, in the preservation of the great eternal truth committed to our custody—the Unity of God; and Israel too, has exclaimed after all her sufferings, "Father, forgive them, they knew not what they did."[87]

In the same year, Brandon, a Sherith Israel congregant, was even more upset when he saw a textbook assigned his children in public school. The *McGuffey Reader,* used throughout America in the second half of the nineteenth century, was to him "blatant sectarianism." In a long letter to the *Daily Alta California,* he quoted an offensive passage, imaginary words of an eyewitness to the crucifixion of "our Savior," as the schoolbook routinely referred to Jesus: " 'We saw the very faces of the Jews; the staring, frightful distortion of malice and rage. My soul kindled with a flame of indignation.' "[88]

Brandon had some notable allies among the Christian clergy in town, such as liberal Reverend William A. Scott of St. John's Presbyterian Church, who had sided with local Jews during the Mortara protest back in 1859. Seeing the public schools as a powerful engine of Americanization, he now urged the removal of "anything . . . obnoxious to any religious, sect, church, or denomination."[89] Even more valued was Brandon's (and Rabbi Bettelheim's) friendship with the famed educator John Swett, the New England progressive known as the "Horace Mann of the Pacific" who was the city's and later the state's superintendent of schools. Swett refused to enforce a board of education regulation requiring Bible reading and prayer to open the school day, "unwise," he said, for "a cosmopolitan city, in which there were large numbers of children of Catholics and Jews."[90] He also heartened the Jewish community by blocking public funding of Catholic schools, routine during the Gold Rush years, and of course he resisted the onslaughts of religious fundamentalists like Hemphill.

No less broad-minded was the president of the fledgling University of California, orientalist Daniel Gilman, who had come to Berkeley from Yale in 1872. So inclusive was his inaugural address that he welcomed the "many among us . . . who look for a Messiah yet to come."[91] The philo-Semitic Gilman was receptive to a petition signed by leading Jews throughout the state asking for Hebrew instruction at the institution. A newly arrived Russian Jew who had spent many years in England, James M. Phillips, was soon hired, becoming one of the few teachers of the ancient language at an American university. In the decade to come, several prominent Jewish businessmen would be appointed to the university's board of regents, and a full-fledged Department of Semitics would be established at the turn of the century.[92]

Despite such gains it was necessary to remain on guard. In 1883, in his influential conservative weekly the *Argonaut,* Frank Pixley leveled a fusillade of charges against the Jews: he combined the time-worn libel that Jews conspired in secret cells with the claim (preposterous in California) that "Jews will not become farmers," accused Judaism of preaching deceit, and held that Jewish merchants committed arson to collect the insurance money.[93]

Pixley, a nativist who also skewered the Catholics and Chinese, had been a state assemblyman, attorney general, and university regent. As founding editor of the *Argonaut,* he was now a leader of the California Republican party, which he vowed to purify of "all impertinent and meddlesome foreign adventurers—Irish, Germans and Jews."[94]

Pixley's assault came during a period that was particularly disturbing for the Jewish elite. Only a year and a half earlier Lewis Gerstle, planning a summer vacation with his family at a Santa Cruz hotel, was informed by letter that Jews were not welcome.[95] There was scarcely a more prominent Jew in San Francisco, and the incident—the first of its kind in Gerstle's life in America—called to mind the exclusion four years earlier of the eminent banker Joseph Seligman, a friend of President Grant, from the Grand Hotel in Saratoga, New York. Perhaps Northern California wasn't that different after all.

Gerstle refused to press the matter—he would forgo Santa Cruz and buy a summer estate in San Rafael instead—but Pixley could not go unanswered. The task of responding to him fell to yet another deft Sephardi, David D'Ancona, a furrier by trade but also an experienced journalist. Born into a well-known London family—his uncle was editor of the respected *Jewish Chronicle*—he immigrated to New York in 1850 and arrived in San Francisco two decades later. There he devoted himself to the B'nai B'rith and in only six years became president of the burgeoning western district. D'Ancona's pride in the fraternal order can be seen in the well-formulated reply he wrote Pixley, which appeared on the front page of the *Morning Call:*

> The B'nai B'rith is a secret Jewish order without a secret. Its chief aim is to gather together in one fold the Israelites of various nationalities, and to weld them into a homogenous mass . . . truly and assuredly American. I may so far violate the secrecy of this non-secret order as to say that all its teachings are strictly moral, whether judged by Christian or Jewish ethics, that it would frown upon anyone who would defraud his creditors, and ruthlessly expel any member convicted of crime. This is the only Jewish "secret tribunal" of which I have any knowledge, and to such secret tribunals I presume even the *Argonaut* will not object.[96]

D'Ancona calmly and skillfully refuted each of Pixley's smears, and while the bigoted editor did not quite apologize, he admitted "the cogency of the argument" and refrained from further anti-Jewish attacks.[97]

It may be a stretch to say, as has one historian, that in the post–Civil War decades "American Jewish activism was . . . invented on the West Coast."[98] In fact, energetic, effective responses to anti-Semitism could be found across the country. But San Francisco Jews seemed to possess a unique motive for their assertiveness; they had been among the city's founders during the Gold Rush, and they were not about to be pushed aside a generation later.

A VOLCANIC PRESS

David D'Ancona was regarded as civil and dignified even by his adversaries. This was not the case, however, for a much better known local Jewish journalist, a rabbi's son from Prussian Poland who had emigrated as a teenager and mastered English in New York and at Yale before coming out West in the mid-1850s.

Isidore Choynski used his considerable literary talent to inflict razor-sharp personal attacks on Jew and gentile alike and actually reveled in being called a blackguard. During the Civil War, as a young interim manager of the *Gleaner* (a journal he regarded as too scholarly and dry), his heedless trumpeting of Jewish superiority resulted in a public relations disaster that ended only when he was disavowed by virtually every prominent Jew in town. Two decades later, facing Pixley's anti-Semitic barrage, Choynski maintained, based on no evidence whatsoever, that the *Argonaut* editor, a Presbyterian of Scottish stock, had been born a Jew and was attacking his own people as a supreme act of self-hatred: "In order to cover his origin and his extraordinary large nose, [Pixley] takes great pains every week to insult the Jews in his paper," which Choynski lampooned as the *Argonose*.[99] Branding Pixley a "scoundrel and a miser" and "dirty coward," he informed his readers that "before this gets into print you may learn that I have spoiled that elongated proboscis of the barren Scotch terrier."[100] This typified Choynski's style: brash, satirical, insulting, even threatening, and without much respect for the facts.

Few were sorry to see Pixley gored in print, but Choynski's merciless flaying of the Jewish community was another matter. From 1874 to 1893, with a few interruptions, he penned the widely read column "San Francisco Letter" in Isaac Mayer Wise's influential weekly *American Israelite,* which was published in Cincinnati and circulated nationally. He signed his articles "Maftir," Hebrew for the concluding section of the Torah portion read on the Sabbath, a fitting pseudonym since he invariably got the last word.

His favorite topics were the hypocrisy and stinginess of the community's wealthiest Jews. A typical item might describe the Concordia Club as filled with diners and poker players on Yom Kippur. After failing to collect a charitable contribution of fifty dollars each from several millionaires, he wrote, "These fellows . . . are more likely to plunk down twice as much on a pair of aces."[101] The San Francisco real estate baron Michael Reese—"a very poor specimen of a man and sad apology for a Jew"—and even Levi Strauss were labeled as tightfisted.[102]

These criticisms were mild, though, compared with some of Maftir's other character sketches. Often naming the principals involved—usually community leaders—he told stories of blackmail, wife beating, adultery, suicide, and even homicide.[103] His worried editor occasionally followed with a disclaimer and sometimes an outright refutation.[104]

Jewish patricians were hardly his only target; the "incessant scold" chastised all of San Francisco Jewry as "a listless, lazy, lukewarm set of people . . . aroused by nothing short of an earthquake or a Mortara abduction."[105] He considered the Reform movement essentially a conspiracy of indolent rabbis wanting to reduce the time spent leading services and, besides, "You can get better sermons and good music in any Unitarian Church."[106] Though an agnostic, he was fairly observant and belonged to Sherith Israel, but he derided its drift toward reform and the sparse attendance at Sabbath services. Not that he approved of Orthodox Beth Israel, "whose ideas belong to the Middle Ages."[107] Although one of his main whipping boys was the local rabbinate, he also lambasted kosher slaughterers and butchers as "mean, miserable wretches" for their price gouging, criticized the city's Jewish teachers for their outdated pedagogy, took the *mohelim* to task for exaggerating their credentials, and even ran down the beloved Orphan Asylum. Not surprisingly, he reprimanded the behavior of Jewish youth at beach and garden parties, "dancing in the heat of the day as if they were Shakers."[108] All this scathing criticism was for local Jewry's own good, claimed Choynski: "If, now and then, I cut deep, I want to cure the sore."[109]

Writing about non-Jews he showed even less restraint. He crusaded against the railroads and their corrupt lawyers but also viciously attacked society's most disadvantaged, the Chinese and Native Americans. Although an early advocate of female suffrage, his attitude toward women was condescending even by late nineteenth-century standards. When the gifted young journalist Henrietta Szold, who would later found Hadassah, wrote the *Israelite* of her fear that Choynki's "vulgar and aggressive" columns could provoke anti-Semitism, he dismissed her as a "pan and pot scourer" and admonished her to "be a good girl . . . remain strong in your faith, but above all, take care of your kitchen utensils."[110]

Most mean-spirited and reckless was his mockery of Christianity, which he engaged in precisely during the period of rising discrimination against American Jewry in the late 1870s and early '80s. He called Jesus "the Hanging One," Christmas the "anniversary of the birth of the little Joker," and pondered aloud if "Mrs. Christ and the second hand carpenter" had any more children, "perhaps another boy, about midsummer," so that Jewish retailers could enjoy a second moneymaking holiday.[111] One of his parodies was translated and reprinted in Germany as an example of the lack of respect Jews had for Christianity.[112]

One wonders why Isaac Mayer Wise, the religious leader of American Jewry, continued to print Maftir. To be sure, he was fired in the mid-1880s, following an "unwarrantable and uncalled-for attack" on Freemasonry, an order that enjoyed Wise's allegiance (and had earlier suspended Choynski for "unmasonic conduct").[113] Yet the rabbi brought him back a few years later not only to boost the *Israelite*'s circulation—the "San Francisco Letter" sometimes appeared on page one—but also perhaps to stab some of his own enemies with Maftir's cutting columns. The B'nai B'rith, for example, angered Wise by refusing to provide funds for his Hebrew Union College; he might have derived some satisfaction from Choynski's attacks on three of its national leaders, "a Holy Trinity . . . grown fat on the order, and constantly sucking the teats of the seven lean cows [i.e., the regional districts]."[114] Choynski himself had served as grand president of B'nai B'rith's District 4 in the mid-1870s, but that meant nothing when a good target came into view.

Wise even stayed with Choynski after the columnist was hauled into court—twice—not only for libel, as might be expected, but also for extortion.[115] The indictments grew out of articles that appeared in *Public Opinion*, a secular political paper Choynski published almost concurrently with his column in the *Israelite*, and for which he wrote nearly all the contents. While it purported to defend the workingman against "soulless corporations and grinding monopolists,"[116] it also served as a scandal sheet, and two individuals accused him of demanding money for suppressing stories of moral turpitude. Nothing came of the first case, but in the second, in 1890, Choynski was jailed during the long trial, convicted, and sentenced to three years imprisonment.[117] He was out on bail during the two-year-long appeal to the state's supreme court, which overturned the conviction. But the ordeal took a heavy toll on his finances and health, and he died, broke and embittered, just before the dawn of the new century.

Most of the other local Anglo-Jewish journalists strove to accentuate the positive in communal life. The best known was Philo Jacoby, who founded the weekly *Hebrew* in 1863 and remained at its helm well into the twentieth century. In San Francisco's tradition of smashing Jewish stereotypes, he was also a consummate athlete, a world-champion marksman and medal-winning strongman who could be seen bending horseshoes at exhibitions. Yet as an editor he was fairly moderate, seeing his role as a unifier of the Jewish community and its judicious defender.

The irreverent Choynski, though, whose column in the *Israelite* probably had as many readers in San Francisco as any of the four local Jewish papers,* went counter to the age-old survival instincts that required avoiding airing dirty linen in public. Peppering his prose with Yiddishisms and nuggets of Jewish folklore, he clearly knew the ways of the shtetl as well as anyone, but he also realized that he inhabited a new territory where self-expression was king. Here Jewish life could be portrayed with all its warts, and Judaism—and even Christianity—could be made the butt of ribald humor, and the world wouldn't come to an end.

Perhaps Choynksi was emboldened by the general virulence of San Francisco's press during the Gilded Age. There are some similarities between Maftir and Ambrose Bierce, the mordant columnist for the *Argonaut, Wasp,* and later Hearst's *Examiner,* who suffered a severe beating from the victim of one of his venomous attacks.

But few reporters spewed more vitriol than the de Young brothers from St. Louis. Michael, Charles, and Gustavus, Jews of Dutch extraction, got their start in the 1860s as typesetters for Rabbi Eckman's *Gleaner.* They then founded the *Daily Dramatic Chronicle,* a theatrical tabloid, which later developed into the *Daily Morning Chronicle* (without Gustavus, who had mysteriously disappeared). The paper routinely resorted to character assassination to boost circulation. When Baptist minister Isaac Kalloch ran for mayor in 1879, the *Chronicle* ran an exposé of the youthful philandering that had earned him the nickname "the Sorrel Stallion." Kalloch's retort, delivered in his church, called the de Youngs "bastard progeny of a whore born in the slums."[118] The next day Charles de Young shot the preacher but succeeded only in wounding him, and Kalloch recovered and won the mayoralty. Early the following year, when the *Chronicle* again accused Kalloch of adultery, his son pumped a bullet into Charles and

---

*By the early 1880s these included the *Jewish Progress,* the *Hebrew Observer* (successor to the *Gleaner*), the *Jewish Times,* and the *Hebrew.*

killed him. Rabbi Elkan Cohn performed the funeral and came close to burying Michael a few years later, when Adolph Spreckels, enraged at the *Chronicle's* ferocious attacks on his family, shot and almost killed the editor in his office. So widespread was hatred toward the de Youngs that many believed young Spreckels had "very nearly rendered a public service." He was ultimately acquitted "on grounds of reasonable cause."[119] Later, muckraker Arthur McEwen founded the weekly *Letter,* which was virtually dedicated to bashing Michael de Young and ruined his bid for a U.S. Senate seat.[120] And yet the public skewering of the de Youngs was rarely mixed with anti-Semitism, a point probably not lost on Choynski.

COURT JESTER

On the eve of the Civil War, San Francisco Jewry also produced the city's most famous eccentric, who amused its residents until his death in 1880. Joshua Norton, a respectable commodities trader who had suffered disastrous reverses in the mid-1850s, briefly went into seclusion before emerging triumphantly as Norton I, Emperor of the United States and Protector of Mexico. An indulgent editor of the *San Francisco Bulletin* saw the humor in the emperor's proclamations, such as those abolishing Congress and the U.S. Supreme Court, and prominently published the decrees, which became the talk of the town.[121]

Finally, his majesty appeared on the streets, decked out in regalia that would be his trademark for the next twenty years: a naval officer's deep-blue dress coat with enormous gold-braid epaulets, a towering white beaver hat sporting peacock feathers, and an ornate walking stick or long military sword.[122] Close by his heels were two stray dogs, Bummer and Lazarus, who themselves became darlings of the press. Norton may have been delusional, but his performance was more likely the calculated survival strategy of a man past forty with few other options to earn a living.

Soon an imitator (a pretender to the throne, Norton called him) appeared on the sidewalks of New York. "Stellifer the King, Reigning Prince of the House of David and Guardian of American Destinies" also issued decrees and claimed to communicate with heads of state.[123] He too declared himself to be protector of Mexico. But the denizens of Fifth Avenue were unimpressed and his reign was brief; he was jailed for nonpayment of a hotel bill and later committed to a mental hospital.[124]

San Francisco, though, even in the mid-nineteenth century had a reputation for indulging oddballs, especially a colorful welter of street people in the downtown area. In revolutionary-era dress, George Washington the Second, a ruined speculator in the Comstock silver mines, used his remarkable likeness to the first president to attract a crowd and ask for handouts. Norton, fearing competition, ordered Washington to be remanded to the insane asylum, but that edict went unheeded and the two remained bitter rivals for years.[125] There were other buffoons: a mysterious dandy called the Great Unknown; a pathetic scavenger named Guttersnipe; and even another Jew, the miserly Money King (Abraham King of New Orleans), who functioned on the street as a sort of pawnbroker to the homeless. Dressed in rags, King spent next to nothing and perfected stinginess as if it were an art form.[126]

But Norton's act was the most elaborate and longest running of all. He was the only one to issue scrip, elegantly engraved bills produced free of charge by the city's best printers and almost always accepted in restaurants and shops.[127] He rode streetcars for free and was admitted to public events without a ticket; sometimes, in a show of respect, the audience rose when he entered. For pocket money he levied taxes on his subjects, visiting businesses once a month for a fifty-cent tribute, generally paid cheerfully and duly noted in his ledger. Choynski, who worked hard for a living, quipped that Norton was "the embodiment of a free pass."[128] A more sympathetic Robert Louis Stevenson, who visited California in the late 1870s, thought the phenomenon shed some light on local mores:

> In what other city would a harmless madman who supposed himself emperor . . . have been so fostered and encouraged? Where else would even the people of the streets have respected the poor soul's illusion? Where else would bankers and merchants have received his visits, cashed his cheques, and submitted to his small assessments? Where else . . . in God's green earth [would he] have taken his pick of restaurants, ransacked the bill of fare, and departed scathless?[129]

The monarch frequently worshipped at Emanu-El or Sherith Israel, but after his death from a stroke in 1880 he was not given a Jewish burial but laid to rest with Episcopalian rites in Lone Mountain cemetery.* His funeral was

---

*Norton received a second Protestant funeral when the city closed the Lone Mountain burial ground in 1934 and his remains were transferred to Woodlawn Cemetery in Colma. But more than a century after his demise, a group of local Jewish history buffs succeeded in memorializing him in the manner of his people. At his grave, kaddish and El Molai Rachamim were said at his third, and likely final, funeral.

attended by thirty thousand people, but no rabbi or cantor played a role in the service nor did any Jewish organization participate.[130] Norton had no local relatives and questions were raised, at the time and ever since, as to why "co-believers did not . . . claim the remains as their own."[131]

It has often been assumed that an embarrassed Jewish community wanted to distance itself from Norton's lunacy. But a Jewish burial was afforded to all sorts of deviants during the Gilded Age, including the repulsive Money King, potentially more harmful to the Jewish image than the beloved Joshua Abraham Norton. Perhaps Christian obsequies could be explained, as one historian has suggested, by the fact that the emperor sometimes denied his Jewish origins, claiming to be a descendant of the Bourbon kings, who "it is very well known were not Jews."[132] Like other San Franciscans, the Jewish community may have wanted Emperor Norton to remain in character to the very end.

ATHENS OF THE PACIFIC

Almost every week Norton crossed San Francisco Bay by steamship to visit his subjects in fast-growing Oakland. He was warmly received along Broadway and further north in Berkeley. In 1869 he proclaimed that a suspension bridge should be constructed linking Oakland with San Francisco.[133]

Almost seventy years would pass before the Bay Bridge became a reality, but the two cities were closely connected even in the nineteenth century. Oakland, however, developed slowly during the Gold Rush decade, its economic growth crippled because its first mayor, Horace Carpentier, claimed the waterfront as his personal property. In 1860 its population was barely 1,500, making it the thirty-eighth largest town in the state. But after the Civil War, with the port controversy resolved, it benefited from a system of horse-drawn streetcars, the new university, and, most of all, the transcontinental railroad, which chose the city as its western terminus. By 1870, with more than ten thousand people, it had become California's second city. Over the next decade its population would triple.

Almost from its founding in 1852 the quiet streets of Oakland were a welcome contrast to the boomtown across the bay, with its saloons, casinos, and brothels. Especially those raising families looked fondly on the area dotted with scrub oaks, which they hoped would become a center of trade in its own right. The East Bay also served as a recreation center for San Franciscans; with its milder climate and natural beauty it was the perfect day trip destination for those seeking relief from the pressures of the big city.

There was a Jewish presence in Oakland from the beginning, when hard-working dry goods dealers lined Broadway between Second and Fourth streets (today's Jack London Square), the town's initial business district. Arriving in 1852, Samuel Hirshberg was probably Oakland's first Jew, a highly educated Posener whose small shop reputedly carried "everything from a needle to an anchor."[134] In the early 1860s Hirshberg built a solid two-story structure on lower Broadway, one of the very first brick buildings in a town whose wooden shacks were often gutted by fire.

In 1862 Hirshberg founded the Hebrew Benevolent Society, for the next thirteen years the only Jewish organization in Oakland. Consisting of a few dozen families, out of a Jewish population of perhaps a hundred households by the early 1870s, it bought land for a cemetery, raised and distributed funds for the needy, and obtained Torah scrolls for Sabbath and holiday services. Also functioning as a fraternal group, it was perhaps the most versatile Hebrew Benevolent Society in the West.[135]

But the rapidly increasing Jewish population, growing in tandem with the town itself, required a greater number of Jewish organizations. The charitable Daughters of Israel Relief Society and the local B'nai B'rith lodge both emerged from the Benevolent Society, but its most important offspring was a congregation.[136] Its eighteen founders, all of them foreign-born merchants, hailed from half a dozen countries, but one group predominated: Prussian Poles, almost all from Posen.[137] The First Hebrew Congregation (today's Temple Sinai), incorporated in 1875, constructed a modest synagogue at Fourteenth and Webster streets three years later and gradually acquired the assets of the Hebrew Benevolent Society.[138]

While Oakland avoided the ethnic rivalry that split San Francisco Jewry—Bavarians were a small minority in the East Bay—there was serious disagreement over questions of ritual. The First Hebrew Congregation, though established along traditional lines and of course using Polish rites, showed reformist tendencies early: a group led by Hirshberg's son, David, introduced a mixed choir of Christians and Jews and organ music in 1881.[139] In that year the congregation engaged its first full-time rabbi, M. S. Levy, who would remain for a decade before taking the pulpit of Beth Israel in San Francisco. Although trained by strictly Orthodox teachers in his native London, the conciliatory Levy was sensitive to the needs of the progressive faction. The traditionalists, mostly former members of the Hebrew Benevolent Society and unhappy about its demise, initiated an alternative to the First Hebrew Congregation in the form of an Orthodox minyan, a worship community meeting in private homes that was the nucleus of Congregation Beth Jacob, formally established in the following decade.[140]

In the economic realm, however, there was little diversity: almost every Jew made a living as a storekeeper or an artisan. The city directory of 1876 lists them as shoemakers and tailors, glaziers and engravers, tobacconists and grocers, and above all clothiers: Jews owned six of the seven stores for men's clothing. Of more than a hundred attorneys and physicians, only one appears to be of Jewish extraction.[141]

The placid community was often compared to Brooklyn, then a suburban and partly rural refuge situated across the water from a "Babylon." Choynski was characteristically dismissive, declaring Oakland "on the wrong side of the bay."[142] But it would be a mistake to think of it as prosaic or provincial. Where rail and water met, close both to San Francisco and the state university, an atmosphere of freedom and creativity permeated the "Athens of the Pacific." It boasted an opera house, a good school system, and an excellent public library.

The immigrant Jewish merchants, rubbing shoulders daily with people from every part of the globe, steadily built up their businesses, and a good number became wealthy by the turn of the century. Before World War I Jews owned most of the city's largest retail establishments, including its major department stores.[143] They were great innovators in buying, displaying, and advertising their wares.

But it was the American-born second generation that was destined to accomplish great things. A community of fewer than a thousand during the 1880s, Oakland Jewry would eventually produce two world-renowned individuals. Judah Magnes, the first West Coast native to become a rabbi, was an effective activist on behalf of immigrant Jews in New York City early in the century and later founded and became the first chancellor of the Hebrew University of Jerusalem.* Gertrude Stein, who migrated to Paris, where she would be at the center of almost every major avant-garde literary and artistic movement of her time, wrote provocative novels, plays, poems, short stories, nonfiction, and criticism that made her one of the most influential authors of the twentieth century.

Raised in observant homes, both Magnes and Stein attended the First Hebrew Congregation's Sabbath School in the 1880s, and one of its young

---

* The Judah L. Magnes Museum, founded in 1962 in Berkeley, was named for the Bay Area's native son.

teachers, Rachel Frank (later Ray Frank Litman), was another pathfinder, who would soon become the nation's first female rabbi.[144] Although not ordained, she led services and delivered sermons up and down the West Coast.

Magnes and Stein left Oakland in the early 1890s, he for Hebrew Union College in Cincinnati and she for Harvard, but both rebels credited their youth in the East Bay for setting them on a course of uncommon personal freedom and uncompromising intellectual honesty. Sustaining Magnes was a vision of democracy and cultural pluralism that he initially formed in the "far West," as he put it, where his "first teachers used to talk of the glories of the real America—no badges, no titles, no special uniforms."[145] Stein's bold experimentation—in language, art, and lifestyle—also owed much to her California roots, as well as her father's business success. Daniel Stein's shrewd investment in a cable car company laid the foundation for the small fortune that allowed Gertrude and her brother Leo to live in Paris and collect the works of some of the world's greatest painters. As they later wrote, their appreciation of beauty originated in the dramatic landscapes they encountered on frequent hikes at sunset in the wooded hills overlooking the shimmering bay.[146] They grew up in the 1880s in a rambling home on an idyllic ten-acre plot in East Oakland, which Gertrude fictionalized in her magnum opus, *The Making of Americans*.

But she took away from Oakland more than vivid memories of an attractive natural setting. As it did for Magnes, who lived for decades in Jerusalem, the diversity of the Bay Area during her youth prepared her well for a life abroad in another great metropolis reflecting a multitude of cultures: "California meant lots of nationalities. And if you went to school with them and knew about their hair and their ways and all you were bound later not to be surprised."[147] At college in the East, and even later in bohemian Paris, Stein felt herself "more worldly and more exotic" than others because of her girlhood home that provided such stimulation, variety, and opportunity.[148] She and Magnes understood they were products of a special environment that brought forth a rare kind of fin de siècle Jew, one who knew no constraints.

THREE

Rooted Cosmopolitans

The Cultural Creativity of the Second Generation

EVEN AFTER THE GOLD RUSH had become a distant memory, the ethnic diversity, physical beauty, and venturesome spirit of the San Francisco Bay Area continued to set it apart. In the late nineteenth century an almost Mediterranean ethos prevailed. Theaters, restaurants, and bars were more numerous per capita than they were back East—and morals looser.[1] In converted lofts around Montgomery Street, a bohemian subculture took root, not merely tolerated, but in some ways imitated throughout the city. Even nearby Chinatown was no longer as forbidding as it had been a generation earlier. The arts flourished as young people in particular sought to express the exuberance they felt.

Native-born sons and daughters of Jewish pioneers were at the forefront of this cultural mecca, their creativity evident on stage and in concert halls, in bookstores and on newsstands, in museums and art galleries, in the architecture of new buildings and the furnishings inside them. And Jews were highly visible as patrons of the arts and impresarios, as consumers of culture and critics.

But the California Jewish imagination of this era resists easy definition. It ranges from the figurative paintings of Toby Rosenthal to the whimsical cartoons of Rube Goldberg. It encompasses the refinement of Alfred Hertz, conductor of the symphony, but also the crass commercialism of Al Hayman, manager of burlesque houses. It is composed of personalities with the loftiest ambitions, like Gertrude Stein, who (comparing herself to Jesus and Spinoza) sought to change human consciousness, and those with modest goals, such as Harriet Lane Levy, whose literary output came second to life's pleasures. It includes individuals born into wealthy families, but also several who grew up poor. And even if these disparate dreamers were all Jews, that category itself meant something different to each of them.

Nonetheless, some common themes may be discerned. Jewish cultural creativity was often rooted in revolt against the older generation's Victorian mores. Harriet Levy described the heavily Jewish Western Addition of her childhood in the 1880s as "a world where variation was perversity," where it didn't take much for "a girl's honor [to fall] from her like a loosely buttoned petticoat."[2] Levy's friend, the poet Flora Jacobi Arnstein, also rebelled against the repressive, overly disciplined, and money-conscious behavior of her upper-middle-class parents and spoke for many of her contemporaries when she said that she had "broken through" all of that with her art.[3] Leo Stein's quip that the death of his overbearing father left him "financially, socially and emotionally self-sufficient" was no joke.[4] Pioneer parents tended to give their children a fine education and expose them to art and music, but the old folks were regarded as hopelessly set in their ways and anything but role models.

Once unleashed from the constraints of bourgeois convention, many of the homegrown artists displayed quirky and irreverent behavior. Gertrude Stein, who made a cult out of nonconformity, is the best known, but the antics of actress Adah Isaacs Menken, the obsessions of sculptor Annette Rosenshine, and the weird carryings-on of playwright Salmi Morse all reflect the streak of eccentricity that runs through this cohort.

More important, though, was the pathbreaking nature of their art. David Belasco—a dramatist, set designer, and producer—was perhaps the most innovative theatrical personality of the American stage. Gertrude Stein interpreted literature in a new light, and when she was in Paris with her brothers Leo and Michael and her sister-in-law Sarah, she was among the first to perceive the genius of some of the world's greatest painters. Abraham Livingston Gump's grasp of Asian art enabled him to change the taste of San Franciscans and countless visitors as well. Illustrator Ernest Peixotto, who published vivid drawings in the avant-garde journal the *Lark,* was at the center of the bohemian circle Les Jeunes, which challenged everything provincial in California culture. Alma Wahrhaftig experimented with fresh forms of photography, and Anna Strunsky developed a new kind of novel. Anne Bremer, departing from the "pretty" style expected of women painters, produced strikingly original watercolors.

Women were well represented among the Jewish artists and intellectuals at the turn of the twentieth century. In small but noticeable numbers they attended the University of California and entered professions almost completely closed to them a generation earlier. There were six Jewish women physicians in San Francisco by 1896, including Adolph Sutro's daughter, Emma, the first female to graduate from the University of California Medical School.[5] One of the first woman architects in the state was Jewish, as were the first University of California–trained woman lawyer and the first female full professor at UC Berkeley.[6] Some Jewish women became scientists and journalists, and of course they were numerous in the occupations traditionally held by women, social work and elementary education. But they were also conspicuous in the arts and letters. Many studied painting at the Mark Hopkins Institute for Art or the more experimental Art Students League. Half a dozen local Jewish women were published novelists at this time; their fiction was reviewed in the press and discussed in literary clubs.

For women no less than men, great foreign cities loomed large in their art and in their lives. Paris was paramount, and a succession of budding Jewish female artists and writers visited the Steins for extended periods and returned home forever changed. The City of Light was also where aspiring architects studied, where thespians toured, and even where commercial artists trained. Europe's other cultural capitals also attracted San Francisco Jews: Toby Rosenthal had a lifelong fascination with Munich (then Germany's center for fine arts); Leo Stein, drawn to Renaissance painting, spent many years in Florence; and Anna Strunsky, a leftist journalist, became enthralled with St. Petersburg. Abraham Livingston Gump, not merely a purveyor but also a connoisseur of Oriental art objects, had connections to Asia.

But as far as they wandered, the dramatic landscape of Northern California usually remained in their minds and inspired their creativity. This comes through in Gertrude Stein's vivid descriptions of her semirural upbringing in East Oakland; it is seen in the landscapes and seascapes of Joseph Raphael, born and raised in the Gold Country and educated in San Francisco. The idyllic artists' colony of Carmel nurtured Anne Bremer, and Piedmont, still a pastoral retreat in 1900, drew authors like Anna Strunsky.

Obviously, Jews also produced a rich and lively culture on the East Coast—one need only think of New York's Yiddish theater—but it was largely an expression of immigrant life. Gotham's Jewish artists often had foreign lands in mind, but these were generally the places from which they had come, not the cultural centers of Western Europe, and certainly not Asia. Nor was nature a theme commonly explored by Jewish artists in the densely settled Atlantic seaports. New York Jewish women were active as writers and actresses, too, but were behind their sisters in San Francisco in the professions and the fine arts. Indeed, in the eastern states few Jewish men or women were serious painters or sculptors until late in the nineteenth century.

In the end, the Jewish muse in Northern California was characterized most by its self-confidence, its brash sensibility. Even if many of the best Jewish minds of the second generation left the Bay Area for good in their early years, they took with them, as was said of Judah Magnes, "the audacious freedom from the fabulous West."[7]

A DARING THEATER

Beginning in 1849, the San Francisco stage, full of energy and variety, was a reflection of the city itself. There was demand for Shakespeare and strip shows, for classical opera and vulgar blackface, and for virtually everything in between. Theater was often covered by the local press and discussed by politicians and clergymen. Impresarios outdid one another in selling tickets, and leading entertainers were the most lionized people in town.

In this charged environment a young Jewish actress was the greatest sensation of her time. Adah Isaacs Menken, with her sensuous acting, flowery poetry, and public romances, conquered San Francisco during the Civil War. Born and raised in New Orleans, she had performed in the East before moving to the West Coast. She had achieved her greatest triumph as the lead in *Mazeppa,* based on a poem by Byron, a role that called for her to ride a live horse over a prop mountain.

In August 1863, the "Napoleon of the San Francisco stage," Tom Maguire, booked Menken into the huge opera house that bore his name, advertising that she would again take her famous ride, this time in the nude. In truth, she wore flesh-colored tights (more bluff than buff, one wit noted), but it hardly mattered; the mostly male audience was enraptured (and at least she remembered her lines, which she didn't always accomplish in her performances back East). Maguire, who paid her an astounding five hundred dollars nightly and drew thirty thousand people in the first two weeks, also presented Menken in other plays, such as *Three Fast Women,* and arranged a wildly successful tour of the mining towns. A handful of newspaper editors called her act scandalous, but overall she was lauded by the drama critics, who were much more accepting of her art than the New York reviewers had been.[8]

She attracted no less attention offstage. Although accompanied to California by her third husband, Menken broke almost all the rules of the day, going out alone in the evening to saloons and even brothels, where she smoked cigars, gambled heavily, and flirted incessantly. She was drawn to a particular type—the dashing young writer—of which there were plenty in San Francisco. She went around with short story author Bret Harte, satirist Artemus Ward, and frontier poets Joaquin Miller and Charles Warren Stoddard (all of them in their twenties then), to name just a few.[9] Miller later recalled "the single garment of yellow silk" that clothed her ravishing body as she moved through the streets: "I doubt if any other woman in the world could wear a dress like that in the winds of San Francisco and not look ridiculous."[10] Mark Twain was similarly overwhelmed and reported that when he arrived in town, "no one was being talked about except . . . 'the Menken.'" Later, he saw her perform and wrote of "a magnificent spectacle [that] dazzled my vision."[11] He, too, took a romantic interest in her.

Menken was also a sculptor, linguist, and poet. Her verse, much of it published by Isaac Mayer Wise in the *American Israelite,* often dealt with Jewish themes.[12] She knew some Hebrew, regularly lit Sabbath candles, and publicly announced that, being a Jew, she would not perform on Yom Kippur.[13]

After rocking the town to its core (much like her idol, the sinuous "Spider Dancer," Lola Montes), Menken left San Francisco in April 1864, after only a nine-month stay, during which she earned fifty thousand dollars.[14] Her destination was London and later the Continent, where again she stunned audiences and took as lovers literary giants.[15] Now with her fourth husband (the previous marriage could not survive her California cavorting), she lived extravagantly but died in her midthirties in Paris, where she was buried in the Montparnasse Cemetery. Although she never returned to San Francisco, Menken was remembered for decades not only by the men of letters whom she had enthralled, but also by her adoring public. In the Sierras, mines and mountains were named for her.

If Menken's brief and brilliant presence resembled a shooting star, another Jewish stage celebrity, David Belasco, enjoyed a career that seemed to shine forever. He was born in San Francisco in 1853, soon after his parents, Orthodox Sephardim from England (the family name had been Valasco), settled in the South of Market district. Shopkeeper Humphrey Abraham

Belasco had difficulty supporting his wife and four sons and moved the family to Victoria, British Columbia, but the Belascos returned in 1865. Their son's "passion for the stage," wrote his biographer, would soon "saturate . . . every fiber" of young David's being.[16]

Belasco attributed his sense of drama to the real-life scenes he witnessed in the pulsating city: "What a conflict of contrasting motives and varying nationalities! Mexican greasers, American squatters, miners, señoras, adventuresses, and the riff-raff that haunted the gambling joints—all of these brushed elbows in the streets." And the youth took it all in: "I knew every infamous and dangerous place in San Francisco."[17]

He dropped out of school to work as a stagehand, prompter, set shifter, ticket taker—anything that would put him in a theater. He acted, too, though the short, squat Belasco landed mostly bit parts and appeared in minstrel shows (in blackface) and farces as often as serious dramas. One of the best reviews he received was of his role as Emperor Norton in a burlesque.[18] At twenty, he had a traditional Jewish wedding, but the "nomadic bohemian" often left his new bride to join troupes touring the mining camps.[19]

It was in San Francisco, though, in the late 1870s that Belasco developed the multifaceted talent that would make him world famous. Maguire, still the town's dominant producer, took over the flashy new Baldwin Theatre on Market and Powell streets and hired Belasco as assistant manager. The collaboration was fruitful, and the Baldwin presented a wide array of stars whose techniques Belasco carefully observed. When the famed tragedian Edwin Booth played the rival California Theatre for two months, the aspirant got himself cast as an extra just so he could watch the master at work.[20]

With unlimited energy Belasco acted, directed, prompted, and also wrote, churning out play after play for Maguire. Although many were mere adaptations (without credit given to the author of the original story, resulting in accusations of plagiarism), his pace was indisputably frantic. In the fall of 1879 alone, the "script carpenter" penned four full-length dramas for the Baldwin.[21]

Unsurprisingly, most of this rushed output was trite; only later would Belasco excel as a playwright. But he demonstrated originality as a set designer, and his special effects revealed, according to one drama critic, a "fearfully realistic" theatrical vision, influenced by the "new naturalism" with which Émile Zola portrayed Parisian street life.[22] The size of the Baldwin Theatre allowed Belasco to simulate an entire Southern plantation for a romance called *The Octoroon,* which used as props actual cannon, live horses, and, for rain, real water. When a script called for a baby he used a real infant, not a doll.

Belasco could masterfully illuminate a set, and he credited the brilliant California sunshine for his ideas about light and shadow.[23] Using colored lights shined onto strips of silk blown around by bellows, he once imitated a fire so realistically that some in the audience bolted for the exits.[24] Other times, with gas lamps hidden behind a layer of glass, he gave the stage a ghostly feel.

For all of this magic at the Baldwin, Maguire was in financial trouble by the early 1880s. In order to cut costs, the aging impresario resorted to amateur actors so desperate for work they would perform without compensation or even pay him to go onstage. The final indignity was a pair of horrid Shakespearean productions that Maguire insisted upon, which broke up the eight-year partnership and led Belasco to leave town.

But a fabulous career was in store for the future Bishop of Broadway. During half a century in New York he was involved in 386 productions, and a playhouse on the Great White Way bears his name to this day. His melodrama *The Girl of the Golden West,* set in a mining town, was seen by the visiting Puccini, who made it the basis of one his most accomplished operas. *La Fanciulla del West,* despite the oddity of Italian-speaking 49ers, enjoyed a sensational opening at the Met in 1910 featuring Caruso.

But perhaps Belasco's highest achievement was his discovery of talented actors. His best find was Paul Warfield (born Paul Wollfeld). The great-grandson of a Polish rabbi and a native San Franciscan, Warfield had been an usher and newsboy at the Bush Street Theater and an unsuccessful vaudevillian. While in New York, throughout the 1890s, he played the burlesque houses, but he remained unnoticed. But Belasco saw potential in Warfield's act, the funny and sensitive mimicking of a Russian-Jewish immigrant, and he commissioned a drama to be written around him, *The Auctioneer.* Warfield prepared by spending a lot of time on the Lower East Side and eventually delivered a captivating performance. It was the first of five phenomenally successful Broadway plays on which the two San Franciscans collaborated in the new century; one of them, *The Music Master,* was seen by more than a million people in New York and on the road.[25] In another, Shakespeare's *Merchant of Venice,* which Belasco took out West, Warfield's rendition of Shylock was so sympathetic that he won the praise of a San Francisco rabbi in the audience who had expected an anti-Semitic caricature.[26] Warfield was forever grateful to his mentor for summoning him to stardom: "What other manager would have taken a clown out of burlesque and develop in him the power to bring an audience to tears?"[27]

Although Belasco would sometimes return to California—to Hollywood, where he worked for Cecil B. DeMille, and to San Francisco, where he would produce an occasional play—Manhattan remained the center of his universe. But in 1879, only a few years before he moved to New York permanently, Belasco and Maguire figured prominently in the greatest theatrical controversy in Northern California history—the first American *Passion,* a "miracle play" on the life of Jesus.

The project was the brainchild of the eccentric Salmi Morse (formerly Samuel Moss). A Jew who was likely from Posen, Morse had immigrated via England to New York and then, in 1848, to San Francisco. He failed as a gold miner and storekeeper but continued to seek adventure, managing first a hotel in Australia and later an import-export firm belonging to his English father-in-law in Constantinople. At the end of the 1850s, Morse, now converted to Christianity, returned to California with his bride and bought a ranch near Mendocino.[28] But in the following decade he sold it, left his wife, and moved to the Caribbean to chase another business opportunity.

In 1875 he showed up in San Francisco again, nearly fifty years old but having lost none of his nerve. Somewhat like Emperor Norton, whom he admired (and like Baron Munchausen, one scholar notes), Morse felt the need to concoct wild stories about himself that fooled virtually no one.[29] He claimed to have been born in England to an Oxford professor and to have been educated at Heidelberg. He bragged that he had built a grand hotel in Melbourne, served heroically in the Crimean War as a British colonel, and personally quashed an insurrection in Santo Domingo, where a grateful nation made his birthday a national holiday. A San Francisco newsman wrote that Morse "had a marvelous fund of erroneous information."[30] And by the late 1870s he was telling another whopper: he was a biblical scholar who had wandered the Holy Land for twenty years.

With this fabrication he hoped to lend credibility to what he trumpeted as a great contribution to American literature, his *Passion.* He first submitted the play to Catholic archbishop Joseph Alemany, who in January 1879 invited Morse to read it publicly at St. Ignatius College. Despite their reservations about Morse's frequent use of California slang, the critics generally responded favorably.[31]

But Morse envisioned something far grander—a lavish theatrical production. He sought out Maguire, of course, who immediately backed it with twenty-five thousand dollars. Rather than stage the *Passion* at the Baldwin, he booked the Grand Opera House, the city's largest theater, with four thousand seats. Maguire then prevailed on young James O'Neill (Eugene O'Neill's father) to play Jesus. He was reluctant at first, but soon grew a beard, wore his hair long, and began to live the part, declaiming his lines on the street and abstaining from tobacco, alcohol, and cursing.[32] Belasco, the obvious choice for lighting and set design, feverishly studied the Bible and artists' renditions of New Testament themes. The extravaganza featured four hundred extras, including a hundred mothers with babes in arms. When Joseph and Mary came down the mountain, Belasco proudly recalled, "We had a flock of real sheep following in their wake."[33]

But weeks before the premiere, scheduled for March 3, a roar of disapproval came from the Protestant ministry. The local preachers had long felt they were fighting a losing battle in Sodom on the Pacific, and, like many in nineteenth-century America, they viewed the theater as a "wicked, unchristian pastime."[34] Nowhere did performers take more liberties than in San Francisco, and although the pastors had failed to mount a concerted attack against Menken's gaudy show the previous decade, they went to war over Maguire's latest and worst offense. While the liberal Episcopalian bishop was appalled ("Think of the Redeemer of the world personified by a play actor"),[35] the Presbyterian reverend John Hemphill became almost apoplectic: "It is enough to make the blood of this so called Christian nation curdle in its veins to see that scene—the holiest and most awful in a Christian religion . . . put on the stage with caricature and burlesque, to be laughed at by the public."[36]

Although Protestant clergy vilified Morse, they said little about his or Belasco's Jewish origins. Even Hemphill, who had earlier publicly attacked Judaism, now held his anti-Semitism in check. Instead, the ministers blasted the Catholic hierarchy because of Archbishop Alemany's early connection with the play, a "Romish" plot, they claimed, to generate funds for a new Jesuit seminary.[37] The *Passion* thus heightened tensions between middle-class Protestants and Irish Catholic laborers, who only two years earlier had torn the city apart in their violent struggle against the Chinese.

One would have expected the Jewish community to oppose the play. Its class interests coincided more with those of the Protestant merchants than the Catholic workers, and, even more important, they might have been concerned about the gruesome crucifixion scenes, which since the Middle

Ages had incited acts of anti-Semitism. Yet San Francisco was different: Jews not only wrote and staged the drama but also defended its showing. Opposing censorship was one motive, certainly, but Rabbi Henry Vidaver also rejected the Protestants' elevation of Jesus as the only figure whose portrayal in the theater ought to be forbidden. "Why should there be more objection . . . than to that of Moses or Elijah?" asked the spiritual leader of Sherith Israel.[38] Even the pugnacious columnist Isidore Choynski discounted the possibility that the *Passion* would trigger an anti-Jewish attack and supported its showing.[39] One of the few Jewish objections came from a letter to the editor of the *Argonaut,* which urged, perhaps facetiously, that Jesus be played by a Jew rather than an Irishman.[40]

The Protestant ministers were not amused and formed a coalition that included like-minded politicians and journalists. San Franciscans became preoccupied with the dispute and "nothing else was thought of or discussed," lamented one of Maguire's rival theater managers.[41] Hours before the premiere, an angry band of religious protestors marched on city hall, entered the offices of the board of supervisors, and demanded it ban the *Passion.*[42] A resolution to that effect passed unanimously, but the district attorney, doubting its legality, refused to enforce it.[43] To the chagrin of the activists, who also demonstrated at the theater's door, the show would go on.

The Grand Opera House was packed. The *Argonaut's* critic claimed that "seven-eighths of the first audience were Jews,"[44] a claim that even if grossly exaggerated further indicates the bizarre nature of this episode. Moreover, local Jews accounted for a good deal of the supporting cast, its directors thinking the Hebrew "type" would best represent ancient Jerusalem's population.

The performance was as solemn as a church service. An austere program printed with a black border contained no cast of characters and requested no applause "until the drop of the curtain." The crowd sat transfixed. "Never have I seen an audience so awed," remembered Belasco at the end of his long career.[45] The script, however, with "few good lines and a great number of ungraceful ones," as one reviewer noted, was weak.[46] Far from having made a decades-long study of the New Testament, Morse relied solely on the King James version. But overall the play was well received. Critics praised the "grand-scale realism" of Belasco's inventive sets, costuming, and lighting and extolled O'Neill's interpretation of Jesus.[47]

Morse's *Passion* demonized the Jewish people only slightly less than its forerunners. On Mission Street as in Oberammergau, Bavaria, all of the guilt for the Savior's death fell on the Jews, none of it on the Romans. But as Alan Nielsen explains, "There is so little dramatic tension [in Morse's work] that it is questionable whether the cumulative effect could ever direct any audience's hatred specifically toward the Jews."[48] San Francisco's tolerant religious atmosphere may also be credited for the apparent lack of anti-Semitic incidents in the wake of the country's first *Passion.**

Benign though it was, the premiere failed to calm the Protestant clergy, who continued their efforts to shut down the play. Maguire himself ended it after one week but sought to revive it six weeks later, for Easter Week. By this time, though, officials had become convinced that the supervisors' ban would indeed hold up in court. After opening night of the second run, a policeman arrested O'Neill "for impersonating Jesus Christ"[49] and jailed the actor, still "wearing sandals, a flowing white robe, and a halo."[50]

Out on bail, O'Neill defiantly played the role again the following night. He was apprehended once more, and nine other cast members and Belasco were carted off with him. They were all released on bail, however, and presented several more shows as they awaited trial. But despite the notoriety, attendance dwindled and Maguire closed the play for good after the performance on April 21. Soon thereafter the actors were required to pay nominal fines, and the courtroom drama, which might have been a test case of freedom of speech, never took place.

Still, the furor spawned by the *Passion* drew national attention. The New York press ridiculed San Francisco as provincial because of the flap the play had caused and because the preachers had succeeded in banning it after about a dozen performances.[51] Of course the Gotham newspapers could not have anticipated that in the following decade Morse would attempt to take his epic to Broadway, where Protestant ministers made sure it would not open at all. Devastated by a failure far worse than the one in the West, the author of the *Passion,* penniless and now without any prospects, jumped to his death in the Hudson River.[52]

Another casualty of the *Passion* was Maguire, who was badly hurt financially and shorn of the vast influence on the local theater that he had enjoyed since the Gold Rush. The fall of his empire in the early 1880s and the

---

*One critic who despised the play did claim that on opening night "ignorant Irish who witnessed [the *Passion*] were so distempered that, on going forth, some of them, from time to time, assaulted peaceable Jews on the public streets." But there is no evidence for this assertion: there are no newspaper reports of such attacks and no mention of them by the *Passion*'s other detractors. According to the *Chronicle,* "the audience . . . quietly withdrew" (Alan Nielsen, *The Great Victorian Sacrilege: Preachers, Politics, and the Passion, 1879–1884* [Jefferson, N.C., 1991], 97).

departure for New York of hugely talented artists like Belasco and Warfield, and even the wacky showman Morse, ushered in a less experimental and duller period for the San Francisco stage, which lasted several decades. The new era was dominated not by risk-taking producers or innovative performers but instead by hard-boiled businessmen who staged low-quality entertainment and cared about little other than the box office.

Jews were among these exploiters as well. In the 1890s Al Hayman founded the Syndicate, a group of theaters that exerted an iron grip on both the local and national stage, squeezing out independent artists. Hayman, his brother Alf, and another of their San Francisco partners, J. J. Gottlob, were often blamed by drama critics for the decline in artistic quality in those years. Of course there had been a profusion of demeaning minstrels, "girlie shows," and animal acts since the Gold Rush, but now even serious theater was forced to bend to the will of the cartel, and too often mediocrity was the result.

The attacks of Harrison Grey Fiske, a reviewer for the San Francisco *Dramatic Mirror,* were so sharp and personal that Al Hayman sued the "Jew hater" for libel (he lost the case).[53] While the monopolistic tendencies of these San Francisco Jewish theater operators did not cause a major anti-Semitic backlash, it was clear that the Syndicate and its investors, such as Marion Leventritt, Herman Shainwald, and Moses Gunst, were contributing to the persistence of negative Jewish stereotypes, even while so many other local Jews were changing that image.[54] The *San Francisco Bulletin,* in summing up Hayman's career, referred to his "shrewd and acquisitive turn of mind."[55]

By the second decade of the new century, the Syndicate, weakened by lawsuits brought by David Belasco and rivaled by other combines (one of them a chain owned by yet another local Jewish businessman, Morris Meyerfeld), lost its hold on the national stage. And even at the height of its power in San Francisco, it could sometimes be bypassed by visiting superstars. None shone more brightly than the fiercely independent Sarah Bernhardt, who often performed in a giant tent rather than split her huge fees with Hayman and his partners. The Parisian actress, the illegitimate daughter of a Dutch Jewish prostitute, herself bore a child out of wedlock, so the private life of the "divine Sarah," like that of Menken a generation earlier, was fodder for the California press.

If anything, the exposés boosted ticket prices for Bernhardt's performances—they went as high as twenty-five dollars. She was immensely popular in San Francisco, to which she returned often during a three-decade period beginning in 1887. Bernhardt loved San Francisco and, with reporters trailing behind, she frequently visited Chinatown—its opium dens as well as its theaters and opera house. At one point she integrated highly complex Chinese dance forms into her act and reportedly "sent the house into convulsions."[56]

Her most memorable Bay Area appearance occurred in May 1906, free of charge to a community still traumatized by the earthquake a month earlier. She played the title role in Racine's classical tragedy *Phèdre* not in a large Syndicate house, nor in her tent, but in the Greek Theater in the Berkeley hills. The audience could gaze above the stage and across the bay and see San Francisco in its hour of crisis. Bernhardt later reminisced that in her entire life, "there is no other day to match it."[57] Almost sixty years old, she delivered, in French, an emotional performance hailed by one leading critic as "immortal."[58] That afternoon in Berkeley constituted one of the most sublime moments in Bay Area theater history—the highest expression of European culture fitting harmoniously into a distinctly Californian setting. Bernhardt, an internationally renowned artist and also a maverick, was identified as a Jew, but her appeal was universal.

"THE STEIN CORPORATION"

Growing up in Oakland in the 1880s, Gertrude Stein and her older brother Leo went to French plays, saw Millet's *Man with a Hoe* on display in San Francisco, and often attended light opera with their father. Bavarian-born immigrant Daniel Stein cared deeply about the education of his five children. Even before moving to the West Coast (he had first settled in Maryland and Pennsylvania), he had lived with his family in Vienna and Paris for two years, largely to broaden the horizons of his offspring. Thus the Steins were trilingual and often played classical music in their rustic East Oakland home. There was much tension between the generations—Daniel was rigid and demanding, not least of all regarding Jewish observance—but the children were grateful for having been raised with a keen appreciation of nature and the arts.

After the early deaths of both parents, Michael, the oldest child and the only one with any business sense, became the head of the family. He augmented his father's estate by improving upon Daniel's plans to consolidate the San Francisco streetcar lines and selling the concept to railroad magnate Collis Huntington. Owning some real estate as well, the young Steins now had an independent source of income for life.

By far the most intellectually inclined of the Stein children, Gertrude and Leo were inseparable. Leo entered Harvard in 1892, and Gertrude joined him there a year later. They plunged into a stimulating world of ideas, studying under George Santayana and William James. The Steins considered themselves advantaged as Californians, because for them the West meant "freedom, imagination, and unconventionality."[59]

Gertrude also left Oakland with a deep sense of Jewish identity. Her circle of friends in Cambridge was almost exclusively Jewish, and her closest companion was the brilliant Leon Solomons, from a noted San Francisco Sephardi family; the two collaborated on psychological experiments in William James's course.[60] She felt almost tribal bonds of friendship with other Harvard Jews as well, and in her junior year wrote a term paper arguing against intermarriage. "The Jews shall marry only the Jew," Gertrude Stein wrote at twenty. "He may have business friends among the Gentiles; he may visit with them in their work and their pleasure, he will go to their schools . . . but in the sacred precincts of the home, in the close union of family and kinsfolk he must be a Jew with Jews; the gentile has no place there."[61] For the rest of her life Stein thought of Jews as the "chosen people," with special abilities and a unique ethical mission in the world. She even claimed that Abraham Lincoln had Jewish ancestry.[62]

But while Gertrude and Leo were intensely proud of being Jewish, as adults they never observed their faith; rather, they worshipped art and literature. Leo left college to travel for a year, broadening his sense of beauty in exotic locales such as Kyoto, Hong Kong, and Cairo. He would eventually finish his formal education at Johns Hopkins, but then went abroad again, to Florence, where he spent two years studying Renaissance painting and initiated a lifelong friendship with Bernhard Berenson, later a renowned art critic and historian. Gertrude also enrolled in Johns Hopkins, completing nearly all the coursework for a medical degree but never graduating. Feeling snubbed there as a Jew and even more as a female, and depressed because of the breakup of her relationship with a young Jewish woman she had met at Harvard, she turned increasingly to writing. In 1903 she decided to join her brother yet again, now as an expatriate. Leo had moved from Florence to Paris, and Gertrude would share his apartment near the Luxembourg Gardens.

Within the year, Leo and Gertrude were joined by their brother Michael and his wife, Sarah, the strong-willed daughter of a San Francisco Jewish lawyer. The Michael Steins, with their young son, set up house only a few blocks from Gertrude and Leo. During the next decade the four Steins— "the Stein Corporation," as they were jokingly known—would be instrumental in transforming Western art.

Paul Cézanne had worked almost in obscurity until the Steins began buying his paintings. When Michael purchased *Portrait of the Artist's Son, Paul* for two hundred dollars, the French press noted the transaction and referred to him as a "crazy American."[63] But it was the young and impoverished Henri Matisse whose career was truly propelled by the Steins. In 1905 Leo bought *Woman with the Hat,* a widely ridiculed work that exemplified the fauves, or "wild beasts," as Matisse and his circle were known.* Viewing the portrait's furious brushstrokes of vivid greens, reds, and purples, "people were roaring with laughter at the picture and scratching at it," as Gertrude remembered.[64] Leo paid 500 francs, barely enough to buy winter clothing for Matisse's daughter.[65]

Sarah Stein did much more for the struggling artist, virtually sustaining him for the three decades she and Michael lived in Paris. Lacking her brother-in-law's background in art history, she judged paintings by instinct and, as Matisse's biographer has written, "delighted in the side of his work that struck others as the wildest and most barbaric."[66] In one eighteen-month period Sarah or Leo bought virtually all of Matisse's output, and she came to own forty of his paintings, displaying about a dozen in her apartment. She also bought his bronze sculptures and ceramic vases. Sarah pleaded Matisse's case with art critics, including Bernhard Berenson, whom she "hypnotized" into buying a picture himself.[67] She introduced Matisse to countless collectors, including the famous Cone sisters, whom Gertrude knew from Baltimore, and a host of wealthy San Francisco buyers passing through Paris. A century later Bay Area museums boast strong holdings of every phase of the master's work.

Soon after the San Francisco earthquake of 1906, Michael and Sarah returned home to assess the damage to the centerpiece of the family fortune, a block of houses on Lyon Street that fortunately—not least of all for Matisse—suffered little damage. She brought along three of his works, including the bold *Portrait with a Green Stripe.* Sarah exhibited the paintings

---

*Later the Steins sold the icon of modern painting to another discerning San Francisco Jewish art collector, Elise Haas, who eventually bequeathed it to the San Francisco Museum of Modern Art.

for her many friends; it was the first time Matisse's work was shown in North America. As she wrote Gertrude, "Since the startling news that there was such stuff in town . . . I have been a very popular lady."[68]

Like Sarah, many of the upper-middle-class Jewish women who came to view the paintings had studied art at the staid Mark Hopkins Institute and were astonished by a style resembling nothing they had ever seen. The young Annette Rosenshine, later a sculptor and psychoanalyst, was left "speechless and nonplussed, [believing] that these paintings were the accepted French art of the day."[69]

Fascinated not only by the art but also by Sarah's tales of Left Bank salons, Annette accepted the Steins' invitation to work for the family in Paris. Her two-year stay would bring her into daily contact with Gertrude and remake Rosenshine's life. Two other young women were also awed by the window on the Seine that Sarah had opened during her visit home: Harriet Levy, then a budding writer; and her intimate companion, the alluring Alice Toklas, an aspiring pianist who had lived with her pioneer Jewish grandparents on O'Farrell Street, next door to the Levys. Harriet and Alice eventually sailed for France, too. Like Rosenshine, Levy returned to California with Matisses (including the captivating *Girl with Green Eyes*) and other outstanding paintings, and continued her life of letters. Toklas, as is well known, put aside her own ambitions and in effect married Gertrude, remaining dutifully at her side until Stein's death in Paris in 1946.* Theirs was the best-known lesbian relationship of the twentieth century, and by writing of its sexual delights, Gertrude broke new ground in modern Western literature.

Several other San Francisco Jewish women artists were drawn across the Atlantic into the Stein circle, remaining for long periods before returning to the city deeply enriched by the experience. Perhaps none was more transformed than nineteen-year-old Theresa Ehrman (later Jelenko), daughter of Temple Emanu-El's sexton. During her year abroad she was in the employ, and under the watchful eye, of Michael and Sarah Stein (close friends of her mother) as their son's music tutor. Ehrman, a pianist, studied with a Parisian virtuoso and composer; later she would work in San Francisco as an accompanist and piano teacher.

In letters home, Ehrman waxes enthusiastic about the paintings in the Louvre, the recitals in the city's great concert halls, and the parade of artists

---

*Toklas stayed on alone until her death in 1967, after which she was buried next to Gertrude's frequently visited grave in Père Lachaise Cemetery.

frequenting the Stein house.[70] She marvels at Leo's intellect and is intrigued by Gertrude's mannish ways. As Sarah reported to the Ehrmans, "The stimulus of a trip like this has done its work."[71] During her year abroad she also resolved her stormy love affair with Pablo Casals. The cellist, still in his twenties but already world famous, had met her in San Francisco while on tour, and though their romance ended in Paris, they would remain friends for the rest of their lives.

In mid-1904 Theresa accompanied the Michael Steins on a long, culture-filled journey through Western Europe, and then, alone, visited her uncle's home in a village outside Frankfurt. Her father's brother had opted not to immigrate to America a generation earlier and, with his large family, lived a traditional Jewish life. Theresa, raised in diverse, liberal San Francisco and for half a year exposed by the Steins to avant-garde European thought, had nothing in common with her aunt, uncle, and cousins. "It was very strange . . . to meet such orthodox people," she wrote home.[72] Theresa knew enough German to communicate with them, but the encounter reflected a gulf of incomprehension. They made their California guest uncomfortable by dwelling on the petty squabbles that plagued their tiny Jewish community and peppering her with religious questions: "whether the *shul* in Paris was big, and if the rabbi was good . . . and whether many Pollakim went to Temple Emanu-El in San Francisco! I started to explain that we were reform Jews, and they didn't know what I meant and [I was told by another guest] sotto voce to shut up."[73] Her uncle also asked if she'd "had to associate much with goyim while traveling."[74] Presumably she revealed nothing about her relationship with Casals. She answered most of his inquiries "falsely" and declined the invitation to extend her visit. "How could I stay in this atmosphere without living a lie?" she wrote her mother.[75]

But if Ehrman left her ancestral village irritated by old-world Judaism, she also witnessed the dark side of modern bohemian life during her year on the Continent; vicious clashes within the Stein circle made her religious relatives' spats seem tame by comparison. Early on there were intense sexual jealousies, usually involving Gertrude and young female visitors from San Francisco. And a profound philosophical disagreement between Gertrude and Leo about the nature of art and literature drove brother and sister apart for the second half of their lives. After 1914 they never spoke to one another again.

The breach stemmed from her close friendship with Pablo Picasso, the indigent twenty-four-year-old who painted Gertrude's portrait soon after they met.* During the ninety sittings the two became virtual soul mates; Gertrude was the most important woman in his life except for his mother and lover.[76] Stein's own art, meanwhile, came to be influenced by the radical cubist style Picasso adopted around 1908. She linked her "struggle" with his: both were out to "kill the nineteenth century."[77]

Leo would have none of this. He thought the young painter's cubism an "utter abomination" and resented the Spaniard's claim on his sister's aesthetic loyalties.[78] But Gertrude continued to champion Picasso and others in his school such as Georges Braque and Juan Gris. She also angered Leo, and of course Sarah, by denigrating Matisse as stuffy and bourgeois. Meanwhile, fierce competitiveness developed between Matisse and Picasso, between the fauves and the artists whose works were even wilder, based on disorder and fragmentation. The two geniuses began "a lifelong dialogue on canvas," writes an art historian, a "polarity . . . defined and fostered by the Steins . . . a rivalry that proved one of the richest and most productive in the history of Western art."[79]

The war between the Steins spread to literature. Leo dismissed Gertrude's repetitive syntax and page-long sentences as nonsense. He vacated their shared apartment in 1914, married, moved to Tuscany, and published several works on aesthetics. But he suffered from a myriad of mental and physical ailments, and, envious of his sister's fame—undeserved, in his opinion—was hurt most by the growing realization that he would be remembered primarily as Gertrude Stein's brother.

Gertrude exaggerated only slightly when in 1928 she called herself "the most famous Jew in the world."[80] Although the Stein family had been known before World War I for its influence on modern painting, in the 1920s Gertrude alone emerged as a celebrity, a grand lady of letters, a mentor of young writers. Hemingway was her guest for a while—Gertrude claimed that she had taught him how to write—and he brought into the Stein orbit F. Scott Fitzgerald and others of the "lost generation" (a term she coined). Sherwood Anderson, Ford Maddox Ford, John Dos Passos, and Ezra Pound all gravitated to her salon between the wars.

Many of Gertrude's numerous works were published in the interwar years, and her odd, rhythmic style, laden with subconscious sexual conno-

---

* The stupendous work was one of only two canvases Gertrude carried with her when she and Alice fled Paris during the Nazi occupation (Linda Wagner-Martin, *Favored Strangers: Gertrude Stein and Her Family* [New Brunswick, N.J., 1995], 237). It was bequeathed to the Metropolitan Museum of Art.

tations, generated confusion and controversy on both sides of the Atlantic. But it was a best seller written in 1932 in her lover's voice, the charming if self-serving *Autobiography of Alice B. Toklas,* a gossipy memoir of Parisian cultural life, that brought Stein the *gloire* she had always sought.[81]

Fresh from this success, Gertrude and Alice sailed to America for a lecture tour, their first visit in three decades. They crossed the country amidst much publicity and were met by curious, though mostly approving, audiences along the way. After reaching the Bay Area, Gertrude issued that most famous rebuke of Oakland, "There is no there there."[82] But it may be read as a lament for the pastoral ten-acre plot that had been her childhood home, now a "shabby and overgrown" housing development: "the house, the big house and the big garden and the eucalyptus trees and the rose hedge naturally were not any longer existing, what was the use."[83] As she said on the lecture platform, with Oakland in mind, "We take our roots with us. . . . I know because you can go back to where they are and they can be less real to you than they were three thousand, six thousand miles away. . . . They will take care of themselves and they will take care of you, too, though you may never know how it has happened."[84]

Late in her life she reflected further upon her formative years in the Bay Area:

> After all anybody is as their land and air is. Anybody is as the sky is low or high, the air heavy or clear and anybody is as there is wind or no wind there. It is that which makes them and the arts they make and the work they do and the way they eat and the way they drink and the way they learn and everything. . . . I have lived half my life in Paris, not the half that made me but the half in which I made what I made.[85]

PARIS OF THE WEST

While Gertrude Stein went to the City of Light to smash conventional thinking, for other Northern Californians Paris meant something else entirely: it was the epitome of old-world refinement, order, and elegance, a thousand-year-old city with much to teach a rowdy town that had emerged overnight. And Jews often had a special connection to *this* Paris.

In the late nineteenth century between 5 and 10 percent of San Francisco's Jewish population had its roots in Alsace or Lorraine.[86] This contingent tended to revere Paris—the cradle of the French Revolution, which had conferred citizenship on the Jews—as a sort of Mount Sinai, and they often spread Gallic civilization with missionary zeal. Daniel Levy, for a while cantor and educator at Emanu-El, furthered French culture in San Francisco more than did anyone else in the second half of the nineteenth century. A teacher of the language at Boys' High School, he was also instrumental in the French Library, Hospital Society, and National League, and was president of the local Alliance Française.[87]

A more flamboyant cultural ambassador—one who spent half of every year in Paris—was Raphael Weill, whose famed White House near Union Square offered matchless French lace and linen. According to local gossip columnists he was the perfect Frenchman: a "boulevardier, club man, arts patron and connoisseur, gourmet chef and perennially eligible bachelor."[88] An officer in the Legion of Honor, he defended *la patrie* during every crisis, from the Franco-Prussian War to World War I, when he hurried overseas to enlist in the French army but was rejected due to his advanced age. San Francisco's German Jews were frequently irked by such demonstrations of Gallic pride and were not sorry to see Weill and his countrymen in distress during the Dreyfus Affair.[89]

The four Godchaux sisters, meanwhile, diligently taught French and classical music in their pioneer parents' dark Victorian home, which was filled with objets d'art. The family was deeply admired, and one of the four brothers, Edmond, was elected state assemblyman and later served as county recorder for a third of a century. In the early 1920s, two generations of grateful alumni from "Little France," as the family's Buchanan Street house was known, presented Edmond and his three unmarried sisters with a trip to Paris (remarkably, only one of the eight Godchaux children ever married).[90] Being tutored by one of the small, squat Godchaux women—"they each resembled an upholstered chair," remembers a former pupil—could be intimidating, and children were as fearful of accidentally knocking a porcelain figurine to the floor as they were of missing a conjugation.[91] But such was the premium placed on learning French that the sisters attracted a steady procession of students for forty years.

The city began to take on a more Continental appearance by the last decades of the nineteenth century, its plain, utilitarian structures gradually giving way to a grander and more ornamental style.[92] As architects and builders, Jews played a major role in this process, and they often looked to Paris for inspiration. Gustave Albert Lansburgh and Alfred Henry Jacobs, both children of pioneers, graduated from Paris's École des Beaux-Arts, the world's leading architectural school at the time. They shared the distinction of being among the few Americans there but otherwise had very different backgrounds. Lansburgh, born in Panama of a Sephardi mother who immigrated to San Francisco, was orphaned at an early age. Emanu-El's Rabbi Jacob Voorsanger arranged for a wealthy congregant to support the youth, who attended the University of California.[93] Jacobs was the privileged son of the dry goods merchant and insurance magnate Julius Jacobs, who served as assistant United States treasurer and overseer of the San Francisco mint.[94] Alfred took two degrees at MIT.

But both youths went through the same rigorous course of study at the École during the first decade of the twentieth century, and Lansburgh graduated with the highest honors. Obviously, the two Californians were molded not only by their eminent French professors but also by the monumental public buildings they saw in Paris, such as the majestic Garnier Opera House, erected a generation earlier during the Second Empire.

After returning to San Francisco, they designed buildings that also fit the California landscape. Lansburgh had apprenticed under Bernard Maybeck, from whom he learned about the use of native woods and handcrafted details. But even more evident in Lansburgh's and Jacobs's work is their Beaux-Arts training, which resulted in stately, symmetrical edifices with a profusion of decoration.[95] Like their French counterparts, they worked closely with engineers and adopted the latest technology, but they also reached back to the Renaissance and the ancient world.

Lansburgh designed the homes of several major Jewish institutions. His plan for the restoration of Emanu-El's Sutter Street Temple after the earthquake won an award from the Grand Salon of the Champs-Élysée, although cost restraints and a shortage of building materials diminished the final product. His preference for classical forms can clearly be seen in Oakland's well-proportioned Temple Sinai. Completed in 1914, it features graceful Corinthian columns supporting a Greco-Roman portico, and an elliptical dome. His Concordia Club on Van Ness Avenue (built in two phases, in 1909 and 1915) sported a typically elaborate Beaux-Arts façade with eight long decorative columns, a prominent pediment, and concrete ornamentation over the doors and windows.*[96]

---

*In 1946, almost all exterior decoration was removed, a casualty of both changing styles and safety concerns (Bernice Scharlach, *House of Harmony: The Concordia-Argonaut's First 130 Years* [Berkeley, 1983], 102). Lansburgh, who lived until 1969, bewailed the boxy glass and steel high-rises that after World War II came to replace the city's more ornamental buildings (Norton B. Stern and William M. Kramer, "G. Alfred Lansburgh," *WSJHQ* 13 [April 1981]: 221).

Lansburgh's patron, Moses Gunst, had him design several downtown commercial buildings in a modern French Renaissance style, but the architect is best known for his many grandiose theaters; his post-earthquake 2,500-seat New Orpheum, on O'Farrell Street near Powell, resembled a French opera house.[97] He was later chosen as one of the architects for the city's neoclassical War Memorial Opera House. Alfred Henry Jacobs was also a prolific designer of extravagant theaters such as the Curran, Granada, and Alhambra in San Francisco, and the Winema, a redwood building in Scotia, California, near Eureka.

Even when it did not engage one of its own as architect, often the case when it constructed its synagogues, the Jewish community appeared to have a preference for École des Beaux-Arts alumni, and for the Continental style. Sherith Israel, designing its new temple in 1905, chose Albert Pissis, an award-winning graduate of the École and advocate in California of the Beaux-Arts method.[98] (The temple would withstand the 1906 earthquake and be the city's grandest synagogue for two decades, until Emanu-El erected its Lake Street Temple.) To be sure, the exterior of the temple, except for its large rose window, is more austere than most great French houses of worship of that period (consider Montmartre's lavishly adorned Sacré-Coeur, as an extreme example), but Pissis's eclectic and luxurious interior, and his brother Emile's magnificent stained-glass windows, reflected the prevailing penchant for ornamentation.

The Victorian houses of the Jewish elite—and Pissis designed several of the greatest—also tended to be heavily decorated both inside and out, though they are not properly considered to represent the Beaux-Arts style.[99] But the best-known Jewish private residence during the first half of the twentieth century could not have been more French. The Pacific Heights home of community leaders and art patrons Marcus and Cora Koshland—the setting for countless Jewish musical events—was a replica of the Petit Trianon, Marie Antoinette's favorite palace on the grounds of Versailles.[100]

THE CREATIVE FRONTIER

The Koshlands, like many in their social circle, were avid collectors of oil paintings, often portraits, the sine qua non of an elegant home. And a group of Jewish artists were among the city's leading painters. Five in particular, all born of pioneers in the quarter century following the Gold Rush and trained across the Atlantic (four in Paris), helped make San Francisco a "creative frontier," even if most of them returned to the Bay Area only sporadically.[101] Their achievements were invariably heralded in the local press, and their best works often exhibited in San Francisco.

Joseph Greenbaum, who produced many fine portraits of the Bavarian Jewish elite (including his own family members) as well as landscapes of the Southwest, won awards in both Europe and America. Joseph Raphael lived most of his adult life in Belgium, but his impressionist oils were regularly shown and deeply admired in California for their depictions of nature and their insights into the human character.

Ernest Peixotto, of an uncommonly gifted Sephardi family, was perhaps the most versatile of this set: he rendered superb oil portraits and landscapes of the Seine River and the Monterey coast, painted murals in the homes of patrons in California and Italy, drew street scenes of San Francisco's China-town, and spent most of his career in New York as an illustrator and commercial artist. In the late 1890s, after his return home from two extended stays in Paris, he was one of Les Jeunes, a coterie of rebellious youths who hoped to create a cultural revolution with an odd little monthly known as the *Lark*.[102] Printed on bamboo paper obtained in Chinatown, it was a California version of fin de siècle European periodicals that experimented in literature and visual arts. It resembled the *Yellow Book* of London (which carried Aubrey Beardsley's drawings) and *La Revue blanche,* which Peixotto had seen in bookstalls along the Seine. The *Lark* covered nature worship, "nonsense" poetry (anticipating the dadaists), and innovations in graphic design, which seem to prefigure the counterculture of the 1960s.

One of Les Jeunes was Frank Norris, a close friend of Peixotto in San Francisco and Paris, where both studied art. Norris was destined to become one of America's greatest novelists, and Peixotto illustrated his first short story, set in France, in the avant-garde literary magazine the *Wave,* which was more serious and influential than the *Lark*.[103]

While Peixotto flirted with *la vie bohème* only as a young man, the painter and poet Anne Bremer remained a nonconformist her entire life. Like so many of her fellow San Francisco artists, Bremer attended the Mark Hopkins Institute, but she soon transferred to the Art Students League, a hotbed of innovation. After a year in Paris at the Academie Moderne, she returned home and began producing portraits and landscapes hailed—and sometimes severely criticized—for their strikingly vivid colors.[104] Often in frail health, she wrote highly original mystical poetry when she could not lift a paintbrush. She never married but enjoyed the close companionship of her bachelor cousin, Albert Bender, who after her death in 1923 would become one of the city's leading art patrons.

The most accomplished and revered Jewish artist produced by pioneer California was Toby Rosenthal, son of a Prussian-Polish tailor. The local press fawned over the "boy of genius" whose lifelike sketches were so promising.[105] At seventeen he journeyed to Munich and enrolled in its prestigious Royal Academy. His proud parents shared photographs of his latest works with local journalists, and some of his paintings, sent from Munich, were displayed in downtown galleries. Coming home in 1871 after six years abroad, he was feted as a celebrity, invited to ostentatious parties thrown by the Jewish elite, and often commissioned to paint their portraits.[106] He painted I. W. Hellman and Sophie Gerstle Lilienthal, but the artist's favorite was the double portrait of Jacob Stern (Levi Strauss's nephew) and his daughter Fanny.[107] He was also commissioned to portray leading non-Jews, including Claus Spreckels and his wife, Alma, and the eminent pioneer historian Hubert Howe Bancroft.[108]

Yet portraiture was not Rosenthal's passion, and he was frustrated that the nouveaux riches lacked the imagination for anything else. He once told his friend and admirer Isidore Choynski of a well-to-do Jewish woman, dubbed "Mrs. Shoddy" by the columnist, who asked "whether smaller-sized pictures might not come a little cheaper."[109] In Munich, though, where he would spend the rest of his life, Rosenthal had many offers to create paintings of grand narratives taken from the Bible, mythology, romantic poetry, or everyday life. The fine detail of his subjects' dress and furnishings, along with the depth of emotion in their faces and gestures, gained him international fame by the mid-1870s.

San Franciscans reveled in his success, and in 1875 the arrival of his masterpiece *Elaine* was acclaimed as no other painting in the city's history had been. Based on a Tennyson poem, the large, haunting canvas features the corpse of a golden-haired beauty, driven to death by her love for Sir Lancelot. The unfounded rumor that an Oakland girl had been the model for Elaine in Munich only heightened the anticipation, and *Elaine* clubs were founded, songs were composed, and Tennyson's epic poem became a local best seller.[110] Having interviewed people who remembered the craze, one historian wrote, "If the murals of the Sistine Chapel had been hung in . . . City Hall they would have caused no greater sensation. After all, a San Francisco boy had painted what . . . was called the greatest painting in the world."[111]

More than a thousand people a day paid to view it in a downtown gallery.[112] But the painting was soon stolen, cut from its frame by a gang of crooks who held it for ransom. The police soon found *Elaine* and easily apprehended the robbers, but San Franciscans could barely think of anything else until the "crime . . . against civilization,"[113] as the *Daily Alta California* put it, was solved.* A long procession of art lovers filed past the empty picture frame as if at a funeral and, according to the *Chronicle,* "some ladies actually shed tears."[114]

The artist was in Munich during the great *Elaine* robbery and returned to San Francisco only one more time, in 1879, primarily to visit his aging parents, who had sacrificed much for his education and that of his brother, who had graduated from Harvard Law School. But Rosenthal, though he married a Bavarian and became a German citizen, remained bound to the city of his youth. He frequently hosted visitors from San Francisco—some of whom sat for their portraits in his Munich atelier—and in 1884 was given a one-man show by the San Francisco Art Association. Seven of his paintings, including the *Trial of Constance de Beverly,* perhaps his greatest work, were exhibited with much anticipation, echoing the clamor over *Elaine.*

Later in the century, however, he fell out of favor with the public, his painstakingly crafted academic style slighted by critics and collectors who gradually came to prefer a more modern and experimental approach.[115] Yet Rosenthal's impact on San Francisco was lasting. It went beyond the quality of his art, impressive though that was, to the self-image he helped provide a frontier town that still lacked a proper art museum. The city's love affair with its favorite homegrown artist and his paintings was an indication of the hunger for high culture in a place on the far side of the continent and yet so much more than a provincial outpost.

At the turn of the twentieth century, painters received the most public attention of all the visual artists, but second-generation San Francisco Jews also gained recognition as sculptors. Best known was the Paris-trained Edgar Walter, son of a highly successful Bavarian-born businessman. A student of Rodin, he created carvings that adorned the War Memorial Opera House and intricate stone lion heads that can be seen today above the courtyard entrance to Emanu-El's sanctuary. Very different was the work of Annette Rosenshine. Influenced by the experimental art she had seen in the Steins' salons, as well as Jungian psychology, she sculpted

---

* But the episode could be overstated, as it was by two contemporary historians of Western Jewry, who called the heist a "cataclysm unparalleled until the ground was split asunder in 1906" and "not a theft or robbery [but] the abduction of a beautiful dead maiden, a kind of necrophilic rape" (William M. Kramer and Norton B. Stern, *San Francisco's Artist Toby E. Rosenthal* [Northridge, Calif., 1978], 32, 36).

highly abstract busts of famous people (like Alice Toklas), as well as tiny grotesque figurines.

Perhaps the most inventive Jewish artist of all was a cartoonist, among the greatest in American history. Son of Max Goldberg, a Prussian-Polish pioneer who served as police commissioner, fire chief, and Republican ward heeler, Rube Goldberg grew up in San Francisco in the 1880s and '90s. Max's colorful—and sometimes corrupt—cronies came over to the family home for a friendly game of poker every Friday night, and these "politicians and windbags" made an indelible impression on the future satirist.[116]

Drawing for the Lowell High School paper, Rube showed talent, but Max, unlike Toby Rosenthal's father, was dead set against his son becoming an artist; he wanted Rube to attend West Point or Annapolis.[117] They compromised on Berkeley's College of Mining and Engineering, and Rube graduated in 1904, but having a cartoon accepted by the *Pelican,* the campus humor magazine, he claimed, was "a greater thrill than a good mark in calculus or geology."[118] He worked one summer in a gold mine, and also put in a brief stint with the city engineer's office in San Francisco designing sewers and water mains, but he felt unfulfilled without a sketchbook in hand. An eight-dollar-a-week job as cartoonist for the *Chronicle* sports page launched him on a career that would ultimately be capped with a Pulitzer Prize. The series of sketches called the *Fan Kid* revealed a young man with a keen sense of human nature. It stripped the pretense from one of the most serious urban endeavors—spectator sports—and skewered manic rooters along with all-knowing commentators. In later decades he would take on theatergoers and tourists, politicians and scientists.

Goldberg was quickly hired away by the San Francisco *Bulletin,* and his caricatures of the world of boxing in particular made him the city's leading humorist while still in his early twenties.[119] Longing to work in a larger media market, he moved to the East Coast soon after the 1906 earthquake and began a long association with the *New York Evening Mail;* his syndicated cartoons lampooning the machine age were seen by millions every day. One of his most famous characters was inspired by two of his teachers at the University of California, one in time-and-motion studies and the other in analytic mechanics. They were the models for the loony Professor Lucifer Gorgonzola Butts, who invented absurdly complicated contraptions to perform the simplest tasks.[120]

An even stronger California memory for Goldberg was a childhood trip he took in 1896 through the Yosemite Valley. It was then an unspoiled game preserve—his well-connected father was one of its directors—and for the rest of his life Rube recalled the "thrilling experience" that included "a stage coach drawn by four fiery horses."[121] According to his biographer, Goldberg "equated the grandeur of Yosemite with Paradise—a tiny indication of the peace and beauty and innocence of divine creation. [It] gave Rube a sense of the beginning of time, before men and machinery had bungled God's masterpiece. Later [his] greatest cartoons dealt with the impact of technology on the world, a concept strongly developed from his vision at Yosemite."[122]

Could not only the unprecedented freedom of the West but also its stunning natural setting have accounted at least in part for the remarkable Jewish achievements in the visual arts? Certainly such a phenomenon was atypical among Jewish communities before the twentieth century. Indeed, scholars have often pointed to a "logocentricity"—an emphasis on language, and especially the printed word—on the part of the People of the Book, and a concomitant weakness in visual aptitude, perhaps stemming from the biblical commandment against graven images.[123] One American Jewish cultural historian believes this dichotomy valid for the period before World War II and uses a line from Oscar Wilde to make his point: Jews "only believe in things you cannot see."[124] But this Jewish "attraction to the impalpable at the expense of the tangible" was yet another generalization stood on its head in the Bay Area.[125]

GUMP'S AND THE BRIDGE TO ASIA

San Francisco's centrally located Chinatown, the most vibrant Asian community in North America, fascinated many second-generation Jewish artists and intellectuals. Leo Stein and his sister-in-law Sarah often visited the alluring quarter, seeking Japanese prints and Chinese ceramics. David Belasco and Toby Rosenthal were repelled by the crowded, unsanitary conditions as well as the gambling, prostitution, and drug trade, but their interest in an exotic culture drew them nonetheless. And one child of a Jewish pioneer—introduced to the food and clothing of the Orient by the family's Chinese cook—made Chinatown his "favorite haunt" and fell in love with Asian civilization.[126] Abraham Livingston Gump suffered from bad eyesight even as a boy and would be nearly blind as an adult, but with "seeing fingers" was able to become the West Coast's most prominent importer of Asian art, jewelry, and fine furniture and change the taste of San Franciscans.

Abe's stern father was Solomon Gump, of Heidelberg, who arrived in America in 1850 and journeyed to San Francisco in 1863. He specialized in large gilt-edged barroom mirrors—always in demand because of the damage done by gunfights. He stocked picture frames as well and soon became a seller of art. He provided paintings for saloons, the "first art galleries of the West," which hung his voluptuous nudes over the bar.[127] But gradually the Emanu-El congregant moved up the ladder of respectability and carried works of the greatest pioneer artists, including grand landscapes by William Keith, a lifelong family friend. Later Solomon made annual trips to Europe, acquiring masterpieces he sold to fabulously wealthy clients such as Collis Huntington, who was furnishing his mansion on Nob Hill. By century's end Gump's was arguably the leading art dealer in the city.[128]

But his store near Union Square, along with much of its art, was destroyed in the earthquake of 1906. Solomon's health, already poor, deteriorated even further after the disaster, but three of his four sons, led by thirty-seven-year-old Abe, borrowed funds from Ignatz Steinhart's Anglo-California Bank and rebuilt the family firm. Abe also sought to point Gump's in a new direction—Asian art. He had to fight hard because his father and brothers believed the public's rampant anti-Chinese and anti-Japanese sentiments would doom the venture.[129]

The family finally agreed that one-third of the temporary store on California Street would become the Oriental Room, filled with the finest porcelain and embroidered brocade that Abe could find in nearby Chinatown. Soon their stock was supplemented by American servicemen returning from China with pieces pilfered during the Boxer Rebellion. But the turning point came when Abe sent plucky Ed Newell to Asia as a buyer for the store. He bought priests' robes in Kyoto, teakwood furniture in Canton, and silk and satin in Shanghai.[130] Next he journeyed to Beijing, becoming one of the first Western buyers to venture into northern China. His purchases proved enormously popular with Gump's clientele, and Abe had Japanese carpenters build a much more elaborate and authentic Oriental Department when the company returned to Union Square in 1909. One room, with rice-paper windows and sliding doors, simulated a Japanese home, while another replicated a Kyoto temple.[131] Kimono-clad Asian women served the customers tea, and Abe always followed the Chinese practice of keeping the highest-quality goods out of sight; they were brought out only for the best clients.

In 1917 Abe accompanied Newell to the Orient on a five-month trip that added the most precious commodity of all to Gump's treasure house: jade. Working in China with a comprador, or go-between, the two Californians bought exquisite jade carvings and became the first Americans to acquire a major part of the eighteenth-century emperor Ch'ien Lung's personal collection.[132] Nothing gave Abe more pride than the Jade Room he installed in Gump's, and in the 1920s the man who assessed the value of a gem only by touch emerged as the world's leading dealer of jade.[133]

But Abe was always more than a mere salesman. Visitors to San Francisco, including many celebrities, flocked to Gump's because of his legendary knowledge of the product line, and the "apostle" of Chinese culture would often dispatch learned consultants to help people decorate their homes with an Asian motif.[134] Many of his acquisitions went into museums across the country, and some adorned the Hearst Castle in San Simeon. Above all, though, he altered the decor of thousands of San Francisco homes belonging to the middle class. "Where the [parlors] of the 'nineties had their gilt cornices, gold-framed mirrors and marble statuary," according to Abe's biographer,

> the early nineteen hundreds saw Japanese screens embroidered to blend with individual color schemes, Chinese rugs on the floor, Japanese and Chinese prints on the walls. Displayed on teakwood stands were small ivories or fine bronzes modeled . . . from animals in the Tokyo zoo. Pianos were draped with mandarin coats from China, a priest robe from Japan, or a "Spanish shawl" from Canton. . . . [A]ttractive trays made from embroidered mats added an Oriental touch to the simplest living room.[135]

Of course there remained an impenetrable social barrier dividing whites from Asians; the vaunted tolerance of the Bay Area did not cross the color line in the early twentieth century. But Abraham Gump, in bringing the beauty and serenity of the Far East into the private living quarters of the West, forged a rare link between his neighbors and the civilizations across the Pacific.

PEOPLE OF THE BODY

Even as they tastefully decorated their homes, Jews, like other Californians, were beckoned—and challenged—by the great outdoors. The memoirs of the second generation abound with references to swimming and sailing, cycling and horseback riding, hiking and scouting, and even mountaineering. And, although the Jewish community comprised only 7 percent of the city's population by the turn of the twentieth century, it produced a bevy of world-class athletes. They competed in sports arenas packed with spectators, which were no less a part of the emergent urban culture than opera houses, theaters, and art galleries.

The feats of the Jewish athletes, like those of the gifted Jewish artists who were their contemporaries, flew in the face of the stereotypical image of the Jew. In 1904 a sportswriter for the *Chronicle* marveled at the physical ability of a group "who are not considered an athletic race" and whose "tendencies have been more to mercantile and financial success than to specialized development for muscular prowess."[136]

Even in the pioneer period an internationally renowned Jewish marksman had appeared. Born and raised in Prussian Poland, Philo Jacoby, who came to San Francisco in his early twenties, held the unlikely day job of editor of the *Hebrew*. Jacoby emphasized his Teutonic roots and joined the local German Turnverein and rifle club; he would be president of both for many decades. A formidable weightlifter, wrestler, and gymnast, he was unsurpassed as a sharpshooter, able to hit a bull's-eye six inches in diameter from 180 yards away. On a European tour in 1873, he captured a championship in Switzerland. Probably the first American to win an international sports competition, he led the field in contests in Germany and Austria-Hungary as well. In Vienna he received the gold medal from Emperor Franz-Josef himself. He competed successfully on the Continent again in 1890, and even after the turn of the century, in his mid-sixties and ailing, he took top honors at a national shooting match held in the Bay Area.[137]

The American-born second generation followed with stars in almost every major sport. Professional baseball was primitive in the nineteenth century, but the most popular player in the city—Reuben Levy, born to Prussian-Polish parents in 1862—was a Jew. A graceful left fielder in the struggling California League, he often played before crowds of ten thousand or more in Golden Gate Park, many of his adoring fans simply sitting behind him on the outfield grass.[138] Jews also excelled in athletics at Stanford and UC Berkeley, in track and field and football.[139]

But there was one sport in particular in which Jews, along with Irish, dominated the city: boxing, the most passionate pastime for many turn-of-the-century Americans, although it was illegal in many locations. Three of the top fighters in the world were San Francisco Jews. On the amateur level, heavyweight Samuel Berger, later a clothing merchant, reigned supreme, winning the gold medal at the Olympiad in St. Louis in 1904.[140] The world featherweight champion throughout the first decade of the century was Abe Attell, the "Little Hebrew," who had grown up in a Russian-Jewish family of nineteen children on the rough streets south of Market. Two of his brothers, Monte and Caesar, were also professional fighters. As one boxing historian put it, Abe "a brilliant ring general . . . knew every trick in the book [and] made the mauling, brawling types look silly when they tried to hit him."[141] But he was also a compulsive gambler with underworld ties and was suspended in New York State for cocaine use and fixing bouts.[142]

In big cities across the country, "tough Jews," usually children of East European immigrants, often saw prizefighting as a way out of poverty. This pattern, however, doesn't fit the greatest Jewish pugilist to come out of San Francisco. Joe Choynski, who many rank as the best heavyweight of his day, reportedly quoted Shakespeare, collected antiques, and neither smoke nor drank.[143] "Chrysanthemum Joe" (so dubbed because of his blond hair as well as his effete lifestyle) was the son of the Yale-educated columnist for the *American Israelite,* Isidore Choynski; while the father's weapon was a merciless pen, the son's was a left hook. And although Joe's cultured mother loathed her son's chosen profession, Choynski *père* took parental pride in the California Terror's success, informing his readers that his boy "fairly wiped the floor" with an Irish opponent to win the Pacific Coast Championship in 1887. The journalist surmised, however, that his own father, a rabbi in Posen, would have been appalled "if he could lift his head from the grave and look upon the arena where mostly the scum of society congregate and behold his grandson slugging and sparring, fighting and dodging."[144]

Joe never won the heavyweight championship, but in a career spanning from 1888 to 1904, he acquitted himself well against five men who at one time or another wore the crown. Choynski's success is all the more remarkable considering that he weighed only about 160 pounds; he would have been a light heavyweight had the category existed then.[145] At five feet, ten inches, "Little Joe" also conceded a height advantage to almost all his opponents. Nonetheless, he fought both Robert Fitzsimmons and the legendary Jim Jeffries to a draw, the latter in a grueling twenty-round bout. In 1901, in Texas, he knocked out two-hundred-pound Jack Johnson, later the first African American heavyweight champion. It was one of only two KOs the mighty Johnson ever suffered, and probably the only honest one.[146] But boxing was banned in the state—an interracial match only made things worse—and Texas Rangers arrested the two fighters, who were imprisoned in Galveston for a month. There they became close friends and, according to Johnson's biography, *Unforgivable Blackness,* the older Choynski taught him the sport's fine points.[147]

But Choynski's best-known fights were against James "Gentleman Jim" Corbett, one of the greatest boxers of all time. Brought together by their boastful older brothers, they had fought several brief, inconclusive bouts before their titanic struggle in May 1889, "an epic of pugilism [that] for the duration of savagery perhaps never had its equal."[148] The marathon lasted twenty-seven rounds. In the midday heat, on a barge moored near Benicia, neither held anything back. Corbett fought half the match with a broken right thumb, and Choynski's blood flowed so freely that both gladiators were in danger of slipping on the "claret" in the ring.[149] Finally, when the men were barely able to stand, the Irishman "let one desperate wallop go . . . in a dying end to finish up matters."[150] The lucky punch knocked Joe out, and Corbett, dazed himself, was declared the winner. It took Choynski half a year to recover, but "America's first great fighting Jew" had many years of prizefighting ahead of him, throughout the country and overseas.[151]

Jack Johnson called Choynski "the hardest hitter, pound for pound, of the last fifty years."[152] But Little Joe's success against much bigger men has been attributed more to his "empirical savvy" than his "brute strength."[153] The crafty Choynski suffered relatively few injuries and never hurt his hands, whether he fought bare-knuckled or gloved. Visits to Chinatown had taught him "to stick [his] fists into a pickling vat, maybe for hours, just to tighten them up."[154] For the Frisco Flash, boxing was a science and an art.

FOUR

Eden on the Pacific

The Challenges to Judaism at the Turn of the Century

ONLY FOR A FEW CULTURAL LUMINARIES in the Bay Area's second generation of Jews was Judaism of primary importance. To be sure, only a handful converted to Christianity, including Alice Toklas and actor David Warfield, who converted long after they left San Francisco.[1] But while the large majority remained Jewish, they tended to be lax in observance, unschooled in the classical texts, and disaffected with the synagogue. Invariably, their religious sensibility was profoundly different from that of their European-born parents.

Nor was the alienation from Judaism among young people in the last third of the nineteenth century limited to artists and intellectuals. Under the California sun, the ancient creed was questioned by Jews in every niche of society. Christianity, too, was on the defensive as people focused more on economics, science, and politics. The Bible was challenged by new methods of scholarship, research into comparative religions, and, of course, Darwin's theory of evolution.

A welter of belief systems competed with traditional religion: Ethical Culture, spiritualism, theosophy, universalism, astrology, fortune-telling, and, above all, Christian Science. In this New Age (the term was already in use), California spawned numerous cults such as the fervent group surrounding naturalist John Muir, which exalted nature and worshipped the mountains.

Local Jews were drawn to these alternative creeds, but many more subscribed to no faith at all. "The City" itself—the nation's ninth largest by 1880—won the hearts and minds of the American-born, often at the expense of the synagogue. Opera and theater had flourished since the Gold Rush, but in the 1870s San Francisco gained international recognition for the variety and quality of its cuisine as well, the plethora of fine restaurants a consequence of the multicultural populace.[2] Urban life became more convenient with the introduction of streetcars and cable cars. San Francisco architecture had become more pleasing, too. But the city's most alluring feature was Golden Gate Park, a thousand-acre showplace stretching all the way to the ocean. Temple Emanu-El found that whether its Sabbath services were held on Saturday or Sunday, its members usually preferred a stroll in the park to a sermon in the synagogue.[3]

The pioneer generation knew its offspring were being seduced by California. As one prominent lay leader declared as early as 1875, "Our children grow up in ignorance of the great truths" of their faith.[4] As a result, both clergy and laymen worked particularly hard in this era to adapt Judaism to an environment radically different from the one in which they had been raised.

The most common response to the malaise was religious reform, which also went hand in hand with Americanization. At Emanu-El the forceful spiritual leader Jacob Voorsanger expounded an ultra-Reform theology rooted in optimism, rationality, and patriotism. In his sumptuous Sutter Street Temple, towering over Union Square, he preached a "religion of reason" shorn of almost all the trappings of traditional Judaism. He defended his position against the Orthodox, of course, but also against those who had given up Judaism altogether and embraced a nonsectarian universalism. Voorsanger's counterpart at Sherith Israel, Jacob Nieto, a London-born Sephardi, also articulated a liberal position and gradually led his congregation into the Reform camp. The First Hebrew Congregation in Oakland was similarly transformed and gravitated to Reform in the 1890s. Its rabbi, Marcus Friedlander, defended an attenuated Jewish education that included almost no Hebrew instruction for the synagogue's youth by asking his congregation's European-born elders, "Can you make your boy do what you were made to do when you were boys?"[5] Even Conservative Ohabai Shalome—formed in 1864 in opposition to Emanu-El's radical innovations—ultimately became a Reform congregation, and Orthodox Beth Israel, headed by the respected M. S. Levy, although remaining bound by Jewish law, showed a great deal of flexibility.

But the younger generation was more interested in the reform of society than the reform of Judaism. In the 1880s and '90s synagogue membership declined, intermarriage grew, and discontent became widespread, particularly among women, who were afforded a marginal role in congregational life and looked elsewhere to channel their energies. By World War I, however, an invigoration of Bay Area synagogues was underway. The local rabbinate had taken note of Christianity's Social Gospel movement but was affected even more by initiatives in New York launched by Rabbis Stephen Wise, Mordecai Kaplan, and Oakland's own Judah Magnes. There emerged a new, lasting vision emphasizing social justice, community service, and inclusiveness.

RELIGION OF REASON

Like many holding pulpits in the nineteenth-century American West—including such giants as Jacob Nieto and M. S. Levy—Jacob Voorsanger had earned neither ordination nor a college degree. His formal education ended with graduation from a Jewish high school in his native Amsterdam.[6] But soon after he became Emanu-El's assistant rabbi in 1886, it became clear that he was more than the equal of his colleagues who had graduated from a seminary or university. Within three years he succeeded Elkan Cohn as senior rabbi, a post he held with great distinction until his death almost two decades later.

He was a stalwart of the Reform movement's radical second generation, along with Emil Hirsch of Chicago, Joseph Krauskopf of Philadelphia, and Kaufmann Kohler of New York. Departing from Isaac Mayer Wise's goals of compromise with the Orthodox and encouraging uniformity in the ranks of American Jewry, these rabbis boldly declared in their Pittsburgh Platform of 1885 their rejection of any law or ceremony "not adapted to the views and habits of modern civilization."

Voorsanger and his colleagues adulated the age in which they lived and fervently believed that things could only get better. Applying Darwin's popular theory of evolution to human society, they sought to synthesize Judaism with the latest scientific advances. Like many other liberal rabbis at the turn of the twentieth century, Voorsanger believed in a Supreme Being but held that evolution was God's plan for the world, and he deemed Judaism "divinely evolved" rather than divinely revealed.[7]

Some of his interpretations of the Bible were radical. Voorsanger founded the Department of Semitics at the University of California, where he not only taught the theory of two Isaiahs but also the nonexistence of Ezra; a Second Commonwealth date for Daniel; and the Gospels as midrash.[8] In one of his annual lectures at Stanford, he suggested that the canonization of the Hebrew Bible was based on crass political considerations.[9]

For Voorsanger, "the religion of reason" also meant that everyday religious practice would have to be conducted in the most dignified and intelligent way possible. He despised "external" ritual performed out of habit or superstition.[10] Attacking "legalism," also referred to as "rabbinism" or "orientalism," was one of the main tasks of the *Emanu-El,* the influential Jewish newspaper he founded in 1895.[11] Confronted with the prediction that the Reform movement would soon fade away, Voorsanger tried to frighten his readers with the prospect of Orthodoxy's return:

> The organ would soon disappear, so would the choir; ladies would be relegated to the galleries, in charge of wardens who would ask them indecent questions. The *tallith* would make its reappearance and the national language would disappear from the prayer book. . . . We would once more sit on the earth on the Ninth of Ab, and pray to return to a country which affords us neither home nor living; we would go unwashed to the synagogue that day. . . . We would sacrifice the barber; have our faces cleansed with lye, as green as grass. We would permit our beards to grow for thirty days in time of mourning and, surely, would wear the *pyes,* which look so interesting. We would recite a hundred benedictions every day, turn our homes topsy turvy before the Passover, appoint *Shomerim*—stewards—who would superintend our meat shops, bakeries, butteries, dairies and vineyards, and level a tax on all victuallers or else pronounce their goods to be *Trefah.* We would reinstate our old prayers; thank God that we were not born women, read unctuously of the Talmudical chapter of the composition of incense, and on Sabbath pray for the continued prosperity of Babylonian universities which went out of existence eight hundred years ago.[12]

Voorsanger not only did not feel bound by dietary and Sabbath laws, but he also led services bareheaded, performed intermarriage, and introduced the revolutionary *Union Prayer Book,* which rendered almost all of the liturgy in English.[13]

The radical reformers almost uniformly opposed Zionism, for Voorsanger "one of the wildest of all wild dreams." Aside from being impractical, a Jewish state in the "Turk-ridden land" seemed to him antithetical to his people's mission: "We refuse to believe that the divine intention is the degradation of the Jew from his present lofty position as a world-teacher to again become the neighbor of mongrel tribes, on the very edge of civilization."[14]

Underlying his objection to Zionism was the love of his adopted land. California was his Zion, and there could be no other, as the following paean testifies. Having chosen to vacation in Monterey over attending a rabbinical conference in Milwaukee, he invited his colleagues, "if they wish to have [a] foretaste of Eden," to convene their conclave in California the following year:

> We will show them the country, rocks that await Alladin's magic key to unlock their treasures, all gold, platinum and quicksilver; plateaux on which the Almighty poured out all the blessings left over from the sixth day of creation. We will show them valleys now growing with fruit and wheat and grain and valleys that know no barrenness in winter time, the only fields in America in which the grass always remains green. We will show them our mountains, white-headed giants watching Hesperidean gardens, in which the golden apples are sweet and rich and luscious; mountains that are the store-houses of floods that rain down to bathe the valleys in their refreshing richness. And we will show them such flowers as they never saw before; our camelias and dandelions, our rich magnolias and jasmines, and our miles of wild flowers, carpeting the unploughed hillsides. . . .
>
> We will remind them that this dear California is a gorgeous *edition de luxe* of Palestine of old of which Midrash says with effusive tenderness that every spot in it has its hills and dales. Our holy land, our promised land is this golden spot, and we want the sages of Babylon to pay us a visit.[15]

Voorsanger's friend Julius Kahn, who represented San Francisco in Congress and worked to block Jewish statehood at the Paris Peace Conference in 1919, was more succinct: "For me the United States is my Zion and San Francisco is my Jerusalem."[16]

Sherith Israel's flock was far more observant than was Emanu-El's, but it, too, was swept along by the powerful tides of reform, American patriotism, and anti-Zionism. The process was slower than at the Sutter Street Temple, and it never led to such extremes as holding Sabbath services on Sunday, or replacing the shofar with a brass instrument, but the end result was similar: an Orthodox congregation became Reform.

By the 1870s Liberal Judaism began to surface at Sherith Israel's Taylor and Post synagogue, which had mixed seating, a choir, and an organ. Liturgical reforms followed, including the introduction of an array of prayers in

English.[17] Yet many members strongly resisted further changes. Although Isaac Mayer Wise spoke there in 1877, Sherith Israel would not formally join the Reform movement. President William Saalburg explained the board's decision by asking, "Are the men who publicly and defiantly trod our most cherished relics underfoot, who boldly denounce the sanctity of the Sabbath Day, who brazenly coquette with Adlerism [Ethical Culture], to be trusted as guides?"[18]

But the charismatic rabbi hired in 1893, the young, olive-skinned Jacob Nieto, would gradually succeed in bringing Sherith Israel into the Reform camp. The descendant of a long line of distinguished Sephardim, Nieto was born in London and raised in Kingston, Jamaica, where his father was a cantor. In his teens Jacob moved to New York. Living with an uncle who served as cantor at that city's Shearith Israel, he enrolled in the public school system, and later City College. He also studied at the Emanu-El Preparatory School in New York, which readied young men for Hebrew Union College, to which he was admitted in 1882.[19]

Yet instead of attending the Reform seminary, Nieto chose to return to England, where he spent the next decade teaching in a variety of Jewish institutions and leading an Orthodox congregation. He also briefly attended traditional Jews' College. But his desire for a more open environment was evidenced by his application in 1893 for the high-profile pulpit of New York's liberal B'nai Jeshurun. He preached a trial sermon, but Stephen Wise was hired instead. Within a few months, however, Nieto was ensconced across the country at Sherith Israel; neither his lack of credentials nor his labeling of himself as "progressive" in his application proved any hindrance.[20]

The ambitious young man drew large, admiring crowds to his sermons, and Isidore Choynski compared the handsome bachelor to Othello: "He has the women on his side . . . a number of promising maids and widows with gold galore who will sacrifice their all—whatever that may be in order to be in the swim—and be a Rebbitzin."[21] The following year he did take a bride,* daughter of a German Jewish stockbroker, and, remarkably,

---

* Nieto's personal life would be marked by tragedy. His attractive wife was left deaf from scarlet fever. Among the couple's four children, one of two sons suffered from Down syndrome and the other drowned in an accident at age fourteen. The rabbi, who compiled his own prayer book for the High Holidays, omitted the phrase referring to "those who shall die by drowning" (Kenneth C. Zwerin, "Rabbi Jacob Nieto of Congregation Sherith Israel," Part 2, *WSJH* 18 [January 1986]: 166–67).

the reception was held at one of the town's fanciest restaurants, Maison Riche, without any thought to the kosher laws. A local newspaper reported that Nieto's father, who officiated at the wedding, refused to be seated until the oysters were removed from the table.[22]

No doubt Nieto regretted that the matter was made public, but he made no effort to hide his "progressive spirit," as a local Jewish paper described the change that had come to Sherith Israel.[23] In 1894, he instituted a short Friday evening service, almost completely in English, with anthems similar to those sung in Protestant churches.[24] Later he made optional the chuppah, or traditional bridal canopy, and made skullcaps optional at synagogue services.[25] He himself officiated at life cycle ceremonies bareheaded.[26] Sherith Israel officially joined the Union of American Hebrew Congregations in 1903, and by the early 1920s did away with worship on the second day of holidays and introduced the *Union Prayer Book.*

Nieto's theology, especially in the optimistic 1890s, was very similar to that of arch-reformer Jacob Voorsanger.* In one of his first sermons at Sherith Israel (at which point it was still considered traditional), he declared that "Liberal Judaism . . . taught only in sympathy with natural and scientific law" was the "grandest and noblest" religious expression, and the one best suited for the "glorious garden" that was the contemporary age.[27] Like his rival on Sutter Street, he frequently delivered Sunday morning lectures on ethics, in which he assigned a much higher priority to personal morality than to ritual observance: "The only sin I know of is an act that does harm to somebody else. I know of no sin between man and God." Nieto taught the Bible using all the tools of critical scholarship and downplayed such time-honored Jewish notions as the "world to come."[28]

Although less vehemently than Voorsanger, Nieto opposed Zionism for decades and held that "to claim nationality, we would isolate ourselves from our surroundings." (He altered his views somewhat only after a visit to Palestine in 1925.) Moreover, without the "national coloring," without the misguided thinking that "the Jewish religion belongs to the Hebrew race

---

*Indeed, one incensed local visitor to the synagogue wrote hyperbolically that Nieto's "religious views are more radical than Rabbis Hirsch or Krauskopf [who were both more extreme than Voorsanger] and his teachings are more dangerous to the younger generation than those of the [Christian] missionaries." There was little dissent, however, from the leaders of Sherith Israel, who were delighted with the increase in attendance (ibid., 162).

alone," Judaism could welcome gentiles into its bosom, and as early as 1893 the rabbi departed from tradition by urging Jews to proselytize.[29]

Nieto never quite avowed that California was Zion, but such thoughts could not have been far from his mind when, in 1905, the congregation opened its new sanctuary on California Street, where he would preach for another quarter century. One of the vividly colored stained-glass windows portrays Moses holding the tablets of the law, but he has not come down from Mount Sinai; rather, he is standing in the Yosemite Valley, with Half Dome and El Capitan appearing unmistakably in the background.

Of course, not every local rabbi would have abided such an image in his synagogue, and not all of them opposed Zionism. One advocate of Jewish nationalism was the Orthodox rabbi M. S. Levy, of Oakland's First Hebrew Congregation and later Beth Israel in San Francisco. Even before the turn of the century Levy was active in a group known as Helpers of Zion.[30] But in other respects even Levy, deeply affected by the enlightened spirit of his day, had much in common with reformers. He delivered lectures with titles such as "Progress of Science" and, while at the First Hebrew Congregation, he invited Oakland's Unitarian minister to give a series of talks at the synagogue.* Levy in turn was well received at the Unitarian Church, where he spoke on the theory of evolution.[31]

Levy also acquiesced to several liturgical reforms proposed by a group of lay leaders at First Hebrew. By the early 1890s, however, he realized that he was unsuited for a congregation whose membership craved even more rapid Americanization. His successor, Marcus Friedlander, had studied at Hebrew Union College and, though not quite as radical as Voorsanger, was firmly in the camp of the reformers. In order to "save Judaism from decay and stagnation," as he put it, the synagogue abolished "antiquated practices [and] unappealing ceremonies," adopted a version of the *Union Prayer Book,* and

---

*A similar pattern prevailed at Ohabai Shalome, where another traditional rabbi made concessions to the reformist spirit. Albert Bettelheim, occupying that pulpit for about a decade beginning in the mid-1870s, dismayed some of his congregants with his interest in modern science and medicine, his close friendship with Isaac Mayer Wise, and his emphasis on ethics, sometimes at the expense of ritual. At one point the rabbi (who had been painted as Jesus by a well-known artist) paraphrased the New Testament, "It is more important to guard that which goes out of the mouth than that which goes in" (I. Harold Sharfman, *The First Rabbi: Origins of Conflict between Orthodox and Reform* [Baltimore, Md., 1988], 616).

joined the Reform movement.[32] Like Sherith Israel, First Hebrew erected a stately house of worship, an attractive white brick structure, in 1914. The inscription from Isaiah above the entrance (chosen by many Reform synagogues in this era) reflected the universalist leanings of both its rabbi and its membership: "My House Shall Be Called a House of Prayer for All People."

Laymen, too, advocated radical religious change. Most influential at the turn of the twentieth century was Harris Weinstock. Half brother and business partner of the visionary agriculturist David Lubin, Weinstock had developed a tremendous dry goods operation but devoted most of his time to public service and was revered throughout the state. Born in London in 1854 to immigrants from Russian Poland and raised in New York, Weinstock was familiar with Orthodoxy and believed it "make[s] of the Jew a slave of meaningless and obsolete forms, and must more or less isolate him from his fellow-men of other faiths."[33] Ever a believer in the Enlightenment, he sought a Judaism that "widens our horizon, broadens our sympathies and extends our fellow-feeling to all humanity. It teaches us, in the broad spirit of the prophet of old, that we have but one supreme Father and that all mankind are his children."[34]

With the same dedication he brought to public policy issues, the California Progressive proposed a far-reaching overhaul of his beloved religion. Like Voorsanger (to whose temple he belonged, though he was more active in Sacramento's B'nai Israel), Weinstock looked forward to a future "when all men [would] worship at the same footstool."[35] Similar to Nieto, he advocated proselytism, and, like both spiritual leaders, he repudiated Zionism.[36] But in his attempt to realize his universalist vision, Weinstock went further than the rabbis. He strongly urged synagogues to adopt Sunday services, for example, an innovation that even Voorsanger ultimately rejected.[37]

Even more controversial were Weinstock's admiration for Jesus and his recommendation that Jewish schools include New Testament teachings in their curriculum. Speaking in churches and synagogues throughout Northern California on his popular book *Jesus the Jew,* he held that the Galilean "preached nothing but Judaism in its purest and simplest form [and] the thought of establishing a new belief or even a new sect was farthest from his mind."[38] Paul was the true founder of Christianity, according to the learned Weinstock, whose work anticipated much scholarship in this vein. While he stressed that he did not consider Jesus the Messiah, nor did he want to "canonize" him, Weinstock credited both Jesus and Paul with speedily spreading the message of Judaism around the world.[39]

Naturally, Weinstock's views were attacked, both by Orthodox Jews, because Jesus had forsaken Jewish law, and by some radical Reform rabbis such as Emil Hirsch, who rejected any embrace of the Nazarene.[40] A number of Christian ministers, meanwhile, voiced their disappointment that the prominent Jewish businessman, although praising Jesus, had not given their Savior his due as the world redeemer. The ecumenical-minded California public, though, generally approved of Weinstock's efforts, and his audiences were large and appreciative.[41]

Yet in the end, the "Progressive Judaism" advanced at the turn of the century by Weinstock, Voorsanger, Nieto, and others failed to revitalize the synagogues. To be sure, the Reform movement, even in this most extreme phase in its history, was an alternative to assimilation that at least maintained Judaism, as a "distinct spiritual entity" in the face of completely secular or liberal Christian options.[42] But in its blanket adoption of the triumphal, rationalist philosophy of the day, more was lost than was gained. As a local journalist described "the religion of the Jew" in 1895, "There is something lacking . . . something so subtle and undefinable. . . . His religion partakes something of that cool, calculating, inaudible expression . . . when the sole demand [of the public] is . . . a certain effusion of 'faith.' "[43]

Of course, the religion of reason had little resonance with the thousands of Russian and Rumanian Jews who arrived in the Bay Area during this period. Even the few who could surmount the class barrier felt uncomfortable at Emanu-El in particular. But more disturbing to Emanu-El's leaders was the failure to pass along the reformed faith to their own children. By the turn of the century the average age of a member of the Sutter Street Temple was fifty-three, and only one congregant in seven was under forty.[44] Nor was Emanu-El (with barely three hundred members the largest Jewish congregation) alone in its struggle to attract younger people; lack of interest was a problem throughout the Bay Area. Much more than doctrinal and liturgical change would be needed to make Judaism meaningful in this Eden on the Pacific.

ONE SYNAGOGUE'S STRUGGLES

A window into synagogue life is opened by the minute books of bellwether Sherith Israel, the oldest congregation in the city (along with Emanu-El, founded in April 1851). Although never possessing the wealth or prestige of its twin sister, Sherith Israel could count dozens of prosperous businessmen in its congregation by the end of the Civil War. In its pews sat Jews from Eastern and Western Europe as well as native-born Sephardim. In contrast to the ultra-Reform tendencies of the Sutter Street Temple, it retained much of the warmth and authenticity of old-world Judaism even as it adapted to the cultural norms of the American West.

But for many decades Sherith Israel was hampered by internal disputes—quarrels that often emitted a whiff of scandal but were essentially power struggles and personality clashes between laymen and clergy. In 1869, the board removed the elderly Rabbi Henry A. Henry, largely for insubordination, and three years later engaged in a much more caustic conflict with his successor, Aaron Messing. The scholarly Midwesterner, like Henry, resisted religious reforms, but the main point of contention was his lack of "integrity," discussed in a series of board meetings.[45] Messing obtained salary advances for personal financial crises that befell him with unusual frequency, and he once received an emergency loan from the congregation to help his in-laws, whom he claimed had lost their home in the Chicago Fire. When a lay leader discovered that all along the rabbi had a substantial bank account, Messing was brought before the board and sharply rebuked.[46] A month and a half later the rabbi "gave vent to *his* passions," as one eyewitness put it, using his sermon to heap "insults upon insults upon the President, Board of Officers, and the Congregation at large, profaning and disgracing the pulpit for his vile purposes."[47] The board suspended him immediately, and President Meyer demanded his dismissal at a rancorous congregational meeting the following month.[48] Because he could marshal a phalanx of defenders, Messing was not fired outright but was instead barred from giving sermons or lectures; he continued, however, to lead services and supervise the religious school until severing all ties with Sherith Israel the following year.

Some members, shaken by the Messing affair and worried about the economic downturn of 1873, recommended the congregation no longer engage a full-time spiritual leader. One powerful trustee, Bahr Scheideman, disagreed and made an impassioned statement about the rabbi's role, asking, "Where I ask you shall we find [the] light? Where shall our children find that knowledge, unless . . . we have someone to look up to as our spiritual guide and religious teacher. A congregation without a minister is alike unto the weary traveler in the gloomy desert without a friend to lead him to his destination."[49]

Scheideman was heeded and Sherith Israel next installed the progressive Dr. Henry Vidaver, a highly regarded rabbi who enjoyed the strong support of the board. Yet he, too, had his detractors among the membership. One mainstay of the synagogue, who sat in the second row on the center aisle every Sabbath, made a big show of getting up and walking out as soon as Vidaver began his sermon.* But overall he was an effective spiritual leader, even amidst the budgetary problems and low membership of the 1870s. His untimely death—from a stroke on the morning of Rosh Hashanah in 1882—was a terrible blow to the institution. Vidaver's successor, his younger brother Falk (who had formerly served in a pulpit in Indiana), proved a far less accomplished pastor, sermonizer, and educator. Although his contract was renewed several times, the lay leadership had little confidence in him. After a decade of discord, capped by a fractious congregational meeting on his tenure that he survived by only three votes, Falk Vidaver finally decided to leave.[50] Only with the arrival of the exceptionally talented Jacob Nieto in 1893 was trust restored between the congregation and its rabbi.

The relationship between the congregation and its cantors was even worse. Sherith Israel employed four *chazanim,* or cantors, in the last quarter of the nineteenth century, and each was fired after a lacerating conflict with the board. In every case the minutes contain lengthy accusations—ranging from financial misconduct and moral turpitude to absenteeism and simply bad singing—followed by rebuttals by the cantor and his defenders. The laypeople themselves were often bitterly divided on personnel issues, and sometimes the president angrily resigned amidst the acrimony, only to be persuaded to return a few weeks later. During one of the most heated disputes, President Scheideman claimed to have been "threatened by some unprincipled men [saying] they would persecute him to the extreme and ruin him and his business if he should testify [before an investigative committee of the board] against the Chazan."[51]

Most embarrassing—because it was covered in painful detail in the *San Francisco Chronicle* on the eve of Rabbi Nieto's installation—was the violent altercation between the secretary of the board, Alexander Badt, and

---

*Harriet Levy's father, Benish, was upset not with the rabbi's reformist tendencies but rather with his apparent insincerity (Harriet Lane Levy, *920 O'Farrell Street: A Jewish Girlhood in Old San Francisco* [Berkeley, 1996], 68).

the wife of Cantor Max Rubin. According to the article (almost certainly written by journalist Gustav Danziger, a Sherith Israel member), Rubin himself coveted the top spot.* Dismayed that Nieto's hiring would deprive him of the fees he had earned for weddings and funerals, reported the *Chronicle,* he was "about as enthusiastic as a man who has been locked in a refrigerator all night"[52] as preparations went ahead for the new rabbi's investiture.

As usual, matters came to a boil over the question of authority. At a gathering to plan the grand occasion Secretary Badt insisted the cantor sing a new version of "Hallelujah," which Rubin refused to do. Rubin's wife, who was present, "detected a derisive inflection in Badt's tone" and immediately punched him in the face. Staggering to a corner, he called his attacker "a miserable woman," words that brought the cantor into the fray, though others restrained Rubin and protected Badt from further harm.[†53] Danziger, referring to both this event and past instances of internecine wrangling at Sherith Israel, concluded, "The congregation has had a remarkably hard time with its spiritual advisers."[54] A few days later he sent a letter to the board members admonishing them to put aside their "petty" differences for the sake of young Nieto. How will he be able to succeed, asked Danziger, "when his brethren are at war?"[55]

Relations with other synagogues in the city were yet another source of friction. Sherith Israel had sold its Stockton Street Synagogue to Congregation Shaare Zedek but was later hit by a lawsuit from the Orthodox shul regarding the property.[56] In 1883, a major rift with Emanu-El occurred when its cantor visited Sherith Israel and was so displeased with the version he heard of "Adon Olam" that he "rushed up on the platform in an excited and uproarious manner."[57] A letter was sent to Emanu-El urging discipline for "the ruffian . . . the aggressor";[58] it is not known how the demand was met on Sutter Street. During a brief period of cooperation in the mid-1890s the two congregations held joint Thanksgiving services, but Nieto and Voorsanger usually behaved icily toward each other during the

---

* Danziger denied authorship of the piece, "Smote Him Real Hard," but it is written in the lively style of the newsman, who was present during the incident (*San Francisco Chronicle,* June 13, 1893).

† Rubin continued as cantor until the following Yom Kippur, when a board member found him smoking in the synagogue lavatory. He was dismissed immediately (Minutes of Congregation Sherith Israel, October 22, 1894).

decade and a half that their careers in San Francisco overlapped. Sherith Israel did graciously offer its building as a temporary home to Emanu-El after the Sutter Street Temple collapsed in the earthquake and fire of 1906. Voorsanger and his board declined; they moved instead to a Presbyterian and later a Unitarian church.[59]

Fiscal difficulties, however, dwarfed everything else at Sherith Israel. In 1873, a desperate year for many institutions in the state, the congregation was "on the verge of bankruptcy," according to its president, and hard times persisted throughout the decade.[60] Although stability was regained later in the century, the temple faced the constant problems of not only attracting new members (the two-hundred-member mark was reached only by World War I), but also collecting the dues from those who were affiliated.

The annual report of 1905 reveals how precarious the synagogue's finances were. Even after the dedication of the new temple and a dozen years into the tenure of an accomplished rabbi, the membership still stood at a disappointing 134, about the same as it was a quarter century earlier.[61] Like Emanu-El, Sherith Israel was aging: thirty-five of its members were widows and only five were "single, young men."[62] The annual income of the temple, derived largely from dues, donations, and the sale of High Holiday seats to nonmembers, barely exceeded $16,000, almost 40 percent of which was needed to pay the $85,000 mortgage.[63] The religious school was allocated a paltry $827 a year, but Nieto's generous salary of $6,000, plus high maintenance costs, led to a deficit of more than $6,000 annually.[64] It was offset only by the profit registered by the cemetery, which was now in Colma.

The synagogue was unscathed by the catastrophe of 1906 and soon derived rental income from displaced institutions, most notably the municipal court. Membership also rose steadily, to 197 households, by the end of that decade. Nevertheless, the fiscal picture worsened because of higher operating expenses related to the new building. Late in 1908, Nieto voluntarily reduced his annual compensation by $1,000 and the congregation dismissed its professional choir, saving another $1,300. Still, it had to borrow $10,000 in 1910 to cover its operating deficit, thus adding to its mountain of debt.[65] As if to suggest a sense of permanence, each annual report after the turn of the century began with the age of the congregation, written in extra-large, flowery script. But on several occasions Secretary Badt (who held his office for more than three decades) declared that survival was no foregone conclusion, and that long-term solvency was dependent on a membership of at least three hundred families.[66]

Although the congregation was preoccupied with monetary and personnel concerns throughout the first decade of the twentieth century, one religious question did embroil Sherith Israel: whether men should be required to wear head coverings during services. Much earlier the board had mandated hats or skullcaps, but the measure was never enforced. Finally, in 1910, a petition requiring compliance was presented to the board, but the liberal faction countered with its own proposal, which would make head coverings optional. A special congregational meeting was convened.[67] The progressive group won almost two to one, the matter deemed so significant that each vote was recorded by name in the minute book. (The last roll call vote, to allow men and women to sit together in the pews, had taken place forty years earlier.) Yet it didn't end there. The defeated minority, claiming that at least three-quarters of the membership was required to enact such a rule, demanded a second congregational meeting, at which they lost sixty-one to seventeen.[68] Again, the vote of each man (women were in attendance but not permitted to cast ballots) was solemnly recorded for posterity. The tedious dispute was now settled, and the following Yom Kippur about half the males prayed bareheaded; the congregation had taken another step toward Reform.[69] But the passion aroused by this issue also highlighted the gulf in San Francisco between the minority of Jews who belonged to synagogues and the majority who did not. It would be hard to imagine that the protracted war over the hats would help efforts to recruit the unaffiliated.

Later in the twentieth century Sherith Israel would attain financial health and be blessed with as much clerical stability as any congregation in America. But success on California Street required an understanding of synagogue life far broader than the one held by the pioneer generation.

A FADING JEWISH IDENTITY

As they had during pioneer times, fraternal and charitable institutions fared better than the synagogues in the new century. Although the B'nai B'rith was not as active as it had been a generation earlier, its ten San Francisco lodges enrolled a thousand men in 1903 (including some East Europeans), two-thirds of its entire membership on the West Coast.[70] The Federation of Jewish Charities boasted 1,675 subscribers only half a decade after its founding in 1910.[71]

To be sure, three of the four major San Francisco congregations constructed impressive new synagogues around the turn of the century. In 1898,

Ohabai Shalome opened a masterfully crafted sanctuary on Bush and Laguna streets, while 1905 saw the erection of Sherith Israel's elaborate synagogue as well as Beth Israel's ample Geary Street Temple. Of course the grandest Jewish house of worship (until its demise in 1906) was Emanu-El's cathedral synagogue, dating from 1866. But while some successful Jewish businessmen had pledged funds to construct these edifices, few Jews were actually dues-paying members of the congregations. As previously noted, only about 17 percent were affiliated at the end of the 1870s.[72] It is unlikely that the percentage was substantially higher a generation later despite the emergence of several small shuls for the newly arrived East European immigrants, who represented a small fraction of San Francisco Jewry until well after World War I. On the eve of the earthquake, Emanu-El and Sherith Israel had fewer than 550 households combined. Ohabai Shalom and Beth Israel were considerably smaller, as were the Orthodox synagogues. In a city of almost 30,000 Jews by 1905, there could not have been more than 1,200 families that were affiliated.*

Of course, there existed a subculture of hundreds of devout families, which included not only East European immigrants but also some Central European Jews with pioneer roots. As evidence, the Jewish press regularly carried ads for kosher butchers and ritual baths and reported weddings conducted with strict Orthodox rites.

But the predominant ethos of the community was decidedly unobservant. Although some leading Jewish retailers had closed their stores on Saturdays in the 1860s, a decade later the visiting Isaac Mayer Wise was disheartened at the lack of Sabbath observance, noting that although their wives often attended services, "the men keep nothing besides Rosh Hashanah and Kippur. . . . 'I take no interest in Jewish affairs' is a remark you hear ten times a day made by men of prominence."[73]

*A study in 1895 quoted an anonymous local rabbi estimating "25% are faithful supporters of synagogues," but even this modest figure may have been based on the inflated claims of one or more congregations (Gustav Danziger, "The Jew in San Francisco," Overland Monthly 25 [April 1895]: 414). For example, a few years earlier the San Francisco Examiner had reported three hundred members at Sherith, double that revealed in the minutes ("California's Hebrews," WSJHQ 4 [July 1972]: 199). More plausible was a synagogue president's estimate of affiliated households in the city in 1916 at somewhere between 1,200 and 1,500 out of 10,000 Jewish families (Minutes of Sherith Israel, October 29, 1916). Similarly, in Oakland, the First Hebrew counted only 115 members even after the construction of its new temple on the eve of World War I (Fred Rosenbaum, Free to Choose [Berkeley, 1976], 53).

First to shed their Jewish folkways was the south German Jewish elite. Even in this group, though, Judaism was passed on to some extent, as the youth of Amy Steinhart Braden reveals. Raised in the 1880s and '90s in the cultured home of her Baden-born father, William, a wealthy dry goods merchant, she notes that the Steinharts at least did not observe Christmas, had annual Passover seders, fasted on Yom Kippur, and observed a "mild form" of the kosher laws.[74] She actually learned some Hebrew at Emanu-El's religious school, and later studied the language at the University of California. Much later in life Amy, a prominent social worker, married a non-Jew, but she stressed that "we were brought up not to be altogether orthodox but to be aware of our Jewish background."[75]

More typical among the Jewish aristocracy, however, were two of Amy's contemporaries, the sisters Florine Haas Bransten and Alice Haas Lilienthal, whose Bavarian father, William, evidently did not impart Judaism to his offspring. In an intimate memoir, Florine's daughter writes that her mother and aunt

> knew little about Jewish rites. We might dine on gorgeously glazed hams but only fish was served on Fridays. As bacon sizzled in the kitchen, Mother worried endlessly about our Catholic nurse's lenten diet. . . . Of course [Florine and Alice] had heard about old Jewish traditions, but they were felt to be part of a different world, a world of old *Tantes* [aunts] living in backwards Bavarian villages. Mother spoke to me about one . . . who refused to light her fire against the bitter cold because of the Sabbath. Her account sounded foreign and fascinating, as though they were speaking of different beings on a faraway planet.
>
> As a child, I never heard my aunt or mother use such words as *yahrzeit, shiva, mikveh,* or *chuppah.*[76]

Alice held lavish Christmas parties in her Franklin Street home, and, according to one historian, the table once held "a glazed sucking pig as its centerpiece with an apple in its open snout."[77] The Gerstles and Slosses, also known for their Christmas celebrations, passed their tree ornaments down through the generations.[78] Easter, "with elaborate egg-rolling parties," was invariably celebrated by the Jewish gentry not in addition to, but instead of, Passover.[79]

Although such behavior characterized only a small, if immensely influential, minority of Bay Area Jews, it appeared that faith was declining throughout much of the community. In the late 1880s, the *San Francisco Examiner* described local Jewry as "a liberal-minded people [who read] the writings of the great Agnostics of the Age," and then enumerated six contemporary philosophers—skeptics, freethinkers, and other radical critics of religion—that Jews "peruse at length."[80] A decade later the point was made even more forcefully by Gustav Danziger, who estimated that 80 percent of the "cultured young [Jewish] men and women" doubted the existence of God.[81]

Intermarriage, rare in the Gold Rush decade, was more widespread later in the nineteenth century. Despite his ultra-Reform orientation, Rabbi Elkan Cohn was pained when his son, a well-known physician, married a Christian in 1879. (It was later rumored that the rabbi was so embarrassed that he tendered his resignation from Emanu-El, but the temple refused to accept it.)[82] Even the respected lay leader Joseph Rodriguez Brandon, according to one newspaper "one of the most pious orthodox Jews in this city," had to confront the marriage of his eldest daughter to an Irish Catholic in 1887. Brandon refused to attend the wedding and expressed his dismay to Isidore Choynski, who quoted him in his column: "What can I do in the matter? My daughter is twenty-eight years old; I brought her up in the religion of her ancestors, and even went so far as to send her kosher meat when, during the summer, she [was away on an outing]."[83] In 1902, Harris Weinstock, after "making out a careful list," concluded that 10 percent of the Jewish community of Sacramento was intermarried;[84] it is doubtful that San Francisco had a lower proportion.

While intermarriage had been roundly condemned in the Jewish press in the late 1850s—"the evil is threatening to grow into an epidemic," wrote Choynski[85]—the community was more evenly divided on the issue a generation later. Even the wounded J. R. Brandon understood his daughter's dilemma: many of the eligible Jewish men expected large dowries, while gentiles tended to be less demanding. "I have the means to give my daughter $50,000," Brandon told Choynski, but she "would not consent to my buying a Jewish husband for her; she preferred a Christian who took her to his manly bosom for her own sake."*[86] He grudgingly came to accept his new son-in-law, and Choynski also reversed his position of thirty years earlier:

---

*A similar lament was voiced two years earlier in the *Jewish Progress* by a young Oakland woman who claimed that Jewish boys have it "drummed" into them "that the dollar must be forthcoming or it's no go" (William M. Kramer, "The Emergence of Oakland Jewry—Part V," *WSJHQ* 11 [January 1979]: 178–80).

I would rather marry my daughter to a respectable, intelligent, sober Christian than to an unwashed Jew who never read a leaf outside the history of the four Kings [playing cards], though his credit was AAA. Never in mourning on account of such a mishap. The world is moving, and intermarriages have ceased to be the wonder of the world.[87]

JEWISH GIRLS AND "SPIRITUAL TRIALS"

Whether or not they married outside the faith, many females in the second generation turned away from Judaism. They accomplished much in the arena of Jewish benevolent work, but they often found little of relevance in the synagogue. True, they were now permitted to sit next to their husbands or fathers in the pews of most houses of worship, but they still could not become members in their own right, and, with the exception of teaching in the religious school, they were allowed but a small role in the congregation.

Their disaffection often began in adolescence, and memoirs abound reflecting the gulf between an American-born girl and her immigrant father, learned in the sacred texts but unable to pass on their meaning, committed to his synagogue but unable to convey its importance. Rebekah Kohut, daughter of Ohabai Shalome's first rabbi, Albert Bettelheim, experienced the most severe "spiritual trials" of her life during the decade she spent in San Francisco beginning in 1875.[88] She became critical of "the unhealthy rivalry among the congregations . . . more concerned with membership drives than with higher values" and saw her dedicated father underpaid and harassed by unfeeling, unappreciative board members.[89] Rebekah herself was allowed no academic freedom as a Sunday school teacher, and when she responded impertinently to the chairman of the school board, she was dismissed, and her father called to account as well.[90] It all pushed her toward Christian friends and teachers, the study of literature at the University of California, and volunteer work for a non-Jewish charity serving the poor. As she later wrote of this "rebellious and irreligious" period, "I had begun to doubt the worthiness of all the sacrifices . . . my father and his family were making for Judaism. . . . Why make a stand for separate Jewish ideals? Why not choose the easier way and be like all the rest? The struggle was too hard, too bitter. . . . Yes, religion oppressed me."[91]

Kohut, later a distinguished social worker in New York, would marry a Conservative rabbi and eventually make Judaism a cornerstone of her existence. But her contemporary Harriet Levy, similarly disinclined toward the ancient faith as a girl, had virtually no connection to the Jewish community for the rest of her long life. An inquisitive child, she nevertheless felt a mixture of fear and repulsion toward Jewish ritual objects in the O'Farrell Street home of her religious parents. Benish Levy's *t'fillin* lay on a shelf in his bedroom closet "coiled like a snake," she wrote.

> I could not talk about the phylacteries and my fingers shunned contact with the long, narrow band of black leather that Father wound around and around his upper left arm, and the two narrower bands with the small, square leather box in the center that he wore every morning in the middle of his forehead while he said his prayers.
>
> The box and its contents puzzled me, but I asked no question, fearing that knowledge might add to my uneasiness. Nobody made mention of the phylacteries. . . . [They] continued alien objects, stirring distaste and an unspoken entreaty that they would disappear from Father's closet forever.[92]

Similarly, the mezuzah "that clung, as by pores" to the bedroom's doorjamb, was so disconcerting that

> years passed before I was able to look at it with free eyes. I asked no questions fearing that here again I entered a forbidden zone. The distrust, awakened by the object itself perched up there like a talisman, was deepened by its name: Mezuzah. Invasion of our intimate life by an object so estrangingly named—Mezuzah—confirmed the accusation that we were a peculiar people, and I did not wish to be peculiar. I wanted to be like. As no question was asked, the explanation was not provided.[93]

Levy and her two sisters accompanied their parents to Sherith Israel on the High Holidays, where she dutifully mouthed the prayers while observing a rigid social pecking order. The flowery supplications read aloud were in stark contrast, she thought, to the whispered gossip and spite. She admired Jacob Nieto's sermons, though felt the "coldly intellectual man . . . curiously misplaced in a . . . congregation of merchants and shopkeepers."[94]

Levy approved of the way the rabbi rebuked his flock for their sins because he provided a message of comfort and hope as well. But for another girl, future educator, musician, and poet Flora Jacobi Arnstein, the High Holidays were a source of dread because of the rabbi's scolding. In a work of autobiographical fiction, the lifelong San Franciscan wrote of being taken by her grandparents to the temple (a composite of Sherith Israel and Emanu-El), where the look from the pulpit "was like a stab" and the whole experience "a horrible ordeal." The rabbi's "eyes were as stiff as an eagle's, and when he spoke, he turned sharply and aimed a sudden finger first at one person and then at another."[95] The sound of the shofar, meanwhile, she compared to "a stupendous burp . . . irresistibly funny."[96] It took all of young Flora's strength to repress her laughter, which, coming at that solemn moment, would have scandalized her.

While girls such as Kohut, Levy, and Arnstein were alienated from the faith of their fathers, another young woman reacted in a different way. Rachel "Ray" Frank (later Ray Frank Litman) devoted herself to curing the ills afflicting her people. She preached in synagogues throughout the West and, with characteristic hyperbole, called herself the first female to occupy a Jewish pulpit since the prophetess Deborah.[97]

Born in San Francisco in 1861 to a Russian-Polish father, Frank followed her older sister's family to Nevada after graduating from high school. For six years Ray taught children as well as adults in a mining town. Around 1885 she settled in Oakland, where she quickly attracted attention as a Bible teacher at the First Hebrew Congregation's Sabbath School. A dynamic instructor, she often drew the children's parents to her classes as well, and soon she was lecturing to most of the membership.[98]

At the same time, Frank embarked on a career in journalism that took her on assignment to the Pacific Northwest. Arriving in Spokane on the eve of Rosh Hashanah in 1890, she sought to attend services but was informed that the town lacked a synagogue. But a lay leader who had heard of her work in Oakland promised that if she would deliver the sermon, services would be held. She consented, and the local opera house was filled for her homily, a plea for the creation of a synagogue and religious school, both of which the local Jews soon undertook.[99]

Thus began a decade during which she was in great demand in the West as a lecturer and preacher. She had hardly mastered the wide variety of topics she addressed—Jewish art, music, literature, philosophy, and history, as well as the Bible—but her rhetorical ability was remarkable. Without notes she was able to mesmerize her audiences. Her success has been credited in part to "the physical attributes most admired of her time—soulful dark eyes, a 'poetic' expression, dark hair swept from a center part in two wings framing her somewhat long face, which bore a marked resemblance to . . . the young Oscar Wilde."[100] She was also propelled by an aggressive press agent who not only arranged her many bookings but also constantly fed information on Oakland's "girl rabbi" to the sensation-seeking western newspapers.[101] Her brief period at Hebrew Union College—a single semester in

1893, during which she took no classes in the rabbinical program—has been characterized by one historian as a publicity stunt.[102] Isaac Mayer Wise, the school's president, was angered to read in the press that she had finished the course of study, been ordained, and been offered rabbinical posts, all falsehoods that the young woman sometimes encouraged reporters to believe.[103] Rabbi Voorsanger invited Frank to deliver a guest sermon at Emanu-El, but he also railed against the "sensational twaddle" surrounding her meteoric rise.* She was brutally satirized by Gustav Danziger and callously patronized by Ambrose Bierce.[104]

None of this, though, should obscure the vital plea for reconciliation she delivered from the pulpit. Like Judah Magnes (probably her student at the First Hebrew's Sabbath School), she was deeply pained by the rampant infighting within the Jewish community and was dedicated to healing the discord—between rich and poor, Germans and Russians, Reform and Orthodox. In several western cities she not only led services but also made peace between feuding factions of liberals and traditionalists. "Drop all dissension about whether you should take off your hats during the services," she implored her listeners, and "in the name of all we Hebrews hold dear . . . be patient with one another."[105]

Yet the outspoken preacher was not a "new woman," as feminists were then called. She opposed universal suffrage, and although she believed females had the right to be rabbis, Frank herself would not accept a calling so "thoroughly masculine."[106] For her, a woman's "noblest work" was in the home.[107] After her marriage, at age forty, to Simon Litman, an economics professor at the University of California, she was preoccupied with wifely duties, and her short, brilliant career as a public figure came to an end.

But Ray Frank Litman was nonetheless a trailblazer. If not actually the first female rabbi, she was the first female *maggid,* or itinerant preacher, as historian William Kramer has pointed out. Her eloquence demonstrated that a woman could be the equal of a man in the pulpit, an example not lost on Jewish females aspiring to the clergy generations later.[108] But perhaps most important was the love for Judaism she fervently conveyed to

---

*Voorsanger also took the opportunity to declare, contrary to Wise, that female rabbis would "usurp an office in which learning, courage, and an infinite amount of self-sacrifice are indispensable" (Reva Clar and William M. Kramer, "The Girl Rabbi of the Golden West: The Adventurous Life of Ray Frank in Nevada, California and the Northwest—Part II," *WSJH* 18 [April 1986]: 223).

her contemporaries. While many Jewish women fled from the religion of their birth, she fought to purify and affirm it. An excerpt from her inspirational speech at the Jewish Women's Congress held at Chicago's Columbia Exposition in 1893 captures her intensity. After invoking the strong and devoted Jewish females of centuries past, she turned to "the poor apology for religious worship" in her own day:

Go to the synagogue on Friday night; where are the people? Our men cannot attend, keen business competition will not permit them. Where are our women? Keener indulgence in pleasures will not permit them. Where are the children? Keenest parental examples of grasping gain and material desires will not permit them, and so the synagogue is deserted. Go there on a Saturday, the day of rest, of holy convocation. Where are the people? Our men are at their shops, our women doing the shopping, calling, or at the theatre; *every one and everything can be attended to but God. For him they have no time.* With whom lies the blame? Where are the wise mothers of Israel today?[109]

ALTERNATIVE BELIEFS

Those apathetic toward Judaism were often lured by other belief systems, and for the well-educated, highly acculturated German Jewish elite, the Ethical Culture Society was an attractive alternative. Founded in the late 1870s by Felix Adler, it leapt far beyond radical rabbis such as Jacob Voorsanger by rejecting any form of Jewish distinctiveness and drawing upon the wisdom of many religions as inspiration for its considerable benevolent work. No lesser a light than Adolph Sutro—who assembled perhaps the greatest private library of Hebraica in the world—favored Ethical Culture over organized Judaism. He left a substantial bequest to Adler, who had visited San Francisco in 1878 and who reflected the philosophy today we might call "secular humanism."[110]

Yet Ethical Culture, perhaps because of its rejection of theism, failed to win mass appeal in California. More popular was spiritualism, which proposed to communicate with the dead, and theosophy, which often delved into Eastern religion to understand extrasensory perception. These cults, along with astrology and fortune-telling, were particularly appealing to women who felt disenfranchised by Judaism or mainstream Christianity. There was no ordained clergy in these alternative movements, and thus no male domination; indeed, women generally held the key roles. Nor was God or the divine spirit considered to be masculine, but rather androgynous or impersonal. And these creeds sanctified neither marriage nor motherhood as the woman's only proper role.[111]

Harriet Levy tells us that in the 1880s her Jewish next-door neighbor, Mabel Lessing, suddenly a widow at age thirty and in need of a steady income, transformed herself into Madame Sybilla, a clairvoyant "whom people consulted for advice and for whose wisdom they paid money."[112] But if Mabel turned to fortune-telling out of financial need, astrology and theosophy became the earnest calling of one of the most politically engaged Jewish women in the state, tireless suffragette Selina Solomons, daughter of Emanu-El's board secretary Seixas Solomons. Along with many other women's rights activists, particularly on the West Coast, Selina eschewed the traditional religion of her birth, feeling more empowered by transcendental beliefs. She corresponded with Carl Jung, joined the Theosophical Society based in Point Loma, and made her living as a "solar biologist," charging $5 for a custom-designed horoscope.[113] Selina had much support in her family for her unconventional views. Her pioneer mother, Hannah Marks Solomons, a founding member of San Francisco's Theosophical Society, used a medium to communicate with her dead brother-in-law.[114]

Selina's brother Theodore, the illustrious family's black sheep who never attended a university, also dabbled in theosophy, but his lifelong passion—which bordered on the religious—was mountaineering. His temple was the High Sierra: "utter wildness, sternness and desolation."[115] In the 1890s, young Theodore made five long expeditions, for more than a month at a time, through "heaven on earth," as he called it,[116] sometimes accompanied by his cousin Sidney Peixotto, sometimes by Ambrose Bierce's son, Leigh, and sometimes alone. He climbed, surveyed, and photographed the range, taking hundreds of pictures and writing extensive reports for the Sierra Club, of which he was a charter member.[117] Theodore named natural landmarks such as Mounts Spencer, Fiske, and Huxley after the agnostic philosophers he admired, and named places like Evolution Basin for his favorite scientific theories. He conceived and charted the breathtaking two-hundred-mile-long crest trail, from Yosemite to Mount Whitney, eventually named (unfairly, believe many naturalists) for John Muir. As did the legendary Scotsman, Theodore believed the Sierras to be virtually sacred. Coming upon the thirteen-thousand-foot, oddly shaped Seven Gables (another mountain he named), he "was too awed to shout. The ideas represented by such words as lovely, beautiful, wild or terrible, cold or desolate fail to compass it. . . . Roughly speaking, one might say the sight was sublime and awful."[118]

In 1897 the adventurer joined the Klondike Gold Rush and lived near Nome for a decade, but he would later settle down with his family on a twenty-one-acre spread in the "transcendently beautiful" Sierras, in sight of El Capitan and Half Dome.[119] He was once more in harmony with the mountains he had discovered in his twenties, feeling "*in* the earth and part of it."[120] Of course, Solomons could have linked his reverence for nature with Judaism, but he chose not to. He avoided Temple Emanu-El from his boyhood, married a non-Jew, and raised his daughter in the Unitarian faith, yet another belief system that drew many Jews.

The rabbis were probably not threatened by the spiritual straying of Selina and Theodore Solomons; neither was likely to cause mass defections among Jews. But the Christian Science movement, led by the celebrated Mary Baker Eddy, was another matter. She asserted that disease could be conquered entirely through faith, and as the centerpiece of her teachings used stories of Jesus as a healer. The Union of American Hebrew Congregations declared Christian Science incompatible with Judaism, and leading San Francisco rabbis voiced dismay that many of their congregants were attracted to Eddy's cause.[121] Within eight months during World War I, the *Emanu-El* printed three front-page essays by nationally known authors, including Rabbi Stephen Wise, stressing that one could not be a Jew and a Christian Scientist at the same time.[122]

But many local Jews, largely women, found comfort in Christian Science, and when reading its texts either whispered or skipped the word "Christ."* Not only lapsed Jews such as art patron Sarah Stein venerated Eddy, but Rabbi Nieto's troubled wife was also drawn in by Christian Science.[123] At Sherith Israel, knowledgeable laymen estimated that one-third of the membership were followers of the movement at one time in their lives, and a storm of criticism and six letters of resignation greeted Nieto's successor when he pointed out its incompatibility with Judaism.[124] Neither Christian Science nor any of the other alternative creeds required formal conversion and renunciation of Judaism, but that made it all the easier for Jews to embrace them.

---

*Trying to woo her mother to Christian Science, Harriet Levy's older sister "made tentative excursions into the gospels, ran back for safety to David and Hosea, and identified the books of the New Testament with the miracles of the Old, artfully avoiding the name of Jesus" (Levy, *920 O'Farrell Street*, 56).

Perhaps the "immense popularity of Christian Science with our people," as one rabbi lamented,[125] reflected the weakness of Judaism in Northern California. But by the second decade of the twentieth century the rabbinate had made a new commitment to make their faith more relevant to people's lives. A central figure in this effort was Martin Meyer, who assumed the Emanu-El pulpit in 1910 and departed completely from his predecessor, Jacob Voorsanger. At Sherith Israel no change in rabbinical leadership was necessary: Jacob Nieto, who would remain until 1930, demonstrated a remarkable ability to adapt to new trends locally and nationally.

Like a number of their Reform colleagues across the country, these leaders, fearing for their movement and indeed for Judaism itself in the new century, reached out to new constituencies. Meyer, only thirty-one when he returned to his native city (his bar mitzvah had been performed at Ohabai Shalome), developed a broad view of both temple and community under the influence of such thinkers and activists as Rabbis Judah Magnes, Mordecai Kaplan, and Stephen Wise. All three enjoyed a high profile in New York, where Meyer had taken his Ph.D. at Columbia and held his first pulpits.[126]

Early on, Meyer tried to reverse what he saw as the excesses of the ultra-Reform Judaism instituted by his predecessor. He brought back ceremonies such as baby naming and praying for the ill, which had fallen into disuse; he recruited Jews for the temple choir; and, most tellingly, he refused to perform intermarriage.[127]

Unlike Voorsanger, he extended a welcoming hand to the East European immigrants, whom he saw as the future of American Jewry not merely because of their numbers, but also because of their deep Jewish feelings. "The German Jew," he wrote bluntly in 1915, "for the most part is a Jew because he can't help it; his neighbors insist he remain a Jew even after he joins the Christian Science Church."[128] So Meyer encouraged the immigration of the Russians, aided the settlement houses that eased their transition to America, and even hired a cantor, Reuben Rinder, who had been born and raised in a Ukrainian shtetl. By World War I the rabbi also broke profoundly with Voorsanger and many of his lay leaders by publicly embracing Zionism, further endearing himself to the East Europeans.[129]

Meyer sought to include many others he felt had been ignored by the city's Jewish establishment. He nurtured small, struggling Jewish communities in the new suburbs and small towns, was instrumental in forming the Menorah Society (forerunner of the Hillel Foundation) at the University of California, and even created an institution to serve Jewish inmates of state prisons and mental hospitals.[130]

Within his congregation he concentrated on two neglected groups: women and youth. He formed the Women's Guild in 1917 to serve the temple, and a few years later he succeeded in winning for females permission to join the synagogue in their own right and even to be elected to the board of directors.[131] Young people, meanwhile, were drawn to the temple by an invigorated and enlarged religious school that met in a newly constructed schoolhouse eight blocks away on Van Ness Avenue. In its ample auditorium, Meyer's advanced students, emulating Stephen Wise's successful initiative in New York, ran a "Free Synagogue" on the High Holidays, intended for non–temple members.[132] The school swelled to more than five hundred by 1921; boasted a slick literary magazine, the *Scroll*; and presented elaborate Hanukkah plays written by Meyer. Beyond that, he formed an athletic league for the city's Jewish schools, founded a cultural and service organization composed of those in their late teens, and sponsored a Boy Scout troop, soon one of the most active in the nation.[133]

Meyer staunchly advocated a new temple even before World War I. But more than an elegant house of worship, he envisaged a complex of buildings bringing Jews together for social, athletic, charitable, and educational purposes, too. He wanted a center that would serve not only Emanu-El's members, but the entire Jewish community as well. He boldly unveiled his concept, "the Temple of the Open Door," in January 1920:

> Community service is the word of the day, not only on the basis of economic waste of a plant which is idle the greater part of the week and the year; but because we feel that any church or synagogue deaf to the possibility of social and community service is doomed. . . . One thing is certain, that just a house-of-prayer idea for weekly services and religious school instruction is apt to be barren.[134]

Not the least important consequence of the construction of this new temple, Meyer realized, would be the lowering of social barriers dividing the city's Jews. His congregants, still numbering fewer than 450 families in the early 1920s, were set apart from the rest of the community by their ability to pay the high dues. A new temple, he reasoned, might accommodate up to a thousand families, a much broader cross section of the population. Arrangements would be made for those in modest circumstances to become members; in any case, they would be permitted to enjoy the temple's facilities. The new structure would thus be the linchpin of an all-embracing Emanu-El—a vision of the temple that was completely different from that of the past.[135]

Meyer's untimely death in 1923 deprived him of the chance to see the majestic Lake Street Temple open its doors. But he was succeeded by his protégé, the intense young Louis I. Newman, who had worked for five years at Stephen Wise's Free Synagogue and shared Meyer's notion that Judaism was more than a faith, and the synagogue more than a sanctuary. The synagogue-center was a widespread phenomenon across America in the mid-1920s, and Newman repeated the often-heard quip about building a "*shul* with a pool."[136] But he was serious about the benefits to be derived from the "basketball games, dramatics, dancing classes and social interests at the temple."[137] He convinced the board to approve a five-story "Temple House," which included a library, gymnasium, and nine-hundred-seat theater.

Of course the exquisite domed sanctuary, with its Byzantine marble columns and resplendent bronze ark, overshadowed the Temple House aesthetically. But the latter, a venue for imaginative cultural programs, was arguably more instrumental than the former in Emanu-El's success in the late 1920s. The new facility and Newman's dynamism resulted in a near doubling of the membership during his six-year tenure; in 1929 it passed the one-thousand-family mark Meyer had envisioned at the beginning of the decade.[138]

Sherith Israel did not experience such startling gains, but it grew steadily in the second and third decades of the century, finally reaching three hundred families by 1928, double its size twenty years earlier.[139] The congregation's indebtedness fell sharply in the prosperous 1920s, when funds became available to engage an assistant rabbi to assist the aging Nieto. Like Emanu-El, Sherith Israel initiated men's and women's auxiliaries and sponsored a Boy Scout troop.

Even before the turn of the century Nieto had articulated his belief that the synagogue should be more than a worship-centered shrine. He advocated that a lecture hall and gymnasium be constructed as part of the new California Street Temple, an idea so abhorrent to Emanu-El's Rabbi Voorsanger that, much to Nieto's chagrin, the Dutchman lobbied Sherith Israel's board members against it.[140] Due to financial considerations neither the lyceum nor athletic facility were incorporated into the new building in 1905, but the notion of a temple house for social activities long remained a goal of both the rabbi and leading laymen.*

Even earlier than Rabbi Meyer, Nieto had sought to bring women into the orbit of the synagogue. In 1908 he induced the congregation to allow females to attend the congregational meetings and make their voices heard. "Intelligence in woman is equal to the intelligence of man," he wrote, and in 1916, looking ahead to a time when females would lead the temple, he declared that "women preside in the chair with a great deal more precision and distinction than many men I know."[141]

Nieto also pleaded for economic justice, inspiring both Jew and non-Jew alike, even if his "socialism" was disconcerting to some congregants.[142] In a city riven by class conflict he identified with the underprivileged. Especially during the second half of his long tenure, he became a strident advocate of trade unionism and public school reform and an opponent of capital punishment. Although he had supported the Spanish-American War in 1898, his views bordered on pacifism by World War I, and along with his close friends in the labor movement, he decried America's arms buildup.[143]

He also spoke out incessantly on behalf of Tom Mooney and Warren Billings, local agitators who, on trumped-up evidence, had been convicted of killing ten people by dynamiting the military preparedness parade in 1916. Mooney personally thanked the rabbi in a letter from San Quentin, noting "Jewish tolerance, generosity and fealty to justice."[144] Other local rabbis, such as Rudolph Coffee, of Oakland's Temple Sinai, and Jacob Weinstein, who succeeded Nieto in 1930, demanded the release of Mooney and Billings, who were finally set free by the governor in 1939.

Nor was this sort of political activism limited to the Reform rabbis. Congregation Beth Israel's M. S. Levy was one of the town's most vocal proponents of prison reform even in the nineteenth century; he was later joined

---

*The synagogue-center idea was also the way that Ohabai Shalome sought to reverse its flagging fortunes. In 1920 its rabbi, Herman Rosenwasser, announced plans for a "huge Temple for study, recreation, religious worship and communal assistance" (*Emanu-El*, March 12, 1920). Unfortunately, the fund-raising drive, headed by the scandal-ridden Abe Ruef, failed miserably. Worse, the city was not able to support a third Reform synagogue, which Ohabai Shalome had become by the 1920s, and the pioneer congregation was forced to sell its fine Bush Street house of worship in 1934. Services were held in the home of its last rabbi, Michael Fried, but ceased at his death six years later.

by Nieto, Meyer, and Coffee, who carried on this struggle after Levy's death in 1916. In their social activism, the rabbis were no doubt impressed by the model of Father Peter Yorke, for decades a key ally of the working class in the Bay Area. Like M. S. Levy, Yorke was a beloved pastor in both Oakland and San Francisco, and the priest's Irish nationalism was analogous to the rabbi's Zionism. Despite Yorke's occasional anti-Semitic lapses, the two frequently traveled the state together speaking on behalf of the disadvantaged.[145]

A boy whose bar mitzvah Levy performed at the First Hebrew Congregation, Judah L. Magnes, would help resuscitate Judaism in California and throughout the world. He was prepared for rabbinical school by Voorsanger, but in many ways his ideas were opposed to what he perceived at Emanu-El: services similar to Unitarian ones, a theology based on cold reason, and a membership isolated by class and ethnicity. At Hebrew Union College, about a year and a half after he left home, Magnes wrote an essay, reprinted in the *Emanu-El*, bemoaning the loss of religious "earnestness" that had structured Jewish life in previous generations. Now, asserted the nineteen-year-old, "Some who have more wealth than anything else, pay their ministers to proclaim them Jews."[146] He did not advocate a return to the "superstitions" of Orthodoxy, but during the next two decades, in Cincinnati, Berlin, and New York, he would be sharply critical of Reform's wholesale rejection of tradition and bewail the superficiality of American Judaism.[147]

Magnes turned his hand to "wiping out the invidious distinctions" among the Jewish people, as historian David Biale has indicated, "between East European and West European, foreigner and native, Uptown and Downtown Jew, rich and poor."[148] As president of one of the most far-reaching organizations in American Jewish history, New York's Kehilla, or "community," he helped direct the resources of the city's leading philanthropists toward the betterment of the huge immigrant quarter on the Lower East Side.[149] Magnes's family background had prepared him well for this role of mediator among the cultures of the Jews: in Oakland he had grown up with an appreciation of German Jewry from his enlightened Posener mother, and a love of Polish-Jewish folkways from his traditionally inclined father, born in a Hasidic village near Lodz.[150]

At the same time, Magnes sought to bridge the gap between Jews and Judaism, to cross the secular-religious divide that challenged Meyer, Nieto, and other Bay Area rabbis. Rather than attempting to turn the synagogue into a Jewish center, he approached the problem from the opposite direction. He helped make New York's large Young Men's Hebrew Association more Jewish by initiating worship services for its young clientele and creating the position of religious director, filled by a rabbi.[151]

Perhaps partly due to the influence of M. S. Levy, the youth also came away from the Bay Area a Zionist (indeed, the germinal essay he penned in Cincinnati was entitled "Palestine—or Death"), which naturally rankled Voorsanger. The Jewish homeland would be the lifelong preoccupation of Magnes, who spent his last twenty-five years in Jerusalem.

Magnes also had an abiding faith in American democracy (another legacy, he claimed, of his childhood in the diverse Bay Area) and was active in numerous human rights and free speech organizations during his two decades in New York. But he also recognized that the open society toward which he strove could weaken the distinctiveness of each racial, religious, or ethnic group. Rather than a melting pot, then, he advocated cultural pluralism for almost half a century.

Such ideas and actions—the critique of ultra-Reform Judaism and the outreach to immigrants, political activism and Zionism, and the linking of the spiritual and social dimensions of Jewish life in a multicultural America—were not Magnes's alone, of course. But in his attempts to synthesize Judaism and humanism he was surpassed by few; as the eminent philosopher Hugo Bergmann has written, Magnes was "one of the crucial figures in the development of Jewish religious thought and life in our time."[152] Perhaps only a Northern Californian could understand so well that while America offered the greatest opportunity to Jews, it also posed the greatest danger to Judaism.

FIVE

Healing California

Jewish Reformers and Revolutionaries in the Progressive Era

EARLY IN THE TWENTIETH CENTURY, Northern California Jews hearkened to their rabbis' pleas for social justice, but they were influenced even more by the clamor for reform outside the synagogue. They were energized above all by the Progressive movement, which transformed California after Hiram Johnson's gubernatorial victory in 1910.

Few states were more in need of reform. By the 1880s, the Southern Pacific Railroad, the "Octopus," to its enemies, controlled much of the natural resources and maintained power by bribing politicians, judges, and journalists. City governments—San Francisco's was an egregious example—were corrupted by the railroad as well as other business interests. Glaring inequities, ranging from child labor to the abuse of migrant farm workers, plagued California. Voters felt powerless, and until 1911 only men enjoyed suffrage.

Bay Area Jews played a major role in challenging and ultimately reining in the oligarchy. Jews, of course, were heavily represented in business, including big business, but the impulse for reform often came precisely from successful merchants, who saw the individual entrepreneur being crushed by corporate giants such as the Southern Pacific. Besides, leading local Jews were well suited to the Progressivist culture of reason and self-reliance, as well as elitism and paternalism. Most of the Progressives were Republicans, belonging to the party that was also favored by the Jewish community for an entire century following the Civil War.[1]

The Progressives were essentially conservative reformers. Most were ambivalent, and a few even hostile, toward the strident labor unions, and the Progressives skirted the state's most blatant injustice, the abominable treatment of its Asians. But the Progressives' effect on California was highly beneficial. They vastly improved the machinery of government, regulated banks and utilities (including railroads), aided farmers and immigrants, and helped women obtain the vote. Jews developed and advocated many of these reforms, and helped to pass them in the legislature, sustain them in the courts, and implement them throughout the state.

Yet the Jewish community was not completely aligned with the Progressives. Leftist Jews viewed their reforms as half measures intended to prop up a rotten capitalist system. Right-wingers, on the other hand, preferred the status quo and opposed almost any social change. A few Jews even symbolized for the Progressives the evil that they hoped to erase.

But if Jews were part of the problem of exploitative capitalism, they were also central to the solution. Jewish men and women at the turn of the century turned to reform with a zeal matched only by one other group: Protestants from New England.* They, too, were known for their Progressives, although they also produced some predators.

FREE ENTERPRISE

Between the Gold Rush and World War I San Francisco produced more Jewish business leaders than any American city except New York. Levi Strauss is the best known, but other Jewish magnates working on Montgomery Street, who extracted natural resources throughout the entire Pacific Basin, were arguably more important.

In his *Imperial San Francisco,* geographer Gray Brechin reveals the complex process whereby the city came to dominate, if not economically subjugate, a hinterland of millions of square miles.[2] This urban conquest required not only acquisitive industrialists but also pliant politicians and opportunistic

---

* Historians were late in understanding the large Jewish contribution to the California Progressives. One classic study focused only on the Protestant affiliation (George Mowry, *California Progressives* [Chicago, 1951], 87), but a convincing reappraisal held that it had "neglected a very important element—the Jews . . . perhaps the most liberal of all, and especially after 1912 . . . much of the major impetus for reform" (Spencer Olin, *California's Prodigal Sons: Hiram Johnson and the Progressives, 1911–1917* [Berkeley, 1968], 181).

media moguls. Brechin describes the venality of Abe Ruef and the jingoism of the de Youngs, but he barely touches on the less notorious Jewish leaders who helped put San Francisco into such a privileged position. As early as the 1860s, Adolph Sutro mined Nevada's Comstock silver lode, and Louis Sloss and Lewis Gerstle monopolized the Alaska seal fur trade.

In the second generation, the San Francisco–born Fleishhacker brothers, Mortimer and Herbert, epitomized the long reach of big business in the West. As one newsman gushed, "Their hand is in practically every recent business venture from Seattle to Los Angeles, and from the Rockies to the Philippines."[3] As youths they worked in their father's paper-box business, but a land deal in Oregon—yielding tenfold their initial stake of $30,000 in just weeks—emboldened them to embark on a myriad of other investments. Their hydroelectric company, Great Western, was eventually absorbed by Pacific Gas and Electric for a huge profit; their mighty paper concern, Crown Willamette, joined with that of the Zellerbachs to form the second largest in the world. The Fleishhackers manufactured chemicals and steel, ran sugar mills in Hawaii and the Philippines, and invested in real estate and insurance, steamship lines and movies. But most San Franciscans knew them as bankers. A few years after the earthquake, their Anglo and London Paris National Bank became the largest in the city, and in the American West they were surpassed only by their bitter rival A. P. Giannini.[4]

Herbert also wielded tremendous political influence after World War I. San Francisco's long-serving mayor James Rolph personally owed him a million dollars—"Sunny Jim" had made some bad investments and was struggling to avoid bankruptcy—and Fleishhacker became one of his closest political advisors and a major force in the Republican Party.[5]

The influence of Jewish businessmen on the city was seen in the Panama-Pacific International Exposition, which in 1915 brought nineteen million visitors to the newly constructed Marina District.[6] The event proclaimed not only the miraculous recovery of San Francisco from the earthquake and fire less than a decade earlier, but also exalted the rise of an empire on the Pacific Rim.

Julius Kahn used his seniority in the House of Representatives to have the exposition awarded to San Francisco (Congress had originally considered New Orleans for the site). He was aided by Leon Sloss, who, along with Michael de Young and I. W. Hellman Jr. were among the six members of the exposition's board of directors. Tobacco importer Alfred

Esberg chaired the budget committee and virtually planned the fair; at the Library of Congress he studied ten prior expositions and returned home with suggestions for the size and placement of pavilions and remarkably accurate attendance predictions. Music was the province of J. B. Levison of the Firemen's Fund. He brought the Boston Symphony Orchestra and other musicians, ranging from Camille Saint-Saëns to John Philip Sousa. The Fleishhackers, of course "threw the force of their considerable influence in support of the project."[7] Fittingly, Rabbi Martin Meyer joined Episcopalian and Catholic bishops in offering the opening prayers.[8]

There was nothing new about such Jewish participation in an exposition showcasing San Francisco and its commercial potential. More than twenty years earlier Michael de Young had organized the Midwinter Fair in Golden Gate Park. Backed by Julius Kahn (then state assemblyman) and the banker Theodore Lilienthal, the bold exercise in boosterism was declared by one hyperbolic journalist as "entirely conceived and carried out by Jews."*[9]

Some Jews sought to align American foreign policy with big business. De Young, for example, used his *Chronicle* to promote the "benefits" of the Spanish-American War, which he ranked second only to the Gold Rush in its importance to California. Under the headline "Trade Will Follow the Flag into the Philippines," in a special issue published on the last day of the nineteenth century, he foresaw "an imperial future" for the state.[10] In agreement were the Fleishhackers, who reaped huge profits in the wake of Admiral Dewey's victory. They, I. W. Hellman Jr., and, above all, Congressman Julius Kahn would be strident advocates for a strong navy and "military preparedness" for decades to come.

The main domestic issue was the seething struggle between labor and capital, and many local Jewish businessmen firmly opposed collective bargaining. Even the relatively benevolent Levi Strauss Company supported the Employers' Association, which sought to prohibit the closed shop and recruited scabs to break the waterfront unions.[11] Rabbi Voorsanger called

---

*Profits from the 1894 fair were used to convert several of its structures into a permanent museum, to which de Young donated much of his personal art collection as well as funds for its expansion. It was officially named for him in 1924 (William Issel and Robert W. Cherny, *San Francisco 1865–1932: Politics, Power and Urban Development* [Berkeley, 1986], 111–12; Gray Brechin, *Imperial San Francisco: Urban Power, Earthly Ruin* [Berkeley, 1999], 184).

all strikes "acts of violence" and "an attack upon the peace of the community."[12] The *Emanu-El* even sided with the business leaders' militant Law and Order Committee, which placed a two-page ad in the Jewish paper declaring "there is no such thing as peaceful picketing any more than there can be lawful lynching."[13] A similar view was probably held by Jesse Lilienthal, who, as president of United Railways (the city's streetcar system), crushed a worker walkout by bringing in strikebreakers.[14]

Were Jews associated in the public mind with the excesses of capitalism? Certainly Michael de Young was a constant target of muckrakers. They revealed that his Midwinter Fair was largely a scheme to drive up the price of land adjacent to Golden Gate Park, sand-covered tracts that he had purchased on the cheap.[15] He was also accused in the press of extortion, which seemed credible when a businessman who had sought a telephone franchise told a grand jury that de Young had demanded $10,000 to "educate the people" about its need.[16] But, despite their well-publicized misdeeds, the de Youngs were rarely the victims of anti-Semitism. Even Abraham Ruef (a much more identifiable Jew), who went to San Quentin for having accepted bribes from some of the city's top corporations, was generally not the object of religious bigotry. Neither was the turn-of-the-century Jewish brothel owner Henry Ach, nor the shady Jewish police commissioner Moses Gunst.[17]

But a popular work of realist fiction published in 1901, written by the West's leading novelist at the height of his fame, was cause for concern. Frank Norris, using the word "Hebraic" as a synonym for "ungenerous," portrays a parasitic Jew who had literally grown fat on the honest labor of Central Valley farmers.[18] S. Behrman, villain of *The Octopus: A Story of California*, is a repulsive, sweaty, mountain of a man who embodies corporate greed. An agent of the despised railroad, he is "much in evidence in and about the San Francisco court rooms and the lobby of the legislature in Sacramento."[19] In the words of one of the story's most sympathetic characters:

> He's the man that does us every time. . . . If there is dirty work to be done in which the railroad doesn't wish to appear, it is S. Behrman who does it. If the freight rates are to be "adjusted" to squeeze us a little harder, it is S. Behrman who regulates what we can stand. If there's a judge to be bought, it is S. Behrman who does the bargaining. If there is a jury to be bribed, it is S. Behrman who handles the money. If there is an election to be jobbed, it is S. Behrman who manipulates it. It's Behrman here and Behrman there. It is Behrman we come against every time we make a move. It is Behrman who . . . will never let go till he has squeezed us bone dry.[20]

The miscreant escapes two assassination attempts but in the final pages falls into a grain elevator and is smothered to death by cascading waves of wheat.

Norris, although he lived mostly in San Francisco, Paris, and New York, echoes the anti-Semitism of the agrarian Populist movement of the 1880s and '90s, which stridently defended western farmers against urban banking and railroad interests often perceived as Jewish.[21] Yet for all the power of his poisonous characterization in the briskly selling *Octopus,* the stereotype of S. Behrman failed to resonate in the Bay Area, which lacked an ingrained tradition of anti-Semitism. Although some Jews were reviled as accomplices of robber barons or foes of the common man, many more were seen to be healing California from its plague of greed and corruption. In fact, in San Francisco the Populist Party, at its zenith in 1894, nominated a Jewish businessman for mayor. Adolph Sutro rallied discontented workers with the slogan "The Octopus must be destroyed!"

ADOLPH SUTRO AND THE COMMON GOOD

He was the city's largest landowner, but he was also long revered by the working class as its champion. After all, back in the mid-1870s, with miners' safety one of his primary considerations, Sutro had prevailed against William Ralston's avaricious "Bank Ring" and built a tunnel through the Comstock Lode.

Sutro also directed much of his time and money toward aiding the city's poor, and in 1878 he embraced the kindergarten movement. Along with Justice Solomon Heydenfeldt and insurance baron Samuel Levy, he initiated the first tuition-free, nonsectarian, privately financed kindergarten in the country, continuing to advance this cause until his death two decades later. The three benefactors assembled an impressive group of contributors, including many leading non-Jews, and secured a building in the teeming South of Market district for the first school; by 1895 there would be forty in the city, enrolling more than 3,500 children.[22] The board recruited Kate Douglas Smith (later Wiggin) as the lead teacher, and her success in the run-down neighborhood she dubbed "Tar Flat" would become a national model.[23] Believing in the potential for human betterment, Sutro understood that kindergartens, first conceived by the German educator Friedrich Froebel, could counter the debilitating effects of the slums on youngsters; it was one of the earliest attempts in America to deal with the plight of urban immigrants.

Similarly, he saw the benefits of recreation for the masses. After acquiring most of San Francisco's northwestern shoreline in the 1880s, Sutro built a relatively modest private home on the rugged heights overlooking the Pacific. The surrounding gardens, though—an immaculately landscaped twenty-acre sculpture park with incomparable views—he opened to the public free of charge. The only public transportation to Sutro Heights, however, was a steam-operated train owned by the hated Southern Pacific, which charged a stiff twenty-cent round-trip fare from downtown. As a result, the philanthropist and his cousin Gustav Sutro countered with a railway of their own, this one electrically powered. It took a scenic route along California Street, turned north at Thirty-third Avenue, and then followed the shore to another Sutro property, the Cliff House, at the base of Sutro Heights—all for five cents each way.[24]

In the next decade the fabled Sutro Baths were constructed, the largest indoor swimming facility in the world.* An entrance resembling a Greek temple led into a cavernous glass-roofed pavilion housing seven pools at different temperatures. The builder of the Sutro Tunnel now performed another engineering feat: seawater came through a bore carved out of the cliff and was pumped into the pools; the water was then frequently drained and piped back out to the ocean. Restaurants, a museum, and palm trees all added to the allure of "Sutro's dream palace of pleasure, entertainment and culture."[25] Also an early environmentalist, he protected the seals off nearby Point Lobos; at his urging Congress passed a law putting Seal Rocks "in trust" for the American people.[26]

The incorruptible civic guardian was the perfect choice to lead a radical third party that would challenge both the Southern Pacific Railroad and the municipal "boodling," or graft, typified by the notorious "Blind Boss," Chris Buckley, who had milked city hall for almost a decade before fleeing the country in disgrace. Sutro, a vigorous campaigner, railed against big business and even backed the unions in the violent Pullman Strike, which had paralyzed the American economy shortly before the election. He ran well among the working class and in a field of six received an absolute majority of votes.[27]

---

*The baths, which could accommodate ten thousand people, were popular through the 1920s, but attendance fell off by midcentury and, in need of costly repairs, they were closed in 1954. A fire in 1966 destroyed the elegant structure, and only stone ruins remain today.

The two-year term of this first Jewish mayor of any major U.S. city was ambitious. Playing to a national audience, Sutro supported women's suffrage, encouraged other reform mayors, and opposed the Southern Pacific.[28] Locally, he fought for a better sewer system, street paving, municipal ownership of utilities, and, with prescience, an improved fire department. But the city charter afforded the mayor little power, and the board of supervisors, which included not one Populist, invariably blocked Sutro, who lacked the artfulness needed to be an effective politician. His mayoralty left few lasting marks, and illness and frustration precluded a try for a second term.

But if he failed in pulling the levers of city government, he continued to work on his own to improve San Francisco. He planted trees throughout town at his own expense, donated twenty-six acres on Mount Parnassus to the University of California for its medical school, and began the process of gifting to the state his stupendous personal library (especially strong in Judaica), with the proviso that it remain in San Francisco. The intrepid bibliophile had journeyed to the Far East, Palestine, Latin America, and Europe in the 1880s, amassing the largest private book collection in the United States, consisting of roughly a quarter million bound volumes and pamphlets. Included were more than three thousand books printed before 1500; they represented around 15 percent of all the incunabula in existence at the time.*

Of course such munificence could not, by itself, resolve the deep conflicts in the urban polity at the turn of the century. But as defender of the common good, and through his attacks on the railroad in particular, this patrician businessman helped pave the way for the Progressives who followed him. They would change California forever.

FIGHTING FOR FARMERS

Although Sutro read the Bible in Hebrew, it is difficult to see it as the philosophical impetus behind his moral crusades. But many other leading turn-of-the-century Jewish reformers credited their heritage at least in part for their social conscience. For one esteemed family that produced three of the

---

*Tragically, most of the collection, which was stored in a downtown warehouse, was destroyed by the catastrophe of 1906. But the remainder, about seventy thousand volumes, comprises the Sutro Library (a branch of the California State Library), now housed near the campus of San Francisco State University.

most exemplary Jews in Northern California's history, the half brothers David Lubin and Harris Weinstock, and David's son Simon, the ethics of the Hebrew prophets were central in understanding society and curing its ills.

David, the internationalist among them, was born in a Polish shtetl in 1849, the youngest of six children. His pious father, whose practice it was to bring home a needy person to share the family's Sabbath meal, died when David was still a toddler.[29] His mother soon remarried and, with her new husband, Solomon Weinstock, immigrated to London, where she bore another son, Harris. The family later moved to New York's Lower East Side. The strong-willed woman instructed her sons in Jewish history, lore, and the Bible while they attended public school, but their education also included a glimpse into America's underside: the New York City Draft Riots of 1863. Amidst the mayhem, the half brothers saved a black man by hiding him in the courtyard of their house while they sent the Irish lynch mob off in the wrong direction.[30]

Harris Weinstock moved to California in the early 1870s, and David Lubin soon followed. There they operated a dry goods store on San Francisco's Washington Street. It prospered, but they were repulsed at the way commerce was conducted. As Lubin remembered, doing business meant

> standing at the door of your store and inviting in customers—sailors and miners formed a goodly percentage of the motley population—and then you would "soak" them for all they were worth. It was the old-world, old-time system of barter . . . bargaining and haggling over prices between salesman and customer, in which the latter was generally worsted. To me it was hateful. I could not square it with my notions of right and wrong.[31]

He and Weinstock resolved to sell their wares differently: with "fixed prices on all goods, marked in plain figures so that all could read."[32] They went to Sacramento and opened what was probably the first store in the West with the words "One Price" over the door. They struggled at first—buyers "knew little or nothing about ethics, but knew very much about beating down the price"—but gradually they built a profitable operation along with an impeccable reputation.[33] When resolving business disputes, the self-taught Lubin would often quote Isaiah, Socrates, Cicero, or Maimonides.

By 1884 the half brothers had developed one of the nation's largest department stores and mail-order houses. It was now time for Lubin to make good on a promise he had made his mother long before: to take her to Palestine, then a barren corner of the Ottoman Empire. Involved in Jerusalem's

The Winter of 1849, by Francis Samuel Marryat. Painted in 1855 by a young artist, this work reflects the hurly-burly atmosphere of Gold Rush San Francisco, with its flooded streets and frenetic commerce. The wood-framed structures were vulnerable to fire, and by 1852 the "cloth and board" city had endured six major conflagrations. (THE BANCROFT LIBRARY OF THE UNIVERSITY OF CALIFORNIA, BERKELEY)

Seixas Solomons's certificate of membership in the vigilantes. Jews were highly visible in the controversial extralegal militias that claimed to save San Francisco from lawlessness in 1851 and again in 1856. Solomons, secretary of the board of trustees of Congregation Emanu-El, was an officer in the vigilantes' five-thousand-man military brigade. (WJHC/JLMM)

Athlete and journalist Philo Jacoby. Founder and longtime editor of the weekly newspaper the *Hebrew,* he countered stereotypes of Jews with his athletic prowess. Shown here in late middle age at the turn of the century, Jacoby was a world-champion marksman and medal-winning strongman. (THE BANCROFT LIBRARY OF THE UNIVERSITY OF CALIFORNIA, BERKELEY)

Glove department at the White House. The bon vivant Raphael Weill's department store near Union Square was among many elegant retail establishments owned and operated by Jews in nineteenth- and twentieth-century San Francisco. (WJHC/JLMM)

The Haas-Lilienthal House soon after its construction in 1887. Originally built by William Haas, a wealthy dealer in imported foods, the Queen Anne–style mansion at 2007 Franklin Street epitomized the magnificent residences of San Francisco's Jewish elite. Haas and his wife, Bertha, and their descendants occupied the home until 1974, when it was donated as a museum to the Architectural Heritage Foundation.

Joshua Abraham Norton, Emperor of the United States and Protector of Mexico. The failed commodities speculator reinvented himself in the late 1850s as a delusional eccentric and was San Francisco's most beloved street person until his death in 1880. He issued his own scrip, which was almost always honored in restaurants and shops, and rode streetcars and attended public events free of charge. (SAN FRANCISCO HISTORY CENTER, SAN FRANCISCO PUBLIC LIBRARY)

Judah Magnes soon after he left the Bay Area in 1894 for Hebrew Union College in Cincinnati. Born in San Francisco and raised in Oakland, Magnes became the first ordained rabbi from the American West and made a career in New York as an advocate for East European immigrant Jews, and in Jerusalem as the founder and first chancellor of the Hebrew University. (WJHC/JLMM)

The Oakland High School baseball team of 1892, with Judah Magnes on the left in the back row. He attributed his lifelong faith in democracy and cultural pluralism to his upbringing in the "far West," where his "first teachers used to talk of the glories of the real America—no badges, no titles, no special uniforms." (WJHC/JLMM)

Gertrude Stein and Alice Toklas traveling in Venice. Stein, whose aesthetic
sensibility was deeply influenced by her youth in East Oakland in the
1880s and early 1890s, transformed modern art in the early twentieth century. She lived with Alice Toklas in France for almost forty years, and
many other San Francisco Jewish women—budding artists, musicians, and
writers—visited them in Paris and returned home forever changed.

A drawing of San Francisco's Chinatown by Ernest Peixotto. A member of an illustrious Sephardi family, he was one of Les Jeunes, rebellious youths who at the turn of the century hoped to create a cultural revolution with an avant-garde monthly, the *Lark,* printed on bamboo paper obtained in Chinatown. Peixotto was one of many Jewish artists and businessmen who were fascinated by the oldest, largest, and most vibrant Chinese community in North America. (THE BANCROFT LIBRARY OF THE UNIVERSITY OF CALIFORNIA, BERKELEY)

Sherith Israel's synagogue on Post and Taylor streets, 1870–1905. Amidst financial difficulties and personnel problems, the mostly Prussian-Polish congregation gradually moved from traditional to liberal Judaism. (WJHC/JLMM)

Emanu-El's Sutter Street Temple, 1866–1906. The imposing sanctuary, one of the costliest in North America, reflected the rapid emergence in San Francisco of a commercial Jewish elite, mostly of Bavarian origin. The "cathedral synagogue" was designed by William Patton, a non-Jew who had grown up among Norman churches in England, but who may have intended the temple's exterior to resemble a Torah scroll. (WJHC/JLMM)

The Sutter Street Temple viewed from Nob Hill. Emanu-El, with its twin towers and bronze-plated domes, was a prominent feature on the San Francisco skyline and could be seen from the Berkeley hills. The congregation's ultra-Reform rabbis replaced the *shofar*, or ram's horn, used during the High Holidays, with a cornet and for a year moved Sabbath services from Saturday to Sunday. (WJHC/JLMM)

Sherith Israel's California Street Temple, erected in 1905. The ornate synagogue, designed by the well-known San Francisco architect Albert Pissis, survived the earthquake and fire a year after its construction. (WJHC/JLMM)

Rabbi Jacob Nieto, spiritual leader of Sherith Israel (1893–1930). The charismatic Sephardi, born in London and raised in Jamaica, was one of the leading voices for social justice in San Francisco. He also brought Sherith Israel into the Reform movement. (WJHC/JLMM)

Handbill from Adolph Sutro's successful mayoral campaign in 1894. One of the wealthiest men in San Francisco, Sutro ran a populist campaign against the Southern Pacific Railroad, "the Octopus." He was the first Jew to be elected mayor of a major U.S. city. (WJHC/JLMM)

Adolph Sutro in his home on San Francisco's northwestern shoreline, overlooking the Pacific. The surrounding grounds of Sutro Heights were open to the public as a pleasure garden. An engineer, environmentalist, real estate developer, philanthropist, and politician, Sutro was also a bibliophile, assembling one of the world's largest private libraries, which was particularly rich in Judaica. (SAN FRANCISCO HISTORY CENTER, SAN FRANCISCO PUBLIC LIBRARY)

Portrait of David Lubin by Giorgio Szoldaticz, 1919. A successful businessman and farmer in Northern California, Lubin sought to improve agriculture throughout the world. In 1905 he initiated the International Institute of Agriculture in Rome, representing forty-six countries tackling the problems of food production and distribution. (WJHC/JLMM)

THE TABLES TURNED
YOU SABE HIM ! KEALNEY MUST GO !

Asians were severely persecuted in California, and one of their most virulent enemies was the demagogue Dennis Kearney, who in 1877 incited crowds with the slogan "The Chinese Must Go." The San Francisco Jewish community, although opposed to violence, expressed strong anti-Chinese sentiments. This card, printed by Isidore Choynski, the city's leading Jewish journalist, is a racist caricature depicting the delight of the Chinese in Kearney's imprisonment. (WJHC/JLMM)

Author and activist Anna Strunsky. The beautiful young Russian immigrant, who had a romantic relationship with Jack London and coauthored a book with him, spoke frequently on socialism before large, adoring audiences. As a foreign correspondent she covered the pogroms in czarist Russia in 1907. (*SAN FRANCISCO EXAMINER*, OCTOBER 3, 1897)

Orthodox community, she remained there for the last decade of her life and was buried in the Holy Land. Lubin himself stayed only a month, but his experience was transformative. Although wandering the hills and valleys did not turn him into a Zionist, he experienced a spiritual if not nationalist epiphany. He came to think of the Jewish people as a light unto the nations, as an instrument of "righteousness" in *every* land. Lubin dedicated himself to this idea of service to the world, which was, according to his biographer, "the underlying motor power of his whole career."[34]

Moreover, in Palestine he conceived of the specific direction of his life's work: worldwide agricultural reform. At home he had focused on the ethical behavior of the merchant, asserting: "The improperly conducted business pulls downward to injustice and barbarism."[35] But contemplating the advanced civilization of ancient Judea, he reasoned that the Jewish state had survived among powerful, hostile nations because of its small land-owning farmers. Lubin found confirmation in his study of the Roman republic, and in Jefferson's writings on freeholders as the backbone of democracy.

Yet he lacked personal experience in agriculture, so, shortly after his return home, he and Weinstock purchased wheat fields and orchards in the Central Valley. Believing that only through unity could the tillers of the soil attain fair prices, the half brothers established the California Fruit Growers' Exchange, a cooperative that sought to change the way farmers brought produce to market. In 1886 Weinstock followed a shipment of his fruit by train to its destination in the East, interviewing every middleman along the way. Lubin, meanwhile, traveled to Europe to see its methods of produce distribution.[36] Shocked at the high shipping costs exacted by West Coast railroads, the two lobbied for rate reductions and government subsidies, later adopted in the form of federal price supports.

They made progress in improving one of the state's most vital industries, but by the turn of the century they had chosen different arenas for their work. Lubin's would be the entire world. In 1905, after many setbacks, he realized his dream: with the backing of the king of Italy, he founded the International Institute of Agriculture (IIA) in Rome,* which represented forty-six countries tackling the problems of food production

---

*Lubin, who lived primarily in Europe until his death in 1919, was the American representative of the IIA. In 1946 his organization would become a part of the Food and Agricultural Organization of the UN. Its million-volume library in Rome is named in Lubin's honor, as is a street in that city's Borghese Gardens.

and distribution on a worldwide basis. The IIA was perhaps the world's first international parliamentary body and a fitting capstone of Lubin's universalism. It would not only gather and disseminate information on wages, products, and plant diseases, but would also coordinate some of the farming policies of member nations.

Weinstock would remain in California and become one of the state's most influential Progressives. Like Lubin, an autodidact, he became a popular lecturer throughout the West in the 1880s, speaking on such topics as civil liberties, agricultural reform, and liberal Judaism, and he rose in the National Guard from private to lieutenant colonel. In 1902 he helped found the Commonwealth Club and became the first president of the prestigious forum dedicated to the serious discussions of civic issues. One of its earliest programs featured Jacob Riis, whose photographs had vividly captured the grinding poverty of the Lower East Side.[37]

Meanwhile, Weinstock (joined by Lubin) endowed a visiting lectureship on business ethics at the University of California. Early in the new century Weinstock also participated in the "City Beautiful" movement, the initiative to remake San Francisco according to the designs of the nation's preeminent urban planner, Daniel Burnham, who had guided Chicago's rebirth after its devastating fire. Weinstock believed nature had blessed San Francisco, where he now had his primary residence—"What other city on the face of the globe combines all the advantages . . . concentrated on this one remarkable spot?"—and he exhorted its citizens to keep aesthetic considerations in mind as they built (and, beginning in 1906, rebuilt) their commercial metropolis.[38]

But no cause engaged him as much as "good government" (the Progressives were often mocked as "goo-goos" for their fixation), and San Francisco's municipal corruption deeply distressed him. Delivering the commencement address at Stanford in 1907, Weinstock did not merely flay Abraham Ruef, who had pleaded guilty to extortion two weeks earlier, but he also explained how his crimes had "undermined the very foundations of government." The "base ingrate," he declared, was "a traitor to the republic in time of peace as was Benedict Arnold in time of war."[39]

A few months later Colonel Weinstock became a charter member of the Lincoln-Roosevelt League, the embryo of California's Progressive movement. Composed mainly of civic-minded Republican businessmen and professionals, it sought to free the party and the state from the railroad and cleanse the political process of corruption. The league advocated direct election of U.S. senators; direct primaries (the 1906 GOP slate had been handpicked by Ruef in the proverbial smoke-filled room); democratic mechanisms such as initiatives, referendums, and recall; conservation of forests; workers' compensation; women's suffrage; and many other positions Weinstock embraced. He traveled the state on behalf of the organization, which virtually owed its existence to the colonel and his Los Angeles counterpart, the more left-leaning Jewish merchant Meyer Lissner.[40]

By 1910, having convinced the legislators to pass the direct primary measure, the Lincoln-Roosevelt League was ready to make a bid for power and sought a candidate for the Republican gubernatorial nomination. Model citizen and compelling orator Harris Weinstock was on the verge of becoming the standard bearer when he removed his name from consideration. He thought that Hiram Johnson, who had gained popularity as prosecutor in the Ruef trial, stood a better chance of success.[41]

Johnson easily won the nomination and the governor's chair, and Weinstock, who appeared with him frequently, was at the center an administration often considered the most reformist in state history. Having recently traveled the world to study workers' rights, Weinstock had become an authority on labor issues and was appointed by Johnson in 1913 as a commissioner of the new Industrial Accident Commission. He administered California's insurance fund and instituted safety measures in factories, mines, and power plants.[42]

Weinstock also successfully implemented the recently passed Workmen's Compensation Act, at the heart of Johnson's agenda. But before the governor and colonel could proceed, the law had to be sustained in the state supreme court (hardly a foregone conclusion, since a similar law had recently been ruled unconstitutional in New York). Fortunately, they had an ally in Louis Sloss's son Marcus, appointed to the court in 1906 at age thirty-six and its most liberal justice throughout the Progressive era. The Harvard-trained jurist, viewing the Workmen's Compensation Act "with the friendliest eye," wrote a sweeping decision upholding it.[43]

To cure the state's economic ills Weinstock often proposed solutions he had encountered abroad. Impressed with the system of rural credits he had investigated in Germany, he convinced Johnson to establish a commission to assist the farmer "who has saved a few hundred dollars," as Weinstock wrote, "to become an independent landowner. . . . [S]urely there is no higher purpose that a government can serve."[44] Joined on the commission by Chester Rowell, the intellectual leader of the California Progressives, and

David Barrows, president of the University of California, Weinstock convinced lawmakers to adopt the plan. It was soon superseded, though, by the Federal Farm Loan Act passed in 1916—inspired in large measure by David Lubin's notions about aiding the small farmer.[45]

Johnson also asked Weinstock to head the State Market Bureau, charged with organizing California's agricultural producers. Just as he and Lubin, as private citizens, had earlier advanced growers' cooperatives, Weinstock urged farmers to unite in order to improve the quality of their products and obtain higher prices.[46]

His deputy in this battle was the aspiring young attorney Aaron Sapiro, who was destined to win nationwide fame in the 1920s as a leader of the agricultural cooperative movement. Sapiro had grown up in wretched poverty, hawking matches on the streets of West Oakland in the 1880s, and spent his adolescence in San Francisco's Pacific Hebrew Orphan Asylum. There his "striking intelligence" was noticed by Rabbi Nieto, an orphanage trustee, who secured admission for the youth to Hebrew Union College.[47] He spent seven years there but in the end refused ordination; he felt Reform Judaism was not yet the "instrument of social service" he had hoped.[48] Instead, he enrolled in Hastings College of the Law, graduating in 1911. Hiram Johnson was in the audience for Sapiro's valedictory speech, "Law as a Training for Citizenship."[49]

Weinstock, who had known Sapiro as a rabbinic intern in Stockton, was impressed with his "great moral courage" and engaged him first as his personal attorney and later, in 1915, as the State Market Bureau's legal counsel.[50] A coterie of other young San Francisco Jewish attorneys, including Leo Rabinowitz, Philip Ehrlich, and Sapiro's brother, Milton, joined in the crusade, but none had the legal mind of Aaron, a pioneer in the new field of jurisprudence. And like his mentor, Harris Weinstock, he was also an enthralling promoter, reportedly able to make the "marketing of a barrel of apples more exciting than a tale from Boccaccio and the signing of a corporate agreement seem as vital to social justice . . . as the Magna Carta."[51]

In just a few years Weinstock and Sapiro organized a significant minority of the state's fruit growers. But the two activists encountered major obstacles, including a "go-it-alone" sensibility among farmers, who looked askance at state help and refused to cooperate with other producers. In 1919 the principled colonel and the ambitious attorney squared off against one another: Weinstock thought Sapiro's legal fees exorbitant and the matter went to the courts.[52] The following year the older man, now in failing health and stymied by Johnson's conservative successor in Sacramento, resigned from his post as director of the State Market Bureau.

Sapiro, though, took agrarian cooperatives into the national arena. He organized tobacco and cotton growers in the South, and wheat and dairy producers in the Midwest. By the mid-1920s, when he had moved to Chicago, he had formed sixty associations encompassing 750,000 farmers.[53]

But the "father of cooperative marketing" was also publicly assailed as an "agricultural Napoleon."[54] Not only were Sapiro's aggressive methods attacked, but, when many of his cooperatives failed, so were his ideas. The thick-skinned orphan from Oakland took the harsh criticism in stride, but nothing prepared him for the assault launched by Henry Ford, who accused him (along with Weinstock, Herbert Fleishhacker, and others) of engaging in an international Jewish conspiracy to exploit the American farmer.

Several years earlier the billionaire industrialist had unleashed the most virulent defamation of Jews in American history. Convinced of a Jewish plot to enslave the world, Ford printed articles in almost a hundred consecutive issues of his weekly *Dearborn Independent,* blaming the Jews for virtually everything he hated: from communism to Wall Street, from Hollywood movies to black jazz. As "evidence" he excerpted large portions of the scurrilous *Protocols of the Elders of Zion.*[55] An anthology of the *Independent's* most hate-filled essays, entitled *The International Jew,* was translated into sixteen languages and sold millions of copies worldwide.

In 1924, after a two-year lull, Ford reopened his attack with twenty articles against agricultural cooperatives, calling them "monopoly traps" manipulated by "a band of Jews—bankers, lawyers, moneylenders, advertising agencies, fruit packers, produce buyers, professional office managers, and bookkeeping experts."[56] Ford's mudslingers named Aaron Sapiro as mastermind of the whole cabal.

The maligned attorney responded with a million-dollar libel suit, despite the lack of support from national Jewish organizations, which were afraid that taking on such a powerful adversary could further inflame anti-Semitism. Sapiro saw no other choice: "I felt that somebody had to call this man. . . . I was there as a representative, first, of the cooperative marketing movement, and second . . . of the Jews who were trying in their own ways to bring social light to disorganized industry in America."[57]

Ford hired scores of detectives to scrutinize Sapiro's life, as well as a team of six trial lawyers headed by a sitting United States senator. Covered on the front page of the *New York Times* throughout the spring of 1927, the case was clouded by a mysterious car accident that Ford used as an excuse for not testifying. Finally, the defendant, tormented by the protracted proceedings, agreed to settle out of court. Ford disingenuously claimed not to have realized the destructiveness of his publications, but he did issue a public retraction of the anti-Semitic accusations, offered an apology to the Jewish people and to Sapiro personally, and paid him roughly $140,000.[58]

Despite that triumph, Sapiro could not slow the agrarian associations' decline, especially during the Depression. In common with Weinstock, he had gained great benefits for the farmer, only to see his handiwork come undone. Lubin, who left a more lasting legacy, was also disappointed: the international body he established proved far less powerful than he had envisioned. Yet whatever the fate of their institutions, the far-sighted thinking of these practical idealists radiated throughout the state, the nation, and the world and affected rural policy for generations.

"CHAMPION OF THE MIGRANTS"

The accomplishments of David Lubin's son Simon were more concrete. In service to Governor Johnson and his successors for a decade as president of the Commission on Immigration and Housing, Lubin drafted and helped pass much of the legislation that made California a national leader in social welfare.

Unlike his father and uncle, Simon received a superb formal education, graduating from Harvard in 1903. There he came under the wing of idealist philosopher Josiah Royce, born in the Sierras and raised in San Francisco, who believed that California, despite its chronic social strife, had the potential to become a model civilization.[59] But Simon was influenced no less by his family's ideas about community service, which were rooted in classical Jewish texts. As he guided his son, David Lubin frequently drew upon Maimonides and other rabbinic sages. In fact, breaking from the pattern of most accomplished second-generation California Jews, Simon became *more* involved in synagogue life than was his immigrant father; he often delivered the Yom Kippur sermon at Temple B'nai Israel in Sacramento.[60] In 1912, when the thirty-six-year-old stood on the brink of joining Johnson's administration, his father revealed a bit about his own pursuit of social justice. Invoking the reluctant prophet Jonah, David wrote:

It is not because I want to be a count, or a duke, or to receive a medal, applause, or thanks; these are of no value, not at least to me. It is because your great-great-grandfathers and mine started out on this work centuries ago. It is the heredity of these ideals, which urges me on in the work, in spite of the many efforts I have made to escape it.[61]

A decade earlier Simon had worked in Boston's South End and New York's Lower East Side, where he compiled data on immigrants.[62] He had traveled extensively in Europe as well, studying the native cultures of the new Americans and helping his father establish the International Institute of Agriculture. Young Lubin returned to Sacramento in 1906 to run the family's mammoth dry goods business, but along with Harris Weinstock, he soon became a full-time advocate of the Progressive platform.*

In 1913, Simon convinced Johnson and the legislature to form the Commission on Immigration and Housing, with himself as its head. The fledgling agency, which included San Francisco's liberal archbishop Edward Hanna and powerful union leader Paul Scharrenberg, was charged with alleviating the poverty afflicting the state's new arrivals.[63]

The commission was barely in existence before Johnson entrusted it with investigating a riot near the Central Valley town of Wheatland. The event had left dead the district attorney, the deputy sheriff, and two migrant farm workers, and many more had been injured. Blame fell upon the Industrial Workers of the World (IWW, or Wobblies, as their members were colloquially known), the radical union aggressively organizing rural laborers in the West. Two of its leaders were convicted of second-degree murder simply for leading the strike.

Lubin's inquiry uncovered the underlying socioeconomic causes of the disaster. The resulting report, authored by the young Carleton Parker, an economist Lubin had recruited from the University of California as the commission's first executive director, portrayed itinerant workers' camps in all their squalor.[64] Laborers, mostly illegal aliens from Mexico, were lured with false promises by landholders who provided neither housing, medical care, nor even enough outdoor toilets. On the day of the Wheatland riot the temperature had topped a hundred degrees, and not only was no drinking

---

* Like his father, who established the state capital's first art museum, Lubin was more a Sacramentan than a San Franciscan. But he was deeply connected to the Bay Area, where he maintained offices for his retail operation and his work on behalf of the state's poor, contributed to the Jewish and general press, and was active in the Commonwealth Club. In 1931, he moved to San Francisco and joined Temple Emanu-El.

water supplied, but workers were refused the right to bring it onto the fields themselves, lest they lower the profits of the lemonade concession operated by the owner's cousin.[65]

Exposing such vile conditions brought Lubin under severe attack by 1918: he was accused in the press of being a Communist, an anarchist, and a German spy. But nothing deterred him from using the Wheatland findings and other investigations to better the lot of the state's immigrants.[66] Over the next ten years he steered through the legislature thirty-four laws mandating inspections and standards for farm labor camps; schooling and recreation for the workers' children; the opportunity to learn English; a grievance procedure against fraudulent employers; and much more.[67]

Lubin sought to ease the immigrants' entry into society, but like his contemporary Judah Magnes, he adamantly rejected the "melting pot" theory that "would make an American of the foreigner by rooting out all he brings with him."[68] He undoubtedly had the rich cultural heritage he had received from his own immigrant father and grandmother in mind when he addressed a multiethnic folk festival in San Francisco shortly before beginning his work for the state:

> Take out of the man the ideas he possesses of social relations, of patriotism, of religion, and you destroy the very man himself, leaving a mere husk, not at all ready to receive our ideals. . . . If you rob a man of the beliefs he acquired in his childhood, if you get him to make fun of his national customs and ideals, you make of him a bitter, discontented and reckless person and by no means a desirable citizen.[69]

While helping California's most disadvantaged, the businessman–social worker spent much of his personal fortune; he served without compensation as commission head and funded much of its staff and research expenses out of his own pocket.[70] By 1923, however, the political climate had shifted far to the right and, despite Lubin's largesse, a fiscally and socially conservative governor crippled the agency, forcing the resignation of its founder and key members.* Even the intervention of influential Herbert Fleishhacker, a

---

*The Commission on Housing and Immigration was restored to its full strength only in 1939, under liberal governor Culbert Olson. He appointed as chief Carey McWilliams, author of the classic *Factories in the Fields,* an exposé of the abuse of farm laborers.

right-winger nevertheless convinced of the commission's usefulness, could not materially affect the outcome.[71]

Lubin remained active in civic life, initiating a council of twenty-one Northern California counties to address on a regional basis such questions as water conservation, land use, and overseas trade. In 1931, he became the director of the state's Bureau of Commerce. But as the Depression deepened, Lubin became increasingly anxious about fresh abuses of farm workers.

In many ways, the violence in the early 1930s was a replay of the agrarian crisis two decades earlier typified by the Wheatland riot, but now the Commission on Immigrants and Housing was too weak to ameliorate the situation. Lubin, on a federal committee investigating the fatal Imperial Valley cotton strike of 1934, spoke out against the growers' rapacity: in a widely broadcast Commonwealth Club address he blamed them for strikes and lockouts, red-baiting and vigilantism.[72] Yet such public preaching could not bring peace to rural California. In his wife's mind, it was the distress of seeing his hard-won reforms go unenforced that claimed his life in 1936 at age sixty.[73] Other activists created the Simon J. Lubin Society to carry on his advocacy work, but "the first great champion of the migrants," as Kevin Starr has referred to him, "was gone."[74]

WOMEN AND PROGRESS

The progressive spirit at the turn of the century had particular appeal for second-generation Jewish women. Better educated, and with more leisure time than their pioneer mothers, they were often drawn to the professions, arts, and business. But they had to break bonds of convention in order to pursue their careers. Along with bettering the lot of women, they frequently sought to improve society as a whole.

The volunteer work of Jewish females in response to the influx of immigrants and the devastation wrought by the 1906 earthquake and fire was extensive and effective. Women's clubs at the turn of the century took on much more responsibility than the charitable "ladies' societies" formed in the Gold Rush decade; running a settlement house required advanced organizational and leadership skills. But the women often had to struggle even to obtain meaningful unpaid positions. As one historian explains, Jewish women nationally had to "radically redefine behavioral norms" as their tasks took them beyond the traditional role of the "enabler," or benevolent nurturer, to a new "sense of selfhood and gender consciousness."[75]

This transition occurred at Mount Zion Hospital, where initially the ladies' auxiliary cooked, visited the sick, and mended hospital linens. Yet within a few years this supportive role had become unacceptable to the women, and when the all-male board rejected their demands for increased responsibility, the auxiliary threatened to disband.[76] The directors capitulated, enlisting females to raise funds in 1903 and appointing them to the committees of the board beginning in 1909. Board president J. B. Levison soon admitted that "the ladies have been of inestimable assistance in all committee work, and have absolutely silenced all apprehension [about] what was considered by some a hazardous experiment."[77]

Many of the same prominent German-Jewish women led the Emanu-El Sisterhood, which ran a busy settlement house in the South of Market district as well as a medical clinic. Established in 1894, the organization also opened in the Fillmore District a dormitory for single, working Jewish women, the forerunner of the well-regarded Emanu-El Residence Club, inaugurated in 1922 in a stately building designed by Julia Morgan, the West's foremost female architect.

But the Jewish organization benefiting most from the surge of female power was the local chapter of the National Council of Jewish Women (NCJW), formed at the dawn of the new century. Outspoken Bay Area women such as Rachel Frank had participated in the Jewish Woman's Conference held at Chicago's Columbia Exposition in 1893, birthplace of the NCJW, and its national secretary, Sadie American, returned the favor by launching the San Francisco chapter with an inspirational address.[78] The council, which represented a broader socioeconomic group than the Emanu-El Sisterhood, emphasized the Jewish and general education of its membership—reportedly a thousand by 1916—and conducted a range of activities helping the elderly, the blind, and the poor.[79] During World War I it initiated a settlement house in the immigrant area known as "Out the Road," in the southeastern corner of the city. A dedicated female social worker molded it into one of the most effective social welfare agencies in the West. Addressing such issues as family stability, health, and childcare, "Progressive action" was a stated goal of the NCJW by 1908, each woman "a factor in the encouragement and promotion of the weal of the commonwealth."[80]

Other Jewish women boldly entered turn-of-the-century politics. One of the most determined was Selina Solomons, the city's leading suffragette. From a Sephardi family of iconoclasts, Solomons emerged as a "new woman" in 1895 when she delivered a radical speech on the "matriarchate" (citing historical examples of females enjoying higher status than males) at the controversial Pacific Women's Congress in San Francisco.[81] She was subsequently preoccupied with caring for her ill mother for many years, but in 1910, past fifty and never married, Selina opened a Votes-for-Women Club on Steiner Street. In a spacious loft festooned with suffrage posters, it contained a cafeteria, reading room, and second-hand clothing store, and was a venue for lectures and plays, including her own lighthearted *Girl from Colorado*.[82] Only five states had thus far opened the ballot box to women, and Solomons, braving ridicule and threats, sought to "sew another star in the suffrage banner."[83]

She led a well-publicized demonstration at the Registry of Voters and was aided by the legendary Caroline Severance, the movement's statewide leader, who was based in Los Angeles. But they labored against the same obstacle that had defeated the measure fifteen years earlier: the strident temperance movement, also backed by women, caused many men in hard-drinking San Francisco (accounting for about a quarter of the state vote) to fear that enfranchising females would result in prohibition.

On October 10, 1911, women's suffrage again lost locally by a wide margin, and its supporters, all but conceding defeat, were despondent. But over the next few days, returns from the rest of the state gave the constitutional amendment a 2 percent majority. In *How We Won the Vote in California*, Solomons wrote, "Now we gave free rein to our emotions, in both manly and womanly fashion, with hand-shaking and back-slapping, as well as hugging and kissing."[84]

Other elements of the Progressive program—including child welfare, the minimum wage, and prison reform—were advanced by a forceful woman from another notable Sephardi family, Jessica Peixotto. Her four brothers included an eminent lawyer, a renowned artist, a four-star general, and an innovative social worker; her uncle, Benjamin Franklin Peixotto, was American ambassador to Rumania. Almost an exact contemporary of her distant cousin Selina Solomons (and likely in the same Sunday school class at Emanu-El), Jessica also remained unmarried throughout her long life.

Whereas Solomons had no higher education, Peixotto became the most accomplished academic woman on the West Coast. But having compiled an excellent record at Girls High School, she waited more than a decade to attend the University of California because of her father's objections.[85] She completed the undergraduate program in three years, majoring in economics and political science. Continuing to pursue a Ph.D., she conducted research for a year at the Sorbonne and returned to write a thesis comparing the principles of the French Revolution with those of modern socialism. She received her doctorate in 1900, only the second the university had awarded a woman.[86]

The mores of her time, however, held her back for a while: it was widely thought that a woman ought not to have "any bread and butter motive" for an advanced degree, as one of Jessica's friends put it.[87] But within a few years she was encouraged by the university's reform-minded president, Benjamin Ide Wheeler, to teach one course, on contemporary socialism. She soon became a regular faculty member in the economics department and a decade later a full professor, becoming the first woman to achieve that position in the university's history. Even in the mid-1930s, when Peixotto retired, she was still one of only six women professors on the campus, and considered by the social philosopher Robert Nisbet, then a graduate student, "undoubtedly the most brilliant of the six."[*][88]

Three of her female colleagues at Berkeley had studied under her, as did dozens of other top academicians across the country, including Clark Kerr, a future president of the university, who contributed to her Festschrift. She also swayed future philanthropists such as Rosalie Meyer Stern, for whom one of Peixotto's courses was an "eye-opener," resulting in a deep commitment to social welfare.[89] "Ro," daughter of the Los Angeles banker Eugene Meyer[†] and wife of Sigmund Stern, president of Levi Strauss and Company, would become the city's greatest supporter of public parks, and her considerable efforts on behalf of children were a "direct result" of her teacher's influence.[90] Developing courses such as "The Control of Poverty," "The Child and the State," and "Crime as a Social Problem," Peixotto was instrumental in creating UC Berkeley's School of Social Work and arranged for an endowment from I. W. Hellman's daughter, Clara Heller—another wealthy admirer—to underwrite research in social economics.

The capstone of her career, though, was public service. Like Simon Lubin, who often consulted with her, Peixotto was appointed by Governor Johnson to a state commission, the Board of Charities and Corrections, on

---

[*] He also quoted a colleague's claim that she was "the most beautiful woman to set foot on this campus" (Robert Nisbet, *Teachers and Scholars: A Memoir of Berkeley in Depression and War* [New Brunswick, N.J., 1992], 69).

[†] Meyer's son, banker Eugene Jr., bought the *Washington Post* at a bankruptcy sale, made it into one of the nation's leading newspapers, and left it to his daughter, Katherine Meyer Graham.

which she served for more than a decade. She helped pass legislation that increased the age limit for children on public assistance, required state certification for midwives, and created a separate women's penitentiary.[91] During World War I, she was tapped by President Wilson for the Council of National Defense, which enabled her to monitor the treatment of women in industry and ensure enforcement of recently passed child labor laws.

One of Peixotto's most trusted partners in the field of child welfare was the pioneering social worker Amy Steinhart Braden. Born into a respected German-Jewish family, she enjoyed a culturally rich girlhood. After graduating from the University of California, she and her two sisters did unpaid work among disadvantaged youth in the South of Market area, and, like many privileged, idealistic young people of their generation, they were drawn "heart and soul" to the Progressives.[92] Amy in particular admired Hiram Johnson's tough stand against the railroad, longed for an end to corruption in government, and, after hearing Susan B. Anthony in San Francisco, joined the cause of women's suffrage.[93]

Having learned much from her visits to Hull House in Chicago and the Henry Street Settlement in New York, Steinhart returned home and took an unpaid position as a social worker with the juvenile court. In 1913, with the Progressives at their peak, she came to the attention of John Francis Neylan, head of the powerful new California Board of Control, who offered her, now thirty-four, one of three recently created posts as a "children's agent." The job—in effect, advocate for youngsters dependent on state aid—required frequent travel and paid $175 a month plus expenses. Amy later recalled her widowed mother's objections: "It disturbed [her] very much, in fact she wept a little about it. She felt it a bit of a disgrace that she wasn't taking care of me. It was rather a reflection on the family."[94] But Steinhart accepted and, traveling by horse and wagon, visited orphanages in remote corners of the state. She did individual casework, checked the certification of nurses and psychologists, and investigated reports of child abuse.

Within two years she had become the chief children's agent and, joining with Jessica Peixotto, she helped to convince lawmakers to increase the amount of state aid to minors and raise the age of eligibility to sixteen years. "We didn't want children to have to go to work at fourteen," Steinhart wrote, adding that she was not averse to using her female sensibility to bring about the desired results: "I found that the direct human appeal, maybe a little bit of a sob thrown in, always won the support of the legislators."[95]

In 1925—a year after she wed for the first time, at age forty-five—Amy Steinhart Braden was appointed chief executive of the state's entire

Department of Welfare, a post she held for five years.[96] Now she focused on the issue of adoption, still unregulated in California. Dismayed by "cases of an iceman, say, arranging for a child from one woman to go to another," she fought for the right of the adopting family to know the background of the birth parents, and for state approval of every adoption, reforms that remained her lifelong concern.[97]

The annals of the Progressive Era describe many other San Francisco Jewish women who sought to give the state's children "a square deal," as Jessica Peixotto put it.[98] Flora Jacobi Arnstein and her sister-in-law Helen Arnstein Salz opened an experimental school in 1915 that emphasized artistic creativity and the great outdoors; it had particular success with disabled and emotionally disturbed youngsters. Selina Solomons's sister, Dr. Adele Jaffa, fought for adequate nutrition, while Helen Hecht (of the shoe manufacturing family) devoted her energies to the Pioneer Kindergarten Society.

Unlike the men of the Lubin-Weinstock family (and Weinstock's protégé Aaron Sapiro), the most active female Jewish progressives did not credit the Bible as the major wellspring of their inspiration. But Selina Solomons, Jessica Peixotto, and Amy Steinhart Braden were each raised in a home where Judaism and its message of communal responsibility were taken seriously. Each also had both a father and a brother who were the president or key officer of a major San Francisco Jewish institution. While the women's idealism was rooted in the spirit of progressivism that swept California, it may also owe something to Jewish messianic hopes.

PUBLIC MORALS, PUBLIC HEALTH

Turn-of-the-century reformers often viewed alcohol, gambling, and prostitution as evils to be eradicated along with other social ills. Yet Bay Area Progressives, and particularly the Jews among them, rarely joined the antivice crusades. They campaigned much more frequently for economic justice than for regulations upon personal behavior.

Rabbis Meyer and Nieto did speak out against "white slavery" but were wary of aligning themselves too closely with Christian ministers who railed against immorality. Nieto received front-page coverage in the *San Francisco Bulletin* for canceling his scheduled appearance at an antivice rally convened by the Reverend Paul Smith; the rabbi said he trusted the authorities to enforce the laws regarding prostitution and saw no reason for a mass meeting.[99]

In fact, the police had been lax in controlling commercial sex since the Gold Rush. Despite ordinances outlawing the world's oldest profession, it thrived in downtown's Barbary Coast. After the earthquake, one brothel—a warren of cubicles featuring more than a hundred harlots of all races and creeds—was so notorious for the bribes it paid politicians, including Abe Ruef, that it was dubbed the "municipal crib."

In the following decade a debate raged between those seeking to legalize prostitution and those (including some Progressives) arguing for its abolition. In 1911, Julius Rosenstirn, longtime chief of staff of Mount Zion Hospital, put forth a third idea: regulate the sex trade and confine it to one area of town. This, too, was a progressive approach, trusting in the government to cope with a social malady.[100] Regulation, claimed Dr. Rosenstirn, would mitigate the most harmful effects of prostitution, such as exploitation, corruption, and, above all, disease. Simply criminalizing it was bound to fail, he wrote in a pamphlet circulated throughout San Francisco. Drawing upon Freud and Havelock Ellis, he asked, "Can we legislate people to become deaf to the passionate call of sex? Do the laws stuff cotton in the ears of men and women as Ulysses put wax into the ears of his crew when his ship passed the isle of sweet singing sirens?"[101]

Mayor P. H. McCarthy agreed with Rosenstirn, and his plan—similar to the policies followed in several European cities*—was implemented. Its centerpiece was a municipal clinic, headed by Rosenstirn, where, for a $1.50 fee, prostitutes were examined twice weekly. Those free of venereal disease were issued a temporary permit to ply their trade; those infected were treated free of charge.[102]

From its inception, the clinic was criticized by priests and ministers, as well as some business leaders who feared legalized prostitution would damage the city's reputation during the upcoming Panama-Pacific International Exposition.[103] In 1913, McCarthy's successor, James Rolph, withdrew support of the clinic, and soon the state legislature enacted the Red Light Abatement Law, outlawing brothels in California.[104] In two years Rosenstirn's clinic had sharply reduced the rate of venereal disease in the Barbary Coast, but, even in free-thinking San Francisco, his experiment could not endure.[105]

*A German-Jewish immigrant, Rosenstirn became a surgeon in California but returned to Europe to study in Paris, Berlin, Vienna, and Milan. In setting up his program of compulsory medical examinations, he received reports from cities in Germany, Austria-Hungary, Russia, and Belgium (Neil Larry Shumsky, "Municipal Clinic of San Francisco: A Study in Medical Structure," *Bulletin of the Journal of Medicine* 52 [Winter 1978]: 542–45).

Yet dealing with prostitution as a health issue rather than a criminal one would remain a concern of Jewish progressives. Lawrence Arnstein, son of a Bavarian-born woolen merchant, worked a dozen years for his father before he was appointed by Mayor Rolph to the city's Board of Health in 1912 and turned his energies to community service. He was encouraged by his forward-thinking wife, educator and writer Flora Jacobi Arnstein. Like many in the second generation, Lawrence and Flora grew up frustrated with their immigrant parents' refusal to speak with them openly about sex.[106] During a long and productive career, "Mr. Public Health," as Arnstein was known, sought to increase awareness about sexually transmitted diseases. For almost two decades, until 1931, he served as chief of the state's Bureau of Venereal Disease. Later, shortly after America's entry into World War II, with the problem more acute than ever, he became executive director of the California Social Hygiene Association, which brought together specialists from many fields to improve testing for syphilis and end the mistreatment of women arrested for sex offenses.

Yet another fixture in the field of public health was Charles Wollenberg, the financial manager of the city's hospitals from shortly after the 1906 earthquake until 1943, when he became the director of the state's Department of Social Welfare. Father of assemblyman and judge Albert Wollenberg, Charles was a Progressive who admired Theodore Roosevelt and Hiram Johnson, and dedicated himself to eliminating the corruption in the municipal infirmaries early in the century. Wollenberg reformed a hospital system rife with graft: his predecessor was the bribable brother of Eugene Schmitz, the unscrupulous mayor whom Boss Abe Ruef coached behind the scenes.[107]

PRISON REFORM

An Oakland attorney of the Progressive era highlighted another issue obscured from public view: the disgraceful penal system. Along with pulpit rabbis such as M. S. Levy, and later Martin Meyer and Rudolph Coffee, Gus Ringolsky cared deeply about Jewish prisoners in state institutions. A knowledgeable Jew and Grand Orator of B'nai B'rith District IV, he often led High Holiday services at San Quentin and Folsom.[108] But it was a highly publicized case that Ringolsky undertook pro bono at age twenty-four that would affect virtually all California prisoners.

His client, who was also a Jew, was an unlikely poster boy for prison reform. Career criminal Jacob Oppenheimer, while serving a fifty-year sentence in Folsom for armed robbery and assault, killed another inmate.[109] Given a life sentence and transferred to San Quentin, "the human tiger," as the press called him, struck again, stabbing a guard who nearly died from his wounds. The State Board of Prison Directors now sentenced Oppenheimer to solitary confinement for life in an almost airless dungeon.[110]

He escaped from his cell seven years later, in 1907; he was caught while still on the prison grounds, but not before he had slashed another convict.[111] After a short trial, Oppenheimer received the death sentence under a law the legislature had passed back in 1901 with his attack on the San Quentin guard in mind. It held that a prisoner serving a life term could receive the death penalty for assault.

Ringolsky now became Oppenheimer's defense attorney, arguing in state appeals courts that it was unconstitutional for this latest felony to be a capital crime. At the same time, he generated pity for "the human tiger" by portraying him as having been driven insane by diabolical jailers.[112] While some papers demanded his swift execution, others described his abuse in solitary confinement, where he was chained to his bed. The revelations came amidst a lively public debate, sparked by the Progressives, on the inhumane conditions in state prisons and the brutal methods employed by San Quentin warden John Tompkins, who was forced to resign in 1906.[113] According to the *Examiner,* Oppenheimer

> was laced up in a canvas straight-jacket, so tightly that the slightest breath caused him great agony and left there for days reeking in filth, with only a cup of water and a bit of bread touched to his lips. . . . He tried to beat his own brains on the stone floor. . . . His body was convulsed with cramps and he was unable to relieve the itching that drove him mad.[114]

There was also sympathy in the press for his frail, elderly Orthodox father, Abie, "whose devotion to his son brought tears to many an eye. . . . In all the sordid affair, the love of the San Francisco merchant for his son was the one beautiful thing."*[115]

---

*Early in Jacob's criminal career, when he was in the Alameda county jail for robbing an Oakland drugstore, Abie tried to smuggle a tiny hacksaw into his son's cell. It was common then for relatives to bring food to prisoners, so the old man concealed the tool in a slab of meat. The mound of bacon he chose to use aroused the guards' suspicions, and the plot was discovered (Gus C. Ringolsky Papers in WJHC/JLMM).

Ringolsky, meanwhile, had little success before the appeals judges, but he was elated when the United States Supreme Court agreed to hear the case in 1911. While finishing his briefs, though, the young attorney was shattered by the news that Oppenheimer had killed again. On Folsom's death row, he had somehow procured an iron bar with which he murdered a longtime rival also scheduled for the gallows.[116]

Nevertheless, Ringolsky refused to concede defeat. He met with Governor Hiram Johnson and presented a petition signed by four thousand people urging Oppenheimer's sentence be commuted on the grounds of insanity.[117] The governor issued a reprieve of five weeks to learn the decision in the Supreme Court case, but the justices dismissed it without a ruling, and Oppenheimer was soon tried and convicted for the fresh homicide at Folsom. Johnson did not intervene, and Oppenheimer was hanged.

Yet if Ringolsky could not save his client, he still accomplished a great deal. He used the Oppenheimer case to focus the public's attention on a range of legal issues, from capital punishment to the insanity defense, from cruelty inside the prison to readjustment following release. Progressive ideals would be applied even to society's most malevolent individuals.

MYSTERIOUS NEIGHBORS

For all the good the reformers did, they had a blind spot when it came to race. Even Harris Weinstock, who spoke out against African Americans being denied the vote in the South, stated at the same time that "in the far west, happily, there is no Negro question and no race problem to solve."[118]

Indeed, there were relatively few blacks in San Francisco at the turn of the century—about 1,500, or less than one-half of 1 percent of the population—and they were comparatively well treated.[119] But Weinstock overlooked the oppression of North America's oldest and largest Chinese community, which comprised 10 percent of the city's population and nearly twice that of its workforce.[120]

The Jews—despite their own suffering in Europe and usually strong record of defending the disadvantaged—evidenced no more sensitivity to the persecution of Asians than did other white Californians. It was noted previously that state supreme court justice Solomon Heydenfeldt ruled in 1854 that no Chinese could testify in a case involving a white. A generation later, during the ugly summer of 1877, anti-Asian agitation peaked as the demagogue Dennis Kearney incited crowds of mostly jobless Irish to beat the Chinese and burn their businesses. Jewish names do not appear on the rosters of the vicious "anti-coolie" clubs; no doubt most Jews feared for the safety of the Chinese, many of whom worked in Jewish-owned shoe, clothing, or cigar factories, or as servants in Jewish homes. To restrain the anti-Chinese mobs, leading Jews supported the extralegal measures of the Committee of Public Safety, a six-thousand-man militia armed with hickory pick handles that, like the vigilantes of the 1850s, tried to impose martial law.[121]

Yet even as it tried to contain racial violence and prevent the insurrection threatening the city, the Jewish community almost uniformly believed the Chinese to be the scourge of California. Among the most biased voices was the widely read Isidore Choynski, who claimed, unfairly, that the state's Chinese were not true settlers but mere sojourners:

All other immigrants assimilate with the dominant race, settle down for good, raise families and take a deep and kindly interest in the body politic. The Chinese are as disgusting as the lowest type of digger Indian. . . . They do not come here to stay. They drive white labor out of cities, they monopolize every industry that requires physical labor, and contaminate the atmosphere where they are packed like sardines in tiers to the depths of thirty feet underground.[122]

Choynski was often marginalized because of his venomous tongue, but on this issue his was the majority opinion, and other Jewish journalists penned their own overwrought tales of the depravity in Chinatown.[123] One justified the anti-Chinese agitation with the grossly exaggerated claim that on the West Coast their women, "live, without a single exception, as prostitutes."[124] In 1878 an editorial in the *Jewish Progress* concluded, "It will be a happy day for California when these disciples of Confucius depart for their Flowery Kingdom, never to return."[125]

At the end of the 1870s, many prominent local Jews—including the three leading rabbis—urged the federal government to end Chinese immigration.*[126] The Exclusion Act was passed in 1882, and its renewal two decades

---

* The otherwise fair-minded Elkan Cohn of Emanu-El, Henry Vidaver of Sherith Israel, and Albert Bettelheim of Ohabai Shalome signed the anti-Chinese petition. David Solis-Cohen, a learned Philadelphian who lived briefly in the Bay Area, wrote to his hometown Jewish newspaper of his outrage toward the rabbis, "professed leaders who have . . . branded 'intolerance' upon [our] faith" (Reva Clar and William M. Kramer, "Chinese-Jewish Relations in the Far West: 1850–1950," *WSJHQ* 21 [October 1988]: 25).

later was sponsored by Congressman Julius Kahn and supported by Rabbi Voorsanger in the *Emanu-El*.[127]

Many eminent Jewish businessmen, meanwhile, refused to hire Chinese. Adolph Sutro, liberal in virtually every other way, bragged that, although he employed fourteen thousand men, he had never engaged a "Chinaman." He wrote, "The very worst emigrants from Europe are a hundred times more desirable than these Asiatics."[128] Even Levi Strauss, intimidated by the riots of 1877, discharged all 180 Chinese workers from his factory.[129] Other Jewish manufacturers either followed suit or, if they chose to retain Asian laborers, moved their operations out of town. A number of Jewish cigar makers, caving in to pressure from a racist union, replaced their Chinese laborers with whites brought out from New York.[130]

Jews in the East, where there was only a tiny Chinese presence, were dumbfounded by the behavior of their San Francisco brethren. Philadelphia's *Jewish Record* pointed to similarities between the hatred toward the Asians in California and anti-Semitism in Eastern Europe: "At first it was said that they were poor, and filthy, and ignorant; that they were religiously perverse, that they were incapable of becoming good citizens; that they did not, would not, or could not 'blend' socially. . . . Now their great fault is that they will not keep down; that they actually aspire to dominate."[131] And a Jewish editor in New York, comparing anti-Chinese hysteria with Russian pogroms, accused his San Francisco counterparts of the same complicity as the St. Petersburg journalists who defended the czar's bloody policies.[132]

Beyond the moral question, the East Coast Jewish press worried that anti-Chinese sentiment could result in demands to curtail Jewish immigration just when Russian Jews were arriving in America in large numbers: "The Chinese today: why not the Jews of tomorrow?"[133] Yet none of this swayed California's Jewish opinion makers, who, to the dismay of the rest of American Jewry, remained "unrepentant."[134]

One obscure local Jew, however, confronted the bigotry of his time. The multilingual socialist Sigismund Danielewicz of Russian Poland played a major role in establishing the powerful Coast Seaman's Union of the Pacific in 1885. Like many other unions threatened by competition from Asian labor, the CSU was virulently anti-Chinese. It urged not merely the exclusion but also the expulsion of Asians, which actually occurred in several California towns in this frenzied period. At a coastwide congress of organized labor held in San Francisco, Danielewicz courageously defied his own union. The recording secretary paraphrased his speech:

He said he belonged to a race persecuted for hundreds of years and still persecuted—the Jews; and he called upon his people to consider whether the persecution of the Chinese was more justifiable than theirs had been. And he left it upon the Irish to say whether it was more justifiable than their persecutions in New York had been; upon the Germans to make a similar comparison.[135]

Before he could finish, Danielewicz was booed off the stage. Many of his closest socialist comrades, like the militant Frank Roney, who chaired the assembly, abandoned him, and the convention easily passed an expulsion resolution.[136] But Sigismund Danielewicz had made his point. A Jew had a special obligation to speak out against the abuse of the Chinese, he believed, even if he had to act alone.

REVOLUTIONARY GOALS

Danielewicz had few allies even among California socialists, who, like the Progressives, assigned a low priority to racial equality. But the Marxists still had a much broader social agenda than did the movement led by Hiram Johnson. Although they tended to be more moderate on the West Coast than in the big industrial cities of the Northeast, socialists supported organized labor, a welfare state, and the social emancipation of women. In the years before America's entry into World War I, the party typically garnered 12 percent of the state vote and had a high profile on the political landscape.[137]

There was no immigrant Jewish proletariat in San Francisco or Oakland, and no Jewish leftist movement such as the one that galvanized the Lower East Side. But individual Jews were highly visible among militant socialist labor leaders in San Francisco, the strongest union town in America. Danielewicz was not active beyond the mid-1880s, but the powerful culinary workers' union was headed for decades, until the 1920s, by the stubborn socialist Hugo Ernst. One of the organization's young members, Selig Schulberg, a waiter, often contributed articles to the combative left-wing paper the *Revolt,* and was a leader of the International Workers Defense League, a radical group providing legal aid to agitators in trouble. In 1913, Schulberg was instrumental in organizing a massive strike against Pacific Gas and Electric, which brought violence and property damage in its wake.[138]

During and after World War I the public would turn against the socialists; in California, as elsewhere in America, they came to be associated with sedition, Bolshevism, and even terrorism. But this was not before a twenty-year-old Jewish woman, a sensitive Russian-born beauty named Anna Strunsky, gained fame in the local press for her deeply felt revolutionary ideals. Like the "girl rabbi" Ray Frank in the early 1890s, the "girl socialist of San Francisco" became an instant celebrity. One long, lavishly illustrated article in the *Examiner* covered a lecture on socialist ethics she had delivered before two hundred people and noted her "pleading, sorrowful voice, vibrant with passion and unremedied wrongs."[139]

Anna had immigrated to America with her large family when she was nine—she would speak English with a slight accent the rest of her life—and lived in New York for seven years, excelling in the public schools. In 1893 the Strunskys moved to San Francisco, where Anna's father opened a liquor store, and their home on Golden Gate Avenue quickly developed into a meeting place for radical East European émigrés passing through the city. One was the fiery anarchist Emma Goldman, who would become Anna's lifelong friend. "This was my best school," Anna wrote later: "From these personalities I got more than I ever got out of books or halls of learning. Here were . . . budding geniuses, refugees, revolutionists; broken lives and strong lives, all made welcome, all met with reverence and warmth."[140]

She also gleaned much from "the Crowd," a loose circle of bohemian artists and writers, including several other Jews, that met in cafes like Coppa's, near a huge building of offices and studios known as the "Monkey Block," on Montgomery Street. But, though she hoped to become a novelist, she found politics even more compelling, and, while still a student at Lowell High School, she joined the local Socialist Labor Party. Later, she served as secretary of its Central Committee for two-and-a-half years, a consuming post that hurt her academic performance at Stanford and led to her suspension.[141]

In 1899, at the party's commemoration of the Paris Commune, she met another young socialist, Jack London, and the two began a tempestuous relationship that would last until his death, at age forty, in 1916. She was drawn to the strapping youth, just returned from the Klondike and on the verge of worldwide fame. "He seemed the incarnation of the Platonic ideal man," she wrote of that first encounter, with "the body of the athlete and the mind of the thinker."[142] They read poetry, frequented the theater, hiked the East Bay hills, and, of course, attended socialist lectures and party meetings. London was overwhelmed by her gravitas—he told a friend "she happens to be a genius"—and smitten by the exotic, "oriental" charms of his black-eyed "Russian Jewess."[143]

While courting Strunsky London married another woman, Bess Maddern, but he and Anna nonetheless decided to coauthor a novel (she would be the only collaborator he ever had) exploring two opposing conceptions of marriage. Published in 1903, the *Kempton-Wace Letters* is a correspondence between an unsentimental economist about to wed for practical reasons and a poet who reveled in romance. London, perhaps reflecting his lack of passion for Bess, argued the pragmatic side; Strunsky defended the desires of the heart.[144]

While editing the book Anna moved into London's Piedmont home for a month (shocking behavior at the turn of the century), and the married man, already a father, proposed to her. She accepted, but two weeks later changed her mind. Not only was she "afraid to take [her] happiness at the expense of his wife and baby,"[145] but Anna also felt him not the pure socialist she sought in a mate.* He angered her with his demeaning attitudes toward women, his stereotyped image of Jews who "haggle and bargain," and, not least of all, his relentless striving for money and celebrity.[146] Still, if she did not "love him enough," she "loved him deeply," and the two exchanged hundreds of letters and poems over the next decade and a half.[147]

After deciding not to marry Jack, Strunsky retreated to a hilltop cabin near Stanford and worked on a novel that had grown out of a youthful trip to Paris. In early 1905, though, she was jolted by the news of the first Russian Revolution, which had been triggered by Bloody Sunday, the massacre of hundreds of peaceful petitioners at the czar's Winter Palace. Inspired by the democratic and socialist insurrection against the tyrannical Nicholas II, she soon organized a group in San Francisco known as Friends of Russian Freedom. Anna became chair, and leading writers, including Jack London, of course, served on the executive board. The society produced persuasive leaflets urging "sympathy and help" for the workers and peasants, whose uprising was growing.[148]

---

* Bess claimed in her divorce petition that Anna had "alienated" Jack's affections, an accusation trumpeted in the local press, causing the entire Strunsky family anguish. Yet the voluminous London-Strunsky correspondence has led scholars to conclude there probably was no adulterous relationship between the two (James R. Boylan, *Revolutionary Lives: Anna Strunsky and William English Walling* [Amherst, Mass., 1998], 40–41; Clarice Stasz, *Jack London's Women* [Amherst, Mass., 2001], 65; Joan London, *Jack London and His Times: An Unconventional Biography* [Seattle, 1968], 218).

London had previously referred to Anna as "exceptionally good copy," and now she received more press attention than ever. And, unlike Ray Frank, she was in no need of a publicist. In *California Woman's Magazine* she wrote about the female leaders of the revolution, a topic that would preoccupy her for decades. The Sunday *San Francisco Bulletin* featured her picture surrounded by breathless dispatches from the czarist capital; she exclaimed to a friend that the piece had the same effect "as if a bomb had been exploded in San Francisco."[149] She spoke fervently on the revolution before a wide array of cultural and political organizations, including the National Council of Jewish Women.

In the late fall, Strunsky and her younger sister, Rose (then a Stanford student and in love with the dashing Mexican artist Xavier Martinez), left for Russia to cover the dramatic developments for the American press. They told their worried father and a *Bulletin* reporter that they were only going as far as Geneva to interview political exiles, but secretly they made plans to journey to St. Petersburg.

Anna would spend more than a year in Russia, the most eventful period of her life. Along with Rose, she worked in a news bureau established by the dapper young William English Walling, a Midwesterner supported by a large trust fund whom she had met briefly in California. Like Anna, English (as he was usually known) was a socialist writer intoxicated by the Days of Liberty of 1905, and they soon fell in love and married in a civil ceremony in Paris.* One of Karl Marx's grandsons was a witness.

The "millionaire socialists," as they were dubbed, would be among the most influential interpreters for the American public of the fast-moving events in Russia, filling a role similar to the one that would be played by John Reed in 1917. With Anna's sister, the couple witnessed violence on the streets and interviewed hundreds of people, from rebels to government officials. On a return trip to Russia in 1907, the three, obviously sympathetic to the revolutionaries, were arrested by the czarist police and jailed overnight.[150] Only their American citizenship saved them from a much worse fate.

---

*They considered waiting until returning home, but Anna wrongly assumed her parents would oppose her marrying a non-Jew: "They would rather see me dead than marry a gentile." She also mistakenly believed "there is no rabbi in the world who could listen to our troth without committing sacrilege" (Boylan, *Revolutionary Lives,* 109; letter of Elias Strunsky to William English Walling, March 31, 1906, made available to the author by Michael Strunsky).

But most distressing for Anna was a side trip she took alone to investigate a pogrom, all too common in this time of turmoil. In the town of Gomel, a mob had burned and looted the Jewish quarter and beaten and killed many of its inhabitants. Anna's fluency in Yiddish enabled her to speak to victims—some maimed by the attackers—and comprehend the depth of their suffering. She also interviewed General Orlov, whose Cossacks had been complicit in the atrocities, and was galled when he claimed that "the Jews burnt the city to get the fire insurance."[151] Her own family had left the Pale of Settlement two decades earlier because of such oppression, and in Gomel she identified with Russian Jewry as never before. At the railway station on her way out of town she was surrounded by Jews asking for her advice on how to immigrate to America. "I dropped my role of objective journalist," she wrote. "I felt I was seeing these people for the last time, and . . . I belonged to them."[152]

Only a few months later, however, Strunsky would say that neither she nor English "belong[ed] to any creed" and that she felt herself a citizen of the world; "provincialism of any kind is distasteful to me."[153] While in Russia, she envisioned a "socialist married life," and in quixotic letters home she described a future of "collaboration and equity" with her "supreme comrade" (she despised the words "husband" and "wife").[154] She wrote, "We will never have a home—except in each other's arms—never let our love stand in the way of the world, in the way of any human association."[155] Like her free-spirited contemporary Gertrude Stein, Strunsky sought lifelong intimacy of the sort that few in her parents' generation could even imagine.

The couple settled in New York in 1908, where they lived for a while in a socialist cooperative.* Walling and Strunsky (she kept her own name, despite the conventions of the day) attacked America's social problems with the same intense brew of journalism and sociology they had produced in Russia. Researching a lynching in Springfield, Illinois, where the black victims were blamed for the violence, stirred Anna's memories of Gomel two years earlier.[156] English's widely read magazine article on the barbarous episode, "Race War in the North," rang an early alarm bell. The couple were in demand as lecturers on the race problem for the rest of the decade, and

---

* The Strunsky liquor store had been destroyed in the San Francisco earthquake, and Anna's father had moved the family back to Manhattan. She would visit the Bay Area only once more, late in her life.

hosted meetings of like-minded intellectuals, both black and white. In 1910 English was instrumental in founding the NAACP.

They continued to write about Russia and put forth a socialist agenda for America as well. But World War I drove a wedge between Anna and English. Once the United States entered the conflict, he branded as disloyal anyone opposing the war. Anna, a staunch internationalist, took a pacifist stance that she attributed to her formative years among San Francisco's left-wingers and bohemians.[157] He moved even further to the right in the 1920s, but she rarely deviated from her youthful ideals. In 1932, when their four children were grown, they separated. She felt increasingly out of place in the middle decades of the twentieth century; neither America nor the Soviet Union had embraced the democratic socialism she had espoused in the innocent years before World War I.

The California-bred Progressives had set more limited goals from the out-set than did socialists like Strunsky, and so ultimately found themselves less marginalized. They did have periods of frustration when conservative gover-nors came to power in the 1920s and when class conflict turned violent in the 1930s, but they also had the satisfaction of seeing much of their reform pro-gram enacted into law. The state's women, children, immigrants, and poor were far better off within one generation; the railroad was tamed and the workings of government vastly improved.

But the more moderate reformers of her generation shared with Anna Strunsky "a social conscience," as Jack London's daughter wrote, "which took upon itself the responsibility for the social sins of the time, [and] which was eager for self-sacrifice."[158] For many a young person, the optimism and innovation permeating California at the turn of the century nurtured dreams of a just society. And for a substantial number of Jews among them, the age-old impulse to "mend the world"—felt as a religious injunction or absorbed in another way—reinforced their commitment to dedicate them-selves to human betterment. The struggle for social justice would remain a central preoccupation of Bay Area Jewry in the century to come.

SIX

Trials

Firestorms and Corruption, Terrorism and World War

FOR ALL THE OPTIMISM DURING the Progressive era, the thirteen years beginning with the earthquake and fire of 1906 were rancorous. Municipal government was discredited throughout much of this period, labor and capital were in combat, and war abroad deepened the divisions at home. In this combustible atmosphere no one could predict who would be the targets of an angry and frustrated populace, and the Jewish community's high standing was tested as never before. Moreover, the social unrest widened existing rifts between Jew and Jew, intensifying class conflict, inflaming political disagreements, and isolating native from newcomer.

Paradoxically, the natural disaster itself had a positive effect, at least in the short term, on intergroup and interfaith relations; the relief work and uplifting words of local rabbis and Jewish lay leaders earned the gratitude of the entire city. And, notwithstanding a few nasty internal spats, Bay Area Jewry demonstrated considerable unity amidst the crisis. The German Jewish establishment rebuilt not only its own shattered institutions but also those of East European Jews. Once the inspiring recovery was underway, some Jewish leaders even pointed to the catastrophe as having been a salutary act of the Divine. But three man-made "aftershocks"—a rampant scandal while the city still lay in ruins and, a decade later, terror downtown and war in Europe—darkened the horizon for Jews.

When one of its own was revealed as the main culprit in the most flagrant example of political corruption in California history, the Jewish community exhibited little fear for its security, even as it became bitterly split. But its characteristic self-assurance waned in the face of another sensational trial, this time of an immigrant Jew accused of complicity in a terrorist bombing that left ten dead. Bay Area Jewry remained on the defensive through World War I, when some of its leaders worried that their German origins might make them suspect, and during the Red Scare, when Bolshevism was linked to the Jews. Northern California Jews emerged from this tense time having actually incurred little wrath from their neighbors, but they were well aware that the new century would be far more complex and dangerous than was the pioneer period.

DESTRUCTION

Of the calamity that struck around dawn on April 18, 1906, Rabbi Voorsanger wrote that "suddenly the abyss yawned at our feet and it seemed that with the overturning of the world we would be lost forever."[1] The earthquake and the resulting firestorms brought down more than half of the city's buildings and claimed more than three thousand lives.[2] It is often considered the worst peacetime disaster in the nation's history.

One of its keenest observers was J. B. Levison, vice president of the huge Fireman's Fund Insurance Company. He wrote of his sedate routine preceding "the most momentous" experience of his life.[3] He had attended the opera on Monday, April 16, but on the following night missed Caruso in *Carmen.* Having to catch up on his paperwork, Levison gave away his tickets and spent a quiet evening at home.

> Wednesday morning I was awakened by something impossible to describe—a crunching of timbers—a roaring, apparently from above and below—and a jumping (the only word that seems to fit) of the house. . . . Not until my wife screamed that it was a dreadful earthquake, and that I should try to get the children, did I awaken to full realization. I leaped out of bed but could not retain my footing because the house was still jumping. . . . It took two or three attempts or lunges before I could get hold of the door leading to the room occupied by my sons . . . nine and seven years of age, who were terrified beyond words.
>
> . . . I found that the telephone wires were broken. And there was neither light nor water. Here for the first time I appreciated the magnitude of the disaster.

Later, on the way to his office, he "could obtain a view of the entire southern portion of the city. . . . Half a dozen distinct conflagrations were raging and roaring in different sections, any one of which would have been a great fire. I realized then that the city was doomed."[4]

Levison sent his family to the San Rafael summerhouse of his in-laws, the Gerstles, and turned his Pacific Avenue home into a refuge for displaced residents and a temporary office for Fireman's Fund.* He saved nearly all the medical instruments of his brother Charles, one of the city's leading physicians.

Voorsanger accomplished even more. Working feverishly as chairman of the mayor's Hunger Relief Committee, he fought to spare the ruined city from famine, which he labeled "the worst anarchist in existence."[5] While monitoring isolated instances of price gouging and looting, he set up food stations throughout San Francisco. With a policeman's badge on his clerical coat, and the mayor's authorization in his pocket, he "commandeered store after store."[6] On one day alone he oversaw the distribution of thirty-five thousand loaves of bread.[7] As he wrote of those first critical days, "I was the biggest thief in the United States. . . . I emptied grocery stores, drug stores, butcher shops, hardware establishments [and] I was able to report to the Mayor that the people were fed and that to the best of my knowledge there was not a hungry soul in San Francisco."[8]

The rabbi's achievement was in stark contrast to blunders committed by Mayor Eugene Schmitz. Likely because of a basic distrust of the masses, he issued an order to shoot looters on sight. The result, according to one study, was the death of hundreds of people, not all of them even guilty of stealing.[9]

Terror also reigned because of aftershocks, advancing fires, and wild rumors that circulated the morning of the disaster, when the city was cut off from communication with the rest of the world. One young Jewish journalist wrote of the dread and delusion that gripped the populace:

How widespread was the shock we wondered. Had it reached Southern California? Had it gone east? How about Chicago, New York, Seattle, Portland?

---

*Levison soon helped salvage the Fireman's Fund Insurance Company itself, which owed roughly $4,000,000 in claims, much more than it had on hand. Rather than liquidate the firm, as his superiors suggested, he proposed to pay half of each claim in cash and the other half in company stock. The plan was accepted by the board of directors and the policyholders and became a model for insurance reorganization throughout the world.

Then came answers to these questions, from whence no one knew. San Jose was destroyed, five thousand killed in Los Angeles, Portland overwhelmed by the river, Chicago wiped out by a tidal wave from the lake and New York swept into the Atlantic. Vesuvius had renewed its activity and eruptions were predicted in San Francisco. You can understand our state of mind with all those stories floating about and no evidence to contradict them.[10]

The fire in San Francisco, though, was all too real; one could feel its heat throughout the city. As the flames spread westward it was hoped that the width of Van Ness Avenue would finally contain the conflagration. But General Frederick Funston, commandant of the Presidio, decided—mistakenly, as recent scholarship has concluded[11]—that many of the mansions along that street would have to be dynamited or burned in order to widen the firebreak further. Among those destroyed were the stately residences of Justice Marcus Sloss and Ernest Lilienthal, head of Crown Distilleries.

The worst of the suffering, however, fell upon the poor. Levison recalls "the grinding noise on the sidewalks of trunks and boxes dragged by the refugees on their way to the western hills." These were the newly homeless from Chinatown, North Beach, the Mission District, South of Market—indeed, the entire eastern part of the city.

Among them were about five thousand Jews living south of Market Street, almost all of them East European newcomers, whose wood-framed shacks and cottages had quickly become fuel for the flames. One young Rumanian Jewish immigrant was giving birth in her ramshackle home precisely when the temblor struck. The midwife fled in horror and fire soon engulfed the kitchen, but the mother and newborn were saved, carried on their mattress out of the burning house and onto the sidewalk by two teenage neighbors.[12] "It's surprising that people didn't step on them," said one eyewitness.[13] Eventually they were taken by horse and wagon to Mount Zion Hospital.

Many South of Market residents retreated to Recreation Park on Harrison Street, in their own neighborhood. But the insatiable inferno threatened even that open space, and soon police cleared the entire district.[14] Some of the displaced stayed with friends or relatives in unburned sections of town such as the Richmond and Fillmore Districts, Hayes Valley, around San Bruno Avenue, and the Western Addition. Others found refuge on the grounds of the Presidio, but most camped out in Golden Gate Park or along the seashore.

More than half the city's inhabitants, over a quarter of a million people, were rendered homeless that April, and forty thousand were still in tents by autumn. But even those fortunate enough to remain in their houses often found their water and gas lines ruptured. Nearly every chimney in town had collapsed, so the use of stoves and fireplaces was prohibited out of fear that the sparks could ignite more fires. Most families, including those "who had always depended upon servants," as one rabbi noted, set up grills on piles of bricks outside and cooked their meals in the rubble-strewn streets.[15] Many of the elite also had to stand for hours alongside paupers in the breadlines, causing the class-conscious city, however briefly, to experience a kind of social leveling.

Jews constituted about 7 percent of the city's population in 1906, but their commercial and residential property accounted for a far greater proportion of the total fire losses, which approached a billion dollars.[16] Jewish communal institutions were ravaged.[17] To be sure, newly built Sherith Israel, on California and Webster streets, sustained only negligible damage and soon began to lease space to the city, as did Ohabai Shalome at Bush and Laguna streets. Beth Israel's nearly completed Geary Street Temple, however, was demolished. In the South of Market district, Keneseth Israel, the Orthodox shul on Russ Street, was lost in the fire, along with seven of its twenty Torah scrolls. In the same neighborhood, the Emanu-El Sisterhood settlement house and clinic and the Jewish Educational Society were also destroyed. The Eureka Benevolent Society, including its trove of records going back half a century, and the B'nai B'rith Hall, with its fifteen-thousand-volume library, were likewise consumed. The Lombard Street Home for the Aged Disabled was gutted, its fourteen elderly residents forced to live in the open air for several weeks; two died, probably from the stress.[18] Destroyed, too, were the plants of each of the city's three Jewish newspapers (although the *Emanu-El* was soon able to publish a special edition from Oakland). Even the Home of Peace Cemetery in San Mateo County was laid waste; eight hundred tombstones were overturned and the chapel wrecked. None of the 190 children in the Pacific Hebrew Orphan Asylum was injured, but that facility was also badly damaged.

The greatest material loss to the Jewish community was Emanu-El's Sutter Street Temple, its proud domes down and only its stone walls standing; they alone survived the fire. Many of Voorsanger's prized books were turned to ashes, as were the entire libraries of his predecessor Elkan Cohn and Cantor Edward Stark. Burned beyond recognition was the Torah scroll that Moses Montefiore had sent the pioneers in 1851, as well as all the minute books and most of the other temple records.[19]

Even as he stood amid the ruins of his synagogue, Voorsanger knew that the membership possessed the means to restore it. But what of the city's other Jewish institutions? And what of the thousands of Jewish families who were now "houseless, helpless, totally ruined, destitute?"[20]

REBIRTH

Voorsanger labored furiously on many tasks. The reconstruction of Emanu-El was left in the hands of a powerful committee that would succeed in re-opening the temple within a year and a half. In keeping with the ecumenical spirit permeating the city in the wake of the cataclysm, the rabbi chose the Calvary Presbyterian Church for his congregation's first temporary quarters and later moved to the Unitarian house of worship. "We are one people at the present time," he wrote, "and sectarian lines are very faint indeed."[21]

For other Jewish needs Voorsanger sought aid from outside San Francisco. Beth Israel would require $75,000 to clear debris and rebuild the under-insured Geary Street Temple, an impossible sum to raise for a congregation composed mostly of East European immigrants.* Adding the costs of reha-bilitating South of Market's Russ Street Shul and the Jewish Educational Society, as well as aid for the homeless, Voorsanger decided that $100,000 would be needed, an estimate with which Rabbi Nieto concurred. But when the Jewish community of Portland sent an unsolicited $5,000, Voorsanger returned it; he wanted the rehabilitation of San Francisco's Jewish institu-tions to be a national priority, not a piecemeal process.[22]

He was disappointed. Jewish periodicals across the country were sympa-thetic, but he had difficulty persuading the newly formed American Jewish Committee to commit itself to reconstruction, even though he was a mem-ber of its executive board. Funds were finally approved in November 1906, following his personal appearance in New York, but by the first anniversary of the tragedy no money had been received. As a result, Beth Israel was re-built with local funds, primarily from Emanu-El congregants.[23]

The rabbi was even angrier with the National Conference of Jewish Char-ities, which a month after the earthquake sent two observers to San Fran-cisco on a fact-finding tour: the Bay Area's own Judah Magnes, now associate

---

*At least Beth Israel's members were spared the need to relocate immediately, as they had not yet moved into their new home. The congregation was able to remain in rented quarters until the reconstruction of its synagogue.

rabbi of New York's Temple Emanu-El, and Lee K. Frankel, superintendent of that city's United Hebrew Charities. The two visitors maintained that the claim of ten thousand homeless Jews was exaggerated, concluded that two thousand seemed the correct figure, and recommended no aid at all.

Voorsanger was incensed. He argued that his former student and Frankel had conducted only a cursory investigation of three tent camps; they did not "take the time" to interview refugees who had found temporary shelter but still needed permanent housing.[24] Earlier, Voorsanger had complained that millions of dollars in federal funds, intended to build homes, had been held up "in the high and mighty East."[25] Rabbi Nieto, meanwhile, vented his frustration with the national Reform movement, which Sherith Israel had recently joined. He had expected its national leaders to "esteem it their most sacred duty" to help prostrate San Francisco Jewry, and in the face of their slow response he publicly demanded "more than lip demonstration of sympathy."[26]

Rabbinical wrath was also directed closer to home. About five hundred people, including many Jews, were sheltered in Oakland's Temple Sinai days after the earthquake, and the Daughters of Israel Relief Society fed hundreds more. But Voorsanger was offended that his Reform colleague, Sinai's Rabbi Marcus Friedlander, never came across the bay to confer with him. Worse was the telegram sent nationwide by Temple Sinai—without consulting San Francisco's Jewish leaders—asking for aid for Oakland since that community had to bear the costs of resettling refugees. Voorsanger, in a wire of his own, described the appeal "indiscreet, injudicious, ill-advised," and in the *Emanu-El* he called the East Bay's leading city "a village."[27]

But none of this squabbling hindered the recovery of San Francisco and its Jewish community. Many leading businessmen soon reopened their firms on Fillmore Street and Van Ness Avenue. Clothiers like the Livingstons, Magnins, and Roos brothers and upscale retailers like the Gumps and Raphael Weill all found business brisk at their new locations. In the summer of 1906, the *Emanu-El* encouraged plans for improved lighting on Fillmore and an electric streetcar line across Van Ness. The newspaper also pointed out that by August the city had already returned to 70 percent of its pre-earthquake population of almost four hundred thousand.[28] Not surprisingly, Voorsanger railed at eastern news reports describing San Francisco as "a total wreck" and its citizens as "a despairing mob."[29]

But it was true that the atmosphere of "Old 'Frisco" had been lost forever. Many of the ethnic neighborhoods would never be the same after the post-earthquake construction, and just as Chinatown became less exotic, the hard-hit South of Market area, bastion of the city's Yiddish-speaking newcomers, lost some of its Jewish character. For decades after the fire the dingy area would continue to house a significant number of poor East European Jews, but it would no longer be the hub of traditional Jewish life. Two new Jewish quarters would arise after 1906: an Orthodox enclave in the remote southeastern part of town known as "Out the Road," and the much larger and more varied immigrant Jewish community in the Fillmore District, about two miles west of downtown.

In addition to forcing the relocation of much of the population, "the re-building," as Kevin Starr has written, "took on dimensions of atonement. Notorious for vice and corruption, the city . . . had been purified, the slate wiped clean."[30] This was the view of Rabbi Bernard Kaplan of Ohabai Shalome, who on the first Sabbath after the earthquake told his flock that God had acted "as a father [who] punishes his children for their own good."[31] It may be that "the cleansing effect of fire," in the words of Hubert Howe Bancroft, was connected in some subliminal way with the decade of sweeping social reform that commenced around the same time.[32]

The crisis also linked early twentieth-century San Franciscans with those who had struggled during the Gold Rush decade half a century earlier. Many of the pioneers who had sailed through the Golden Gate in the 1850s passed away during the period just before the earthquake, and newspapers prominently featured their obituaries, which were filled with stories of resourcefulness and resilience. At the rededication of Emanu-El in September 1907, Voorsanger focused on the first generation's legacy: "We inherited more than their names, their wealth or achievements; we inherited their faith, their courage, their unequaled patience, their inflexible piety, their high moral character—else how could we have withstood that awful time of trial?"[33]

These were also Harris Weinstock's sentiments. The admired business-man and civic leader was elected president of the Policy Holders League, a powerful association of bankers, merchants, manufacturers, and shippers determined to collect about $100,000,000 from insurance companies, which were often slow to pay. He also sought to give hope to the city's residents, delivering an inspiring sermon to Emanu-El's worshippers at the Calvary Presbyterian Church that was reprinted in the *Call:* "The same strength of heart and mind, the same body and brains that built one San Francisco will build another and build it better."[34]

The Great Earthquake and Fire was not the only affliction visited upon San Francisco in 1906. On November 15, the city's political boss, Abraham Ruef, son of a prosperous Alsatian dry goods dealer active in several Jewish organizations, was indicted for extortion. Charged, too, was Mayor Eugene Schmitz, whose political career Ruef had made and manipulated. For the next three years the fast-spreading scandal would convulse the city.

Ironically, the man who came to symbolize everything the Progressives despised began his public life as a reformer. A prodigy, Ruef entered the University of California in 1879 at age fourteen, wrote a senior thesis called "Purity in Politics," and helped organize a Berkeley students' cooperative designed to lower the price of textbooks.[35] He graduated near the top of his class, went on to Hastings College of the Law, and was admitted to the bar at twenty-one.[36] The fledgling attorney Ruef and future Progressives such as Franklin K. Lane established the Municipal Reform League, which was in frequent contact with its counterpart in New York, led by another young idealist, Theodore Roosevelt.[37]

But the cultivated Ruef soon adopted the rough-and-tumble ways of big-city politics. He first served as a Republican ward heeler in one of the coarsest parts of town, North Beach, which included the Barbary Coast. Here he was schooled in voter fraud, bribes from shady businesses, and even physical intimidation.[38] At his service was a gang of brass knuckle–carrying toughs known as "the push."

With city hall controlled by the Populists and Democrats in the 1890s, Ruef bided his time as a leader of the unruly opposition. But the bitter transportation strikes of 1901, which caused several deaths and ignited city-wide resentment, created an opportunity. Although he had never been interested in organized labor and would later even become its enemy, Ruef joined and soon assumed control of the nascent Union Labor Party. Appealing to union members, it was perhaps the only instance in American history that labor entered politics as a party and reflected the unique power that unions wielded in San Francisco. For his mayoral candidate, Ruef recruited the personable head of the musicians' union, Eugene Schmitz, who had no political experience. Coached by Ruef at every turn, "Handsome Gene" led this strange third party to an improbable victory in November. From the day Schmitz was sworn in, it was obvious that Ruef—neither elected nor appointed to any office—was in charge. He would never command a machine that reached into the daily lives of the masses, as did Boss Tweed's

Tammany Hall, but Ruef, who was also known as "the Boss," exercised an iron grip on San Francisco.

Anyone seeking to do business with the city was directed to "see Mr. Ruef," and, one of his biographers explains, "'Seeing Ruef' involved the payment of a legal fee."[39] For the next half a decade, a panoply of special interests—utility companies, real estate developers, restaurant owners, and others—collectively paid millions for "legal expertise" in one of the most brazen influence-peddling schemes in American history. Ruef kept much of the boodle for himself, over $1,000,000, but he also funneled sizable kickbacks to the mayor and, after 1905, to all but one of the supervisors.[40]

Seeking reelection in 1903, Schmitz waged a dirty campaign, and Ruef pandered to the racism infecting the working class. He accused the opposing candidate (his old friend Franklin K. Lane) of hiring a Chinese cook—whom Ruef openly mocked as "Ah Chew"—while white chefs were unemployed.[41] But while the Union Labor Party triumphed again, the second administration saw a dogged effort by the great muckraker Fremont Older, editor of the *Evening Bulletin,* to expose Ruef and Schmitz and bring them to justice.

In articles, editorials, and political cartoons, Older revealed protection money going to city hall from gamblers and pimps, drug peddlers and whiskey dealers.[42] Most payoffs occurred in Chinatown, raising little public concern. But the *Bulletin,* the largest afternoon daily in the West, also broke the story of an association of "French restaurants" that had bribed the Boss to retain their liquor licenses.[43] The dozen establishments, which included Delmonico's and the famous Poodle Dog, were called San Francisco's "peculiar institutions" because they not only served food on the first floor, but also provided bedrooms, and sometimes prostitutes, upstairs.[44] Fearful of police raids, these houses of fine dining and discreet assignation simply bought off Ruef as the price of doing business.

Despite the criminality unearthed by Older, the tarnished administration handily won a third term in 1905. Not only was Schmitz reelected, but the Union Labor Party also garnered all eighteen seats on the board of supervisors.* Fremont Older now worried that the newly elected candi-

---

*The sweeping victory was largely due to the questionable introduction of complicated new voting machines, which made it difficult to cast ballots for a split ticket during the mere two minutes that voters were allowed (Walton Bean, *Boss Ruef's San Francisco: The Story of the Union Labor Party, Big Business and the Graft Prosecution* [Berkeley, 1952], 65).

dates, most of them unknown and uneducated, would act as if they had won the lottery rather than a public office and simply loot the municipal coffers.

He enlisted formidable allies both locally and nationally. In Washington, D.C., he met with President Roosevelt, long a foe of big-city corruption, and persuaded him to lend two key federal employees to the San Francisco district attorney's office: the combative U.S. prosecuting attorney Francis Heney, and the famed Secret Service agent William Burns. Heney, a native San Franciscan already on record as opposing Ruef, would head the prosecution without compensation. But to fund the prosecution's staff, Older convinced the civic-minded sugar magnate Rudolph Spreckels (from whom the Boss had earlier tried to extort a bribe) to contribute $100,000.[45] The group was rounded out by another incorruptible individual: former mayor and future U.S. senator James Phelan. The "unarmed vigilance committee" feared that if Ruef and his cronies were not driven from power, the city might see a return of the anarchy of 1856.[46]

The earthquake, meanwhile, provided Ruef with fresh opportunities to line his pockets, and he took bribes for the issuance of every type of city permit. In the summer of 1906 it was evident that he exerted great influence on state politics as well local, as he personally anointed the Republican candidate for governor (a pawn of the Southern Pacific Railroad) at the party's convention in Santa Cruz. A photograph of that conclave, showing statewide candidates and other GOP stalwarts huddled around a seated Abe Ruef, was published in the *Call* and widely circulated under the caption "The Shame of California."[47] But the Boss still seemed untouchable; both friend and foe thought he might eventually run for the U.S. Senate.

Yet within a few months Ruef's world would be crumbling. A grand jury stood ready to indict him and Schmitz on multiple counts of extortion in the French restaurant matter. In desperation, the Boss arranged for the firing of Heney's superior, District Attorney Langdon (one of the few honest officeholders in the city), and had himself appointed the new DA. He then removed Heney, no doubt intending to end the prosecution and muzzle Older. The press and public were appalled by the brash ploy (the *Bulletin*'s front-page story was bordered in black), and Ruef needed the protection of his bodyguard in the face of a menacing mob.[48] In short order a judge quashed the attempted usurpation of power, and Ruef was soon indicted and arraigned.

As his lead defense attorney he engaged Henry Ach, a distinguished-looking Emanu-El congregant and Ruef's silent partner in the notorious brothel known as the "municipal crib." Ach arranged Ruef's bail and infuriated Heney and the judge with delay tactics and dismissal motions. But the determined prosecutor moved ahead, and in March 1907 he named Ruef in dozens of new indictments, for bribery as well as extortion.

The trial took place in May, in the sanctuary of Sherith Israel. Because so many municipal buildings had been destroyed a year earlier, the new domed synagogue was the temporary venue of the superior court.* Ohabai Shalome was similarly used as a courtroom—for Mayor Schmitz's trial.

Before the proceedings Ruef had been subjected to a grueling interrogation by William Burns.[49] As much as Heney wanted to convict the Boss, he was even more eager to punish the tycoons who had bribed him, such as the United Railroads' executives Tirey Ford, a former California attorney general; and Patrick Calhoun, patrician grandson of the renowned U.S. vice president and South Carolina senator John C. Calhoun. Shortly after the earthquake, Ford and Calhoun had delivered a staggering $200,000 in cash to Ruef in exchange for a twenty-five-year trolley franchise, for which the ravaged, strapped city received nothing.[50]

But pressure on Ruef failed to produce a deal of immunity, such as those struck with the venal members of the board of supervisors. For agreeing to testify against the Boss and the mayor, the supervisors not only avoided prosecution but also remained in office and were even allowed to keep their ill-gotten gains. Ruef, though, would neither admit to his own wrongdoing nor incriminate others.

Rabbi Nieto, a close friend of Ruef's elderly parents, came forward to break the logjam and spare the defendant's family and the city further pain. He had also overheard some anti-Jewish remarks made by Heney when the prosecutor was interviewing potential grand jurors at Sherith Israel, and he may have believed that a lengthy trial might trigger an outbreak of anti-Semitism.[51] In a series of meetings—including secret encounters in his

*The judge's desk was set up alongside the pulpit, and the lawyers and defendant sat in the front pews. For the grand jury hearing, a large classroom on the ground level was used because another graft trial was being held in the sanctuary upstairs (Lately Thomas, *A Debonair Scoundrel: An Episode in the Moral History of San Francisco* [New York, 1962], 210).

temple at midnight—he and Rabbi Bernard Kaplan of Ohabai Shalome, where the Ruefs had been active members for decades, brokered a deal between the defense and prosecution. On the rabbis' advice—indeed, their solemn assurance "as men and ministers"—Ruef reluctantly agreed to turn state's evidence and plead guilty to one count of extortion (the shakedown of the French restaurant association) in exchange for immunity on all other charges.[52] He read a dramatic statement to that effect early in his trial, bringing it to an abrupt halt.

But the deal fell through. The prosecution was not satisfied that Ruef, in custody as he awaited his sentence, had "told all he knew." The Boss had expected to avoid prison, but Heney now claimed that he had never agreed to that. Heney cancelled the immunity contract in January 1908, making it clear that Ruef would have to enter the dock again, on any and all charges of the district attorney's choosing.

Nieto and Kaplan, "stunned" at this turn of events, went to a *Chronicle* reporter and accused the prosecutor of duplicity. Then the *Emanu-El*, breaking its silence on the case, ran a rare banner headline: "Startling Revelations in the Graft Prosecutions as Disclosed by Rabbi Nieto." Its front-page editorial, by Voorsanger, was fierce even by his standards. Describing "a chapter of disgrace unequaled in the history of San Francisco," it accused the prosecution of suborning perjury and claimed that the promise of immunity was withdrawn because Ruef had not implicated innocent men.[53]

Ruef's second trial ended in a hung jury, and Heney was convinced that those jurors holding out for acquittal had been fixed.[54] But at Ruef's third trial, held in Carpenter's Hall in late 1908, the Boss was convicted of bribery for the huge trolley franchise kickback. He received the maximum sentence of fourteen years, to be served at San Quentin.

The trials of Ruef, Schmitz, Calhoun, Ford, and many, many others deeply divided the city and the Jewish community, and the rift ran through the privileged classes as well. According to the Progressive Amy Steinhart Braden, "The feeling was so high that you were either for or against the graft prosecution. The Cabots never talked to the Lodges at that time. . . . We all felt that we were living on a keg of dynamite. We didn't know what was going to happen next and to whom it was going to happen."[55]

Prominent Jews such as J. B. Levison, Raphael Weill, and, of course, Harris Weinstock saw municipal corruption as the bane of the city; they wanted Ruef, Schmitz, the supervisors, and those who had bribed them sent to jail.[56] But the town's leading rabbis, along with highly influential

Jews such as I. W. Hellman and Jesse and Ernest Lilienthal, regarded the aggressive prosecution waged by Heney as a mortal threat to big business and thus the true danger to San Francisco.[57] Hellman was the major financial supporter of a new daily newspaper, the *Globe,* the raison d'être of which was opposition to the graft trials.[58]

The *Emanu-El* also became one of the most vociferous anti-prosecution papers in town. Beyond his anger that his rabbinical colleagues had been deceived, Voorsanger saw himself as a spokesman for the city's beleaguered captains of industry. As a result, he lauded the civic contributions of Ford and Calhoun and demanded "a square deal for the indicted."[59] Pleasure at their acquittal—as well as the overturning of Mayor Schmitz's conviction on a technicality—was expressed by Rabbi Kaplan, who wrote the *Emanu-El* editorials after Voorsanger's death in 1908.*[60]

Both men also delivered blistering attacks on the "perverse" press, namely the *Call* and *Bulletin,* which had "poisoned the public mind against those charged with wrong-doing."[61] In January 1907 Voorsanger reported from Paris that due to the "exposure of all the political filth," San Francisco was "considered one of the most infamous communities extant."[62] He predicted that the economy would suffer as a result, a theme that Kaplan reiterated in two dozen articles. Of course the *Emanu-El* opposed Heney's bid for district attorney in 1909; by then much of the electorate was weary of the prosecution, and he was soundly defeated.

One young local Jewish Progressive, Miriam Michelson, sister of the Nobel Prize–winning physicist Albert Michelson, voiced her disgust with the *Emanu-El*'s prodefense stance. "In this contest between Right and Wrong," she declared in a short-lived journal called the *Liberator,* "most disheartening is the attitude of editor-priests, Jew and Christian."[63] Turning Voorsanger's argument on its head, she asserted that "the thing that will hurt business in the long run [is that] San Francisco does not punish her thieves."[64]

Ruef's conviction and sentencing were ignored by the *Emanu-El,* no doubt to spare the Jewish community further embarrassment, but the journal did carry letters by leading Jews urging his parole and demanded his early release in an editorial.[65] The weekly even took exception to Stephen Wise's comment that "Israel is not responsible for Ruef's sins," chiding the New York rabbi for assuming the convicted man guilty: "Wise is a brilliant

---

*Voorsanger died of heart failure at fifty-six, which was perhaps brought on by his unrelenting relief work after the earthquake.

and eloquent young man but not of a well balanced frame of mind."[66] Whereas another Jewish community might have tried to distance itself from a scoundrel such as Ruef, in turn-of-the-century San Francisco he had many distinguished defenders among his own people.

While the prodefense camp's comparison between Ruef and Dreyfus was ludicrous,* there *was* a bit of anti-Semitism injected into the trials of the political boss, who was the only one to go to prison of the hundreds accused.[67] At the defendant's second trial, in April 1908, Heney had needlessly revealed the prison record of one potential juror, Morris Haas, a record that the obscure middle-aged family man had long kept secret. Pointing a finger at the humiliated Haas and holding up his prison photo, Heney shouted, "He is an ex-convict and he is a Jew, and this defendant Ruef is a Jew."[68]

The *Emanu-El* expressed deep sympathy for Haas—even after he returned to court in November and shot Heney in the head before taking his own life a few days later.[69] Heney survived but was unable to finish the trial;[†] he entrusted the case to his assistant, young Hiram Johnson, who would use the prosecution of Ruef as the springboard of his stellar political career. Johnson made an impassioned closing argument about the corrosive effects of municipal corruption, which heartened Progressives throughout the West, but his labeling of Ruef as a "Judas" caused some discomfort in the Jewish community.[70]

More upsetting were comments in the *Bulletin* by a local Protestant minister who, in an open letter to Schmitz, rebuked the disgraced mayor for associating with Ruef: "'If you lie down with dogs you will get up with fleas'—but you knew that. You willingly became the servant of the Jew. Now both master and slave may go to the penitentiary."[71] But the reverend

---

*In a recent book on the social dislocation following the earthquake, journalist Philip Fradkin also equates Ruef with the French army captain—a false analogy given that Dreyfus, who was convicted of treason by a secret military tribunal and abused for years on Devil's Island, was completely innocent (Philip L. Fradkin, *The Great Earthquake and Firestorms of 1906* [Berkeley, 2006], 307–8). Moreover, in stark contrast with the Ruef case, the Dreyfus Affair triggered a wave of violent attacks against Jews and long remained a rallying cry for anti-Semites.

†Heney's life was saved because he happened to be laughing at the moment the gun went off; the bullet entered his mouth and lodged in the jaw muscles below his left ear. After Haas committed suicide in his jail cell, suspicion fell on Police Chief Biggy, who himself soon drowned mysteriously. The nightmarish case also saw the bombing of a key witness's home and the kidnapping of Fremont Older.

was quickly put in his place by stinging rejoinders from Voorsanger and Weinstock and soon wrote an apology.[72]

The relative lack of anti-Semitism overall is telling, considering that, during a series of sensational trials, "a small, weak, nervous Jew," as Ruef was characterized by a Midwestern priest, had come to symbolize the city's degradation.[73] Indeed, with his prominent nose, short stature, and dark, curly hair, the money-hungry defendant perfectly fit the anti-Jewish stereotype. On top of that, another Jew had shot and nearly killed the prosecuting attorney. Coming on the heels of a horrendous physical disaster, and coinciding with a period of violent labor unrest, the seamy Ruef affair certainly had the potential to generate a wave of Judeophobia throughout Northern California.

But it did nothing of the kind. Not only were anti-Semitic utterances few and scattered, but the public refrained even from retaliating against Jewish politicians. Congressman Julius Kahn was reelected as usual. Edward Wolfe, a member of Congregation Beth Israel, was again sent to the state senate, and Lippman Sachs, vice president of Emanu-El, received the second largest number of votes of the twelve men elected to the "reform" board of supervisors in 1907.

Even Ruef received an absolution of sorts. It came from an unlikely source: Fremont Older, who had second thoughts soon after he had won his crusade. He publicly admitted "pandering to many low instincts to sell newspapers," and that the prosecution "in the heat of enthusiasm [had] done questionable things" and "was full of evil too."[74] Indeed, at the height of the struggle, in 1907, Older (using a pseudonym) had penned a piercing article on the Boss's character in the *Overland Monthly*.* But now he showed deep personal sympathy for the incarcerated Ruef, "one poor, miserable, helpless human being," and a tragic victim.[75] In an emotional speech before the San Francisco chapter of the National Council of Jewish Women, Older stretched the truth in claiming that one man had unfairly been made to pay with his freedom for a sordid system he had not created but "found around him."[76] The editor frequently visited Ruef in San Quentin and asked for,

---

*The odd piece contains both high praise for the "wonderful" Jewish people, "among the finest and noblest . . . in history," as well as sharp barbs, referring to some Jews as "men of low cunning" ("Q," "Ruef—A Jew Under Torture," *Overland Monthly* 37 [November 1907], 518). It skewers Ruef but is hardly the "vicious diatribe" described by Philip Fradkin (Fradkin, *The Great Earthquake*, 307).

and received, his former enemy's forgiveness.[77] He published the Boss's vivid (though unrevealing) memoirs in the *Bulletin* and lobbied for his release after only a year of confinement. With Ruef's former prosecutor Hiram Johnson now governor, Older's efforts were fruitless, but in 1913, after four and a half years behind bars, Ruef's good behavior earned him parole, and he was pardoned by the state's next chief executive.*

Again, it was the Asians who were abused during the turbulent post-earthquake years; they, and not the Jews, became the scapegoats. Ruef, for example, before his fall had tried to prevent their return to Chinatown, a desirable section of the city near Nob Hill, which they had occupied since pioneer times.[78] He and Schmitz attempted to create a new Chinese quarter in Hunters Point, or even beyond city limits in Colma.

His plan ultimately failed, but an even greater controversy erupted later in 1906 over the more recently arrived Japanese, who were often depicted in the press as shrewd and conniving. Resentful of their rapid success, San Francisco officials used the disruption caused by the earthquake as an opportunity to segregate Japanese children from whites. The newly rebuilt Chinese School was renamed the Oriental Public School, becoming the only one in the city allowed to admit Japanese students. Mayor Schmitz and the board of education, headed by Ruef's brother-in-law, Aaron Altman, eventually rescinded the order, but only after a promise—the infamous "Gentleman's Agreement"—made to them by President Theodore Roosevelt that Japanese laborers would be excluded from California in the future.[79]

"DYNAMITERS"

Just as the graft prosecutions had been the touchstone of social conflict in the immediate post-earthquake years, so did a terrorist act in downtown San Francisco during World War I arouse class consciousness. In 1916 the city was split over the question of America's entry into the war in Europe: big business favored military intervention, while much of the working class hoped the country would remain neutral. When a "military preparedness" parade along Market Street was scheduled for July 22, the left

*Ruef continued to live in San Francisco. Disbarred, he was nonetheless active in real estate and other business ventures and a mainstay of Congregation Ohabai Shalome. He was financially crushed during the Depression, however, and in 1936 the lifelong bachelor died almost penniless.

wing countered with a stormy rally in the Fillmore's Dreamland Rink two days earlier. Jewish leaders of the culinary workers union such as Hugo Ernst and Selig Schulberg were among the sponsors, but front-page coverage the next day went to Rabbi Jacob Nieto, who energized the crowd of four thousand: "Picture . . . the well-fed paunches from Montgomery Street signing up for a musket to go out and fight. Theirs is not to reason why. Theirs but to do, and for *you* to die!"[80]

Nieto's barb was no doubt aimed at the conservative businessmen on the executive committee of the Preparedness Parade, which included the Jews Herbert Fleishhacker, I. W. Hellman Jr., Jesse Lilienthal, and Michael de Young.[81] Modeling their march on a grand procession that took place along New York's Fifth Avenue several months earlier, organizers planned for a crowd of one hundred thousand.

The patriotic pageant began on a hot Saturday afternoon at 1:30 P.M. Thirty-six minutes later a tremendous explosion on Steuart Street just south of Market killed ten and injured forty. Law enforcement officials soon became frantic in their attempt to root out those responsible. Newspaper editors cast a wide net of blame, and some journalists even felt that Rabbi Nieto and other Dreamland Rink speakers were guilty of incitement.[82] But most attention was focused on a local circle of anarchists and radical socialists, several of whom had been suspects in attacks against the property and personnel of Pacific Gas and Electric (PG&E) amidst a viciously fought labor dispute several years earlier.

The investigation of the Preparedness Day bombing was headed by District Attorney Charles Fickert. In 1909 he had defeated Francis Heney with the aid of a committee of twenty-five top businessmen led by I. W. Hellman and his son, I. W. Jr., and had quickly dismissed the graft prosecutions still roiling the city.[83] Now, in 1916, backed by a frenzied press (including even Fremont Older's *Bulletin* at the outset),[84] Fickert sought to use the shocking act of terror as a way to destroy radicalism in the city, cripple the unions, and propel his political career.

A few days after the explosion he ordered a wave of arrests and indicted five individuals, including young labor agitators Tom Mooney and Warren Billings, who were charged with planting the bomb; and Mooney's wife, Rena, and militant union leader Ed Nolan, who were charged as accomplices. The identity of the fifth defendant stirred great anxiety in Jewish ranks. Israel Weinberg, of the Mission District, was a thirty-two-year-old jitney operator from czarist Russia who had lived in San Francisco about a decade. He was accused of having driven Mooney and Billings with their dynamite-packed suitcase to the explosion site.

Worse, Fickert alleged that the five were part of an anarchist conspiracy masterminded by another Russian Jew, Alexander Berkman,[85] who, along with his close companion Emma Goldman, was the most widely recognized anarchist in the world. Berkman had been living in San Francisco since early 1916, working as editor of a radical weekly unfortunately entitled the *Blast*. Goldman was in town during the bombing as well; she had recently delivered a series of lectures on the West Coast and spoke against militarism on the night of the Preparedness Day march. Fickert, without a search warrant, immediately raided the offices of the *Blast*, but he did not indict Berkman until a year after the bombing; by then the revolutionary was back East and able to avoid extradition.[86]

Billings was tried first, but Fickert's case was weak. It depended upon eyewitnesses of dubious credibility who placed the defendants at the scene of the crime with a heavy suitcase. But the DA, declaring the offense "far more serious than any other ever submitted to any jury," invoked the anarchist menace in his closing remarks: "This American flag was what they desired to offend . . . by killing the women and men that worshipped it . . . and if that flag is to continue to wave, you men must put an end to such acts as these."[87] Billings was convicted, but clearly the jurors had some doubts: they voted for life imprisonment rather than death by hanging.

Attempting to strengthen his next case, that against Tom Mooney, Fickert added another eyewitness, Oregon cattleman Frank Oxman. He testified that, in San Francisco on business, he had seen Weinberg drive up to the corner of Steuart and Market streets before the explosion. Mooney, Billings, and a man with a mustache (perhaps this was supposed to be Berkman) got out, Oxman said, and deposited a suitcase on the sidewalk. The witness also claimed he jotted down the Ford jitney's license number. Of course, it turned out to be owned by Weinberg.[88]

Oxman's testimony was later revealed to be deceitful, motivated by his desire for the reward money. In fact, he had not even arrived in the city until the evening of July 22, after the explosion. He would later be tried for perjury, but his testimony severely damaged Mooney, who was found guilty and sentenced to death. Israel Weinberg's wife, Blanche, was in the courtroom and fainted when she heard the pronouncement.[89]

Her husband was in prison awaiting his own trial. He was an official in the Jitney Operators Union but, unlike Mooney and Billings, was no radical and had no police record. Fickert had called Weinberg as a witness in the Mooney case, and tried to portray him as a friend of Emma Goldman, but they had no such relationship. As for the Mooneys, Weinberg was merely an acquaintance: he had driven the couple to an anarchist picnic on July 4.[90]

Around the time of that excursion, private detective Martin Swanson, employed by PG&E and by Jesse Lilienthal's United Railroads, hounded Weinberg for information about Mooney, whom the utility companies strongly suspected of industrial sabotage. Swanson attempted to bribe Weinberg for incriminating information and, when that failed, threatened to get his jitney license revoked.[91] On July 22, only hours following the disaster, Swanson was hired by the DA's office to assist in the investigation.

Arrested soon after the bombing and charged with multiple counts of murder, Weinberg was now under infinitely greater pressure to implicate Mooney. He was visited in prison by a friend he had known in Russia named Farber, who told Weinberg that he was acting as a go-between for three powerful local Jews who feared the anti-Semitic repercussions the case might cause. Farber said they had authorized him to offer Weinberg $20,000 for testimony against Mooney, and that turning state's evidence would also result in immunity. When Weinberg suspected that it was really Fickert who had concocted the story of the Jewish money, Farber admitted the district attorney's ruse but insisted that the deal was legitimate. Weinberg came close to accepting this Faustian bargain but in the end refused: "They can hang me to a post," he reportedly said, "but I will not do that."[92]

Weinberg suffered terribly for his honesty. He had been arrested without a warrant, interrogated under a searchlight, and not been permitted to meet with counsel for weeks. Repeatedly denied bail, he remained incarcerated for fourteen months before his trial, while he lost his life savings, regular customers, and modest home. His wife and son were housed and fed by friends.[93]

At first it appeared that, in an echo of the Ruef scandal, the leading rabbis would come to Weinberg's defense. Unsettled by newspaper reports that sometimes labeled Weinberg "a Russian Jew," several San Francisco rabbis*

---

*The rabbis' identities remain unknown, but they likely included prolabor Jacob Nieto, who obviously was not averse to working behind the scenes on behalf of a high-profile Jewish defendant. Emanu-El's activist rabbi Martin Meyer may also have been involved.

engaged two outstanding attorneys to represent their coreligionist.[94] Edwin McKenzie had defended two anarchists in a similar case, the bombing of the *Los Angeles Times* building in 1910, which had killed twenty. He was joined by Thomas O'Connor, a well-known civil liberties advocate.

But within days the rabbis withdrew from the case; they would neither raise funds for Weinberg's legal battles nor help him in any other way. Fickert had summoned the Jewish spiritual leaders to his office and shown them some "evidence" against Mooney and Weinberg. It is unclear whether the DA genuinely convinced them of the culpability of the two or simply pressured them to retreat.[95] In any case, the rabbis, who had ardently supported a guilty Jewish racketeer in 1907, now turned their backs on an innocent family man facing the death penalty.

Of course, Weinberg was an immigrant with anarchist sympathies who made his living a nickel at a time, and Ruef was a wealthy public figure with pioneer roots and was active in his synagogue. But the major difference in their two cases was the nature of the crime. Early in the century the self-confident, almost brash Jewish community judged correctly that graft trials would provide little traction for anti-Semites. But in the fevered climate of World War I, the accusation that a foreign-born Jew had killed for the cause of revolution was another matter entirely. The *Emanu-El* reported not a word on the case, nor did any mainstream Jewish leader speak out for the defense.

Nor did the defendants receive support from many other quarters. For months after the explosion even organized labor chose to distance itself from Mooney, Billings, and Weinberg because it feared big business would attempt to tie the unions to the "dynamiters." Only Selig Schulberg's International Workers Defense League came to Weinberg's side; it kept on McKenzie and O'Connor as his lawyers after the rabbis dropped out.[96]

However, by October 1917, when Weinberg entered the courtroom, the prosecution had sustained major setbacks. Fickert had lost his case against Rena Mooney in July and, even more damaging, Frank Oxman, the star witness in her husband's trial earlier in the year, had lost all credibility when some of his personal correspondence had been made public. He was acquitted of perjury in late summer, but the *Bulletin* headline cried "whitewash" and "farce";[97] he would not be called to testify against the jitney driver. Meanwhile, Fickert was widely perceived to have been aware of Oxman's lies as well as the dishonesty of other prosecution witnesses. While most San Franciscans probably still believed Mooney and Billings guilty, they also felt that the district attorney had acted unscrupulously, and enough signatures were collected in 1917 to make him face a recall.*

Undaunted, he pressed his feeble case against Weinberg. During a seven-week trial, covered daily in the local press, Fickert and his team proved little beyond that the defendant had subscribed to the *Blast,* long excerpts from which were read in court. About twenty defense witnesses testified they had seen him far from downtown during the early afternoon of July 22, and no criminal connection was made between him and Mooney and Billings.[98] On top of that, Weinberg's lawyers showed how absurd was the prosecution's claim that he had driven down Market Street during the parade, an artery choked with people marching in the opposite direction and blocked to all traffic save emergency vehicles.

The jury acquitted him after deliberating for twenty-three minutes. As one juror said, "I'm against anarchists . . . and I was ready to convict on any kind of adequate evidence—but not on a wild-eyed, astral-bodied, wine-bum case like that—never!"[99]

Yet Weinberg's ordeal was not over. The bullheaded Fickert, intending to retry him on other charges, opposed bail even in the face of a petition signed by all twelve jurors urging his release. The judge agreed with the DA, and Weinberg later lost his bid in the appellate court as well. Only a state supreme court ruling set him free on bail—$15,000, which his already hard-pressed friends had to raise in cash—in March 1918, four months after his acquittal and twenty months after his arrest. He was not retried, but, a broken man, he soon left with his family for the Midwest.

If Fickert doggedly pursued Weinberg, he was obsessed with bringing to trial Alexander Berkman, whom he considered the "brains" behind the bomb plot.[100] The activist and writer was hardly an implausible suspect. Like Emma Goldman, whom he had met on the Lower East Side when both were youthful new immigrants (he from Vilna, she from St. Petersburg), Berkman embraced the Russian revolutionary tradition known as anarchism.[101] Rejecting American socialism as too "middle class," the anarchists sought to sweep away virtually all laws and create a classless society free of government, religion, and private property.[102]

To destroy the old order anarchists perpetrated some spectacular acts of violence. Provoked by the deaths during Pennsylvania's Homestead Strike

---

*Fickert would remain in office because of a mysterious explosion at the governor's mansion on election eve that once again raised the specter of anarchism. He was defeated in the regular election of 1919, however, and trounced again four years later.

of 1892, Berkman shot and seriously wounded the union-busting industrialist Henry Clay Frick, later serving fourteen years in prison for the act. Like-minded terrorists followed suit. A deranged man with anarchist leanings assassinated President McKinley in 1901, and later in the decade a wave of deadly attacks took place in big cities across the country. In 1914 a homemade bomb accidentally exploded in a New York City apartment, killing four of Berkman's anarchist friends.[103]

Fear and anger swept the country. "San Francisco, with its cosmopolitan and relatively tolerant traditions," writes social historian Richard Frost, "was less susceptible to hysteria than other communities."[104] But the murder of two Bay Area policemen eight months apart, by Russian immigrants thought to be anarchists, added to the sense of foreboding by the summer of 1916.

The very presence of Berkman, who had come to the West Coast the year before, increased tensions. After a few months in Los Angeles (where he aided the defendants in the *Times* bombing case) he moved to San Francisco, established connections with an Italian anarchist group, and soon founded his revolutionary paper. With biting political cartoons, incisive social criticism, and thunderous radical proclamations, it was perceived as a threat by the authorities despite its low circulation. Three months into the journal's existence, the U.S. Post Office suspended its second-class mailing permit, dealing a heavy financial blow to the "Blasters," as the editorial staff referred to themselves.[105] Still, for another year the organ continued to highlight the plight of the working class and vehemently argue against conscription and censorship, and in favor of one of Emma Goldman's favorite causes, birth control.

She joined Berkman in San Francisco in early July 1916 for a month-long stay. No stranger to the city, she had made about a dozen visits in the previous decade as a popular speaker. Although usually tolerated by law enforcement officials, she and her lover Ben Reitman had been harassed in 1909 by Police Chief William Biggy, who claimed she had arrived "to blow up the American fleet now in the harbor."[106] He shadowed them with numerous detectives, placed scores of policemen in her lecture halls, and soon arrested the two for "conspiracy and riot."[107] Released on bail only upon payment of $16,000 each, they were soon indicted for "unlawful assemblage, denouncing all organized government, and preaching Anarchist doctrines."[108] But the case was quickly dismissed and she spoke to overflowing crowds in the Fillmore District and elsewhere for the rest of her Northern California trip. As she later wrote, "Never in all the years since I had first gone on tour, with the exception of [New York's] Union Square demonstration in 1893, had I seen masses so eager and enthusiastic. It was all due to the stupendous farce staged by the authorities at huge expense to the San Francisco taxpayers."* [109]

In the summer of 1916, opposition to "military preparedness" was high on Goldman's agenda. She had scheduled a talk on the subject for July 20 but postponed it—to the evening of the fateful 22nd—because she wanted to avoid a conflict with the rally of the "liberal and progressive labor elements" at Dreamland Rink (where Rabbi Nieto delivered an impassioned address).[110] She went ahead with her lecture, hours after the bombing, but only fifty people attended, she recalled, not counting the many detectives present.[111]

The poor turnout was the first sign, she wrote, "of the lack of courage, not only of the average person but of the radicals and liberals as well . . . [who] ran to cover like a pack of sheep at the approach of a storm."[112] Indeed, after the explosion and the arrest of the union militants the city was so paralyzed with fear that Goldman barely exaggerated when she later stated, "Only Sasha [Berkman] and I dared speak up for the prisoners."[113]

Not surprisingly, the *Blast* decried the prosecution's case as "preposterous," the only paper in town to take such a position.[114] Berkman, himself a target of the investigation, accused detective Martin Swanson of having framed the defendants on behalf of the utility companies that employed him. Meanwhile Goldman, a veteran of many such struggles, sought legal counsel for Billings, and was stymied when no qualified local attorney would agree to take the case. Berkman, however, had success in finding representation for Mooney; through his many connections he was able to persuade an eloquent former New York congressman to head the defense team.

Berkman, in Manhattan in the fall of 1916, attempted to convince the public that a travesty was taking place in California, and he found deep sympathy among Jewish garment workers on the Lower East Side. The United Hebrew Trades, a federation of unions comprised mostly of socialists, backed him in organizing lectures, demonstrations, and fundraising events benefiting the San Francisco defendants.[115]

In July 1917, as Rena Mooney's trial was coming to a conclusion and Israel Weinberg's was still several months away, Fickert indicted the absent Berkman with the intent of bolstering the prosecution's conspiracy theory. But

---

*The two received much rougher treatment in San Diego in 1912, when vigilantes tarred and feathered Reitman and branded his body with the letters "IWW."

the anarchist was already in federal prison in Atlanta, having been convicted, along with Goldman, of interfering with the draft. Freed on bail in September, Berkman returned to New York and successfully fought extradition to California. So much pressure was exerted in Albany by leading socialists (several of them state legislators) that Governor Whitman refused to release Berkman to the custody of Fickert's agent. It was the beginning of a bitter cross-country disagreement on the Mooney case that would last for decades.

Goldman and Berkman also sent word of the case to fellow anarchists in Russia, then in the throes of revolution. In April 1917 the American embassy in Petrograd (the new name for St. Petersburg) was threatened by an angry mob.[116] The demonstration worried the Wilson administration, which was trying to keep its Russian ally in the war. Fearing that anti-American agitation could undermine his overtures to Alexander Kerensky's Provisional Government, the president asked California governor William Stephens to spare Mooney's life. The convict received a stay of execution pending his appeal before the state supreme court.

Even beyond potential damage to Russo-American relations, Wilson worried that a martyred Mooney might inflame labor disputes in the western states and hamper production. The White House ordered an investigation of the case and appointed Harvard Law School professor and assistant secretary of war Felix Frankfurter as counsel to the commission. After a two-week visit to San Francisco in November 1917, during which the commissioners interviewed many of the key figures and examined a raft of documents, they concluded that the utility companies, having regarded Mooney as a threat, had tried to "get" him through Detective Swanson. "An injustice was done," they wrote, and they recommended a new trial.[117]

Fickert was enraged. He claimed he had not been allowed to address the commission, a charge Frankfurter emphatically denied. The eminent legal scholar (later to be the third Jew appointed to the United States Supreme Court) was also attacked as a "Bolshevik"[118] by Frank Dunne, trial judge in the Billings, Rena Mooney, and Weinberg cases.

Meanwhile, in letters to Governor Stephens citing "the many complicated interests involved," Woodrow Wilson pleaded for Mooney's life, an especially urgent entreaty after the California Supreme Court let stand the death sentence in March 1918.[119] Two weeks before the sentence was to be carried out, Stephens reduced the punishment to life imprisonment, but Mooney's supporters, who had hoped for a pardon, vowed to continue the fight. It would take more than twenty years for him and Billings to be released, a struggle that, particularly during the strife-ridden 1930s, would see prominent local Jews, from Rabbi Nieto on the left to Herbert Fleishhacker on the right, passionately arguing the question.*

RED SCARE

The Mooney case was soon eclipsed by a sweeping crackdown on suspected radicals directed by U.S. Attorney General A. Mitchell Palmer and his young assistant J. Edgar Hoover. In November 1919, federal agents conducted raids in a dozen cities and arrested more than 650 people. The following month, without a court hearing, they deported 249 of them to Russia. Aboard the "Soviet Ark" were Alexander Berkman and Emma Goldman.[†]

Palmer characterized the leadership of the alleged insurrectionists as "a small clique of outcasts from the East Side of New York," and historians of the Red Scare have noted its anti-Semitic component.[120] As early as 1917, Leon Trotsky's presence in New York, as well as the strong bid for mayor by the socialist, antiwar candidate, Morris Hillquit, raised fears that the Jewish immigrant quarter was a hotbed of subversion. In October of that year, only days before the Weinberg trial began, seven Jewish radicals from Lower Manhattan were tried under the newly passed Espionage Act for distributing leaflets opposing U.S. intervention in Russia. Most of them received long sentences, and one died from the harsh prison conditions even before the trial commenced.[121] Indeed, concern about alien radicalism persuaded Congress in 1917 to tighten the immigration laws for the first time in a third of a century. The notion that Bolshevism was a specifically Jewish invention was spread widely: through a periodical based in Brooklyn, a Senate

---

*In 1931, Aaron Sapiro, representing Mooney for the ACLU, lobbied Governor James Rolph for a pardon. He failed because Herbert Fleishhacker, who wielded enormous influence over Rolph, declared that "Mooney was an S.O.B. and that Rolph should keep him where he was," according to Charles Erskine Wood, an eminent attorney and one of the banker's closest friends. Wood claimed that when he told Fleishhacker to "care more about civil rights because he was a Jew," the magnate "blanched and said nothing" (quoted in Richard H. Frost, *The Mooney Case* [Stanford, 1968], 403–4).

†The Criminal Syndicalist Law, passed by the California legislature in 1919, initiated a statewide suspension of civil liberties. Hundreds of alleged conspirators—most of them IWW activists from Southern California—were arrested, and many incarcerated for years in San Quentin.

committee hearing in the Capitol, an organization of right-wing business-men in the Midwest, and Christian churches throughout the nation.[122]

Could a similar dread of foreign-born Jewish agitators have motivated Fickert's overly zealous prosecution of Weinberg and Berkman in San Francisco? A young Jewish reporter covering Mooney's trial for the *Call* referred to Fickert many decades later as a Red-baiter and the most anti-Semitic public official he had seen in his entire career.[123] But evidence is lacking for the claim that Fickert's vendetta was motivated by hatred of the Jews. One of the prosecution's "star witnesses," prostitute Estelle Smith, did describe Berkman as a "very repulsive looking man [with a] long mustache. I would say he was a Russian Jew or something that way."[124] Yet Fickert ignored the innuendo, and social historians have found no further anti-Semitic utterances in the voluminous trial transcripts, nor in the prosecutor's numerous statements to the press.[125]

The local dailies were anything but restrained in their coverage of the trials; accepting as fact Fickert's story of an anarchist conspiracy, they inflamed public opinion for years. But despite the obvious Jewish origin of Weinberg, Berkman, and Goldman, as well as other well-known radicals such as union leaders Selig Schulberg and Hugo Ernst and Communist Party chief Emanuel Levin, anti-Semitism played only a minor part in demonizing the extreme left. To be sure, a large political cartoon printed on the first page of Hearst's *Examiner* in the midst of the Weinberg trial is defamatory. Under the heading "The Root of the Evil," it depicts a squat man with an oversized nose reading a newspaper entitled *Seditious Press*. In the background a U.S. Army warehouse is ablaze, and the caption reads, "Well done fellows, keep the home fires burning."[126] Yet this offensive image—and the figure is less luridly drawn than many an anti-Semitic caricature—was evidently one of a kind in the Bay Area. A survey of the local press conducted by the Emma Goldman Papers Project revealed nothing similar, and in the news coverage of his case Weinberg is usually referred to as an "anarchist" and only occasionally as a Russian Jew.[127]

HYPER-PATRIOTISM

Still, the Weinberg case alarmed local Jews, and America's declaration of war on Germany further heightened fears of anti-Semitism. San Francisco's long-serving congressman, Julius Kahn, advised his coreligionists, "Jews have always done their share. . . . But we must do more now, we must see that we do not fall short of the number of our volunteers."[128]

Despite—or perhaps because of—his German birth, Kahn emerged as arguably the most hawkish member of the House of Representatives. As the ranking Republican on the Military Affairs Committee, he broke with the leadership of his own party to back the Selective Service Bill in 1917. Due to his skillful efforts to pass it, the legislation enacting the military draft, which added millions of men to the armed services, is sometimes known as the "Kahn Amendment."[129] Looking back on his role in instituting conscription, he "took especial pleasure," a magazine interviewer wrote, "in showing that the thinking men of his race [the Jews] were prepared to uphold American honor and American resistance to insult and aggression."[130]

Kahn was also "foremost among congressmen," according to a glowing report in the *Emanu-El,* "to offset the spirit of dissent fostered by pacifists, anti-Americans, and all those acting as a clog in the machinery of government."[131] The weekly devoted almost its entire front page to a speech he delivered in Congress soon after America entered the war, full of praise for the Justice Department's suppression of "sedition and treason wherever it attempts to raise its treacherous head. . . . [I]t is well that the snake is being crushed at the very outset of this struggle." Evoking the crackdown on Copperheads during the Civil War, Kahn quoted Lincoln: " 'Must I shoot a simple-minded soldier boy who deserts, while I must not touch a hair of a wily agitator who induces him to desert?' "[132] The following year, in another oration on the House floor, Kahn went even further, claiming, "Whenever any voice is raised in this country—a seditious voice, a traitorous voice—I hope that the strict arm of the law will reach out for that man or woman . . . and that we shall have a few prompt hangings. We will have to make an example of some of these people and do it quickly."[133]

During and immediately after war, the *Emanu-El* (now edited by its founder's brother, A. W. Voorsanger) felt compelled to deny repeatedly the connection between radicalism and the Jewish people: it prominently featured articles under such headlines as "Are the Jews Responsible for Russian Bolshevism?"[134] In a rare mention of Berkman and Goldman by name, shortly after the former was indicted by Fickert, an editorial argued that only a "jaundiced mind" would generalize that because they are "the most prominent of the anarchists, therefore all or most Jews are foes of government and order."[135] In a similar vein, the piece held that the presence of Jewish socialists in Congress, such as Lower Manhattan's Meyer London and Milwaukee's Victor Berger, did not mean "all or most Jews are endeavoring to radically reconstruct the social fabric."[136] It asserted, too, that Jews as a whole ought not to be tainted by "the most extreme and revolutionary pacifist views" held by Morris Hillquit and Oakland's "unpatriotic" Rabbi Judah Magnes, a pacifist during World War I.[137]

Not surprisingly, the journal made frequent mention of local Jews "called to the colors" and, in a special box headed "Jews in War Work," ran profiles of community leaders helping the Allied cause.[138] Mortimer Fleishhacker, for example, was California's federal mediator for industrial disputes during the war; he settled the prolonged strikes of shipbuilders and ironworkers. His cousin Albert Schwabacher served as the state's top federal fuel official. Rosalie Meyer Stern turned an entire floor of her elegant home into a workshop where Red Cross volunteers sewed hospital dressings.[139]

The *Emanu-El* proudly recorded that Jews were "foremost in generous subscriptions" to Liberty Loans[140] and published many full-page ads for war bonds. At the same time it featured numerous stories on Jewish patriotism throughout American history, starting with the Revolutionary War.[141]

The paper was careful to downplay parochial Jewish interests in this time of national crisis (as it would again during the early 1940s). Even before America entered World War I, an editorial disapproved of handbills endorsing Wilson because he had appointed Jews to high posts. "There is no Jewish vote," the *Emanu-El* insisted: "Our Jewish citizens [ought not] form a political unit."[142]

The editor felt, too, that he had to address the thorny issue of the German origin of most of his readers. This was of special concern in San Francisco, where, more than any other major American city, Jewish life was dominated by those who had gloried in Teutonic culture as much as had any German gentile. The potential problem of mixed loyalties during the war was raised in an article referring to a local Jew whose son had been drafted but whose nephew fought for the Kaiser. "But now he has become reconciled to the situation," wrote the *Emanu-El,* which held that despite the German extraction of so many local Jews, "they will always be ready to defend their hearths and houses from aggression or menace from any quarter."[143]

As an additional proof of their fidelity a number of venerable German Jewish families anglicized their names soon after the United States joined the Allies. Sinsheimer became Sinton; Brandenstein was now Bransten. But here the *Emanu-El* drew the line. It ridiculed the new appellations as "cowardice, snobbishness, ignorance."[144] It would be "unworthy" to "change an old and respected Jewish family name," A. W. Voorsanger wrote. "Looking back on almost three quarters of a century of Jewish achievement and acceptance on the West Coast," he saw "no prejudice against mere names."[145]

Indeed, despite the vulnerability they felt, Bay Area Jews were hardly ever suspected of divided loyalties during the war. And, as a group, they were neither tarnished by the real crimes of Abe Ruef nor by the false charges brought against Israel Weinberg and Alexander Berkman. But the specter of Jewish radicalism—Rabbi Voorsanger had accused Emma Goldman of "moral insanity" as early as 1908[146]—was of no minor concern to prominent Jews with Gold Rush roots. It served to deepen the Jewish elite's long-standing suspicion of the East European immigrants, whose numbers in the Bay Area were now rising.

SEVEN

With a Yiddish Accent

East European Jewish Neighborhoods

VISITORS TO THE BAY AREA often note the lack of a Jewish neighborhood such as Los Angeles's Fairfax District or Chicago's Devon Avenue. But in earlier days there were four traditional Jewish areas: South of Market, the San Bruno Avenue area, Fillmore-McAllister, and West Oakland. There was also a rural Jewish colony composed of chicken farmers in Petaluma. These communities were filled with East European Jews—not the half Germans from Prussian Poland who had arrived in the decades after the Gold Rush, but Yiddish-speaking immigrants mostly from Russia, Austria-Hungary, or Rumania.

In addition to housing a high concentration of Jews, the urban enclaves were home to synagogues and *minyanim* (worship groups that met in private homes), kosher butchers and bakeries, mutual aid societies, and Hebrew schools. Orthodox abounded, but there were also socialists, communists, Yiddishists, and Zionists. These neighborhoods added up to something greater than the sum of their parts, and children in these areas—whether they felt nurtured or smothered—grew up with a keen sense of Jewish identity.

Yet in Northern California "there were no ghettos" (meaning an area of density, isolation, or squalor), according to one observer in the 1920s, a communal worker on both sides of the bay who was also intimately familiar with New York's Lower East Side.[1] Indeed, the East European immigrant experience in the Bay Area differed markedly from that in most other big American cities. First, the number of Jews was relatively low. By World War I there were more than half a million immigrant Jews and their children on the Lower East Side, and more than one hundred thousand in Chicago and Philadelphia, but probably fewer than ten thousand in San Francisco and less than a thousand across the bay.* In the Bay Area, the Yiddish speakers and their offspring comprised perhaps a third of the Jewish community by 1918; among major U.S. cities, only New Orleans, where the German Jewish aristocracy was also well entrenched, had such a low percentage.[2] In the interwar period, the population of East European Jews in the Bay Area would increase somewhat (especially in the Fillmore), but their number would not surpass that of Jews of German origin, as happened almost everywhere else.

Naturally, the paucity of East European Jewish immigration held back the overall growth of the Bay Area's Jewish population. During the half century between 1878 and 1927, San Francisco Jewry barely doubled, and its numbers grew more slowly than the city's population as a whole. By contrast, America's twenty-five other largest Jewish communities increased, on average, seventeenfold during that period.[3]

The small size of the Bay Area's East European Jewish neighborhoods created a kind of intimacy that was impossible to achieve in New York City, where immigrants often endured loneliness and anonymity along with poverty. This sense in San Francisco's Jewish neighborhoods that everyone knew everyone else may also have contributed to the relative

---

*A survey of San Francisco's public and private schools in 1908 revealed only 863 children born of "Hebrew, Russian" or "Hebrew, Polish" fathers—a mere 2.3 percent of all the city's youngsters (David George Herman, "Neighbors on the Golden Mountain" [Ph.D. diss., University of California, Berkeley, 1981], 294). In 1920, the government census listed only 5,800 Jews in the city born in the Russian Empire, the country that sent the overwhelming majority of *Ostjuden* (East European Jews) to America (Michael Kazin, *Barons of Labor* [Urbana, 1989], 201n). A demographic survey in 1938 concluded that almost eleven thousand San Francisco Jews (roughly 27 percent of the Jewish community) were born in Eastern Europe (Samuel Moment, *The Jewish Population of San Francisco* [San Francisco, 1939], n.p.). Including their native-born children and grandchildren, they likely approached parity with the German Jews by that point.

lack of crime. While Jewish prostitution did exist in freewheeling San Francisco,* it was negligible compared with the "abomination" of vice in Lower Manhattan that had shocked Judah Magnes when he moved East.[4] Absent, too, in the Bay Area were the infamous rings of Jewish extortionists, arsonists, and thieves that preyed upon their own people. Even the juvenile delinquency problem was "comparatively small" concluded a study undertaken in 1922.[5] In sum, in Oakland and San Francisco, Jews felt safe in their homes and on the streets.

They also enjoyed mild winters and expansive parks. Their aging wooden houses, substandard in the South of Market area in particular, were nonetheless preferable to the horribly congested tenements of New York City's Hester, Delancey, and Rivington streets, which suffered from bad ventilation and inadequate plumbing. Tuberculosis, the "white plague" that ravaged immigrant New York, was far less of a killer in California, and some Jews made the journey westward for reasons of health.

Very few Bay Area Jews toiled in the garment industry, and no other contrast with the eastern cities was more significant. By avoiding the needle trades immigrants were not only spared the rigors of the sweatshop, but they also were likely to become acculturated more quickly. Jews who slaved over sewing machines—whether in a dimly lit factory or at home— often had little connection with anyone other than Yiddish speakers. A peddler or storekeeper, on the other hand, was more likely to enjoy contact with a broader range of people.

These were, after all, not the dislocated Jews who had just come ashore at Ellis Island; they had migrated not only from Eastern Europe, but also from the eastern United States. By the time they arrived in California, an interval of several years and the distance of an entire continent had usually considerably blunted the trauma of immigration.

Still, the Northern California newcomers—usually poorly educated, low on funds, and barely fluent in English—formed distinct neighborhoods and were easily marked by their old-world background. And while some immigrants did realize their dreams, thousands remained impoverished, even in the prosperous Bay Area. They presented a problem that, if not considered

*Fremont Older wrote of a Jewish newcomer from the Lower East Side, "Helen of Bartlett Alley," who sold her body in the Tenderloin (Fremont Older, *My Story* [New York, 1926], 295–306).

acute by the general public, was taken seriously by the established Jewish community.

"AN INVASION FROM THE EAST"

Even before the turn of the century, the teeming South of Market neighborhood elicited the concern and contempt of local Jewish leaders. Like their counterparts across America, they thought the best remedy was moving the immigrants out of the city and onto farms, and in 1891 they proposed to raise $1,000,000 for that purpose.

Attempts to create Jewish agricultural colonies a few years earlier, such as the one in New Odessa, Oregon, had been unsuccessful. But the plan conceived in San Francisco added a twist: a semitropical location. At a mass meeting in B'nai B'rith Hall, eighteen prominent Northern California Jews, led by the progressive David Lubin, unveiled a "magnificent humanitarian enterprise."[6] They proposed the desolate Mexican territory of Baja California as the prime spot to absorb large numbers of East European Jews and thus solve the problem of their concentration in San Francisco.

Lubin, himself of Polish birth, was well intentioned; he genuinely understood the benefits of rural life and favored Baja California because that was where "the highest-priced plant products are produced . . . almonds, apricots, olives, oranges, lemons, citrons, figs, raisins, table and wine grapes."[7] But Jacob Voorsanger, who chaired the huge gathering, supported the Mexican scheme for other reasons. Emanu-El's influential rabbi was swayed by the remoteness of Baja California (more than six hundred miles from San Francisco) and that it lay outside the United States.* Unlike Lubin, he opposed colonization attempts in the Salinas Valley, Colusa County, and Nevada, and he was one of the very few American Jewish leaders to urge the federal government to end, or at least suspend, immigration.[8]

"We are confronted by an invasion from the East," Voorsanger warned, "that threatens to undo the work of two generations of American Jews."[9] He feared that the immigrants' tendency to "herd together and refuse to scatter" would cause "social and economic problems" for their

---

*The Baja plan failed because of the vast funds needed and the legal obstacles faced by private American citizens attempting to colonize part of another country.

coreligionists—"Israelites" whom the public would confuse with "Yiddish mumblers."[10]

Of course, such prejudice infuriated some local Jews. One letter to the *Emanu-El* accused "rich Jews" of being "the first to kick at their own kith, kin and kind." Was the elite "worried," the writer wanted to know, "that the Russian Jews are apt to overwhelm us here in San Francisco and . . . lower the social status of the Jews in this city and state?"[11]

In fact, few attacks on East European Jewish immigrants emanated from non-Jews, although Frank Norris's fictional portrayal, in his novel *McTeague,* of a Polish Jewish rag picker who kills his Hispanic wife for money exceeded even his demonizing of the craven German Jewish railroad agent in *The Octopus.* Zerkow of Polk Street

> had the thin, eager cat-like lips of the covetous; eyes that had grown keen as those of a lynx from long searching amidst muck and debris, and claw-like prehensile fingers—the fingers of a man who accumulates and never disburses. It was impossible to look at Zerkow and not know instantly that greed—inordinate insatiable greed—was the dominant passion of the man . . . groping hourly in the muckheap of the city for gold, for gold, for gold.[12]

A critically acclaimed best seller, *McTeague,* published in 1899, may have strengthened Voorsanger's argument, but the rabbi was nevertheless unable to divert the flow of East European immigrants away from his city. Even before the earthquake, he believed that a "seething and sickening center of Slavic Jewish immigration" had already come into existence in San Francisco.[13]

Yet even as he voiced his disgust for the "riff raff of Europe,"[14] Voorsanger and his lay leaders worked to alleviate the suffering of the immigrants—and to Americanize them. In 1890 he joined banker and industrialist Philip Lilienthal in forming the Jewish Alliance, an employment agency for East European Jews, which was effective in finding jobs statewide for the considerable contingent of Rumanians who arrived around 1900.[15] With other rabbis and businessmen, Voorsanger sought to provide Jewish education and training in civics to "the children of the proletariat," and in 1897 he launched the Jewish Educational Society, forerunner of today's Bureau of Jewish Education.[16] The Emanu-El Sisterhood for Personal Service, initiated three years earlier, had an even broader reach. Emulating the ambitious settlement houses of the East, the Emanu-El Sisterhood opened a building with classrooms, a kindergarten, and a gymnasium for the immigrants on

Folsom Street, in the South of Market area.[17] In 1905, Voorsanger's son William, a German-trained physician specializing in tuberculosis, inaugurated the Emanu-El Sisterhood Polyclinic on Seventh Street, heading a staff of a dozen doctors.[18] The temple's leading females also founded the local branch of the National Council of Jewish Women, which later instituted a highly effective settlement house on San Bruno Avenue.

Still, there would be antipathy toward the East European Jews, emanating not only from the largely Bavarian elite at Emanu-El, but also from Poseners at Sherith Israel. The Prussian Poles were not yet fully accepted socially by the Bavarians, but with the wave of Yiddish-speaking newcomers, the front line in the internal Jewish ethnic conflict shifted further to the east. Most Prussian Poles, by now long established in California, joined with those from west of Berlin to form a solid "German" front against the "Russians."

If anything, the ill will between Jews of different origins ran deeper in the Bay Area than in most other American cities, and it likely contributed to the small number of East European Jews who settled near the Golden Gate, as the records of a national Jewish organization indicate. In 1901, a New York–based agency with the unappealing name of the Industrial Removal Office (IRO), funded by Baron Maurice de Hirsch, began a concerted program of relocating Jews from the Northeast to the rest of the country. Unlike the ill-conceived agricultural projects, it sought manufacturing and retail jobs for the immigrants, and over two decades successfully transferred nearly eighty thousand Jews.[19] The IRO subsidized the train fares, but the project depended on cooperation in the receiving cities from B'nai B'rith lodges, prospective employers, rabbis, and communal workers.

San Francisco, with more than twenty-five thousand Jews in 1900, took in a meager number from the IRO—fewer than two thousand—during the first twenty years of the century.[20] Obviously, the great distance from New York was a hindrance, but Los Angeles, with a Jewish population of just 2,500, accepted considerably more immigrants from the IRO than did its big sister to the north.[21] In L.A., a large Jewish-owned department store, Hamburger's, not only offered jobs to new arrivals but even helped pay their transportation expenses.[22] In 1909, the IRO chairman praised Los Angeles along with Portland and Seattle for their "very cordial" relationship with his organization.[23]

A different spirit prevailed in San Francisco, however, reflected not only by Voorsanger's attitude, but also that of other leaders. In 1904, Philip Wascerwitz, grand president of B'nai B'rith District 4, insisted that "only proper material for good citizenship shall be given the opportunity for immigration [by] the order."[24] He warned, "Much caution must be exercised that the evil now existing in the East be not merely transplanted to our shores."[25]

That this attitude soured relations with the IRO may be seen in the following note—among several of its kind—penned in the spring of 1905 by the secretary of the local Jewish Alliance. Among a group of twelve skilled workers arriving in San Francisco under IRO auspices, eight were deemed "incompetent" or "unsatisfactory" and sent back. Isaiah Choynski, the journalist Isidore's brother and a Posener, wrote, "These people do not speak English, refuse to learn, and have little knowledge of the trades they profess. It is very hard to find work for them, and if employed, are lacking in every essential, to make good workmen."[26] Of course, there were similar cases across the country, but they were rare; nationally, fewer than 2 percent of the IRO's placements ended in this sort of failure.[27]

To be sure, in 1917 the San Francisco Federation of Jewish Charities established and liberally funded a new employment agency aimed at helping both Jewish and non-Jewish newcomers. But even though it successfully placed hundreds of job seekers, the federation's president, I. W. Hellman Jr., abruptly closed the bureau only two years later. He accepted the jaundiced report of a consultant: "The Jewish applicant, who offers a much lower grade of service as a rule, demands disproportionate wages and almost impossible opportunities and it is only after a great deal of explanation and cajoling that they can be persuaded to consider available openings."[28]

Michael Goldwater of Posen, grandfather of the Arizona senator Barry Goldwater and president of San Francisco's Hebrew Benevolent Society at the turn of the century, not only put forth the "bootstraps," or self-help, argument, but also suggested that his agency

be empowered to return [a new arrival] at once to his former place of residence which course will serve a double purpose: first, Eastern communities will know they cannot use this city as a dumping ground for their poor and sick; and secondly, our expense for the support of newcomers will be lessened to such a degree that more adequate assistance could be given to our own unfortunates.[29]

Those who successfully relocated from the Lower East Side often attracted their friends and relations, who arrived independently of the IRO, so the lack of success in San Francisco of the national resettlement effort had serious and long-term repercussions. To be fair, the tepid response of the local German Jewish establishment to such relocation efforts was not the only factor in making the Bay Area, for all its charms, an unpopular destination. San Francisco was simply not viewed as the beacon of economic opportunity it had been by Central European Jews half a century earlier in the wake of the Gold Rush. By the 1890s, the skilled craftsmen among the newcomers faced the challenge of breaking into the strongest unions in the country, while those in the needle trades found the industry largely in the hands of the Chinese and Irish. Opening one's own business was of course the dream of many immigrants, but in that regard, too, Los Angeles, which was expanding more rapidly than San Francisco, was generally considered more promising. Also weighing against San Francisco was the devastation wrought by the earthquake and fire precisely during the years that saw the highest number of Jews entering the country.*

Besides, the town hardly had a reputation for Jewish observance, which the Orthodox took into account. Until the late 1920s many secular Jews were equally put off by the dearth of Yiddish cultural life. And for no one did San Francisco—known around the country for its sin and scandals—seem to be an especially good environment for raising children.

Yet a welcoming Jewish community might have overcome all these concerns. And certainly if fifty thousand instead of ten thousand East European Jews had settled in San Francisco by the 1920s—a reasonable number given the experience of other big cities—Bay Area Jewry would have had a profoundly different future.

SOUTH OF THE SLOT

"The Slot was an iron crack that ran along the center of Market Street," wrote Jack London, who claimed that it "expressed the class cleavage of Society." He continued, "From the Slot arose the [cable] hitched at will to the cars it dragged up and down. . . . North of the Slot were the theatres,

---

*Los Angeles surpassed San Francisco in accepting immigrants through the IRO for the first time in 1908, no doubt reflecting the difficult conditions in the Bay Area. However, the earthquake and fire cannot have remained a major factor by 1912 and 1913, when L.A. drew more than three times the number settling in the San Francisco (IRO Records, 1899–1922).

hotels, and shopping districts, the banks and the staid, respectable business houses. South of the Slot were the factories, slums, laundries, machineshops, boiler works, and the abodes of the working class."[30]

The densely populated two square miles between Market and Townsend streets and from the waterfront to Eleventh Street, filled with saloons and boardinghouses, drew single men: migrant farm laborers, factory workers, miners, fishermen, and, above all, sailors. There were also many vagrants. But, especially before 1906, it was also a neighborhood of families, packed tightly into two- or three-story wooden row houses. In 1900, the average flat in this area held 10 people, compared with 6.4 citywide.[31]

East European Jews had lived south of the Slot since the mid-1870s. One was the future New York City congressman Sol Bloom, the youngest of five children, brought by his Orthodox mother from the Midwest in 1875. Bloom's father had come to San Francisco earlier, found a menial job, and rented a small house on Brannan Street. Sol was forced to drop out of school at age seven and for years worked twelve-hour days, six days a week, in a brush factory. His wages—$1.25 a week—were supplemented by hawking food at Sunday sports events, and if he had a spare moment he scavenged the nearby railway yards for lumps of coal to burn in the family's stove. "The one thing completely lacking in my boyhood," he wrote, "was play."[32]

There were other immigrant groups living south of the Slot, too—Irish, Scandinavians, and Germans, and later Portuguese, Italians, and Greeks—but certain pockets, like the alleys Harriet, Russ, and Moss, between Sixth and Seventh and from Howard to Folsom, were overwhelmingly Jewish. Another concentration could be found half of a mile away on Minna, Natoma, Tehama, and Clementina streets between Third and Fourth (today occupied by the Moscone Convention Center and the Yerba Buena Center for the Arts). The Jews were "inclined to isolate themselves," observed one journalist in 1895, who remarked that they were slow to learn English, adding, "they are industrious and frugal, but unable to compete with the advanced requirements of society."[33]

A cohesive, religiously observant community, unlike any the city had seen before, took hold south of Market Street. Numbering perhaps five thousand before the earthquake,[34] it supported kosher butcher shops run by families like the Shensons, bakeries such as Waxman's and Frisch's, and dairies like the one owned by the "*milchik* Shensons," not to be confused with the "*fleishik* Shensons," who presided over the meat market.[35] The Diller family had a grocery that did a brisk business, and other Jews ran fruit markets, clothing shops, and candy stores. The junk and scrap iron dealers were invariably Jewish as well; a few, like Gershon Sugarman from Vilna, became respected community leaders.*

Saturdays most of the Jewish-owned businesses closed, and "nearly everybody went to the synagogue . . . there was no separation of church and state," remembered Art Rosenbaum, the *Chronicle* sports page editor who grew up south of the Slot.[36] His father, who ran a modest secondhand shop, was learned in the Talmud and a mainstay of Chevra Tillim, then on Russ Street. Congregation Keneseth Israel, later the hub of the Fillmore-McAllister neighborhood, was another of the Orthodox synagogues in the area. The pioneer Congregation Beth Israel began south of the Slot as well, and although it moved a few blocks above Market in 1879, it still attracted residents from the area. While spiritual life centered on these shuls, smaller groups of worshippers could also be found in *shtieblach*, prayer rooms complete with Torah scrolls, inside a rabbi's house.

Jews south of the Slot, seeking to replicate communal institutions they had known in eastern Europe, created two that have served Bay Area Jews ever since. In 1897 they founded Chevra Gemilus Chasodim, later called the Hebrew Free Loan Association (HFLA). By 1910, a thousand members each paid dues of three dollars a year, which, along with the money generated from frequent fundraising events, was used for small interest-free loans to needy Jews, often newly arrived immigrants or breadwinners who had lost their jobs in the disaster of 1906.[37]

In 1901, leading neighborhood Jews such as Gershon Sugarman and Bernard Diller established an Orthodox burial society, Chevra Kadisha, that a generation later was reorganized as Sinai Memorial Chapel. Like the HFLA, Chevra Kadisha was much concerned with the poor: indigent Jews were laid to rest without charge.

An old-world atmosphere permeated the South of Market district even as late as in the Depression. William (Ze'ev) Brinner, later chairman of the Department of Near Eastern Studies at UC Berkeley, grew up on Moss Street in the 1920s and early '30s and recalls Jewish peddlers selling ice, fruit, and vegetables from horse-drawn carts.[38] Housewives picked out live

---

*Soon after coming to San Francisco Sugarman befriended a shipping clerk, James Rolph, who would become mayor from 1911 to 1932. The two remained "inseparable," enabling the kindhearted Sugarman to aid many Jewish immigrants in trouble over the years (*Emanu-El*, June 1, 1934, 7).

chickens in the market and brought them to the *shochet* to have them ritually slaughtered. The modern, well-stocked department stores of Market Street were only blocks away, but they could just as well have been in another world.

As a child, Art Rosenbaum sold newspapers on the corner, earning twenty cents an evening, and his father worked interminable hours to support a family of eight.[39] Youngsters on their way to school often saw homeless people and drunks in the streets, and Rosenbaum recalled the time when an alcoholic came into his father's store and tried to sell his shoes in order to buy liquor.[40] Yet, as seedy as it was, according to its former residents, the neighborhood was safe, especially for children.[41] People left the doors of their houses unlocked.

Fistfights between members of different ethnic groups were not unknown in this rough end of town, but there was also a lot of friendly mingling at school, on the playgrounds, and even in one another's homes. Young Brinner's closest friends were a Japanese boy and a Portuguese youngster, in whose house Ze'ev ate unkosher food (horrifying his mother when she learned of it).[42] In the end, "we didn't feel that different" as Jews, said Rosenbaum; "there was a sense that *all* of us were the descendants of immigrants."[43]

OUT THE ROAD

Not unlike the denizens of the Lower East Side, Jews sought to leave the decaying South of Market district as soon as they had the means to do so. Other, more recently arrived immigrants took their places over nearly three generations. But one event caused a sudden exodus of many hundreds of Jewish families. The fire of 1906, which remade San Francisco in many ways, quickly consumed the flimsy wooden dwellings south of the Slot and led to the creation of two new Jewish neighborhoods.

The refugees from the inferno had few options. One largely Orthodox group relocated in the remote southeastern part of town, five miles from their original homes, in the area around San Bruno Avenue, known as "Out the Road." The eight-square-block district (bordered by San Bruno Avenue to the east, Bowdoin to the west, Sweeny to the north, and Olmstead to the south) would contain a lively, traditional Jewish community until World War II. At its height, in the 1920s, there were more than a thousand Jews there, around a quarter of the neighborhood's total population, which also included Italian, Portuguese, and Maltese immigrants.[44]

Jews operated shops on San Bruno and Silver avenues, but this area was better known for its peddlers, who drove horse-drawn wagons from which they sold the cheapest household wares. There were numerous scavengers, too, who rode through San Francisco or the farm towns on the Peninsula, calling out "rags, bottles, sacks," and at the end of the day delivering their hauls to a junk dealer.[45]

The little community in this area regarded itself as distinct from the downtown East European Jews and in 1912 established its own free loan society, which had 130 members by the end of World War I. With a few hundred dollars lent by the association, a destitute Jew could at least acquire a horse and wagon and go into business as a hawker.

Even the poorest Jews tended to dress up for the Sabbath after a visit to the popular Russian bathhouse on Silver Avenue. One woman who grew up in the neighborhood remembered her "ragged" grandfather, who rummaged in the city's refuse all day but still donned a cutaway coat, striped pants, and derby hat every Friday afternoon, an outfit "he must have taken off a dead butler."[46]

The most active synagogue in the Out the Road neighborhood, Mokum Israel, founded in 1907, soon engaged the Russian-born rabbi Morris Block, who served for eighteen years. Supporting eleven children, he was also the neighborhood's bar mitzvah tutor, *shochet,* and *mohel.*[47] There were other small Orthodox synagogues in the area, but the most important Jewish institution by far was the Esther Hellman Settlement House, known as "the Club." Here, in a plain two-story house on San Bruno Avenue, an immensely successful experiment in Jewish social service struck just the right balance between the twin goals of Americanizing the immigrants and respecting their native culture.

The Club was begun in 1918 by the local chapter of the National Council for Jewish Women, and underwritten by society women like the late Esther Hellman's daughter, Clara Heller. Yet it owed most of its success to its indefatigable founding director, Grace Wiener. The daughter of Temple Emanu-El's sexton was "a prim lady who never hugged anyone," but for two decades she devoted herself to the neighborhood's Jews.[48] Under her supervision, the tastefully furnished Club provided a well-baby clinic staffed by a nurse and visiting pediatricians from Mount Zion Hospital, a small gymnasium and library, and classes in music and dance, sewing and cooking, weaving and painting.[49]

The Club's Hebrew school was directed by another selfless, unmarried woman, Annette Levy, principal of a public school for wayward boys.[50]

Educator Moshe Menuhin (Yehudi's father) taught Hebrew, while Emanu-El's cantor, Reuben Rinder (himself an East European immigrant), taught Jewish religious practice and its meaning, always remaining sensitive to the Orthodox rites that his students saw at home.[51] At the Club's annual confirmation ceremony, the stage was exquisitely decorated, just as it was at Emanu-El, and each girl was presented a great bouquet of flowers. "We thought everyone lived this way," remembers one former student. "Even if [the German Jewish elite] would not imagine us mixing with their children . . . they were trying to give us the same kind of upbringing."[52] Miss Wiener expected her charges to know how to use a finger bowl at a fancy restaurant and much more:

> We had the Eastern European parent . . . whose values were what they brought from Europe, and they were Orthodox. The second parent figure was Miss Wiener, whose ambitions for us were to get a higher education and go on to college, and she nudged, and pushed, and nagged, and looked very disapprovingly. We were all afraid of her disapproval; we excelled because of her. We would have excelled because of our parents, but in a different direction. Their ambitions were economic security and not much else.[53]

When the speaker of that tribute informed Miss Wiener that she was going to Commerce High instead of top-rated Lowell, her second Jewish mother grew "absolutely furious."[54]

Safe and nurturing, and more pleasant than the crowded South of Market neighborhood, the San Bruno Avenue area still could not retain most of the Jews who had grown up there. Although the neighborhood (about a mile north of Candlestick Park) is easily reached by freeway today, it was isolated before World War II. Even in the mid-1930s, "we'd have to take three streetcars to get downtown," remembers a resident, "and when a young man offered to drive me home from a dance, he often changed his mind when he found out how far away I lived. 'Nobody's ever going to come out there,' we thought, 'We'll never get married!'"[55]

By 1940 only a few hundred Jews remained "Out the Road," and after the war the Club and synagogues closed down. Coincidentally, though, a Jewish community of another sort took root just to the east beginning in 1923. After more than two decades of legal wrangling over the bequest of businessman Julius Friedman, the Hebrew Home for the Aged Disabled finally received funds to construct a nursing home on a wooded ten-acre tract along Silver Avenue. Today's highly regarded Jewish Home San Francisco, having added buildings almost every decade, still occupies the site, keeping alive the sounds of Yiddish in this corner of San Francisco.

THE FABULOUS FILLMORE

Like the San Bruno Avenue area, the Fillmore District began to draw a substantial number of Jews from the South of Market quarter starting in 1906. But unlike the Out the Road area, the Fillmore boasted every manner of amusement. As a result, it grew far more populous than the neighborhood in southern San Francisco and kept some of its distinctive flavor into the 1960s.

The Fillmore, as it has long been called, is near the geographical center of the city, but early in the twentieth century it sat on the western edge of the developed part of town and was spared serious damage from the earthquake and fire. In 1906, many of its Victorian houses were quickly converted into multifamily dwellings, with their ground floors housing businesses whose downtown locations had been destroyed. For a year or two after the calamity, Fillmore Street was the city's busiest commercial thoroughfare, and the area remained a mercantile hub even after the largest stores returned to Market Street and Union Square.

Jews resided largely in the neighborhood's southern end, on Fillmore and the streets running parallel to it like Steiner, Webster, Buchanan, Octavia, and Laguna, from Haight to Geary streets. The blocks near the intersection of Fillmore and McAllister streets were filled with Orthodox Jewish institutions. But the Fillmore was also the most ethnically diverse district in San Francisco. In addition to housing immigrants from Italy, Ireland, Russia, Rumania, it was also home to a good number of blacks by the 1920s and to Japanese immigrants even earlier.[56]

The wide range of cuisine available reflected the diversity of the neighborhood. The Jewish eateries included tempting bakeries like Langendorf's, Waxman's, and the Ukraine, known for their rye and pumpernickel breads; kosher restaurants, of which Diller's was the most highly regarded; and sumptuous delicatessens such as Goldenrath's.[57] Yet on the same streets one could also find delicious Hungarian, Greek, Mexican, Italian, and Chinese food.

The Fillmore was an entertainment mecca for the entire city. Just north of where the Jews were concentrated, on Ellis Street, was a popular vaudeville house, the Princess Theatre, which on one bill would present five routines, such as jugglers, acrobats, magicians, comedians, or even dog acts. A few blocks away, on Fillmore Street, the Dreamland Rink stood until 1927, when it was torn down and replaced by the Winterland Arena, which lasted until late in the century. The wooden Dreamland, a roller-skating rink and boxing arena, also hosted world-famous lecturers such as Emma Goldman and Rabbi Stephen Wise, who spoke there during World War I. Around the corner was an ice-skating rink, home for a while to a professional hockey team. But the greatest draw was the "picture shows." Along one eight-block stretch of Fillmore Street were seven movie theaters, offering everything from first-run talkies to silent films accompanied by an organ.[58]

The streets themselves had the aura of an amusement park, resembling Coney Island more than Hester Street. Just after the earthquake local merchants erected tall, curving metal arches, which gracefully swept upward from each of the four corners of the fourteen intersections along Fillmore from Fulton to Sacramento streets, a full mile. The arches were dotted with dozens of electric bulbs, and where the four branches came together, high above the intersection, great globes of light hung down.* They were "like the illuminated ribs of a great umbrella,"[59] wrote one former resident, describing what was the most brilliantly lit street in the country in 1907.

By the early 1940s people were coming to the Fillmore for jazz. Dave Rosenbaum, Art's youngest brother, married a black woman, and he also shocked his father by opening a record shop on Sutter near Fillmore specializing in New Orleans–style "hot jazz" as well as Negro spirituals.[60] Every Sunday he presented superb black musicians such as Turk Murphy, Saunders King, and Buck Johnson.

The Fillmore set many temptations in the path of Jewish immigrant children from observant homes. Ze'ev Brinner and Art Rosenbaum, whose families had moved here from south of the Slot, were now grudgingly permitted by their parents to go to the movies on Saturday afternoons. But they were still required to attend services on Saturday mornings.[61]

No less than its worldly attractions, the fervent religious life of the Fillmore remained in the minds of many of those raised there. There were three major synagogues, each with roots south of Market Street. Keneseth Israel, or the Webster Street Shul, was just off McAllister in the heart of Jewish Fillmore, with two kosher restaurants on the same block. Its rabbi during

---

*The arches remained until 1943, when dim-out regulations and the wartime need for scrap metal led to their demise.

most of the interwar period was Wolf Gold, a spellbinding preacher active in the Mizrachi movement (of Orthodox Zionists) and a powerful advocate for Jewish education. On the High Holidays the good-sized synagogue overflowed with worshippers, the men on the main floor and the women occupying the large balcony to the last row. "It was a noisy place with a lot of side-talking," said Art Rosenbaum, who also recalled "the musty smell, especially during Yom Kippur. People would arrive at six in the morning and stay all day long. Body odor and bad breath were pretty evident. They didn't open the windows."[62]

Around the corner was Anshe Sfard (so named despite its paucity of Sephardim), under the leadership of the austere Lithuanian Talmud scholar Rabbi Mayer Hirsch. The Golden Gate Avenue Shul, as it was called, was smaller, poorer and even more rigidly Orthodox than Keneseth Israel but would outlive its rival by moving to the Richmond District after World War II.[63]

The third congregation, founded at the end of the Gold Rush decade, was quite different. Beth Israel erected an imposing brick-and-steel synagogue on Geary Street just before the earthquake and, after its destruction, rebuilt it on the same site. With its elaborate wood-carved *bimah* (elevated platform in front of the ark), stained-glass windows, and imposing exterior, the Geary Street Temple was the most visible symbol of traditional Judaism in the city for more than half a century.[64] But Beth Israel, with its pioneer roots, was *in* but not *of* the Jewish Fillmore of poor immigrants. Located six long blocks from McAllister Street, it drew its members not only from the neighborhood but also from better parts of the city, people who in New York would have been called *alrightniks*. One Beth Israel president, Isidore Golden, served as a superior court judge in the 1930s.

The congregation was already Modern Orthodox during the quarter-century rabbinate of civic-minded M. S. Levy, which ended in 1916. Under the long leadership of Rabbi Elliot Burstein (1927–69), a political liberal and Zionist ordained at the Jewish Theological Seminary, the Geary Street Temple gravitated toward Conservative Judaism. Burstein even had a connection with Emanu-El after his daughter married a Zellerbach. Near the end of Burstein's tenure, Beth Israel abandoned its home in the drastically changed Fillmore and merged with a Reform synagogue on the city's southern edge, Temple Judea on Brotherhood Way.

One cantor, the learned and beloved Joseph Rabinowitz, served Beth Israel from 1891 to 1943, for nearly half of its independent existence. Rabinowitz had inherited a traditional musical style from his famous family of

Lithuanian cantors.[65] But on Geary Street, his rich baritone voice, accompanied by an organ and a choir of men and women, harmoniously blended old and new.

Rabinowitz, an eloquent advocate of Zionism even before the turn of the century, had considerable influence on Jewish youth. But it was another Litvak (Jew from Lithuania), Rabbi David Stolper, a small man with piercing eyes and a Vandyke beard, who profoundly affected hundreds of Jewish children in the Fillmore and transformed Hebrew education in San Francisco.

Before the 1920s, Jewish learning in the immigrant quarters was in chaos. Struggling freelance "Hebrew experts" with no pedagogical training prepared boys for their bar mitzvah ceremonies but provided little grounding in Jewish history, ethics, or religious practice.[66] The Jewish Educational Society operated schools south of the Slot, Out the Road, and in the Fillmore, but these institutions were underfunded and devoted more classroom hours to civics and hygiene than Jewish learning.

In 1918, the Russian-born, Jerusalem-educated Moshe Menuhin, an excellent Hebraist, was hired to direct the Jewish Educational Society, now supported with funds from the Federation of Jewish Charities. But Menuhin, perhaps rebelling against his Hasidic upbringing, showed scant respect for Jewish law—little Yehudi reportedly let slip to Wolf Gold that the family ate ham—and the traditional rabbis lost all trust in him.[67] Disaffected, too, by Menuhin's anti-Zionism (a position that would only harden during his long lifetime), they organized a rival network of religious schools, the Talmud Torah Association. As its director they chose the newly arrived Rabbi Stolper, who was thoroughly versed in classical Jewish texts and committed to teaching synagogue skills. In 1927, with Menuhin in Europe managing the career of his extraordinary son, the rabbis agreed to merge the Talmud Torah Association into the Jewish Educational Society, with Stolper as its head.[68] He would remain at his post until his death two decades later.

For all his outward piety and emphasis on ritual, Stolper was at heart a modern Jew, an adherent of the Russian Haskalah, or Jewish Enlightenment, who had pursued secular studies at the University of Vienna. He spoke to his wife, who seemed little interested in Judaism, in Russian.[69] (Their only son died before they came to America.) The adventurous Stolper had moved to Siberia after the October Revolution and opened a Jewish school there before crossing the Pacific. In San Francisco, on a walk home from Sabbath services one day, he confided he was "not a believer" to one of his star pupils, who himself doubted God's existence. "In Judaism you don't believe, you do," the rabbi told him.[70]

And Stolper was nothing if not a doer. He ran six schools across the city but accomplished most at the Jewish Educational Society's flagship, the Central Hebrew School, housed in a substantial brick building on Grove and Buchanan streets.* To be sure, student records were disorganized and a couple of the teachers incompetent. Stolper himself was a fine instructor but temperamental: "He sometimes threw an eraser at a kid who wouldn't behave," remembers Ze'ev Brinner.[71] Yet the community he created, of several hundred boys and girls and their families, demonstrated what was possible even in the *"midbar,"* or wasteland, that the rabbi called San Francisco. Stolper provided the only opportunity for intensive Jewish learning in the city, and for Brinner's mother, sending him and his sister to the Central Hebrew School was the main reason for moving from South of Market to the Fillmore.[72]

"We were there seven days a week," recalled a future attorney and Jewish community leader. Classes met for two hours a day after public school (Stolper was interested in what the children were learning there, too) and focused on Hebrew, Jewish history, prayer, the Bible, and esoteric texts as well.[73] On the Sabbath pupils conducted their own services; only on the High Holidays would Stolper, a sweet-singing tenor, himself lead the young congregation. Whether or not their parents were affiliated with a synagogue, students participated in bar mitzvah ceremonies at the Central Hebrew School.[74]

The school had an active youth group, a drama club, and an annually published student-run magazine with articles in English and (with the rabbi's help) Hebrew. A high degree of parental involvement was encouraged. Every Sunday, after students finished their morning prayers and studies, the Mothers Club prepared a hearty breakfast for them. It all served to endow Jewish learning with importance, and grateful alumni include local clergy such as Rabbis David Teitelbaum and David Robbins and Cantor Henry Greenberg; lay leaders such as George Karonsky, Art Zimmerman, and Daniel Goldberg; the philanthropist Sanford Diller; and, of course, Professor Ze'ev Brinner. During the war, graduates of the Central Hebrew

---

*Constructed in 1925, on land acquired by the Federation of Jewish Charities and with funds from the estate of a local businessman, Aaron Alper, it also housed the Hebrew Free Loan Association. The structure is today a Korean senior center.

School were scattered all over the globe in the armed forces, often far from a rabbi, and some wrote to Stolper that the training they received as teenagers enabled them to lead services.[75]

To maintain the Jewish Educational Society, Stolper needed to supplement the nominal tuition he charged and the modest allocation received from the Jewish National Welfare Fund (and later the Federation of Jewish Charities). He solicited donations not only from affluent East European families like the Dillers, but also from German Jewish philanthropists active in Emanu-El. Its ultra-Reform rabbi, Irving Reichert, and Cantor Reuben Rinder were members of Stolper's board.

But though he benefited from their largesse, the rabbi had no love for the Emanu-El crowd. Brinner recalls him saying, "They think that without the school we'd all be criminals."[76] Several of the teachers railed against liberal Judaism, and Brinner and his classmates were taught to spit every time they walked past a Reform temple.[77] Art Rosenbaum told of similar venom spewed from the pulpits of Keneseth Israel and Anshe Sfard: "They cursed the modern Reform Jews as sinners and predicted total hell for us if we adopted that attitude. . . . We learned literally to hate Fleishhacker, Haas, and Temple Emanu-El."[78] The enmity ran so deep, he claimed, that soon after the Nazis came to power, some immigrants in the Fillmore were "not sorry to see the German Jews get their comeuppance."[79]

But the attacks against the city's Jewish elite cut both ways. The teenaged Rosenbaum wondered

why we had to go to services from 8 to 1 and they went [only] to Sunday school from 10 to 11:50, why, on Yom Kippur, they only went from 10 to 5 and were home before sunset while we had to stay until dark, why they all had nice suits and came to the synagogue in automobiles, some with chauffeurs, why the Jewish newspaper was called the *Emanu-El,* and ran wedding announcements mostly for the Reform families, why the church page of the *Chronicle* would always have something on them and never Keneseth Israel, [why their] public relations [and fundraising efforts] consisted of printed literature while ours was some old rabbi knocking on the door and asking for a donation to a yeshiva back in a place we never heard of.[80]

"Maybe they knew something we didn't," he concluded.[81] He married a German Jewish woman who had her own prejudices against East European immigrants. Before her first visit to Art's home she was "frightened and thought [his] parents wouldn't be able to speak English and that [his] father had a long beard."[82]

ter the war the rift between the two groups would narrow. The nbaums joined a Reform temple, Sherith Israel, and many of his childhood friends became members of Conservative synagogues. But they rarely forgot their roots in the traditional Fillmore. "It took me ten or fifteen years to get accustomed to the Reform [liturgy]," said Art, and even then he found it "sterile and plastic."[83]

This was part of the complex legacy the Fillmore bequeathed to the young people it sent into the world: a creative tension between Orthodoxy and liberal Judaism, between Jewish pride and a respect for other cultures, and between high ideals taught in school and survival instincts learned on the street. It all occurred in the middle of a city that, despite some hard times, seemed a unique spot with a limitless future. "From the rooftops of the Fillmore even during the Depression," says Brinner, "we could see the Bay Bridge rising."[84]

A VARIETY OF IDEOLOGIES

Like the rest of Jews in prewar America, those in the Fillmore enjoyed a rich secular Jewish culture apart from—and in some ways opposed to—its synagogues. As soon as Jews moved to the neighborhood, many joined the Workmen's Circle (or Arbeiter Ring, in Yiddish), a mutual aid society that provided funds for emergency medical needs and death benefits, and held weekly lectures and discussions. It also advocated socialism, opposed Zionism, and often ridiculed religion.

The group was organized in 1908 by a fiery agitator from Kishinev, Harry Koblick, who owned a bookstore on Fillmore near McAllister. He made more money selling comic books than revolutionary literature, but his passion was the political empowerment of the working class.[85] Koblick ardently campaigned for the socialist presidential candidate Eugene Debs and presented a series of militantly prounion speakers.

But, like many chapters across the country, the San Francisco Arbeiter Ring split in two after the Bolshevik Revolution, and a handful of Jewish communists tried to take over its headquarters on O'Farrell near Fillmore. So dogmatic were the Leninists that they gave up all Jewish culture save the Yiddish language, and retained that only so they would be able to communicate with the immigrant workers. Koblick tried to mediate between the socialists and Communists, but the rancor was so great that police were often needed to restore order.[86] Ultimately he lost control of the facility to the Communist International and moved the Workmen's Circle into the busy Yiddish cultural center on Steiner Street. It was a painful choice, but in the end he was unwilling to jettison his Jewish sensibilities from his Marxist ideology.

Left-wing politics abounded on Steiner Street, but Yiddish culture was paramount. One couple in particular, Philip and Bassya Bibel, were instrumental in fostering the language, literature, music, and drama of East European Jewry in the Fillmore through the 1930s. When Phil Bibel, in his early twenties, arrived in San Francisco from Poland in 1927, he discovered many opportunities to communicate in his mother tongue.[87] New York newspapers like the *Forward, Freiheit,* and *Tog* were sold at two local bookshops, and a Yiddish literary and drama club met occasionally at the YMHA on Haight Street. There was even a cafe, the Europa on Fillmore Street, which could have been on the Lower East Side or in Warsaw. Over glasses of tea, immigrants discussed the world's problems in their native language day and night.

But the furniture maker felt more could be done to advance Yiddish in the "assimilated, almost gentile" city.[88] With other enthusiasts he organized lectures, staged amateur dramas, and began to invite well-known playwrights from New York. Bibel and his friends caught an early break when Rabbi Louis Newman of Emanu-El, himself a playwright and lyricist, attended their events and decided to stage a major Yiddish production in his synagogue's new Temple House on Lake Street.[89]

Newman's idea took Bibel by surprise. "We were like oil and water then," he said. "We were the oil—effervescent and sparkling. They were the water—placid."[90] But he could not have been more pleased with the "blending of the two cultures" that in the fall of 1928 produced *The Dybbuk,* S. Ansky's gripping drama of an exorcism, drawn from medieval Jewish folklore.[91] To direct it, Newman engaged Nahum Zemach, who had founded the celebrated Habima troupe in Moscow during the Russian Revolution but had fled the Soviet Union with his company in 1926. The cast of about fifty included both temple members and Jewish immigrants from the Fillmore. Although the unquestioned star was Carolyn Anspacher, the granddaughter of pioneers, Zemach wrote a special part for the twenty-year-old Ukrainian refugee who would soon marry Phil Bibel.* The play drew

---

*Bassya Bibel believed that Zemach would have preferred her over Anspacher in the lead role, but that the Emanu-El leadership pressured him into choosing one of their own as the headliner (Philip Bibel, "San Francisco Jews," oral history project of the WJHC/JLMM, 1978, Marcia Frank, interviewer, tape 1).

more than eight thousand people during its two-week run, and critics were unanimous in their praise of the detailed sets, eerie lighting, and inspired acting.[92]

The success of *The Dybbuk* emboldened the Bibels to produce Yiddish plays by H. Leivick, Sholom Aleichem, and Peretz Hirshbein, usually at Scottish Rite Hall on Van Ness Avenue.[93] The Russian-born Hirshbein, whose greatest play, *Green Fields,* extols the pleasures of the countryside, eventually moved from New York to the artist colony of Carmel, and the Bibels developed a deep friendship with him and his wife. They often invited Hirshbein to speak at Steiner Street, where they also presented other popular Yiddish authors, including dramatist David Pinski, poet Abraham Reisen, and novelist Sholem Asch.[94]

In 1934 Maurice Schwartz, the frenetic producer who had built the greatest Yiddish repertory company in America, came to town. At the Tivoli Theatre he both directed and played the title role in *Yoshe Kalb,* based on I. J. Singer's critical portrait of Hasidic life. Schwartz's success was in sharp contrast to the apathy he had encountered more than a decade and a half earlier when he had been "warned by friends against playing San Francisco, because of the apparent diffidence of its Jewish citizens."* By the mid-1930s, though, Yiddish culture in the city was flourishing, and Philip Bibel had a large enough readership to publish the weekly *Yiddishe Presse.*† Characteristic of San Francisco journalism, it not only carried news and cultural criticism but also revealed local scandals.[95]

The Yiddish culture that sprang to life during the Depression left little room for Judaism. The Bibels celebrated their son's bar mitzvah in a synagogue—his speech and much of the ceremony were in Yiddish—but some went further and forswore any connection to a Jewish house of worship. They sent their children to a socialist-oriented Yiddish school as an alternative to the education offered by Stolper and the other rabbis. The Ukrainian dressmaker and union organizer Zena Druckman was a founder

---

* He came to San Francisco anyway in 1918, and not only was attendance at the play he produced abysmal, but Schwartz also encountered "absurd" opinions about Yiddish in B'nai B'rith circles and at Temple Emanu-El. He was told his native tongue was "simply a jargon . . . mixed with German, Polish and having many confused sources" (*Jewish Journal,* August 7, 1929, 3).

† The *Yiddishe Presse,* however, was not the city's first Yiddish newspaper; the short-lived *Yiddishe Shtimme* (Jewish Voice) had appeared before World War I.

of the local *kindershul* in 1939, where roughly sixty children learned Yiddish instead of Hebrew and celebrated May Day rather than most of the Jewish holidays. Anything could be taught, recalled a proud Druckman, even the story of Passover, as long as it was "without God."[96]

For all of their initiatives though, the Yiddishists were waging a war they could never win. Even Phil Bibel granted that few of the immigrants' American-born children would speak and read, much less write, their parents' language.[97] And the relatively small size of the East European Jewish community before the war, compared to that of, say, Los Angeles, made the struggle even harder.*

Also facing long odds, it surely seemed at the time, were dreamers of a different stripe, the Zionists of the Fillmore, who sought to create a Hebrew-speaking nation in Palestine. A stronghold of Jewish nationalism was Congregation Beth Israel, where Rabbi M. S. Levy had founded the Helpers of Zion back in the nineteenth century. It had long been dormant, but Zionist activity in San Francisco resumed during World War I, invigorated not only by the Balfour Declaration but also by the presence of thousands of East European Jewish newcomers in the city. They were much readier to embrace the concept of a Jewish homeland than were the descendants of the German-speaking pioneer Jews.

In the 1920s, Leo Rabinowitz, son of Beth Israel's long-serving cantor, emerged as the leader of the San Francisco District of the Zionist Organization of America (ZOA) and deftly worked to secure funds for Palestine from the city's Jewish National Welfare Fund. Another ZOA president, Judge Isidore Golden, was well served by his close ties with local Sinn Féin members when he sought support for Zionism among Irish politicians.[98]

But the ZOA was constantly battling the powerful anti-Zionist forces in town. While Emanu-El rabbis Martin Meyer and Louis Newman and of course Cantor Rinder and his wife Rose (who founded the local Hadassah chapter) were enthusiastic supporters, many leading temple members feared that the creation of a Jewish state might cast doubt on their loyalty to America. Chaim Weizmann's request to speak at Emanu-El was turned down in 1924, and the city's Jewish elite caused the ZOA "great difficulty" even in

* By the 1920s, when L.A.'s Jewish population passed that of San Francisco, the heavily Orthodox neighborhood of Boyle Heights alone contained about ten thousand Jewish families (Vorspan and Gartner, *Jews of Los Angeles*, 118).

presenting him at the Civic Center.[99] The event drew a massive crowd, though, and he also spoke at Keneseth Israel.[100] Yet Zionism remained weak until after World War II. The pulpit rabbis of the Fillmore, particularly Wolf Gold (who later moved to New York to head the national Mizrachi movement) and Elliot Burstein at Beth Israel were articulate advocates. But in the 1930s they had to contend with a fiercely anti-Zionist spiritual leader at Emanu-El, Irving Reichert, who sounded the "dual loyalties" alarm throughout the West.

And there might have been another factor, perhaps stronger in San Francisco than elsewhere, that inhibited Zionism among East European Jews, even though most felt an affinity for the movement. It was the notion, left unspoken, that the promised land was under their feet.

FARMER-INTELLECTUALS

Perhaps the Jewish immigrants' most heated ideological arguments took place not in San Francisco but in the old farming town of Petaluma, forty miles north of the Golden Gate. By the early 1920s, a close-knit community of about a hundred East European Jewish families emerged, nearly all of them raising chickens. "It was the strangest thing," said a visitor: "Here the Kelleys live in town and the Cohens live on the farms."[101]

The easy availability of credit enabled people to get started in the business, but chicken ranching was "backbreaking work," as one old-timer recalled, requiring

> hauling sacks of feed, picking kale for making feed, taking care of sick chickens. All hours, seven days a week, no vacations, in all kinds of weather. You got that chicken-killing heat in the summers when [they] would drop like flies, and then the freezing rains in the winter. . . . The chicken house floods—can you imagine thousands of chicks swimming for their lives? Just cleaning those chicken houses . . . a lot of prominent people in this community began by hiring themselves to shovel chicken shit.[102]

But as hard as they toiled during the day, these poultry farmers enjoyed a rich political and cultural life in the evenings. For most had chosen a life on the land out of idealism—Zionist, socialist, communist—and the first generation generally held on to their aspirations. "The only thing similar I have seen," said Ze'ev Brinner, who taught Sunday school there in the 1930s, "was the early kibbutzniks in Israel. They too were farmer-intellectuals."[103]

Many Petaluma Jews were preparing for *aliyah,* or immigration to the Jewish homeland, and in 1925 about a dozen families whom the British had barred from Palestine actually formed a kibbutz in Petaluma.[104] As the years passed and their obligations grew, few actually left the bucolic Sonoma community, but the energetic chapters of Hadassah, Pioneer Women, and Poale Zion made it a bastion of Jewish nationalism in the West.[105] Golda Meir spoke there before the War of Independence, as did other Zionist luminaries.

Yet Petaluma's Jewish communists—also well informed and well organized—doggedly opposed Zionism. There was also a tiny Orthodox contingent in the small town, and ferocious clashes among the various groups continued for decades. The opening round was the furor over the Jewish Community Center (today's Congregation B'nai Israel), which opened in 1925 with the aid of a gift of Fannie Haas (widow of the grocery magnate Abraham Haas), who aided the Jewish poultry farmers in a myriad of ways.[106] The modest structure, still standing on Western Avenue, would house almost all of the town's many Jewish organizations, but the project almost foundered over the question of whether it ought to include a synagogue. Half a century after the bitter dispute, a religious Jew was still angry at "the radicals," who

> said the *shul yidn* [synagogue Jews] are parasites who do nothing but *davn* (pray) and study like in the Old Country. You know, *benkl kvetchers*—people who just sit [on a bench and complain]. They said the *shul yidn* are religious fanatics . . . but these radicals [were] the fanatics. They think [they're] gonna get some disease if there's a shul in the Center.[107]

As a compromise, one small room in the building was reserved for prayer. But when the communists' demand that worshippers enter and leave through a separate entrance was rejected, many of the leftists bolted the new center, not to return for decades. During the McCarthy era, the fight over the use of the JCC between the *linke* (left) and *rechte* (right) was even more acrimonious; a county judge was called in to settle it.[108]

Yet, as Brinner points out, despite their internecine warfare, Petaluma's immigrant Jews shared more than they realized.[109] They were bound together by Yiddish, their love for outdoor labor, and, above all, their commitment to transforming society. Whatever their ideology, they were invariably well versed in Jewish history, literature, and philosophy. The chicken ranchers kept up with events in Washington and New York, the Soviet Union and

Palestine. And in turn, the little Jewish farming community was known all over the world.

Oakland, too, gave rise to a Yiddish-speaking Jewish community, in the area west of Broadway between Third and Twelfth streets.[110] Pioneers, including some Jewish merchants, had built fine Victorian homes in this tranquil section a generation earlier. But, by the turn of the century, uncontrolled industrial growth had begun to take its toll in the flatlands: factories and new railroad lines added to the noise and congestion, and the busy commercial district drew closer. Those who could moved east or north.

Their places were taken by Mexicans, Italians, and, conspicuously, East European Jews. Frequently seen on Castro, Chestnut, and Myrtle streets were bearded, black-coated peddlers, uncomfortable in the warm sun. Women, their hair in scarves, hurriedly compared prices among the half dozen kosher butchers. Small boys, Hebrew books under their arms, made their way from public school to the daily Talmud Torah on Brush Street.

There were two major Orthodox congregations, Beth Abraham and Beth Jacob, but, as in San Francisco, many rabbis, like Yitzchak Rabinowitz, operated not in a synagogue but at home. The descendant of a long line of Rumanian rabbis, he was brought to California during World War I by his enterprising son Max, himself a cantor. At 1440 Chestnut Street, until his death in 1929, Rabbi Rabinowitz led services, arranged and performed marriages, fed the needy, sheltered transients, and counseled the troubled.[111]

One of his colleagues, the ultra-Orthodox Ephraim Garfinkle, pored over the holy books in his cluttered library on Linden Street. He had come from San Francisco after the earthquake and, although never ordained, was the spiritual leader of Congregation Zemach Zedek, a tiny synagogue to which he walked wearing a frock coat and a wide-brimmed hat.[112] But the community's wisest Talmud scholar was the prosperous businessman Marcus Parker (originally Pacher). He left West Oakland in the early 1920s for a large home overlooking Grand Avenue, where learned men would gather to discuss the subtleties of the sacred texts.[113]

Those not religiously inclined gravitated toward the Workmen's Circle. Oakland's Jack London branch held "Russian tea parties," sponsored educational and cultural evenings, and disseminated socialist literature. And, as in San Francisco, there were altercations between the Arbeiter Ring, which met at the Jewish Community Center on Brush Street, and the communists.[114] Yiddish theater troupes, which visited frequently from Los Angeles and New York, were well received, and there was also a degree of Zionist activity: a local Mizrachi group was founded in the late 1920s and soon followed by the socialist Poale Zion.

While some East European Jews joined Oakland's B'nai B'rith lodge, they felt more at ease in their own fraternal order, the Judaeans. Begun in 1908 with more than 150 members, the group organized casual picnics that were in sharp contrast to the expensive, formal, and unkosher dinners of B'nai B'rith.[115]

Most of the Yiddish speakers made a living by selling a line of goods, everything from fruit (as did Shapiro, "the Watermelon King") to jewelry (sold by men with names such as Riskin, Shane, Goldstein, and Samuels). Those less fortunate were peddlers, who were still a common sight in the late 1920s on the state's back roads. Like Charles Kushins, who came from the Lower East Side in 1911, they carried their goods in their cars or by rail, hoping eventually to open a store. Kushins succeeded, inaugurating the first of a chain of shoe stores in 1929. But most typical were those who bought and sold used merchandise. Immigrant Jews were the city's pawnbrokers, appraisers, auctioneers, and junk dealers; by the 1920s they ran almost a hundred surplus and secondhand stores in the East Bay.[116]

Many of the first East European Jews to establish themselves in Oakland were Hungarians, like the resourceful Bercovich clan, in business as early as 1883. Admired figures in the community, they thrived as scrap iron dealers, auctioneers, cigar distributors, and, ultimately, furniture sellers. After the death of the family's patriarch, Abraham, a gift from his widow to a worship group of Hungarians in 1908 enabled the acquisition of a modest old building near the foot of Harrison Street, formerly a Chinese temple. The new congregation—Bais Avruham, or Beth Abraham—was named in his memory.[117] Women sat in the balcony of this strictly Orthodox synagogue, which for two decades relied on its members to conduct services until it could finally afford a rabbi.

The late 1920s finally brought prosperity to a good number of these Hungarians, such as Sam Katzburg, who was in the "fruit game," Sol Quittman, who ran two haberdasheries, Kalman Gluck, owner of the Union Hide Company, and Maurice Learner, a scrap metal and hardware dealer.[118] They had arrived earlier than the Russian Jews and would leave the area of primary settlement earlier, too, forsaking West Oakland for the Grand Lake District, where they erected a spacious synagogue in 1929.

Beth Jacob, though, didn't move out until almost a generation later; it remained in a plain building on Ninth and Castro streets through the early 1950s and counted barely seventy dues-paying families during the Depression. The congregation's handwritten minutes, in broken English, reveal the tribulations of a poor immigrant synagogue. Board meetings were boisterous, full of accusations and countercharges, laughter and tears. Often the stormy sessions had to be "closed, there being too much discussion on the sobject; the President not being able to control the siduation."[119]

A meeting in the mid-1920s might begin with the report of an "investigation committee" on some alleged wrongdoing. Was all the money collected for the Book of Life actually turned over to the shul? What happened to the cemetery's ledger books? How legal was the recent reelection of the rabbi? Then complaints were aired: a professional mourner's threat of litigation for lack of payment, a member's claim that his father's grave had been improperly maintained. Finally came directives, like, "A new *puscka* [poor box] should be brought, with a good lock, that no one can tamper with."[120]

At the center of every issue was Rabbi B. M. Paper (1922–40), an accomplished Lithuanian Talmudist. Neither he nor his full-time cantor ever earned an adequate salary from the congregation. But, as was typical during this period, the rabbi did well by selling wine for "religious purposes" during Prohibition. He sold a gallon for $6.50 (the cost to him is unclear), of which Beth Jacob received seventy-eight cents.[121] Two hundred gallons appears to be the average amount sold every month in the early 1930s.

A number of members felt gouged by this arrangement, and in 1930 one declared that the permit might be revoked were the Prohibition office to learn of the excessive profits. Another suggested that the congregation, not the rabbi, handle the transactions and that a cheaper brand be obtained from the wholesalers, thus netting the shul a larger profit. Then a Mr. Moscowitz rose to state that if the quality of the wine were "lowered one bit, the majority of the members [would] resign."[122]

Even if he did profit from the arrangement, Beth Jacob's spiritual leader was a minor offender compared to some of Oakland's other Orthodox "wine rabbis," who, unlike Paper, sold mostly to non-Jews.* One rabbi, who made deliveries from a horse-drawn "laundry wagon," included among his

---

*In Oakland, as in other cities, "Orthodox bootlegging" was considered scandalous by Reform leaders. Temple Sinai's Rabbi Rudolph Coffee used grape juice rather than wine to avoid even the suggestion of impropriety.

customers a few influential Irish politicians,[123] which kept the police far from his door.

The repeal of Prohibition in 1933 amidst the depths of the Depression caused a financial crisis in Orthodox ranks. At Beth Jacob, which charged only fifty cents a month in dues, a steady salary had to be generated for Paper now that the sacramental wine business was over. To raise money the congregation bought a Torah for $190 and raffled it off. One thousand seven hundred one-dollar tickets were sold by December 1934.[124] Beth Jacob survived the hard times, but just barely.

MUSICAL GENIUS

In both good times and bad the Jewish neighborhoods were a breeding ground for brilliant young musicians. As Rose Rinder later recalled, "One child after another sprang up—out of the blue, with this talent. . . . This hasn't happened since."[125] While no explanation for such an explosion of musical genius is satisfactory, clearly the Bay Area Jewish community cultivated its uncommonly gifted youngsters in every way: visionary leaders discovered them, dedicated music teachers tutored them, wealthy patrons subsidized them, and the awestruck Jewish masses adored them.

The pianist Ruth Slenczynski—so tiny at age four that her father had to devise an extension for the foot pedal—stunned European audiences before she was seven; twelve-year-old Miriam Solovieff gave a violin recital in the Hollywood Bowl; and Leon Fleisher became an internationally known concert pianist at fifteen following his debut with the city's symphony orchestra. And, of course, two of the best-known violinists in the world came out of San Francisco: Isaac Stern and Yehudi Menuhin.

Like so many local prodigies, Stern was discovered by Reuben Rinder. Born in the Ukraine in 1920, he had been brought to San Francisco while still a baby. His father, an artist, became a house painter in California, although he suffered from chronic heart disease. Isaac's mother, noticing her son's flair for the piano, brought him before the cantor. Rinder, observing the child's fingers were somehow unsuited for the keyboard, suggested the eight-year-old try the violin.[126] Mrs. Stern bought the instrument, Rinder the bow.

The boy, who attended Emanu-El's religious school, studied violin with Robert Polak, concertmaster of the city's symphony orchestra. Rinder found a patron for Isaac, Jennie Baruh Zellerbach, and also arranged for a physician-friend to treat Isaac's ailing father.

Diligent though he was, Stern did not make lightning-fast progress, and Mrs. Zellerbach eventually gave up on him. But Rinder, never at a loss for backers, contacted the elderly Miss Lutie Goldstein, who resided at the Mark Hopkins Hotel, where she dispensed the fortune of her late brother, a Southern California businessman. She heard Stern at the cantor's house and doubted he would succeed, but after Rinder "begged her," she agreed to support him for a trial period.[127]

Goldstein's enthusiasm had to be periodically rekindled, but she lived to see her "investment" pay off handsomely. Stern, who left Polak to study at the city's new Conservatory of Music with Naoum Blinder, a Soviet refugee who ultimately succeeded Polak as concertmaster, played at the age of eleven with the local symphony orchestra. He gave his first concert in New York four years later, in 1935; his Carnegie Hall debut in 1943 enhanced his reputation even further. In later decades, his tours to distant nations such as China made him the world's premier ambassador of classical music.

Rinder, along with other prominent San Francisco Jews, also nurtured the career of the greatest child prodigy of the century, Yehudi Menuhin. Interviewing Moshe Menuhin for a teaching job at Emanu-El, the cantor discovered the three-year-old* in the cluttered two-room Berkeley shack the family occupied upon their arrival from the East Coast in 1918. Rinder heard the tot singing a Hebrew arpeggio on key and was awed.

Yehudi's parents, who soon moved to San Francisco, would smuggle their little son into the Curran Theater, where he became enraptured by the violin solos of the young Coloradan Louis Persinger, concertmaster of the symphony orchestra. For his fourth birthday Yehudi wanted a violin, and Persinger to teach him how to play it. Both wishes would be granted, but not without initial frustration. His first instrument was a metal toy (a gift from one of his father's colleagues) and, sobbing with disappointment, he threw it on the ground. And his first teacher was not Persinger but the workmanlike Sigmund Anker, from Austria-Hungary, who, stressing the fundamentals, taught about thirty children in the city. The boy's development as a virtuoso was slow at first, something he later attributed to Anker's lack of subtlety.[128] But before age six he performed at his instructor's annual studio recital, and within a year he played at the Civic Auditorium, enthralling the *Examiner*

---

* Rinder, though, believed he was only two, because Moshe, already a wily promoter, claimed his son was born on January 22, 1917; in reality, Yehudi entered the world nine months earlier (Humphrey Burton, *Yehudi Menuhin* [Boston, 2000], 4).

music critic: "He has learned the fiddle for a year and already he plays it with prophecy of the master that is to be."[129] But the child was soon crestfallen when, at a competition at the Fairmont Hotel, he saw the gold medal won by another of Anker's prize students, twelve-year-old Sarah Krindler. Rinder, who witnessed the defeat, presented Yehudi with a children's book about Mozart—small comfort to the youngster and his demanding parents.[130]

But the cantor also arranged for the reluctant Persinger to take on the boy wonder. With Moshe and Yehudi, Rinder drove to the concertmaster's home. He asked the often-hotheaded father to wait downstairs while he led the lad up to the study. There Yehudi began to play a Lalo concerto from memory, and Persinger interrupted him midway and immediately agreed to be his teacher. Persinger, "who [set] high my sights from the beginning," Menuhin wrote, "took extraordinary pains with me."[131] The weekly lesson eventually became a daily one, every morning for three hours, until Yehudi went to Europe in 1926.

More than three years before they went overseas, the Menuhins had moved from their home in run-down Hayes Valley into an ample two-story house, with a practice room and a backyard, on Steiner Street. The fanatically protective Moshe would not allow his son or two daughters, both budding pianists, to play with the neighbors' children; his offspring lived "in a cocoon," and when Yehudi went out he usually wore gloves.[132] Except for their music lessons and the French they learned from Rebecca Godchaux, the children were essentially homeschooled by Moshe and their almost equally headstrong mother, Marutha.*

Yet anyone who walked by 1037 Steiner Street in the mid-1920s might hear the magic of Yehudi's violin, and following the eight-year-old's triumphant professional debut at the Civic Auditorium, a frenzy gripped the Fillmore:

All cheap and medium-priced violins were sold out overnight, and the beginners flooded McAllister and the adjoining streets with hideous sound. Attendance in Hebrew schools was cut in half, to be restored only after several weeks when the grind of practice dulled the ambition of the would-be Yehudi Menuhins who returned lamb-like to the school bench. But the little boy who started it all went on playing the violin.[133]

* Crimean-born, she added to the Menuhin mystique by claiming not only Jewish but also Tartar ancestry.

In 1926, his first concerto performance with an orchestra so impressed the critics that, as one Menuhin scholar puts it, "their praise verged on blasphemy."[134] Indeed, the *Chronicle* rhapsodized, "What built the world in six days is what contrived the genius of Yehudi. He walks on the waves."[135]

He was now ten and ready, Moshe decided, to advance even beyond Persinger and be taught in Europe by a world-renowned violinist. That long sojourn, during which he would study with Georges Enesco and gain international fame, was financed by the philanthropist Sidney Ehrman. The tall, urbane attorney, grandson of pioneers, learned of the marvelous child not from Rinder but from another respected clergyman and educator, Rabbi Samuel Langer, who directed the Pacific Hebrew Orphan Asylum. Ehrman heard Yehudi perform and was overwhelmed, but his offer of a year on the Continent was initially vetoed by Marutha, who dreaded the breakup of her family and also felt ashamed of the need for outside donations. Ehrman overcame the first objection by offering to underwrite the expenses for the entire family to spend the year abroad. The second doubt he erased with his noble, selfless manner. "He adopted us," wrote Yehudi, "not simply for a subsidized year or so, but unto his heart for life, and we children promptly recognized the bonds of kinship by calling him Uncle Sidney. My own father apart, no man has had greater title to my filial affection, not even my revered masters Enesco and Persinger."[136]

By 1929, barely a teenager, Menuhin, played the great cities of Europe and enchanted audiences with his heartfelt, emotional style. Receiving about $3,500 a concert, he was unsurpassed at the box office by any violinist. He also recorded countless works, often accompanied by his sister, Hephzibah.[137] The family spent a great deal of time in London and, in the 1930s, moved their Northern California base of operations from Steiner Street to a serene estate in Los Gatos, near the Santa Cruz Mountains.

But while the Fillmore's Jews took pride in Yehudi's achievements, his unconventional family offended some members of the community when, in 1938, Moshe announced that all three children would wed non-Jews. Yehudi married the Australian aspirin heiress Nola Nicholas, and Hephzibah accepted the proposal of Nola's brother. The youngest Menuhin, Yaltah, took as her husband a St. Louis businessman.* Many were further inflamed when

---

*Yehudi's London agent, meanwhile, asserted that if the star "had loved a Chinese or an Eskimo it would have been alright with his father," and added that the great musician had never been inside a synagogue (Burton, *Yehudi Menuhin,* 192).

Moshe, with the Nazi menace in mind, argued in the *Emanu-El* that joining people of different faiths could "contribute to the sunshine so badly needed now."[138]

Within a decade Yehudi divorced Nola and married another gentile, Diana Gould, an English ballet dancer, but in the late 1940s the Fillmore's Jews were more distressed to read of his quick forgiveness of postwar Germany. He publicly defended, and performed with, the head of the Berlin Philharmonic, Wilhelm Furtwängler, who had remained at his post throughout the war.[139] Menuhin claimed the conductor had protected a number of Jewish musicians. But the violinist's strong support of a high-profile servant of the Third Reich so soon after the Holocaust earned him the rebuke of Jews throughout the world.[140] Menuhin did not echo his father's unceasing denunciation of Israel, but neither was he an avid Zionist. After the War of Independence he visited the Jewish state and performed there several times, but his invitation to play with the Israeli Philharmonic was withdrawn because of the Furtwängler controversy.

In his later years, as his talent declined and he accepted fewer bookings, Menuhin became interested in Eastern religion, yoga, and numerous human rights causes. "I was born old and shall die young," he said of this turn in his life.[141] He gave up his American citizenship to become a British subject and a knight, which raised eyebrows even in the cosmopolitan Bay Area. But like Gertrude Stein, another expatriate genius who belonged to the whole world, he remained proud of his Jewish patrimony, as his very name indicated ("a Jew" in Hebrew). And he chose his epitaph—he died in 1999—from the Talmud: "He who makes music in this life makes music in the next."[142]

MOVING OUT AND MOVING UP

While the Menuhins traveled the globe, most immigrant families simply sought to move to a better part of town, to newer sections of San Francisco and Oakland that offered more pleasant surroundings and more personal space.

By the late 1920s, those in the East Bay who had climbed a couple of rungs up the economic ladder were able to purchase modest stucco homes around Lake Merritt, or further east in the Fruitvale District. By 1950, only 10 percent of the Jewish community remained in West Oakland.[143]

Beth Abraham was the first Jewish institution to leave West Oakland for the Grand Lake District, and the synagogue it opened in that neighborhood just before the Depression clearly reflected the Hungarian Jews' advancement. The hulking red-brick building on Perry Street (renamed MacArthur Boulevard in 1942) houses a grand sanctuary seating well over a thousand. The move was also accompanied by a religious shift. The congregation would now be known as Temple Beth Abraham and as "Traditional Conservative" rather than Orthodox, a change that was intended to attract new members, according to Sam Katzburg, as well as "to keep the children of the old members."[144]

There were still rough times ahead for the congregation of only a hundred families. In the 1930s its teachers often went unpaid, and the county sheriff even padlocked the doors at one point, but an emergency sale of lifetime seats kept the congregation afloat.[145] By the late 1940s, propelled by returning war veterans starting new families, the membership grew to almost six hundred households.[146]

While many Jews vacated West Oakland, most of the Jewish institutions—the strapped community center, Talmud Torah, and Congregation Beth Jacob—remained in the old neighborhood well past midcentury, even as it fell into deep decline. And the Jews who moved to more comfortable areas around Lake Merritt, though they constituted a considerable percentage of the population there, never re-created the dense, vibrant Jewish quarter with the sights and smells they had known earlier.

A similar pattern can be seen in San Francisco's Fillmore District, which lost many of its Jews to better neighborhoods in the 1930s and '40s. Many moved a couple of miles west to sturdy three-bedroom row houses in the diverse Richmond District, just north of Golden Gate Park. Already by 1938, the Richmond contained about three thousand Jewish families, roughly the same as the Fillmore.[147] The trend accelerated soon after the attack on Pearl Harbor, when Japanese residents, many of whom had lived in the Fillmore for decades, were forced to evacuate and spend most of the war's duration in remote detention camps. African American defense workers from the South often took their places, and, especially after 1945, when that community was ravaged by unemployment, crime in the area rose markedly. One stretch of Fillmore Street frequented by winos was labeled "Muscatel Drive" by its denizens.[148]

Congregation Beth Sholom built a sizable new synagogue on Fourteenth Avenue and Clement Street in 1934, at the beginning of the demographic shift to the Richmond. Started as an informal group of worshippers after Jews first trickled into the neighborhood following the earthquake, Beth Sholom initially met in a church on Fourth Avenue near Geary, where it drew a good portion of its members from the more traditional Keneseth Israel.[149] As their small businesses succeeded—furniture stores, laundries, produce markets—and as more Jews moved into the area, hopes rose for the formation of a major congregation. With a membership of only several dozen households, a lot was purchased and construction began.

The turning point for Beth Sholom came when it hired its first full-time rabbi, twenty-seven-year-old Saul White, in 1935. Born and raised in Russian Poland, White had immigrated to New York with his family at age twelve and received an excellent education in the humanities at New York University before being ordained by Stephen Wise at the Jewish Institute of Religion. But the clean-shaven young man hardly "looked like a rabbi," White recalled, when he was met at the train station by a delegation of the congregation's leaders. Their image of a spiritual leader was a bearded, mature man, realized White, but though "let down," they had him conduct High Holiday services since they had already paid his railway fare from the East.[150]

He remained with the congregation for almost half a century, and in his last decades no one had more of the bearing of a traditional rabbi than the leonine, hoary-headed White. Early in his tenure, inaugurating Friday evening services, he skillfully led Beth Sholom, still ostensibly Orthodox, toward Conservative Judaism, and the congregation formally joined the movement soon after the war. By 1949 membership had risen almost tenfold from a decade earlier, to 460.[151]

He was the city's foremost spokesman for Zionism during and after World War II, leading public protests and rallies, battling Rabbi Reichert's anti-Zionist American Council for Judaism, and raising funds for the beleaguered Jews of Palestine. In 1938, with Rabbi Elliot Burstein of Beth Israel, White organized the local chapter of the American Jewish Congress, the progressive pro-Zionist organization. Comprised largely of East European Jews, the group aimed to advance social justice both at home and abroad. But most of all, he reached thousands of households each week through a hard-hitting weekly op-ed column in the *Emanu-El*, in which he voiced sharp criticism of a local Jewish establishment he felt too timid and assimilationist.

The newspaper, under new management since 1932, now reflected the concerns of a broad spectrum of Jews in the city, even as it still carried the name of the elitist temple whose rabbi had founded it. The community paper highlighted events at most of the other synagogues in town, took a moderately pro-Zionist position, and devoted much coverage to Yiddish cultural activities. The growing East European middle class now had to feel well served by the Anglo-Jewish press.

This group, too, benefited the most from the well-equipped Jewish Community Center (JCC) that opened in 1933 and soon became the most active Jewish organization in the city. Replacing the old and inadequate YMHA, it registered a thousand members its first year and quickly tripled its rolls.[152] Despite the free memberships extended in the mid-1930s to those in need, few of the poor, traditional Jews took advantage of the rambling Mission-style facility on California Street and Presidio Avenue, a long mile from Fillmore-McAllister. But for the more Americanized East Europeans, the JCC became a beehive of social activity. The Saturday and Sunday night dances, "*the* place to be," typically drew hundreds of young people and gave them a sense that they counted for something in San Francisco.[153]

Rabbi Saul White, meanwhile, articulated what many East Europeans felt. With his blend of Jewish and secular learning, his New Deal liberalism (which had supplanted socialism as the immigrants' political creed), and his combative style, he was just the right voice for those who had grown up in the city's vigorous Jewish neighborhoods. His modern Yiddishkeit, a hearty embrace of all things Jewish, was especially welcomed during the upheavals of the 1940s.

By World War II, the East European Jewish immigrants had come far since their nineteenth-century beginnings in the coarse South of Market area. In the early days they had been derided as a "pauper element" that would never adapt to America, and even many Jews themselves had hoped to transfer their greenhorn kinsmen to Baja California.[154] Less than two generations later, however, they had spread across many neighborhoods of the Bay Area, established benevolent associations, and erected substantial synagogues.

And yet, East European Jewish influence was still limited in San Francisco compared to other American cities. The reins of community leadership would remain in the hands of the German Jews of pioneer origin for decades to come.

EIGHT

Good Times

The Jewish Elite between the Wars

THE GERMAN JEWISH MERCHANT CLASS had dominated the American Jewish community since the mid-nineteenth century, but after World War I its power began to erode. By 1924, the flood of East European immigration had rendered those of German origin only a tenth of American Jewry. The Reform movement, with its Americanized liturgy and refusal to embrace Zionism, held little appeal for Yiddish-speaking newcomers and faced a dwindling membership. Moreover, East European Jews were finally entering politics. Following Meyer London's election to the House from the Lower East Side in 1914, an increasing number won seats in Congress and state legislatures. East European Jews founded important advocacy groups such as the American Jewish Congress, and they penetrated the leadership of major organizations such as the B'nai B'rith.

Yet in San Francisco and Oakland the old guard seemed rock solid in the 1920s. German Jews remained in the majority (as almost nowhere else) and their synagogues thrived. In the middle of the decade Emanu-El constructed one of the world's most exquisite sanctuaries, as well as a five-story Temple House serving the cultural and recreational needs of members and nonmembers alike. While the congregation's innovative rabbi, Louis I. Newman, reached across denominational and class lines, its cantor, Reuben Rinder, established himself as a potent catalyst in the realm of Jewish music, proving Reform Judaism anything but sterile in the arts.

Membership at Emanu-El, Sherith Israel, and Oakland's Sinai soared in the 1920s. To be sure, spiritual ardor, Zionism, and Jewish education were decidedly weak outside the Yiddish-speaking community, but the temples' cultural and youth programs were superb, especially at Emanu-El. Philanthropy abounded as well. As so often happened in Bay Area Jewish history, the most influential families devoted themselves to helping the disadvantaged, bettering their city, and fostering the arts. Walter Haas and Daniel Koshland, at the helm of Levi Strauss and Company, were headed in this direction by the 1920s and would continue to follow this path for the next five decades. Many other Jewish benefactors made vital contributions as well. By the beginning of the 1930s, a museum, aquarium, swimming pool, zoo, and outdoor concert hall in San Francisco all bore well-recognized Jewish names. Taken together, they constituted a recreational bonanza for the city.

Among the leading Jewish families, a third generation—the pioneers' grandchildren—was now coming of age. They enjoyed all the advantages of their native-born parents: exclusive private schools, mansions filled with servants, the opportunity to take a yearlong tour of Europe. Their behavior was more relaxed than during the Victorian years—young men and women drove cars, saw movies, listened to jazz, and spent less time at home with their families—but they still tended to be "sheltered" and "snobbish," adjectives that frequently appear in their own memoirs.[1] Like the upper echelon of New York's Jews described in Stephen Birmingham's *Our Crowd,* the world generally remained divided between "people we visit and people we don't visit."[2] While a good number of them broke out of their gilded cocoons in various ways, they did not exhibit the creativity demonstrated by Bay Area Jewry's extraordinary second generation.

Despite their high level of acculturation and well-publicized largesse, the Jewish aristocracy was not untouched by anti-Semitism. Even in tolerant San Francisco, the prejudices engendered during World War I caused some social clubs that had freely admitted Jews in the past to restrict their membership. Many college fraternities barred Jews, and top private schools now set Jewish quotas. Still, the hatred spewed by Henry Ford's *Dearborn Independent* and the resurgence of the Ku Klux Klan—the major worries of national Jewish leaders in the 1920s—seemed far from the Golden Gate. Locally, the main concern of the Jewish establishment was Christian fundamentalism, but, unlike in Southern California, in the Bay Area able rabbis and prominent lay leaders invariably won their battles to preserve the separation of church and state.

One reflection of the continued acceptance of Jews was their uniquely high profile in political life. Not only did a Jew, and later his widow, represent the city in Congress for well over a third of a century, until 1937, but local Jews were also highly conspicuous in the state legislature, where one served as assembly Speaker. Some were supervisors, while others received choice appointments to municipal commissions and still others were highly influential behind the scenes.

These Jewish politicians were invariably of South German origin, from pioneer families, and Republican. They came from a tiny elite, but their success gave many Bay Area Jews a relative sense of security that lasted well into the 1930s, even while other American Jews were feeling more vulnerable than ever.

A GOLDEN DOME

Emanu-El's Lake Street Temple epitomized the style of the city's Jewish gentry: dominating but graceful, stately yet not showy. The edifice also reflected the congregants' great wealth, which swelled in the postwar years. The complex cost more than $1.3 million—fifteen times the average price of constructing an American synagogue in this period—and, after selling their Sutter Street Temple for $450,000, Emanu-El paid the balance in cash.[3] About fifty families, nearly all with Gold Rush roots, accounted for the great bulk of the money raised.

The status-conscious lay leaders established sixteen categories for lifetime seats, which precisely reflected the congregation's socioeconomic stratification. Rows two through eleven were considered most desirable, but even within this choice section there were further distinctions: a seat on the aisle cost $850, while one in the middle of the row could be had for a hundred dollars less. The last four rows on the main floor went for $75 a chair, the back rows in the balcony for only $50.[4]

Dedicated on April 18, 1926, exactly twenty years after the earthquake, the new house of worship was designed by Arthur Brown Jr. in the prime of a sterling career. He had been the architect of San Francisco's splendid City Hall in 1915 and would later design the War Memorial Opera House, Coit Tower, the Bay Bridge, and Stanford University's Hoover Library. A non-Jew, Brown nevertheless chose the medium of the synagogue to express his personal religious feelings. His main motif would be an imposing dome "of all the architectural forms yet imagined . . . the most superb, the most noble and most deeply inspiring."[5]

He was influenced by St. Peter's Basilica, the Église du Dôme at Les Invalides in Paris, and, above all, Hagia Sophia in Istanbul, considered the finest product of the Byzantine age. Like the sixth-century shrine, Emanu-El's dome—150 feet high—appears to float, "a great, golden bubble, lofty, soaring in the sky."*[6] But the new temple was also distinctly Californian. The open-air cloistered court, where worshippers gather before services, recalls a Spanish mission. One of the consultants on the project was Bernard Maybeck, Brown's former teacher, and he contributed this seemingly effortless blending of indoor and outdoor spaces.

Brown and his associates anticipated the most common criticism: the cold feeling engendered by the sparse interior of the immense sanctuary. The soaring walls and ceiling—sweeping curves of colorless concrete—would remain unbroken by any decoration until stained-glass windows were installed in 1973. But the stark rendering was precisely Brown's intention. As Rabbi Newman explained, "There is a rugged and potent barbaric splendor in the edifice . . . vast and almost primitive power."[7]

The austere interior focuses attention on the ark, for which Brown created a large, pyramid-topped stone canopy, or ciborium, held in place by four columns of the same dark antique marble used along the room's sides. The ark, a three-thousand-pound masterwork in the form of a nine-foot-high bronze jewel box, stands freely, as did the Ark of the Covenant that the ancient Israelites carried in the desert.[†]

The sanctuary, which soon won the American Institute of Architects award as the finest building in Northern California, fulfilled Newman's prediction that "here shall stand one of the rarest buildings in the land."[8] But regardless of its splendor, the rabbi had more in mind than just a shrine. Attempting to manifest the vision of his late predecessor and mentor, Martin Meyer, he convinced the board of directors to erect a large multipurpose Temple House as well.

---

*Also impressed was Louis Mumford, for whom the geometric relationship of the dome to the cubical Temple House seemed to prove "everything in architecture is either a cube or an egg" (Louis Mumford, "Toward a Modern Synagogue Architecture," *Menorah Journal* 11 [June 1925]: 222).

[†]California artists George Dennison and Frank Ingerson studied biblical specifications before beginning a year's work on the ark in London, at a centuries-old foundry on the Thames. Their finished product created a sensation in British art circles before it was shipped to San Francisco (Fred Rosenbaum, *Visions of Reform: Congregation Emanu-El and the Jews of San Francisco* [Berkeley, 2000], 148–49).

Emanu-El's Sutter Street Temple after the 1906 earthquake. All of the synagogue's contents were destroyed, including the Torah scroll donated by Moses Montefiore in 1851, the libraries of Rabbi Jacob Voorsanger and Cantor Edward Stark, and the congregational minutes and records. Emanu-El reconstructed its home within a year and a half, during which it held services in temporary quarters in the Calvary Presbyterian Church and the Unitarian Church. (WJHC/JLMM)

A Jewish family (the Lehners) living in Golden Gate Park after the earthquake. More than half of the city's residents, about a quarter of a million people, were rendered homeless in April 1906, and especially hard hit was the city's immigrant Jewish quarter south of Market Street. Many of its residents were forced to camp out for months in Golden Gate Park, on the grounds of the Presidio, or along the seashore. (WJHC/JLMM)

Attorney Henry Ach whispering to his client Abraham Ruef. The sensational graft trials involving Ruef, San Francisco's Jewish political boss, polarized the city and the Jewish community for three years beginning in 1906. One of the trials was held in Temple Sherith Israel, used as a municipal courtroom after the earthquake. Ruef was convicted and served more than four years in San Quentin. (THE BANCROFT LIBRARY OF THE UNIVERSITY OF CALIFORNIA, BERKELEY)

EX-CZAR NAMED RULER OF

ENEMY
ROL IS
GHT IN
TRAP

nfantrymen, Assisted
h, Hide at Deserted
e, Catch Enemy and
ll for Recent Losses

Outnumber Franco-
Two to One, but
r Heavy Fire; Ameri-
ches Heavily Shelled

Associated Press.]
THE AMERICAN
Y IN FRANCE, No-
ber 14.—American in-
acted a part revenge
t trench raid by am-
e German patrol in No
during a recent night
wounding a number of

an patrol, in which
me Frenchmen, ar-
mbuscade near the Ger-
a shell ruined farm.
in the mud nearly all
lence of the watchers
by the sight of a large
ol, its number more
that of the Franco-

were permitted to pass,
ricans and Frenchmen
opened a hot fire from
nd other shelters where
reted.

SURPRISED,
ASTE

ns were taken com-
prise and bolted, car-
m their men who had

of dead and wounded
certain, but none of the
h was hit by the bul-
ns later sent in from a

congratulations all
the Americans and
red their trenches.
on both sides is be-
active, as is also the
The Germans during
ar-hour period of a re-
t over at least three

THE ROOT OF THE EVIL By Louis Raemaekers
Famous Dutch Artist, Who Is Drawing for the Hearst Papers
Copyright, 1917, by Louis Raemaekers.

FOOD FOR THE ARMY
SEDITIOUS Press
Nov. 5.
(Popular song of Tommy in France)
Well done fellows! „Keep the home-fires bur-ning,

LLOYD GEO
QUIETS CR
OVER SPE

Hastens to Explain to
That Allied Council \
No Executive Power

FATE RESTS WITH

Storm Over Paris Addres
by Explanation, bu
Debate Is Expected

LONDON, November
"Globe" says that great p
being brought on Northcli
ter the government, wh
"he alone is deemed capal
stering up."

LONDON, November
storm warning of a minist
which flared up suddenly
of Premier Lloyd Georg
in Paris subsided almos
denly. Challenged in the
Commons to-day to ex
speech, the premier conte
self by reading the actua
the agreement creating
council, which, he declare
clear that the council was
visory and possessed of
tive power and, therefore,
override decisions of the
governments or their mili
The premier further
submit a letter in the for
next Monday if the Hou
and with this offer the n
dropped. It is assumed th
bate will have a lively cha
although the possibility
is not excluded, it is suspe
next week.

LONDON, November
with the most hostile
newspaper criticism since
Premier, David Lloyd Geo
made an explanation in
on the aims, scope and in
the proposed inter-allied
which is to sit in France
and direct military policies
tente.
The Premier truly talke
the government from the
defeat by a vote showing la
fidence. Whether Parlia
accept his explanation o
the ministry must fall
forecast now.
For his speech in Paris
evening, in which he spok
defeats as being the resu
close regard for traditions
tige and not enough unity
the German west front

VIGILANTES TO TRACE SPIES

Only Six Ships Lost by British; Divers Curbed

FAMED VENICE

Wartime caricature of a Jewish traitor. Although anti-Semitism was usually milder in San Francisco than in other parts of America, this widely syndicated political cartoon, drawn by Louis Raemaekers, a Dutch artist living in exile in London, was printed on the front page of the *San Francisco Examiner*. The image implies wartime disloyalty on the part of the Jews, and after the United States entered World War I a number of venerable German Jewish families tried to prove their patriotism by Anglicizing their names. (*SAN FRANCISCO EXAMINER*, NOVEMBER 15, 1917)

Joseph Strauss photographed by Ralph Stackpole. Strauss, a diminutive German Jew from the Midwest, was obsessed with building the Golden Gate Bridge for more than twenty years. His dream became a reality in 1937, a year before his death. (THE BANCROFT LIBRARY OF THE UNIVERSITY OF CALIFORNIA, BERKELEY)

On the Marin side of the Golden Gate, Joseph Strauss is second from the right and Leon Moisseiff is at the far right. Although Strauss was the leading promoter and public face of the project, he did not design the Golden Gate Bridge. A far greater role in the engineering was played by Moisseiff, a Jewish immigrant from czarist Russia, who was one of the world's experts in the area of wind stress. (SAN FRANCISCO HISTORY CENTER, SAN FRANCISCO PUBLIC LIBRARY)

Albert Bender photographed by Ralph Stackpole. The son of a Dublin rabbi, Bender was one of San Francisco's leading patrons of the arts and its unofficial greeter between the wars. In 1928 he helped bring Diego Rivera to the city for a major commission. (THE BANCROFT LIBRARY OF THE UNIVERSITY OF CALIFORNIA, BERKELEY)

Photographer Alma Lavenson Wahrhaftig. Born and raised among
Oakland's German Jewish aristocracy, she was influenced by Edward
Weston, Consuelo Kanaga, and Imogen Cunningham. In 1932 Wahrhaftig
participated in the seminal "f.64" photography exhibit at the de Young
Museum. A photo she later took in New Mexico, "San Ildefonso Indians,"
was selected by Edward Steichen as part of his "Family of Man" exhibit
that toured the country in the mid-1950s. (WJHC/JLMM)

EMANU-EL

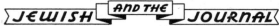

JEWISH [AND THE] JOURNAL

"FEAR NOT, FOR I AM WITH THEE"
(ISAIAH: 43:5)
A Passover Drawing by Allen Simon

PASSOVER EDITION

March Twenty-seventh   ·   ·   ⚹   ·   ·   1942   ·   5702

Cover page of the special Passover edition of the *Emanu-El,* March 27, 1942. In the early 1940s, in the face of accusations of "tribalism" and self-interest, the Jewish community often trumpeted its American patriotism. In this illustration, President Franklin Roosevelt is seen at the right hand of Moses in the war against the Axis. The Four Freedoms are shown as a companion to the Ten Commandments. (WJHC/JLMM)

Children's Synagogue of the Central Hebrew School, May 1928. The colorful Fillmore District was home to a vibrant community of East European Jews between the wars, and many of its children attended this traditional Jewish supplementary school on Grove and Buchanan streets. The dedicated director, Rabbi David Stolper, is third from the left on the back row, and one of its leading financial supporters, the immigrant businessman Bernard Diller, is on the far left. (WJHC/JLMM)

Rabbi Mayer Hirsch of Congregation Anshe Sfard. During Prohibition many traditional synagogues generated income through the sale of "sacramental" wine, which the authorities permitted. (WJHC/JLMM)

Diller's Kosher Delicatessen and Restaurant in the Fillmore. The diverse Fillmore District was known for its fine cuisine in the 1920s and '30s, and this establishment, on Golden Gate Avenue, was widely considered the most popular of the many kosher eateries. (WJHC/JLMM)

Political cartoon of Congresswoman Florence Prag Kahn in the *San Francisco Examiner,* December 19, 1928. The first Jewish woman elected to Congress, she succeeded her husband, Julius Kahn, in 1925 and served until her defeat eleven years later. The image on the left reflects her forcefulness on Capitol Hill; the drawing on the right portrays her advocacy of a strong military. She was the first woman to serve on the House Military Affairs Committee. (WJHC/JLMM)

Louis Persinger, concertmaster of the San Francisco Symphony, and Yehudi Menuhin around 1924. Persinger taught the child prodigy until Yehudi and his family left for a year in Europe at the end of 1926. Destined to become one of the greatest violinists of all time, Yehudi grew up on Steiner Street in the Fillmore District under the watchful eye of his protective father, Moshe Menuhin, director of San Francisco's Jewish Educational Society. (COURTESY LAWRENCE RINDER)

The banking tycoon Herbert Fleishhacker. A member of one of
San Francisco's earliest Jewish families, he wielded a great deal of
political influence during the mayoralty of "Sunny Jim" Rolph
(1911–30). One of the city's leading philanthropists, Fleishhacker
donated the famous pool bearing his name, as well as a zoo, and in
1934 was at the center of the bitter controversy over the murals in
Coit Tower. (SAN FRANCISCO HISTORY CENTER, SAN FRANCISCO PUBLIC
LIBRARY)

Emanu-El's Lake Street Temple soon after its construction in 1925. The design of the temple by Arthur Brown Jr., widely considered one of the most beautiful in the world, caused critic Lewis Mumford to remark, "Everything in architecture is either a cube or an egg." (WJHC/JLMM)

Jacques Schnier working on a quarter-size clay model of *Dance of Life* for the Golden Gate International Exposition in 1939. Born in Rumania and raised in San Francisco, Schnier traveled widely in Asia and was greatly influenced by Buddhist art and sculpture. He later pursued psychoanalysis, both for its therapeutic uses and as a means of probing the meaning of art.

A demonstration in San Francisco in the 1970s against the oppression of Soviet Jewry. Joan Baez is in the center; Regina Bublil (later Regina Bublil Waldman) holds the sign; and Harold Light, founder of the Bay Area Council for Soviet Jewry, is on the left wearing a jacket and tie. The Bay Area was in the forefront of the struggle for Soviet Jewry, and many young Jews were first introduced to political activism through this movement. In 2003 Waldman, herself a refugee from Libya, founded an advocacy organization for Jewish refugees from the Middle East and North Africa. (WJHC/JLMM)

Particularly in the late 1920s, the Temple House would be the hub of many successful community programs, including the elaborately staged play *The Dybbuk*. On the floorboards of the new Martin Meyer Auditorium, children of some of town's wealthiest families mixed with the offspring of Yiddish-speaking immigrants as had never happened before in the city. Unlikely matches were made. Rehearsing *The Dybbuk,* Mortimer Fleishhacker Jr. met his future wife, Janet Choynski, granddaughter of Isidore Choynski, the incorrigible pioneer journalist from Posen who had excoriated San Francisco's largely Bavarian Jewish establishment for decades. On the other side of her family were Russian Jews, further convincing the Fleishhacker parents of a "misalliance," but young Morti would not be deterred.[9]

Louis Newman's six-year tenure as rabbi, which ended in 1930, contributed much to this era of good feeling. Jews throughout the city admired him not only for his embrace of Yiddish culture, but also for his militant Zionism and his refusal to perform intermarriage.[10] Not until the middle of the century would an Emanu-El rabbi again be such a unifying figure in the Jewish community.

SACRED SERVICE

The late 1920s also saw Cantor Reuben Rinder emerge as a force in the world of Jewish music. Connecting musical prodigies to moneyed patrons, as described in the previous chapter, he cultivated extraordinary talents such as Yehudi Menuhin and Isaac Stern and propelled the careers of many other virtuosos as well. He also commissioned some of the finest synagogue music of the twentieth century. Hoping to produce a "Jewish Palestrina,"[11] he came close to that goal with his first invitation—to Ernest Bloch to write *Avodath Hakodesh,* or *Sacred Service.*

The cantor was instrumental in bringing the eminent composer to the Bay Area and would play a central role in Bloch's career during its most fertile years. In 1924, Rinder visited the Swiss immigrant in Cleveland, where he directed that city's Institute of Music. Already world famous, Bloch was unhappy in Ohio and interested when Rinder told him a director was being sought for the new San Francisco Conservatory of Music. Upon his return home, the cantor spoke to the school's cofounders, who soon convinced Bloch to accept a teaching position at the conservatory, and later its directorship.[12]

The composer's five years in the West constituted a rare period of contentment in a life marked by deep ruts of hypochondria and depression. As

Bloch wrote in 1927, "I have felt around me, in Frisco, an atmosphere of kindness, friendship, good camaraderie, which have gone to my heart. Like a desiccated plant—and this is what I was when I came—I feel life come back again to me, as if fresh, good, healthy water was uplifting me."[13]

His professional life flowered as well with the completion of *America: An Epic Rhapsody,* in mind from the day he had landed in New York in 1916. For the sweeping tribute he appropriated a wide range of folk music— Native American songs, Negro spirituals, sea shanties, and jazz—unified organically with his own "Anthem." In 1928 it was performed in seven cities, and in San Francisco it drew twelve thousand people to Exposition Auditorium. At its conclusion, Bloch was lifted over the footlights by his fans and carried onto the stage amidst thunderous applause. The *Examiner* proclaimed it "the greatest symphonic work thus far written in this century."[14]

Yet a number of New York critics ridiculed the piece, wondering if a foreign-born Jew ought to be writing American music.[15] That must have seemed a jarring question in the Bay Area, where Jews dominated classical music. In addition to the celebrated Bloch and the adored Yehudi Menuhin, the conductor of the symphony, Alfred Hertz (who would be succeeded in 1935 by the French Jew Pierre Monteux), was also Jewish, as were four of its concertmasters in the interwar period, including Menuhin's teacher, Louis Persinger. Alexander Fried, Alfred Frankenstein, and Alfred Metzger were among the leading local music critics, and Professor Albert Elkus of UC Berkeley, a descendant of pioneers, was the preeminent musicologist.

Rinder aimed to channel some of that reservoir of talent toward synagogue music, and in 1928 he sought to interest Bloch in composing a Sabbath service. Yet Bloch was ambivalent. Several of his works had been on Hebraic themes, and one reviewer of *America* had written, "The Indians in the symphony dance with Hasidic feet."[16] But sacred music was altogether different. Bloch's Jewish education was minimal, his deepest convictions universalist. In 1916 he had written, "It is not my purpose, not my desire to attempt a 'reconstruction' of Jewish music. . . . I am not an archaeologist. I hold it of first importance to write good, genuine music."[17] Yet he followed those lines with a declaration bordering on Jewish tribalism:

It is the Hebrew spirit that interests me—the complex, ardent, agitated soul that vibrates for me in the Bible; the vigor and ingenuousness of the Patriarchs, the violence that finds expression in the books of the Prophets, the burning love of justice, the desperation of the preachers of Jerusalem, the sorrow and grandeur of the Book of Job, the sensuality of the Song of Songs. All this is in us, all this is in me, and is the better part of me. This is what I seek to feel within me and to translate in my music—the sacred race-emotion that lies dormant in our souls.[18]

He took home the *Union Prayer Book* and told Rinder he would study it. When the cantor succeeded in obtaining a $3,000 stipend from the Haas and Koshland families, Bloch finally embarked on *Sacred Service,* often considered his most enduring work.

Ten thousand dollars was soon added by New York philanthropist Gerald Warburg, himself a cellist, whom Rinder informed of the project.[19] It enabled Bloch to leave San Francisco for a remote mountain village in the Swiss Alps. For two years he remained in seclusion mastering Hebrew, analyzing Jewish liturgy, and writing the first Jewish service by a composer of stature.

In long letters to Rinder he described having "literally to *fight* for each note" and discussed not only an outline of the emerging piece but also its underlying philosophical—indeed cosmological—premises.[20] The cantor provided the title, and a portion of the Sabbath service that Rinder had set to music—"Rock of Israel"—appeared in toto in Bloch's final manuscript.[21]

Avodath Hakodesh, unveiled in Turin, Italy, in 1934, would not be performed at Emanu-El until March 28, 1938, nearly a decade after its inception. The evening was a stunning triumph, causing the *Chronicle* virtually to canonize Bloch, who, the paper claimed,

speaks at times with an epic grandeur paralleled only in Handel and Bach, with an awful, subdued sense of mystery and wonder akin to the final meditations of Beethoven, with a soft, lyric breath like that in the "German Requiem" of Brahms. All of which it resembles not the slightest for it is altogether Bloch [brooding] for a while over an age-old poem that has a thousand meanings or one meaning and is here revealed in a new and supremely beautiful context.[22]

Bloch, still in Europe when he learned of his San Francisco success, poured out his feelings of gratitude in a typically agitated letter to Rinder:

It seems *yesterday* to me that *you* approached me with the idea of the Service—you are the godfather of this work—you felt instinctively that it would liberate in me, from me, within me, a whole world which (wanted?) needed to take

shape . . . and you know what happened then! And how, amidst terrific sufferings and pains of childbirth . . . this work . . . was born.[23]

Beginning in the 1920s, Rinder was as committed to presenting great music as he was to developing it. Open to the public free of charge every year
were productions at Emanu-El of Handel, Mendelssohn, Gaul, and many
others. The oratorios and cantatas were usually performed by an ensemble
from the San Francisco Symphony and a chorus, directed by the cantor, of
about a hundred voices, the professional Emanu-El choir joining that of one
of the local universities.[24]

The sumptuous home of Marcus Koshland's widow, Cora, was the venue
of other memorable performances. Beginning in 1928, about a hundred of
her guests, including many non-Jews, would gather around the fountain
in the marble hall of her mansion, the Petit Trianon, each Hanukkah.
Throughout the afternoon sublime liturgical and folk music would be performed by Rinder, the temple choir, leading local soloists, and the temple
organist, who played a grand organ that she had permanently installed in her
home.[25] Then scores of menorahs would be kindled, flooding the house
with light, and hot spiced wine, a Bavarian delicacy, would be served.
Recitals of child prodigies were also presented in the Petit Trianon. It was
there that Ernest Bloch first heard Yehudi Menuhin perform; he would later
write a work specifically for the boy genius.[26]

THE THIRD GENERATION

Cora Koshland was perhaps the leading benefactor of music in the city in
the 1920s. But other women at the pinnacle of the Jewish elite, such as Rosalie Meyer Stern and Justice Sloss's wife, Hattie, were also major supporters of the symphony, opera, and individual artists. The diminutive Hattie
Hecht Sloss, a witty Bostonian, did not have the physical presence of Cora
or Rosalie—she was described by her contemporaries as "all chin"[27]—but
her knowledge of classical music was unsurpassed by anyone in her circle. In
the 1940s she would host a popular weekly radio show entitled "Know Your
Symphony."

The Jewish aristocracy passed on the appreciation of great music to the
third generation, which reached intellectual maturity after World War I. Of
course, the three Koshland children, who grew up in the Petit Trianon, were
frequently treated to concerts in their own home, and all were tutored in

piano, as were most of the privileged youngsters of this era. As in the late nineteenth century, in the 1920s it was common for parents and children to gather around the ivories in the evening and play four- or eight-handed piano.[28]

Similarly, the elders felt obliged to have their offspring schooled in French.[29] Many youngsters regularly visited the home of Rebecca Godchaux and her sisters for that purpose—the dedicated, quirky family continued to be a beacon of Gallic culture throughout the 1920s—while others received a French teacher at their door. In addition, children typically took dance and horseback riding lessons. Girls in particular often attended fine private day schools, like Miss Murison's, Madame Ziska's, or, the most exclusive one of all, Katharine Delmar Burke's. The elite's young were also set apart by their yearlong trip abroad, generally to Europe but sometimes around the world.

Jewish education was not a prominent ingredient in this extracurricular mix. Although Jewish youth groups abounded, Sunday school, which met for less than two hours weekly, was an ineffective vehicle for conveying the Jewish heritage. One distinguished Jewish educator remembered his own Sunday school experience at Emanu-El in the late 1920s as "just horrible" and even spoke of a food fight in the middle of a model Seder.[30] A teacher recalled the great emphasis placed on "social life" in those days, noting that many of the older girls came to Sunday school wearing orchids their boyfriends had given them on Saturday night: "I'm not sure it was religious fervor that brought them. . . . [I]t was rather to talk over what happened the night before."[31]

Rabbi Newman felt he was losing to "the California out of doors."[32] Swimming, at the Sutro Baths, the new Fleishhacker Pool, or an athletic club, claimed the attention of young people, as did sports of all sorts. Scouting became enormously popular, and starting in 1922 Emanu-El sponsored one of the most active groups in the nation, Troop 17, the "Eagle Machine."[33] It met at the temple on Friday nights, when school was farthest from the boys' minds. Newman strenuously objected, but neither he nor any of his successors prevailed.

Even more troubling was the obsession, as Newman put it, with jazz, alcohol, and sexuality.[34] He voiced his fears that "nature worship" might replace religion and that the balmy Golden State, with its fads and cults, was especially vulnerable. "Jewry, like other religious groups," he warned, "is being overborne by the threat of prosperous, ease-loving, pagan pleasure-seeking."[35]

Intermarriage also imperiled the Jewish people, according to the rabbi, and he would not marry Jew to non-Jew. His policy cost him the support and friendship of the temple president, whose daughter wed a Christian without Newman's blessing.[36] But while intermarriage was not uncommon, it was hardly rampant in the 1920s even among the Emanu-El elite, and it was not nearly as widespread as it would become later in the century. Conversions to Christianity were also less frequent in San Francisco's Jewish community than they were among New York's German Jews, whose chroniclers reported pangs of self-hatred when the third generation was caught between the pressures of acculturation and social anti-Semitism.[37] The Jewish patriciate in the Bay Area was more relaxed; being Jewish perhaps engendered apathy, but rarely agony.

The San Francisco Jewish aristocracy largely retained its insularity. The social lives of well-to-do Jewish men of German and French origin continued to revolve around two highly selective Jewish social clubs, the Argonaut and Concordia, which merged in 1939. The Concordia rehabilitated its stately Van Ness facility in the mid-1920s and at decade's end reached its highest enrollment yet, almost five hundred. There were some members of Prussian Polish extraction, but "a paucity" of Russians or Rumanians, whom the club president disdained as the "Ishmaelites [i.e., outcasts] of McAllister Street" as late as 1935.[38] According to one clubman, the Concordia was "a German-Jewish hangout" in the late 1920s and early 1930s, and the leadership, "didn't want to let outlanders in."[39]

The much smaller Argonaut was even more high-hat. "Individually they were all fine men," recalled the widow of a longtime president, "but as a club the Argonauts were the biggest snobs in the world," a characterization corroborated by several former members.[40]

Temple Emanu-El, of course, was much more inclusive under Rabbis Meyer and Newman than it had been in the days of Cohn and Voorsanger. But with the arrival of Rabbi Irving Reichert in 1930, the congregation once more assumed a haughty and elitist posture.

Yet if the third generation was generally status-conscious and conventional, it also produced several nonconformists, including intellectuals, artists, and adventurers. Leo Eloesser, whose grandfathers were German-speaking pioneers, was one of the city's most prominent thoracic surgeons during the interwar period, but he also exhibited a restless curiosity about foreign cultures and languages his entire life. As a youth he traveled throughout Mexico; for his medical training he chose Heidelberg and explored Eastern Europe (learning Russian in the process); in middle age he journeyed across the Soviet Union on the Trans-Siberian Railway and served as a surgeon in the Spanish Civil War; and in his late sixties he went to China and aided the forces of Mao Tse-tung against the Nationalists.[41] Beyond all of that, Dr. Eloesser was an accomplished violinist in a quartet whose members included the symphony's Pierre Monteux and Naoum Blinder. Comfortable among the bohemian artists who lived and worked near the downtown "Monkey Block" on Montgomery Street, he often provided them medical services free of charge.

Oakland, too, produced an original in this period, the photographer Alma Wahrhaftig. The East Bay had formed its own German Jewish aristocracy by the turn of the century, comprised mostly of department store owners who belonged to Temple Sinai, the increasingly Reform congregation that erected an elegant synagogue in 1913. Its president, Albert Lavenson, son of pioneers from Frankfurt am Main, developed the huge Capwell's department store while his brother-in-law Frederick Kahn presided over another gigantic retail operation bearing his name.[42] Lavenson's daughter Alma grew up in a privileged environment similar to that of her counterparts across the bay. She attended an exclusive private school, Miss Horton's in Oakland; was tutored in piano by one of the Bay Area's most respected music teachers; and, after graduating from the University of California, embarked on a seven-month grand tour of Europe with her whole family in 1922. She associated almost exclusively with the children of her parents' friends and relatives—the Furths, the Jonases, the Mosbachers, and of course the Kahns, who lived next door. But in 1933, at age thirty-six, Alma married a son of Russian Jewish immigrants, Matthew Wahrhaftig, who would become a local judge.

In the late 1920s she began photographing Marin's Mount Tamalpais and the coast near Mendocino, developing the pictures in a darkroom in her backyard. She met several of the era's greatest photographers, including Edward Weston, Consuelo Kanaga, and Imogen Cunningham, who became her lifelong friend. On Weston's advice, which she initially resisted, her work lost its "fuzzy, romantic" quality and soon became "clearer and straighter."[43] In 1932, she exhibited her photos in one of the most seminal photography shows in San Francisco's history, called "f.64" after the smallest aperture setting of their cameras. Featuring Weston, Cunningham, and Ansel Adams, among others, the sharply focused images—a modernist "visual manifesto" rebelling against the prevailing "pictorialism"—helped transform the public's taste for photography.[44] Alma next undertook a multiyear project in the Mother Lode, work shown at the San Francisco

Museum of Modern Art in 1948. A few years later, "San Ildefonso Indians," which she had taken in New Mexico, was selected by Edward Steichen for his famed "Family of Man" exhibit that toured the country in the mid-1950s.

There were other grandchildren of pioneers who went against the grain. Prominent attorney Henry H. Hart closed his practice in midlife and turned to Chinese literature; by the late 1930s he had amassed the largest private Chinese library in the country and would later translate dozens of works into Mandarin.[45] A. L. Gump's daughter Marcella married Tahitian royalty and lived on an island in French Polynesia.[46] J. B. Levison's son, who went by the name Charles Lane, enjoyed a career as a Shakespearean and Hollywood actor. Ellis Levy showed San Francisco its first newsreels (with perfect timing at the start of World War II) and soon founded one of the Bay Area's earliest chains of movie houses. Flora Jacobi Arnstein, as has been mentioned, was a progressive educator and proficient poetess. And, during the Depression, a number of bluebloods even became Communists.

Yet despite such risk taking, the cultural achievements of Bay Area Jewry's third generation lagged far behind those of the second. One looks in vain, among those born after 1880 of California-born parents, for as penetrating a thinker as Judah Magnes, a painter as accomplished as Toby Rosenthal, a multifaceted genius such as Gertrude Stein, or even a satirist on the level of Rube Goldberg. It may be that the tension between the pioneer German-speaking parents and their native-born children was essential for the near renaissance at the turn of the century. Indeed, the Jewish community's most brilliant artists in the 1920s and '30s, Yehudi Menuhin and Isaac Stern, were also the offspring of immigrants, East Europeans who lived in the Fillmore and Richmond. In 1927, the *Emanu-El* recognized the intellectual ascendancy of the newcomers' children with a proud piece on the third East European Jew in a row to win the gold medal for superior scholarship at UC Berkeley.[47]

Moreover, San Francisco and Oakland were no longer the exuberant frontier towns that they had been in the decades following the Civil War. Of course, the Bay Area would remain a stimulating, multicultural metropolis but, especially after the devastation of 1906, some of the romance was gone, especially from neighborhoods such as Chinatown and North Beach. Beyond that, the city's golden age of theater and opera was over by the early twentieth century. Much of the dynamism in the state could be found in booming Southern California, as the population of Los Angeles passed that of San Francisco, something unthinkable just a generation earlier. Russian-born

Jewish immigrants and their children poured into the Southland, some of whom would display a genius in laying the foundations for the American movie industry.

WALTER HAAS AND DAN KOSHLAND

The German Jewish elite in Northern California largely remained preoccupied with its long-established family businesses. Of course innovation was required here too, and after the First World War one firm, Levi Strauss and Company, was on course to become the largest apparel maker in the world. Two disciplined and discerning corporate executives were largely responsible for the transformation. Walter Haas and Dan Koshland were first cousins, brothers-in-law, and business partners (and died within three days of one another, in 1979).

They were both scions of pioneers who had built thriving firms. Their grandfather, Simon Koshland, founded a woolen company operating in San Francisco and Boston that came under the control of Dan's father, Marcus. Walter's father, Abraham Haas (who had married Marcus Koshland's sister, Fannie), made shrewd investments in oil and gas and developed a statewide wholesale grocery chain. The cousins Walter and Dan attended the University of California, where each was inspired by progressive professors. Both also traveled extensively (Koshland even visited Palestine on his yearlong tour abroad) and served as army officers during World War I.

Before entering the service, the urbane and reserved Walter married Elise Stern, the only child of Sigmund Stern, head of Levi Strauss and Company.* Strauss, a lifelong bachelor, had died in 1902, after which the firm passed to his four nephews, sons of his partner and brother-in-law, David Stern. By the time Walter was demobilized, Sig Stern needed help because two of his brothers had died, his brother Jacob was nearing retirement, and he himself had grown weary of the business. So he approached his thirty-two-year-old son-in-law, who had gained valuable experience in his father's produce business and in a New York bank, and asked him if he

*Soon, Haas's cousin Charles married Elise's cousin Fannie Stern, further cementing the ties between the Haases and the Sterns. Charles and Fannie's daughter was the magnanimous Madeline Haas Russell, who along with Dan Koshland and Walter Haas was one of the leading Jewish philanthropists in Northern California in the mid-twentieth century.

would direct the clothing company. Decades later, Haas laughed as he recalled Sig's offer of a two-year trial period: "If you don't like it . . . the company will be liquidated."[48]

In January 1919, when Walter came on board, Levi Strauss and Company operated only in the West and recorded annual sales of around three million dollars; there was little evidence of the multinational giant to come. Haas first introduced cost analysis, which revealed that the company's vaunted full-body Koveralls for children were actually a money loser. He went head-to-head with factory manager Simon Davis, whose father had applied for the patent for jeans with Levi Strauss back in the 1870s. Other employees backed Davis, who led a group that gave Sigmund Stern an ultimatum: End Haas's "meddling" or lose their services. It was a "confrontation," remembered Walter, between "the man who married the boss's daughter and the people who had been running the business."[49]

Stern backed his son-in-law and the firm suffered the resignation of Davis and other key workers, but Haas was undaunted. He filled the vacancies with capable people, shifted from manufacturing Koveralls to durable adult overalls, and maintained a sizable advertising budget even when clothing prices fell in 1920 and the corporation posted its first loss.

In 1922, Haas invited Dan Koshland, who had married Walter's sister, Eleanor, four years earlier, to codirect Levi Strauss. Dan was then unhappily working as an investment banker on Wall Street and eagerly accepted his brother-in-law's proposal, but he doubted whether he and Eleanor would have the same opportunities in San Francisco they had in New York to "help others who haven't our advantages."[50]

For the young Koshland had already made good works a cornerstone of his life. Some of his commitment stemmed from his Jewish values. His parents took Judaism more seriously than did most other pioneer families; they were active at both Ohabai Shalome and Emanu-El, where Dan learned about civic responsibility from the community-minded Rabbi Martin Meyer. But his sense of social justice owed even more to his student years at Berkeley, when he came under the influence of the left-leaning, somewhat bohemian economist Carleton Parker. The professor, as has been noted, wrote the seminal report on the Wheatland riot for Simon Lubin's state commission and was a leading advocate for impoverished farm workers. Koshland later said that entering Parker's orbit, at the height of the Progressive era, was "the most important thing in my college career."[51] Dan not only took Parker's popular courses but also established a warm relationship with him and his wife.* The youth who had grown up in the Petit Trianon was now part of "a circle of people who subscribed to the *New Masses*."[52]

As a banker in post–World War I New York, Koshland had attended the Free Synagogue, known for its social activism. Its crusading rabbi, Stephen Wise, officiated at his wedding. The San Franciscan met Herbert Lehman (the future governor and senator who belonged to one of the most prominent German Jewish families in the nation), whose liberal philosophy was similar to his own.[53] Lehman, who headed the business division of New York's Federation of Jewish Charities, enlisted Koshland as a fundraiser and put him on the committee dealing with community centers and settlement houses. Every week Dan visited the bustling University Settlement House on the Lower East Side, where he monitored the operation on behalf of the federation and volunteered as a coordinator of activities for disadvantaged immigrant youth.

After joining Haas at the helm of Levi Strauss, Koshland participated in the key decisions that would propel the company to unimaginable heights. He and Haas cut out almost everything but the production of pants; after World War II, of course, the allure of the jeans spread across the country and later the world, becoming one of the most recognizable American products ever. But no matter how large the company grew—the brothers-in-law lived to see it approach two billion dollars in annual sales—Haas and Koshland kept in mind the welfare of their employees, the Jewish community, and, most important, society as a whole.

THE PUBLIC GOOD

Like Harris Weinstock, who advocated the "City Beautiful" movement early in the century, many leading Jewish businessmen in the 1920s directed their energies and resources toward civic improvement. Early in the decade

---

*Koshland once invited the Parkers to meet his parents. Because Dan dressed casually on campus, the academic assumed he came from a family of modest means, so Parker left his suit and tie at home. He was stunned when Marcus and Cora Koshland greeted him in the marble entryway of a lavish mansion ("Levi Strauss and Company: Tailors to the World," interviews with Levi Strauss executives Walter A. Haas Sr., Daniel E. Koshland, Walter A. Haas Jr., and Peter E. Haas, 1976, Bancroft Library, Regional Oral History Office, University of California, Berkeley).

Herbert Fleishhacker, prominent attorney Emanuel Heller, and cigar manufacturer Milton Esberg worked closely with the mining and oil magnate William Crocker in guiding the War Memorial project. The complex, near the Beaux Arts–style Civic Center, would house an opera house as well as symphony hall, art museum, and veterans' center. Esberg, who had married into the Lilienthal-Sloss family and was active in the Republican Party, was later praised by President Hoover for exemplifying the way corporate leaders had literally changed the face of America: "The greatest good fortune . . . is a citizen outside its government who gives that leadership."[54] Businessmen were, in many respects, society's heroes in the 1920s, and Jewish descendants of pioneers were among San Francisco's leading businessmen.

Of course, the "leadership" lauded by Hoover also involved large financial contributions. The Bavarian-born pioneer banker Ignatz Steinhart set the tone as early as 1917 with a $250,000 bequest to the new California Academy of Sciences for an aquarium, "as fine and complete as anywhere in the world," in Golden Gate Park.[55] It was the largest donation the city had received since the earthquake.

Steinhart named the project for his late brother, Sigmund, a stockbroker who had long wanted to establish an aquarium in San Francisco and who had enlisted the help of David Starr Jordan, president of Stanford University and a prominent ichthyologist. In 1916, six years after Sigmund's death, Ignatz negotiated the terms of his mammoth gift with Barton Evermann, director of the Academy of Sciences. Although they encountered critics who would have preferred a location on the ocean or bay,[56] avid support for the Golden Gate Park site came from Michael de Young; no doubt he thought the aquarium would help his own art museum, which would be built nearby the following year. Ignatz Steinhart died in 1917, and when his will was made public Evermann was "flabbergasted" by the extent of his generosity. The aquarium, "filled with the life of the Pacific Ocean," opened half a decade later.[57]

Yet in bettering San Francisco no one in the Jewish community and few in the entire city could match the Fleishhacker brothers, now at the peak of their success. The "fun-loving and backslapping" Herbert[58] made huge donations to the War Memorial Opera House and the California Palace of the Legion of Honor, the elegant museum largely housing French art that opened in scenic Lincoln Park in 1924. His greatest passion, though, was outdoor recreation, and while president of the Park Commission he donated a colossal swimming pool to the city as well as a zoo.

The six-million-gallon outdoor pool, where Sloat Boulevard meets the beach, was the world's largest when it opened in 1925; lifeguards crossed it by kayak. It featured a Renaissance-style bathhouse as well as sixty acres for hiking, picnicking, tennis, and children's playgrounds. The entry fee was minimal, and the Fleishhacker Pool was initially popular with residents and movie stars such as Johnny Weissmuller and Esther Williams. But, as one local historian has written, it "proved to be a mistake."[59] The ocean breezes chilled swimmers, and an elaborate heating system had little effect on the ice-cold saltwater pumped in from the ocean. Besides, complained an aquatic champion, "half the time you were diving through the fog, and couldn't see the pool or the water."[60] "An economic monster," the pool deteriorated and would burden the city financially until it closed in 1971.[61]

But Fleishhacker was successful with the zoo. Bears, goats, elk, and bison had already been exhibited in the meadows of Golden Gate Park, but he envisioned a full-scale zoo, housing lions, tigers, apes, and especially elephants. Park superintendent John McClaren feared the exotic animals would mar the naturalistic setting, so Fleishhacker made available part of the sprawling acreage near the pool, brought over some of the animals from Golden Gate Park, and personally donated three elephants.[62] On a cruise in 1929, he met the famed animal collector George Bistany and hired him first to augment the collection and later as the zoo's founding director. Bistany arranged for a shipment to San Francisco of exotic animals and quickly upgraded the fledgling institution's makeshift facilities. During the Depression, a WPA grant allowed for the erection of ten animal houses. Fleishhacker personally worked with an architect to design the zoo; its moated enclosures, among the nation's first, helped simulate the animals' native habitats. The zoo was named in the banker's honor, but in 1941, hoping to attract a larger base of donors, he recommended it be called the San Francisco Zoological Gardens.*

Rosalie Meyer Stern made a similarly outstanding contribution to her city. After her husband, Sigmund, died in 1928, she purchased and then

*All told, Fleishhacker donated about a million dollars to the city, but his level of giving dropped sharply in the late 1930s, when he faced charges, brought by the Lazard banking family, of fiduciary mismanagement. He was ultimately exonerated, but the legal costs "and floodgate of other lawsuits" ruined him. His share of the family bank went into receivership, he lost his lavish home, and legend has it that "even his diamond cufflinks had to be tossed into the pot to satisfy creditors" (Irena Narell, *Our City* [San Diego, 1981], 236).

donated a twenty-five-acre parcel—the Trocadero, a former beer garden with a checkered past—later enlarging it to sixty-five acres. Although near the chilly, foggy western end of town, the Sigmund Stern Grove sits in a vale of towering eucalyptus trees protected from the elements. Rosalie donated funds for an outdoor pavilion and established a tradition, continued by her descendents to this day: music festivals free of charge to the public on summer Sundays.

Walter Haas and Daniel Koshland, meanwhile, focused on helping the needy. In 1922 they became charter board members of the Community Chest, an umbrella organization (in some ways a forerunner of the United Way) that allocated funds to dozens of relief organizations in San Francisco. They would also frequently lead the organization's fundraising drives.

A beneficiary of the Community Chest throughout most of the interwar period was the Federation of Jewish Charities, which supported the Hebrew Home for the Aged Disabled, Mount Zion Hospital, the Eureka Benevolent Society, and Homewood Terrace (as the orphanage was now known), among other Jewish institutions. The federation thus conducted no annual campaign of its own, an arrangement that perfectly suited Koshland's notion of "the inter-relation of Jewish and non-Jewish [philanthropic] activities [to meet] the requirements of a progressive community."[63]

It was usual in the West at this time for the Jewish Federation to be a subsidiary of the Community Chest. But virtually nowhere else did Jews—about 6 percent of San Francisco's population—contribute so much of the total raised (typically one-third) relative to the amount allocated to Jewish organizations (16 to 20 percent). Yet this "fortunate situation, wherein the Jews give much more than they receive," filled Koshland with pride;[64] when he dispensed charity, neither religion nor ethnicity counted in the slightest.

Walter Haas turned his attention toward local institutions of higher learning. His mother-in-law had donated a much-needed women's dormitory to the University of California, Berkeley, in 1940. Later, with aid of the trust fund of Rosalie's sister-in-law, Lucie Stern, he provided the University of California with the sprawling Strawberry Canyon Recreation Center. This merely foreshadowed the much grander philanthropy of the Haas family near the end of the century, when they endowed both the business school and a new sports arena on the Berkeley campus. And the School of Social Work fittingly bears the name of Richard and Rhoda Goldman. Walter and Elise Haas's daughter and Dan Koshland's niece, Rhoda accurately described herself as having been "bred" for benevolence.* [65]

Did the cascade of giving stem from ulterior motives such as attempting to preserve the family name, counter anti-Semitism, or curry favor with gentiles? Such thoughts probably crossed the minds of even the most altruistic Jewish benefactors. But the scope and creativity of their philanthropy, and the devotion as well as money they gave to their favorite causes, point to more idealistic motives. Dan Koshland, who was surprisingly modest and even self-effacing, epitomized those Jewish—and, even more so, Progressive era—ideals. In 1935, he wrote:

> Perhaps our financial contributions are generous in a comparative way. But should we not strive to do more than our share? Not because we want to buy peace and good will (they cannot be purchased), not because we can thus overcome the age-old accusations of avarice—but because we thereby increase our own self-respect, and because we help to alleviate pain and suffering among our neighbors in a troubled world.[66]

TAKING CARE OF ONE'S OWN

For all of their efforts to improve the lot of all San Franciscans, the Jewish elite was also concerned about the plight of their coreligionists, both at home and abroad. Of course, an extensive network of philanthropic agencies had already been formed by the second half of the nineteenth century. In 1910, community leaders brought the major Jewish welfare organizations together under the umbrella of the Federation of Jewish Charities, an attempt to coordinate and control the myriad of local agencies, especially their fundraising efforts. The federation's strongest advocate, Rabbi Jacob Voorsanger, predicted that allowing contributors to write one check covering all Jewish causes would "free every contributor from promiscuous begging, from unauthorized collections, from the constant annoyance of being interrupted by solicitors of the thousand and one charities which claim to have just title to support."[67] A decade later a similar federation

---

*Similarly, Mills College received the funds to build Lucie Stern Hall and the Walter A. Haas Pavilion. Other Jewish "first families" were also munificent toward the local universities: the Zellerbachs erected a spacious auditorium and playhouse at UC Berkeley, while the Dinkelspiels donated an auditorium at Stanford.

was formed in Oakland, and a lay leader spoke even more bluntly: "There were quite a few *shnorrers* [beggars] in town bothering private people."[68]

Not surprisingly, those at the apex of the Jewish aristocracy held the reins of power. Justice Marcus Sloss was the first president of the San Francisco federation, and was succeeded by I. W. Hellman Jr. The wool merchant Henry Sinsheimer (brother-in-law and business partner of Simon Koshland) and J. B. Levison were founding vice presidents.* In the East Bay, too, the Jewish Relief Federation was headed by the most prominent German Jewish lay leader, Frederick Kahn. His family would later be a major benefactor of the Oakland Art Museum.

As early as 1922, a decade and a half before the San Francisco–Oakland Bay Bridge would be completed, Temple Sinai's Rabbi Rudolph Coffee and others advocated a merger of the two federations. Sam Kohs, who became director of the Oakland federation a few years later, shared that goal. But the effective young social worker who would soon direct Brooklyn's huge federation and engineer its consolidation with wealthy Manhattan was unsuccessful in uniting the two federations in the Bay Area, which have remained separate to this day.[69] No doubt Kohs was impressed by the strength of the federation in San Francisco: by 1921, it had more than three thousand subscribers contributing almost a third of a million dollars.[70]

But early in the decade, when the federations became subsidiaries of their respective cities' Community Chests, a new vehicle was needed to meet Jewish needs nationally and internationally. In the mid-1920s each federation launched a separate corporate body, the Jewish National Welfare Fund (JNWF), to raise money and channel most of it outside the Bay Area. The lay leaders vividly recalled fundraising drives in both cities during World War I to aid starving Jews trapped between the German and Russian armies. Led by Justice Sloss, Mortimer Fleishhacker, and I. W. Hellman Jr., the San Francisco effort yielded a quarter of a million dollars, a sum second only to that collected by New York.[71] The creation of the JNWF a decade later was an attempt to institutionalize that effort.

The Jewish National Welfare Funds in San Francisco and Oakland were among the first in the country, but the one in the East Bay proved a

---

*A mere 3.5 percent of the funds raised was needed for the federation's own expenses, which suggests a great deal of lay involvement. A full-time director, I. Irving Lipsitsch, was not appointed until 1917 (Minutes of the Executive Committee of the San Francisco Federation of Jewish Charities, 1912, in WJHC/JLMM).

disappointment: it averaged barely $29,000 in annual donations before World War II, with only about twenty families contributing $200 or more in a typical year, and only four giving $500 or above.[72] A "small town" atmosphere prevailed, much to the chagrin of Kohs and others, who later spoke of an "unwritten agreement" among Oakland's Jewish donors to keep pledges low.[73] San Francisco, with its "old money" and its leadership in the national and international spotlight, did far better, raising about twelve times as much as the East Bay (and twice per capita).[74] Yet even the San Francisco JNWF fell short of expectations in the mid-1930s, when German Jews were in dire need of funds from America.

Much like the federations, the JNWFs sought to eliminate the "chaos," as a local historian described it, that resulted from the profusion of Jewish fundraising appeals.[75] The forty-six founding board members of the San Francisco Fund examined proposals from fifty agencies and decided to allocate funds to twenty-four. Although two-thirds of the board consisted of Emanu-El congregants, the beneficiaries crossed denominational, ideological, and ethnic lines. They included Jewish hospitals and rabbinical seminaries across the country, the Menorah Society (forerunner of the Hillel Foundation), the Jewish Publication Society, the American Jewish Congress, yeshivas in Eastern Europe and Ethiopia, and the "United Palestine Budget," which encompassed Hadassah, the Hebrew University, and the Jewish National Fund. The Mizrachi movement, comprised of Orthodox Zionists, was supported, too, reflecting the influence of Rabbi Wolf Gold of the Fillmore's Webster Street Shul, a JNWF board member from the outset, as were three other pulpit rabbis.[76]

The most powerful figure in San Francisco's JNWF was Lloyd Dinkelspiel, a third-generation San Franciscan who married into the Hellman family and was a partner in the prestigious law firm of Heller, Ehrman, White & McAuliffe. He led two of the early annual campaigns, eventually became president of the JNWF, and in 1955 would oversee its merger with the federation, by then long independent of the Community Chest. A similar consolidation of JNWF and federation took place several years earlier in Oakland. Thus was born the modern federation, an institution of local, national, and international reach that, especially on the San Francisco side of the bay, was destined to exert great influence on Jewish life in the last third of the century and beyond.

But through the early 1930s there would only be a hint of the future power and orientation of the federation. Zionist organizations were funded by the JNWF, but only modestly. Moreover, neither the fund nor the federation yet acted as a policy-making body, or even attempted to speak for the Jewish community.

"Our Jewish residents know very little about anti-Semitism," wrote Rudolph Coffee in 1927; the rabbi of Oakland's Temple Sinai considered the recent rebirth of the Ku Klux Klan a distant phenomenon, despite some incidents of cross burning in Napa County, about fifty miles from his synagogue.[77] But while the Bay Area was largely free of such hate groups in the 1920s, discrimination was felt at the highest levels of society as well as the lowest. There was no sudden shift in attitudes, but Northern California was no longer quite as welcoming to the immigrant and even to the native Jew as it had been in the nineteenth century.

The Jewish elite, unsettled by the Weinberg case, World War I, and the Red Scare, now sensed a change in their exclusive haunts as well. At the Bohemian Club, which had admitted numerous Jewish pioneers and their sons, a much tougher policy prevailed by the third generation. Longtime member J. B. Levison reportedly felt snubbed as early as 1917, and though he remained active until his death thirty years later, he did not propose any of his four sons for the club, fearing that as Jews they would be turned down.[78] Worse was the experience of Raphael Weill, a founding Bohemian who enjoyed preparing Sunday breakfasts for his many friends at the club.[79] He angrily resigned when his nephew and heir was blackballed.[80] Nor could he switch allegiance to the posh Burlingame Country Club, which accepted no Jews, although its menu featured "Frogs' legs à la Raphael Weill."[81] As the cruel joke went, "At least he made it as an entrée."[82]

Golf gained popularity after World War I, and although the venerable Presidio Golf Club included J. B. Levison and Justice Sloss (also a Bohemian), it added no new Jewish members during nearly the entire interwar period. That policy led to the founding in 1922 of the Lake Merced Golf and Country Club, which reportedly had Jews as half of its charter members.[83] Similarly, the San Francisco Yacht Club counted a couple of Jewish bluebloods accepted before World War I—a Lilienthal and an Ehrman—but barred any more Jews until the 1940s.[84]

Even the leading day schools became more selective. Although Mortimer Fleishhacker and Sigmund Stern had helped Katharine Delmar Burke establish her top-rated girls' academy, it set a quota of only two Jewish students a year in the 1920s. By the following decade, when Rhoda Haas attended Miss Burke's, she was the only Jew in her class.[85]

Few corners of Bay Area life exhibited more prejudice than did higher education. At Stanford University and Mills College Jews were limited to just a few percent of the student body. At the University of California this was not the case, and by 1927 more than five hundred Jews were enrolled as undergraduates, the highest representation at a university in the West. But the atmosphere on campus was sometimes hostile, and in the mid-1920s the fraternities' policy of excluding Jews led to the formation of several Jewish frats and even played a role in the birth of a Hillel Foundation, the fifth in the nation.[86] Jews also found themselves barred from leadership positions in some student activities, and when one improbably became the editor of the *Daily Californian* in 1935, he found himself the subject of an anti-Semitic caricature in the form of a float in the annual fall parade known as the Big "C" Sirkus.[87] Despite the presence of distinguished Jewish professors such as Jessica Peixotto and Provost Monroe Deutsch, a number of departments, such as English and history, refused to hire Jews until well after World War II. At Stanford, meanwhile, Herbert Fleishhacker Jr. was the football team's star quarterback in 1927, no minor celebrity in a period when the "Big Game" against Cal (whose team also had some Jewish stalwarts) transfixed the Bay Area.[88] A few years later, however, another Stanford Jewish student complained publicly of the "almost complete exclusion of Jews from non-sectarian fraternities and fairly complete restriction . . . from the more desirable campus offices."[89]

The Jewish community's response to such anti-Semitism was measured in the 1920s. In the middle of the decade, as we have seen, Aaron Sapiro, who had long before moved to the Midwest, boldly and successfully sued Henry Ford, but prominent Bay Area residents attacked in the *Dearborn Independent* refused to join the fray. The *Emanu-El* occasionally noted difficulties on the Berkeley campus and protested the exclusion of Jews from summer resorts in the Santa Cruz Mountains, but not until the appearance of several American fascist groups during the Depression did local anti-Jewish prejudice become a major story. And only in the late 1930s were professionally run "defense" organizations formed on each side of the bay; before that anti-Semitism was countered by a committee of laymen constituting the local branch of the B'nai B'rith Anti-Defamation League and, of course, individual rabbis.

In the post–World War I decade, the top priority of Jewish leaders (as it was in the nineteenth century) was the separation of church and state. When evangelical Christians tried to persuade state lawmakers to end the teaching of evolution and to grant release time for religious education, Rabbis Newman and Coffee lobbied aggressively in Sacramento against any penetration of Christianity into public schools. Both bills failed to make it out of committee, and the rabbis continued in the same vein, campaigning against a ballot measure to allow Bible reading in the classroom.[90] It went down in defeat despite winning a majority in ten counties in Southern California. Coffee expressed pleasure that in "three clashes . . . with the fundamentalist forces, liberals have been successful each time."[91]

The rabbis had mixed results, however, in countering the depiction in popular culture of the Jew as Christ-killer. In 1929, a half-century after his passion play had plunged San Francisco into turmoil, David Belasco, now world famous, returned with an even more defamatory drama that graphically depicted the crucifixion. Rabbis Newman and Nieto sought to convince the board of supervisors that if they did not ban the production outright, they should at least deny the producers the use of the municipally owned Civic Auditorium.[92] After a series of contentious hearings—unlike during the bizarre 1879 controversy, many Protestant ministers sided with the play—the promoters saw they would be outvoted and pulled their proposal for a permit. Belasco's passion play was staged, but in a downtown theater where it had a short, uneventful run.

More dangerous, though, was Cecil B. DeMille's epic movie *King of Kings,* which opened nationwide in the fall of 1927. Newman and Coffee joined lay leaders of the Anti-Defamation League (ADL) and pulpit rabbis in Los Angeles in an attempt to pressure the director to drop his project or tone down its inflammatory scenes. But they had little influence on the final product, which Coffee termed "a crucifixion of truth."[93] A frustrated Newman publicly lashed out against his Southern California colleagues, including Rabbi Edgar Magnin of the Wilshire Boulevard Temple, for not having made stronger efforts to block the film.[94] The ADL fired back in print with a stinging criticism of the Emanu-El rabbi's "baseless, factless accusations."[95] The internal clash pointed to the need for unity and better coordination in the realm of community relations, which would become far more urgent in the next decade.

That the internal flap was covered in the *Emanu-El* was unusual, however, for nothing was more characteristic of the Jewish establishment in the 1920s than discretion. Throughout most of the decade the community's main forum for news and opinion, the *Emanu-El* was guided not by a forceful editor, as it had been earlier in the century (and would be in the 1930s and early '40s), but rather by a committee of pulpit rabbis that did not even include the assertive Louis Newman. Tending to avoid controversy, the weekly ran bland editorials, few op-ed pieces, and no letters to the editor.*

Virtual silence was the rule whenever there was a risk that the community's image might be tarnished, such as in 1923, when the shocking and potentially scandalous deaths of two pulpit rabbis occurred only ten weeks apart. Early on April 5, Ohabai Shalome's spiritual leader, the young San Francisco native Alfred Lafee, who had occupied his post for almost a year and lived with his parents, was discovered nude, dazed, and bludgeoned in a cheap, disreputable hotel.[96] Rushed to Mount Zion Hospital, he died a short time later from a fracture to his skull. The rabbi had checked into the hotel under a false name the night before, accompanied by a sailor. Evidently expecting a homosexual tryst, Lafee was instead robbed and killed. The *Emanu-El* reported only the conclusions of "friends that [he] was the victim of a man whom he befriended in distress and whom he probably accompanied on an errand of mercy," but the *Examiner* and *Chronicle* supplied lurid details and followed the case closely over the next two months.[97] Within three weeks the murderer was found: an eighteen-year-old seaman who confessed to the crime and was implicated by a mountain of evidence, including his own diary and the victim's bloodstained clothing.[98]

Yet after extraditing the killer, who had fled to Arizona, the district attorney dropped the charges against him on June 29, and newspaper coverage of the case abruptly ceased. Philip Zwerin, at the time a trial attorney and an active member of Sherith Israel, was convinced—as was his son, who later became a lawyer and a Reform rabbi—that "Jewish department store owners . . . threatened" the major dailies with the loss of advertising revenue if they continued reporting on the Lafee matter, and pressured the authorities

---

*A more serious and probing weekly, the *Jewish Journal,* appeared near the end of the decade, but financial difficulties required it to merge with a transformed *Emanu-El* a few years later.

to dismiss the charges.*[99] If true, the conduit may have been the head of the local ADL, Isidore Golden, a college classmate and close friend of District Attorney Matthew Brady, as well as his chief deputy.[100] Lafee's killer went free only two days after Emanu-El's Rabbi Martin Meyer committed suicide, so the Zwerins may have had a point about the fear of "unhappy publicity," as they put it, weighing heavily on the minds of Jewish leaders.[101]

The demise of forty-four-year-old Meyer, one of the leading rabbis in the West, was no less disturbing than that of Lafee. His wife had discovered his lifeless body late one night after entering his study in their home. Because he had delivered a lecture only hours before and had played golf earlier in the day, his family and friends first hypothesized a sudden stroke.[102] But the coroner found in Meyer's stomach potassium cyanide, a chemical he used to mount butterflies.[103]

The *American Israelite* suggested that someone had poisoned the rabbi, and there also exists the possibility—accepted by the San Francisco police after a cursory investigation—that he drank the lethal substance by mistake. Much more likely, though, in the opinion of those who knew him well, was that he was driven to suicide by an agonizing crisis in his personal life.[104]

One of his closest colleagues felt that he had returned from service with the Red Cross during World War I "a disillusioned man."[105] When eulogizing his lifelong friend, Rabbi Coffee noted that "harrowing labors with the wounded and dying burned their impress on his soul."[106] Meyer was also depressed due to poor health: he was hospitalized for several months in 1920 from "stress and exhaustion" and then required a lengthy vacation outside the city.[107] Afterward he had operations for gallstones and appendicitis.

He was also suffering from a severe hearing loss, which some said contributed to his despondency.[108] Others believed that he had an inoperable brain tumor as well, the diagnosis of which led to his suicide.[109] There was also a more disconcerting rumor spread at the time—like the other theories, circulated over the decades by highly regarded temple leaders—that he had had sexual relations with a teenaged boy and was unable to face the prospect of being found out.†[110]

---

*There were rumors as well that the Lafee family, shamed by the newspaper coverage, agreed that the case should be dropped.

†In hindsight, questions were raised about the all-male Pathfinders, a club that the rabbi had formed in 1921. He had close relationships with several of its young members, who frequently came to his home, and even watched him shave on Sabbath mornings, before walking with him to the synagogue.

Needless to say, neither the Jewish press nor the synagogue would even raise the possibility that Meyer had committed suicide, much less speculate on its possible causes. The Meyer and Lafee tragedies were discussed behind closed doors, as was so much else in the 1920s.

There was nothing restrained, however, about the role played by Jews in San Francisco politics. During the 1920s and even more so in the 1930s, precisely when anti-Semitism was increasing nationwide, local Jewish politicians showed remarkable success at winning elections. In contrast to nineteenth-century office seekers such as Michael de Young or Adolph Sutro, Jewish candidates in the early twentieth century rarely downplayed their Jewish origins, which was sometimes an asset, as voters in the ethnically diverse town were seeking to loosen the grip on politics held by Irish Catholics. No other American city during the interwar years could match the high proportion of Jews holding elective and appointed offices, nor the influence that the Jews had on the choice of candidates.

The baker's son Julius Kahn, who first worked as an actor directed by David Belasco, became one of the most popular congressmen in American history. The staunchly pro-military Republican was initially sent to Washington in 1898, when San Francisco was still heavily Democratic, and served almost without interruption until his death in 1924. Only seven representatives (none of them from a big city) had ever been elected to more terms.[111] Beloved in his district, Kahn was also highly regarded on Capitol Hill: he became chairman of the Military Affairs Committee and almost became Speaker of the House.[112]

After he died in office, his widow won a special election to serve out his term. Florence Prag Kahn, the first Jewish woman in Congress, then won five successive elections, until she succumbed to the Roosevelt landslide in 1936.* In 1852 her grandparents, the Isaac Goldsmiths, and her mother, Mary, then age six, had come to San Francisco on a frightening journey via

---

*She was one of the first widows to succeed her husband in Congress, a pattern that has often been repeated since. When Kahn first joined the House in 1925 she had only two women colleagues, but while she hoped to see more females in public office, she was hardly a constant advocate of women's rights, having opposed universal suffrage as a "fad" as late as 1908 (*San Francisco Chronicle*, April 12, 1983, 2).

Nicaragua. Mary Goldsmith Prag became a leading public school educator and teacher at Emanu-El, and her daughter was one of only nine women to graduate from the University of California in 1887. Florence married Kahn soon after he was first elected and became almost as absorbed by politics as he was.

Utterly without glamour—the stout Florence donned "sack-like dresses" and wore no makeup—but energetic and sharp-witted, she wielded much influence during her eleven-year tenure on Capitol Hill.[113] The long friendships she had established with House leaders early in the century, when many of them were freshmen, partly offset her lack of seniority, and she was appointed to the Military Affairs and the Appropriations Committees, in each case breaking a new barrier for women.[114]

Not surprisingly, she carried forward her husband's right-wing agenda, advocating a giant defense budget, continued exclusion of Chinese immigrants, and a crackdown on pacifists and Communists.[115] President Hoover dubbed her the "mother of the FBI" because she was instrumental in securing funding for the new bureau.[116] She favored tax cuts and staunchly opposed the New Deal as too costly, causing critics to call her "the most astute and dangerous anti-liberal in Northern California."[117] But though she represented a relatively conservative district in the northern part of the city, she was, after all, a San Francisco politician, prounion and broad-minded on social issues. She worked to repeal Prohibition (drawing the rebuke of several women's groups) and the blue laws mandating Sunday closings of certain businesses.[118] Endearing her to the voters, too, was the river of federal dollars she channeled to the Bay Area. Massive projects such as the San Francisco–Oakland Bay Bridge and the Alameda Naval Air Station owe much to her legislative skill.[119]

While the Kahns were virtual fixtures in Washington, Jesse Colman set a record for longevity on the board of supervisors that still stands. First elected in 1921, the grandson of Emanu-El's pioneer rabbi Elkan Cohn did not retire until 1947. Then, in 1961, past the age of eighty, he returned to finish the term of another supervisor. Like almost all the Jewish politicians of his day, Colman was highly active in Jewish causes; he was a longtime board member of Emanu-El, the federation, and the Jewish Community Relations Council.[120] In the late 1920s and early '30s he was joined on the board of supervisors by Jefferson Peyser, Grand President of B'nai B'rith's District 4.

Peyser was also one of several local Jews sent to the state legislature in the interwar period. Edgar C. Levey was assemblyman for a dozen years beginning in the mid-1920s, spending half of that period as speaker. But no less influential was B. J. Feigenbaum, grandson of prosperous German Jewish pioneers, elected to the state assembly at the age of twenty-six. A moderate Republican, as was Peyser and Levey, he won the endorsement of the Democratic Party as well, and during the Depression he helped balance the budget by supporting a sales and income tax.[121] The most progressive Jewish politician in the GOP was Albert C. Wollenberg, yet another third-generation German Jew. Elected in the late 1930s, he served as the floor leader for much of the liberal legislation of Governor Earl Warren in the following decade. In 1947, after nearly a decade as a powerful lawmaker, Wollenberg embarked upon a second distinguished career as a superior court judge.

Jews had an even higher profile as appointed office holders than they did as elected officials. One political scientist, analyzing the city's major boards and commissions, showed that during the administration of Mayor James Rolph (1911–30) Jews held nearly 15 percent of the municipal appointments.[122] His successor, Angelo Rossi, who served until 1944, raised the level to almost 30 percent, a ratio that continued until the early 1960s.[123] The board of education was typical: beginning in 1921, two of the seven seats were always held by Jews until 1971, when it became an elected body.[124] Of course, many of these positions, especially the presidencies of the Recreation, Library, and Art commissions, were rewards to philanthropists or campaign supporters. Besides, for the Italian Rossi, the Jewish community was a natural ally in his rivalry with the Irish, and the Protestant mayors who succeeded him may have seen Jews as partners in their struggle against Catholic political rivals. Whatever the reasons for the plethora of Jewish appointments, the interwar period saw the dawn of a golden age of civic leadership for San Francisco Jewry.[125]

Jews were also powerbrokers as never before, even in San Francisco. Herbert Fleishhacker virtually controlled Mayor Rolph, as has been seen, and remained a valued advisor of Angelo Rossi. But other prominent Jews, such as I. W. Hellman Jr., Walter Haas, Marcus Sloss, Milton Esberg, and Jesse Steinhart, were also kingmakers and fundraisers in the Republican Party, which dominated the city and the state.

Jesse Steinhart wielded the most clout of all. Distantly related to the philanthropists Ignatz and Sigmund, his father was William Steinhart, who had founded the first B'nai B'rith lodge on the West Coast. Jesse grew up in a home that esteemed Jewish tradition as much as it did French and German culture, but, like his sister, Amy Steinhart Braden, he was molded primarily by the Progressive movement early in the century. An avid "Bull Mooser," he attended the convention in 1912 that nominated Theodore Roosevelt for President and Hiram Johnson as his running mate, and for the rest of his long life "good government" would be the cornerstone of his political philosophy.

Steinhart never faced the voters himself, but, focusing on the "absolute integrity of the man holding office," he propelled the political careers of numerous others.[126] B. J. Feigenbaum, a Harvard-trained lawyer in Steinhart's prestigious firm, and Albert C. Wollenberg were two exceptional young men whom he convinced to run for the State Assembly, and he contributed liberally to the campaigns of Jefferson Peyser and Jesse Colman.[127]

Steinhart also operated on the statewide level. In 1926 he was instrumental in the gubernatorial campaign of the progressive C. C. Young, a low-key former English teacher at Lowell High School, whom Walter Haas, his former student, also admired. Steinhart supplied Young with money and advice, and the unlikely candidate was elected in 1926.[128] Steinhart's greatest coup would come during World War II, when he helped convince a reluctant Earl Warren, then state attorney general, to run for governor.

Although the state Democratic Party was weak until the late 1930s, and roundly despised by San Francisco's German Jewish elite, a blueblood was nevertheless its chief fundraiser as well. Edward Heller, grandson of I. W. Hellman and son of Emanuel Heller, founder of the law firm Heller, Ehrman, White & McAulliffe, was also a first cousin of New York governor Herbert Lehman. Ed, an executive of Wells Fargo, "the family bank," and his civic-minded wife, Elinor, were delegates to many Democratic national conventions beginning in 1928 and major supporters of Culbert Olson's successful bid for governor in 1938. He rewarded Heller with an appointment to the Board of Regents of the University of California. In the early 1940s, Elinor became a national Democratic committeewoman and Ed Heller a close confidant of legendary Democratic state chairman Bill Malone. The two met after work almost every day in a Market Street bar, where they discussed campaign contributions, federal appointments, and patronage. People spoke of the "Heller-Malone machine."[129]

The best-known Jew in San Francisco was not a philanthropic titan whose name adorned a famous landmark, nor was he a gifted artist or an influential politician. He did not hail from an old German Jewish family, but neither was he an East European immigrant. Fully consistent with the Jewish community's idiosyncratic tradition, the beloved Albert (Micky) Bender was an Irishman—and proud of it.

Son of a Dublin rabbi, Micky never lost his brogue, or his love of Celtic poetry. Arriving in San Francisco as a teenager in the late 1880s, he soon prospered as an insurance broker, winning the accounts and friendships of many leading Jewish businessmen. He then turned to improving the quality of cultural life in his adopted city. A bibliophile from the beginning, he served as board member of the San Francisco Library and as president of the library commission, and was a major donor of rare books and manuscripts to the University of California, Stanford, and Mills College.[130] The latter two named their rare book rooms in his honor.

Bender lived as a bachelor in a tasteful apartment in the Studio Building on Post Street near Franklin, then a neighborhood filled with artists. He cherished his younger first cousin Anne Bremer, the talented painter known for her innovative use of color. Also unmarried, Bremer occupied a studio apartment in the same building. The precise nature of their relationship is impossible to determine, but her death in 1923, at the age of fifty-one, was a life-changing event for Bender, who "maintained her apartment as a shrine."[131] Until he passed away in 1941 he devoted himself to helping aspiring artists, and he set up a fund in Anne's memory for that purpose.

He also brought artists and patrons together, and sometimes he initiated meetings among the artists themselves. Bender's close friend Ansel Adams first met Edward Weston in Micky's apartment.[132] When retailer Albert Lavenson died in 1930, recalled his daughter Alma, who was then experimenting with photography, Bender, "instead of bringing flowers . . . gave me cards of introduction to Edward Weston, Imogen Cunningham, and Consuelo Kanaga."[133] He introduced the Rumanian-born sculptor Jacques Schnier to Jesse Lilienthal Jr.; it led to a commission for the struggling artist and also to a marriage between Schnier and Lilienthal's daughter.

Bender refused to let political vagaries stand in the way of good art. In the mid-1920s, interested in Mexico's monumental public murals, he sought to bring Diego Rivera to San Francisco for a major commission. The refined insurance man began a correspondence with the flamboyant Communist, bought and donated many of Rivera's controversial works to the San Francisco Art Museum, and used his influence to obtain the painter's visa.[134] November 1928 saw his hard work rewarded; he went to the train station to welcome Rivera and his wife, Frida Kahlo.[135]

Now Bender worked closely with William Gerstle (son of the pioneer magnate Lewis Gerstle), president of the San Francisco Art Association and himself a painter. The two, both members of the Bohemian Club and allies in other cultural battles, had hoped Rivera's art would grace the walls of a public building. But in the face of angry opposition—led by the all-powerful Herbert Fleishhacker—Bender and Gerstle changed the location to a private and unlikely site, the Stock Exchange Lunch Club.[136] Fortunately for Bender, Rivera did not take the opportunity to ridicule American capitalism (as he done before and would do in the future); his 1931 mural *Allegory of California* primarily depicted the state's abundance of natural resources. But the presence of one of the world's leading political artists in San Francisco galvanized a cadre of radical young painters who would soon stir up the town in ways no one could have foreseen.

Bender also came to the aid of nonpolitical artists victimized by world events. In the 1930s he showed deep sympathy for local Japanese artists (many of them American-born), who had been economically devastated by a boycott resulting from the savage war waged by Japan against China. Bender "patronized them heavily," his friend, the historian Oscar Lewis, recalls, making up for their loss of business.[137]

Nearly every kind of art intrigued him, and he purchased works on an almost daily basis, admiring them in his apartment for a few weeks before invariably donating them to a local institution or one in Ireland. The museum in the new Veterans Building benefited most: during one five-year period in the 1930s Bender donated eleven hundred objects to the grateful institution, which annually held a special exhibit of his gifts.[138] He donated treasures to the University of California's museum, the de Young, and the Legion of Honor. To the National Museum in Dublin he contributed a fine collection of Asian art, perhaps to remind those in his native land that he had attained prominence on the shores of the Pacific.[139]

By 1930 Bender was acting in another capacity as well, as "unacknowledged greeter of the city," prefiguring the role later played by another Jewish bon vivant and civic booster, Cyril Magnin, San Francisco's first official chief of protocol.[140] Bender was stocky, barely five feet tall, and had a slight speech impediment, but no one was more likely to charm out-of-towners or, for that matter, local residents. Kevin Starr captures Micky's inimitable blend of polish and warmth:

> Elegantly attired in his tailored double-breasted suit with extra-wide and finely pointed lapels, his tie impeccable against a gleamingly white starched shirt, his hat at a jaunty angle (the right brim raised, the left brim rakishly lowered), Bender negotiated the streets of the city as if on a family visit. He knew everyone and they knew him. To walk with him in the downtown . . . was to have the opportunity to experience San Francisco as a cohesive community, even a small town.[141]

Bender was a founding board member of the Federation of Jewish Charities and a longtime congregant of Emanu-El, whose cavernous sanctuary could not hold all who came to his funeral. But his significance lay in the ease and grace with which he moved among both the most prominent Jews and non-Jews in the Bay Area. Proof of that are the mixed guest lists for his St. Patrick Day parties, an annual "civic institution, covered in the press like opening day at the races . . . occasions [for which] Bender dressed in the robes of a cardinal."[142] In few other places in America were social boundaries crossed and stereotypes questioned as they were at those events.

Bay Area Jewry's "prosperity, sense of well being, philanthropic commitment to Jewish and non-Jewish causes alike, [and] leadership in business and the arts" caused Starr to make the bold claim that "San Francisco was a Jewish city" in the interwar period, but he added, "not like New York was a Jewish city."[143] Perhaps as much as the obvious demographic differences, he had in mind the phenomenon of Micky Bender.

NINE

Both Sides of the Barricades

Jews and Class Conflict during the Depression

THE DEPRESSION HIT THE DIVERSE Bay Area economy with less ferocity than it struck the cities of the East and Midwest, or even Southern California. In 1931 unemployment in San Francisco was 12.5 percent, compared with 15.3 percent nationwide and almost 17 percent in Los Angeles.[1] Jews in the Bay Area were also less reliant on the hard-hit manufacturing sector than were their neighbors, and thus not as vulnerable to the steep economic decline.[2]

Nevertheless, thousands of Jews—professionals and small business owners as well as blue-collar workers—lost their jobs. In 1932 the *Emanu-El* reported that one in ten San Francisco Jews required help in the form of cash, food, or lodging, compared with one in forty a few years earlier.[3] The sociological profile of the Jewish poor had quickly changed as well. Before 1929 the destitute were primarily elderly, disabled, or widowed. By 1932, however, they included many that had recently had jobs, homes, and savings.[4] Beyond that was the problem of Jewish transients, mostly young males, who arrived in town without any means.

The Eureka Benevolent Society found jobs for the unemployed and distributed meal tickets, vouchers for shelter, and clothing on a level unprecedented in its eighty-year history.[5] In 1932, the National Council of Jewish Women opened the "Opportunity Shop," staffed by volunteers on Sutter Street in the Fillmore. Several times a week more than a hundred needy women sold food they had cooked or garments they had made in their homes.[6]

Beyond the material hardships it caused, the Depression altered the political and cultural landscape of Northern California, affecting Jews along with every other group. Class conflict worsened, making San Francisco, already known for strife between labor and capital, perhaps the most polarized metropolis in the nation.

To be sure, some employers protected their workers. Levi Strauss and Company, for example, after three consecutive years of losses in the early 1930s, reduced salaries and hours but dismissed no wage earners. Even when production had to be halted, Dan Koshland and Walter Haas put their employees to work refurbishing the factory.[7] But such concern for labor was the exception among both Jewish and non-Jewish owners; overall, big business showed little sympathy for workers and aggressively tried to break strikes. In 1934 the *Emanu-El* declared "Jewish unity impossible" because of the self-interested actions taken by the community's corporate executives.[8]

Leading pulpit rabbis took the side of labor, and the vehement attack on capitalism by one spiritual leader, the young Jacob Weinstein at Sherith Israel, cost him his post. Max Radin, a distinguished law professor at UC Berkeley, was denied a seat on the state supreme court in 1940 because of his views favoring unions and free speech.[9] Other Jews joined strikes and demonstrations or created left-leaning works of art and literature. Many of them, too, paid a high price. And while most Bay Area Jews fully approved of FDR's New Deal as the proper remedy for the Depression, a small segment lost all trust in the American system and joined the Communist Party, which reached the peak of its popularity in the mid-1930s. Several local Jewish Communists were shadowed by the FBI through World War II and may well have been Soviet spies.

For all the suffering and rancor of the 1930s, the decade nonetheless witnessed a strengthening of Jewish institutions. Although the pioneer congregation Ohabai Shalome closed, a new synagogue, Beth Sholom, arose to serve the rapidly growing Jewish population of the Richmond District. Mount Zion Hospital raised nearly a million dollars in 1931 to transform itself into an institution for research and teaching as well as medical care.[10] And San Francisco's first Jewish Community Center opened on California Street in 1933, offering a wide range of recreational, cultural, and educational programs.

Government was the largest engine of growth in the second half of the decade, which saw the construction of the city's two great bridges as well as a world's fair on Treasure Island. Jews were deeply involved in those endeavors as promoters and civic boosters, artists and engineers. Public works, too, were a defiant response to the Depression.

"DRIVE THE SMUGNESS OUT OF THE STRONG"

Rabbi Jacob Weinstein, the most radical advocate for social justice ever to hold a major synagogue pulpit in Northern California, led Sherith Israel in the early 1930s. Born in Russia and raised by Orthodox parents in Portland, Oregon, he attended Columbia University in the 1920s, where he engaged in the fierce debates that gripped New York Jewish intellectuals.[11] An ardent Zionist and socialist, he entered Hebrew Union College intending to apply prophetic ethics to society's socioeconomic problems. Less than a year after his ordination in 1929, at age twenty-seven, Weinstein succeeded the venerable Rabbi Nieto.

From the beginning he showed little interest in the congregation's finances or administration, and he was only marginally effective as a pastor. But his sermons were extraordinary: with his passionately delivered critiques of the capitalist system ("our barbarous economic order"), he sought to "comfort the weary and worn, and yet drive the smugness out of the strong."[12] His message resonated among those who felt victimized by the deepest economic slide in American history. Friday evening services now drew a good number of non-Jews, some of them dressed in the overalls they wore during the day as teamsters.[13]

But Weinstein angered some of the congregants with a humanist approach that seemed to leave out God. He assailed the "false trust on the Heavenly Arms," which, he told his flock, "sapped your energies, and turned your eyes from the sources of strength within yourself."[14] Others were appalled at the depth of his pacifism. In a front-page article in the Jewish press he put forth the Quakers as a model:

Suppose we fill the jails! Suppose some of us get shot for refusing to fight! . . . In the past war, let it be said to our glory, there were many Jews among the conscientious objectors in the federal penitentiaries. But these Jews were considered outcasts from the body of respectable Jewry. Let us reverse the tables in the next war. Let the body of Israel be in the prisons and the outcasts in uniforms.[15]

Perhaps the greatest affront to Sherith Israel's lay leadership was the rabbi's embrace of Tom Mooney's cause, which was the theme of his Yom

Kippur sermon in 1931 (see chapter 6). As has been noted, in 1917, the labor agitator had been convicted, on highly questionable evidence, of planting a bomb that killed ten people. Weinstein, having studied the case since his college days, and having obtained a press pass to sit in the gallery of the state supreme court while it heard—and rejected—Mooney's appeal, concluded that Mooney's sentence was "a perfect example of social injustice."[16] He and his alleged coconspirator, Warren Billings, had suffered, Weinstein proclaimed from the pulpit, "because their fellow men were too cowardly or too avaricious to tell the truth."[17]

According to one local historian, "some of the most influential members" of the congregation walked out in the middle of the Mooney homily, and a committee of the board insisted that in the future he submit his sermons for review.[18] He refused, demanding the freedom "to preach the ideals of prophetic Judaism."[19] As he wrote the board, "The ten million unemployed among which are thousands of fine elderly middle-class people such as join our Temple are the victims of this economic warfare. The religious organization which does not bend its energy toward eliminating the brutal factors of modern industry is derelict in its moral obligation to the people."[20]

The minute books of Sherith Israel, so revealing of personnel problems at the temple a generation earlier, are uncharacteristically mute on Weinstein's departure; the board met in executive session, its deliberations unrecorded. But the caustic correspondence between the rabbi and lay leaders in the spring of 1932 indicates that his resignation in June, a year before his contract was to expire, was mutually agreed upon, the result of "irreconcilable" differences.[21]

The *Emanu-El* erroneously reported that he had taken an indefinite leave of absence for an operation on his vocal chords, but Weinstein would not slink away under such a veil.[22] In a thunderous farewell sermon he squarely addressed the reasons for his departure: "I insisted on . . . pointing out definite ways in which people of this very congregation could do their share in putting an end to the savage conditions about us, [and this] was most unwelcome to many of you."[23]

Later in the year Weinstein wrote a candid article for a national magazine on his turbulent two-year tenure. Still filled with anger and frustration, he parodied the typical temple board member as a crude social climber. Weinstein recalled the "counsel" he received:

"Pardon the language, [rabbi] . . . but you've got an easy racket. You don't have to sell a thing but yourself. You've got a good show here—a beautiful

Temple, a fine choir, a swell cantor, and the pull of religion. If you will only fit into the scheme and show the people how really good the stuff is, you're made. There is no reason why in five years you can't have fifteen to twenty thousand a year, a nice car, a home, and a congregation that will eat out of your hands. The people of this [synagogue] . . . have played second fiddle to the other Temple and many of us have been snubbed at public occasions by people who lay claim to leadership because their parents peddled around here before ours. Now we have a chance to get back at them. You're much brighter than their rabbi and you can steal the show from him. Prepare a couple of swell addresses on patriotic themes for general consumption and the people of this congregation will be your friends for life."

I thanked my friend for his advice and promised that I would give it most careful consideration.[24]

Now with time to travel, Weinstein and his wife visited Palestine, a trip that further deepened his commitment to socialist Zionism. During his eventful stay in San Francisco he had married Janet Harris, daughter of Dr. Henry Harris, one of the town's staunchest Jewish nationalists. The couple settled in New York, where he directed the Jewish student center at Columbia and assisted Mordecai Kaplan with his monumental *Judaism as a Civilization.*

Returning to San Francisco in the spring of 1935 to deliver a series of lectures on Kaplan's thought, Weinstein was impressed by the interest in contemporary Jewish philosophy. He decided to move back and establish an independent nondenominational school for adult Jewish education—the first in Bay Area history—and quickly raised the necessary funds among his many admirers.

The Institute of Jewish Studies opened in October with much fanfare. Housed in the vibrant new JCC, the institute enrolled more than three hundred people in seven courses during its inaugural semester. Predictably, Weinstein's curriculum tacked far to the left. The rabbi had undergone a spiritual crisis after leaving Sherith Israel; what little faith he had in God was now extinguished. His new school stressed "rational humanism," downplayed prayer and ritual, and emphasized the ethical and cultural dimensions of Jewish life.[25] Weinstein recruited Marxist instructors such as the refugee scholar Carl Landauer, who viewed Jewish history through an economic lens, and UC Berkeley professor Alexander Kaun, whose course painted a sparkling portrait of Jewish life in the Soviet Union. On the eve of his institution's birth Weinstein bluntly wrote in the *Emanu-El* that "the Jewish people might assert its selfhood by accepting the economic postulates of Communism—planned production for use and not for profit."[26]

The school flourished, but in 1939 the pressures of fundraising led Weinstein to resign.[27] By then, against the darkening background of world events, he had lost his trust in secular humanism and regained his emotional ties to Judaism. He returned to the pulpit, accepting the call of Chicago's Kehilath Anshe Maariv, a large progressive congregation where he remained for more than a quarter of a century.*

In 1932 Weinstein had been replaced at Sherith Israel by the able pastor Morris Goldstein, who would attract many new families to the temple, particularly after World War II. Yet he was not outspoken on the major issues of the day, and Sherith Israel—though it had been at the center of controversy since Rabbi Nieto's arrival in the 1890s—was largely disengaged from politics during Goldstein's long tenure. Had Weinstein remained in town, he would have joined rabbis such as Saul White and Elliot Burstein in advocating Zionism and an assertive response to the Holocaust.

But it would be unfair to conclude that Sherith Israel was too narrow-minded to keep Weinstein as its rabbi. Weinstein himself bore some of the blame for the bad ending, since in the early 1930s he still lacked a measure of prudence and patience. His subsequent success in Chicago's Hyde Park occurred only after a process of maturation: an unbridled radical while at Sherith Israel (he later admitted the "inadequacy of his years" during his tenure there), he became a judicious, if still courageous, liberal a decade later.[28] In any case, Weinstein's influence continued to be keenly felt in the Bay Area decades after his departure. In 1948, Temple Emanu-El engaged as its rabbi Alvin Fine, Weinstein's protégé and first cousin. Remaining for seventeen years, Fine, too, was a crusader for social equity and advocate of Labor Zionism.

Fine's predecessor on Lake Street, Rabbi Irving Reichert, arrived in 1930, the same year that Weinstein came to Sherith Israel. At first glance the two young rabbis (Reichert was thirty-six) seemed worlds apart. Reichert abhorred Zionism and would later become one of its most vitriolic American detractors. While Weinstein loved Yiddish and reveled in Jewish folkways, Reichert derided East European Jewish culture as "either a phrase

---

*A steadfast defender of civil rights and a vociferous critic of the Vietnam War, Weinstein capped his career with the presidency of the Central Conference of American Rabbis.

or a fetish . . . dependent on kitchen recipes, musicians, painters and story-tellers, but not on God."[29] He constantly repeated the axiom of the late nineteenth-century "classical" reformers, that "Judaism is a religion *and a religion only.*"[30] Moreover, the personal style of the two rabbis could not have been more different: Weinstein was gregarious and down to earth, Reichert aloof and elitist. If the Sherith Israel rabbi paid little heed to his board members, Emanu-El's spiritual leader was perhaps overly solicitous to a handful of leading families.

But Reichert shared Weinstein's burning anger toward injustice, and during the Depression he spoke out on behalf of the disadvantaged with no less eloquence or conviction. His homilies were filled with the searing ethical message of the Hebrew prophets. In one of his many nationally broadcast sermons, Reichert related Amos's indictment of ancient Israel to his own inequitable society: "How much liberty do we want?" he cried out. "Do we want it only for white men and not for others? How much justice do we want? Do we want it only for people of wealth and power, or for the humble and friendless too? . . . [O]nly an angry social conscience will get results."[31]

Like Weinstein, Reichert subordinated administrative, teaching, and even pastoral duties ("time and energy-consuming activities . . . a digression") to "preaching" of a particular kind. He wrote, "Preaching that claims to be interested in the spiritual welfare of men but ignores the slums that degrade them, the politics that exploit them, the industrial conditions that enslave them, the international relations that slaughter them—well . . . that kind of preaching is the apotheosis of futility, the superlative illustration of sanctimonious ineffectiveness."[32]

Like Weinstein, he supported Tom Mooney. He was active, too, in the ACLU and the National Committee for the Defense of Political Prisoners.[33] Emanu-El's board of directors consisted primarily of Republican businessmen, but Reichert openly admired the New Deal. In fact, in the summer of 1933 he was appointed to the state advisory board of the National Recovery Act (NRA) as vice president for Northern California, and in this capacity arbitrated dozens of labor disputes.

Upon assuming his NRA position, Reichert's concern for the rights of striking Filipino, Mexican, and Dust Bowl cotton pickers in the Central Valley caused him to clash openly with Governor James Rolph. When vigilantes and local police terrorized twelve thousand farmworkers—through arrests, beatings, and even murder—Reichert and his friend Lincoln Steffens sent telegrams of protest to Rolph and the press. "Gangsterism has replaced law and order in the cotton area," they declared, claiming that they would hold the governor "responsible for any further outrages."[34] The rabbi then publicly threatened the growers, a few of whom were his own congregants, with the cutoff of federal farm relief if the migrant workers were abused.

The strike was settled before the harvest, but another bloody incident later in 1933 caused Reichert again to denounce the governor, no longer the genial, consensus-building "Sunny Jim" Rolph of his San Francisco years but now a cranky, dangerous reactionary. In San Jose a mob dragged two confessed kidnappers and murderers out of jail, lynched them in the town square, and set their bodies afire—hours after Rolph proclaimed that he would not call out the National Guard to protect the prisoners. He then commended the hangmen for "the best lesson California has ever given the country," adding, "If anyone is arrested for the good job, I'll pardon them all."[35]

With the nation appalled by the Lindbergh kidnapping case, public opinion may well have been in Rolph's favor. For Reichert, however, the deed brought "humiliation and shame" to California, where lynchings occurred more frequently than anywhere outside the South.[36] Along with Justice Sloss and twenty-three other prominent citizens, the rabbi issued a statement deploring the action and its "laudation" by the state's chief executive.[37]

Included among the signers were two local clergymen who were allied with Reichert on many occasions: Caleb S. S. Dutton of the Unitarian Church and Catholic archbishop Edward Hanna. Rabbis of conscience such as Reichert, Saul White, Elliot Burstein, and others were also backed by Episcopalian bishop Edward Parsons and Dr. Howard Thurman, the black minister who led an interracial church in the Fillmore. Indeed, as one urban historian writes, a Jewish-Christian "coalition [emanating] from the liberal center" arose in response to the threat to civil rights during the Depression and became even more effective in the following decade.[38] Its members included not only younger leaders influenced by the New Deal, but also those weaned on Progressivism, such as Archbishop Hanna, who had worked closely with Simon Lubin to improve conditions on the farms as early as 1913. The interreligious bonds against discrimination in the Bay Area, dating back to the Gold Rush, were among the strongest in the country.

In the early 1940s, Irving Reichert also bravely came to the aid of the Japanese American community of the West Coast, interned in detention camps following Pearl Harbor.[39] This struggle, however, was one of the rare instances he lacked a broad interfaith coalition.

As much as any rabbi's sermon in Depression-era San Francisco, the life and work of an immigrant Jewish artist vividly reflected the class war on the streets. Bernard Boruch Zakheim, a Yiddishist and a Communist, a portraitist and a muralist, would be at the center of the greatest controversy over public art in the city's history.

Born into a wealthy Hasidic family in Warsaw in 1898, Zakheim was sent to a yeshiva but cut class in order to explore the city's colorful neighborhoods. He developed an aversion toward both Judaism and capitalism, dropping out of the yeshiva and later a business school intended to groom him to run the family's enterprises.[40] Instead he gravitated toward painting and, over the objections of his widowed mother, entered the prestigious Warsaw Art Academy.

World War I, however, forced him to postpone his dreams. He fought against the German invaders, was captured, and spent nearly a year in a POW camp. After the armistice Zakheim had high hopes for the new Polish republic, but he soon became disillusioned when a right-wing dictatorship took power. Hoping to put the trauma of the war and its aftermath behind him, he and his new bride immigrated to San Francisco, "as far away from Europe as they could possibly go."[41]

They had a daughter in 1921, and economic necessity forced Zakheim to put painting aside and work as a designer and manufacturer of fine furniture. Business was brisk, but, lacking the time or energy for his true passion, he despaired and sought refuge in alcohol.[42]

An opportunity came in 1929, when Diego Rivera, to whom Zakheim had sent some sketches, invited him to Mexico City to work as an assistant muralist. During his six months there—during which he left his business and child in his wife's care—he learned about Mayan and Aztec art and studied wall painting at the feet of a master.

Zakheim returned to San Francisco with a deepened understanding of the relationship between art and ethnicity. Before leaving for Mexico he had been active in the left-leaning Folkschule at the Steiner Street Yiddish cultural center, where he occasionally taught woodcarving, sculpture, and painting, and organized Jewish art exhibitions.[43] His experience in Mexico confirmed his belief that "an artist's native soil will always impress a certain character on his work."[44] Like Marc Chagall, who retained his East European sensibility after he immigrated to a modern Western metropolis, Zakheim would produce art that reflected the yearnings of the Jewish people.

Despite the birth of a second daughter, Zakheim left his family again, this time to study in Paris and travel throughout Europe for a year. Returning in 1932, he discovered that his wife had lost the furniture factory in the Depression, so he scratched out a living as an upholsterer, continued to paint, and battled his drinking problem. Finally, a fresh opportunity arrived: he won a competition to create a fresco in the courtyard of the new Jewish Community Center.

Completed in mid-1933, *The Jewish Wedding* would be one of the most notable works of art in any Jewish building in the American West. The local press lauded the hundred-square-foot representation, indeed celebration, of life in ancient Israel with human figures that seemed to originate in Africa, Europe, and the Far East as well as the Holy Land. Zakheim's multicultural vision was also eclectic in form, combining geometric techniques he had learned in Mexico, modernist styles he had just seen in Paris, and, of course, Jewish symbols with which he had grown up in Warsaw. For Joseph Danysh, arguably the city's most influential art critic and dealer, Zakheim had "made his wall come alive" with Jewish "movement" that ranged from religious to recreational activity, creating a work especially befitting a JCC:*

> Jugglers so dexterous as to keep eight full glasses of wine constantly in the air without spilling a drop; drummer, fiddler and piper playing the dithyrambic chants of the Hasidim; singing maidens, hasty weddings, archers and judges, prayers and dancers, all contribute life and conviction to a finely executed picture.[45]

After years of struggle and pain, recognition had finally come Zakheim's way. At the gallery he co-owned with Ansel Adams, Danysh scheduled a one-man show of the enchanting watercolors, many of them on Jewish themes, that the artist had painted in Europe. But that accomplishment was soon dwarfed by the commission to create a huge wall painting, and indeed to conceptualize the entire "mural program" executed by twenty-six local artists, for San Francisco's newest public building, Coit Tower.[46] Funded

---

*In 2001, as the JCC planned to raze its outmoded building and replace it with a new facility at the same site, it appeared that the beloved mural would be demolished. Only a last-minute plea from Zakheim's family saved it. The wall containing the mural was removed, restored, and in 2004 triumphantly installed in the new building.

through a bequest seeking to honor San Francisco's firefighters, the tall, cylindrical, fluted landmark, with its dazzling marine views, was destined to become a popular attraction. The 3,700 square feet of its interior walls—providing more space than all the murals in the state combined—were to carry scenes of everyday life in California.

The offer came from an unexpected source: Herbert Fleishhacker. The conservative banker had not only overseen construction of the tower as president of the Park and Art Commission, but he was also the most powerful member of a committee recently formed to allocate federal funds to arts projects on behalf of the New Deal's WPA. He invited Zakheim to his mansion, and the Communist noted the "exquisite wines" and "wonderful goodies" that "this Fleishhacker" served in the depths of the Depression.[47]

Fleishhacker was likely familiar with the political sympathies of Zakheim, now active in the left-wing Artists' and Writers' Union and the John Reed Club, both organized by his close friend, Kenneth Rexroth, the city's best-known bohemian poet. But Fleishhacker, who had staked his reputation on the oddly shaped tower, which was opposed by many neighborhood residents, felt that a lively, engaging decoration of the interior might quiet the critics.

Presiding over the largest federally funded arts project in the country, Fleishhacker sought to retain artistic control over the murals. He knew that the compensation of a dollar an hour would mean a great deal to the painters during the Depression, to say nothing of the publicity they would gain. Predictably, however, Zakheim would come to resent his patron's interference, dubbing the tower "Fleishhacker's last erection."[48] The tycoon, meanwhile, would demand that a good number of the murals be removed.*

The battle over the frescoes of Telegraph Hill might never have occurred had it not been for events on the waterfront below. In the late spring of 1934, while the artists worked in Coit Tower, the city was torn apart by its largest and most violent labor dispute ever. As one art historian has said, the muralists "had clear sight lines [to] the bloody hand-to-hand battles between strikers, scabs, the National Guard and the city police."[49]

---

*Ironically, Zakheim's and Fleishhacker's descendants cooperated much better seventy years later, when the Fleishhacker family's foundation supported the Jewish Community Center's project of saving *The Jewish Wedding.*

Accordingly, class struggle was a major theme of the Coit Tower artists, and Zakheim's own mural, innocuously titled *Library,* was one of the clearest examples. Near the center of the composition sat the artist himself, intently studying the Bible in Hebrew. But his reading room also included a well-known local Communist reaching for *Das Kapital.* Perhaps most striking was a welter of people perusing newspapers, including the *Western Worker* (the Pacific Coast edition of the *Daily Worker*), with inflammatory headlines mirroring the current crisis of American capitalism. One with grave portents announced the recent destruction of Rivera's mural in New York City's Chrysler Building; his patron, Nelson Rockefeller, had objected to a portrait of Lenin, which the Mexican would not expunge.

In the combative context of July 1934, the Coit Tower murals led to a "grudge" match, as one journalist wrote, "between Kid Capital and Kayo Communism."[50] Three artists in particular, John Langley Howard, Clifford Wight, and Zakheim, all members of the Communist Party, were singled out in the press for having "indulged in a little Communist propaganda, and at the expense of the U.S. government."[51]

In an effort that resembled their bumbling response to Emma Goldman's visit two decades earlier, the police raided artists' studios, searching in vain for explosives behind canvases and sculptures. But the height of Red-baiting occurred on July 5 (coincidentally "Bloody Thursday," the day police shot dead two strikers on the docks), when the *Examiner* published a reproduction of Zakheim's *Library.* Across the top of the picture the Hearst paper superimposed a hammer and sickle, encircled by the slogan "Workers of the World Unite," an icon the artist never used. The headline read "Soviet Symbol in Tower," and the caption below declared "Here is the painting in the Coit Memorial Tower that has caused a bitter dispute."[52]

The doctored photo dampened enthusiasm for Zakheim's exhibition at the Adams-Danysh Gallery—many shunned the painter they now believed to be a hard-line Stalinist—and further inflamed the Coit Tower imbroglio. In reality, Zakheim, like his mentor Rivera and companion Rexroth, frequently strayed from the party line, and the American Communist Party leaders considered all three renegades. But this fact was lost on the press, the art critics, and, of course, Herbert Fleishhacker.

Fleishhacker used his influence to padlock the tower in early June—its public opening had been scheduled for July 7—and to keep it closed until October, when tensions finally eased after the waterfront strike ended. (One wonders how the *Examiner* photographer gained access to the premises.) The Artists' and Writers' Union picketed against the closure, but their actions had no effect on the "Fleishhacker group," for whom some of the wall paintings were "wholly unacceptable and . . . dangerous."[53] In the end, however, the murals remained almost entirely intact and may be viewed today nearly exactly as painted.*

Despite his sullied reputation, Zakheim would be commissioned for other monumental frescoes, including *The Story of California Medicine,* in the amphitheater of Toland Hall on the UC medical school campus in San Francisco. Finished toward the end of the 1930s, the ambitious twelve-panel painting reflects the influence on Zakheim of another leftist Mexican muralist, José Clemente Orozco, and delivers a Marxist message about the exploitation of indigenous peoples.

But this proletarian art caused none of the turmoil generated by the Coit Tower murals.[54] By the late 1930s left-wing artists and intellectuals in the city were internally divided ideologically and, most important, had lost their fleeting link to the working class. The establishment no longer perceived Zakheim and other radical artists as the mortal threat to society that they had seemed in 1934.† That year, punctuated by violence on the waterfront, stands alone in San Francisco history as the apogee of class conflict.

1934

Among the workers hurt most by the Depression were longshoremen, who constituted a major segment of the city's laborers. Fifteen hundred of their union representatives from Seattle to San Diego met in San Francisco on May 9, 1934, and, despite the intense efforts of federal mediators, they voted to strike. They were joined by the teamsters, seamen, and virtually every other maritime and waterfront association, and within a week Pacific Coast shipping was halted. The owners countered with strikebreakers, and for the next five months labor and capital fought each other mercilessly.

---

*Wight's mural did in fact include a hammer and sickle, and he reluctantly agreed to remove it.

†Zakheim faded from public view by World War II but was productive almost until his death in 1985. During his last decades he created sculptures in his studio in an orchard near Sebastopol, north of San Francisco. His *Genocide,* composed of six huge wooden figures, was one of the earliest Holocaust memorials in North America. It graced the entryway of Berkeley's Judah L. Magnes Museum in the 1960s and is currently at Mount Sinai Memorial Park in Los Angeles.

The work stoppage escalated to an unprecedented mass strike that for four days in mid-July paralyzed the city and panicked the populace.

Like others in the city, most Jews, even while they sympathized with the dockworkers, feared the violent labor dispute, which during the mass strike resulted in acute shortages of food and other essentials. Even in immigrant neighborhoods pummeled by the Depression, such as the Fillmore, some parents scraped together the funds to send their children away from the city, to summer camp in Marin County.[55] But Jews were also major actors in the Big Strike, as it was called: they were both key labor leaders and conspicuous among the *anti*-union forces as well. Not least of all, they rank among the keenest chroniclers of the episode.

The Communist Party exerted its own influence on the strike, and Jews were noticeable among both the party's leadership and its rank and file. To be sure, there were more Jewish Communists in Los Angeles, host to a far larger Yiddish-speaking community working in the needle trades.[56] But even among Bay Area union organizers, Jewish Communists were highly visible. Louis Goldblatt, a quick-witted Bronx-born Marxist who later became one of the most effective Pacific Coast labor leaders, got his start in the 1934 waterfront strike while in his mid-twenties.[57] Having attended City College of New York before he was seventeen, the son of Lithuanian immigrants gravitated toward Trotskyism. After his family moved west in the late 1920s, Goldblatt studied law at Berkeley and led campus protests. He ran for a seat on the city council as a Communist in 1931, receiving six hundred votes in a losing effort. Aiding the longshoremen in 1934, he came to the attention of the strike's leader, the steely Australian immigrant Harry Bridges and would eventually become his chief deputy—invariably more analytical and ideological than his boss.

Samuel Adams Darcy (born Shmuel Dardeck in a Ukrainian shtetl) played a much larger role in the strike. He was radicalized when his father, a garment worker on the Lower East Side, was badly beaten by police in the course of a labor dispute.[58] Darcy went to the Soviet Union for sixteen months of indoctrination. Then, in 1931, he became head of the Communist Party's San Francisco–based Western District, succeeding another Jew, Emanuel Levin, who had held that post for a dozen years.[59]

But Darcy, no blind follower of the party line, broke with the national Communist Party and involved the western region in seething labor disputes throughout rural and urban California. The Communists had generally refused to make common cause with trade unionists, viewing them as cogs in the capitalist system, but Darcy saw an opportunity in the 1930s to revitalize the party by focusing on workers' current grievances. He was open to collaboration with militant labor organizers such as Harry Bridges, and during the strike the party, through its publications and rallies, wielded much power on the docks. The inclusive Darcy also welcomed into the fold free-spirited leftist artists such as Bernard Zakheim. Membership in the Communist Party swelled to more than twenty thousand, and Darcy was instrumental in creating a "united front," in the words of one insider, "entirely and absolutely against the official course of the Party."[60]

One union virtually controlled by the Communists was the seamen's. It, too, had a Jewish leader, the abrasive Harry Jackson, another local Communist at odds with the national office. Jackson, who had changed his name from Gliksohn, was born and raised in San Francisco but affected a gruff Brooklyn accent, perhaps to blend in with the many New York Jewish radicals in town.[61]

A key role in the strike was played by Communist Party member Elaine Black, born Rose Elaine Buchman on the Lower East Side. In 1934, when she was in her late twenties, she was the local leader of International Labor Defense, a legal society for arrested demonstrators and strikers. That summer the Red Angel, as the *Western Worker* called her, solicited food for the picketers' families and raised cash used to bail dozens of people out of jail.[62] But Black, who spoke Yiddish to her assistant Ida Rothstein to circumvent police wiretaps, was herself soon put on trial—in front of hundreds of spectators in City Hall—for distributing the "subversive" pamphlet "What to Do When under Arrest."[63] She was convicted and sentenced to six months in prison.*

Not all militant Jewish union organizers were Communists. Rose Pesotta, an anarchist, retained an antipathy toward the rigid Communist Party even during the rare period of good feeling among leftists in 1934. Like Emma Goldman, whom she knew and admired, Pesotta immigrated to New York as a teenager and became active in revolutionary politics while finding "support for a sexually free lifestyle embedded in anarchist tenets of personal freedom."[64] A dressmaker in the 1920s, she joined the International Ladies Garment Workers Union (ILGWU) and became one of its vice presidents— the first woman on its executive board—by 1933.[65]

---

*Black ran for the board of supervisors in 1939 but narrowly lost. She remained popular in left-wing circles until her death in 1988 (Vivian Ranieri, *The Life and Times of Elaine Black Yoneda* [New York, 1991], 164).

After passage of the National Industrial Recovery Act, ILGWU president David Dubinsky dispatched Pesotta to California, and after a brief stint in Los Angeles she arrived in San Francisco in 1934. Her first task was to unionize Chinatown's garment workers, who were toiling in atrocious conditions, often in crowded, dank cellars beneath expensive stores and restaurants that catered to tourists. It was "worse than in the old tenement sweatshops of New York's East Side," Pesotta wrote, and she took federal officials on a tour of some of the most congested and foul-smelling subterranean factories.[66] But for once in her long career she failed to make any progress. In a widely reprinted article she exposed the exploitation of the Chinese laborers, but she could not bring them the benefits of collective bargaining.[67] In addition to facing language and cultural barriers, she learned that in Chinatown the workers were often related to their employers, so union activity could be considered an attack on one's family.

It was different on the waterfront, though, and Pesotta was electrified by the strike. She wrote, "We of the ILGWU talked with groups of the strikers, pledged our financial and moral support, urged them to call upon us for advice if needed, offered our headquarters to them for meetings, and promised that we would bring the strike to our International convention in Chicago."[68]

There was much sympathy for the strikers among East European Jews in the Bay Area, particularly in the Fillmore District and in ideologically charged Petaluma. Funds poured in from the "Jewish people on the farms," according to Harry Bridges, who later noted their "reputation for raising money for trade unionism and human rights. Those farmers knew what it meant for a worker to be out on strike."[69]

But there were also Jews—businessmen and civic leaders—on the opposite side of the picketers. The mainstream press, most elected officials, the police, and even federal mediators all tended to portray the strike as a Communist plot, so it is not surprising that the town's commercial elite— ill-disposed toward the unions to begin with—were mortified. In addition there were legitimate fears about the health and safety of San Franciscans, particularly during the mass strike in mid-July, the only one of its scale in American history. A majority of the workforce—150,000 people—walked off their jobs, closing down the city's transportation system and jeopardizing its food supply. The strike's leaders effectively ran the town; they permitted only nineteen restaurants out of three thousand to remain open and decided which trucks could enter or leave.[70] A humbled Mayor Rossi likened the crisis to that of 1906.[71]

These were also the sentiments of the *Emanu-El*, which hailed the appointment of three prominent Jews to the mayor's twenty-five-man executive committee "to find ways and means of running the gauntlet of strike pickets guarding the arteries to the city."[72] Federation of Jewish Charities president Walter Haas, civic leader Alfred Esberg, and Adrien Falk (chief executive of the S&W Fine Foods Company and formerly president of the Concordia Club) gave the impression that they were operating above the fray and concerned only with the public welfare. But their efforts, fully approved and supported by the probusiness Industrial Association, were also aimed at undermining Bridges's tactics.[73] The mass strike ultimately exhausted both sides and they submitted to federal arbitration on July 19. By October they reached a compromise that met most of the longshoremen's demands.

Slowly the Bay Area returned to normal, but the killing of strikers on July 5, which prompted the mass strike ten days later, would embitter the working class for years to come. Several of the most penetrating (if one-sided) accounts of that summer of terror were penned by a young woman destined to become one of the century's leading Jewish feminist authors.

Tillie Lerner (who later took the last name of her activist husband, Jack Olsen) was one of six children of unmarried Russian immigrants living in poverty in Nebraska and Wyoming while they pursued radical politics. An unwed teenaged mother, Tillie journeyed to California in the early 1930s and wrote the evocative "The Iron Throat," a short story about the miserable lot of female factory workers. Printed in the *Partisan Review* in early 1934, it was considered by the journal the best story appearing in the "little magazines" that year.[74] Tillie's tale was part of an unfinished novel, and several publishers tried to locate the gifted writer to offer her a contract.

They failed to find her because she was in the San Francisco county jail, arrested in a raid on suspected subversives at the height of the strike. She soon wrote a nonfictional account of that experience. Published in the *New Republic*, it was entitled "Thousand Dollar Vagrant" because of the exorbitant bail demanded by the judge. In taut prose she described the police brutality visited on the "Reds."

[The police] rounded us back into the kitchen. There were five of them. Only two harness bulls looked a little human. The other faces were distorted and bestial. I wouldn't have been surprised if they had ripped out knives or irons and started torturing us. . . . Words were lurching out of the head bull's mouth. . . . He whipped out a blackjack and beat Dave over the head and chest. . . . They began searching the place. Flinging up curtains, peering in the garbage can, looking in the stove, ransacking the drawers.

They tell me to go to the other room. . . . I know why they want me out of the kitchen. I hear the questions: Where were you born? In Russia? Silence. A thud of something soft on a body. . . . Who's the girl? Silence. A thud. . . . How many times you been arrested? Who's the head guy around here? What nationality are you? Come on—lie, we all know you're all Jews, or greasers, or niggers.[75]

Later in the year Tillie again wrote of the turmoil in San Francisco, focusing on "monstrous" Bloody Thursday for the *Partisan Review.* With barely controlled rage she described the "battlefield" on which a thousand police, facing five thousand picketers, clubbed or gassed forty-two, shot thirty-one, and killed two: "Guns spat death on us that a few dollars might be saved to fat bellies. . . . My fists clench at the remembrance and the hate congests so I feel it will burst."*[76]

One of the casualties of Bloody Thursday was Joe Rosenthal, of the San Francisco *News,* his ear pierced by a police bullet. A decade later the heroic photographer would take one of the most famous pictures of the century—the flag raising at Iwo Jima—but he was more afraid, he always said, on July 5, 1934.[77]

By the fall of that year the struggle had shifted from the street to the ballot box. A socialist, the crusading novelist Upton Sinclair, had won the Democratic nomination for governor and promised to make his own revolution from Sacramento. His utopian plan—one of many floated during the Depression—called for the state to establish cooperative farms and factories and distribute monthly pensions to the elderly and disabled. Sinclair, author of *The Jungle* and dozens of other books exposing the excesses of capitalism, was a hero to the working class and perceived as a grave threat by the establishment. His program, End Poverty in California, or EPIC, was assailed by those who claimed that poor people throughout America would descend on the Golden State for "easy pickings." But the deteriorating economic picture

* Olsen's political work and the demands of raising four daughters resulted in a meager literary output during the 1930s and '40s. In 1953, however, at age forty-one, she enrolled in a creative writing course at San Francisco State and soon thereafter went to Stanford on a fellowship. The economic freedom enabled her to write a novel and many acclaimed short stories, most notably "Tell Me a Riddle," about an aging Jewish immigrant couple, which won an O. Henry Award.

made his ascent to the governor's chair—occupied by Republicans for almost a generation—a distinct possibility.

In its coverage of the bellicose gubernatorial contest, the *New York Times* reported that a "sense of Armageddon hangs in the bland California air."[78] Jewish kingmakers like Herbert Fleishhacker operated behind the scenes to ensure that the GOP would field as strong a ticket as possible. Concerned that the colorless incumbent, conservative Frank Merriam, would have little appeal among moderates, Fleishhacker met with party wheelhorse Chester Rowell, editor of the *Chronicle,* in an effort to replace Merriam with a younger, more liberal Republican.[79] In the end Merriam remained the nominee and Fleishhacker contributed handsomely to his campaign. The self-made real estate magnate Louis Lurie had enormous influence over Merriam's running mate, George Hatfield, and poured money into GOP coffers as well.[80]

In Southern California, meanwhile, Jewish studio heads sought to ruin Sinclair because of an exposé he had written about Hollywood. Led by Louis B. Mayer, they inaugurated a new level of negative campaigning. Picking through Sinclair's voluminous writings, they ripped passages out of context to portray him as "an atheist, a Communist, and a believer in free love."[81] Irving Thalberg of Metro-Goldwyn-Mayer produced a "newsreel," distributed free of cost to movie theaters statewide, in which actors posing as average citizens explained why they supported Merriam or Sinclair. Advocates for the former were well dressed and articulate, while those of the latter appeared "disheveled and disreputable . . . many of them with thick foreign accents." One repulsive Sinclair "voter" asked: "His system worked vell in Russia, vy can't it vork here?"[82]

In mid-September Joseph Schenck of United Artists publicly threatened to move the film industry to Florida if Sinclair were elected. The *Emanu-El* did not endorse any candidate but deemed the Hollywood producer's "ultimatum to the voters . . . an offense to basic American rights."[83] Sinclair countered with fearmongering of his own, warning that a Merriam victory would lead to "a Fascist State that [would] put even Huey Long to shame."[84]

Sinclair's claim resonated among the state's Jewish community in particular, which for more than a year and a half had watched Hitler persecute German Jews. Raymond Dannenbaum, senior reporter for the *Emanu-El* and head of the Liberal Forum, a political discussion group, brought Sinclair to San Francisco to debate one of the foremost proponents of American fascism. Lawrence Dennis advocated an "authoritarian" executive, unchecked by the legislature, while Sinclair forcefully argued for power to be vested in the people through popularly elected officials.[85] Held two about weeks before the election, and thoroughly covered by the Jewish press, the well-attended event raised the Democratic candidate's standing among local Jews.[86]

Yet while Sinclair naturally energized the left, he elicited little passion among working-class Jews in the Bay Area. For one thing, the wealthy writer, a quirky food faddist and avid tennis player with homes in Pasadena and Beverly Hills, seemed aloof from the concerns of everyday people, despite his principled ideology. Liberal Jews were also disappointed when Sinclair failed to win President Roosevelt's endorsement, and even as zealous a Democrat as Edward Heller voted for Merriam.[87] Jews on the extreme left, meanwhile, felt that Sinclair was not a true Marxist, some of them preferring to vote for Sam Darcy, whom the Communist Party had put up for governor.

There was the question, too, of whether Sinclair was an anti-Semite. William Fox, head of the studio bearing his name, had hired Sinclair to ghostwrite his memoirs and, although Fox was a Jew, the final product depicted the movie business as a kind of Jewish mafia.[88] Fox decided not to publish the autobiography, but Sinclair printed it himself, igniting his feud with Hollywood and unnerving Jews throughout California.

On November 6, 1934, Sinclair lost the gubernatorial election by about a quarter of a million votes. His quixotic bid for office, though, had been more successful than expected, and, because of the strong showing of a third candidate, the incumbent had not received a majority. But socialism would not come to California after all, and the year that had been filled with so much class warfare—a scathing controversy over public art, a crippling mass strike, and an apocalyptic electoral clash—was finally nearing its end.

TAR AND FEATHER JUSTICE

The surge of left-wing activity in the Bay Area generated a ferocious anti-Communist backlash that sometimes included anti-Semitism. In 1934 the *Emanu-El* revealed the following hate letter, sent to a local Jewish physician who merely subscribed to the *Western Worker:* "We members of a committee of San Francisco citizens organized for the purpose of purging the city of communists, Bolsheviks, radical agitators and their sympathizers, hereby notify you that you—greedy, red Jews of jackel's [sic] blood—are known to be directly linked with them. . . . Leave this community immediately or drastic means will be taken."[89]

The extreme right, however, struck hardest in rural California, often with shocking acts of violence. In addition to those belonging to fascist groups such as the Silver Shirts and the Ku Klux Klan, members of such mainstream organizations as the American Legion evicted, robbed, clubbed, and even killed striking farm workers, all in the name of saving the country from communism.[90]

The great agrarian reformer Simon Lubin, now nearing the end of his life and despondent over the violation of farm workers' rights throughout California, warned *Emanu-El* readers in 1934 that Red-baiting and Jew-hating could go hand in hand. Referring to a smear in the state's leading agricultural publication blaming the Jews for the plight of the farmer, Lubin lamented, "Unfortunately, Nature's Nobleman, the man of the soil, is not always so intelligent that he can discern the absurdity in such an explanation." His warning: "Today, the scapegoat is the Communist, the Red, the Radical. Tomorrow it may be some other element in our population—even the Jew."[91]

Especially vulnerable was the small, left-wing immigrant Jewish community of Petaluma. Many of the Yiddish-speaking chicken farmers had openly voiced Communist sentiments for decades. They were ardent supporters of the migrant apple pickers who came to Sonoma County every summer, and who in 1935 went on strike for a minimum wage of thirty-five cents an hour. Tensions rose when vigilantes broke up workers' meetings and encircled their camps with armed patrols. The *Santa Rosa Press Democrat* endorsed the "war on communism" waged by "the grim and determined" militants and printed the demand made by the "anti-red vigilantes" to every radical: "Get out and stay out!"[92]

Late on the evening of August 21, an armed mob of more than a hundred men, mostly American Legion members, surrounded the remote farmhouse of the middle-aged Russian Jew Sol Nitzman, an outspoken Communist who had aided the strikers. For hours the crowd shouted, "Lynch him!" while his horrified wife fruitlessly called the Petaluma police and county sheriff (who, as was revealed later, were likely complicit in the crime).[93] Nitzman held off the vigilantes with a shotgun, but the night riders fired tear gas canisters through his windows, forcing the couple and their young son out of the house.

Masked men then abducted Nitzman, taking him to a warehouse in Santa Rosa where, along with four others accused of Communism (all non-Jews), he was forced to kneel and told to kiss the American flag while a rabble of drunken vigilantes looked on. He refused and, according to testimony he later gave in court, told his tormentors he had fought for the flag as an American soldier in World War I. It did not save him from a beating. Next he and one of the others were stripped naked, smeared with hot tar, and covered with feathers. Before dawn he was made to walk down Santa Rosa's Fourth Street and out of town.*[94]

Whether Nitzman's punishment was the result of his being Jewish or "just" a Communist would long be debated in Petaluma, where Jews remained shaken by the incident for a generation. One local resident, sixteen years old at the time, later recalled, "It brought back our parents' memories of persecution in the Old Country. . . . We were aware of southern lynchings, the Mooney Case, all the attacks on strikers. . . . But we never thought that a thing like this could happen in our town! We wondered if we could trust the people around us."[95]

Nine days after the outrage, Rabbi Weinstein wrote an article that appeared on the front page of the *Emanu-El* under the headline "Beware of Tar and Feather Justice Here." He declared mob rule "an avalanche of fury" that could "pave the way for a Hitler or Mussolini."[96]

The vigilantism of the mid-1930s gave rise to the Northern California Branch of the American Civil Liberties Union. While there had been a number of abortive attempts to organize an ACLU office in the Bay Area, dating from World War I and the Red Scare, the local chapter took root only after the bloody altercations on the state's docks and farms during the Depression. Its courageous cofounder was Helen Arnstein Salz, privileged daughter of Bavarian Jewish pioneers and an educator, poet, and painter.

Helen Salz and her civic-minded husband Ansley, a wealthy businessman, had underwritten initiatives of a founder of the national ACLU, Alexander Meikeljohn, president of Amherst College and an expert on the first amendment. By late 1934, shocked by "the terrific injustices . . . done to the people," Salz joined Meikeljohn in establishing the ACLU locally.[97] The organization was small at first; a decade after its inception membership was fewer than a thousand and the annual budget less than $7,000. In its earliest years it was often reviled as a Communist front, and many of its members preferred their affiliation not be made public.[98] But with an active board that included Rabbi Reichert, the ACLU accomplished a

---

*Nor was Nitzman's ordeal over. The poultry farmer soon had difficulty obtaining credit and insurance. Except for a brief period, however, he and his family remained in Petaluma for the next four decades (Kenneth L. Kann, *Comrades and Chicken Ranchers: The Story of a California Jewish Community* [Ithaca, N.Y., 1993], 119).

great deal. In its first year it filed civil suits on behalf of the victims of vigilante "justice," intervened in violent labor disputes, and prodded the state to take action against a lynching. The ACLU was also instrumental in bringing criminal charges against the perpetrators of the tar and feather incident in Santa Rosa. Sadly, that trial ended in acquittal, and Nitzman also lost the civil case against his kidnappers.

REDS

Threats from the ultraright hardly dampened the Jewish romance with Communism in the 1930s. To be sure, only a tiny percentage of Bay Area Jewry sympathized with Stalin, and fewer still actually joined the Communist Party. In the Fillmore District one could discern a shift from the immigrant radicalism that Emma Goldman had tapped toward the Democratic Party of FDR. Yet Communism continued to influence some of the most creative Jewish minds in Northern California even after the Moscow show trials of 1936 and 1937 and the German-Soviet Nonaggression Pact between Stalin and Hitler on the eve of World War II.

Bernard Zakheim and Tillie Olsen admired the Soviet Union until well into the 1950s. They had personally experienced the harsh side of capitalism and longed for its destruction. But other devoted Jewish Communists came from wealthy Bay Area families, and, as one historian has concluded, their "guilt over their class origins" made them susceptible to the allure of Marxist-Leninism.[99] The avant-garde objectivist poet George Oppen (a Pulitzer Prize winner in 1968), son of an affluent San Francisco Jewish businessman, joined the Communist Party in 1935. He infiltrated a right-wing group for the party and, at its insistence, gave up his poetry for years to focus on his political work.[100] Even the illustrious Bransten family produced a Communist. Richard Bransten, grandson of the pioneer Joseph Brandenstein (and great-grandson of Lewis and Hannah Gerstle) wrote editorials for the Communist Party's *New Masses* in the 1940s and backed the paper financially.[101] In the 1930s Bransten was married to Louise Rosenberg, whom the FBI suspected of being a Soviet spy during World War II;[102] she was a socialite descended from a pioneer Jewish family that had prospered in the dried fruit business. Yet another extreme leftist was the talented writer Edith Arnstein Jenkins, Helen Salz's niece and the daughter of respected progressives Lawrence and Flora Jacobi Arnstein. Edith, the radical child of a liberal family, married a tough Communist waterfront labor organizer and became, in her own words, "totally immersed in the Movement."[103]

Perhaps the greatest concentration of Jewish Communists in the Bay Area in the late 1930s and early '40s was in Berkeley. Many of them, including Edith Jenkins, gravitated to the intense young physics professor J. Robert Oppenheimer. Born to wealthy, cultured German Jewish parents on New York City's Riverside Drive, Oppenheimer was destined to lead a group of scientists in constructing the world's first atomic bomb.

Oppenheimer and his younger brother Frank (a physicist of lesser note) arrived in Berkeley in 1929. "Oppie," as Robert was known, worked closely with the eminent nuclear physicist Ernest Orlando Lawrence, who had come to UC around the same time and soon built the world's first cyclotron. Despite the differences in their backgrounds and temperaments—Lawrence was a plainspoken Lutheran from South Dakota raised by Norwegian immigrants—the two became friends.

There was some social bias against Jews in the physics department and "Rad Lab" (Radiation Laboratory) in the 1930s, as was seen in a personal letter written by Lawrence describing a colleague: "He is Jewish and in some quarters, of course, that would be held against him, but in his case it should not be, as he has none of the characteristics that some non-Aryans have. He is really a very nice fellow."[104]

Clearly the cultivated Oppenheimer, who had been brought up in the Ethical Culture movement and felt ambivalent toward Judaism,[105] fell into that category for Lawrence. But if the senior scholar was little bothered that Oppie was Jewish, he was seriously perturbed about the New Yorker's left-wing politics. Oppie was a leader in the movement to unionize the faculty, including the scientists at the Rad Lab; sympathized openly with the migrant farm workers; and expressed his admiration for Harry Bridges and the longshoremen.[106]

By the late 1930s Oppenheimer's redwood house, high in the Berkeley hills, became a kind of Marxist salon, regularly drawing left-wing intellectuals from the campus and the community. In addition to French literature professor Haakon Chevalier, arguably the most radical individual on campus, the group's members included Lou Goldblatt, activist East Bay attorney Aubrey Grossman, and prominent anthropology professor Paul Radin, son of a Lithuanian rabbi and brother of liberal jurist Max Radin.[107] Evidence recently unearthed has led several historians to conclude that everyone in the group, including Oppenheimer, secretly belonged to the

Communist Party and that the Shasta Road coterie operated as a "closed unit" or "cell."*

By the early 1940s Oppenheimer had, probably unwittingly, assembled another Communist clique—of Jewish graduate students and teaching assistants who had come to work under his direction in the Rad Lab. Rossi Lomanitz, Joseph Weinberg, Max Friedman, and David Bohm were all promising disciples of Oppie, and Bohm in particular—a prodigy whom Einstein would later call his eventual successor—seemed headed for greatness.[†][108] Yet the four close friends were also Marxists and highly active in radical politics. Lomanitz was the only Zionist in this circle; he joined the left-wing Hashomer Hatzair in 1940 as well as the Communist Party.[109]

Due to the urgent need to develop the atom bomb, all were granted interim security clearances in 1942 so that they could conduct theoretical work on the secret weapon. But they soon came under FBI surveillance, suspected of funneling classified information to Grigory Kheifitz, the Soviet vice-consul in San Francisco—perhaps with the assistance of Louise Rosenberg Bransten, whom wiretaps revealed to be the diplomat's paramour—and were removed from the project.[110] At the end of the 1940s Oppenheimer's four former students, now physics professors at different institutions, were called to testify before the House Committee on Un-American Activities (HUAC). Lomanitz, Bohm, and Weinberg were eventually indicted on charges of contempt of court or perjury but acquitted at trial. Yet another Berkeley Jewish scientist tracked by the FBI was the young chemist Martin Kamen, who also worked closely with Oppenheimer at the Rad Lab in the early 1940s. G-men claimed he had passed secret documents to Soviet diplomats in the Bernstein Fish Grotto in San Francisco, and he was hauled before the HUAC, where he denied being a spy. Recently

---

*Despite the affiliation of his mistress Jean Tatlock (who committed suicide in 1944), as well as his brother, wife, landlady, and many of his students and colleagues, Oppenheimer always denied he was a party member. Although there is irrefutable evidence of the physicist's payments to the Communist Party's San Francisco bagman, the Latvian immigrant Isaac "Pop" Folkoff, it may be that these funds were not dues but rather donations for particular causes, such as that of the Spanish Loyalists. As a biography of Oppenheimer points out, the line between party member and sympathizer was often blurred (Kai Bird and Martin J. Sherwin, *American Prometheus: The Triumph and Tragedy of J. Robert Oppenheimer* [New York, 2006], 135–37).

†Bohm's lover was yet another high-powered left-wing Jewish intellectual on campus, Betty Goldstein, the future Betty Friedan (Bird and Sherwin, *American Prometheus*, 187).

declassified FBI files reveal that it intended to charge Kamen and Weinberg with conspiracy to commit espionage,[111] but the bureau evidently deferred to the Army, which oversaw the Manhattan Project and wanted to shield its top officials from the embarrassment such a trial would doubtlessly bring.[112] Although the government held extensive preliminary hearings for a criminal case against Oppenheimer himself, no charge was ever brought. But the Atomic Energy Commission revoked his security clearance in 1954, stressing his "associations" with known Communists.[113]

FBI and KGB documents indicate that the case against Joe Weinberg was the strongest, but it was built upon warrantless wiretaps that would likely have been inadmissible in court.[114] It remains unclear whether any of the four graduate students or Oppenheimer was actually a spy. As for Kamen, according to two authoritative historians, the allegations against him were simply "false."[115] They cite "a series of misunderstandings" on the part of the prosecution, but the HUAC and the Justice Department were so politicized during these years that a full-fledged witch hunt against Berkeley's Rad Lab scientists is hardly an implausible scenario.[116]

The issue of espionage aside, it is indisputable that a significant number of Jewish writers, artists, and scientists—rich and poor, bluebloods and immigrants—were infatuated with Communism and the Soviet Union during the Depression and the war. Certainly one reason was the class warfare of the mid-1930s, which had rendered the Bay Area the most left-leaning corner of the country, "a little Russia, completely isolated and insulated," according to Kenneth Rexroth.[117] Obviously, the poet did not mean to be taken literally, but in fact the combination of a mass strike, inflammatory political murals on public buildings, and an avowed socialist nearly elected governor were unique in America.

Beyond that, Jews in particular were often drawn to Communism. Some, like Lou Goldblatt, consciously associated the "messianic expectancy" in the Jewish tradition with the Marxist goal of creating a new world free of economic exploitation.[118] By contrast, David Bohm, raised in a religious home, embraced science as a child, and later communism, in part to distance himself from his overbearing father, a Talmud scholar and cantor. Dialectical materialism became David's new faith, as his biographer explains, for under Marxism, "humanity would finally be free of endless cycles of hatred, irrationality, cynicism, and warfare."[119]

Foremost in the minds of Bohm and other Jewish Communists was the Soviet Union's unwavering stand against fascism in the late 1930s, when the Western democracies were appeasing Hitler. As late as August 14, 1939, two eminent Jewish professors at UC Berkeley, Paul Radin and Alexander Kaun, signed a widely published open letter calling the Kremlin a supporter of democracy and world peace.[120]

One week later, the Molotov-Ribbentrop Treaty rendered the USSR a virtual ally of Germany, giving the Nazis a green light to invade Poland and eventually ghettoize and terrorize millions of Jews. Party hacks such as William Schneiderman*—the third Jew in a row to lead the Communist Party's California district—wrote hollow propaganda pieces minimizing the significance of the German-Soviet Nonaggression Pact, pointing instead to British and French capitulation at Munich the year before, which had allowed Hitler to annex the Sudetenland. Remarkably, many Jewish party members and sympathizers agreed with that reasoning and continued to support Stalin unequivocally. The poet Edith Jenkins exhibited just this sort of blind faith. "I want to be part of the cleansing wave that will change the world," she thought at the time, and "would not be shaken in my political loyalties."[121]

A TIME TO BUILD

If communism was one response to the Depression, public works was another, a concerted effort to create jobs and stimulate the economy in bleak times. The most challenging Depression-era construction project in the state was the Golden Gate Bridge, at the time the longest suspension bridge in the world. According to a plaque beneath his statue near the entrance to the iconic span, "the man who built the bridge" was Joseph Baerman Strauss, a diminutive and intensely ambitious German Jew born and raised in the Midwest, where he had always felt himself an outsider. In his adopted San Francisco he would feel more at home.

Strauss, chief engineer of the decade-and-a-half-long project, was obsessed with bridge building his entire life. For his senior thesis at the University of Cincinnati he proposed spanning the Bering Strait. While that remained a fantasy, during his career he constructed more than four hundred

---

*Like the more independently minded Samuel Adams Darcy before him, Schneiderman came to America as a child from an East European shtetl, was raised in the home of a garment worker, and returned to the Soviet Union for indoctrination in the early 1930s. Assuming his post in 1935, he remained California's Communist Party chief for twenty-one years (*Biographical Dictionary of the American Left,* ed. Bernard K. Johnpoll and Harvey Klehr [Westport, Conn., 1986], 350).

bridges, mostly of the "bascule" variety: short, counterbalanced, tilted-up drawbridges such as those across the Chicago River. Strauss used some of the same engineering principles to erect a popular amusement ride, the Aeroscope, at San Francisco's Panama-Pacific International Exposition in 1915. From its site in the newly built Marina, he looked out at the Golden Gate and had an almost mystical vision: "Perhaps . . . the Master Artist who stretched the canvas for that vast picture . . . intended that, in time to come, presumptuous man might trace upon it his greatest etching in steel."[122]

In the same year as the exposition, he constructed San Francisco's Fourth Street Bridge over the China Basin water channel, in collaboration with city engineer Michael O'Shaughnessey. That span was short and squat, but the partnership soon led to the venture that would preoccupy Strauss for the rest of his years.[123] O'Shaughnessey, who would later become Strauss's archrival, invited him to devise a plan to bridge the Golden Gate.

Strauss, who never actually received a degree in civil engineering—although he often implied that he had—initially proposed a bulky design that was nothing like the marvel that would eventually be built.[124] The plans he submitted in 1921 called for a dense cantilever framework, resembling that of a railroad bridge from the early industrial era, only longer.

But if Strauss was no design genius—his concept would be scrapped by the end of the decade—he proved a masterful promoter of the project. Deep into middle age, and with serious health and marital problems, he nevertheless tirelessly made the case for the bridge. Real estate developers, auto dealers, and hoteliers were naturally in favor, but he faced opposition from the ferryboat interests, as well as public officials anxious about the project's cost. The Sierra Club sought to protect the pristine North Bay, and the War Department worried that an attack on the bridge could cause it to collapse and block navigation.[125] Still others doubted whether the towers could withstand the ocean winds or an earthquake. Strauss adroitly countered all these concerns and, largely due to his persuasiveness, five counties—Marin, Sonoma, Napa, Mendocino, and Del Norte, near the Oregon border—joined San Francisco in forming the Golden Gate Bridge and Highway District to issue bonds for the project. The little dynamo was the public face of the bridge until the start of construction in 1933 and through its completion four years later.

Strauss sacrificed much to realize his dream. His million-dollar fee was eaten up by numerous lawsuits and tax problems, and he publicly complained that he had built the bridge "for nothing."[126] He suffered a nervous breakdown just as work on the span began and died of a heart attack in 1938, less than a year after it opened. But he succeeded in literally changing the face of San Francisco Bay, and during the Depression he was one of the most admired men in town.

Yet the imperious Strauss, who frequently took credit for the work of others, did not design the Golden Gate Bridge. Although he wangled the title of chief engineer,* he was not the "poet in steel" he made himself out to be. In reality, the slender, soaring span was the concept of two individuals who avoided the limelight: Charles Ellis, formerly professor of engineering at the University of Illinois, and Leon Solomon Moisseiff, a Latvian Jewish immigrant who had graduated from Columbia and was the leading theoretician of bridge design in the country.† Ellis, whom Strauss fired on the eve of the construction phase, may rightfully be credited with the plan of the masterwork. Moisseiff, the "consulting engineer," provided the theories and calculations, especially in the critical area of wind stress, that Ellis relied upon.[127]

The Golden Gate Bridge was the culmination of two decades of Moisseiff's original work on suspension bridges. His understanding of metallurgy and mathematics enabled him to design spans that were successively longer, taller, and lighter, including the Philadelphia–Camden Bridge (later renamed the Benjamin Franklin), the Ambassador Bridge in Detroit, and the majestic George Washington Bridge, linking upper Manhattan with northern New Jersey. As the leading historian of the Golden Gate Bridge has explained, Moisseiff's pathbreaking ideas allowed Ellis and others to design the towers with their signature feature: "great open rectangles, huge windows or portals framing the intense blue sky, the scudding clouds, and the frequent swirling fogs."[128]

---

*Late in his life, Strauss settled a lawsuit brought by his shady longtime associate, H. H. "Doc" Meyers, who alleged that Strauss owed him the balance of a $110,000 "commission" for landing him the job of chief engineer in 1929. The go-between in this scheme was likely the Polish-born Jew Abraham "Murphy" Hirschberg, a flamboyant San Francisco businessman and horseracing enthusiast. As the right-hand man of political boss Tom Finn between the wars, Hirschberg, known as the "Twelfth Supervisor," was a "near legendary influence peddler and bagman" at city hall and was fully enmeshed in the murky deal making that led to the construction of the bridge (John van der Zee, *The Gate: The True Story of the Design and Construction of the Golden Gate Bridge* [New York, 1986], 72; *San Francisco Chronicle,* January 15, 1959, 16).

†Unlike Strauss, Moisseiff, who spoke with an East European accent, was active in many national Jewish organizations, such as the Hebrew Immigrant Aid Society and the Jewish Publication Society. In 1915 he served as an editor of *Der Tog,* a Yiddish newspaper published on the Lower East Side (*Emanu-El,* July 27, 1934, 6).

Moisseiff was also a consulting engineer on the San Francisco–Oakland Bay Bridge, a mighty four-and-a-half-mile span dismissed by Strauss as a mere "trestle."[129] Unlike its more beautiful sister, the long link to the East Bay was a hybrid of suspension, cantilever, and truss sections. The recipient of massive federal funding (due in part to the clout of Congresswoman Florence Prag Kahn) and posing fewer engineering challenges than the Golden Gate, the construction of the Bay Bridge proceeded more quickly than that of its rival. Although work on the Bay Bridge began after the Golden Gate Bridge was already underway, it was completed in November 1936, many months ahead of Strauss's project.

To mark the completion of "the greatest bridge yet constructed in the world," as Herbert Hoover described the Bay Bridge at its dedication,[130] the federal government commissioned a commemorative half-dollar. The sculptor Jacques Schnier, a Rumanian-born Jew raised in San Francisco's South of Market neighborhood early in the century, was selected to design the coin. On one side he rendered a detailed scene of the bridge and a ferryboat, with the Berkeley hills in the distance; on the other he depicted a California grizzly bear.[131] A hundred thousand of the fifty-cent pieces were minted in San Francisco.[132] Two years later he was invited to create an array of large sculptures for the third great project to grace the bay in the 1930s, the Golden Gate International Exposition. Held on newly constructed Treasure Island, the expo would attract seventeen million visitors.

Like his nearly exact contemporary Bernard Zakheim, Jacques Schnier emerged from obscurity to become a well-known experimental artist in San Francisco during the Depression. But the creativity of Schnier, who arrived in the country much earlier and was far more acculturated, owed little to the class conflict that animated Zakheim. Rather, Schnier looked inward to unlock basic truths about art and life; prefiguring the interests of many Bay Area Jews decades later, he pursued Freudian psychoanalysis and Buddhism. And throughout his long career, he was much more inspired by the images of Asia than those of Europe.

The son of a middle-class vintner, Schnier attended Stanford but felt out of place there, not because he was a Jew, but because his father did not wear a "starched collar."[133] He graduated in 1920 with a degree in civil engineering, a field that bored him. But his first job was in Hawaii, where for two years he lived on Kauai and Maui, as well as on Oahu in Waikiki.[134] In Hawaii, reading Somerset Maugham's novel based on the life of Gauguin, *The Moon and Sixpence,* Schnier began to identify with the French master who journeyed to the South Seas for art and adventure. Returning home, he soon enrolled in the

Department of Architecture at UC Berkeley and took drawing courses. He preferred sculpture, however, and by the mid-1920s he had left the university and rented a studio in San Francisco's fabled Monkey Block, where he rubbed shoulders with Kenneth Rexroth, painter and sculptor Ralph Stackpole, and photographer Dorothea Lange.[135] Evenings he wandered through nearby Chinatown, fascinated by the exotic objects in the antique stores.

His career was propelled by the big-hearted collector Albert Bender, who aided a plethora of struggling artists between the wars.[136] Bender bought numerous woodcarvings, usually in teak, from the budding sculptor and donated them to institutions ranging from Temple Emanu-El to the San Francisco Art Institute. The Irishman also helped him line up other prominent Jewish patrons, such as Jesse Lilienthal, who much later would become Schnier's father-in-law.

Eager to see the source of the art he had viewed in Chinatown, Schnier, with a knapsack and blanket, embarked on a Wanderjahr through Asia in 1932. He shipped home small jade pieces from China, little bronze Buddhas from Thailand, and countless artworks from Japan, India, and Burma. In Asia he became deeply interested not only in the art and sculpture of Buddhism, but also in its "quietness and freedom from strife."[137]

When Schnier returned to the Bay Area, his fertile mind was soon attracted by another current of thought, psychoanalysis, both for its therapeutic value and for its use in probing the meaning of art.* For his own analyst Schnier chose Joseph Thompson, who shared his patient's ardor for Buddhism. For more than half a decade Schnier saw Thompson almost every day, receiving "an entirely new kind of education . . . far more important than anything I had experienced before."[138]

The varied strands of Schnier's background are reflected in the work that made his reputation as a sculptor, the eight huge statues for the Golden Gate International Exposition. The world's fair of 1939 celebrated the completion of the two great bridges, of course. But, like the Panama-Pacific International Exposition nearly a quarter of a century earlier (also built on land reclaimed from the bay), it marked San Francisco's recovery—this time from an economic rather than a natural disaster. Treasure Island provided thousands of jobs, drew millions of tourists, and was intended to become a

---

* Although never a practicing analyst, Schnier wrote several juried journal articles in the field and won the praise of Freud's biographer Ernest Jones (Jacques Schnier, "Jacques Schnier," in *There Was Light: Autobiography of a University: Berkeley, 1868–1970*, ed. Irving Stone [Garden City, N.Y., 1970], 98).

regional airport. And in common with its illustrious predecessor, the Golden Gate International Exposition looked toward Asia. One of its major goals, as Kevin Starr has noted, was "boosting [San Francisco] . . . as the financial, trading, travel, and cultural capital of the Pacific Basin. . . . No city could sit so superbly on the edge of this vast ocean and not dream such dreams."[139]

The point was not lost on civic leaders such as Herbert Fleishhacker, still president of the Park and Art Commission, who played a major role in the extravaganza along with other politically connected Jews such as the Democratic powerbroker Edward Heller. A. L. Gump, now in the last decade of a career devoted to placing Asian art and furniture into American homes, was elated about the fair. He was entrusted with the sale of many of the objects on display—in particular, exquisite pieces of jade—and "helped to prolong [the] sentiment" of the expo, just as he had done by selling bronze sculptures from the Far East during and after the exposition of 1915.[140]

In the mid-1930s Gump had occasionally called in Schnier, who was soon to join the faculty of UC Berkeley, as a consultant on the provenance of ancient Asian sculpture.[141] Schnier's wide knowledge of Asian art, the primacy he accorded it, and, of course, his talent in creating works with Far Eastern motifs led to the invitation he received in early 1938 to be one of the fair's artists.

He worked in clay, producing models that others would enlarge and cast in concrete before Schnier applied the finishing touches. His sculptures were immense, one of them twenty-six feet high and more than eighty feet in length. The bas-relief *Dance for Life* was strongly influenced by reliefs at Angkor Wat and Angkor Thom, which he had seen in Cambodia several years earlier.[142] But his most important contribution, which has remained on Treasure Island to this day, is *Spirit of India,* two tall figures at an entrance to the Court of Pacifica, the part of the exhibition where the theme of Pacific fellowship was strongest.[143]

Although the Golden Gate International Exposition opened for a second season in 1940, the war in Europe mocked its theme of international harmony and prosperity. A year later the United States entered the worldwide conflict. Second Lieutenant Schnier, more fortunate than most, was able to pursue his interests while in uniform. The army sent him to Yale to learn Chinese and then to Asia as an intelligence officer.

By the end of the 1930s the Depression had been overcome, but a far darker time was being ushered in. For the Jewish community of the Bay Area, the war years would prove the most disconcerting and divisive period in its entire history.

TEN

Cataclysms

Responses to the Holocaust and Zionism

WORLD WAR II AFFECTED CALIFORNIA MORE than any other state. The defense industry became the mainspring of the state's economy, and the population grew 30 percent in the first half of the 1940s alone. The boomtown atmosphere led newsmen (and, later, historians) to speak of a "Second Gold Rush."[1]

As in the rest of America, life now included gasoline rationing, women at work in factories, victory gardens, and war bond drives. But West Coast cities also contended with the fear of enemy attack. Soon after the bombing of Pearl Harbor, sensational news headlines spurred people to sign up as air raid wardens, first aid providers, and ambulance drivers.

Bay Area Jews, naturally, adjusted to wartime conditions like everyone else, and almost every Jewish institution did its part for civil defense. The Jewish Community Center was in the forefront. By early 1942 it served as a shelter during blackouts; conducted classes in home nursing, first aid, and air raid precautions; and launched a "Physical Fitness for Victory" campaign.[2] It now held its popular dances in cooperation with the USO.[3]

But while local Jews were preoccupied by the *American* war effort, they were also confronted by two cataclysmic *Jewish* events—the Holocaust and the struggle for Palestine—and bitterly divided in their responses to both. The twin crises laid bare the extent to which the German Jewish dynasties that had led the community since the Gold Rush were now out of sync with the rest of world Jewry. Despite nearly a century of acceptance and achievement matched almost nowhere else, the old guard was intimidated in the early 1940s by shrill accusations of Jewish self-interest—stinging barbs for a group priding itself on its universalism. They expressed little solidarity with the East European victims of the Shoah, and made anti-Zionism a major priority.

Already in the late 1930s the Jewish aristocracy in Northern California was being attacked as timid and apologetic by a stirred-up group of rabbis and laymen of East European origin who made their own bid for leadership based on an assertive reaction to Hitler and a ringing endorsement of Zionism. The "furious battle . . . the large-scale collision," as the *Emanu-El* put it in 1943, tore Bay Area Jewry apart.[4]

Yet even in this most contentious hour in its history the Jewish community found common ground in the fight against racial discrimination. That cause grew more urgent with the huge influx of black job seekers, and later with the return of Japanese Americans from wartime detention camps.

And in the 1940s, as so often in its past, the Bay Area was graced with creative Jewish artists in its midst. They both reflected and helped to shape the Jewish and general community's identity as California's first American century came to an end.

THE WHITE JEW

Contending with the Depression and fearful of being branded as ethnocentric, San Francisco Jews reacted to the abuses of their brethren in Nazi Germany with little sense of urgency. Although Rabbi Stephen Wise convened a mass protest meeting in Madison Square Garden less than two months after Hitler's seizure of power, and similar gatherings occurred that spring in West Coast cities (including Oakland), San Francisco did not follow suit. "What are we waiting for then?" bemoaned the *Emanu-El,* which advocated a major rally to arouse public interest in the cause.[5]

The local weekly tried, mostly in vain, to shake the community out of its lethargy. Published and edited by the young attorney Sol Silverman, a Zionist and Conservative Jew, the periodical *Emanu-El* now gave scant coverage to Congregation Emanu-El (which reached its members through its own weekly). Throughout Silverman's thirteen-year tenure, which ended in 1945, his publication would largely serve the growing East European Jewish middle class concentrated in the Fillmore and Richmond districts, many of whom belonged to Beth Israel, Sherith Israel, Beth Sholom, and, of course, the new JCC.

Silverman had no qualms about taking the German Jewish establishment to task for its quiescence toward the outrages perpetrated by the Nazis. In 1933 he ran a series of front-page articles by his top reporter, Raymond Dannenbaum, skewering the smug "white Jew . . . a gentleman, a good guy [who] knows how to repress his Jewish instincts."[6] No doubt the portrait caused discomfort on Pacific Heights:

> He belongs to a San Francisco *Club,* of which the chief membership is Jewish. He is a member of a *Temple.* Occasionally, he attends meetings of the *Temple's Men's Club.* He gives, within what he considers reason, to the *Jewish National Welfare Fund* and to various other Jewish organizations. Right now, he is thinking about joining the *Center* because he likes the handball courts.[7]

But he "takes all of these activities for granted," wrote Dannenbaum, who ascribed the following dinner party banter to his white Jew: "Don't you think that this whole business about German persecution of the Jews is exaggerated? You know that Jews always howl before they're struck . . . they always complain."[8]

Emanu-El's Rabbi Irving Reichert, who traveled to Germany in mid-1933, also tried to prod the elite families into action. He returned telling of "600,000 of our fellow-Jews . . . condemned as a cancerous growth to be excised and destroyed."[9] At a time when several eminent Bay Area academics still made light of Hitler's anti-Semitism,* Reichert's prescience was uncanny. On Rosh Hashanah, a mere eight months after the Nazi takeover, he told his flock, "There is no further hope. . . . [T]he more fortunate thousands will emigrate and the more miserable hundreds of thousands will be killed, or shunted off into social if not actual ghettos, condemned to degradation by a constant stigma of inferiority."[10]

Reichert urged a much higher level of giving to the Jewish National Welfare Fund (JNWF), of which he soon became the campaign chairman. "The very least we can do," he pleaded, "is to protect [German

---

*In the spring of 1934, the recently retired president of Stanford University, Robert Swain, called Hitler "an apostle of peace," and UC Berkeley political science professor General David Barrows claimed that in Germany Jews were treated no differently than non-Jews (*Emanu-El,* May 25, 1934, 1; June 1, 1934, 1, 6).

Jewry] from the ravages of famine, disease, and destitution, and to make it possible for some of them to escape the living hell of Germany."[11] Second, he implored his listeners to join the national boycott of German-made goods, a tactic advocated by the *Emanu-El* as well.[12]

But Reichert's sermon also revealed his frustration. "There are among you some who object to this macabre theme," he said as he faced the worshippers. "There are many people . . . who would fain close their eyes to all that is sordid and ugly in the world, and flee before the presence of tragedy as they would from a pursuing specter."[13]

He was deeply disappointed with the results of the JNWF drive the following spring. To meet the new overseas needs, the fundraising goal was set at $400,000—double the amount raised in early 1933.[14] The organization's "most intensive campaign ever" included a gala pageant at the Tivoli Theater featuring celebrities such as Paul Muni.[15] Reichert spoke of the "haunted expressions" he had seen among German Jews the year before. But, even taking the bad economy into account, the campaign failed miserably. It generated only $180,000, less than it had in 1933.[16] Reichert publicly deplored the poor showing as evidence of "defeatism."[17]

The rabbi also pointed to another threat related to the rise of Nazism in Germany: anti-Jewish hate groups springing up on American soil.[18] This was also of great concern to the *Emanu-El*, which for the first time in its history covered local anti-Semitism as a major news story.

In 1933 and 1934 the paper focused on the San Francisco branch of the Silver Shirts, a national movement led by the fanatic William Dudley Pelley. Combining fascism with spiritualism, the group allied itself with the Ku Klux Klan. Dannenbaum went undercover to many of their hate-filled meetings, held in a dingy room on Divisadero Street. The *Emanu-El* printed a dozen articles on the group in six months, quoting vehement attacks on Jews as both Communists and capitalists and claims that Jesus was an Aryan.[19]

But just as Dannenbaum was dispirited by the Jewish community's tepid response to Nazism across the Atlantic, he was also frustrated by the listlessness greeting his exposé of fascist stirrings at home. Midway through the long series on the Silver Shirts he wrote an article bringing back his imaginary friend (the "good guy," the "white Jew") who "subscribes to the doctrine of 'letting well enough alone.' 'Don't cross your bridges before you come to them,' describes a portion of his philosophy. That is very dangerous philosophy these days."[20]

If many Northern California Jews failed to heed the ominous events of the mid-1930s, they could not ignore the increasing number of Central European refugees in their midst. At first only a handful arrived, many of them accomplished artists and intellectuals who enriched the Bay Area's professional and cultural life. Émigré scholars such as economist Carl Landauer and art historian Albert Simony accepted positions at local universities. Heinz Berggruen became the art critic for the *San Francisco Chronicle* in the mid-1930s; after the war he would return to Europe and become one of its leading modern art collectors. The multitalented Viennese pharmacologist Leon Kolb, an art collector, music critic, and student of ancient history, in 1937 bought a grand home on Pacific Avenue, where he hosted visiting luminaries and held cultural events. Prominent Freudian psychiatrists from Central Europe also settled in San Francisco. Bernard Berliner, later a leader in the local psychoanalytic institute, was in a circle that included Erik Erikson, who was just beginning to break with Freud's orthodoxy. At UC Berkeley Erikson conducted research that led to his pathbreaking *Childhood and Society,* published in 1950.[21] During the war he also worked at Mount Zion Hospital treating U.S. veterans suffering from emotional battle scars.

The prewar German transplant who would make the greatest impact on Jewish life in the Bay Area was the lavishly gifted Ludwig Altman, organist for the ornate Oranienburgerstrasse synagogue in Berlin, who landed a similar position at Temple Emanu-El soon after he came to town.[22] He would remain for half a century, earning worldwide acclaim as a composer and virtuoso.*

By the late 1930s a broader cross-section of German Jewry had begun to arrive, a migration that peaked in the new decade and then abruptly ceased when America entered the war. By then, more than three thousand German-speaking Jewish refugees had moved to San Francisco, constituting perhaps 7 percent of the city's Jewish population.[23] They required food, housing, and jobs in difficult economic times.

---

*The Bay Area was also the refuge of a coterie of German rabbis arriving after the war. Among them were Theodore Alexander, who founded a synagogue in the Sunset District, B'nai Emunah; and Leo Trepp, John Zucker, Moritz Winter, and Gunther Gates, who took pulpits in East Bay cities.

The Jewish community leadership met this challenge with alacrity. In 1936 the Federation of Jewish Charities inaugurated the Committee for Service to Émigrés, one of the earliest and best-run programs of its kind in the country. It attracted hundreds of volunteers and skillfully coordinated the services of many of the federation's constituent agencies, such as Mount Zion Hospital, which offered refugees free medical care, and the Hebrew Free Loan Association, which helped many start businesses.[24] The committee's substantial budget—$65,000 by 1940—was funded entirely by San Francisco's Jewish National Welfare Fund.[25]

Most agreed that the committee's success was largely due to the resourcefulness and persistence of its director, Sanford Treguboff, himself an immigrant. "Treg," as nearly everyone called him, was of Ukrainian origin, but his father was an industrialist in Manchuria, where the family was exposed to both Chinese and Russian culture. Treg left the lively Jewish colony of Harbin, China, to attend UC Berkeley, and after graduating in 1931 joined the staff of the Eureka Benevolent Society. The urbane young man succeeded as a caseworker and also ingratiated himself with powerful lay leaders such as Walter Haas and Robert Sinton, who remained his lifelong friends. In 1946, after he returned from the U.S. Army, Treguboff would serve as director of the JNWF and, when it merged with the federation in 1955, he would be the top executive of the new institution, the Jewish Welfare Federation, for another fifteen years.

In 1936 the popular Treg was the consensus choice to head the Committee for Service to Émigrés.* His top priority was job placements, and he found positions for hundreds of refugees annually. Several of Northern California's leading employers met weekly, reviewed the detailed profiles Treg prepared, and then interviewed job seekers. A physicians committee, meanwhile, helped refugee medical practitioners find the one-year placement as interns required for foreign doctors, dentists, and nurses.

To be sure, about half the refugees for whom Treg landed work toiled as live-in domestics, securing lodging along with employment. Many were trained in an eight-week course in home economics conducted by

---

* He worked under the federation's leading executive, Hyman Kaplan, according to Treg "a truly brilliant social engineer." Kaplan had been his supervisor earlier, too, as director of the Eureka Benevolent Society, but his lack of "emotional attachment" to those in need would render him Treguboff's "teacher but not mentor" (Sanford Treguboff, "Administration of Jewish Philanthropy in San Francisco," 1988, p. 28, Bancroft Library, Regional Oral History Office, University of California, Berkeley).

the Emanu-El Residence Club.[26] But hundreds of others were placed as salespeople, clerks, bookkeepers, seamstresses, janitors, and gardeners, and Treg tirelessly approached local merchants and unions to find openings. During the war the committee established its own "Utility Workshop" to provide half-time employment for almost a hundred elderly and disabled refugees, an innovative program that won national recognition.[27]

Many of Treg's clients would have been eligible for public assistance but, as he proudly recalled, "We did not test it. . . . We relied on strictly private contributions to Jewish fundraising organizations for our budget."[28] In the sensitive atmosphere of the late 1930s and early '40s, the last thing the federation and the JNWF wanted was for Jewish refugees to be considered a burden on taxpayers.

SEEKING A LOW PROFILE

Though anti-Semitism was less pronounced in the Bay Area than in other parts of America, it was on the upswing in the 1930s. The class conflict of 1934 triggered anti-Jewish sentiment from Petaluma to the San Francisco waterfront, and groups such as the Silver Shirts and German-American Bund gained in strength. Finally, in 1937, the top rung of the Jewish aristocracy formed the community's first defense organization, the Survey Committee. The influential Jesse Steinhart initially convened an ad hoc group to deal with a small but vitriolic anti-Jewish paper published in the Mission District. Soon he asked the group's seven prominent members, including Rabbi Reichert, Justice Sloss, Walter Haas, and Dan Koshland, to constitute the board of an agency that would monitor the mass media and, usually behind the scenes, respond to anti-Semitism.[29]

Newspaperman Eugene Block was appointed executive director of the Survey Committee, which scored some impressive victories. Reichert, for example, succeeded in removing the anti-Jewish Father Coughlin from the airwaves. The radio station carrying his Sunday diatribe was controlled by a Protestant minister, and Reichert approached him "as one man of the cloth to another," a more effective approach, it was felt, than a public campaign to pressure the station's advertisers.[30] Block also worked quietly to fight prejudice in housing and hiring. He saw to it that the loathsome sentence often found at the end of a newspaper ad for a job or an apartment on the East Coast—"Only Christians Need Apply"—remained out of the Bay Area press.[31]

But the Survey Committee, although it gave the impression it was speaking for the whole Jewish community, was really the representative of the German Jewish establishment. Only in the fall of 1943 did it join forces with the B'nai B'rith Community Committee (local laymen representing their fraternal order's Anti-Defamation League), and not for a year after that did it join a community-wide forum with a broad cross-section of the city's Jewish organizations. (That group, the Association of Jewish Organizations, may be said to be the forerunner of today's Jewish Community Relations Council.) But during the critical years of 1938 to 1944 the powerful Survey Committee would remain aloof from first- and second-generation East European Jews, dividing San Francisco Jewry and crippling its response to the Holocaust.

Late in the 1930s Oakland, too, established a task force of well-connected laymen to fight anti-Semitism. That group's name, the Americanism Commission, reflected its strategy of downplaying Jewish distinctiveness, and, like the Survey Committee, it sought a low profile. Its 1939 "Guide for Publicity," approved by the Jewish Welfare Federation of Alameda County, cautioned Jewish organizations:

Common interest now demands modest use of the general press for Jewish purposes. Therefore, be moderate with your publicity. . . .

Bear in mind that nationally the Jews are less than 4% of the total population—and the interests of the vast majority . . . may differ from ours.

Avoid emphasizing large Jewish needs because in doing so the general public comes to believe we are a burden on the community. Public resentment has already appeared against fund-raising for overseas purposes in the face of so much need in our own country. . . .

Avoid sensational statements about the spread of anti-Semitism in the United States. It is better to stress the privileges Jews, as well as people of all faiths, enjoy in our democracy.[32]

In 1938 the JWF literally waved the American flag, ordering that the colors be raised daily at the Oakland JCC. The following year a framed copy of the U.S. Constitution was hung in the center's library during an elaborate ceremony organized for the press.[33] Across the bay, the *Emanu-El* was not far behind. Beginning in 1940, its masthead proclaimed the paper's mission: "To preserve the ideals of American democracy."

While most Northern Californians knew little about the Holocaust because it was afforded meager coverage by the local and national media,*
Jews were regularly informed of the unfolding catastrophe in the pages of
the *Emanu-El*. But Silverman's paper—like much of the rest of the
Anglo-Jewish press—was caught in a double bind: reports of genocide
were often downplayed in an attempt to deflect the charge of "tribalism"
or self-interest.[34]

At times the *Emanu-El* editor was unflinching. In mid-1942 he declared,
"Nothing short of mass extermination is now going on in Warsaw. There are
400 Jews dying every day from . . . hunger and disease, their bodies picked
up by Nazi trucks as so much litter."[35] At the end of that year he printed
Stephen Wise's appalling revelation that two million Jews had already been
killed and a plan was underway to murder millions more.[36]

And yet such reports were the exception. Many other vital stories on the
destruction of the Jews were assigned a low priority or even ignored.
Remarkably, Silverman barely mentioned Kristallnacht, the pogrom in
November 1938 during which almost all the synagogues in Germany were
burned. Shmuel Zygielbojm's pivotal dispatch from London in June 1942,
providing city-by-city details of Polish and Lithuanian Jews massacred by
the SS, was afforded less than one column on page four.[37] There was no
coverage of the march on the White House of four hundred Orthodox
rabbis in October 1943.[†] Nor was any notice given to the most widely circulated Holocaust story of all: an eyewitness account of Auschwitz that
had come to American officials through Switzerland, which many metropolitan dailies ran on page one.

More frequently than news of the systematic murder of European Jews,
the *Emanu-El* featured articles on the achievements of American Jews,
beginning with Haym Solomon, who sold government bonds to finance

---

*A study that surveyed nineteen big city newspapers, including the *Chronicle* and *Examiner*, concluded that the major dailies "ignore[d] the news [of the Final Solution] or
[gave] it cursory coverage at best" (Deborah Lipstadt, *Beyond Belief: The American Press
and the Coming of the Holocaust* [New York, 1986], 219).

†The event was sponsored by the strident antiestablishment Emergency Committee
to Save the Jewish People of Europe, headed by a young Jew from Palestine, Peter Berg-
son. None of its many activities—marches, musical presentations, congressional lobbying, and full-page ads in the *New York Times*—was reported by the *Emanu-El*.

the Revolutionary War.[38] But the most attention was given to current U.S. Jewish heroes in the form of countless stories of Jewish bravery on the battlefield as well as service in remote locations. In the second half of 1944 it seemed that the paper's primary goal was to "answer the anti-Semitic infamy that the American Jew is fighting the war with the blood of others."[39] The campaign began with a nationally syndicated column, printed in extra-large, bold type on page one, that listed twenty facts about the Jewish contribution to the war effort, each in the form of a question beginning with the drumbeat of "Did you know . . ." Typical was: "Did you know that a house to house canvas in . . . representative cities shows that the percentage of Jewish men in the service is in excess of the ratio of Jews to the general population?"[40] In an unusual front-page editorial the paper asked its readers to help document this claim for the Bay Area, urging them to send it information on their friends and relatives in the armed services. For the next six months nearly every issue contained a two-page spread under the headline "Local Boys on Duty in Far-flung Areas," consisting of about fifty photographs, each accompanied by a brief story. This feature alone took up a quarter of each edition.

When the war itself was covered, great pains were taken to ensure it would not be seen as a war for the Jews, but rather as a defense of Western civilization and even the Church. So eager was the *Emanu-El* to find Christian allies that it gave undue weight to the vaguest expressions of sympathy from Pope Pius XII and even from a group of German bishops.[41] Nazi atrocities against non-Jews, such as the bombing of a nursery school in London in 1943, were frequently reported and the subject of editorials.[42] The weekly also carried huge ads for war bonds, devoted much space to the downtown USO run by the Jewish Welfare Board, and hailed the many local Jews active in San Francisco's civil defense efforts.

President Roosevelt was virtually deified. A full-page drawing on the cover of the Passover edition of 1942 depicted him gallantly holding the Four Freedoms alongside Moses carrying the Ten Commandments, with Japanese prime minister Hideki Tojo and Hitler drowning in the Red Sea. Below was the caption "Fear Not for I Am with Thee."[43]

While the *Emanu-El*'s display of wartime patriotism literally pushed the Holocaust off the front page, the top Jewish lay leaders were even more cautious than was Silverman about focusing attention on the developing disaster. Inactivity in the face of calamity abroad was uncharacteristic of San Francisco Jewry, which had held mass meetings to protest the Mortara kidnapping in 1859 and the pogroms in Russia during and after World

War I. Christian ministers and politicians were featured at these rallies, reflecting their rock-solid bonds with Jews, which were exceeded nowhere else. And beginning in 1936, as has been noted, the federation had conducted an exemplary program to settle German Jewish refugees in the Bay Area.

But the elite families were uncomfortable acting in concert with the East European Jews, now the majority of the town's Jewish population. The eloquent Rabbi Reichert, who had vividly portrayed the plight of German Jewry in the mid-1930s, would have been the logical person to galvanize the community in the face of the destruction of Yiddish-speaking Jewry during the war. Yet he exhibited no personal warmth toward the Bay Area's East European Jews, and the feeling was mutual. Far more important was his animosity toward Zionism, full-blown by 1942, which made cooperation with Jews outside his synagogue almost impossible during the Holocaust. Emanu-El was isolated as never before.

In addition to its estrangement from the Jewish masses, the old guard felt increasing pressure from American anti-Semites. The leading families had lost some of their sense of security as early as World War I as a result of the Weinberg terrorism trial and even their German origins. They briefly regained their assertiveness in mid-1919, with a mass meeting protesting the "butchery" of Jews during the civil war raging on the borders of the new Soviet Union.* But confidence was soon eroded by the Red Scare and postwar social discrimination, and later by the bigotry born of the Depression. After the rise of Hitler, and particularly during the first two years of the war, when most of European Jewry became trapped in the Nazi net, American Jews came under attack for yet another reason: putting Jewish concerns ahead of the common good. With the United States still neutral in the war, and the public opposed to intervention, the canard that Roosevelt, the British, and the Jews were "pushing" America into the war gained traction.

That was the message of the America First Committee, which stridently opposed U.S. military involvement in Europe. Its chief exponent was the wildly popular Charles A. Lindbergh, whose articles, radio addresses, and mass gatherings beginning in 1940 electrified millions of Americans and wor-

---

*Justice Sloss presided over the gathering of two thousand in Scottish Rite Hall, which approved tough resolutions to be sent to President Wilson and Congress. Sponsors spanned the political spectrum, ranging from the socialist bookseller Harry Koblick to corporate titans I. W. Hellman Jr. and Mortimer Fleishhacker (*Emanu-El,* June 13, 1919, 4, 16).

ried many Jews. His appearance in San Francisco on July 1, 1941, generated one of the most enthusiastic welcomes for a visitor in the city's history. The Civic Auditorium was filled hours before his speech, and thousands listened to it on loudspeakers outside the hall. Broadcast nationally and rebroadcast on local stations, the address was also printed in its entirety the next day in the *Chronicle* and *Examiner*.[44] The Hearst paper supported the Lone Eagle with a glowing editorial and also ran a page of photos featuring celebrities who had appeared with him, including film star Lillian Gish.[45]

Lindbergh did not mention the Jews by name in San Francisco—he would several months later in Des Moines, Iowa, labeling them "warmongers" and threatening that instead of "pressing America towards the war . . . they should be opposing it in every possible way for they will be among the first to feel its consequences."[46] But the speech in the Civic Auditorium was disconcerting nonetheless. To thunderous applause he declared, "A refugee who steps off the gangplank and advocates war is acclaimed a defender of freedom. A native born American who opposes war is called a fifth columnist."[47] Hitler had invaded the USSR only nine days earlier, affording Lindbergh his first opportunity to play the anti-Communist card: "I would a hundred times rather see my country ally herself with England, or even with Germany with all her faults, than with the cruelty, the godlessness, the barbarism that exist in Soviet Russia."[48]

The *Emanu-El* rebuked Lindbergh and his allies in the U.S. Senate like Burton K. Wheeler of Montana, who thinly veiled his anti-Semitism by referring to "New York warmongers" and international bankers including the Rothschilds, Warburgs, and Sassoons.[49] Wheeler addressed a capacity crowd of 6,500 in the Oakland Civic Auditorium in late September and also spoke at the Commonwealth Club.[50] The condescending comments of another isolationist senator, Gerald P. Nye, were also denounced by Silverman, who no doubt feared that timid local Jewish leaders might heed the South Dakotan: "If I were [a Jew]," Nye said, "I should try not to let my natural hatred blind me to the first and best interests of my country."[51] The America First Committee collapsed after Pearl Harbor, of course, but the charge of Jewish self-interest retained its potency in the minds of Jews and gentiles alike.

A RABBI'S WRATH

The local Jewish community's apprehensiveness was reflected in the long delay before a rally was held to protest the ongoing genocide. On July 21, 1942, Rabbi Stephen Wise's meeting in Madison Square Garden drew twenty thousand people, including the mayor and governor, and elicited telegrams of sympathy and support from Roosevelt and Churchill. Many other cities, including Los Angeles, soon held similar events, but Oakland and San Francisco did not follow suit until the following spring. And when San Francisco finally held its mass meeting in the Civic Center, virtually all of the old guard chose not to participate, opting for near silence in the face of the greatest tragedy ever to befall the Jewish people.

By the end of the 1930s there emerged a loose coalition that openly objected to the pioneer families' passive response to Hitler, and that during the war would attempt not only to change that policy but also to democratize Jewish community governance. These insurgents, not surprisingly, were East Europeans immigrants or their American-born offspring. They tended to be middle or working class, left of center politically, Conservative and sometimes Orthodox religiously, and, not least of all, avid Zionists.

Their most powerful voice was that of Beth Sholom's rabbi, Saul White, a native of Poland and protégé of Stephen Wise. Having taken the helm of his new Richmond District synagogue in 1935 while still in his twenties, White quickly set his congregation on an upward course and then turned his attention to the grave events overseas.

The rabbi's main forum was his trenchant op-ed column published in the *Emanu-El* almost every week for six years, coinciding almost exactly with the duration of World War II. His Friday missive to the Jewish community was prominently featured: except for Silverman's editorial, it was usually the only opinion piece in an eight-page paper that ran no political cartoons and rarely any letters to the editor.

Other rabbis were cowed by the German Jewish dynasties, but White, president of the Board of Rabbis of Northern California by 1940, held nothing back as he lambasted a Jewish establishment he felt was doing the community a shameful disservice. In attacks that were more focused and sustained than those of the sardonic Dannenbaum almost a decade earlier, and more honest and substantive than the columns of the scandalmongering Choynski in the prior century, White exposed the failings of the German Jewish gentry as no one had before or since. Early on he expressed his exasperation with a "self-appointed and self-perpetuating" leadership, "distrustful of the masses, suspicious of all manifestations of Jewish life . . . opposed to Yiddish . . . mortally afraid of Zionism."[52] He seldom attacked lay leaders by name, and even composed a warm tribute to Marcus Sloss on the occasion of the justice's seventy-fifth birthday.[53]

But as a group he castigated the Jewish "city fathers, the well-born aristocrats" whose "innermost wish is to assimilate, to disappear as Jews."[54]

White bewailed the overall weakness of Yiddishkeit in San Francisco, especially in comparison with Los Angeles, "where Jewish life . . . refuses to be chloroformed."[55] He took the local JCC to task for its classes in opera, flower arranging, and film history "when millions of Jews are being decimated on the European front."[56] He railed at the sorry state of Jewish education, the lack of even one Jewish bookstore in the city, and the small sum of money raised by the Jewish National Welfare Fund. In one column in mid-1942, entitled "The Woes of My People," he lamented, "We have been infected with the disease of self-hatred and its active virus is felling countless victims."[57]

The interminable delay in holding a mass meeting to protest the Nazi extermination of the Jews showed White "how deeply the acid of decay has eaten into our souls."[58] After describing for his readers the stirring rally in New York mounted by Wise, the rabbi excoriated San Francisco's leading Jews for fearing to call attention to a specifically Jewish tragedy. And even while his own editor made patriotism the dominant issue, White criticized the notion that Jewish defense agencies needed to prove to the general public the loyalty of the Jews.[59] White himself had no qualms about openly reproaching the American government during the war; he exposed anti-Semitic consular officials who were insensitive to Jewish refugees seeking asylum.[60] Above all, he rejected the argument that Jews needed to line up gentile support for any mass meeting:

> How unnatural a people we have become that, to express our sympathy with the tortured Jewish communities of Europe, our leaders urge that we must do so only if we can enlist non-Jewish organizations in the planning, that we dare not express our sorrow for the Jewish victims without doing so for others, that it would be best if non-Jews would eulogize our slain brothers and sisters. Such counsel you give us! Only against us has the enemy declared a policy of extermination, and is now well on his way to realizing it. How lowly we have fallen! . . . How poor in spirit we have become![61]

"DEEP BREACH"

But the old guard was more inflexible than even White imagined. Despite his constant urging, and that of Silverman and Congregation Beth Israel's Rabbi Elliot Burstein, the mass meeting would not occur for another ten months. And even then the town's leading Jews would not agree to be involved, even though prominent non-Jews were included as speakers and sponsors and due weight was given to the Nazi persecution of "other minorities."

The Civic Center event of June 17, 1943, represented virtually every segment of the city's Jewish population *except* the bluebloods. More than fifty organizations participated, including every major synagogue aside from Emanu-El and every main pulpit rabbi other than Reichert.*[62] No less conspicuous was the absence of the Survey Committee, headed by Jesse Steinhart. And while numerous public officeholders appear on the list of sponsors—including Governor Warren, Mayor Rossi, and state senator (and later mayor) Jack Shelley—leading *Jewish* politicians, such as the third-generation San Franciscan Jesse Colman, president of the board of supervisors, refused to take part.[†]

Two months prior to the big night, Sol Silverman, event chairman, began planning meetings with representatives of dozens of Jewish groups. But even within this nonestablishment forum there was much disagreement over the program. In the end, moderates such as Silverman and Sherith Israel's Rabbi Morris Goldstein prevailed over those like White and others who hoped the evening would send a potent and unambiguously Jewish message.

One of those who was disappointed was Ze'ev Brinner. Only nineteen years old at the time, but a member of the event's executive committee, Brinner represented Hashomer Hatzair, a spirited socialist Zionist youth group.[‡] The choice of the main Jewish speaker, popular bug-eyed comedian Eddie Cantor, "trivialized" the event according to Brinner.[63] Although Thomas Mann (in exile in Southern California since 1936) also spoke, the main thrust of his remarks was that the overwhelming majority of Germans opposed anti-Semitism; engaging in some wishful thinking,

---

*The best-known lay leader backing the event was the real estate magnate Louis Lurie, a transplant from Chicago who belonged to no synagogue. Emanu-El's organist, Ludwig Altman, was on the program; he accompanied several vocalists.

†The mass meeting held at the Oakland Auditorium Theatre on May 5, 1943, drawing about 1,500, showed none of the divisiveness of the San Francisco rally. The mayor and state attorney general were present and the featured speaker was Rabbi Edgar Magnin of Los Angeles's Wilshire Boulevard Temple (*Emanu-El*, May 14, 1943, 1).

‡It was founded several years earlier by a charismatic young Jew from Palestine, Zelic Braverman, who was aided by a "very sympathetic" Saul White. The youths held dances and songfests, studied Hebrew, set up summer camp in the Santa Cruz Mountains—and never ceased talking world politics. At its height, the Northern California *ken*, or circle, included ninety youngsters. In 1948 a small chapter of the right-wing Zionist youth group Betar came into existence as well (Hashomer Hatzair Collection, in WJHC/JLMM).

he stated that the Wehrmacht might overthrow Hitler by going on strike.[64] In keeping with the patriotic spirit of the times, the "Star Spangled Banner" opened the proceedings and "God Bless America" was the finale. The event committee rejected Brinner's request to include "Hatikvah," but, at a pre-arranged moment, he and his friends began singing the Zionist anthem, and most of the crowd joined in.[65]

The resolution adopted by those assembled and sent to the president and State Department was relatively tame. It urged Britain to open Palestine to Jewish refugees but failed to endorse Jewish statehood. Likewise, it recommended admitting more immigrants to the United States, but only to the extent that empty slots in the existing quotas be filled, quotas that for Eastern Europeans were extremely small. Silverman exaggerated when he declared the mass meeting of June 17, 1943, "the most significant event in the history of San Francisco Jewish community."[66]

Still, the gathering, attended by almost eleven thousand and covered by the local press and the *New York Times,* drew much-needed attention to the Holocaust.[67] Coupled with a smaller rally held in Oakland the previous month, it added the Bay Area, albeit quite late, to the large number of American metropolitan areas demanding U.S. action to impede Hitler's genocide. As recent scholarship has confirmed, the Roosevelt administration did little to hinder the machinery of death. But the collective weight of mass meetings such as occurred in the Bay Area may have helped push Congress toward the "rescue resolution" of late 1943, which led FDR to approve the creation of the War Refugee Board, the only government agency with a creditable record of saving Jews.

While it is unclear what difference, if any, the mass meeting of June 17 made in Washington, it unquestionably shifted the landscape of Jewish community politics in San Francisco. The event's coalition of Jewish organizations remained largely intact, and ten weeks later presented a second mass meeting before another capacity crowd at the Civic Auditorium. Also spearheaded by Sol Silverman, the August 31 gathering was a tribute to the suffering and heroism of the Russian people. The featured speakers were the renowned actor (and founding director of the Moscow Jewish State Theater) Solomon Mikhoels and the beloved Yiddish poet (and Red Army colonel) Itzik Feffer. They had been sent by Moscow on a forty-six-city goodwill tour to unite American and Russian Jews in the struggle against fascism. They spoke in Yiddish, and many in the audience did not understand them, but in San Francisco they drew their largest crowd west of Chicago.[68]

The event marked the pinnacle of Silverman's pro-Soviet efforts, which also included touting Paul Robeson's local concerts benefiting Russian war relief, and hailing the twenty-fifth anniversary of the Bolshevik Revolution.[69] Beyond the goal of restoring cross-Atlantic ties between the world's two largest Jewish communities, the *Emanu-El* editor may have been motivated by the belief that Mikhoels's and Feffer's tour heralded a positive new stance of the Kremlin toward Zionism.

Needless to say, the German Jewish elite would not take part in this mass meeting either, "the Soviet stigma lending them added conviction," according to social scientist and communal worker Earl Raab, who a few years later wrote of San Francisco Jewry's "deep breach" of the mid-1940s.[70]

In the fall of 1943, the groups that had mounted the two huge rallies formed their own United Council, posing a clear institutional challenge to the Survey Committee and the entire venerable organizational network of the elite. The following year, after much wrangling, the two sides came together, creating the Association of Jewish Organizations, but any spirit of mutual trust and cooperation was short-lived. As Raab indicated, "cries of 'aristocracy' and 'no representation' were undiminished in vigor."[71] This was much more than a "petty scrap for power," he explained in *Commentary,* but rather "sharp differences in approaching the fundamental problems of Jewish identity in America."[72]

"WHERE DO YOU STAND" ON ZIONISM?

While profoundly split over the proper response to the Holocaust, the Jewish community was plagued by a related and even more malevolent clash—over the merits of Jewish nationalism. For nearly all of the old German Jewish families joined with their rabbi in vigorously opposing the creation of a Jewish state, and anti-Zionism soon became more strident in San Francisco than anywhere else in the country.

Rabbi Reichert, an apostle of Classical Reform Judaism, fervently believed nationalism "alien" to Judaism. As he proclaimed in 1936, the Jews took upon themselves "the yoke of the Law, not in Palestine but in the wilderness at Mount Sinai, and by far the greater part of its deathless and distinguished contribution to world culture was produced not in Palestine but in Babylon and the lands of the Dispersion."[73]

But this widely published sermon was more than a theological tract. It also contained the political premise Reichert would put forth for decades to come: the "dual loyalties" argument. Reichert writes, "One wonders what the Gentile world makes of all this [Zionism]. It is notorious that anti-Semites, when other arguments fail, sometimes succeed in prejudicing even friendly Christians against the Jew by quoting this type of nationalistic propaganda to convict us out of our own mouths for being a nationality imbedded within a nation. We may live to regret it."[74] The rabbi also objected to the "truculent" style of the Zionists. Three years after Hitler had taken power he compared their "provocative language" to the posturing of a "swashbuckling, saber-rattling Nazi."[75]

In the *Emanu-El* Rabbi Jacob Weinstein exposed the contradictions of Reichert's position: he "violates all the canons of logic and fairness," the young Labor Zionist wrote. "The same chauvinism, which the rabbi so bitterly assails in [Zionism], he seems so anxious to placate in the American hundred percenter. This is part of the screaming inconsistency of many Reform Jews."[76]

Reichert held his anti-Zionist sentiments in check for the next six years. By 1942, however, a large number of his younger Reform colleagues, including Rabbi William Stern of Oakland's Temple Sinai, had come to embrace Jewish nationalism; for them the need of a refuge in Palestine now outweighed all other considerations. That year, at its annual conference, the Central Council of American Rabbis endorsed the creation of a Jewish army in Palestine. The decision not only angered Reichert but also triggered the revolt of ninety-two non-Zionist Reform rabbis who convened their own conference in Atlantic City.[77] That rabbinical conclave, in which Reichert played a major role, countered with a manifesto holding that "The day has come when we must cry, 'Halt.' A dual citizenship in America is more than we can accept."[78]

The gathering also led to the formation of the American Council for Judaism (ACJ), underwritten by the philanthropist Lessing Rosenwald, former chairman of the board of Sears, Roebuck and Company.[79] Reichert became vice president and official spokesman for the ACJ in the West and by mid-1943 had organized the San Francisco Section, soon to be the organization's largest. Only in Houston, where the leading Reform congregation actually barred Zionist congregants from full, voting membership, did the level of ACJ activity approach that of the Bay Area.[80]

Reichert drew his leadership almost exclusively from the board of directors of Emanu-El. Monroe Deutsch, born in San Francisco of pioneer parents, served as the first head of the local chapter. A classics professor, he was provost of the University of California, Berkeley, and president of the Commonwealth Club. A local ACJ vice president was Hattie Sloss, who often hosted meetings in her home.[81] Each board member person-ally solicited a hundred people, and the ACJ sent a packet of information along with a membership application to three thousand others.*

Reichert, meanwhile, stunned the Jewish community by using his Kol Nidre sermon of 1943 to unveil the ACJ program and attract members. En-titled "Where Do You Stand?" his exhortation reiterated the dual loyalties argument and stressed the duplicity of the Zionists. On the holiest night of the year the rabbi demanded that his listeners "make a decision . . . take a place on one side or the other," and join either the Zionist Organization of America (ZOA) or the American Council for Judaism.[82]

No one actually walked out on the sermon, but the highly charged speech resulted in several resignations from the temple. Also distressed were most of the servicemen in attendance, many of whom were on their way to the Far East.[83] Heated exchanges ensued, such as on the following Sabbath when the ardent Zionist Rose Rinder, wife of Emanu-El's revered cantor, in a most uncharacteristic fit of anger, compared the rabbi to Hitler in earshot of many worshippers.[84]

But on the whole Reichert was sustained by his congregants, many of whom joined the ACJ; by February 1944 the San Francisco Section boasted a thousand members. By the time membership peaked the following year, at around 1,400, it constituted almost one-third of the national rolls and surpassed the local ZOA, which claimed about 1,100.[85] The San Francisco chapter also sent the main office roughly $20,000 annually in the mid-1940s, a figure that constituted nearly 30 percent of the operating budget and (leaving aside Lessing Rosenwald's personal largesse) almost one-half of the funds raised by all the chapters combined.[86] Although opposed by Rabbi Stern, an Oakland branch of the ACJ emerged as well, composed of leading members of Temple Sinai, including its president, Lionel Wachs.[87]

The San Francisco Section drew large crowds to events such as Memo-rial Day services at Emanu-El and speeches by Rosenwald and the feisty national director of the ACJ, Rabbi Elmer Berger, at the Jewish Commu-nity Center. A program devoted to the contributions of the Jews of Cali-fornia featured distinguished speakers, as well as young ushers in cowboy

---

*Other executive committee members included Mrs. Joseph Ehrman Jr., Reichert's fu-ture wife; Dan Koshland; J. D. and Harold Zellerbach; Sydney Ehrman; Mrs. I. W. Hell-man Jr.; and Robert Levison, whose brother George would later head the ACJ. One influ-ential temple board member, Madeline Haas Russell, refused to join the ACJ.

costumes. In explaining the strength of California Jewry from the Gold Rush to the present day, one lecturer quoted Emanu-El's pioneer rabbi Elkan Cohn, who had written that, "while Israelite, it had known no other nationality than that of American."[88]

Clearly, the Jewish elite viewed Zionism as a threat to that sentiment, and as a wedge that would drive apart the Jew and his neighbors. He would now be seen as more distinct and self-interested. And there were no guarantees that a Jewish state would not be Communist or theocratic, or anything else that could cause American Jewry embarrassment at the very least.

The attraction anti-Zionism held for the leading families also exposed their limited understanding of the inherent dangers of the Diaspora and the high price exacted by Jewish powerlessness. The extent of their naïveté was virtually unmatched during this terrible time and may also have contributed to their sluggish response to the genocide in Europe. "Having been blessed with more than nine decades of prosperity and peace," as Silverman explained the elite's mindset, it seemed to them that, without a Jewish state to bar the way, integration of the Jews into the host country anywhere in the world was the natural order of things, and anything else was an aberration.[89]

Of course, in the mid-1940s most other San Francisco Jews angrily dismissed both the hand-wringing about dual loyalties and the Pollyanna-like predictions about Jews abroad, and were infuriated by the ACJ. Yet several rabbis were wary of tangling with Reichert, most notably Sherith Israel's Morris Goldstein, even though his brother Israel, spiritual leader of New York's B'nai Jeshurun, headed the national ZOA.

Saul White, of course, refused to hold his fire. "The masses of the Jewish people still pray for the return to Zion," he exclaimed, "and if the Council wants to make a case of it, we will accept the challenge!"[90] Throughout 1943 the rabbi berated the ACJ in the strongest possible terms in nearly every *Emanu-El* column he wrote. By turns he described them as "traitorous," "disruptive," "destructive," "holier than thou," and "self-hating."[91] "It is enough to make God shed tears," he grieved.*[92] In personal conversations, meanwhile, White mocked Reichert, "who smoked expensive cigars and spent too much time on the golf links," as out of touch with the Jewish masses.[93]

---

*Rabbi Burstein, White's closest ally among local rabbis, expressed a similar opinion in the *Emanu-El,* attacking the "religionists" (i.e., those that held Judaism was a religion only) for their fear that Zionism might "impair their positions of wealth and power in the community . . . might threaten to unloosen their age-old stranglehold on most Jewish communal institutions and philanthropic funds" (*Emanu-El,* November 12, 1943, 8).

But White did not merely take the anti-Zionists to task; he also force-fully articulated the arguments *for* Jewish nationalism, emphasizing both its ancient origins and its present necessity. "Is anyone so naïve to believe," he asked in 1942, "that the people of Poland and Germany will open their gates and reestablish the exiled Jews into jobs and positions which have since been filled by others? The only effective answer to the plight of the Jew is a homeland."[94]

White, who headed the United Palestine Fund, the Jewish National Fund, and the Zionist Organization of America, organized and led many public protests. Perhaps most eventful was the picketing of the consulate of Great Britain, which had virtually shut the doors of Palestine to the Jews with its White Paper of 1939, refusing to lift it even after the Holocaust. In March 1946 the rabbi led several Zionist groups and labor unions in a demonstration outside the downtown consular offices. A few days later, however, the Survey Committee condemned the protest and published an open letter apologizing to the British consul general.[95] "You do not speak for the San Francisco Jewish community," retorted White and other Zionist leaders in an open letter of their own. "By what right do you act to nullify this effort in San Francisco? Yours is not a democratically elected body. You certainly do not represent us. . . . Your letter to the consulate is in our minds a betrayal of the Jewish people. Your people lie sick and bleeding and you apologize to the British government."[96]

But by this time White was no longer a columnist for the *Emanu-El;* his last regular op-ed piece appeared on April 6, 1945. His and Silverman's forum became a casualty of the Jewish community's civil war. At the beginning of the year Walter Haas, Dan Koshland, and Philip Lilienthal, fearing the *Emanu-El* might fall into "irresponsible" hands, had bought the paper and turned it into an organ of the federation and the Jewish National Welfare Fund.[97] Silverman, undercapitalized and drawing little advertising revenue, was unable to resist their offer.[98] Eugene Block of the Survey Committee became the new editor of the weekly, now called the *San Francisco Jewish Community Bulletin.* One of Block's first actions was to drop White unceremoniously and replace him with a series of less controversial writers.[99] Gone, too, were Silverman's pointed and timely opinion pieces, replaced now by the blandest filler. Block even boasted that, before taking a long vacation, he wrote three months of editorials in advance.[100] And in a setback for the Zionists, the town's only Jewish paper now increased its coverage of the American Council for Judaism.

In the immediate postwar years the ACJ entered the diplomatic arena but had little success. Reichert, along with George Levison, sought out and met with Bartley Crum, the San Francisco attorney appointed to the Anglo-American Committee of Inquiry, charged by London and Washington with devising a solution to the Middle Eastern crisis. Yet the two ACJ leaders failed to budge Crum's pro-Zionist leanings, perhaps because an articulate local ZOA leader, Morris Lowenthal, lobbied him even more assiduously.[101]

Of course, the Zionists also benefited from the fast-moving events in Palestine. In October 1946, even the *Jewish Community Bulletin* featured on its front page a poignant eyewitness account of the British internment of Jewish emigrants on Cyprus, many of them death camp survivors.[102] The following year, when the UN voted to partition Palestine and create the first Jewish state in nineteen centuries, Zionist organizations held a large "meeting of thanksgiving" at the War Memorial Opera House, with Bartley Crum as the main speaker.[103] Meanwhile, donations to the San Francisco Jewish National Welfare Fund, most of which went to Palestine through the United Jewish Appeal (UJA), doubled in 1946 to almost $1,500,000.[104] The list of fundraising speakers was stellar: Eleanor Roosevelt in 1946, former treasury secretary Henry Morgenthau Jr. in 1947, and Golda Meyerson (later Meir) as part of her triumphant American tour in February 1948.

Meyerson spoke at Emanu-El, but it was no longer Rabbi Reichert's synagogue. While White had lost his newspaper column in the struggle, Reichert had lost his pulpit. On November 29, 1947—the day the UN voted for partition—he received a call from influential board member (and soon-to-be president) Harold Zellerbach urging him to resign.[105] With supporters such as Monroe Deutsch, Hattie Sloss, and Lloyd Dinkelspiel, he initially opted to fight for his job, but the board of directors soon voted to end Reichert's seventeen-year tenure.[106]

There was more at issue than his stubborn stance against Zionism. Dissatisfaction with his avoidance of pastoral duties had long been brewing, and the august institution was deteriorating.[107] Membership had declined steadily, from more than a thousand families in 1929 to fewer than seven hundred by the end of the war, a period when other Reform temples made tremendous strides. Sherith Israel, for example, under Rabbi Goldstein had tripled its membership from 1932 to 1946, surpassing its wealthier rival in numbers for the first time.[108]

But Reichert's anti-Zionist crusade doubtlessly contributed greatly to his fall. By the time his fate was decided, Jewish statehood had become a strong possibility. Were Reichert to be retained the temple would be frozen in a militantly anti-Zionist posture, whatever the years ahead might bring. It was a risk most of Emanu-El's lay leaders, already pained by the bruising battle, preferred not to take.

Reichert, now fifty-three, chose to leave the rabbinate and work full-time for the American Council for Judaism as executive director of the western region. For the next five years, from an office on Market Street, he conducted a publicity campaign to prevent American Jewish youth from being "indoctrinated" by a foreign country. In the face of fierce opposition from the rest of the Jewish community, the ACJ placed anti-Zionist display ads in the *Bulletin* and openly objected to pro-Israel textbooks in synagogue religious schools.* [109]

But many of the ACJ's most respected backers dropped out in May 1948, after independence and American recognition of the Jewish state. As Lloyd Dinkelspiel put it, "If it's good enough for my country, it's good enough for me."[110] Yet doubts about the AJC did not translate into a universal acceptance of Jewish nationalism on the part of Northern California Jewry. Exultant Zionist organizations held celebrations to mark the birth of the state, but—in contrast with the annual Independence Day extravaganzas of later decades—there was no communitywide event on either side of the bay in May 1948. The *Bulletin*'s editorials continued to take seriously the dual loyalties argument. "Now that a Jewish state is a *fait accompli*," wrote Block, "let us remember that the United States has recognized the State of Israel and we must support our government. Naturally we Jews in America will continue to serve our own country as we have in the past—as loyal citizens of our great land."[111]

To be sure, the arrival in the late 1940s of two dynamic individuals boded well for the future of Zionism in Northern California. In 1946 real

---

*He also publicly accused the Zionist movement of "extortion, character assassination, intimidation, and blackmail" and likened it to Nazism and McCarthyism (Irving Reichert, "Getting Back to Fundamentals," April 4, 1952, in *Judaism and the American Jew: Selected Sermons and Addresses of Irving Frederick Reichert* [San Francisco, 1953], 142). But when the national ACJ established ties with Arab governments in the mid-1950s, he broke with the organization, "recognized" the fact of Israel's existence, and encouraged Jews to contribute to the UJA (*San Francisco Jewish Community Bulletin*, June 15, 1956, 8). Yet he still considered Zionism the most pernicious force in the Jewish world. Except for a three-year period as rabbi of the small Temple Judea, on the southwestern edge of the city, he was ostracized by the Jewish community until his death in 1968, by his own hand (Fred Rosenbaum, *Visions of Reform: Congregation Emanu-El and the Jews of San Francisco* [Berkeley, 2000], 212–13).

estate magnate Benjamin H. Swig moved from Boston to San Francisco to develop an empire that would include the Fairmont and St. Francis hotels. Son of a Lithuanian immigrant, Swig, a fervent Zionist, was the first "outsider" to gain access to the inner circle of Jewish community leadership and distinguished himself as a UJA fundraiser even before the War of Independence. Beginning in 1948, he worked closely with Emanu-El's young new rabbi, who had been raised by East European Orthodox Jews in Portland, Oregon. Alvin Fine's orientation could not have been more different from Reichert's: the silver-tongued spiritual leader proudly advocated Labor Zionism throughout a highly successful rabbinate that lasted until 1964.[112] Nevertheless, it would take Swig and Fine many years to kindle genuine enthusiasm for Israel among the old families, most of whom would not embrace it fully until the Six Day War.

COMMON GROUND

For all of the dissension of the 1940s, the decade witnessed a broad Jewish consensus on civil rights issues. Unlike in the 1930s, when class conflict bitterly divided the community, Bay Area Jews now came together for social justice.* Jews of East European and German origin ranging from right-wingers to Communists led an interfaith and interracial movement that, in its goals if not its tactics, prefigured the more intense struggles of the 1960s and beyond.

Before World War II blacks constituted only a small segment of Northern California's population, and their condition—good in comparison with the rest of the country—was not a top priority for civil rights activists. In the 1940s, though, the insatiable demand for defense workers, especially in Henry J. Kaiser's shipbuilding plants, quickly drew more than a hundred thousand African Americans, mostly from rural Texas, Arkansas, and Oklahoma. Not unlike during the Great Migration following World War I, when eastern and Midwestern cities were transformed by an influx of Southern blacks, the demography of the Bay Area changed

---

*An exception occurred in Oakland, however, in mid-1946. In an echo of the violent Depression-era strikes, Kahn's Department Store, owned by the city's most prominent Jewish family, stubbornly resisted a month-long walkout of its employees over the right to bargain collectively (Robert O. Self, *American Babylon: Race and the Struggle for Postwar Oakland* [Princeton, N.J., 2003], 36–40).

markedly. The African American population soared in San Francisco (increasing eightfold in the decade, to almost forty-five thousand), as well as in Marin City, Oakland, Alameda, and especially Richmond.[113]

The newcomers, marked even among other blacks by their accent and clothing, encountered serious discrimination in the workplace, a problem that intensified after the war, when the defense industry contracted and many had to find new jobs. Housing was a severe problem from the beginning, in part because many landlords, aware of wartime race riots in other cities, refused to rent apartments to blacks; the only San Francisco neighborhood where they resided in large numbers was the tolerant, diverse Fillmore. Many Bay Area restaurants and nightclubs instituted segregation as well.[114]

The Survey Committee, formed earlier against the background of increasing anti-Semitism, was convinced that racism weakened democratic institutions and threatened not only Jews but ultimately all citizens. The organization's leaders, such as Jesse Steinhart, Justice Marcus Sloss, and Dan Koshland, had been deeply affected by the Progressive movement a generation earlier and were committed to working toward a more equitable society. Steinhart in particular was concerned about the plight of blacks, an issue he discussed frequently with his close friend Earl Warren.*[115]

As early as 1942 the Survey Committee assigned a young staff member, journalist David Selvin, who had grown up in the only Jewish family in a small Utah town, as its representative on the Bay Area Council Against Discrimination. The BACAD implored city hall to ensure African Americans access to municipal services and urged the local press not to inflame prejudice by identifying criminals by race.[116] It was one of the earliest and most effective such multiracial groups in the country. Selvin joined liberal Catholic clergy as well members of the NAACP from both sides of the bay; he worked with trade unionists such as the militant head of the

*To be sure, Steinhart's views were shaped by the pragmatic and somewhat paternalistic notions held by many who had come of age early in the century. "If twenty million Negroes in the country were going to be disenfranchised," he told Warren, "it was silly not to expect them to become friendly toward the people who urged them to become communists" (Sam Ladar, in "Earl Warren's Campaigns: Oral History Transcripts and Related Material, 1969–1976," vol. 2, p. 80, Bancroft Library, Regional Oral History Office, University of California, Berkeley). Steinhart is credited by his legal colleague Sam Ladar with stimulating the thinking on race relations of the chief justice who struck down the laws segregating the nation's public schools (ibid., 83).

sleeping car porters union, C. L. Dellums (uncle of the future congressman), and activists such as Walter Gordon, Berkeley's first black policeman.[117] And the new organization also included Jewish leaders, such as the heads of the American Jewish Congress, Rabbis Saul White and Elliot Burstein.

Burstein held that the liberal activists' "big positive guns are persuasion and education," and if these were not successful the group would resort to legislation.[118] It was an apt summary of the work of the organization that succeeded the BACAD, the Council for Civic Unity, which was formed in 1944 and would remain a force in San Francisco politics for the next two decades. The CCU, in which Jews again played the leading role, sought to break down prejudice not only among employers and but also within unions, which often opposed equality for blacks. It ran display ads against bigotry, sent speakers to schools and other venues, and, beginning in the 1940s, backed laws mandating fair employment practices (legislation that, however, did not pass until the 1960s).[119] A similar organization in the East Bay, the Berkeley Interracial Committee (which also included Selvin among a group of Jews of varied backgrounds) fought against segregated housing. In 1948 it helped elect one of the state's first black assemblymen, Byron Rumford, who would use his seat in Sacramento to wage a fifteen-year struggle against the restrictive covenants that blocked many nonwhites seeking to purchase homes.[120]

Toward the end of the war the *Jewish Community Bulletin*, too, focused on racial prejudice. Editor Eugene Block was active in the Council for Civic Unity (later becoming its executive director) and devoted much of the paper's coverage to its work on behalf of the city's minority groups. The paper supported the Fair Employment Practices Bill in the face of Mayor Roger Lapham's opposition, and ran a long series of cartoons ridiculing a "Mr. Bigott," a stupid and ignorant, although not mean-spirited, character who would let his house burn down rather than allow a black fireman to save it.[121]

No doubt the trauma just suffered by their brethren across the sea added to the affinity American Jews felt toward blacks, who were still enduring lynchings in the South, another issue covered by the *Bulletin*. Bay Area Jews were also affected by the birth of the United Nations in San Francisco over a heady two-month period in mid-1945. The central venue of the founding conference was the War Memorial Opera House, where a recital by Yehudi Menuhin opened the proceedings, and Sherith Israel was the location of one of the meetings.* The city seemed engulfed in good will as Rabbi Burstein spoke of "humanity as one great family—a family of equals in its own eyes and in the eyes of God."[122] On the eve of the momentous gathering of delegates from fifty nations he implored Jews to "link their fight with the general fight for decent living conditions for all men and against discrimination against any man."[123]

No small factor in the ability of the "liberal coalition" to advance civil rights was the financial support garnered by groups like the CCU and the Berkeley Interracial Committee from the Haas family's Columbia Foundation, Rosenberg Foundation (founded by the owners of the huge dried fruit concern), and San Francisco Foundation, all of which were established through Jewish leadership.[124] Inaugurated in 1948 largely through the efforts of Dan Koshland, the San Francisco Foundation became a powerful catalyst for improving the lives of the city's disadvantaged residents in areas such as housing, public health, and education.

The Jewish community also sought to achieve racial harmony by "policing its own."[125] In the East Bay, in particular, Southern blacks were sometimes easy marks for Jewish pawnbrokers and jewelers hawking shoddy goods at inflated prices. In May 1944, following a Cab Calloway dance in the Oakland Auditorium, hundreds of blacks went on a violent rampage along Broadway below Twelfth Street. This "spontaneous outburst," in the words of the police, had no anti-Semitic impetus but nevertheless resulted in damage to Jewish-owned stores.[126] The authorities and the press came down hard on the rioters, while Oakland's Jewish Welfare Federation discreetly pursued its own methods of easing racial tension: it called the handful of Jewish merchants who were known price-gougers into the office of federation head Harry Sapper.[127] There, two Jewish assistant district attorneys threatened the businessmen with jail time if they persisted in their predatory ways.[128] This strategy of confronting Jewish merchants may have contributed to one of the best climates of black-Jewish relations in the country.

Late in the war Jews also addressed the welfare of their Japanese American neighbors, the Nikkei, who were returning from detention camps. The

*Walter Haas, meanwhile, almost succeeded in securing the Presidio as the permanent site of the world body. He traveled to London and other cities to make his case, but most European delegations objected to the Pacific Coast as too distant from their home countries ("Levi Strauss and Company: Tailors to the World," with Levi Strauss executives Walter A. Haas, Sr., Daniel E. Koshland, Walter A. Haas Jr., and Peter E. Haas, 1976, p. 39, Bancroft Library, Regional Oral History Office, University of California, Berkeley).

Jewish concern was in stark contrast to their behavior immediately after the executive order for the internment of the Japanese in February 1942. No Jewish organization spoke out against the evacuation of more than a hundred thousand people of Japanese origin, about two-thirds of them U.S. citizens. While the *Emanu-El* expressed concern about the government's treatment of "friendly enemy aliens," it explicitly meant refugees from Germany or Italy and not "Japs" or "Nips," as the Jewish paper sometimes called the Nikkei.[129] No doubt many Jews, fearful of putting their patriotism in question, were wary of criticizing a military policy ostensibly implemented for reasons of national security.

Jews on the far left seldom spoke out against the relocation, and even in radical Petaluma some "took advantage" and bought Japanese property on the cheap.[130] The young socialist Ze'ev Brinner, who lived in the Fillmore, witnessed a long line of evacuees on Sutter Street—among them one of his closest friends at Lowell High School—holding their suitcases and being loaded into buses. "I was terribly upset, I was taken aback," Brinner recalls, "but we had so many issues going on at once—the war, Jews in Europe, above all Palestine—this was down the list. I had contacts at the time with Trotskyists and Communists and they never mentioned it."[131] Indeed, the Communist Party in California expelled all its Japanese members in 1942.[132]

No Jew had greater reason to condemn the internment than local Communist organizer Elaine Black Yoneda, a veteran of the waterfront strike. During the war she was one of the few whites married to a Japanese— because of California's miscegenation laws they had wed in Seattle—and was the mother of a Eurasian three-year-old whom callous government officials required to join his father in the forlorn Manzanar detention center. In order to be with her family Elaine had to fight the authorities for permission to reside in the camp, where she remained for nine months, until Karl Yoneda joined the army and she was allowed to return to San Francisco with their son.[133] But neither of the Yonedas, both lifelong activists, spoke out against the evacuation.[134] They hewed to the Communist Party line of focusing exclusively on defeating the fascist enemy.

Yet even in the frenzied period following the attack on Pearl Harbor a number of leading Jews, as individuals or representing secular organizations, defended the Nikkei and later spoke out against the mass removal. Rabbi Reichert, in a courageous sermon only a week after America's entry into the war, expressed his dismay at the "unpardonable attacks and outrages upon American citizens of Japanese parentage whose loyalty to our country is as unyielding and assumed as that of President Roosevelt himself. . . . We Jews ought to be among the very first to cry down the unjust persecution of the foreign-born in our midst whose patriotism is equal to ours."[135]

Reichert joined the board of the Fair Play Committee, which lobbied government officials to reverse the internment policy and worked for the smooth reentry of the Japanese into American society. According to David Selvin the organization resembled the BACAD, which was founded around the same time but focused primarily on protecting blacks.[136] University of California provost Monroe Deutsch, who tried to intervene on behalf of many Nikkei students, faculty, and staff, was also active in the Fair Play Committee, and along with Dan Koshland wrote Secretary of War Henry Stimpson urging swift restoration of full citizenship to the Japanese Americans.[137]

Many of the prominent Jews seeking to help the internees were also members of the American Council for Judaism, and therefore particularly sensitive to the charge of dual loyalties leveled against a minority group.[138] Yet, as they did in the battle to aid blacks, Jews from many other corners of the community also raised their voices against injustice. Lou Goldblatt, the militant Marxist labor leader, testified before the Tolan Committee investigating the origins of the internment for Congress in 1942, "The wolf pack was in full cry . . . the old flames of racial suspicion were fanned to full blaze. Publicity seekers spouted ill-considered and vigilante-inciting epithets against the Japanese born in this country. The Hearst press found new field for its rantings about the 'yellow menace.' Politicians saw a good occasion to garner publicity."[139] Inspired by the Hebrew prophets, Goldblatt came forward, he later said, because "somehow the Jews don't have the right to be cruel sons of bitches the way other people have."[140]

But the most effective protestor was maritime union organizer Morris Weisberger, who in 1942 intervened on behalf of forty Nikkei sailors who were members of his union and faced detention. They were necessary for the war effort, he argued, and, after many attempts Weisberger convinced the government to let them remain on their ships.[141] It was the same union in which Sigismund Danielewicz made his lonely stand against the Chinese Exclusion Act in 1885, the Sailors' Union of the Pacific.

Other Jews were active in the various legal challenges filed on behalf of the internees. In 1942 Helen Arnstein Salz, defying the national American Civil Liberties Union, insisted that the local chapter, which she had cofounded, fight the mass evacuation in the courts.[142] The Northern California branch represented Oaklander Fred Korematsu in the U.S. Supreme Court, but the case was lost in August 1944. After the war another ACLU suit, however, was successful: appeals court judge Louis Goodman (an Emanu-El congregant) ruled in favor of five thousand Japanese who had renounced their American citizenship in the camps and now petitioned for the right to reverse their decision. Goodman held that many of them had not understood the complicated questionnaire and could hardly have been expected to pledge unconditional loyalty to America in the midst of their ordeal.[143]

By mid-1944 the *Emanu-El* finally sided with the evacuees. An editorial published in July praised University of California president Robert Gordon Sproul, honorary chairman of the Fair Play Committee, for advocating an end to the incarceration and a return of civil rights to the Nikkei.[144] Two months later, near the end of an eventful career in Jewish journalism, Silverman raised the internment issue again in one his boldest editorials: "The reason assigned for moving the Japanese Americans en masse was the military exigency. Tomorrow the excuse for taking parallel action against another racial minority will be the preservation of law and order."[145] He concluded with a quotation from state supreme court justice Frank Murphy: "Japanese removal here was painfully remindful" of the early treatment of Jews in Nazi Germany.[146]

The *Emanu-El* closely monitored the return of the Nikkei, "the most serious racial factor on the West Coast."[147] Silverman lauded the town of Cupertino, where James Yamamoto was warmly welcomed home by his former high school classmates and neighbors.[148] And the Jewish paper expressed shock at the firebombing in San Jose of the home of nine Japanese Americans.[149]

COSMOPOLITANS

Even as they were caught up in the foreign and domestic upheavals of the 1940s, Jews continued to enrich the Bay Area's varied cultural life. Gifted artists who had come of age the decade before—including painter Bernard Zakheim, sculptor Jacques Schnier, and photographer Alma Wahrhaftig— continued to be productive. Yehudi Menuhin and Isaac Stern were often on tour in these years, but both returned to the Bay Area for major performances. Pierre Monteux conducted the San Francisco Symphony Orchestra and Naoum Blinder was concertmaster.

A deep impact was also made by three Jewish newcomers from vastly different backgrounds: French refugee Darius Milhaud, one of the century's most prolific and eclectic composers; New Yorker Muriel Rukeyser, a major poet with striking insights into her times; and Sacramento native Herb Caen, whose newspaper column helped shape San Francisco's sense of itself.

Caen's first man-about-town column debuted in the *Chronicle* in mid-1938, when he was only twenty-two, and its immense popularity in the 1940s was credited with raising the circulation of the newspaper above that of its rivals.[150] He set a national record for journalistic longevity—nearly six decades—and a year before his death in 1997 won a Pulitzer Prize.

His column contained juicy gossip and cultural criticism, vignettes of city life and nuggets of local history, a collection of aphorisms and a string of jokes. In terms of his influence—his witticisms could make or break a restaurant, a play, or even a politician—Caen has often been compared to New York's Walter Winchell, also a Jew. But the latter had a hard-boiled edge missing in the Californian. Caen styled himself as the ultimate urban connoisseur but exhibited an informal, easygoing nature suited to the cool, fog-bound city at midcentury.

He evoked the charm and zest of Old San Francisco while at the same time bemoaning its erosion through soulless modernization. Even before the war he wrote of "the grotesque sight of this jumbled city from Twin Peaks, a sardonic, hysterical travesty on the dreams of those who stood there after the Great Fire and planned the Perfect City. . . . Long forgotten cable car slots wandering disconsolately and alone up steep hills that are now flattened, with a contemptuous snort, by high-powered, twin-engined buses."[151]

But his "Baghdad-by-the-Bay," a nickname he coined in 1940, was still the best place in the world.[152] With the possible exception of Paris, everyplace else was hopelessly provincial in comparison. Herb Caen, of course, did not create this smugness about the city; San Franciscans were often accused of this attitude in the 1940s, especially after the two stupendous bridges went up and a world's fair was held on Treasure Island. But he certainly reinforced it. He depicted the seamy side of town as well as the breathtaking vistas from the mansions on Pacific Heights. It all added up to "an indescribable conglomeration of beauty and ugliness . . . a poem without meter, a symphony without harmony, a painting without reason, a city without equal."[153]

Caen, the product of an interfaith marriage, "felt Jewish" according to several who knew him well, but he had little connection to Jewish organizations and rarely mentioned his roots.[154] He reveled in the city's ethnic and religious diversity but personally refrained from identifying himself with any group. As his public persona took shape in the troubled 1940s, he certainly did not want to be labeled the town's "Jewish columnist." A secular humanist, he seemed to worship nothing except San Francisco.

Caen, however, admitted to being a Francophile and welcomed the arrival in the Bay Area of one of France's leading composers, Darius Milhaud, in 1940. Nearing fifty, Milhaud had written more than two hundred musical works—operas, symphonies, ballads, and film scores—when the Nazi invasion forced him to flee with his family to the United States. Having been a member in the 1920s of the group of young, experimental French composers known as "les Six," Milhaud occupied the highest rung of Gallic culture.

He accepted a job teaching musical composition at Mills College, which, grateful to have such a luminary on its faculty, built a house on campus for Milhaud and his wife, Madeleine. They loved the natural setting of the East Bay—in Darius's words, "a garden of enchantment"—but had their "ears glued to the radio" as they thought of their friends and family enduring the German occupation.[155] Yet living in exile affected Milhaud's productivity not at all; he composed dozens of works in the 1940s, including string quartets, ballets, concertos, and an opera.

Each Passover the Milhauds attended the Seder at the home of Emanu-El's cantor Reuben Rinder, where Darius would charm those present by singing traditional melodies in his native Provençal. During the Passover meal of 1948, the cantor mentioned that Milhaud would be an excellent choice to write a Sabbath service for the temple. Another guest, the ambitious philanthropist Clara Heller, hastily offered to fund the project.[156] Without hesitation the Frenchman accepted. In stark contrast to Ernest Bloch, who had struggled for years to complete his masterwork, Milhuad would compose his *Sacred Service* in a mere two months.[157]

Aware of the composer's breezy, popular style, the cantor consulted closely with the prodigy of Provence (as he had with Bloch a decade and a half earlier), persuading him to work out in intricate depth at least one portion of the service, the prayer for returning the Torah scroll to the Ark. Highly developed contrapuntally, the segment was written for a large number of voices.[158] The premiere, conducted by the composer himself despite his painful arthritis, was held at Emanu-El in the spring of 1949. The performance, taking place near the end of a turbulent decade, was especially welcome as a link to earlier presentations of serene artistic grandeur in that venue. Critics praised *Sacred*

Service for its "magnificently fluent melody," "classic clarity," and "subtle beauty."* [159]

Soon after the war the Milhauds journeyed home to their beloved Aix-en-Provence, where they discovered what had been destroyed and what remained. But by then they had also established an unbreakable bond with California. The couple would spend part of every year in France, but Darius would continue to teach at Mills College almost until his death in 1974.

While Caen and Milhaud moved in San Francisco's most rarefied social circles, Muriel Rukeyser frequented bohemian and working-class settings. She lived most of her life in Manhattan but spent six years, beginning in early 1944, in the Bay Area. She was overwhelmed by the dramatic physical setting and awed by the Golden Gate Bridge—its construction had triggered her first visit the decade before. Although she formerly considered herself a "skyscraper poet," her work would come to reflect the natural beauty of Northern California, including its animals and insects. [160] But most of all she was attracted by the stimulating social and intellectual environment, and in turn she augmented the lively literary scene with her own daring and visionary voice.

Thirty years old when she arrived in San Francisco, Rukeyser had already experienced the Spanish Civil War (where she lost a lover in the fighting), reported on a bloody strike of West Virginia coal miners, and been arrested in Scottsboro, Alabama, where she was covering the ordeal of nine blacks wrongly convicted of raping a white woman. Her poetry had garnered major awards, and she had also written a biography of an early American physicist. Born to upper-middle-class parents who lived on Riverside Drive, she had gone to Vassar and Columbia, and in Northern California she would attend flight school. [161]

In San Francisco she soon befriended Kenneth Rexroth, who adored her fresh, powerful verse, which, according to one of her contemporary admirers, Adrienne Rich, "ran formidably counter to existing traditions of feminine lyricism." [162] One feels even in Rukeyser's early work the intensity of the famous lines she would write decades later: "What would happen if one

---

*Milhaud, whose Sephardi origins reached back to the Middle Ages, later composed another work on a Jewish theme, the opera *David*, which he considered one of the highlights of his career. It was first performed in Jerusalem in 1954 and at the Hollywood Bowl in 1956, the latter a dazzling production before an audience of twenty thousand people (Seymour Fromer, interview with the author, December 14, 2002).

woman told the truth about her life? The world would split open."[163] Some of her poetry reflected the turmoil in her personal life in the Bay Area: she married but got an annulment two months later; she had a son out of wedlock with another man and raised the child by herself.[164]

In the early 1940s she taught at the California Labor School, a kind of front for the Communist Party, but she was a fiercely independent thinker and probably never actually joined the party.[165] During the war she drew the ire of the left-wing *Partisan Review* for an "overly-patriotic" poem.[166] Still, her closest friends were Marxists, and, like Rexroth, they were among the most creative minds in town. She socialized with the Oppenheimer brothers, like herself raised on Morningside Heights and alumni of the Ethical Culture School, and she spent time with Oppie's ill-starred mistress, Jean Tatlock, her former classmate at Vassar. In Berkeley she also met the great Mexican poet Octavio Paz, and she undertook a multidecade project of translating his works. One of her best friends in those years was Ella Winter, the Jewish widow of Lincoln Steffens, and Rukeyser also knew the militant labor leaders Harry Bridges and David Jenkins.[167] Activists and artists, including many a jazz musician, appeared on a popular radio show she hosted, *Sundays at Eight*, on KDFC, then a commercial left-wing station.[168]

Rukeyser also explored her evolving Jewish identity against the backdrop of the genocide in Europe. In a national Jewish journal she described her rebellion against the "torpor and conservatism" of the Classical Reform Judaism of her childhood to which her mother subjected her every Saturday morning for seven years.[169] But Muriel's mind was stimulated by reading the Bible—"its clash and poetry and nakedness, its fiery vision of conflict resolved only in God"—and biblical themes would inform her poetry until her death in 1980.[170] Her Jewish heritage became entwined with everything else she cared about, and at age thirty-one she wrote, "To live as a poet, woman, American, and Jew—this chalks my position. If the four come together in one person, each strengthens the others."[171]

She may not have closely followed the heated debate among local Jewish leaders over the proper response to the Holocaust or the merits of Zionism; Jewish organizations held little attraction for her. But Rukeyser was all too aware of the timidity of many prominent Jews "who refused to be involved in suffering that demanded resistance, and refused to acknowledge evil." With revulsion she spoke of the recent "leaning over backward to be 'American' at its most acceptable." She recalled the Jews with whom she had grown up in the previous decade, "who wished, more than anything else, I think, to be invisible. They were playing possum . . . they were the people who felt that Hitler would be all right if he would leave the Jews alone."[172]

But she also celebrated Jewish heroism, including the Zionist struggle, albeit by evoking left-wing causes to do so: "One thinks of the men and women in the Warsaw ghetto, standing as the Loyalists stood in Spain, weaponless against what must have seemed like the thunder and steel of the whole world; one thinks of the men and women, Jews moving freely in Russia; one thinks of the men and women, planting Palestine and taking a fierce oath never to put down their arms."[173]

For Rukeyser, though, only a poem could suffice in extreme times. The opening lines of her sonnet of 1944, published in her slender volume *Beast in View,* captured the dilemma and anguish of Jews in the Bay Area and around the world:

> To be a Jew in the twentieth century
> Is to be offered a gift. If you refuse,
> Wishing to be invisible, you choose
> Death of the spirit, the stone insanity.

The octet grants that "The gift is torment," yet concludes by offering hope:

> The whole and fertile spirit as guarantee
> For every human freedom, suffering to be free,
> Daring to live for the impossible.[174]

An ocean and a continent away from the Holocaust, a young female poet looked into the abyss when few other American artists were willing to do so. Through her art she also affirmed the Jewish yearning to seek deliverance for all humanity. Near the end of her life the Reform and Reconstructionist movements included "To Be a Jew" in their prayer books. Rukeyser was "astonished,"[175] but she herself had asserted in 1944 that "poetry and politics" are "two phases of religion."[176] That statement was true for Bay Area Jews more than she knew.

Epilogue
Legacies of the First Century

IN AN ARTICLE IN 1950, Earl Raab referred to "a mysterious ingredient . . . an 'x' factor," to explain the Bay Area Jewish community's often unconventional behavior. He related an adage then making the rounds: "If half a dozen Jews of similar background, Jewish intensity, and ideology were settled three in Los Angeles and three in San Francisco, they would be found to be very different groups in outlook and activity after five years."[1] Fresh in Raab's mind was the near-assimilationist, ultra-Reform mentality of the overwhelmingly German Jewish leadership, which had rejected Zionism and responded timidly to the Holocaust. But he wrote as well about the high Jewish profile in business, civic, and political life and the comparatively mild degree of anti-Semitism.[2] He was struck, too, by the remarkable emphasis local Jews placed on social justice and the arts. Pulling it all together, he entitled his essay " 'There's No City Like San Francisco.' "[3]

The notion of Bay Area Jewry as an exception among American Jewish communities would seem to have been warranted at the end of its first century. But how have the community's distinguishing traits—most of which may be subsumed under the rubric of cosmopolitanism—fared over the subsequent six decades of profound socioeconomic and cultural change?

Since the 1940s thousands of Jews have arrived in the Bay Area every year, the great majority of them of East European origin, the group that since 1880 had been markedly underrepresented in San Francisco and Oakland compared to other American cities. In the first postwar wave came veterans of the armed services, many of whom had become enthralled with the physical beauty of the area during their tours of duty. They were joined by young families from the Northeast or Midwest seeking a better life in Northern California, as well as Holocaust survivors, hundreds of whom sailed directly from the wartime refuge of Shanghai. The 1960s and '70s saw an inflow of young, mostly single Jews to San Francisco and to Berkeley in particular. In more recent decades the pace of growth has accelerated, with newcomers tending to be businesspeople or professionals, well along in their careers, who have settled in the suburbs as well as the cities.

The massive influx has caused the local Jewish population, which has grown at an even faster pace than the Bay Area as a whole, to increase about sevenfold since midcentury.[4] A demographic survey in 2004 estimated the Jewish community at roughly 425,000, making it the fourth largest in the country and the seventh largest in the world.[5] (Early in the 1950s, after a seventy-year period in which its growth rate had lagged behind that of the rest of American Jewry, the Bay Area Jewish population ranked only eleventh nationally and twenty-second in the world.[6])

In the hugely expanded postwar community the German Jews lost the majority status they had enjoyed as late as the 1930s. More importantly, East European Jews and their descendants, and newcomers from other parts of the world as well, have finally become more conspicuous than the old guard in the local Jewish federations and their endowment funds and in cultural and educational organizations. The hotel owner Ben Swig, for example, born in Boston to immigrants from czarist Russia, reached the highest echelons of Jewish lay leadership by the late 1940s and began to guide the community in a new direction. He raised funds for Zionist causes on an unprecedented scale, and in the mid-1960s he established a popular Jewish camp in the Santa Cruz Mountains that helped invigorate Reform Judaism throughout Northern California. In recent decades other potent family foundations have been established by philanthropists such as Joseph Koret, Bernard Osher, Tad Taube, Jim Joseph, and Jacques Reutlinger, all born and raised outside the Bay Area (and in most cases outside the United States).*

In their ambition and creativity, particularly in the Jewish sphere, these and other munificent newcomers to the establishment have rivaled the pioneer dynasties, epitomized by the Haas and Goldman families, which set up mighty foundations as well. As a result, Jewish education, culture, and social services have been supported on an unprecedented scale. The power sharing took more than a generation longer than it did in the rest of the country, but certainly by the 1980s a sturdy social barrier was leveled, one that for more than a century had excluded nearly all but the German Jewish aristocracy from the seats of communal authority.

Suburbanization, too, has transformed Jewish life and vaulted many first-generation Bay Area Jews into leadership positions in new synagogues and community centers. The urban areas did not empty out of Jews, however, as sometimes occurred in the Midwest. Despite an exodus of families with school-age children in the 1960s and '70s, San Francisco's Jewish population has increased by almost a quarter since the war and is home to the region's largest synagogue, Emanu-El, with about 2,600 households. And although Oakland lost its JCC and Home for Jewish Parents, it has retained the same three congregations (one Reform, one Conservative, and one Orthodox) for more than a hundred years.

Still, none of the old, colorful, urban Jewish neighborhoods on either side of the bay survived past the mid-1960s, and the lion's share of the astonishing growth in the Jewish population has occurred in the suburbs. In 1948 more than 80 percent of Bay Area Jews lived in San Francisco or Oakland, but by the beginning of the twenty-first century the ratio was nearly reversed, the Jewish population in the outlying areas having soared exponentially.[7] The South Peninsula (extending from Redwood City south to Sunnyvale, and including Stanford University and much of Silicon Valley) was reportedly home to only 5,500 Jews as late as 1959. In 2004 its Jewish population was estimated at 72,500, outstripping that of San Francisco.[8]

---

*Another group in the circle of major benefactors in the past generation consists of families such as the Dillers, Shensons, and Rabins, of East European origin but deeply rooted in San Francisco. Before the war, though, their influence was largely confined to charities serving the immigrant Jewish neighborhoods of South of Market, the Fillmore District, and West Oakland.

Especially in the past quarter of a century, many of the Jewish communities ringing San Francisco and Oakland have not only grown large but have also become very vibrant and, in many respects, independent of Jewish institutions in the big cities. The roughly sixty suburban synagogues enjoy a higher rate of affiliation than do their urban counterparts. And the commodious, well-equipped, and in almost all cases recently built or newly remodeled Jewish Community Centers—there are six in the suburbs—are hubs of social and recreational activities and Jewish and general learning.*

The satellite communities reflect a Jewish population that is ever more widely dispersed, now encompassing a nine-county area of about seven thousand square miles, nearly as large as New Jersey. Indeed, the fastest-growing areas are those furthest from San Francisco: Sonoma County, the South Peninsula, and the Tri-Valley area, twenty miles southeast of Oakland. A geographically broad cross-section of Jews can still be assembled in one place, as at the lively Israel Independence Day celebration every spring, usually held in downtown San Francisco or Golden Gate Park. But given worsening traffic and increasing distances, it is much more challenging than ever before to draw people to a central location.

In the suburbanized, decentralized Bay Area, in which four out of every five Jewish adults (including most of the leading philanthropists) hail from somewhere else,[9] part of the distinctiveness of prewar San Francisco and Oakland Jewry and its institutions has necessarily given way to more generic forms. Moreover, although the region had been anything but isolated since the Gold Rush, the revolution in communication and transportation of the past generation has linked Northern California with the rest of America and the world in ways previously unimaginable. This has affected everyone from new immigrants to fifth-generation San Franciscans. Visits to Auschwitz or the Western Wall; conferences in New York or Washington, D.C.; news bulletins and opinion pieces on television or online have blunted the differences among regional Jewish identities throughout the country. In the Bay Area, a largely newly arrived population with ever-closer ties to the rest of American and world Jewry has led to the embrace of some of the basic elements of Jewish life that had been given short shrift in its first century.

---

*The massive eight-acre Taube Koret Campus for Jewish Life now under construction in Palo Alto, a kind of "Jewish town square," will include not only a grand new JCC and regional offices of the federation and other organizations, but also a large residence for Jewish seniors under the auspices of the Jewish Home San Francisco.

One of the most marked changes among Bay Area Jews has been a renewed sense of assertiveness. Although papal anti-Judaism and czarist anti-Semitism had been forcefully opposed in San Francisco in the pioneer period and beyond, Bay Area Jewry was increasingly timorous after World War I and nearly paralyzed in the face of the destruction of European Jewry during World War II. Yet by the 1970s and '80s the community had again distinguished itself nationally in fighting for oppressed Jews. Missions from San Francisco to Ethiopia highlighted the plight of the Falashas, local Jewish leaders urged U.S. congressmen to intervene on behalf of Syrian Jews, and the Bay Area Council for Soviet Jewry (BACSJ) held vigils and rallies outside the USSR's consulate on Green Street. One demonstration in 1987 featured Natan Sharansky soon after his release from the gulag; he told the crowd that even in a remote prison camp he had learned of the efforts to free him emanating from the Bay Area.

While nonestablishment groups like BACSJ have generally taken the lead in such causes—and today a local grassroots organization aggressively advocates for the rights of Jewish refugees from Arab lands—a supportive and coordinating role has been played by the San Francisco Federation's Jewish Community Relations Council (JCRC). Under the direction of Earl Raab beginning in 1951, the community activist Rita Semel in the late 1980s, and Rabbi Douglas Kahn in recent decades, the inclusive JCRC has borne no resemblance to its narrowly constituted and aloof predecessor, the Survey Committee.

The attitude toward Zionism has also undergone a sea change. Support for Jewish nationalism was notably weak in the Bay Area for well over a century and gained a consensus among local Jews only after the Six-Day War. But the community that produced the country's most powerful branch of the anti-Zionist American Council for Judaism has in recent decades emerged as a bulwark of pro-Israel activism. Although traditional Zionist organizations have not always fared well—Israel Bonds, the Jewish National Fund, the Zionist Organization of America, and the American Friends of the Hebrew University of Jerusalem have had to close their local offices for years at a time—by the 1980s and '90s the Bay Area showed a great deal of enthusiasm and innovation in supporting the Jewish state. Under its young, dynamic director, Cleveland-born rabbi Brian Lurie, who took the reins in 1975, the San Francisco Jewish Welfare Federation, as it was then called, was among the first in the country to open an office in Israel to monitor its several initiatives there. Later, in a bold experiment, the federation channeled considerable resources toward improving the living conditions of Arab communities in the Galilee and other regions. The Bay Area was also the birthplace of the progressive New Israel Fund, which aims to strengthen civil society in the Jewish state. Most striking, though, has been the rapid growth of the Northern California region of the American Israel Public Affairs Committee (AIPAC), founded by the tireless community organizer Naomi Lauter, who molded it into one of the strongest chapters in the nation for the Israel lobby. San Francisco native Amy Friedkin, active for decades in Jewish life in the East Bay, became the first woman national president of AIPAC in 2002.

To be sure, there have been sharp rebukes of Israel's policies voiced by leading Bay Area Jews in every decade since the 1970s, when Rabbi Joseph Asher of Congregation Emanu-El (1968–85) joined the national board of Breira, an organization highly critical of the Jewish state's treatment of the Palestinians.[10] Similarly, Rabbi Martin Weiner of Sherith Israel (1972–2002) held several well-publicized meetings with Palestinians in San Francisco and in 1982 delivered a Yom Kippur sermon taking Israel to task for its complicity in the Sabra and Shatilla massacres. Later in the decade, ninety prominent local Jews—many of them rabbis and university professors—signed a petition presented to Israel's consul general decrying his country's "iron fist" response to young Arab stone throwers in the Occupied Territories.[11] More recently, longtime Berkeley resident Marcia Freedman, a former Knesset member and one of Israel's earliest feminists, founded Brit Tzedek v'Shalom (Jewish Alliance for Justice and Peace), a national organization imploring both Israel and America to do more to bring about a Palestinian state. And the East Bay–based periodical *Tikkun,* since its birth in 1986, has taken every opportunity to condemn the occupation, repeatedly declaring it "immoral and self-destructive."[12] But such dissent, infuriating as it has been for many local Zionists, is seen by others as a sign of healthy engagement with Israel, a dialogue about the merits of the Jewish state's policies rather than a debate about whether the state should exist at all, as occurred among local Jews during World War II. Indeed, studies reveal that the "emotional attachment" to Israel of Bay Area Jews, whatever their political perspective on the Mideast crisis, is far higher than that of American Jews as a whole.[13]

Another realm in which the community has reversed course in the past generation has been Jewish learning. Fundamentally inadequate during the community's first century (Rabbi David Stolper's fine Central Hebrew School notwithstanding), Jewish education has made dramatic gains.

Whereas a survey undertaken in San Francisco in 1938 revealed that only 39 percent of Jewish children aged five to fourteen were receiving any formal Jewish training, that percentage for the entire Bay Area had doubled fifty years later, comparing favorably with other American communities.[14] The majority of these children were enrolled in synagogue-run supplementary schools, far more professionally conducted than they were in past generations. Among many examples is the religious school of Congregation Emanu-El. As late as the 1950s the school provided less than two hours of instruction on half the Sundays in the year and was plagued by absenteeism, discipline problems, and an uninspired curriculum.[15] Since the late 1980s, however, under the direction of rabbi-educator Peretz Wolf-Prusan, a much more comprehensive educational program has encompassed Hebrew, liturgy, social action, and the arts and has mandated parental involvement for bar and bat mitzvah training.[16] On both sides of the bay, meanwhile, well-staffed and well-funded bureaus of Jewish education have provided the schools with curricular resources, in-service teacher training, and other assistance. In the East Bay such an agency did not even exist until 1957.

The Bay Area's thirteen Jewish day schools—there was none until the early 1960s—now enroll 10 percent of all Jewish schoolchildren.[17] While that ratio is still less than half of the national average,[18] it reflects a major shift in thinking since midcentury, when the top lay leaders of San Francisco's federation opposed the creation of day schools on the grounds they would "ghettoize" the Jewish community.[19] In the past decade the day schools have collectively been allocated well over a million dollars annually by the federation. But the schools have benefited even more from private foundations, which in the early years of the twenty-first century invested tens of millions of dollars to create two new state-of-the-art Jewish high schools. One, which also houses the extensive Jewish Community Library, administered by the Bureau of Jewish Education, occupies an entire square block in San Francisco's Fillmore District, and the other enjoys a well-equipped facility in Palo Alto.

Adult education has also taken long strides. Since 1974 Lehrhaus Judaica, modeled after the school of Franz Rosenzweig and Martin Buber in Weimar Germany, has offered courses, workshops, and conferences at dozens of sites throughout the Bay Area, enrolling thousands annually. The region has also been a fertile field for intensive national adult education initiatives such as the Wexner Heritage Program; CLAL–The National Jewish Center for Learning and Leadership; and the Florence Melton Adult Mini-School.

But perhaps the most startling change is in higher education. Although Northern California lacks a rabbinical seminary, full-scale Judaica programs have mushroomed at seven local universities—including the Jesuit-run University of San Francisco, a national pioneer in Jewish studies among Catholic schools—and the region now rivals New York and Boston as a center of Jewish scholarship. At San Francisco State University, for example, as recently as the early 1990s only a few scattered courses in Judaica were offered. Today the Jewish Studies Program, which serves hundreds of students, boasts three full-time faculty members, including one holding an endowed chair, and three adjunct lecturers.

Stanford University and the University of California, Berkeley, meanwhile, have emerged as world-class institutions in the field, and the towns of Palo Alto and Berkeley have become hothouses of Jewish intellectual creativity. In one eighteen-month period, the fall of 2002 through the spring of 2004, three scholars living in the Berkeley hills published works that will reverberate for decades and perhaps generations. Professor David Biale of UC Davis edited *Cultures of the Jews: A New History,* a compendium of twenty-three essays by internationally renowned scholars exploring Jewish identity from its ancient origins to the modern world.[20] Daniel Matt, formerly a professor at Berkeley's interfaith and intercultural Graduate Theological Union, produced the first two volumes of a projected eleven-volume translation and line-by-line annotation of the Zohar, a collection of texts that is central to Jewish mysticism.[21] And UC Berkeley's Professor Robert Alter unveiled a monumental translation of the Torah, with copious commentary, that ranks among the greatest ever written in the English language.[22] Beyond that, local scholars have produced probing histories of the Jews of czarist Russia and the Ottoman Empire, penetrating translations of Hebrew poetry and Yiddish fiction, intriguing studies of early Christianity and Talmudic culture, and a welter of other important works.

As might be expected, some of the Jewish scholarship generated in the Bay Area in the past two decades has been highly controversial, sometimes critical of traditional Judaism and Zionism or adopting postmodernist and feminist theories. In 1998, writing in *Commentary,* the essayist and translator Hillel Halkin expressed his irritation with what he was "tempted to call . . . the California School," although he pointed out that it has many proponents elsewhere.[23] He directed some praise and a good deal of criticism at five local professors, reserving his sharpest rebuke for Howard Eilberg-Schwartz, formerly of Stanford and San Francisco State University, who had recently completed a provocative anthropological study entitled

God's Phallus.[24] But Halkin concluded that the new breed of skeptical scholars would have a profound and long-lasting impact on American Jewry.[25]

THE COSMOPOLITAN CONSTANT

With its concern for Israel and oppressed Jewry, its renaissance in Jewish education and scholarship, and its explosive growth in population and philanthropy, the Bay Area has taken a new turn in the past generation. Yet even as the community has moved from the periphery to the center of American Jewish life, and many peculiarities of the past have disappeared, strong echoes of the nineteenth and early twentieth century can still be heard.

For the Jewish community, like the Bay Area of which it is an integral part, remains deeply influenced by the diverse cosmopolitan culture that was born in the pioneer period, enhanced by the vast wealth of the region, and perpetuated by self-selection. The flood of newcomers, even as they have arrived with beliefs and opinions shaped by their former habitats, have often chosen to journey to the Golden Gate in order to experience a way of life they thought was available virtually nowhere else.

For Jews, like many others, strict religious observance was usually not at the heart of the Northern California dream. The laxity of Jewish practice was noted with alarm by visitors throughout the entire century following the Gold Rush,[26] and has been reflected more recently in contemporary demographic studies. Now, as then, Bay Area Jews light Hanukkah candles, attend Passover Seders, and fast on Yom Kippur far less frequently than their coreligionists across America, and even less than in the West as a whole, which itself trails the rest of the nation by a wide margin.[27]

Throughout the country the Orthodox comprise roughly one-tenth of the Jewish population,[28] but they account for only about 3 percent locally,* a

---

*The number of Orthodox may be lower still among younger Jews in the Bay Area; when denominational preference was disaggregated by age in the 1986 demographic study conducted by Gary Tobin, it was reported as hovering around 1 percent among those under forty-five (Gary A. Tobin and Sharon Sassler, *Bay Area Jewish Community Study, Special Report: Jewish Identity and Community Involvement* [Waltham, Mass., 1988], 28). In a study by the same researcher in 2000, the Orthodox were too few to constitute a category, while the Reconstructionist and Renewal movements, at 3 percent and 2 percent respectively, made the cut (Gary A. Tobin, *A Study of Jewish Culture in the Bay* proportion unchanged for many decades, even while other major American cities have experienced a sharp increase in traditional movements such as Young Israel. As elsewhere, the Orthodox are disproportionately represented among the community's lay leaders, but in the Bay Area they have had only a modest impact in shaping the federations, Jewish Community Centers, and cultural institutions. To be sure, since 1969 the Orthodox rabbi Pinchas Lipner has been at the helm of a K–12 San Francisco Jewish day school and widely praised for educating many of the children of immigrants from the former Soviet Union and for offering high-quality conferences on medical ethics. The Bay Area also houses over a dozen Chabad centers (run by the worldwide Lubavitch Hasidic movement), whose Hanukkah candle-lighting ceremonies in Union Square and other public sites have become a tradition, drawing thousands of people each year.[29] Chabad has also made inroads into several campus communities. But the paucity of kosher butchers and restaurants in the region—about one of each for every hundred thousand Jews—suggests that, for all of their zeal, neither Lipner nor the Hasidic missionaries have substantially increased the observance of Jewish law. Lipner's influence on the larger community may also have been limited by his open feuds with San Francisco's federation and one of its past presidents.[30]

Fully a third of Jewish households currently identify themselves as secular or nondenominational and an additional 38 percent as "Reform or Liberal."*[31] In the Bay Area, as in the rest of the nation, the Reform movement has adopted some formerly scorned traditional practices in recent decades, but by also endorsing patrilineal descent and same-sex marriages it has hardly moved closer to Orthodoxy. At Emanu-El, the decorous Americanized devotions born in the nineteenth century had become only one of several worship options by the 1990s, and even many of the descendants of the pioneer families now prefer services with more Hebrew and communal singing. Yet, significantly, Emanu-El's Classical Reform service, one of the few still left in the country, lives on under the direction of operatic cantor Roslyn Barak, who is accompanied by a professional choir and a giant pipe organ.

Area [San Francisco, 2002], 22). Bruce Phillips's survey of 2004, based on a larger sample, estimates the "Orthodox-Traditional" at 3 percent (2004 Jewish Community Study/Full Findings [San Francisco, 2005], 53).

*Using the term "Reform" rather than "Reform or Liberal," Gary Tobin's 2002 study yielded 45 percent for that category (Tobin, A Study of Jewish Culture in the Bay Area, 26).

The Conservative movement, the preference of about 17 percent of the Jewish community[32] (far below the national norm),[33] is relatively progressive in the Bay Area, where several rabbis have received national attention for their outreach to interfaith families and for controversial rituals such as same-sex marriage ceremonies.[34] As another marker of the region's liberalizing influence on Conservative Judaism, the Jewish Theological Seminary recently chose as its chancellor Stanford religious studies professor Arnold Eisen, who has been instrumental in bringing about the matriculation of openly gay rabbinical and cantorial students.

The progressive posture of most of the synagogues has generally not filled the pews, however. Synagogue affiliation in the Bay Area stands at a mere 22 percent of all Jewish households[35]—less than half the national average[36]—calling to mind the lament voiced by pulpit rabbis and lay leaders a century ago, when membership was even lower. Participation in most other Jewish institutions is relatively low as well, reflecting both the individualism of local Jews and their distrust of community organizations, traits that demographers and sociologists have found ingrained throughout the American West and in Northern California in particular.[37]

Consistent with the region's long history of religious experimentation, Bay Area Jewry includes many "seekers," who borrow liberally from Eastern religions and other beliefs and are likely to experiment with mysticism, meditation, and movement. Although interest in these subjects is increasing nationwide, it has been especially strong in the Bay Area, where almost three-quarters of the Jews feel "it is good to explore many differing religious teachings" and only 7 percent believe "one should stick to a particular faith."[38] In Marin County, abounding with people on personal, emotional quests for divine contact, more than half the Jews surveyed in 2002 affirmed the statement: "I am spiritual but not religious."[39]

Centers for nontraditional Jewish spirituality have thrived in the Bay Area since Rabbi Shlomo Carlebach's House of Love and Prayer attracted Jewish hippies to the Haight-Ashbury district in the late 1960s. In the following decade, Rabbi Zalman Schachter-Shalomi's New Age or Renewal Judaism began to draw many young Bay Area Jews disaffected with the religious services they had experienced as children. The charismatic former Lubavitcher Hasid, who had experimented with psychedelic drugs, conducted a month-long Kabbalah workshop in Berkeley, which led to the establishment of the Aquarian Minyan in 1974, at first an informal prayer group and later a congregation in his Renewal Movement.[40]

In the 1970s the Aquarian Minyan introduced elements of Eastern religions into its services, while in recent decades Bay Area figures such as Sylvia Boorstein and the late Rabbis Alan Lew and David Wolfe-Blank have sought to refresh Jewish prayer by infusing it with Zen Buddhism in particular. The mysteries of Asia have continued to hold a special allure for Bay Area Jews.

The JuBus, as Jewish Buddhists are sometimes known, gained publicity in 1990, when the San Francisco ophthalmologist Marc Lieberman arranged a trip to India on which he and seven other prominent Jews, including Schachter-Shalomi, met with the Dalai Lama.[*][41] Dr. Lieberman, a knowledgeable Jew who is fluent in Hebrew, has referred to Judaism as his roots and Buddhism as his wings.[42] But others, although remaining proud of their Jewish ancestry, have turned almost exclusively to Buddhism for their spiritual nourishment, in the process making major contributions to that community. As early as 1969 Sam Bercholz, a son of Holocaust survivors, established Shambhala Booksellers in Berkeley, which soon became the largest publisher in North America of texts devoted to dharma. By the late 1990s, individuals of Jewish birth served as abbess and co-abbot of the San Francisco Zen Center as well as co-abbot of the Berkeley Zen Center. Anecdotal accounts suggest that at some Zen centers on the West Coast as many as half of the members may be Jewish-born.[43]

Jews have also been disproportionately represented in the Hare Krishna movement, Scientology, Transcendental Meditation, and est.[44] Neo-paganism, encompassing witchcraft and earth worship, is currently led in San Francisco by a Jewish-born woman named Starhawk.

As leading scholars of contemporary American religion such as Wade Clark Roof and Robert Wuthnow have pointed out, much of the attraction of these spiritual communities for both Christians and Jews may be related to the baby boomers' experiences in the late 1960s and their distrust of traditional institutions.[45] Clearly this has been the case in the Bay Area, but there were also much earlier antecedents: the "spiritual trials" of the younger generation at the turn of the last century and the alternatives to organized religion that were then so popular such as Ethical Culture,

---

[*]Lieberman's contact among the Tibetans was another Bay Area Jew, Michael Sautman, who had been studying with the Dalai Lama for many years. The seminal encounter became the subject of a documentary film and a popular book, *The Jew in the Lotus,* by Rodger Kamenetz, who accompanied the travelers and interviewed them along the way.

theosophy (which also drew upon the wisdom of the Far East), spiritualism, Christian Science, and even the veneration of the Sierra Nevada mountains.

Unlike these earlier sects, Buddhism and its offshoots, while no doubt still considered alien by many local Jews, have penetrated some of the most mainstream synagogues. Rabbi Alan Lew, who studied for almost a decade in Zen monasteries and centers, held the pulpit of one of the Bay Area's oldest and largest Conservative congregations, San Francisco's Beth Sholom, for fifteen years beginning in 1991. The "Zen rabbi," as he often referred to himself, successfully introduced yoga and meditation before Sabbath services and directed Makor Or, a center for Jewish meditation, adjacent to the synagogue.[46] Daniel Kohn, for four years a rabbi at the Conservative Kol Shofar in Marin County and currently a Jewish day school educator, is a third-degree black belt in aikido; in his sermons, workshops, and his book *Kinesthetic Kabbalah* he speaks of a new syncretism of Jewish spirituality and the Japanese martial arts.[47] At Emanu-El, Associate Rabbi Helen Cohn made meditation a central part of her rabbinate from 1994 through 2006, coleading workshops with the abbess of the San Francisco Zen Center and holding weekend programs in the serene, austere setting of the Zen mountain retreat at Tassajara.

Of course meditation, and even more so mysticism, has Jewish roots independent of Buddhism, and many Northern California teachers have sought to recover that experiential, nonrational side of Judaism.* Berkeley's Chochmat HaLev (Wisdom of the Heart), founded in 1995 by Avram Davis, is an alternative learning and worship community of hundreds of Jews. Although it occasionally borrows from Eastern religions, it primarily mines the rich veins of Jewish mysticism. At Congregation Kol Shofar, meanwhile, Senior Rabbi Lavey Derby has conducted a semimonthly Neshama (soul) Minyan for almost fifteen years using experimental spiritual "tools and techniques to deepen connectedness to the divine."[48] And for its first permanent, full-time scholar-in-residence, Congregation Emanu-El chose Rabbi Lawrence Kushner, one of the leading interpreters of Jewish mysticism in the country.

---

*Rabbi Burt Jacobson, founder of Berkeley's Kehilla Community Synagogue, perhaps the largest Renewal congregation in the movement, has lamented the "innocent and over-romanticized view of Buddhism" by many of its Jewish adherents, "and a lack of knowledge about the spiritual depth of Judaism" (Judith Linzer, *Torah and Dharma: Jewish Seekers in Eastern Religions* [Northvale, N.J., 1996], 233).

The new spirituality is only one among many innovations in Bay Area Judaism. Other initiatives have included the creation of Sha'ar Zahav (Golden Gate), one of the nation's earliest and most active gay congregations; the country's first Jewish healing center; feminist Seders and liturgy; and several synagogues devoted primarily to social action. Such wide-ranging spiritual experimentation recalls the restless searching that took place a century ago, when local leaders—taking advantage of the freedom and flexibility of the West—sought fresh ways to rejuvenate Judaism and reach new constituencies. Civic leader Harris Weinstock advocated the use of Jesus' teachings in Jewish school curricula, Rabbis Martin Meyer and Louis Newman of Emanu-El presided over the erection of a magnificent Temple House for cultural and recreational programs, and Rabbis Jacob Nieto and Jacob Weinstein of Sherith Israel made human rights the cornerstone of their rabbinates.

Rabbis Meyer and Nieto strove to provide women a greater role in Jewish life commensurate with the remarkable progress they had made since the pioneer period in business, the professions, and the arts. By 1922 the spiritual leaders of the two oldest and largest congregations had predicted that women would one day lead the Jewish community, and recent decades have seen the attainment of that goal.[49] Although there were no females officially serving as rabbis anywhere in America until the beginning of the 1970s—even though an unordained Oakland woman, Rachel Frank, had led services up and down the West Coast as early as the 1890s—they currently account for almost 30 percent of the Bay Area's rabbinate and hold senior posts at several of the largest suburban congregations. One of them, Janet Marder of Congregation Beth Am in Los Altos Hills, in 2003 became the first woman president of the Reform movement's Central Conference of American Rabbis. Women are also counted among the most powerful Jewish communal executives, heading such large and dynamic agencies as the Jewish Community Center of San Francisco, Jewish Family and Children's Services, the Jewish Vocational Center, and both of the Bay Area's Jewish museums. And no individual has held greater sway in the contemporary community than Phyllis Cook, who presided over the Jewish Community Federation's Endowment Fund for a quarter century, almost since its inception in 1982; with more than two billion dollars in assets, it is possibly the largest Jewish endowment in the United States.

In other respects as well the Jewish community is more diverse than ever before, even more so than it was in Gold Rush era, when it consisted of disparate groups such as Bavarians and Poseners, Russians and Hungarians,

French and Sephardim. The contemporary subgroups include many new immigrants: the contingent from the former Soviet Union—at least 8 percent of the total Jewish population in the Bay Area and a far higher percentage in San Francisco and the South Peninsula—is one of the largest in the country,* and the number of Israelis, around 4 percent, is significant, too.[50] There is also a high proportion of gays relative to other American Jewish communities, as well as a comparatively large number of single, single-parent, and disabled Jews.[51] Because of interracial marriages—Rabbi Helen Cohn recalls at least one nonwhite in each of the fifteen conversion courses she taught at Emanu-El[52]—as well as interracial adoptions, the color of the Jewish community is beginning to change as well. Among Jewish children in particular one now finds a noticeable number of blacks and especially Asians, the latter group comprising about half the population of the city of San Francisco.

The intermarried are the fastest-growing subgroup of all, and more than 40 percent of the area's married Jews now have non-Jews as spouses.[53] Of course, intermarriage rates at this level—more than half of all Jewish households in the region and 75 percent in Sonoma and Marin†—are unprecedented.[54] But exogamy in Northern California had already become fairly widespread in the late nineteenth century, according to the leading San Francisco Jewish journalist of his day, who urged his readers to accept it. "The world is moving," Isidore Choynski wrote in 1888, "and intermarriages have ceased to be the wonder of the world."[55] A century later the Bay Area's intermarriage rate was one of the highest in the country,[56] and it has doubled in the past twenty years.[57]

For the most part community leaders have viewed the phenomenon not as a crisis but rather as an opportunity for outreach and connection. Pointing to the roughly hundred thousand non-Jews living in Jewish households, some speak of an "enlarged" Jewish community that is well over half a million strong.[58] Rosanne Levitt, the founder of the San Francisco Federation's Interfaith Connection in 1986, was for two decades a national pacesetter in this field, offering courses, workshops, and events. Today more than half a

* Several Bay Area communal workers believe that the Jews from the former Soviet Union were undercounted in the demographic study of 2004 and that they could number almost 100,000, constituting as much as 20 percent of the region's total Jewish population (Elina Kaplan, interview with the author, April 29, 2007).

† Because two individual Jews marrying each other create one household, the household intermarriage rate is higher than the individual rate.

dozen organizations throughout the Bay Area and almost all of the region's synagogues work collaboratively to make intermarried families more knowledgeable about Judaism. Probably because of these efforts more than a third of the local interfaith couples raise their children as Jewish, a higher percentage than the national average.[59]

There is also a relatively large number of converts to Judaism in the Bay Area, a region that has a comparatively large number of inhabitants switching from the religion of their birth. Converts account for at least 7 percent of the Jewish population and are active in almost all aspects of community life.[60] It was thus not surprising that the "Who is a Jew?" controversy in Israel, triggered by the religious political parties' attempt to exclude non-Orthodox converts from automatic citizenship under the Law of Return, produced especially deep concern and anger in the Bay Area. In 1988, at the height of the dispute, a group of communal leaders traveled to Jerusalem: Rabbi Robert Kirschner of Emanu-El; Rabbi Brian Lurie, executive director of San Francisco's federation; its president, Annette Dobbs; and Mayor Dianne Feinstein. After lobbying members of the Knesset they returned home to address a packed community forum, at which Feinstein, born of a non-Jewish mother, voiced "pain and outrage at the prospect of having [her] Jewish legitimacy challenged."[61]

Today's religiously liberal, highly diverse, and largely intermarried Bay Area Jewish community contends with relatively little anti-Semitism, as has been the case since 1849, when many Jews almost instantaneously became part of the original frontier aristocracy. Nevertheless, the discrimination in housing, jobs, social clubs, and university admissions that became evident in the 1920s continued in some instances until well after World War II. And for a hundred and sixty years local Jews have been the targets of disturbing, if scattered, anti-Semitic incidents. In the past few decades these incidents have ranged from the opening in the Sunset District of a Nazi bookstore in 1977 (soon wrecked by a group of enraged Holocaust survivors) to the 1994 unveiling at the student union of San Francisco State University of a mural of Malcolm X, filled with anti-Jewish symbols (it was sandblasted a week later on the order of the university president, Robert Corrigan, after discussions with Jewish communal leaders). Harder to quell was a widespread eruption of vandalism and arson in 2002, triggered by the Middle Eastern crisis and rendering vulnerable the area's many Hillel Foundations in particular.

A demographic survey conducted only two years later, however, concluded that the large majority of Jewish residents believed "anti-Semitism to be more serious in the United States overall than in the Bay Area."[62] More than two-thirds of respondents felt there was little or no animus toward Jews locally, and of those who had encountered bigotry, most described negative remarks about Jews or unfair criticism of Israel.[63] Only 6 percent of all respondents held that being Jewish deprived them of a club membership or social relationship; a mere 1 percent stated that it prevented them from obtaining a job or promotion.[64]

Surely Jewish identity continues to be no bar to elective office in the Bay Area, a pattern in evidence in San Francisco since the nineteenth century, when Adolph Sutro became the first Jewish mayor of a major American city. In the tradition of Florence Prag Kahn, in 1925 the first Jewish female elected to Congress, two Bay Area Jewish women were elected to the United States Senate in 1992 without a trace of anti-Semitism, and Barbara Boxer and Dianne Feinstein have been reelected multiple times since. Local Jews have distinguished themselves in the House, the state legislature, and on the San Francisco Board of Supervisors.* Even the pattern of the powerful Jewish political fundraiser, epitomized by Herbert Fleishhacker and Jesse Steinhart in the first half of the twentieth century, was evident well after the war when Ben Swig became the national treasurer of Adlai Stevenson's presidential campaign in 1956, and later the cochair of Pat Brown's two successful gubernatorial runs. Another local real estate magnate, Walter Shorenstein, was one of Jimmy Carter's major backers in 1976, and Don Fisher has emerged more recently as a key funder of campaigns throughout California. Until 1948 the many Jewish political figures were almost exclusively of German Jewish origin and Republican, and in the past sixty years they have largely been East European and Democrat, but the high visibility of Jews in political life has remained a constant.

The recent success of Jews in the business world has been no less impressive, in a reprise of the stunning achievements of the community's first hundred years, when Jewish enterprises like the Alaska Commercial Company played a key role in San Francisco's meteoric economic rise. While most of

---

* Leading members of Congress from the Bay Area have included Polish-born Sala Burton of San Francisco and Holocaust survivor Tom Lantos of San Mateo. The popular Milton Marks Jr. represented San Francisco in the state senate for three decades, Jackie Speier of San Mateo won a rare nomination by both Republicans and Democrats for an assembly seat in 1994, and Dion Aroner led the Democratic caucus of that body in 2002. Harold Dobbs served as president of the San Francisco Board of Supervisors in the late 1950s and early '60s, and Dianne Feinstein was elected to that post in 1977, as was Aaron Peskin in 2004.

the firms dating from the Gilded Age are no longer in existence, Levi Strauss and Company continues to be a worldwide force in the apparel industry, and its principal owners, especially the magnanimous Haas, Goldman, and Koshland families, remain at the pinnacle of the Jewish community. In the last generation many new global businesses have been created in the Bay Area by Jews, including Don and Doris Fisher of the Gap, Larry Ellison of Oracle, and Andy Grove of Intel, among many others. In 1998 Moscow-born Sergey Brin and Lawrence Page of Michigan, both students at Stanford University, cofounded Google. And just as they have since the days of I. W. Hellman and the Fleishhacker brothers, contemporary Jews have been leaders in banking and finance. In the 1960s, Herbert and Marion Sandler created Golden West Financial, the parent company of World Savings. For the first six years of the 1990s, Richard Rosenberg was chairman and CEO of the rapidly expanding Bank of America. And one of the West's foremost private equity investors is Warren Hellman, great-grandson of the pioneer titan.

Few sectors of the Bay Area economy have been more important since the war than biotechnology, and Jews have played an enormous role in that field. They range from Arthur Levinson, since 1995 the president and CEO of Genentech, to the eminent Berkeley professor of molecular and cell biology Daniel Koshland Jr., who commuted to Washington, D.C., to edit the journal *Science*. Since 1948, fifty-four individuals from UC Berkeley, Stanford University, and the UC San Francisco Medical Center have won Nobel Prizes, and about a third of these laureates, the large majority in medicine or the sciences, have been Jews. In 2006 Stanford's Roger Kornberg won the award for chemistry; his father, Arthur Kornberg, who worked at the same institution, won the Nobel Prize for medicine forty-seven years earlier, both scientists having made breakthroughs in genetics.*

Jewish real estate developers, meanwhile, have been influential in remaking the Bay Area in another way. Homebuilder Joseph Eichler was a pioneer in the construction of open, airy, modernist suburban homes that would profoundly affect the California lifestyle by "letting the outside in." Later, developers such as Ben Swig and Walter Shorenstein built a forest

---

*There is no equivalent of such achievement during Bay Area Jewry's first century, but a forerunner can be found in the person of Albert Michelson, born in the Prussian province of Posen and raised in the California Gold Country in the 1850s. In 1907 he won the Nobel Prize in physics, becoming the first American Nobel laureate in the sciences.

of downtown high-rises, causing some to speak of the "Manhattanization" of San Francisco.*

One well-known real estate man, Bob Lurie, owned the San Francisco Giants for many years, and their opponent in the Bay Bridge World Series of 1989, the Oakland A's, was also owned by a Jewish businessman, Walter Haas Jr. Haas, like Lurie, had bought the club to prevent it from moving out of town. As in prior generations, Jewish civic-mindedness has often gone hand in hand with corporate success and has hardly been limited to the local sports teams. From public health to public television, from the universities to the museums, Jewish philanthropy has been highly conspicuous. Perhaps the grandest of many recent examples was announced in 2007: Don and Doris Fisher offered to build a new public museum in the Presidio to house their extraordinary collection of contemporary art, a project requiring a donation from the family possibly exceeding a billion dollars according to a grateful Mayor Gavin Newsom.[65]

Other Jews have been catalysts as well as patrons of the arts. Like Albert Bender before the war, Cyril Magnin, the debonair chief of protocol, greatly enhanced the cultural life of his beloved city from the 1950s through the '70s. The third-generation San Franciscan helped convince Avery Brundage to donate his famed collection of Asian art to the local Asian Art Museum, and Magnin was also instrumental in establishing the American Conservatory Theater in San Francisco. His son-in-law, Walter Newman, presided over the complex and delicate merger of the de Young and Legion of Honor museums and arranged for a series of blockbuster shows, including the King Tut exhibit, one of the greatest attractions in the city's history.

Jews have also been some of the leading contemporary impresarios, offering the Bay Area public even more verve and variety than did their turn-of-the-century counterparts. Among many examples are Bill Graham, who presented rock concerts in the Fillmore West in the 1970s and '80s; Carole Shorenstein Hays, responsible for award-winning theatrical productions; and Berkeley-based Saul Zaentz, a producer of music and movies who has seen three of his films win the Academy Award for best picture.

---

*Other leading developers and real estate investors have included Gerson Bakar; the Holocaust survivors Joseph Pell, William Lowenberg, and Tad Taube; and, in the East Bay, Donald Chaiken, Morton and Gerald Friedkin, and Moses Libitzky, to name only a few.

Moreover, the innovation and irreverence of nineteenth-century theatrical personalities such as Adah Isaacs Menken, David Belasco, and Salmi Morse have reverberated in San Francisco with the audacious poetry readings by Allen Ginsberg, who debuted *Howl* on Fillmore Street in 1955; the brazen nightclub routines of Lenny Bruce, Mort Sahl, and Paul Krassner in the 1960s; and currently the quirky riffs of comedic monologuist Josh Kornbluth of *Red Diaper Baby* fame. Not unlike during the Bay Area's nineteenth-century cultural renaissance, with its decidedly bohemian overtones, today's Jewish nonconformists are again thriving in a metropolis that celebrates nonconformity.

The accomplished classicism once represented by artists such as Yehudi Menuhin and Isaac Stern has also been in evidence in recent years: Michael Tilson Thomas, grandson of the revered Yiddish actor Boris Thomashevsky, has been the conductor and musical director of the San Francisco Symphony since 1995. Meanwhile, the literary scene in the postwar Bay Area has been immeasurably enriched by legendary newspaper columnists such as Herb Caen and Art Rosenbaum, master short-story writers Tillie Olsen and Leonard Michaels, the incisive film critic Pauline Kael, and imaginative novelists such as Herb Gold and twenty-first-century sensations Michael Chabon and his wife, Ayelet Waldman.

Beyond the manifold achievements of individual creators of culture, the arts have been central to the very experience of being Jewish in the Bay Area, surpassing even Jewish education in importance according to the respondents in the 2004 demographic survey.[66] Another recent study reported that local Jews attend Jewish cultural events (including lectures as well as performances) almost as often as they celebrate Jewish holidays and with much greater frequency than they go to synagogue.[67] It identified more than three hundred Jewish cultural events in the Bay Area organized in 1999, held at more than fifty Jewish venues and an even larger number of non-Jewish sites such as bookstores, theaters, cafes, clubs, art galleries, museums, universities, and even churches.[68] The arts were paramount, too, in the early decades of the twentieth century, when the priorities of the Jewish community were expressed through the sublime liturgical music commissioned by Cantor Reuben Rinder, the architectural splendor of Temples Emanu-El and Sherith Israel, elaborate productions of Yiddish drama like *The Dybbuk,* and vivid public murals such as Bernard Zakheim's *Jewish Wedding* at the JCC on California Street.

Today the San Francisco Jewish Film Festival, the oldest and largest in the world, draws tens of thousands of people to its annual summer screenings;

for many Jews it constitutes their primary Jewish activity. In addition, the region boasts the nationally recognized repertory company A Traveling Jewish Theatre; an annual Jewish music festival; a host of klezmer bands; several cultural street festivals; and two major Jewish museums, the Judah L. Magnes Museum in Berkeley and the Contemporary Jewish Museum in San Francisco, the latter housed in a new downtown facility designed by the world-renowned Daniel Libeskind.

The calligrapher David Moss, one of the many young artists and scholars nurtured in the 1970s and '80s by the Magnes Museum's resourceful co–founding director Seymour Fromer, helped ignite a worldwide interest in illustrated *ketubot,* Jewish marriage contracts. Ori Sherman was a pioneer in producing gouache paintings of Jewish holidays and life cycle rituals, and Victor Riess created highly original ceremonial objects and sanctuary interiors, as have the Mendocino glass artists David and Michelle Plachte-Zuieback.*

While the arts have loomed large, the fight for social justice—the other main preoccupation of Bay Area Jewry—has also been as pronounced in the community's second century as it was in the first. In the tradition of Jacob Nieto, many contemporary spiritual leaders have made the defense of human rights essential to their rabbinates. Foremost among them in the early postwar decades was Emanu-El's Alvin Fine, chair of the regional ACLU in the 1950s. He opposed the loyalty oath required of UC faculty and staff and later vigorously defended the principle of the separation of church and state. In 1960 Fine publicly deplored the strong-arm tactics of Mayor George Christopher and the San Francisco police in breaking up a peaceful demonstration of college students protesting hearings held in City Hall by the House Committee on Un-American Activities. He also influenced the city to launch the Fair Employment Practices Commission (the predecessor of the Human Rights Commission), of which he became a charter member, and he brought Martin Luther King Jr. to his temple in 1961.[69]

Fine's successors at Emanu-El continued to speak out for the disadvantaged. Robert Kirschner, in his first Yom Kippur sermon as senior rabbi in 1985, boldly called attention to the AIDS crisis, and a year and a half later he

---

*Additionally, Ira Nowinski has emerged as a recognized photographer of Holocaust landmarks, and local printmaker Joseph Goldyne and painter Anthony Dubovsky have won national acclaim for their works on Jewish themes.

marched in rural Georgia against the Ku Klux Klan. Rabbi Stephen Pearce and his colleagues have helped at-risk inner-city youth and fought hunger and the despoiling of the environment.[70] At Sherith Israel the long-serving Rabbi Martin Weiner, who succeeded Fine on the Human Rights Commission, addressed such issues as gun control and domestic violence, and at Beth Sholom Rabbi Alan Lew tackled the stubborn problem of homelessness in San Francisco. In the East Bay, Rabbi Harold Schulweis of Temple Beth Abraham focused on the plight of economically exploited blacks in his city. Other local rabbis journeyed to Mississippi with the Freedom Riders and marched with Dr. King in Selma, Alabama. In more recent decades, even as the community has commemorated the Holocaust each year with elaborate Yom Ha-Shoah ceremonies, Jewish organizations have been in the forefront in deploring apartheid in South Africa and genocide in such places as Bosnia and Darfur.*

On almost all of these issues of social conscience the Bay Area rabbinate has worked side by side with outspoken non-Jewish clergy, solidifying the interfaith bonds that have prevailed since the 1850s. The number of local African American pastors collaborating with Jewish leaders has been particularly remarkable. Their ranks include, among others: Howard Thurman of the Fellowship Church of all Peoples, in the early postwar years; then Amos Brown of the Third Street Baptist Church; and Cecil Williams of Glide Memorial.

Beginning in the late 1960s, as black leaders became more militant, many local Jews turned away from their former allies and focused their energies on specifically Jewish causes such as Soviet Jewry and a newly vulnerable Israel.[71] But blacks and Jews showed greater cooperation in the Bay Area than in most other big cities, taking part in interracial coalitions that helped to prevent the race riots that erupted elsewhere in urban America. When, at the end of the 1970s, many blacks felt that Jewish pressure on the White House had caused Andrew Young's resignation as ambassador to the United Nations (because he had held unauthorized meetings with the PLO), calm prevailed in Northern California. A concerned Earl Raab called

---

*Rabbi Joseph Asher of Emanu-El, a member of the United States Holocaust Memorial Council and himself a German refugee, was a universalist voice on that issue as early as the 1980s. Despite opposition he would refer to the eleven million rather than six million victims of the Holocaust, calling attention to the many non-Jews who had perished (Fred Rosenbaum, *Visions of Reform: Congregation Emanu-El and the Jews of San Francisco* [Berkeley, 2000], 258).

a meeting of African American organizations and was relieved to learn that "the issue didn't touch our relationships in the city."[72]

Another longtime builder of interreligious and intercultural alliances, frequently collaborating with the preeminent black public intellectual Cornel West, has been Michael Lerner of the progressive magazine *Tikkun*. Privately ordained by Zalman Schachter-Shalomi and two other rabbis in 1995, Lerner also serves as spiritual leader of a local Renewal synagogue, Beit Tikkun, as devoted to social justice as it is to Jewish spirituality.

But during the past half century, like the Progressive era and the turbulent Depression years, when so many young local Jews dedicated themselves to reform or revolution, the synagogue pulpit and classical Jewish texts have been only one spur to social action. Jews have also been responsive to the calls for improving the world emanating from secular society. This was clear on the Berkeley campus in the 1964, when primarily non-religious Jews, some of them children of New York Communists, constituted a majority of the steering committee of the Free Speech Movement, which sparked campus activism throughout the country.[73]

Within a few years, though, other Jewish students at Berkeley, dismayed at the Israel bashing of the far left and influenced by the ethnic pride seen in the Black Power movement, formed the Radical Jewish Union. The RJU based its antiestablishment politics on prophetic ethics and even more so on the notions of early socialist Zionist thinkers such as Ber Borochov.* But whether they organized themselves along sectarian lines or not, the political preference of most Jewish students was clear: a poll of freshmen at Berkeley conducted in 1971 revealed that 58 percent of the Jews considered themselves "leftist," more than twice the percentage for non-Jews.[74]

Not surprisingly, the campus revolts of the 1960s and early '70s, at San Francisco State as well as at Berkeley, created a backlash against the left, just as did Bay Area radicalism during the Depression. Once again, Jews could be found on both sides of a momentous and bitter political debate. Although in the minority, Jews on the right were highly vocal and articulate. Berkeley professors Nathan Glazer and Seymour Martin Lipset, as well as

---

*The organized American Jewish community was frequently targeted in the RJU's journal, the *Jewish Radical*, which bestowed an annual Golden Calf Award for shallowness and hypocrisy. In 1971 the RJU and several other Jewish youth groups participated in a sit-in at the offices of San Francisco's federation, during which they demanded more funds for Jewish education.

Sidney Hook, later of the Stanford University's Hoover Institution—all born of East European immigrants and themselves Marxists in the 1930s—now chastised the young demonstrators and upheld the universities' prerogatives. These thinkers and others, later dubbed "neocons," ensured that leftist thought would not thoroughly dominate Bay Area intellectual life, and they have been joined in the past decade by writers such as David Horowitz, another former Marxist who has been fiercely critical of the current crop of left-wing academics. One of his main targets has been a Jewish professor of Middle Eastern history at Stanford, Joel Beinin, a strident defender of the Palestinian cause.[75]

In the 1960s the challenge to the establishment was hardly limited to college campuses or the field of politics, and Jews played a major role in the fast-emerging counterculture. The actor Peter Coyote (born Pinchas Cohon), for example, was active in the guerrilla theater performed throughout the Bay Area by the San Francisco Mime Troupe. Other Jews were among the founders of the Diggers, an anarchist group in Haight-Ashbury providing free food, medical care, and temporary housing; no doubt Emma Goldman would have approved. Across the bay, shaggy Max Scherr published and edited the underground antiwar *Berkeley Barb,* hawked by street people on Telegraph Avenue. Advocating not only political but also social and sexual revolution, it was not that different from Alexander Berkman's *Blast* during World War I, and it also incurred the wrath of the authorities.

In the 1960s and '70s local Jews also edited more sophisticated left-wing periodicals, such as *Ramparts* magazine and *Mother Jones.* In these and other publications, and through demonstrations, petitions, and the courts, they were conspicuous as advocates for the Black Panthers, Native Americans, and Mexican farm workers. In such areas as affirmative action and labor law, the liberal rulings of Jewish California supreme court justices Matthew Tobriner (1962–82) and Joseph Grodin (1982–87) call to mind the early twentieth-century Progressive Justice Marcus Sloss.* Jews have fought, too, against capital punishment, nuclear power, and the criminalization of marijuana. It would be hard to find a progressive cause or countercultural trend in the Bay Area in which Jews were not represented in the leadership as well as the rank and file.

---

*In 1996 Steven Breyer, born, raised, and educated in San Francisco, ascended to the U.S. Supreme Court, where he has usually been part of the liberal bloc.

Jews have also been among the major historians of the social movements roiling the Bay Area and the nation; they have not only recorded the tumultuous events but also taught their import to two generations of college students. Todd Gitlin, an early president of Students for a Democratic Society and a popular professor of sociology at Berkeley for several decades, has written authoritatively on the Free Speech Movement and the turbulent 1960s in general, as has the eminent Berkeley political science professor Sheldon Wolin. The activist Ruth Rosen (who taught for many years at UC Davis) has analyzed the women's movement, while professors Lawrence Levine and Leon Littwack published pathbreaking works on black folk culture and pioneered in offering courses in African American history at UC Berkeley. Other local Jews have extensively chronicled labor history, anarchism, the civil rights and antiwar movements, and gay liberation.

In the movement for gay rights, of particular importance in the Bay Area, Jews have also been some of the leading protagonists. Even before New York's famous Stonewall riots, Jews were active in San Francisco's Committee for Homosexual Freedom, which was among the first gay rights organizations in the country, founded in 1969.[76] Less than a decade later Harvey Milk, owner of a camera shop in the Castro District, was elected to the San Francisco Board of Supervisors after several unsuccessful attempts, becoming the first openly gay office holder in the country. In 1978 he was assassinated in City Hall, along with Mayor George Moscone, by former supervisor Dan White. The shocking tragedy and moving memorial service held at Temple Emanu-El energized many homosexuals, and since then there have been an increasing number of gay religious and political leaders in the Bay Area, including several Jews. Roberta Achtenberg and Mark Leno are Jewish gays who have served on the board of supervisors, and Achtenberg later became the first openly gay person to be confirmed by the United States Senate for a major political post, assistant secretary of Housing and Urban Development. Leno (a former rabbinical student at Hebrew Union College) is currently a state senator. In 2005, as assemblyman for eastern San Francisco, he championed a bill to legalize same-sex marriages, which was passed by the legislature but vetoed by Governor Arnold Schwarzenegger.

As they have since the nineteenth century, when they championed the rights of women and children, migrant workers and small farmers, and even prisoners and prostitutes, Jews in the Bay Area continue to be highly visible on the political frontier, often testing limits and igniting controversy. And the Jewish public, as it has since the tumultuous Gold Rush decade, remains deeply involved in the political and social issues of the day.

Observers of Jewish identity on the national level, such as Steven M. Cohen and Arnold Eisen, have pointed to a declining engagement of Jewish citizens in the public sphere in the past few decades, largely due to a shift in emphasis to the inner spiritual life.[77] But according to two recent surveys, Bay Area Jews in almost all age groups still consider social justice as their main concern among "issues of Jewish passion."[78]

Perhaps Rabbi Alvin Fine, the lifelong fighter for civil liberties and human dignity, who followed a stellar career at Emanu-El (1948–64) with a decade and a half of distinguished teaching at San Francisco State, understood best the irresistible appeal that *tikkun olam,* or healing the world, has had for Bay Area Jews. "The universal principles are like windows that let in the light," he declared from the pulpit in 1949.[79] But in the same breath the staunch Zionist who would lead his sedate, ultra-Reform congregation into the mainstream of Jewish life seemed to intuit something that would become increasingly clear in the next half century and beyond: "If the house is fallen," he said, "woe to the windows."[80]

In the past generation the Bay Area Jewish community has become more conscious of the vulnerability of Israel and Jews around the world, and of the imperative for Jewish education. But it has also maintained its easygoing, eclectic religious tone, its artistic creativity, and its broadminded concern for all peoples. It continues to be one of the widest windows in the house that is American Jewry.

NOTES

ABBREVIATIONS

WSJH   *Western States Jewish History* (formerly *Western States Jewish Historical Quarterly*)

WSJHQ   *Western States Jewish Historical Quarterly*

WJHC/JLMM   Western Jewish History Center of the Judah L. Magnes Museum

PREFACE AND ACKNOWLEDGMENTS

1. Gary A. Tobin, *A Study of Jewish Culture in the Bay Area* (San Francisco, 2002), 22.

2. Fred Rosenbaum, *Free to Choose: The Making of a Jewish Community in the American West* (Berkeley, 1976); *Architects of Reform: Congregation and Community Leadership, 1849–1980* (Berkeley, 1980); *Visions of Reform: Congregation Emanu-El and the Jews of San Francisco, 1849–1999* (Berkeley, 2000).

3. For example, Irena Narell, *Our City: The Jews of San Francisco* (San Diego, 1980); Robert E. Levinson, *The Jews in the California Gold Rush* (Berkeley, 1978); Peter F. Decker, *Fortunes and Failures: White Collar Mobility in Nineteenth-Century San Francisco* (Cambridge, Mass., 1978); Harriet and Fred Rochlin, *Pioneer Jews: A New Life in the Far West* (Boston, 1984); and Ava F. Kahn, *Jewish Voices of the California Gold Rush: A Documentary History, 1849–1880* (Detroit, 2002). Important issues in both nineteenth- and twentieth-century Bay Area Jewish

history are covered in William Issel and Robert W. Cherny, *San Francisco, 1865–1932: Politics, Power and Urban Development* (Berkeley, 1986); Kevin Starr, *The Dream Endures: California Enters the 1940s* (New York, 1997), 125–130; and a recent anthology with a statewide focus, Ava F. Kahn and Marc Dollinger, *California Jews* (Hanover, N.H., 2003).

4. David Hollinger, cited in Glenna Matthews, "Forging a Cosmopolitan Civic Culture: The Regional Identity of San Francisco and Northern California," in *Many Wests: Place, Culture, and Regional Identity,* ed. David M. Wrobel and Michael C. Steiner (Lawrence, Kans., 1997), 231.

5. Ibid.

6. R. A. Burchell, *The San Francisco Irish, 1848–1880* (Berkeley, 1980); Douglas Henry Daniels, *Pioneer Urbanites: A Social and Cultural History of Black San Francisco* (Berkeley, 1990); Yong Chen, *Chinese San Francisco, 1850–1943: A Trans-Pacific Community* (Stanford, 2000).

CHAPTER I

1. Carey McWilliams, *California: The Great Exception* (Berkeley, 1998), 65; Gunther Barth, *Instant Cities: Urbanization and the Rise of San Francisco and Denver* (New York, 1975).

2. Hubert Howe Bancroft, *The Works of Hubert Howe Bancroft* (San Francisco, 1888), 222.

3. Robert E. Levinson, *The Jews in the California Gold Rush* (New York, 1978), 4.

4. R. A. Burchell, *The San Francisco Irish, 1848–1880* (Berkeley, 1980), 3.

5. Norton B. Stern and William M. Kramer, "What's the Matter with Warsaw?" *WSJH* 17 (July 1985): 177–85.

6. Norton B. Stern and William M. Kramer, "The Turnverein: A German Experience for Western Jewry," *WSJH* 16 (April 1984): 228; Norton B. Stern and William M. Kramer, "The Major Role of Polish Jews in the American West," *WSJHQ* 8 (July 1976): 326–44.

7. Stern and Kramer, "The Major Role of Polish Jews," 328–29; Rudolph Glanz, "Vanguard to the Russians: The Poseners in America," *YIVO Annual of Jewish Social Service* 18 (1983): 1–37.

8. Avraham Barkai, *Branching Out: German-Jewish Immigration to the United States, 1820–1914* (New York, 1994), 25.

9. Hasia R. Diner, *Time for Gathering: The Second Migration, 1820–1880* (Baltimore, 1992), 43.

10. J. S. Holliday, *The World Rushed In: The California Gold Rush Experience* (New York, 1981).

11. Abraham Abrahamsohn, "Interesting Accounts of the Travels of Abraham Abrahamsohn," *WSJHQ* 1 (April 1969): 138.

12. Peter R. Decker, *Fortunes and Failures: White Collar Mobility in Nineteenth-Century San Francisco* (Cambridge, Mass., 1978), 12; Stephen Birmingham, *Our Crowd: The Great Jewish Families of New York* (New York, 1967), 84–85.

13. Ava F. Kahn, ed., *Jewish Voices of the California Gold Rush: A Documentary History, 1849–1880* (Detroit, 2002), 105–10.

14. Annegret S. Ogden, ed., *Frontier Reminiscences of Eveline Brooks Auerbach* (Berkeley, 1994), 36.

15. Ibid., 36–46.

16. Kevin Starr, *Americans and the California Dream, 1850–1915* (New York, 1973), 52.

17. Kahn, *Jewish Voices*, 121.

18. Ibid., 124.

19. Abrahamsohn, "Interesting Accounts," 138.

20. Ibid., 139.

21. Robert E. Stewart Jr. and Mary Frances Stewart, *Adolph Sutro: A Biography* (Berkeley, 1962), 22–23.

22. Ibid., 24.

23. Mary Prag, "Early Days," in *Birth of a Community: Jews and the Gold Rush,* ed. Leslie Brenner (Berkeley, 1995), 259.

24. James P. Delgado, *To California by Sea: A Maritime History of the California Gold Rush* (Columbia, S.C., 1996), 63.

25. Peter R. Decker, "Jewish Merchants in San Francisco," in *The Jews of the West: The Metropolitan Years,* ed. Moses Rischin (Berkeley, 1979), 21.

26. Abrahamsohn, "Interesting Accounts," 140.

27. Daniel Levy, "Letters about the Jews of California, 1855–1858," *WSJHQ* 3 (January 1971): 101.

28. Irena Narell, *Our City: The Jews of San Francisco* (San Diego, 1981), 124.

29. Decker, *Fortunes and Failures,* 211.

30. Herbert Asbury, *The Barbary Coast: An Informal History of the San Francisco Underworld* (New York, 1933), 32.

31. J. B. Barnhart, *The Fair but Frail: Prostitution in San Francisco, 1849–1900* (Reno, 1986), 20.

32. Abrahamsohn, "Interesting Accounts," 141.

33. Daniel Levy, "Letters," 101.

34. Ibid.

35. Abrahamsohn, "Interesting Accounts," 190.

36. Kramer and Stern, "Some 'Warts' on the Face of Early Western Jewry," *WSJHQ* 14 (October 1981): 82–87; Albert M. Friedenberg, "Letters of a California Pioneer," *Publications of the American Jewish Historical Society* 31 (1928): 159.

37. Decker, "Jewish Merchants," 21.

38. Henry J. Labatt, "The Commercial Position of the Jews in California," in Kahn, *Jewish Voices,* 256.

39. Daniel Levy, "Letters," 100.

40. *Daily Alta California,* December 11, 1851, quoted in Stern and Kramer, "Anti-Semitism and the Jewish Image in the Early West," *WSJHQ* 6 (January 1974): 135.

41. Friedenberg, "Letters of a California Pioneer," 135–71.

42. Ibid., 140.

43. Ibid., 145.

44. Roger W. Lotchin, *San Francisco, 1846–1856: From Hamlet to City* (Urbana, 1997), 175.

45. Friedenberg, "Letters of a California Pioneer," 150.

46. Ibid., 153.

47. Ibid., 157.

48. Ibid., 158.

49. Ibid., 162.

50. Ibid., 166.

51. Ibid., 170.

52. Abrahamsohn, "Interesting Accounts," 142.

53. Ibid.

54. Kahn, *Jewish Voices,* 382.

55. Abrahamsohn, "Interesting Accounts," 194–95.

56. Michael Reese, "Biographical Sketch," typescript ca. 1883, Bancroft Library, University of California, Berkeley.

57. Stewart and Stewart, *Adolph Sutro,* 32.

58. Malcolm J. Rohrbaugh, *Days of Gold: The California Gold Rush and the American Nation* (Berkeley, 1997), 160.

59. August Helbing, "How the Eureka Was Founded," unpaginated manuscript in the 80th anniversary yearbook of the Eureka Benevolent Society, in Eureka Benevolent Society Records, WJHC/JLMM.

60. Stern and Kramer, "A Search for the First Synagogue," *WSJHQ* 7 (October 1974): 3–20; Jacob Voorsanger, *Chronicles of Emanu-El* (San Francisco, 1900), 16.

61. Voorsanger, *Chronicles,* 17–18.

62. Lewis Franklin, "The First Jewish Sermon in the West: Yom Kippur, 1850, San Francisco," *WSJHQ* 10 (October 1977): 8.

63. Ibid., 10.

64. Kahn, *Jewish Voices,* 147–61; Alexander Iser, *The California Hebrew and English Almanac for the Year 5612, Corresponding with the Years 1851–1852* (San Francisco, 1851), in WJHC/JLMM.

65. Franklin, "The First Jewish Sermon," 12.

66. Stern and Kramer, "A Search for the First Synagogue," 6.

67. Ibid., 9.

68. Ibid., 10.

69. Leon A. Jick, *The Americanization of the Synagogue, 1820–1870* (Hanover, N.H., 1976), 102–3.

70. Barkai, *Branching Out,* 98.

71. Lotchin, *San Francisco,* 129.

72. Voorsanger, *Chronicles,* 24–25.

73. Ibid., 26–28.

74. Minutes of Congregation Sherith Israel, 1851. These minutes are kept at the WJHC/JLMM.

75. Alan Silverstein, *Alternatives to Assimilation: The Response of Reform Judaism to American Culture, 1840–1930* (Hanover, N.H., 1994), 13–14.

76. Voorsanger, *Chronicles,* 26–28; Minutes of Congregation Sherith Israel, 1851.

77. Voorsanger, *Chronicles,* 26–28; Minutes of Congregation Sherith Israel, 1851.

78. Brenner, *Birth of a Community,* 195.

79. Rudolf Glanz, *Jews of California: From the Discovery of Gold until 1880* (New York, 1960), 37.

80. Edgar F. Kahn, "The Saga of the First Fifty Years of Congregation Emanu-El, San Francisco," *WSJHQ* 3 (April 1971): 131.

81. Levy, "Letters," 96.

82. Lotchin, *San Francisco,* 134.

83. Ibid., 322–23.

84. Starr, *Americans,* 69–109.

85. Michael A. Meyer, *Response to Modernity: A History of the Reform Movement in Judaism* (New York, 1988), 242–43; James G. Heller, *Isaac Mayer Wise: His Life, Work, and Thought* (New York, 1965).

86. Voorsanger, *Chronicles,* 38–39.

87. Ibid., 40–45.

88. Ibid., 46.

89. Letter of Henry J. Labatt to Isaac Leeser in Kahn, *Jewish Voices,* 170–71.

90. Joshua Stampfer, *Pioneer Rabbi of the West: The Life and Times of Julius Eckman* (Portland, Ore., 1988), 25–57.

91. Quoted in ibid., 173.

92. Reva Clar, "Women in the *Weekly Gleaner,*" Part 1, *WSJH* 17 (July 1985): 338.

93. Ibid., 343.

94. Stampfer, *Pioneer Rabbi,* 190–91; Voorsanger, *Chronicles,* 143.

95. Reva Clar, "Rabbi Julius Eckman and the Elephants," *WJSH* 20 (October 1987): 39–40.

96. Ibid., 40.

97. Ibid.

98. *Daily Herald,* December 20, 1854.

99. Stampfer, *Pioneer Rabbi,* 71–72.

100. Robert E. Levinson, "Julius Eckman and the *Weekly Gleaner,*" in *A Bicentennial Festschrift for Jacob Rader Marcus,* ed. Bertram Korn (New York, 1976), 323–40.

101. Ibid., 334.

102. Levy, "Letters," 96.

103. I. Harold Sharfman, *The First Rabbi: Origin of the Conflict between Orthodox and Reform* (Malibu, Calif., 1988), 649.

104. Ibid., 323.

105. Henry A. Henry papers, WJHC/JLMM; and Marcus Henry, "Henry Abraham Henry: San Francisco Rabbi 1857–1869," *WSJHQ* 10 (October 1977): 31–37.

106. Henry, "Henry Abraham Henry," 57.

107. Minutes of Congregation Sherith Israel, April 30, 1869.

108. Reva Clar and William Kramer, "Julius Eckman and Herman Bien: The Battling Rabbis of San Francisco," Part 1, *WSJHQ* 15 (January 1983): 107–30; Part 2, *WSJHQ* 15 (April 1983): 232–53; Part 3, *WSJHQ* 15 (July 1983): 341–59.

109. Clar and Kramer, "Julius Eckman," Part 3, 344.

110. Clar and Kramer, "Julius Eckman," Part 2, 249, 252.

111. Decker, *Fortunes and Failures,* 32.

112. I. J. Benjamin, *Three Years in America, 1859–1862,* vol. 1 (Philadelphia, 1956), 232.

113. Barkai, *Branching Out,* 136.

114. Kahn, *Jewish Voices,* 199; Norton B. Stern, "Cholera in San Francisco in 1850," *WSJHQ* 5 (April 1973): 200.

115. Benjamin, *Three Years,* 210–27.

116. "From the Mayor of San Francisco—1854," *WSJHQ* 7 (October 1974): 21.

117. Tony Fels, "Religious Assimilation in a Fraternal Organization," *American Jewish Historical Quarterly* 74 (June 1985): 375.

118. Bernice Scharlach, *House of Harmony: Concordia-Argonaut's First 130 Years* (Berkeley, 1983), 13.

119. Ibid.

120. Benjamin, *Three Years,* 1:233.

121. Robert M. Senkewicz, *Vigilantes in Gold Rush San Francisco* (Stanford, Calif., 1985).

122. Kahn, *Jewish Voices,* 417–18.

123. Irena Narell, *Our City,* 44. On the substantial involvement of the Jews in the vigilantes of 1851, see Glanz, *Jews of California,* 41.

124. *Marysville Herald,* July 26, 1856, quoted in "Support for the Vigilantes—1856," *WSJH* 20 (April 1988): 277–78.

125. Walton Bean and James J. Rawls, *California: An Interpretive History* (New York, 1983), 124.

126. Decker, *Fortunes and Failures,* 138, 300; William Issel and Robert W. Cherny, *San Francisco, 1865–1932: Politics, Power, and Urban Development* (Berkeley, 1986), 207–8.

127. Norton B. Stern, "The First Jewish California State Legislator: Elcan Heydenfeldt, 1850," *WJSH* 16 (January 1984): 123.

128. William M. Kramer, "The Earliest Important Jewish Attorney in California, Solomon Heydenfeldt," *WSJH* 23 (January 1991): 154–55; Stanley Mosk, "A Majority of the California Supreme Court," *WSJHQ* 8 (April 1976): 227–31.

129. Earl Raab, "There's No City Like San Francisco," *Commentary* 10 (October 1950): 371.

130. "Anti-Jewish Sentiment in California, 1855," *American Jewish Archives* 12 (April 1960): 15–33.

131. William M. Kramer, "Pioneer Lawyer of California and Texas: Henry J. Labatt (1832–1900)," *WSJHQ* 15 (October 1982): 9.

132. "Anti-Jewish Sentiment," 22–23.

133. Ibid., 23.

134. Decker, *Fortunes and Failures,* 100.

135. Kahn, *Jewish Voices,* 394.

136. Rudolf Glanz, "Where the Jewish Press Was Distributed in Pre–Civil War America," *WSJHQ* 5 (October 1972): 11.

137. Kahn, *Jewish Voices,* 473.

138. Ibid., 463.

139. Ibid., 465; Bertram W. Korn, *The American Reaction to the Mortara Case* (Cincinnati, 1957); David I. Kertzer, *The Kidnapping of Edgardo Mortara* (New York, 1997), 126.

140. "Proceedings in Relation to the Mortara Abduction," in WJHC/JLMM, 5.

141. Ibid., 13.

142. Ibid., 8–9.

143. Ibid., 11.

144. Ibid., 10.

145. Korn, *American Reaction,* 24.

146. "Proceedings," 13–16, 18–19.

147. Ibid., 28–29.

148. Ibid., 27.

149. Benjamin, *Three Years,* 1:232–33.

150. Decker, *Fortunes and Failures,* 254.

151. Decker, "Jewish Merchants," 22.

152. Levy "Letters," 110.

153. Benjamin, *Three Years,* 1:233.

CHAPTER 2

1. Gray Brechin, *Imperial San Francisco: Urban Power, Earthly Ruin* (Berkeley, 1999), 1–9.

2. William Issel and Robert W. Cherny, *San Francisco, 1865–1932: Politics, Power, and Urban Development* (Berkeley, 1986), 23.

3. Jacob Voorsanger, *Chronicles of Emanu-El* (San Francisco, 1900), 101.

4. Albert Friedenberg, "Solomon Heydenfeldt: A Jewish Jurist of Alabama and California," *Publications of the American Jewish Historical Society* (1902): 138.

5. Robert J. Chandler, "Some Political and Cultural Pressures on the Jewish Image in Civil War San Francisco," *WJSH* 20 (January 1988): 150–51.

6. Ibid., 157.

7. Bertram Wallace Korn, *American Jewry and the Civil War* (Philadelphia, 1951), 172.

8. Ava F. Kahn, ed., *Jewish Voices of the California Gold Rush: A Documentary History, 1849–1880* (Detroit, 2002), 395.

9. Chandler, "Some Political and Cultural Pressures," 159.

10. Ibid., 160.

11. Ibid., 160–61.

12. Ibid., 161.

13. Ibid., 164.

14. William B. Kramer, " 'They Have Killed Our Man but Not Our Cause': The California Jewish Mourners of Abraham Lincoln," *WSJHQ* 2 (April 1970): 203.

15. Ibid., 194–95.

16. "Mucho Dinero," *Daily Morning Call*, August 6, 1871, 1.

17. Edgar F. Kahn, "Pioneer Jewish San Francisco Stock Brokers," *WSJHQ* 1 (January 1969): 50, 58.

18. William M. Kramer, ed., *The Western Journal of Isaac Mayer Wise, 1877* (Berkeley, 1974), 62.

19. Irena Narell, *Our City: The Jews of San Francisco* (San Diego, 1981), 89–93.

20. Ibid., 90.

21. "The Grain King of California," *WSJHQ* 10 (October 1977): 60.

22. Ibid.

23. A. W. Voorsanger, ed., *Western Jewry: An Account of the Achievements of Jews and Judaism in California* (San Francisco, 1916), 117–19.

24. Lin Weber, *Under the Vine and the Fig Tree: The Jews of the Napa Valley* (St. Helena, Calif., 2003), 48–51.

25. Frances Dinkelspiel, *Towers of Gold: How One Jewish Immigrant Named Isaias Hellman Created California* (New York, 2008), 200.

26. Robert E. Stewart Jr. and Mary Frances Stewart, *Adolph Sutro: A Biography* (Berkeley, 1962), 34.

27. Ibid., 36–37.

28. Ibid., 59–67.

29. Ibid., 67, 78.

30. Ibid., 168–69.

31. Ibid., 171.

32. Fred Rosenbaum, *Visions of Reform: Congregation Emanu-El and the Jews of San Francisco, 1849–1999* (Berkeley, 2000), 71.

33. Voorsanger, *Chronicles*, 61n.

34. Rosenbaum, *Visions*, 48.

35. Ibid., 48–49.

36. First Minute Book of Congregation Ohabai Shalome, November 6, 1864, to October 13, 1870, 1.

37. Rosenbaum, *Visions*, 47.

38. Allan Temko, "Temple Emanu-El of San Francisco," *Commentary* 26 (August 1958): 114–15.

39. Minutes of Congregation Sherith Israel, October 24, 1867; April 9, 1868.

40. Ibid., October 30, 1870.

41. Ibid., November 21, 1868.

42. Ibid., October 3, 1869.

43. Ibid., April 15, 1869; April 18, 1869.

44. Ibid., August 28, 1870.

45. Ibid., October 3, 1869.

46. Ibid., September 7, 1871.

47. *American Israelite*, May 6, 1870, quoted in Norton B. Stern, "An Orthodox Rabbi and a Reforming Congregation in Nineteenth-Century San Francisco," *WSJHQ* 15 (April 1983): 237.

48. Morris B. Margolies, "The American Career of Rabbi Henry Vidaver," *WSJH* 16 (October 1983): 38.

49. Ibid., 43.

50. Raymond Dannenbaum, "Glorious History of Congregation Beth Israel," *The Jewish Journal*, August 30, 1930, 2.

51. Ibid.

52. Ava F. Kahn and Marc Dollinger, *California Jews* (Lebanon, N.H., 2003), 12.

53. Tony Fels, "Religious Assimilation in a Fraternal Organization," *American Jewish Historical Quarterly* 74 (June 1985): 392; *2004 Jewish Community Study: Full Findings* (San Francisco, 2005), 76–77.

54. Kramer, *Western Journal*, 58.

55. Gunther Barth, *Instant Cities: Urbanization and the Rise of San Francisco and Denver* (New York, 1975), 177.

56. "Annual Report of the Eureka Benevolent Society 1890," in Eureka Benevolent Society Records, WJHC/JLMM.

57. *Emanu-El,* September 27, 1935, 42.

58. Barbara S. Rogers and Stephen M. Dobbs, *The First Century: Mount Zion Hospital and Medical Center, 1887–1997* (San Francisco, 1987).

59. William M. Kramer, "David Solis-Cohen of Portland: Patriot, Pietist, Litterateur and Lawyer," *WSJHQ* 14 (January 1982): 145.

60. Mary Watson, *San Francisco Society* (San Francisco, 1887), 27.

61. Homer S. Henley, "Yom Kippur in the Temple Emanu-El," *WSJHQ* 4 (October 1971): 11–19.

62. Harriet Lane Levy, *920 O'Farrell Street: A Jewish Girlhood in Old San Francisco* (Berkeley, 1996), 177.

63. Narell, *Our City,* 213.

64. "Six Jewish San Franciscans Gather for Reunion," *Emanu-El,* May 31, 1935, 1.

65. Alan Silverstein, *Alternatives to Assimilation: The Response of Reform Judaism to American Culture, 1840–1930* (Hanover, N.H., 1994), 76, 81.

66. B'nai B'rith District Grand Lodge No. 4, Records, in WJHC/JLMM.

67. Philo Jacoby quoted in Kramer, "They Have Killed Our Man," 204–5.

68. Levy, *920 O'Farrell Street,* 151.

69. Ibid., 153.

70. Rebekah Kohut, *My Portion (An Autobiography)* (New York, 1927), 47.

71. Narell, *Our City,* 111–12.

72. Gertrude Atherton, *My San Francisco: A Wayward Biography* (Indianapolis, 1946), 152.

73. Quoted in Charlene Akers, introduction to Levy, *920 O'Farrell Street,* viii.

74. Robert W. Cherny, "Patterns of Toleration and Discrimination in San Francisco," *California History* (Summer 1994): 138; J. B. Levison, *Memories for My Family* (San Francisco, 1933), 235; Isidore Choynski, *American Israelite,* March 24, 1882, 309.

75. *The Elite Directory for San Francisco and Oakland, 1879;* Peter R. Decker, "Jewish Merchants in San Francisco," in *The Jews of the West: The Metropolitan Years,* ed. Moses Rischin (Berkeley, 1979), 22.

76. *The San Francisco Blue Book 1888.*

77. Atherton, *My San Francisco,* 152.

78. Barth, *Instant Cities,* 174.

79. Chandler, "That Lurking Prejudice," *WSJH* 27 (July 1995): 205–13.

80. Ibid., 206.

81. Ibid., 211–12.

82. Ibid., 207.

83. Ibid., 209.

84. William M. Kramer, "Joseph R. Brandon, Activist Lawyer," in *Sephardic Jews in the West Coast States,* ed. William M. Kramer (Los Angeles, 1996), 78.

85. Ibid., 79.

86. Ibid., 80.

87. Ibid., 79.

88. Joseph R. Brandon, letter to the editor, *Daily Alta California,* March 26, 1875; Joseph R. Brandon, "A Protest against Sectarian Texts in California Schools in 1875," *WSJH* 20 (April 1988): 234.

89. Kramer, "Joseph R. Brandon," 79–80.

90. R. A. Burchell, *The San Francisco Irish, 1848–1880* (Berkeley, 1980), 163.

91. Harold Wechsler, "Jewish Learning at UC, 1870–1920," *WSJH* 18 (January 1986): 132

92. Ibid., 139.

93. David A. D'Ancona, "D'Ancona's Answer to Anti-Semitism: San Francisco, 1883," in *Sephardic Jews,* ed. William M. Kramer, 112.

94. John L. Levinsohn, *Frank Morrison Pixley of the Argonaut* (San Francisco, 1989), 55.

95. Narell, *Our City,* 167.

96. David A. D'Ancona, "The Jewish Question," *The Morning Call,* January 26, 1883, reprinted in *Western States Jewish Historical Quarterly* 8 (October 1975): 59–64.

97. William M. Kramer, "David A. D'Ancona, 1827–1908: A Sephardic B'nai B'rith Leader and His Family," in *Sephardic Jews,* ed. William M. Kramer, 101.

98. Kramer, "Joseph R. Brandon," 78.

99. Robert Singerman, "The San Francisco Journalism of I. N. Choynski: 'He Flatters None and Displeases Many,'" Part 2, *WSJH* 24 (April 1997): 174.

100. *American Israelite,* February 2, 1883, 261. See also Singerman, "San Francisco Journalism," Part 2, 187.

101. *American Israelite,* April 21, 1882, 341.

102. Singerman, "The San Francisco Journalism of I. N. Choynski: 'He Flatters None and Displeases Many,'" Part 1, *WSJH* 29 (January 1997): 31.

103. *American Israelite,* September 15, 1882, 90; May 5, 1882, 355; February 17, 1882, 270; September 8, 1882, 82; January 1, 1881, 210.

104. Singerman, "San Francisco Journalism," Part 2, 177.

105. Ibid., Part 1, 32.

106. *American Israelite,* January 13, 1882, 299.

107. Singerman, "San Francisco Journalism," Part 1, 33.

108. Ibid., Part 2, 176.

109. Ibid., 175.

110. Ibid., 172–73.

111. Ibid., 170–71.

112. Ibid., 171.

113. Ibid., 177.

114. Robert Singerman, "The San Francisco Journalism of I. N. Choynski: 'He Flatters None and Displeases Many,'" Part 3, *WSJH* 29 (July 1997): 273.

115. Ibid., 267.

116. Ibid., Part 2, 185.

117. Ibid., Part 3, 267.

118. Brechin, *Imperial San Francisco,* 173.

119. Ibid., 177.

120. Ibid., 181–82.

121. Allen Stanley Lane, *Emperor Norton: Mad Monarch of America* (Caldwell, Idaho, 1939), 53–71.

122. Ibid., 11.

123. Ibid., 163.

124. Ibid., 119–20.

125. Ibid., 141.

126. Ibid., 161–63.

127. Ibid., 78–79.

128. William Kramer, *Emperor Norton of San Francisco* (Santa Monica, Calif., 1974), 54.

129. Robert Louis Stevenson, *The Wrecker,* quoted in Lane, *Emperor Norton,* 80.

130. Narell, *Our City,* 80.

131. Kramer, *Emperor Norton,* 54.

132. Ibid., 66.

133. Ibid., 191.

134. Fred Rosenbaum, *Free to Choose: The Making of a Jewish Community in the American West* (Berkeley, 1976), 3.

135. Ibid., 3, 5, 9.

136. William M. Kramer, "The Emergence of Oakland Jewry," Part 1, *WSJHQ* 10 (January 1978): 108–11.

137. Rosenbaum, *Free to Choose,* 4–5.

138. Ibid.

139. Ibid., 44–45.

140. Ibid., 48, 59, 64, 69–71.

141. Ibid., 4.

142. Kramer, "The Emergence of Oakland Jewry," Part 3, *WSJHQ* 11 (July 1978): 370.

143. Rosenbaum, *Free to Choose,* 26–40.

144. Ibid., 11–24.

145. Quoted in Arthur Goren, ed., *Dissenter in Zion: From the Writings of Judah L. Magnes* (Cambridge, Mass., 1982), 8.

146. Elizabeth Sprigge, *Gertrude Stein: Her Life and Work* (London, 1957), 15.

147. Quoted in Linda Wagner-Martin, *Favored Strangers: Gertrude Stein and Her Family* (New Brunswick, N.J., 1995), 13.

148. Ibid., 28.

CHAPTER 3

1. Oscar Lewis, *Bay Window Bohemia: An Account of the Brilliant Artistic World of Gaslit San Francisco* (Garden City, N.Y., 1956), 8–9.

2. Harriet Lane Levy, *920 O'Farrell Street: A Jewish Girlhood in San Francisco* (Berkeley, 1996), vii.

3. Flora Jacobi Arnstein, interview with the author, 1978.

4. Hilary Spurling, *The Unknown Matisse: A Life of Henri Matisse, the Early Years, 1869–1908* (New York, 1998), 343.

5. Rebecca Gradwohl, "The Jewish Woman in San Francisco" (1896), in Jacob Rader Marcus, *The American Jewish Woman, 1654–1980,* vol. 1 (Cincinnati, 1981), 365.

6. "First Woman Law Graduate of the University of California," *WSJHQ* 14 (October 1981): 36; "First Jewish Lady Architect of the West," *WSJH* 17 (October 1984): 19–25.

7. Norman Bentwich, quoted in Fred Rosenbaum, "San Francisco-Oakland: The Native Son," in *Like All the Nations? The Life and Legacy of Judah L. Magnes,* ed. William M. Brinner and Moses Rischin (Albany, N.Y., 1987), 19.

8. Bernard Falk, *The Naked Lady: A Biography of Adah Isaacs Menken* (London, 1934), 66.

9. Misha Berson, *The San Francisco Stage, 1849–1869* (San Francisco, 1989), 75.

10. Ibid.

11. Ibid.

12. Falk, *Naked Lady,* 25.

13. Ibid., 69.

14. Berson, *San Francisco Stage,* 78.

15. Irena Narell, *Our City: The Jews of San Francisco* (San Diego, 1981), 82.

16. William Winter, *The Life of David Belasco* (New York, 1925), 14.

17. Herbert Leo Kleinfield, "The Theatrical Career of David Belasco" (Ph.D. diss., Harvard University, 1956), 72.

18. Berson, *San Francisco Stage,* 29; Craig Timberlake, *The Life and Work of David Belasco, the Bishop of Broadway* (New York, 1954), 32–34.

19. Timberlake, *The Life and Work of David Belasco,* 14.

20. Edmond M. Gagey, *The San Francisco Stage: A History* (New York, 1950), 45.

21. Berson, *San Francisco Stage,* 32.

22. Ibid., 33.

23. Harriet and Fred Rochlin, *Pioneer Jews: A New Life in the Far West* (Boston, 1984), 194.

24. Gagey, *San Francisco Stage,* 148.

25. "David Warfield" (Obituary), *New York Times,* June 28, 1951.

26. Lewis, *Bay Window Bohemia,* 120.

27. David Warfield, "My Beginnings," *Theatre Magazine,* February 1906, 42.

28. Alan Nielsen, *The Great Victorian Sacrilege: Preachers, Politics, and the Passion, 1879–1884* (Jefferson, N.C., 1991), 33–40.

29. Ibid., 29.

30. Quoted in ibid., 33.

31. Ibid., 56.

32. Ibid., 120.

33. Ibid., 68.

34. Ibid., 8.

35. Ibid., 74.

36. Ibid., 75.

37. Ibid., 77.

38. Norton B. Stern and William M. Kramer, "The Strange Passion of Salmi Morse," *WSJH* 16 (July 1984): 343.

39. Ibid.

40. Nielsen, *Victorian Sacrilege,* 76.

41. Ibid., 70.

42. Ibid., 87–88.

43. Ibid., 89–91.

44. Quoted in ibid., 91.

45. Quoted in Winter, *Life of David Belasco,* 125.

46. Nielsen, *Victorian Sacrilege,* 98.

47. Ibid., 94.

48. Ibid., 59.

49. Ibid., 105.

50. Berson, *San Francisco Stage,* 38.

51. Nielsen, *Victorian Sacrilege,* 99.

52. Ibid., 1.

53. Michael B. Leavitt, *Fifty Years in Theatrical Management* (New York, 1912), 646.

54. Ibid.

55. *San Francisco Bulletin,* Nov. 16, 1897, quoted in ibid.

56. *San Francisco Examiner,* April 26, 1891, quoted in Berson, *San Francisco Stage,* 50.

57. Quoted in Berson, *San Francisco Stage,* 139.

58. Quoted in ibid.

59. Brenda Wineapple, *Sister Brother: Gertrude and Leo Stein* (New York, 1996), 56.

60. Ibid., 56–57.

61. Quoted in Linda Wagner-Martin, *Favored Strangers: Gertrude Stein and Her Family* (New Brunswick, N.J., 1995), 34.

62. Wineapple, *Sister Brother,* 57.

63. Wagner-Martin, *Favored Strangers,* 69.

64. Wineapple, *Sister Brother,* 230.

65. Ibid.

66. Spurling, *The Unknown Matisse,* 348.

67. Ibid., 386.

68. Diana Souhami, *Gertrude and Alice* (London, 1991), 78.

69. Ibid.

70. Leon L. Strauss, ed., "Beloved Scribe: Letters of Theresa Ehrman," Part 2, *WSJHQ* 12 (January 1980): 142–43.

71. Ibid., 154.

72. Ibid., 150.

73. Ibid., 150–51.

74. Ibid., Part 3, *WSJHQ* 12 (April 1980): 236.

75. Ibid.

76. Wagner-Martin, *Favored Strangers,* 72–73.

77. Leon Katz, "Matisse, Picasso and Gertrude Stein," in *Four Americans in Paris: The Collections of Gertrude Stein and Her Family Museum of Modern Art* (New York, 1970), 60, 62.

78. Wagner-Martin, *Favored Strangers,* 87.

79. Spurling, *The Unknown Matisse,* 404–5.

80. Wagner-Martin, *Favored Strangers,* 185.

81. Gertrude Stein, *The Autobiography of Alice B. Toklas* (New York, 1933).

82. Gertrude Stein, *Everybody's Autobiography* (New York, 1937), 298.

83. Ibid., 300.

84. Quoted in Souhami, *Gertrude and Alice,* 218–19.

85. "What Are Masterpieces?" quoted in Fred Rosenbaum, *Free to Choose: The Making of a Jewish Community in the American West* (Berkeley, 1976), 20.

86. William M. Kramer and Norton B. Stern, "French Jews in the Early West: An Aristocratic Cousinhood," *WSJHQ* 13 (July 1981): 322.

87. A. W. Voorsanger, ed., *Western Jewry: An Account of the Achievements of Jews and Judaism in California* (San Francisco, 1916), 119–20; Ava F. Kahn, ed., *Jewish Voices of the California Gold Rush: A Documentary History, 1849–1880* (Detroit, 2002), 81.

88. Leon Harris, *Merchant Princes: An Intimate History of Jewish Families Who Built Great Department Stores* (New York, 1979), 240.

89. Kramer and Stern, "French Jews," 335.

90. Flora J. Arnstein and Susan B. Park, "The Godchaux Sisters," *WSJHQ* 15 (October 1982): 42

91. Ibid., 43.

92. Christopher H. Nelson, "The Architecture of Albert Pissis and Arthur Brown, Jr." (Ph.D. diss., University of California, Santa Barbara, 1986), 151.

93. Norton B. Stern and William M. Kramer, "G. Alfred Lansburgh," *WSJHQ* 13 (April 1981): 212–14.

94. *Western Jewry,* 114–15, 195.

95. Nelson, "Architecture," 60.

96. Bernice Scharlach, *House of Harmony: The Concordia-Argonaut's First 130 Years* (Berkeley, 1983), 201.

97. *Western Jewry,* 201.

98. Nelson, "Architecture," 151–52.

99. Ibid., 101.

100. Narell, *Our City,* 335–36.

101. "The Creative Frontier" is the title of a joint exhibition of five California Jewish artists marking the 125th anniversary of Congregation Emanu-El in 1975, cosponsored by the JLMM and Temple Emanu-El Museum.

102. Stephen Schwartz, *From West to East: California and the Making of the American Mind* (New York, 1998), 128.

103. Exhibition catalog, "Creative Frontier."

104. Ibid.

105. William M. Kramer and Norton B. Stern, *San Francisco's Artist Toby E. Rosenthal* (Northridge, Calif., 1978), 15.

106. Ibid., 94–95.

107. Ibid.

108. Ibid.

109. *American Israelite,* March 21, 1879, 6.

110. Kramer and Stern, *San Francisco's Artist,* 22.

111. Quoted in ibid., 30.

112. Ibid., 31.

113. Quoted in ibid., 21.

114. Ibid., 36.

115. Rochlin, *Pioneer Jews,* 188.

116. Peter C. Marzio, *Rube Goldberg: His Life and Work* (New York, 1973), 5.

117. Ibid., 15.

118. Irving Stone and Jean Stone, eds., *There Was Light: Autobiography of a University: Berkeley, 1868–1996* (Berkeley, 1996), 47.

119. Marzio, *Rube Goldberg,* 32, 37.

120. Maynard Frank Wolfe, *Rube Goldberg: Inventions* (New York, 2000), 16.

121. Marzio, *Rube Goldberg,* 7.

122. Ibid., 7–8.

123. Stephen J. Whitfield, *In Search of American Jewish Culture* (Hanover, N.H.), 23; Margaret Olin, *The Nation without Art* (Lincoln, Neb., 2001), 1–6.

124. Ibid., 24.

125. Ibid.

126. Carol Green Wilson, *Gump's Treasure Trade: A Story of San Francisco* (New York, 1949), 17.

127. Narell, *Our City,* 398.

128. Wilson, *Gump's Treasure Trade,* 27–49.

129. Ibid., 80.

130. Ibid.

131. Ibid., 94.

132. Ibid., 138.

133. Ibid., 139.

134. Ibid., 95.

135. Ibid., 100.

136. Archie Rice, *San Francisco Chronicle,* January 31, 1904, quoted in "Jews in Sports in California—1904," *WSJHQ* 14 (October 1981): 50.

137. William M. Kramer and Reva Clar, "Philo Jacoby: California's First International Sportsman," Part 2, *WSJHQ* 22 (January 1990): 246.

138. Joel S. Franks, "Rube Levy: A San Francisco Shoe Cutter and the Origin of Professional Baseball in California," *WSJH* 25 (October 1992); "Jews in Sports in California," 52.

139. Rice in "Jews in Sports in California," 52–53.

140. Ibid.; Jack Fiske, "The 1904 Olympic Games Heavyweight Boxing Champion," *WSJHQ* 16 (July 1984): 348–50.

141. Ken Blady, *The Jewish Boxers Hall of Fame* (New York, 1988), 45.

142. Ibid., 45–46.

143. Daniel Bezmozgis, *Natasha and Other Stories* (New York, 2005), 114; Geoffrey C. Ward, *Unforgivable Blackness: The Rise and Fall of Jack Johnson* (New York, 2004), 35.

144. Quoted in Blady, *Jewish Boxers,* 30.

145. Ibid., 27.

146. Harold Ribalow, *The Jew in American Sports* (New York, 1948), 151.

147. Ward, *Unforgivable Blackness,* 38.

148. Quoted in Blady, *Boxers,* 32.

149. Ribalow, *Jew in American Sports,* 150.

150. Ibid.

151. Bezmozgis, *Natasha,* 114.

152. Quoted in Blady, *Jewish Boxers,* 27.

153. Ibid.

154. Ibid.

CHAPTER 4

1. "David Warfield" (Obituary), *New York Times,* June 28, 1951, 63.

2. Oscar Lewis, *San Francisco: Mission to Metropolis* (San Diego, 1980), 146.

3. *Emanu-El,* November 20, 1896, 5.

4. Quoted in Avraham Barkai, *Branching Out: German Jewish Immigration to the United States, 1820–1914* (New York, 1994), 168.

5. Quoted in Fred Rosenbaum, *Free to Choose: The Making of a Jewish Community in the American West* (Berkeley, 1976), 50.

6. Kenneth Zwerin and Norton B. Stern, "Jacob Voorsanger from Cantor to Rabbi," *WSJHQ* 15 (April 1983): 195–200; Fred Rosenbaum, *Visions of Reform: Congregation Emanu-El and the Jews of San Francisco* (Berkeley, 2000), 79n.

7. Rosenbaum, *Visions,* 82; Marc Lee Raphael, "Rabbi Jacob Voorsanger of San Francisco on Jews and Judaism: The Implications of the Pittsburgh Platform," *American Jewish Historical Quarterly* 63 (December 1973): 188.

8. Raphael, "Rabbi Jacob Voorsanger," 187.

9. Ibid.

10. Rosenbaum, *Visions,* 82–83.

11. Raphael, "Rabbi Jacob Voorsanger," 195–200.

12. *Emanu-El,* December 27, 1895, 6–7.

13. Rosenbaum, *Visions,* 83–84.

14. *Emanu-El,* January 15, 1904, 8; December 2, 1898, 5.

15. *Emanu-El,* July 10, 1896, 6.

16. *Emanu-El,* February 14, 1919, 11, quoted in Ava F. Kahn, *Jewish Life in the American West: Perspectives on Migration, Settlement, and Community* (Los Angeles, 2002), 13.

17. Morris B. Margolies, "The American Career of Rabbi Henry Vidaver," *WSJH* 16 (October 1983): 41–42.

18. Minutes of Congregation Sherith Israel, October 5, 1879.

19. Kenneth C. Zwerin, "Rabbi Jacob Nieto of Congregation Sherith Israel," Part 1, *WSJH* 18 (October 1985): 35–36.

20. Ibid., 39; Letter of Jacob Nieto to the Board of Trustees of Congregation Sherith Israel, April 20, 1893, in Sherith Israel Papers, WJHC/JLMM.68/8 f. 6.

21. Zwerin, "Rabbi Jacob Nieto," Part 1, 42.

22. Zwerin, "Rabbi Jacob Nieto," Part 2, *WSJH* 18 (January 1986): 166.

23. Ibid., 164.

24. Ibid., 163–64.

25. Minutes of Congregation Sherith Israel, October 16, 1911.

26. Zwerin, "Rabbi Jacob Nieto," Part 3, *WSJH* 18 (April 1986): 253.

27. January 26, 1893, handwritten notes for sermon in Sherith Israel Papers, WJHC/JLMM 68/8 f. 6, p. 7.

28. Quoted in Fremont Older, "Jacob Nieto," *Jewish Journal,* October 28, 1931, 1.

29. Sermon of January 26, 1893, quoted in Jacob Nieto, "Liberal Judaism," *Jewish Journal,* January 13, 1932, 2.

30. Fred Rosenbaum, *Free to Choose,* 11.

31. William M. Kramer, "The Emergence of Oakland Jewry," Part 5, *WSJHQ* 11 (January 1979): 175.

32. Quoted in Rosenbaum, *Free to Choose,* 48.

33. *Jewish Progress,* September 8, 1893, clipping without page number, in Harris Weinstock Papers, vol. 1, Bancroft Library, University of California, Berkeley.

34. Ibid.

35. Harris Weinstock, *Jesus the Jew and Other Addresses* (New York, 1902), 141.

36. Ibid., 63, 86.

37. *Emanu-El,* November 10, 1905, in Weinstock Papers, vol. 8, p. 70; Jacob Voorsanger, "The Sabbath Question," in *Sermons and Addresses* (New York, 1913), 258.

38. *Emanu-El,* January 7, 1902, in Weinstock Papers, vol. 6, 1902.

39. Weinstock, *Jesus the Jew,* 30, 34.

40. Editorial in *Reform Advocate,* August 24, 1901.

41. Oakland Tribune, April 15, 1907, in Weinstock Papers, vol. 9, 1907.

42. Voorsanger, *Sermons,* 258.

43. Gustav Danziger, "The Jew in San Francisco," *Overland Monthly* 25 (April 1895): 390.

44. Alan Silverstein, *Alternatives to Assimilation: The Response of Reform Judaism to American Culture, 1840–1930* (Hanover, N.H.), 79.

45. Minutes of Congregation Sherith Israel, November 20, 1871; January 9, 1872; February 5, 1872.

46. Ibid., November 20, 1871.

47. Ibid., January 9, 1872.

48. Ibid., February 5, 1872.

49. Ibid., October 19, 1873.

50. Norton B. Stern, "A San Francisco Synagogue Scandal of 1893," *WSJHQ* 6 (April 1974): 198.

51. Minutes of Congregation Sherith Israel, December 5, 1881.

52. Quoted in Stern, "A San Francisco Synagogue Scandal," 198–99.

53. Ibid., 200.

54. Ibid., 198.

55. Quoted in ibid., 202.

56. Minutes of Congregation Sherith Israel, December 13, 1885.

57. Ibid., June 4, 1883.

58. Ibid.

59. Rosenbaum, *Visions,* 100.

60. Minutes of Congregation Sherith Israel, October 19, 1873.

61. Ibid., October 29, 1905.

62. Ibid., September 16, 1906.

63. Ibid., October 29, 1905.

64. Ibid.

65. Ibid., April 17, 1910.

66. Ibid., October 25, 1908.

67. Ibid., March 27, 1910.

68. Ibid., May 2, 1910.

69. Ibid., October 17, 1910.

70. IOBB District Grand Lodge 4 in WJHC/JLMM; "California's Hebrews—1887," from the *San Francisco Daily Examiner,* reprinted in *WSJHQ* 4 (July 1972): 200.

71. Minutes of the Executive Board of the San Francisco Federation of Jewish Charities, March 24, 1915.

72. Tony Fels, "Religious Assimilation in a Fraternal Organization," *American Jewish Historical Quarterly* 74 (June 1985): 392.

73. William M. Kramer, ed., *The Western Journal of Isaac Mayer Wise, 1877* (Berkeley, 1974), 61–62.

74. Amy Steinhart Braden, *Child Welfare and Community Service* (Berkeley, 1965), 17.

75. Ibid.

76. Frances Bransten Rothmann, *The Haas Sisters of Franklin Street: A Look Back with Love* (Berkeley, 1979), 71.

77. Irena Narell, *Our City: The Jews of San Francisco* (San Diego, 1981), 166.

78. Ibid., 165.

79. Ibid.

80. "California's Hebrews—1887," 198.

81. Danziger, "The Jew in San Francisco," 395.

82. "The Editor's Page," *WSJHQ* 13 (January 1981): 191.

83. *American Israelite,* December 30, 1887, quoted in William M. Kramer, *Sephardic Jews in the West Coast States, Vol. I: The San Francisco Grandees* (Los Angeles, 1996), 80.

84. Harris Weinstock, "Shall Jew and Christian Intermarry?" in *Jesus the Jew,* 138.

85. Quoted in Dana Evan Kaplan, "Judaism and Intermarriage: A Discussion in 19th Century California, 1857–1859," *WSJH* 31 (Summer 1999): 357.

86. Quoted in Kramer, *Sephardic Jews,* 81.

87. Quoted in ibid., 82.

88. Rebekah Kohut, *My Portion (An Autobiography)* (New York, 1927), 63.

89. Ibid., 47.

90. Ibid., 51–52.

91. Ibid., 62–63.

92. Harriet Lane Levy, *920 O'Farrell Street: A Jewish Girlhood in Old San Francisco* (Berkeley, 1996), 123.

93. Ibid., 124.

94. Ibid., 180.

95. Flora Jacobi Arnstein, "No End to Morning," unpublished manuscript, ca. 1934, p. 14, in Bancroft Library, University of California, Berkeley.

96. Ibid.

97. Fred Rosenbaum, *Free to Choose* (Berkeley, 1976), 21.

98. Ibid., 20.

99. Ibid., 20–21.

100. Reva Clar and William M. Kramer, "The Girl Rabbi of the Golden West: The Adventurous Life of Ray Frank in Nevada, California and the Northwest," Part 2, *WSJH* 18 (April 1986): 230.

101. Ibid., Part 3, *WSJH* 18 (July 1986): 346.

102. Ibid.

103. Ibid., Part 2, 228.

104. Ibid., 234, 236.

105. Ray Frank, "Yom Kippur Sermon," in *Four Centuries of Jewish Women's Spirituality,* ed. Ellen M. Umansky and Dianne Ashton (Boston, 1992), 129.

106. Clar and Kramer, "Girl Rabbi," Part 1, *WSJH* 18 (January 1986): 111.

107. Umansky and Ashton, eds., *Four Centuries,* 131.

108. Clar and Kramer, "The Girl Rabbi," Part 1, 111; Part 3, *WSJH* 18 (July 1986): 350.

109. Umansky and Ashton, eds., *Four Centuries,* 131.

110. Robert E. Stewart Jr. and Mary Frances Stewart, *Adolph Sutro: A Biography* (Berkeley, 1962), 192–93; Kevin Starr, *Inventing the Dream: California through the Progressive Era* (New York, 1985), 221.

111. Catherine Wessinger, "Introduction," and Ann Braude, "The Perils of Passivity: Women's Leadership in Spiritualism and Christian Science," in *Women's Leadership in Marginal Religions: Explorations outside the Mainstream,* ed. Catherine Wessinger (Urbana, 1993).

112. Levy, *920 O'Farrell Street,* 34.

113. Shirley Sargent, *Solomons of the Sierras* (Yosemite, Calif., 1989), 88.

114. Ibid., 8.

115. Ibid., 18.

116. Quoted in Shirley Sargent, "Theodore Solomons, An Unlikely Mountaineer," *WSJH* 18 (April 1986): 201.

117. Ibid., 200.

118. Sargent, *Solomons of the Sierras,* 30.

119. Ibid., 31.

120. Ibid., 27.

121. Michael A. Meyer, *Response to Modernity: A History of the Reform Movement in Judaism* (New York, 1988), 314; Martin Meyer in *Emanu-El,* June 23, 1911.

122. Joel Blau in *Emanu-El,* June 30, 1916; Stephen M. Wise in *Emanu-El,* December 29, 1916; Frederick Cohn in *Emanu-El,* February 2, 1917.

123. Albert Bennett, ed., *Just a Very Pretty Girl from the Country: Sylvia Salinger's Letters from France, 1912–1913* (Carbondale, Ill., 1987), xiii; Zwerin, "Rabbi Jacob Nieto," Part 2, 167.

124. Jacob Weinstein, "A Rabbi's Farewell," *Life and Letters* 7 (November 1932): 8.

125. Ibid.

126. Rosenbaum, *Visions,* 115–19; Daniel J. Moscowitz, "Martin Meyer: His Life and its Lessons," Part 1, *WSJH* 26 (April 1994): 194–216.

127. Rosenbaum, *Visions,* 117.

128. *Emanu-El,* February 5, 1915, 2.

129. Rosenbaum, *Visions,* 118–24.

130. Ibid., 124–31.

131. Ibid., 127.

132. Ibid.

133. Ibid., 129.

134. Quoted in ibid., 131.

135. Ibid., 131–32.

136. David Kaufman, *Shul with a Pool: The "Synagogue-Center" in American Jewish History* (Hanover, N.H., 1999).

137. Louis I. Newman, *Biting on Granite: Selected Sermons and Addresses* (New York, 1946), 37.

138. Rosenbaum, *Visions,* 149.

139. Minutes of Congregation Sherith Israel, October 27, 1928.

140. Zwerin, "Rabbi Jacob Nieto," Part 2, 167.

141. Jacob Nieto, "Woman!" sermon quoted in *Jewish Journal,* November 25, 1931.

142. Weinstein, "A Rabbi's Farewell," 8.

143. Irena Narell, "Old Traditions on a New Frontier: San Francisco Jews, A Bicentennial Portrait Prepared by the WJHC/JLMM" (Berkeley, 1976), unpaginated.

144. Ibid.

145. Mrs. Sol Kahn, "Rabbi Myer Levy's Memory," *Emanu-El,* April 3, 1936, 72.

146. *Emanu-El,* January 10, 1896, 12.

147. David Biale, *Judah L. Magnes: Pioneer and Prophet on Two Continents* (Berkeley, 1977), 18, in WJHC/JLMM.

148. Ibid., 21.

149. Arthur Goren, *New York Jews and the Quest for Community: The Kehilla Experiment, 1908–1922* (New York, 1970).

150. Fred Rosenbaum, "San Francisco-Oakland: The Native Son," in *Like All the Nations? The Life and Legacy of Judah L. Magnes,* ed. William M. Brinner and Moses Rischin (Albany, N.Y., 1987), 22; Arthur Goren, ed., *Dissenter in Zion: From the Writings of Judah L. Magnes* (Cambridge, Mass., 1982), 5.

151. Kaufman, *Shul with a Pool,* 82–86.

152. Quoted in David Meyers, "In Search of the 'Harmonious Jew': Judah L. Magnes between East and West," The 1992 John S. Sills Memorial Lecture (Berkeley, 1993), 7–8, in WJHC/JLMM.

CHAPTER 5

1. David G. Dalin, "Jewish and Non-Partisan Republicanism in San Francisco, 1911–1963," in The Jews of the West: The Metropolitan Years, ed. Moses Rischin (Berkeley, 1979), 108–32.

2. Gray Brechin, Imperial San Francisco: Urban Power, Earthly Ruin (Berkeley, 1999).

3. B. C. Forbes, Men Who Are Making the West (New York, 1923), 41.

4. Irena Narell, Our City: The Jews of San Francisco (San Diego, 1981), 234.

5. William Issel and Robert W. Cherny, San Francisco 1865–1932: Politics, Power and Urban Development (Berkeley, 1986), 180.

6. John B. McGloin, San Francisco: The Story of a City (San Rafael, Calif., 1978), 160.

7. Narell, Our City, 302.

8. Issel and Cherny, San Francisco, 169.

9. Gustav Danziger and K. M. Nesfield, "The Jew in San Francisco," Overland Monthly 25 (April 1895): 398.

10. Brechin, Imperial San Francisco, 185.

11. Stephen Schwartz, From West to East: California and the Making of the American Mind (New York, 1998), 143.

12. Emanu-El, December 4, 1903, 2.

13. Emanu-El, November 20, 1903, 2.

14. Narell, Our City, 192.

15. Gunther Barth, Instant Cities (New York, 1975), 197.

16. Brechin, Imperial San Francisco, 190; Narell, Our City, 292.

17. Philip J. Ethington, The Public City: The Political Construction of Urban Life in San Francisco (Cambridge, 1994), 376; Narell, Our City, 293.

18. Frank Norris, The Octopus (New York, 1986), 65.

19. Ibid., 67.

20. Ibid., 109.

21. Richard Hofstadter, The Age of Reform: From Bryan to FDR (New York, 1955), 77–81.

22. Kevin Starr, Inventing the Dream: California through the Progressive Era (New York, 1985), 223; Carol Roland, "The California Kindergarten Movement: A Study in Class and Social Feminism" (Ph.D. diss., U.C. Riverside, 1980), 93–94.

23. Kate Douglas Smith Wiggin, My Garden of Memory: An Autobiography (Boston, 1923), 110.

24. Robert E. Stewart Jr. and Mary Frances Stewart, *Adolph Sutro: A Biography* (Berkeley, 1962), 200, 208.

25. Jerry Flamm, *Good Life in Hard Times: San Francisco's '20s and '30s* (San Francisco, 1988), 96.

26. Stewart and Stewart, *Adolph Sutro,* 183.

27. Cherny and Issel, *San Francisco,* 135.

28. Ethington, *The Public City,* 375.

29. Olivia Rossetti Agresti, *David Lubin: A Study in Practical Idealism* (Boston, 1922), 15; Gotthard Deutsch, "David Lubin: A Remarkable Jew," *WSJHQ* 14 (July 1982): 318–19.

30. Agresti, *David Lubin,* 21–22.

31. Ibid., 38–39.

32. Ibid., 39.

33. Ibid., 42.

34. Ibid., 69.

35. Ibid., 52.

36. Grace H. Larsen, "A Progressive in Agriculture: Harris Weinstock," *Agricultural History* 32 (July 1958): 189.

37. Harris Weinstock Papers, Bancroft Library, vol. 8, University of California, Berkeley, January 1905.

38. *San Francisco Bulletin,* March 15, 1906.

39. *San Francisco Call,* May 23, 1907.

40. David George Herman, "Neighbors on the Golden Mountain" (Ph.D. diss., U.C. Berkeley, 1981), xxvii.

41. Ibid., 256.

42. Spencer Olin, *California's Prodigal Sons: Hiram Johnson and the Progressives, 1911–1917* (Berkeley, 1968), 75.

43. Frank Sloss, "M. C. Sloss and the California Supreme Court," *California Law Review* 46 (December 1958): 729.

44. Quoted in Larsen, "A Progressive in Agriculture," 190.

45. Olin, *California's Prodigal Sons,* 106.

46. Larsen, "A Progressive in Agriculture," 192.

47. Grace H. Larsen and Henry E. Erdman, "Aaron Sapiro: Genius of Farm Co-operative Promotion," *Mississippi Valley Historical Review* 49 (September 1962): 243.

48. Ibid.

49. Ibid., 244.

50. Ibid., 245–47.

51. Ibid., 247.

52. Ibid., 250–51.

53. Ibid., 257–58.

54. Ibid., 242.

55. Neil Baldwin, *Henry Ford and the Jews: The Mass Production of Hate* (New York, 2001).

56. Albert Lee, *Henry Ford and the Jews* (New York, 1980), 69.

57. Aaron Sapiro, "An Experience with American Justice," *Free Synagogue Pulpit* 8, no. 5 (1927–28): 10.

58. Lee, *Henry Ford and the Jews,* 80–81.

59. Kevin Starr, *Inventing the Dream,* 257–58.

60. *Sacramento Union,* October 6, 1908.

61. Agresti, *David Lubin,* 277.

62. Samuel Edgerton Wood, "The California State Commission of Immigration and Housing: A Study of Administrative Organization and the Growth of Function" (Ph.D. diss., U.C. Berkeley, 1942), 84.

63. Ibid., 105, 113.

64. Ibid., 120; Kevin Starr, *Endangered Dreams: The Great Depression in California* (New York, 1996), 44–45.

65. Walton Bean and James J. Rawls, *California: An Interpretive History* (Berkeley, 1983), 223.

66. Simon Julius Lubin Collection, in WJHC/JLMM.

67. Starr, *Inventing the Dream,* 258; Wood, "The California State Commission," 143–66.

68. Wood, "The California State Commission," 167.

69. Ibid.

70. Ibid., 89–90.

71. Ibid., 134.

72. Simon Lubin, "Can the Radicals Capture the Farms of California?" lecture delivered at the Commonwealth Club of California, March 23, 1934, in Bancroft Library, University of California, Berkeley.

73. Kevin Starr, *Endangered Dreams,* 231.

74. Ibid., 232.

75. Beth S. Wenger, "Jewish Women and Voluntarism: Beyond the Myth of Enablers," *American Jewish History* 79 (Autumn 1989): 17.

76. Barbara S. Rogers and Stephen M. Dobbs, *The First Century: Mount Zion Hospital and Medical Center, 1887–1987* (San Francisco, 1987), 16.

77. Ibid., 17

78. A. W. Voorsanger, *Western Jewry: An Account of the Jews and Judaism in California* (San Francisco, 1916), 32.

79. Ibid., 33.

80. Josephine Cohn, "Communal Life of San Francisco Jewish Women in 1908," *Emanu-El,* April 17, 1908, reprinted in *WSJH* 20 (October 1987): 19.

81. *San Francisco Examiner,* May 26, 1895.

82. M. K. Silver, "Selina Solomons and Her Quest for the Sixth Star," *WSJH* 31 (Summer 1999): 310.

83. Ibid., 306.

84. Quoted in ibid., 313.

85. Henry Rand Hatfield, "Jessica Blanche Peixotto," in *Essays in Social Economics in Honor of Jessica Blanche Peixotto,* ed. E. T. Grether (Berkeley, 1935), 5.

86. Ibid., 8.

87. Ibid.

88. Robert Nisbet, *Teachers and Scholars: A Memoir of Berkeley in Depression and War* (New Brunswick, N.J., 1992), 69.

89. Narell, *Our City,* 362.

90. Ibid.

91. Hatfield, "Jessica Blanche Peixotto," 10.

92. Amy Steinhart Braden, *Child Welfare and Community Service* (Berkeley, 1965), 93.

93. Ibid., 95.

94. Ibid., 98.

95. Ibid., 149.

96. Ibid., 98.

97. Ibid., 215.

98. Ibid., 165.

99. *San Francisco Bulletin,* January 25, 1917.

100. Ruth Rosen, *Lost Sisterhood: Prostitution in America, 1900–1918* (Baltimore, Md., 1982), 14–19.

101. Julius Rosenstirn, *Our Nation's Health Endangered by Poisonous Infection through the Social Malady* (San Francisco, 1913), 11.

102. Neil Larry Shumsky and Larry M. Springer, "San Francisco's Zone of Prostitution, 1880–1934," *Journal of Historical Geography* 7 (January 1981): 82.

103. Ibid., 84.

104. J. B. Barnhart, *The Fair but Frail: Prostitution in San Francisco, 1849–1900* (Reno, Nev., 1986), 26–27.

105. Herbert Asbury, *The Barbary Coast: An Informal History of the San Francisco Underworld* (New York, 1933), 276.

106. Lawrence Arnstein, *Community Service in California Public Health and Social Welfare* (Berkeley, 1964), 9.

107. Albert Charles Wollenberg, *To Do the Job Well: A Life in Legislative, Judicial, and Community Service* (Berkeley, 1981), 2.

108. Gus C. Ringolsky Papers in WJHC/JLMM.

109. *San Francisco Bulletin,* September 20, 1911.

110. Gus C. Ringolsky Papers in WJHC/JLMM.

111. Ibid.

112. Ibid.

113. Shelley Bookspan, *A Germ of Goodness: The California State Prison System, 1851–1944* (Lincoln, Neb., 1991), 88.

114. Gus C. Ringolsky Papers in WJHC/JLMM.

115. Ibid.

116. Ibid.

117. Ibid.

118. "Future of the American Negro: Extract from a Feeling and Instructive Address by H. Weinstock of Sacramento," in *Stockton Record* in Weinstock Papers, vol. 4, 1901.

119. Douglas Henry Daniels, *Pioneer Urbanites: A Social and Cultural History of Black San Francisco* (Berkeley, 1990), 18.

120. Yong Chen, *Chinese San Francisco, 1850–1943: A Trans-Pacific Community* (Stanford, Calif., 2000), 59–60.

121. William M. Kramer, ed., *The Western Journal of Isaac Mayer Wise, 1877* (Berkeley, 1974), 30, 33.

122. Quoted in Rudolf Glanz, "Jews and Chinese in America," in *Studies in Judaica Americana* (New York, 1970), 323; Robert Singerman, "The San Francisco Journalism of I. N. Choynski: 'He Flatters None and Displeases Many,'" Part 2, *WSJH* 24 (April 1997): 189.

123. Reva Clar and William M. Kramer, "Chinese-Jewish Relations in the Far West: 1850–1950," Part 1, *WSJHQ* 21 (October 1988): 32, 24.

124. Ibid., 23; Chen, *Chinese San Francisco,* 82.

125. Quoted in Clar and Kramer, "Chinese-Jewish Relations," Part 1, 28.

126. Ibid., 24.

127. Ibid., Part 2, *WSJHQ* 21 (January 1989): 149.

128. Quoted in ibid., 125.

129. Glanz, "Jews and Chinese in America," 316; Karl Schoenberger, *Levi's Children: Coming to Terms with Human Rights in the Global Marketplace* (New York, 2000), 35.

130. Alexander Saxton, *The Indispensable Enemy: Labor and the Anti-Chinese Movement in California* (Berkeley, 1995), 217–18.

131. Clar and Kramer, "Chinese-Jewish Relations," Part 1, 24.

132. Glanz, "Jews and Chinese in America," 326.

133. Quoted in ibid., 324.

134. Ibid., 326.

135. Quoted in Saxton, *Indispensable Enemy,* 221.

136. Ibid., 267.

137. Bean and Rawls, *California,* 287.

138. Richard H. Frost, *The Mooney Case* (Stanford, Calif., 1968), 36.

139. "Girl Socialist of San Francisco," *San Francisco Examiner,* October 3, 1897.

140. Quoted in James R. Boylan, *Revolutionary Lives: Anna Strunsky and William English Walling* (Amherst, Mass., 1998), 8.

141. Ibid., 9–11.

142. Ibid., 12.

143. Ibid., 19.

144. Jack London and Anna Strunsky, *The Kempton-Wace Letters* (London, 1903).

145. Boylan, *Revolutionary Lives,* 24.

146. Ibid.; Joan London, *Jack London and His Times: An Unconventional Biography* (Seattle, 1968), 216.

147. Boylan, *Revolutionary Lives,* 24.

148. Ibid., 80.

149. Ibid., 81–82.

150. Ibid., 133–35.

151. Ibid., 101.

152. Ibid.

153. Ibid., 107.

154. Ibid.

155. Ibid.

156. Ibid., 154.

157. Ibid., 218.

158. London, *Jack London,* 218.

CHAPTER 6

1. *Emanu-El,* September 6, 1907, 6.

2. Gladys C. Hansen and Emmet Condon, *Denial of Disaster: The Untold Story and Photographs of the San Francisco Earthquake of 1906* (San Francisco, 1989), 153.

3. J. B. Levison, *Memories for My Family* (San Francisco, 1933), 120.

4. Ibid., 122.

5. Jacob Voorsanger, "Relief Work in San Francisco after the 1906 Earthquake and Fire: An Overview," in *California: Earthquakes and Jews,* ed. William M. Kramer (Los Angeles, 1995), 194.

6. Ibid., 196.

7. Dan Kurzman, *Disaster! The Great San Francisco Earthquake and Fire of 1906* (New York, 2001), 230–31.

8. Voorsanger, "Relief Work in San Francisco," 196.

9. Kurzman, *Disaster!,* 129–31.

10. "Paul Sinsheimer's Letter on the San Francisco Earthquake-Fire of 1906," in Kramer, ed., *California: Earthquakes,* 165–66.

11. Philip L. Fradkin, *The Great Earthquake and Firestorms of 1906* (Berkeley, 2006), 74–79.

12. Kurzman, *Disaster!,* 122.

13. Ibid.

14. Harry Meyer, "Harry Meyer Remembers the Earthquake-Fire of 1906," in Kramer, *California: Earthquakes,* 151.

15. Bernard Kaplan in *Emanu-El,* May 11, 1906, 3.

16. Hansen and Condon, *Denial of Disaster,* 127.

17. *Emanu-El,* December 28, 1906, 4.

18. Rudolph I. Coffee, "Jewish Conditions after the Earthquake-Fire of 1906: An Overview," in Kramer, *California: Earthquakes,* 201.

19. *Emanu-El,* May 18, 1906, 3.

20. Ibid., May 4, 1906, 1.

21. Kurzman, *Disaster!,* 245.

22. *Emanu-El,* November 16, 1906, 3.

23. Ibid., April 19, 1907, 2.

24. Ibid., March 13, 1908, 1.

25. Ibid., August 24, 1908, 2.

26. Jacob Nieto, "Nieto's San Francisco Protest and Appeal," in *Sephardic Jews in the West Coast States, Volume I: San Francisco's Grandees,* ed. William M. Kramer (Los Angeles, 1996), 228.

27. *Emanu-El,* June 8, 1906, 2.

28. Ibid., August 10, 1906, 1; July 13, 1906, 1.

29. Ibid., August 17, 1906, 1–2.

30. Kevin Starr, *Americans and the California Dream, 1850–1915* (New York, 1973), 294.

31. *Emanu-El,* May 18, 1906, 8.

32. Starr, *Americans,* 294.

33. *Emanu-El,* September 6, 1907, 1.

34. *San Francisco Call,* August 8, 1906, 28.

35. Lately Thomas, *A Debonair Scoundrel: An Episode in the Moral History of San Francisco* (New York, 1962), 8.

36. Ibid.

37. Walton Bean, *Boss Ruef's San Francisco: The Story of the Union Labor Party, Big Business and the Graft Prosecution* (Berkeley, 1952), 1–2.

38. Thomas, *Debonair Scoundrel,* 10.

39. Ibid., 21.

40. Ibid., 205.

41. Bean, *Boss Ruef's San Francisco,* 38.

42. Fremont Older, *My Own Story* (New York, 1926), 69.

43. Ibid., 70.

44. Bean, *Boss Ruef's San Francisco,* 50–51.

45. Ibid., 75.

46. Ibid., 77.

47. Walton Bean and James J. Rawls, *California: An Interpretive History* (New York, 1983), 265.

48. Thomas, *Debonair Scoundrel,* 96, 107.

49. Bean, *Boss Ruef's San Francisco,* 202.

50. Thomas, *Debonair Scoundrel*, 230.

51. Bean, *Boss Ruef's San Francisco*, 203.

52. Thomas, *Debonair Scoundrel*, 231.

53. *Emanu-El*, January 31, 1908, 1–2.

54. Thomas, *Debonair Scoundrel*, 329.

55. Amy Steinhart Braden, *Child Welfare and Community Service* (Berkeley, 1965), 90.

56. Irene Narell, *Our City: The Jews of San Francisco* (San Diego, 1981), 291; Bean, *Boss Ruef's San Francisco*, 263.

57. Bean, *Boss Ruef's San Francisco*, 159, 304.

58. Frances Dinkelspiel, *Towers of Gold: How One Jewish Immigrant Named Isaias Hellman Created California* (New York, 2008), 276–77.

59. *Emanu-El*, June 7, 1907, 1.

60. Ibid., August 14, 1908, 5.

61. Ibid., September 13, 1907, 3.

62. Ibid., January 11, 1907, 2.

63. *The Liberator*, February 27, 1909, 4.

64. Ibid., December 12, 1908, 4.

65. *Emanu-El*, July 3, 1914, 5; August 7, 1914, 2, 62–63.

66. Ibid., October 15, 1909, 1.

67. Bean, *Boss Ruef's San Francisco*, 309.

68. *Emanu-El*, October 1, 1909, 5.

69. Ibid.

70. Thomas, *Debonair Scoundrel*, 361.

71. Scrapbooks, vol. 7, p. 46, in Harris Weinstock Papers, Bancroft Library, University of California, Berkeley.

72. Ibid.; *Emanu-El*, April 4, 1907, 2.

73. *Emanu-El*, July 19, 1907, 2.

74. Older, *My Own Story*, 162, 174, 179.

75. Ibid., 174.

76. Ibid., 162.

77. Ibid., 164–65.

78. Bean, *Boss Ruef's San Francisco*, 126; Yong Chen, *Chinese San Francisco: A Trans-Pacific Community* (Stanford, 2000), 165–66.

79. Chen, *Chinese San Francisco*, 182–83; Roger Daniels, *The Politics of Prejudice: The Anti-Japanese Movement in California and the Struggle for Japanese Exclusion* (Berkeley, 1962), 31–44.

80. *San Francisco Bulletin*, July 21, 1916.

81. Richard H. Frost, *The Mooney Case* (Stanford, 1968), 8, 80.

82. Ibid., 89.

83. Ibid., 61.

84. Older, *My Own Story*, 335.

85. Frost, *The Mooney Case,* 176.

86. Ibid., 174.

87. Ibid., 138.

88. Ibid., 180.

89. Curt Gentry, *Frame-up: The Incredible Case of Tom Mooney and Warren Billings* (New York, 1967), 193.

90. Frost, *The Mooney Case,* 75–76.

91. Ibid.

92. Estolv E. Ward, *The Gentle Dynamiter* (Palo Alto, Calif., 1983), 202.

93. Frost, *The Mooney Case,* 256.

94. Ibid., 199.

95. Ward, *Gentle Dynamiter,* 37; Richard H. Frost, telephone interview with the author, January 16, 2004.

96. Frost, *The Mooney Case,* 252; Ward, *Gentle Dynamiter,* 37.

97. Frost, *The Mooney Case,* 250.

98. Gentry, *Frame-up,* 86.

99. Frost, *The Mooney Case,* 256.

100. Ibid., 192.

101. Kenneth C. Wenzer, *Anarchists Adrift: Emma Goldman and Alexander Berkman* (Malden, Mass., 1996).

102. John Chalberg, *Emma Goldman: American Individualist* (New York, 1991), 30.

103. Frost, *The Mooney Case,* 47.

104. Ibid., 46–47.

105. Ibid., 45.

106. Emma Goldman, *Living My Life* (New York, 1970), 426.

107. Richard Drinnon, *Rebel in Paradise: A Biography of Emma Goldman* (Chicago, 1982), 126.

108. Ibid.

109. Goldman, *Living My Life,* 427.

110. Ibid., 577.

111. Ibid., 578.

112. Ibid., 577.

113. Ibid., 580.

114. *The Blast,* September 15, 1916, in *Life of an Anarchist: The Alexander Berkman Reader,* ed. Gene Fellner (New York, 1992), 139; Frost, *The Mooney Case,* 145–47.

115. Frost, *The Mooney Case,* 252.

116. Ibid., 284.

117. Quoted in ibid., 293.

118. Ibid., 300.

119. Ibid., 318.

120. David H. Bennett, *The Party of Fear: From Nativist Movements to the New Right in American History* (Chapel Hill, N.C., 1988), 193; John Higham, *Strangers in the Land: Patterns of American Nativism* (Westport, Conn., 1980), 278–79.

121. Stanley Feldstein, *The Land That I Show You: Three Centuries of Jewish Life in America* (Garden City, N.Y., 1978), 255–56.

122. Higham, *Strangers,* 279.

123. Eugene Block, "San Francisco Jews of East European Origin," oral history project of the WJHC/JLMM, 1976–77, Jill Lerner Hallinan, interviewer, tape 5.

124. Frost, *The Mooney Case,* 131n.

125. Frost, telephone interview.

126. *San Francisco Examiner,* November 15, 1917, 1.

127. Barry Pateman, associate editor of the Emma Goldman Papers, telephone interview with the author, January 18, 2004.

128. William M. Kramer and Robert J. Hoffman, "Congressman Julius Kahn of California," Part 2, *WSJH* 19 (January 1987): 144.

129. Ibid., 143.

130. Ibid., 144.

131. *Emanu-El,* September 21, 1917, 1.

132. Ibid., 8.

133. Kramer and Hoffman, "Congressman Julius Kahn," 143.

134. *Emanu-El,* September 14, 1917, 1; November 30, 1917, 1; December 13, 1918, 1.

135. Ibid., September 14, 1917, 12.

136. Ibid.

137. Ibid.

138. Ibid., June 22, 1917, 2.

139. Fred Rosenbaum, *Architects of Reform: Congregational and Community Leadership, Emanu-El of San Francisco, 1849–1980* (Berkeley, 1980), 68.

140. *Emanu-El,* June 22, 1917, 2.

141. *Emanu-El,* March 15, 1918, 2.

142. Ibid., October 27, 1916, 2.

143. Ibid., August 17, 1917, 2; March 30, 1917, 2.

144. Ibid., March 29, 1918, 10.

145. Ibid.

146. Ibid., March 27, 1908, 1.

CHAPTER 7

1. Sam Kohs, "San Francisco Jews of East European Origin," oral history project of the WJHC/JLMM, 1976–77, David Kagel, interviewer, tape 1.

2. Lee Shai Weissbach, "The Jewish Communities of the United States on the Eve of Mass Migration: Some Comments on Geography and Bibliography," *American Jewish History* 78 (September 1988): 84.

3. Ibid.

4. Arthur Goren, *New York Jews and the Quest for Community: The Kehilla Experiment, 1908–1922* (New York, 1970), 143.

5. Louis H. Blumenthal, *Report on the Recreational-Cultural Problem of the Jewish Community of San Francisco* (New York, 1923), 32–33.

6. "Articles of Incorporation of the International Society for the Colonization of Russian Jews," in Bancroft Library, University of California, Berkeley; Norton B. Stern, *Baja California: Jewish Refuge and Homeland* (Los Angeles, 1973), 11–17.

7. "The Occupation of Agriculture as a Means for the Betterment of the Condition of the Russian Jews" (San Francisco, 1891), p. 7, in Bancroft Library, University of California, Berkeley.

8. *Emanu-El,* May 21, 1897, 7; October 15, 1897, 6–7; June 24, 1904, 25; November 12, 1897, 5; Fred Rosenbaum, *Visions of Reform: Congregation Emanu-El and the Jews of San Francisco* (Berkeley, 2000), 94–95; *Emanu-El,* February 24, 1905, reprinted in *WSJHQ* 6 (July 1974): 278–89.

9. *Emanu-El,* June 17, 1904, 5.

10. Marc Lee Raphael, *Profiles in American Judaism: The Reform, Conservative, Orthodox, and Reconstructionist Movements in Historical Perspective* (San Francisco, 1984), 28.

11. *Emanu-El,* February 3, 1905, 2.

12. Frank Norris, *McTeague: A Story of San Francisco* (New York, 1982), 42–43.

13. *Emanu-El,* June 17, 1904, 5.

14. *Emanu-El,* August 24, 1904, 5.

15. *Western Jewry: An Account of the Achievements of the Jews and Judaism in California* (San Francisco, 1916), 124; "No Ghetto in San Francisco—1903," *Hebrew,* October 2, 1903, 4, reprinted in *WSJHQ* 15 (October 1982): 21.

16. Quoted in Michael M. Zarchin, *Glimpses of Jewish Life in San Francisco* (Berkeley, 1952), 168.

17. *Western Jewry,* 32.

18. Barbara S. Rogers and Stephen M. Dobbs, *The First Century: Mount Zion Hospital and Medical Center, 1887–1997* (San Francisco, 1987), 42–43.

19. Robert A. Rockaway, *Words of the Uprooted: Jewish Immigrants in Early Twentieth-Century America* (Ithaca, N.Y., 1998).

20. Industrial Removal Office Records (hereafter cited as IROR), 1899–1922, Library of the American Jewish Historical Society at the Center for Jewish History, New York, N.Y.

21. Ibid.

22. Max Vorspan and Lloyd P. Gartner, *History of the Jews of Los Angeles* (Philadelphia, 1970), 112.

23. "Ninth Annual Report of the Industrial Removal Office," 1909, IROR, p. 5.

24. Philip Wascerwitz, "Proceedings of District Grand Lodge #4 International Order of the B'nai Brith," San Francisco, 1904, in WJHC/JLMM.

25. Ibid.

26. Letter of Isaiah Choynski, March 7, 1905, in IROR, box 15, folder 4; box 93, folder 2.

27. IROR, 1899–1922.

28. "Report on the Employment Bureau," in the Minutes of the Executive Committee of the San Francisco Federation of Jewish Charities, September 1, 1918, in WJHC/JLMM.

29. Letter of Michael Goldwater, January 15, 1899, in *WSJHQ* 13 (January 1981): 160–67.

30. William Issel and Robert W. Cherny, *San Francisco, 1865–1932: Politics, Power, and Urban Development* (Berkeley, 1986), 53.

31. Ibid., 59.

32. Sol Bloom, *The Autobiography of Sol Bloom* (New York, 1948), 51.

33. K. M. Nesfield "The Jew in San Francisco," *Overland Monthly* 25 (April 1895): 465.

34. Judah L. Magnes and Lee K. Frankel, "San Francisco Jewry Following the Earthquake and Fire," in *California: Earthquakes and Jews,* ed. William M. Kramer (Los Angeles, 1995), 209.

35. Lilan Cherney, "San Francisco Jews," oral history project of the WJHC/JLMM, 1978, Yehudit Goldfarb, interviewer, tape 1.

36. Art Rosenbaum, "San Francisco Jews," oral history project of the WJHC/JLMM, 1977, Jane Field, interviewer, tape 2.

37. Zarchin, *Glimpses,* 129.

38. William M. (Ze'ev) Brinner, interview with the author, June 13, 2001.

39. Rosenbaum, "San Francisco Jews," tape 2.

40. Ibid.

41. Ibid.; Brinner, interview.

42. Brinner, interview.

43. Rosenbaum, "San Francisco Jews," tape 6.

44. Steven A. Leibo, "Out the Road: The San Bruno Avenue Jewish Community of San Francisco, 1901–1968," *WSJHQ* 11 (January 1979): 100.

45. George Edelstein, "San Francisco Jews," oral history project of the WJHC/JLMM, 1978, William S. Bregoff, interviewer, tape 1; Ida Block Smith, "San Francisco Jews," oral history project of the WJHC/JLMM, 1977, Steven A. Leibo, interviewer, tape 1.

46. Vivian Dudune Solomon, "San Francisco Jews," oral history project of the WJHC/JLMM, 1977, Ruth Kelson Rafael, interviewer, tape 1.

47. Leibo, "Out the Road," 103.

48. Jean Braverman–La Pove, "San Francisco Jews," oral history project of the WJHC/JLMM, 1977, Susan Green, interviewer, tape 2.

49. Leibo, "Out the Road," 106.

50. *Emanu-El,* September 7, 1934, 27.

51. Rosenbaum, *Visions,* 122.

52. Solomon, "San Francisco Jews," tape 1.

53. Ibid.

54. Ibid.

55. Ibid.

56. Jerry Flamm, *Good Life in Hard Times: San Francisco's '20s and '30s* (San Francisco, 1988), 72.

57. Ibid., 75–76.

58. Ibid., 80–83.

59. Ibid., 72.

60. Rosenbaum, "San Francisco Jews," tape 2.

61. Ibid.; Brinner, interview.

62. Rosenbaum, "San Francisco Jews," tape 3.

63. Ibid.

64. *Western Jewry,* 53–54.

65. Ibid., 219.

66. Moshe Menuhin, "Jewish Communal Education in San Francisco," *WSJH* 21 (January 1989): 100.

67. Humphrey Burton, *Yehudi Menuhin* (Boston, 2000), 30.

68. Zarchin, *Glimpses,* 172.

69. Brinner, interview.

70. Ibid.

71. Ibid.

72. Ibid.

73. Daniel Goldberg, "San Francisco Jews," oral history project of the WJHC/JLMM, 1977, Tess Schwartz, interviewer, tape 1.

74. George Karonsky, telephone interview with the author, March 26, 2001.

75. David Stolper Collection, in WJHC/JLMM.

76. Brinner, interview.

77. Ibid.

78. Rosenbaum, "San Francisco Jews," tape 5.

79. Ibid., tape 10.

80. Ibid., tape 5.

81. Ibid.

82. Ibid.

83. Ibid.

84. Brinner, interview.

85. Flamm, *Good Life in Hard Times*, 76–77; Reuben Waxman, "San Francisco Jews," oral history project of the WJHC/JLMM, 1976–77, Janet Mohr, interviewer, tapes 2–3.

86. Celia Alperth, "San Francisco Jews," oral history project of the WJHC/JLMM, 1976, Adele Donn, interviewer, tape 2.

87. Philip Bibel, "San Francisco Jews," oral history project of the WJHC/JLMM, 1978, Marcia Frank, interviewer, tape 1.

88. Letter of Philip Bibel in Philip Bibel Collection 67/47, in WJHC/JLMM.

89. Rosenbaum, *Visions*, 138, 151–52.

90. Bibel, "San Francisco Jews," tape 2.

91. Ibid.

92. Rosenbaum, *Visions*, 151–52.

93. Bibel, "San Francisco Jews," tape 3.

94. Ibid.

95. Ibid.

96. Zena Druckman, "San Francisco Jews," oral history project of the WJHC/JLMM, 1977, Sally Hanelin, interviewer, tape 2.

97. Bibel, "San Francisco Jews," tape 3.

98. Marvin Lowenthal Collection 67/7, in WJHC/JLMM.

99. Michael Zarchin, *Glimpses of Jewish Life in San Francisco*, 2nd rev. ed. (Berkeley, 1964), 223.

100. Flamm, *Good Life in Hard Times*, 78.

101. Kenneth L. Kann, *Comrades and Chicken Ranchers: The Story of a California Jewish Community* (Ithaca, N.Y., 1993), 56.

102. Ibid., 56.

103. Brinner, interview; Kann, *Comrades and Chicken Ranchers*, 83.

104. Kann, *Comrades and Chicken Ranchers*, 236.

105. Ibid., 26.

106. *Emanu-El*, December 8, 1944, 4; Philip Naftaly, "Jewish Chicken Farmers in Petaluma, California 1904–1975," *WSJH* 23 (April 1991): 235n.

107. Kann, *Comrades and Chicken Ranchers*, 59.

108. Ibid., 199–220.

109. Brinner, interview.

110. Fred Rosenbaum, *Free to Choose: The Making of a Jewish Community in the American West* (Berkeley, 1976), 58.

111. Ibid., 59–60.

112. Ibid.

113. Ibid.

114. Ibid., 99.

115. Ibid., 61.

116. Ibid.

117. Ibid., 64–65.

118. Ibid., 65.

119. Minutes of Congregation Beth Jacob, quoted in ibid., 69.

120. Ibid.

121. Ibid., 70.

122. Ibid.

123. Ibid.; Waxman, "San Francisco Jews," tape 2.

124. Rosenbaum, *Free to Choose,* 70–71.

125. Rose Rinder, "Music, Prayer and Religious Leadership," 1971, 66, in Bancroft Library, Regional Oral History Office, University of California, Berkeley.

126. Ibid., 67.

127. Ibid.

128. Ibid., 19.

129. Quoted in ibid., 21–22.

130. Robert Magidoff, *Yehudi Menuhin: The Story of the Man and the Musician* (London, 1973), 35.

131. Yehudi Menuhin, *Unfinished Journey* (New York, 1976), 29, 33.

132. Burton, *Yehudi Menuhin,* 29.

133. Magidoff, *Yehudi Menuhin,* 48.

134. Ibid., 53.

135. Quoted in ibid.

136. Menuhin, *Unfinished Journey,* 59.

137. Terry Teachout, "The Riddle of Yehudi Menuhin," *Commentary* III (June 2001): 54.

138. *Emanu-El,* September 23, 1938, 15.

139. Teachout, "The Riddle of Yehudi Menuhin," 55; Burton, *Yehudi Menuhin,* 262.

140. *San Francisco Jewish Bulletin,* October 31, 1947, 8.

141. Burton, *Yehudi Menuhin,* 508.

142. Ibid.

143. "Population and Jewish Community Center Study, Oakland, California, 1951," Oakland, 1951, p. 22.

144. Rosenbaum, *Free to Choose,* 67.

145. Ibid.

146. Ibid., 68.

147. Samuel Moment, *The Jewish Population of San Francisco* (San Francisco, 1939), unpaged, in WJHC/JLMM.

148. Druckman, "San Francisco Jews," tape 2.

149. *Emanu-El,* September 27, 1935, 49.

150. Saul E. White, "San Francisco Jews," oral history project of the WJHC/JLMM, 1978, Jill Hallinan, interviewer, tape 1.

151. Ibid., tape 2.

152. Zarchin, *Glimpses* (1952 ed.), 164.

153. Rosenbaum, "San Francisco Jews," tape 6.

154. Jacob Voorsanger, *Emanu-El,* August 26, 1904, 5.

CHAPTER 8

1. Alma Lavenson Wahrhaftig, oral history interview conducted by Elinor Mandelson for the WJHC/JLMM, 1978–80, p. 18; Bernice Scharlach, *House of Harmony: Concordia-Argonaut's First 130 Years* (Berkeley, 1983), 93–94.

2. Stephen Birmingham, *Our Crowd: The Great Jewish Families of New York* (New York, 1967), 15.

3. Fred Rosenbaum, *Visions of Reform: Congregation Emanu-El and the Jews of San Francisco* (Berkeley, 2000), 141; David Kaufman, *Shul with a Pool: The "Synagogue-Center" in American Jewish History* (Hanover, N.H., 1999), 244.

4. Rosenbaum, *Visions,* 142.

5. Arthur Brown Jr., "Building a Temple," *Pacific Coast Architect* 30 (September 1926): 31.

6. Harris Allen, "Sermons Cast in Stone," *Pacific Coast Architect* 30 (September 1926): 10.

7. Louis I. Newman, "The New Temple Emanu-El of San Francisco," *Pacific Coast Architect* 30 (September 1926): 55.

8. *Temple Chronicle of Temple Emanu-El* (San Francisco), February 27, 1925.

9. Irena Narrel, *Our City: The Jews of San Francisco* (San Diego, 1981), 322.

10. Rosenbaum, *Visions,* 155–57.

11. Reuben R. Rinder, "The Society for the Advancement of Synagogue Music: Its Aims and Scope," in Reuben R. Rinder Collection, in WJHC/JLMM.

12. Ruth Rafael, "Ernest Bloch at the San Francisco Conservatory of Music," *WSJHQ* 9 (April 1977): 195.

13. Ibid., 201.

14. Alfred Frankenstein, quoted in ibid., 202.

15. Ibid.

16. David Ewen, quoted in ibid.

17. Quoted in ibid., 213.

18. Ibid.

19. Ibid., 207.

20. Ernest Bloch's letters to Reuben Rinder, November 26, 1930, and March 5, 1931, in Reuben R. Rinder Collection, in WJHC/JLMM.

21. Rose Rinder, "Music, Prayer and Religious Leadership," 1971, p. 51, in Bancroft Library Regional Oral History Office, University of California, Berkeley.

22. Alfred Frankenstein, *San Francisco Chronicle,* March 29, 1938, 14.

23. Ernest Bloch's letter to Reuben Rinder, May 18, 1938, in Letters of Ernest Bloch, Music Library, University of California, Berkeley.

24. Rosenbaum, *Visions*, 162.

25. Ibid., 160.

26. Narell, *Our City: The Jews of San Francisco* (San Diego, 1981), 336.

27. Ibid., 209.

28. Frances Bransten Rothmann, *The Haas Sisters of Franklin Street: A Look Back with Love* (Berkeley, 1979), 24.

29. Ibid.

30. Marshall Kuhn, "Catalyst and Teacher: San Francisco Jewish and Communal Leader, 1934–1978," oral history typescript, WJHC/JLMM, 1978, p. 187.

31. Louis Heilbron, interview by Anita Hecht for Congregation Emanu-El, May 21, 1998, in Congregation Emanu-El, San Francisco, California.

32. Quoted in Rosenbaum, *Visions*, 154.

33. Ibid., 129, 151–52.

34. *Temple Chronicle of Temple Emanu-El* (San Francisco), August 16, 1929.

35. Ibid.

36. Rosenbaum, *Visions*, 155.

37. Birmingham, *Our Crowd*, 403–4.

38. Scharlach, *House of Harmony*, 80, 90.

39. Quoted in ibid., 90.

40. Quoted in ibid., 93–94.

41. Michael Zarchin, *Glimpses of Jewish Life in San Francisco*, 2nd rev. ed. (Berkeley, 1964), 36; Leo Eloesser Collection, Bancroft Library, University of California, Berkeley.

42. Fred Rosenbaum, *Free to Choose: The Making of a Jewish Community in the American West* (Berkeley, 1976), 28–32.

43. Wahrhaftig, oral history transcript, 48.

44. Patricia G. Fuller, *Alma Lavenson* (Riverside, Calif., 1979), 7.

45. *Emanu-El*, January 12, 1934, 5.

46. Carol Green Wilson, *Gump's Treasure Trade: A Story of San Francisco* (New York, 1949), 179.

47. *Emanu-El*, May 5, 1927, 3.

48. "Levi Strauss and Company: Tailors to the World," interviews with Levi Strauss executives Walter A. Haas, Sr., Daniel E. Koshland, Walter A. Haas Jr., and Peter E. Haas, 1976, p. 3, Bancroft Library, Regional Oral History Office, University of California, Berkeley.

49. Ibid., 14.

50. Narell, *Our City*, 343.

51. "Levi Strauss and Company," 14.

52. Ibid., 16.

53. Narell, *Our City,* 341.

54. Quoted in William Issel and Robert W. Cherny, *San Francisco, 1865–1932: Politics, Power, and Urban Development* (Berkeley, 1986), 34.

55. John E. McCosker, *The History of Steinhart Aquarium* (Virginia Beach, Va., 1999), 15.

56. Ibid., 16.

57. Ibid., 17.

58. Narell, *Our City,* 237–38.

59. Jerry Flamm, *Good Life in Hard Times: San Francisco's '20s and '30s* (San Francisco, 1989), 105.

60. Quoted in ibid.

61. Ibid.

62. San Francisco Zoo, "About the Zoo: History," www.sfzoo.org/about/gen History.htm (accessed 2003).

63. *Emanu-El,* September 27, 1935, 5.

64. Ibid.

65. Rhoda H. Goldman, remarks upon receiving Lehrhaus Judaica's Genesis Award for community service, November 7, 1993, San Francisco, California.

66. *Emanu-El,* September 27, 1935, 5.

67. *Emanu-El,* November 13, 1903, 6.

68. Quoted in Rosenbaum, *Free to Choose,* 76.

69. Ibid., 81.

70. Minutes of the Executive Committee of the San Francisco Federation of Jewish Charities, 1921, in WJHC/JLMM.

71. *Emanu-El,* February 4, 1916, 2.

72. Rosenbaum, *Free to Choose,* 84.

73. Ibid., 85.

74. Ibid.

75. Michael M. Zarchin, *Glimpses of Jewish Life in San Francisco* (Berkeley, 1952), 145.

76. Ibid., 149–50.

77. *Emanu-El,* April 15, 1927, 11; Lin Weber, *Under the Vine and Fig Tree: The Jews of the Napa Valley* (St. Helena, Calif., 2003), 71, 74.

78. Narell, *Our City,* 304.

79. Leon Harris, *Merchant Princes: An Intimate History of Jewish Families Who Built Great Department Stores* (New York, 1980), 229.

80. Narell, *Our City,* 404.

81. Ibid.

82. Harris, *Merchant Princes,* 229.

83. Narell, *Our City,* 404.

84. Ibid.

85. Ibid., 405.

86. *Emanu-El,* October 1, 1926, 2; September 9, 1927, 1.

87. Rosenbaum, *Free to Choose,* 91.

88. *Emanu-El,* September 27, 1935, 50; Narell, *Our City,* 239.

89. *Emanu-El,* October 14, 1932, 3.

90. Rosenbaum, *Visions,* 154.

91. *Emanu-El,* April 15, 1927, 11.

92. *San Francisco Examiner,* November 13, 1929, 5.

93. Rosenbaum, *Free to Choose,* 93.

94. *Emanu-El,* December 2, 1927, 1; Felicia Herman, "Jewish Leaders and the Motion Picture Industry," in *California Jews,* ed. Ava F. Kahn and Marc Dollinger (Hanover, N.H., 2003), 100.

95. *Emanu-El,* December 9, 1927, 5.

96. Kenneth C. Zwerin, "A Rabbinical Tragedy," *WSJHQ* 15 (January 1983): 167.

97. Quoted in ibid., 168–69.

98. Ibid.

99. Ibid.

100. Zarchin, *Glimpses* (1952 ed.), 17.

101. Zwerin, "A Rabbinical Tragedy," 170.

102. *Emanu-El,* June 29, 1923, 1.

103. Eugene Block, interview with the author, 1978.

104. Rosenbaum, *Visions,* 134.

105. Rudolph Coffee in Daniel J. Moscowitz, "Martin A. Meyer: His Life and its Lessons," Part 1, *WSJH* 26 (April 1994): 213.

106. Ibid.

107. Ibid., Part 2, *WSJH* 24 (July 1994): 350.

108. Narell, *Our City,* 408; Block, interview.

109. Louis Heilbron, interview with the author, October 25, 1997.

110. Louis Freehof, interview with the author, 1978; Rosenbaum, *Visions,* 135, 446n.

111. David G. Dalin, "Jewish and Non-Partisan Republicanism in San Francisco, 1911–1963," in *The Jews of the West: The Metropolitan Years,* ed. Moses Rischin (Berkeley, 1979), 116.

112. Ibid.

113. *San Francisco Chronicle,* November 17, 1948, 1.

114. "The Military Congresswoman," *Jewish Tribune,* December 28, 1928, 1.

115. Julius Kahn and Family Collection, WJHC/JLMM, 75–9 Box 1.

116. *San Francisco Chronicle,* November 17, 1948, 3.

117. John J. McGrath, letter to the editor, *Today,* September 21, 1935, 1.

118. "No Wonder California Is Proud of Congresswoman Florence Prag Kahn," *Pacific Coast Independent Exhibitor,* February 15, 1928, 10.

119. Michael Harris, "The Famous Widows of Congress," *San Francisco Chronicle,* April 12, 1983, 2.

120. Dalin, "Jewish and Non-Partisan Republicanism," 116.

121. B. J. Feigenbaum, oral history in "Earl Warren's Campaigns: Oral History Transcripts and Related Material, 1969–1976," vol. 2, p. 41, in Bancroft Library, Regional Oral History Office, University of California, Berkeley.

122. Dalin, "Jewish and Non-Partisan Republicanism," 122–24.

123. Ibid.

124. Ibid., 124–25.

125. Earl Raab, quoted in ibid., 123–24.

126. John H. Steinhart, oral history in "Earl Warren's Campaigns: Oral History Transcripts and Related Material, 1969–1976," vol. 2, p. 53, in Bancroft Library, Regional Oral History Office, University of California, Berkeley.

127. Ibid.

128. Feigenbaum in "Earl Warren's Campaigns," vol. 2, 58.

129. Elinor Raas Heller, oral history in "A Volunteer Career in Politics, in Higher Education and on Governing Boards," 1984, pp. 230–31, in Bancroft Library, Regional Oral History Office, University of California, Berkeley.

130. Oscar Lewis, *To Remember Albert (Micky) Bender: Notes for a Biography* (Oakland, 1973).

131. Kevin Starr, *The Dream Endures: California Enters the 1940s* (Oxford, 1997), 129.

132. Ibid., 214.

133. Wahrhaftig, oral history transcript, 60.

134. Anthony W. Lee, *Painting on the Left: Diego Rivera, Radical Politics, and San Francisco's Public Murals* (Berkeley, 1999), 54–56.

135. Ibid., 58.

136. Ibid., 62–63.

137. Lewis, *To Remember Albert (Micky) Bender,* 25.

138. Ibid., 18.

139. Starr, *The Dream Endures,* 129.

140. Ibid.

141. Ibid.

142. Ibid.

143. Ibid., 125.

CHAPTER 9

1. Max Vorspan and Lloyd P. Gartner, *History of the Jews of Los Angeles* (Philadelphia, 1970), 193.

2. Beth S. Wenger, *New York Jews and the Great Depression: Uncertain Promise* (New Haven, Conn.), 15–17.

3. *Emanu-El,* September 30, 1932, 16.

4. Ibid.

5. Ibid.

6. *Emanu-El,* December 2, 1932, 1.

7. Ed Cray, *Levi's* (Boston, 1978), 84.

8. *Emanu-El,* June 8, 1934, 1.

9. Robert E. Burke, *Olson's New Deal for California* (Westport, Conn., 1982), 212.

10. Barbara S. Rogers and Stephen M. Dobbs, *The First Century: Mount Zion Hospital and Medical Center, 1887–1987* (San Francisco, 1987), 77.

11. Janice J. Feldstein, *Rabbi Jacob J. Weinstein: Advocate of the People* (New York, 1980), 22–24.

12. Ibid., 45, 51.

13. Michael M. Zarchin, *Glimpses of Jewish Life in San Francisco* (San Francisco, 1952), 92.

14. Feldstein, *Rabbi Jacob J. Weinstein,* 46.

15. *Jewish Journal,* February 10, 1932, 4.

16. Feldstein, *Rabbi Jacob J. Weinstein,* 47.

17. Ibid.

18. Zarchin, *Glimpses,* 92.

19. Feldstein, *Rabbi Jacob J. Weinstein,* 48.

20. Ibid., 49.

21. Ibid., 49; Jacob Weinstein Collection, Papers, 1930–1940 (photocopies from the Chicago Historical Society), in WJHC/JLMM.

22. *Emanu-El,* June 3, 1932, 7.

23. Feldstein, *Rabbi Jacob J. Weinstein,* 51.

24. Jacob Weinstein, "A Rabbi's Farewell," *Life and Letters* 7 (November 1932): 8.

25. Feldstein, *Rabbi Jacob J. Weinstein,* 60

26. *Emanu-El,* September 27, 1935, 6.

27. Feldstein, *Rabbi Jacob J. Weinstein,* 61. The Institute for Jewish Studies soon closed, and adult Jewish education would not revive on that scale for another generation.

28. Ibid., 50.

29. Irving Reichert, "Getting Back to Fundamentals," April 4, 1952, in *Judaism and the American Jew: Selected Sermons and Addresses of Irving Frederick Reichert* (San Francisco, 1953), 9.

30. Ibid.

31. Reichert, "The Duty of Hating," May 1, 1937, in ibid., 73.

32. Reichert, "The Spoken Word as Part of Worship," January 15, 1937, in ibid., 19, 24.

33. Fred Rosenbaum, *Visions of Reform: Congregation Emanu-El and the Jews of San Francisco, 1849–1999* (Berkeley, 2000), 184.

34. Kevin Starr, *Endangered Dreams: The Great Depression in California* (New York, 1996), 77.

35. Ibid., 149.

36. *San Francisco Chronicle,* November 30, 1933, 1.

37. Ibid.

38. William Issel, "Jews and Catholics against Prejudice," in *California Jews,* ed. Ava F. Kahn and Marc Dollinger (Hanover, N.H., 2003), 124.

39. Rosenbaum, *Visions,* 188.

40. "Bernard Zakheim," ed. Gene Hailey, Abstract from *California Art Research* 20, part 2 (W.P.A. Project 2874) (San Francisco, 1937), 37–39.

41. Ibid., 47.

42. Ibid., 50.

43. Ibid., 54.

44. Ibid., 53.

45. Ibid., 61.

46. Anthony W. Lee, *Painting on the Left: Diego Rivera, Radical Politics, and San Francisco's Public Murals* (Berkeley, 1999), 143.

47. Ibid., 130.

48. Ibid., 135.

49. Ibid.

50. Ibid., 145.

51. "Bernard Zakheim," vol. 20, part 2, p. 71.

52. Masha Zakheim Jewett, *Coit Tower, San Francisco: Its History and Art* (San Francisco, 1983), 50.

53. Lee, *Painting on the Left,* 135.

54. Ibid., 181.

55. William M. (Ze'ev) Brinner, interview with the author, June 13, 2001.

56. Vorspan and Gartner, *Jews of Los Angeles,* 201–3.

57. Louis Goldblatt, "Louis Goldblatt: Working Class Leader in the ILWU, 1935–1977," 1980, p. iii, in Bancroft Library, Regional Oral History Office, University of California, Berkeley.

58. Bruce Nelson, *Workers on the Waterfront: Seamen, Longshoremen, and Unionism in the 1930s* (Urbana, Ill., 1988), 108.

59. Ibid.; "Darcy, Sam," in *Biographical Dictionary of the American Left,* ed. Bernard K. Johnpoll and Harvey Klehr (Westport, Conn., 1986), 82–83.

60. Quoted in Lee, *Painting on the Left,* 102.

61. Nelson, *Workers on the Waterfront,* 110.

62. Vivian Ranieri, *The Life and Times of Elaine Black Yoneda* (New York, 1991), 68.

63. Ibid., 91.

64. Ann Schofield, "Introduction," in Rose Pesotta, *Bread upon the Waters,* ed. Nicholas Beffel (Ithaca, N.Y., 1987), vii.

65. Ibid., ix; Elaine J. Leeder, *The Gentle General: Rose Pesotta, Anarchist and Labor Organizer* (Albany, N.Y., 1993).

66. Pesotta, *Bread upon the Waters,* 74–75.

67. Ibid., 76.

68. Ibid., 89.

69. Kenneth L. Kann, *Comrades and Chicken Ranchers: The Story of a California Jewish Community* (Ithaca, N.Y., 1993), 91.

70. Starr, *Endangered Dreams,* 113.

71. Ibid., 112.

72. *Emanu-El,* July 20, 1934, 1.

73. Ibid., 8; Starr, *Endangered Dreams,* 92.

74. Constance Coiner, *Better Red: The Writing and Resistance of Tillie Olsen and Meridel LeSueur* (New York, 1995).

75. Tillie Lerner, "Thousand Dollar Vagrant," *New Republic* 25, August 29, 1934, 69.

76. Tillie Lerner, "The Strike," *Partisan Review* 1 (September–October 1934): 3–9, reprinted in Jack Salzman and Barry Wallenstein, eds., *Years of Protest: A Collection of American Writings of the 1930's* (New York, 1967), 141.

77. Starr, *Endangered Dreams,* 108.

78. Ibid., 150.

79. Greg Mitchell, *The Campaign of the Century: Upton Sinclair's Race for the Governor of California and the Birth of Media Politics* (New York, 1992), 169.

80. Ibid., 275.

81. Walton Bean and James J. Rawls, *California: An Interpretive History* (New York, 1983), 343.

82. Starr, *Endangered Dreams,* 148.

83. *Emanu-El,* September 21, 1934, 6.

84. Quoted in Starr, *Endangered Dreams,* 150.

85. *Emanu-El,* October 21, 1934, 1, 8.

86. Ibid.

87. Elinor Raas Heller, oral history, "A Volunteer Career in Politics, in Higher Education and on Governing Boards," 1984, p. 81, in Bancroft Library, Regional Oral History Office, University of California, Berkeley.

88. Starr, *Endangered Dreams,* 147–48. According to Starr, the novelist "had edged into anti-Semitism." Ibid., 148. But a recent biography points out that he similarly skewered other groups, such as the Mormons and the British aristocracy. Moreover, his large body of fiction contains many Jewish characters portrayed in a favorable light. Anthony Arthur, *Radical Innocent: Upton Sinclair* (New York, 2000), 187–88, 247–48.

89. *Emanu-El,* August 10, 1934, 8.

90. Starr, *Endangered Dreams,* 161.

91. *Emanu-El,* September 7, 1934, 4.

92. Kann, *Comrades and Chicken Ranchers,* 103.

93. Ibid., 112–13.

94. Ibid., 106–7.

95. Ibid., 114.

96. *Emanu-El,* August 30, 1935, 1.

97. Helen Arnstein Salz, oral history, "Sketches of an Improbable Ninety Years," 1973–75, p. 104, Bancroft Library, Regional Oral History Office, University of California, Berkeley.

98. Ibid., 106.

99. Stephen Schwartz, *From West to East: California and the Making of the American Mind* (New York, 1998), 329.

100. Ibid., 285.

101. Irena Narell, *Our City: The Jews of San Francisco* (San Diego, 1981), 382.

102. Gregg Herken, *Brotherhood of the Bomb: The Tangled Lives and Loyalties of Robert Oppenheimer, Ernest Lawrence, and Edward Teller* (New York, 2002), 122.

103. Edith A. Jenkins, *Against a Field Sinister: Memoirs and Stories* (San Francisco, 1991), 24.

104. J. L. Heilbron and Robert W. Seidel, *Lawrence and His Laboratory: A History of the Lawrence Berkeley Laboratory* (Berkeley, 1989), 251.

105. Kai Bird and Martin J. Sherwin, *American Prometheus: The Triumph and Tragedy of J. Robert Oppenheimer* (New York, 2006), 9–10.

106. Ibid., 106, 172–75.

107. Ibid., 120; Herken, *Brotherhood of the Bomb,* 31, 59.

108. F. David Peat, *Infinite Potential: The Life and Times of David Bohm* (Boston, 1996), 1.

109. Hashomer Hatzair Collection, in WJHC/JLMM.

110. Herken, *Brotherhood of the Bomb,* 93.

111. Ibid., 144.

112. Ibid.

113. Ibid., 297.

114. Bird and Sherwin, *American Prometheus,* 627n; Jerrold and Leona Schecter, *Sacred Secrets: How Soviet Intelligence Operations Changed American History* (Washington, D.C., 2002).

115. Bird and Sherwin, *American Prometheus,* 627n.

116. Ibid.

117. Schwartz, *From East to West,* 300.

118. Goldblatt, *Louis Goldblatt,* 291.

119. Peat, *Infinite Potential,* 58.

120. Schwartz, *From East to West,* 290.

121. Jenkins, *Against a Field Sinister,* 18, 27.

122. John van der Zee, *The Gate: The True Story of the Design and Construction of the Golden Gate Bridge* (New York, 1986), 31.

123. Ibid., 20.

124. Ibid., 40.

125. Starr, *Endangered Dreams,* 331–32.

126. Van der Zee, *The Gate,* 309.

127. Ibid., 92.

128. Ibid., 113.

129. Ibid., 232.

130. Starr, *Endangered Dreams,* 328.

131. Jacques Schnier, "Jacques Schnier," in *There Was Light: Autobiography of a University: Berkeley, 1868–1970,* ed. Irving Stone (Garden City, N.Y., 1970), 98.

132. Jacques Schnier, oral history, "A Sculptor's Odyssey," 1987, p. 163, Bancroft Library, Regional Oral History Office, University of California, Berkeley.

133. Ibid., 8.

134. Schnier, "Jacques Schnier," 92–93.

135. Schnier, "A Sculptor's Odyssey," 56–60.

136. Ibid., 93.

137. Ibid., 107.

138. Schnier, "Jacques Schnier," 98.

139. Starr, *Endangered Dreams,* 340–41.

140. Carol Green Wilson, *Gump's Treasure Trade: A Story of San Francisco* (New York, 1949), 227.

141. Ibid., 212.

142. Schnier, "A Sculptor's Odyssey," 150.

143. Starr, *Endangered Dreams,* 352.

CHAPTER 10

1. *San Francisco Chronicle,* April 25, 1943, 6; Marilynn S. Johnson, *The Second Gold Rush: Oakland and the East Bay in World War II* (Berkeley, 1993).

2. *Emanu-El,* January 2, 1942, 2; February 20, 1942, 3.

3. Ibid., April 10, 1942, 3.

4. Ibid., October 29, 1943, 2.

5. Ibid., April 14, 1933, 4.

6. Ibid., May 5, 1933, 2.

7. Ibid., December 15, 1933, 1.

8. Ibid.

9. Irving Reichert, "The New Year and the Nazi Terror," September 20, 1933, in *Judaism and the American Jew: Selected Sermons and Addresses of Irving Frederick Reichert* (San Francisco, 1953), 9.

10. Ibid.

11. Ibid., 120.

12. *Emanu-El,* May 25, 1934, 6.

13. Reichert, "The New Year and the Nazi Terror," 117.

14. *Emanu-El,* April 27, 1934, 3.

15. Ibid.

16. Ibid., April 27, 1934, 3.

17. Ibid., April 20, 1934, 1.

18. Fred Rosenbaum, *Visions of Reform: Congregation Emanu-El and the Jews of San Francisco* (Berkeley, 2000), 189–90.

19. *Emanu-El,* November 17, 1933, 1; March 9, 1934, 1; May 26, 1933, 4; June 2, 1933, 5.

20. Ibid., December 15, 1933, 1.

21. Lawrence J. Friedman, *Identity's Architect: A Biography of Erik H. Erikson* (New York, 1999), 160.

22. Rosenbaum, *Visions,* 177–78.

23. *San Francisco Committee for Service to Emigres, January 1936–June 1941* (San Francisco, 1941), in Sanford Treguboff, "Administration of Jewish Philanthropy in San Francisco," 1988, p. 204, Bancroft Library, Regional Oral History Office, University of California, Berkeley.

24. Ibid.

25. Ibid., 208.

26. Ibid., 34.

27. Ibid., 36, 209.

28. Ibid., 34.

29. Eugene Block, "San Francisco Jews of East European Origin," oral history project of the WJHC/JLMM, 1976–77, Jill Lerner Hallinan, interviewer, tape 4.

30. Eugene Block, interview with the author, 1978.

31. *San Francisco Jewish Community Bulletin,* May 31, 1946, 8.

32. Fred Rosenbaum, *Free to Choose, The Making of a Jewish Community in the American West* (Berkeley, 1976), 100–101.

33. Ibid., 99.

34. Gulie Ne'eman Arad, *America, Its Jews, and the Rise of Nazism* (Bloomington, Ind., 2000), 103–224; Haskell Lookstein, *Were We Our Brothers' Keepers? The Public Response of American Jews to the Holocaust* (New York, 1985).

35. *Emanu-El,* June 19, 1942, 2.

36. Ibid., December 11, 1942, 2.

37. Ibid., July 3, 1942, 4.

38. Ibid., December 26, 1941, 5.

39. Ibid., July 28, 1944, 1.

40. Ibid.

41. Ibid., January 16, 1942, 1.

42. Ibid., January 30, 1943, 2.

43. Ibid., March 27, 1942.

44. *San Francisco Examiner,* July 1, 1941, 1, 6; *San Francisco Chronicle,* July 1, 1941, 5.

45. *San Francisco Examiner,* July 1, 1941, 10.

46. Arad, *America, Its Jews, and the Rise of Nazism,* 212.

47. *San Francisco Examiner,* July 1, 1941, 6.

48. Ibid.

49. *Emanu-El,* October 17, 1941, 2.

50. Ibid., September 26, 1941, 8.

51. Ibid., 5.

52. Ibid., January 17, 1941, 3.

53. Ibid., March 3, 1944, 2.

54. Ibid., January 17, 1941, 3.

55. Ibid., March 27, 1942, 3.

56. Ibid., October 9, 1942, 3.

57. Ibid., August 14, 1942, 3.

58. Ibid., August 28, 1942, 3.

59. Ibid., November 28, 1941, 3.

60. Ibid., May 15, 1942, 3.

61. Ibid., August 28, 1942, 3.

62. "Mass Meeting Against Nazi Extermination of Jews and Other Minorities, June 17, 1943," made available to the author by William M. (Ze'ev) Brinner.

63. William M. (Ze'ev) Brinner, interview with the author, June 13, 2001.

64. *San Francisco Examiner,* June 18, 1943, 7.

65. Brinner, interview.

66. *Emanu-El,* June 11, 1943, 2.

67. *New York Times,* June 18, 1943, 14.

68. *Emanu-El,* September 6, 1942, 2.

69. Ibid., October 20, 1943, 1; December 19, 1941, 2.

70. Earl Raab, "There's No City Like San Francisco," *Commentary* 10 (October 1950): 373.

71. Ibid.

72. Ibid., 372.

73. Irving Reichert, "One Reform Rabbi Replies to Ludwig Lewisohn," January 11, 1936, *in Judaism and the American Jew,* 133.

74. Ibid., 132.

75. Ibid.

76. *Emanu-El,* January 24, 1936, 12.

77. Rosenbaum, *Visions,* 195.

78. *Temple Chronicle of Temple Emanu-El* (San Francisco), October 9, 1942; Samuel Halperin, *The Political World of American Zionism* (Detroit, 1961), 78.

79. Thomas A. Kolsky, *Jews against Zionism: The American Council for Judaism, 1942–1948* (Philadelphia, 1990).

80. Records of the American Council for Judaism, San Francisco Section in WJHC/JLMM, 1943.

81. Ibid.

82. Reichert, "Where Do You Stand?" May 1, 1937, in *Selected Sermons and Addresses,* 142.

83. Rose Rinder, interview with the author, 1978.

84. Ibid.

85. Kolsky, *Jews against Zionism,* 246; Records of the American Council for Judaism, San Francisco Section in WJHC/JLMM.

86. Records of the American Council for Judaism; Fred Rosenbaum, "Zionism vs. Anti-Zionism: The State of Israel Comes to San Francisco," in *Jews of the West,* ed. Moses Rischin and John Livingston (Detroit, 1991), 123.

87. Rosenbaum, *Free to Choose,* 110.

88. Quoted in ibid., 124.

89. *Emanu-El,* February 18, 1944, 2.

90. Ibid., November 19, 1943, 2.

91. Ibid., January 15, 1943, 2; January 22, 1943, 2; October 13, 1944, 2.

92. Ibid., November 6, 1942, 3.

93. Saul E. White, "San Francisco Jews," oral history project of the WJHC/JLMM, 1978, Jill Lerner Hallinan, interviewer, tape 2; Saul White, interview with the author, 1978.

94. *Emanu-El,* January 16, 1942, 3.

95. *San Francisco Jewish Community Bulletin,* March 8, 1946, 1.

96. Ibid.

97. *Emanu-El,* September 15, 1945, 1.

98. Rita Semel, interview with the author, January 18, 2001.

99. White, "San Francisco Jews," tape 2.

100. Eugene Block, "San Francisco Jews," tape 4.

101. Morris Lowenthal Collection, 67/7, WJHC/JLMM.

102. *San Francisco Jewish Community Bulletin,* October 18, 1946, 1.

103. Ibid., December 12, 1947, 1.

104. Ibid., July 5, 1946, 1.

105. Harold Zellerbach, interview with the author, 1978; Louis Freehof, interview with the author, 1978.

106. Zellerbach, interview; Freehof, interview.

107. Gene K. Walker, "Report to the Board of Directors," May 15, 1947, typescript in the Temple Emanu-El Archives; Rosenbaum, *Visions,* 201–6.

108. Michael M. Zarchin, *Glimpses of Jewish Life in San Francisco* (San Francisco, 1952), 94.

109. Rosenbaum, "Zionism vs. Anti-Zionism," 125–29.

110. Marshall Kuhn, interview with the author, 1978.

111. *San Francisco Jewish Community Bulletin,* December 5, 1947, 8.

112. Rosenbaum, *Visions,* 215–49.

113. Douglas Henry Daniels, *Pioneer Urbanites: A Social and Cultural History of Black San Francisco* (Berkeley, 1990), 165.

114. Johnson, *The Second Gold Rush,* 93, 109, 169, 231.

115. Sam Ladar, oral history in *Earl Warren's Campaigns: Oral History Transcripts and Related Material, 1969–1976,* vol. 2, p. 77, in Bancroft Library, Regional Oral History Office, University of California, Berkeley.

116. Kevin Allen Leonard, "'Brothers Under the Skin?': African Americans, Mexican Americans and World War II in California," in *The Way We Really Were: The Golden State in the Second Great War,* ed. Roger W. Lotchin (Urbana, Ill., 2000), 199.

117. David Selvin, telephone interview with the author, March 18, 2003.

118. William Issel, "Jews and Catholics against Prejudice," in *California Jews,* ed. Ava F. Kahn and Marc Dollinger (Hanover, N.H., 2003), 129.

119. Ibid.

120. Johnson, *The Second Gold Rush,* 206; Selvin, telephone interview.

121. *San Francisco Jewish Community Bulletin,* March 9, 1945, 1; January 4, 1946, 2.

122. Ibid., quoted in Issel, "Jews and Catholics against Prejudice," 128.

123. *Emanu-El,* March 30, 1945, 15.

124. Issel, "Jews and Catholics against Prejudice," 124.

125. Rosenbaum, *Free to Choose,* 100.

126. Johnson, *The Second Gold Rush,* 169.

127. Frieda (Mrs. Harry) Sapper, interview with the author, 1975; Rae (Mrs. William) Stern, interview with the author, 1975.

128. Rosenbaum, *Free to Choose,* 100–101.

129. *Emanu-El,* December 19, 1941, 3; March 27, 1942, 5.

130. Kenneth L. Kann, *Comrades and Chicken Ranchers: The Story of a California Jewish Community* (Ithaca, N.Y., 1993), 142.

131. Brinner, interview.

132. Vivian Ranieri, *The Red Angel: The Life and Times of Elaine Black Yoneda* (New York, 1991), 199.

133. Ibid., 207–8.

134. Ibid., 199.

135. *Temple Chronicle of Temple Emanu-El* (San Francisco), December 19, 1941.

136. Selvin, telephone interview.

137. Ellen Eisenberg, "Civil Rights and Japanese American Incarceration," in *California Jews,* 119.

138. Ibid., 121.

139. Quoted in Ranieri, *Red Angel,* 197.

140. Louis Goldblatt, "Louis Goldblatt: Working Class Leader in the ILWU, 1935–1977," 1980, p. 292, in Bancroft Library, Regional Oral History Office, University of California, Berkeley.

141. Stephen Schwartz, *Brotherhood of the Sea: A History of the Sailors Union of the Pacific, 1885–1985* (San Francisco, 1986), 125.

142. Helen Arnstein Salz, oral history, "Sketches of an Improbable Ninety Years," 1973–75, p. 100, in Bancroft Library, Regional Oral History Office, University of California, Berkeley.

143. Address of Eric L. Muller at Congregation Emanu-El, October 19, 2001. See also Eric L. Muller, *Free to Die for Their Country: The Story of the Japanese American Draft Resisters in World War II* (Chicago, 2001).

144. *Emanu-El,* July 21, 1944, 2.

145. Ibid., September 29, 1944, 2.

146. Ibid.

147. Ibid., September 29, 1944, 2.

148. Ibid., December 24, 1944, 2.

149. Ibid., March 16, 1945, 2.

150. Zarchin, *Glimpses,* 53.

151. *San Francisco Chronicle,* October 1, 1940, 33.

152. Herb Caen, *Baghdad-by-the-Bay* (Garden City, N.Y., 1949).

153. *San Francisco Chronicle,* October 22, 1940.

154. Leslie Katz, "Herb Caen Thought All People Should Be Brothers," *Jewish Bulletin of Northern California,* February 7, 1997, 8.

155. Darius Milhaud, *My Happy Life* (London, 1994).

156. Rose Rinder, *Music, Prayer and Religious Leadership: Temple Emanu-El, 1913–1969,* Bancroft Library, Regional History Office 1971, p. 72.

157. Rosenbaum, *Visions,* 169.

158. Ibid.; Ludwig Altman, interview with the author, 1978.

159. *San Francisco Chronicle,* May 20, 1949, 8; *San Francisco Examiner,* May 20, 1949, 77.

160. Jan Heller Levi, telephone interview with the author, October 28, 2005; William Rukeyser, telephone interview with the author, October 7, 2005.

161. Levi, telephone interview; Rukeyser, telephone interview; Adrienne Rich, "Introduction," in *Muriel Rukeyser: Selected Poems,* ed. Adrienne Rich (New York, 2004), xix.

162. Rich, "Introduction," xvii.

163. Muriel Rukeyser, "The Outer Banks," in ibid., 147.

164. Rich, "Introduction," xx; Rukeyser, telephone interview.

165. Rukeyser, telephone interview; Stephen Schwartz, *From West to East: California and the Making of the American Mind* (New York, 1998), 382, 395.

166. William Phillips, Philip Rahv, and Delmore Schwartz, "Grandeur and Misery of a Poster Girl," *Partisan Review* 10 (September–October 1943): 472–73.

167. Levi, telephone interview.

168. Rukeyser, telephone interview.

169. Muriel Rukeyser, "Under Forty: A Symposium on American Literature and the Younger Generation of American Jews," *Contemporary Jewish Record* 7 (February 1944): 7.

170. Ibid.

171. Ibid., 8.

172. Ibid., 6.

173. Ibid., 8–9.

174. Muriel Rukeyser, "Beast in View," in *Muriel Rukeyser: Selected Poems,* 103.

175. Janet Kaufman, "But Not the Study: Writing as a Jew," in *How Shall We Tell Each Other of the Poet? The Life and Writing of Muriel Rukeyser,* ed. Anne F. Herzog and Janet E. Kaufman (New York, 1999), 47–48.

176. Rukeyser, "Under Forty," 6.

EPILOGUE

1. Earl Raab, "There's No City Like San Francisco," *Commentary* 10 (October 1950): 372.

2. Ibid., 373.

3. Ibid., 369.

4. *2004 Jewish Community Study/Full Findings* (San Francisco, 2005), 15.

5. Ibid. There were 228,000 Jews reported to be living in San Francisco, Marin, and Sonoma counties and the North and South Peninsula, 91 percent more than a similar study found in 1986. Assuming that the East Bay and greater San Jose, included in the earlier survey, also experienced growth rates of 91 percent—a conservative estimate, albeit one based on anecdotal evidence—those two regions would add an additional 183,000 Jews. Adding Napa and Solano counties would account for roughly 25,000 more. With a population of about 425,000 Jews, the Bay Area likely trails only New York, Los Angeles, South Florida, Tel Aviv, Jerusalem, and Haifa. Based on the data of the 2004 demographic survey, the Jewish weekly *j.* estimated the local Jewish population at 450,000, making it the third largest in the nation, ahead of South Florida. Joe Eskenazi, "And the Survey Says," *j.,* June 9, 2005, 1.

6. *American Jewish Year Book 1955* (Philadelphia, 1956), 171–81, 297.

7. *2004 Jewish Community Study,* 20; Fred Massarik, *The Jewish Population of San Francisco, Marin County and the Peninsula, 1970–1973* (San Francisco, 1974), 2; Population and Jewish Community Center Study, Oakland, California (Oakland, 1951), 16.

8. *2004 Jewish Community Study,* 18.

9. Ibid., 21.

10. Fred Rosenbaum, *Visions of Reform: Congregation Emanu-El and the Jews of San Francisco* (Berkeley, 2000), 266–67.

11. Winston Pickett, "Ninety Prominent Jews in Bay Area Criticize Israel—with Regrets," *Northern California Jewish Bulletin,* February 5, 1988, 1, 41.

12. Michael Lerner, "The Occupation: Immoral and Self-destructive," *Tikkun Online,* May 12, 2007, http://files.tikkun.org/current/article.php/20070611230447290/print (accessed 2007).

13. *2004 Jewish Community Study,* 116. For a national perspective, see Steven M. Cohen and Arnold M. Eisen, *The Jew Within: Self, Family, and Community in America* (Bloomington, Ind., 2000), 142–44.

14. Leo L. Honor, *Survey of Jewish Education in San Francisco* (San Francisco, 1938), 1–3; Gary A. Tobin and Sharon Sassler, *Bay Area Jewish Community Study, Special Report: Jewish Identity and Community Involvement* (Waltham, Mass., 1988), 112, 117.

15. Rosenbaum, *Visions,* 241–42.

16. Ibid., 429–32.

17. *2004 Jewish Community Study,* 70.

18. Laurence Kotler-Berkowitz, "The Jewish Education of Jewish Children," in *United Jewish Communities Report on the National Jewish Population Survey 2000–01* (New York, 2005), 8.

19. Natalie Weinstein, "Candid S.F. Leaders Recall Controversies," *Northern California Jewish Bulletin,* November 21, 1997, 48.

20. David Biale, ed., *Cultures of the Jews: A New History* (New York, 2002).

21. Daniel C. Matt, *The Zohar: Pritzker Edition* (Stanford, Calif., 2004).

22. Robert Alter, *The Five Books of Moses: A Translation with Commentary* (New York, 2004).

23. Hillel Halkin, "Feminizing Jewish Studies," *Commentary* (February 1998): 40.

24. Howard Eilberg-Schwartz, *God's Phallus and Other Problems for Men and Monotheism* (Boston, 1994).

25. Hillel Halkin, "Feminizing Jewish Studies," 44.

26. William M. Kramer, ed., *The Western Journal of Isaac Mayer Wise, 1877* (Berkeley, 1974), 61–62; Kenneth C. Zwerin, "Rabbi Jacob Nieto of Sherith Israel," Part 2, *WSJH* 18 (January 1986): 162.

27. Tobin and Sassler, *Bay Area Jewish Community Study,* 103–4; *2004 Jewish Community Study,* 54–55;

28. Jonathan Ament, "American Jewish Religious Denominations," in *United Jewish Communities Report,* 9.

29. *Resource: A Guide to Jewish Life in the Bay Area, 2006/5766* (San Francisco, 2005), 161–68.

30. Joe Eskenazi, "Rabbi Pinchas Lipner Seeks $10 Million for 'Defamation,'" *j.,* November 22, 2002, 1.

31. *2004 Jewish Community Study,* 53.

32. Ibid.

33. Ament, "American Jewish Religious Denominations," 9.

34. "California Rabbis Back Gay Vows," *Forward,* June 12, 1998, 1.

35. *2004 Jewish Community Study,* 76.

36. "Jews in the West," in *National Jewish Population Survey, 2000–01* (New York, 2001), 16.

37. Ibid., 20, 43; *2004 Jewish Community Study,* 80–83.

38. *2004 Jewish Community Study,* 56.

39. Gary A. Tobin and Patricia Y. C. E. Lin, *Religious and Spiritual Change in America: The Experience of Marin County, California* (San Francisco, 2002), 27.

40. Marc Dollinger, "The Counterculture," in *California Jews* (Hanover, N.H., 2003), 162.

41. Rodger Kamenetz, *The Jew in the Lotus* (San Francisco, 1994).

42. Ibid., 255.

43. Judith Linzer, *Torah and Dharma: Jewish Seekers in Eastern Religions* (Northvale, N.J., 1996), 2.

44. Marc Dollinger, "Counterculture," 156.

45. Wade Clark Roof, *A Generation of Seekers: The Spiritual Journeys of the Bay Boom Generation* (San Francisco, 1993), 63; Robert Wuthnow, *After Heaven: Spirituality in America since the 1950s* (Berkeley, 1998), 57.

46. Alan Lew, *One God Clapping: The Spiritual Path of a Zen Rabbi* (New York, 1999), 286.

47. Daniel Kohn, *Kinesthetic Kabbalah: Spiritual Practices from Martial Arts and Jewish Mysticism* (Charleston, S.C., 2004).

48. Alexandra Wall, "Minyan Fuses Tradition, Soul for Experimental Davening," *j.,* April 6, 2001, 15.

49. *Emanu-El,* June 2, 1922, 1; Nieto, writing in 1916, quoted in *Jewish Journal,* November 25, 1931, 3.

50. *2004 Jewish Community Study,* 104.

51. Ibid., 107–8.

52. Rabbi Helen Cohn, telephone interview with the author, May 6, 2007.

53. *2004 Jewish Community Study,* 62.

54. Ibid.

55. *American Israelite,* December 30, 1887, quoted in William M. Kramer, *Sephardic Jews in the West Coast States, Volume I, The San Francisco Grandees* (Los Angeles, 1996), 82.

56. Tobin and Sassler, *Bay Area Jewish Community Study,* 139.

57. *2004 Jewish Community Study,* 62. Nevertheless, the Bay Area rate of intermarriage is no longer among the highest in the country.

58. Dawn Kepler, telephone interview with the author, September 5, 2007.

59. Ibid.; *2004 Jewish Community Study,* 64.

60. *2004 Jewish Community Study,* 51.

61. Winston Pickett, "Who Is a Jew? Forum with Four Jewish Leaders Draws 800," *Northern California Jewish Bulletin,* February 5, 1988, 3.

62. *2004 Jewish Community Study,* 116.

63. Ibid., 112.

64. Ibid., 113.

65. Cecilia M. Vega, "Don and Doris Fisher Keep a Low Profile in Art World, Not Politics," *San Francisco Chronicle*, August 9, 2007, A-13.

66. *2004 Jewish Community Study*, 123.

67. Gary A. Tobin, *A Study of Jewish Culture in the Bay Area* (San Francisco, 2002), 42.

68. Ibid., 44–47, 58.

69. Rosenbaum, *Visions*, 227–37.

70. Ibid., 305–14, 388–89, 420–21.

71. Marc Dollinger, "Counterculture," 157–61.

72. Earl Raab, "Earl Raab, Executive of the San Francisco Jewish Community Relations Council, 1951–1987: Advocate of Minority Rights and Democratic Pluralism," interview conducted by Eleanor Glaser, in Bancroft Library, Regional Oral History Office, University of California, Berkeley, 1998, pp. 121–22.

73. Marc Dollinger, "Counterculture," 154.

74. Ibid.

75. David Horowitz, *The Professors: The 101 Most Dangerous Academics in America* (Washington, D.C., 2006).

76. Leo Laurence, telephone interview with the author, June 18, 2007.

77. Cohen and Eisen, *The Jew Within*, 137.

78. Tobin, *A Study of Jewish Culture*, 41; *2004 Jewish Community Study*, 123.

79. Alvin Fine, "The State of Israel and the American Jew," October 14, 1949, in Alvin I. Fine Papers, in WJHC/JLMM.

80. Ibid.

INDEX

Text: 11.25 / 13.5 Adobe Garamond
Display: Adobe Garamond
Compositor: Westchester Book Group
Indexer: Ruth Elwell
Printer and binder: Thomson-Shore, Inc.